International Energy and Resources Law and Policy Series

International Oil and Gas Investment
Moving Eastward?

Editors

General Editor

Professor Thomas W. Wälde, *Executive Director, Centre for Petroleum & Mineral Law & Policy (CPMLP), University of Dundee, UK*

Editorial Working Committee
(All of the Centre for Petroleum & Mineral Law & Policy)

Ayesha Dias, *Senior Research Fellow*
David Mac Dougall, *Lecturer*
James Gunderson, *Honorary Lecturer; General Counsel, Schlumberger Electricity Management*
James Otto, *Senior Lecturer*
Professor Paul Stevens

Consulting Editors

Dr. Emilio J. Cárdenas, *Ambassador, Permanent Representative of Argentina to the United Nations, New York, USA*
Dr. Istvan Dobozi, *Technical Department, Energy Division, The World Bank, New York, USA*
Dr. Fereidun Fesharaki, *Director, Program on Resources, East-West Center, Honolulu, Hawaii, USA*
Professor William F. Fox, *Columbus School of Law, Catholic University of America, Washington DC, USA*
Professor Rosalyn Higgins, QC, *London School of Economics, London, UK*
Dr. Kamal Hossain, *Dr. Kamal Hossain and Associates, Dhaka, Bangladesh*
Philippe Kahn, *Director, CREDIMI, Université de Bourgogne, Dijon, France*
Dr. Amanda Niode Katili, *Agency for the Assessment and Application of Technology, Jakarta, Indonesia*
Professor Eugene M. Khartukov, *Ministry of Foreign Affairs, Moscow, CIS*
Professor Alain Lapointe, *Director, Oil & Gas Company Management Programme, Centre d'Etudes en Administration Internationale, Ecole des Hautes Etudes Commerciales, Université de Montréal, Quebec, Canada*
Dr. Ole Anders Lindseth, *Director General, Oil & Gas Department, Royal Ministry of Industry and Energy, Oslo, Norway*

International Energy and Resources Law and Policy Series

International Oil and Gas Investment
Moving Eastward?

Editors
Thomas W. Wälde
and
George K. Ndi

Graham & Trotman/Martinus Nijhoff
Members of the Kluwer Academic Publishers Group
LONDON/DORDRECHT/BOSTON

Graham & Trotman Limited
Sterling House
66 Wilton Road
London SW1V 1DE
UK

Kluwer Academic Publishers Group
101 Philip Drive
Assinippi Park
Norwell, MA 02061
USA

ISBN 1-85333-963-6
Series ISBN 1-85333-796-X

British Library Cataloguing in Publication Data
International Oil and Gas Investment:
Moving Eastward? – (International Energy & Resources Law & Policy Series)
  I. Walde, Thomas   II. Ndi, George
  III. Series
  332.673

  ISBN 1-85333-963-6

Library of Congress Cataloging-in-Publication Data
International oil and gas investment: moving eastward? / editors,
  Thomas W. Wälde, George K. Ndi.
    p.   cm. – (International energy and resources law and policy
  series)
    Includes bibliographical references and index.
    ISBN 1-85333-963-6
    1. Petroleum law and legislation. 2. Oil and gas leases.
  I. Waelde, Thomas W.   II. Ndi, George K.   III. Series.
  K3915.4.I57   1994
  343'.0772–dc20   93-42911
  [342.3772]   CIP

Typeset in 10/11pt Times by BookEns Ltd, Baldock, Herts.
Printed and bound in Great Britain by Hartnolls Ltd, Bodmin, Cornwall.

Contents

Part II: THE TREND EASTWARD: RUSSIA, CIS AND EASTERN EUROPE

List of Authors

Introduction
> *Thomas W. Wälde*
> Executive Director and Professor of Petroleum and International Investment Law, Centre for Petroleum & Mineral Law & Policy, University of Dundee, Scotland;

> *George K. Ndi*
> Research Associate and Teaching Fellow
> Centre for Petroleum & Mineral Law & Policy, University of Dundee

Part I – INTERNATIONAL FRAMEWORK

1. International Petroleum Investment and Policies: Green, Privatising and Moving Eastward

   Thomas W. Wälde and *George K. Ndi*, Centre for Petroleum & Mineral Law & Policy, University of Dundee

2. Structuring Legal Relationships in Oil & Gas Exploration and Development in 'Frontier' Countries

   Sheila Slocum Hollis, Senior Partner, Metzger, Hollis, Gordon & Mortimer, Washington D.C.

   John W. Berresford, Partner, Metzger, Hollis, Gordon & Mortimer, Washington D.C.

3. Competitive Bidding Tactics for New Exploration Concessions

   P.W. Hawley, A.D. Bramley, and *J.M. Castellani*, Arthur D. Little, London

4. Restructuring or Privatisation? – State Petroleum Enterprises and the Global Economic Adjustment Process

    George K. Ndi, and *Leon E. Moller*, Centre for Petroleum & Mineral Law & Policy, University of Dundee.

5. International Petroleum Licensing, Exploration Activity and Fiscal Terms

    Susan Hodgshon, Director, Petroconsultants (UK) Ltd, London

6. China's Petroleum Industry: Oil and Gas Development Policy and Legislation

    David D. Peng, Manager, China Division, MINET Asia Ltd, Hong Kong

7. The Production Sharing Contract in Indonesia

    T.N. Machmud, Legal Adviser, Atlantic Richfield (ARCO) Indonesia Inc, Jakarta, Indonesia

8. Recent Developments in Legal Structuring of Petroleum Investment Agreements in Nigeria

    Sena Anthony, Head, Corporate Legal Services, Nigeria National Petroleum Corporation (NNPC), Lagos, Nigeria

9. Oil Investment in Latin America

    Maria Kielmas, Editor, "LATOIL", Surbiton, Surrey, England

10. The Law of Offshore Petroleum Development: Basic Concepts and Main Issues

    Jeremy P. Carver, Head, Public International Law Group, Clifford Chance, Solicitors, London

11. Negotiating Dispute Settlement in the International Petroleum Industry: The International Chamber of Commerce

    Stephen R. Bond, Former Secretary General, ICC International Court of Arbitration; Attorney-at-Law, White & Case, Paris, France

Part II – CIS, RUSSIA & THE EAST

22. Natural Gas from Russia/CIS for Europe

   Jochen Alsleben, Senior Legal Adviser, Ruhrgas AG, Essen, Germany

23. International Petroleum Exploration and Exploitation Agreements: A Comprehensive Environmental Appraisal

   Zhiguo Gao, Post-doctural fellow, East-West Centre, Honolulu, USA

Acknowledgement
The editors would like to express their gratitude to all the contributors for their generosity in devoting their time and giving their knowledge and expertise towards the production of this volume. The views expressed in the book are the personal opinions of the authors and do not necessarily reflect the position of their professional affiliations.

Foreword

This book represents an important and timely contribution to the varied subjects it attempts to cover. It is *important* because it addresses the twin phenomena of the risk in foreign direct investment flows noticed since 1987 (both on a worldwide scale and in particular towards the East Asian, Eastern European and former Soviet Union countries) and the continued transformation of the economies of many of the latter countries from command to market structures. And it is *timely* because it does so while these important changes are taking place and at a time when foreign investors in increasing numbers are considering new exploration, development and rehabilitation activities in the oil and gas sectors of these countries. These same developments have led the World Bank to direct a good part of its attention, and lending, to the oil and gas sectors, especially in the Russian Federation. They have also caused the Bank to revise its policy regarding its insistence on securing for itself the same protection provided by its borrowers to other creditors in the form of liens or other priorities over public assets (under its negative pledge clause) so as to facilitate foreign private lending for investment purposes in the ex-socialist countries in transition.

The various topics covered in the 23 chapters of this book are treated by recognized experts and practitioners. By compiling them in one volume, the editors, Professors Thomas W. Wälde and George K. Ndi, offer a unique service to the legal profession and to the wider readership of those interested in the oil and gas industry and in the legal treatment of foreign investment in general. This is a welcome addition to legal literature for which the editors and authors are to be commended.

Ibrahim F.I. Shihata
Vice President and General Counsel,
The World Bank
Secretary-General, International
Centre for Settlement of
Investment Disputes,
Washington, D.C.
August 1993

Introduction

Thomas W. Wälde and George K. Ndi

Transnational investment policies have been undergoing a profound evolution in recent years – from previously restrictive tendencies on the part of host governments to investment promotion and protection. Mirroring this transformation has been the gradual evolution in national oil and gas policies with the change in investment conditions in the petroleum sector worldwide. More recently, there have also been indications of emerging new geographical patterns in transnational petroleum investment in the impending movement eastward of transnational resource companies to the former eastern block countries. The still-unfolding situation in the international petroleum industry holds significant future implications for industry structure and for the pattern of transnational investment in the industry for quite some time to come. In particular, the break-up of the former Soviet Union and the movement eastward of international oil and gas ventures has acted as a catalyst for a stimulating debate on evolving trends in international energy investment. This debate has been marked by perceptive reflections on the growing significance of the transition economies within the emerging paradigm of the international oil and gas industry. Energy law and practice must continue to respond to, and keep pace with, these diverse and complex developments. It must seek to identify those issues which are of current relevance to the continuing evolution and development of the international energy industry. Hence a distinguished faculty from industry, the public sector, private practice and academia – with between them global experience in international energy issues – has been assembled to identify key issues underlying current trends in international oil and gas investment and policies, and to analyse their long term implications for the global industry.

The contributions to this book – some of which have been developed from various papers presented at the summer programmes on International

Petroleum Investment organised by the University of Dundee's Centre for Petroleum & Mineral Law & Policy – were written against the background of the momentous political and economic changes currently still taking place in the ex-centrally planned economies in transition (the republics of the former Soviet Union and the newly-liberalised economies of Eastern Europe) and the worldwide evolution in investment conditions and policies in the petroleum sector.

Part I of the book addresses current issues which are of specific relevance to the development of oil and gas resources from an international perspective. In the opening chapter, Thomas W. Wälde and George K. Ndi appraise the dominant themes currently driving international oil and gas investment and policies: evolution in investment conditions, policies affecting the restructuring or privatisation of state energy enterprises, the oil and gas industry in transition in the former communist countries, and the environmental protection aspects of international petroleum investment and policies. The limited availability of investment capital following the slump in commodity prices, coupled with the shattered paradigm of ever-increasing oil prices and the worldwide recession of the late 1980s, has since led to an intensification of the international competition for scarce exploration and development investment funds. In our view, the global competition for oil and gas investment and technological resources seems set to continue for a long time to come – by reason mainly of the massive prospective acreage potentially on offer in Russia and the new CIS republics. With reference to the increasing availability of investment opportunities for the international petroleum industry in the ex-socialist countries following the opening up of these countries to private foreign investment, Chapter 1 poses the question whether international oil and gas investment may now be regarded as irreversibly committed to the process of moving eastward.

The rapidly changing international economic and political landscape of today, as well as generating new investment opportunities in areas hitherto closed to foreign investment, also has worrying implications for investors. The prevailing instability and uncertainty associated with these developments appreciates considerably the non-commercial risk aspect associated with transnational oil and gas investment. While it is as yet uncertain to what extent the political risk factor will have an impact on the scope and magnitude of the impending movement eastward of transnational oil and gas investment, the recent (April 1993) cancellations of petroleum contracts by the government of Azerbaijan invariably makes potential investors apprehensive of the prospect of future unilateral state actions involving property and investment deprivation. In view of this uncertainty, concerns as to the stability of international oil and gas investment in the frontier regions is bound to be accentuated. Much of the discussion in Part II focuses on this aspect of uncertainty with specific reference to the ongoing associations of transnational resource companies with the development of the oil and gas resources of the transition economies.

One of the major issues of the 1980s has been the environment. With the worsening ecological situation worldwide, hydrocarbons have come to acquire a rather dubious reputation with the various environmental lobby groups.

Whereas traditional energy thinking appreciates less fully the demands on the industry from such lobby groups, hydrocarbons – on the other hand – are viewed with suspicion by environmentalists, some of who refuse even to consider an economic criteria when advocating environmental protection policies. However, even with the acknowledged existence of these fundamentally opposed and seemingly irreconcilable schools of thought, the principal consequence of heightened environmental awareness in the 1980s has been the growing convergence between oil and gas development policies and environmental protection objectives. As a result, the environmental component has come to acquire a higher profile in oil and gas operations over the years and has tended to leap-frog, even if only sometimes with less conviction, from one oil and gas jurisdiction to another. Environmental impacts and environmental protection and regulatory issues in the petroleum sector therefore continue to occupy an important place in the formulation of oil and gas policies. As far as we can see, they will continue to do so for a long time to come.

Successful implementation of environmental protection policies in the oil and gas sectors will tend to depend on the sound implementation and pragmatic application of prescribed standards. Even in the absence of full environmental-costing and pricing of petroleum products, the application of such standards will inevitably lead to higher costs and additional investments in appropriate technologies. The implications of this for Russia and the other transition economies in terms of oil and gas development could be far-reaching. Over the past decades oil and gas operations in the region are known to have had a significant adverse impact on environmental resources. As such, the need, as well as the demand, for appropriate environmental protection safeguards in Russia and some of the oil producing CIS states can not be overemphasised. Chapter 1 identifies some of the key environmental issues facing the international petroleum industry of today – and contemplates those which are likely to arise in the near future. In Chapter 18, Nicholas A. Robinson examines, from an environmental perspective, the technological, infrastructural and legal challenges facing the Russian petroleum industry and outlines the possible scope for Russian environmental legislation. And in Chapter 23 Z. Gao builds further on the environmental theme with a comprehensive appraisal of the environmental protection aspects of both concessionary and modern petroleum agreements.

Petroleum development agreements provide the key legal instrument and medium for the development of oil and gas resources on a transnational scale. One of the main products of the nationalistic policies and growing self-assertiveness on the part of petroleum-producing developing countries in the 1970s was the emergence of a variety of legal forms and contractual arrangements governing the exploration for and development of hydrocarbon resources. Designed to facilitate the implementation of the concept of national ownership and to promote the policy of sovereign control over natural resources, such agreements ranged from concession contracts to risk/service and management contracts, joint ventures and production-sharing arrangements. Critical analysis of these various forms of arrangements ultimately leads us to an enquiry into the extent of the correlation between the form and the substantive content of the different types of petroleum contracts. In Chapter 2, Sheila S. Hollis and John Beresford consider and assess the principal issues involved in formulating and drafting modern oil and gas development agreements in 'frontier' countries.

Notwithstanding the profound evolution which international oil and gas policies have undergone in recent years with regard to investment promotion and protection, the fact that no significant new contractual forms have so far emerged from this trend is quite remarkable. On the contrary, hybrid forms of the familiar contractual arrangements of the 1970s have continued to be used flexibly to accommodate new terms and conditions. The substantive content (essential fiscal terms and investment conditions) of today's agreements, on the other hand, continue to be responsive to specific industry – and general economic – conditions. Hence, in the absence of new contractual forms and arrangements for oil and gas development, a survey of international petroleum licensing, exploration and fiscal terms (Susan Hodgshon – Chapter 5) provides one of the best possible indications of evolving practice in the area of international petroleum investment and policies.

Following the evolution in investment regimes, investment conditions generally and fiscal terms in particular have improved considerably for transnational oil and gas companies worldwide. Not only have more investor-friendly investment regimes come into being than ever before; various fiscal incentives are on offer with contractual and legal guarantees of long-term stability of essential investment conditions attached. Even so, exploration remains a highly uncertain and risky business. This element of uncertainty increases considerably when companies have to go through competitive bidding or auction procedures (now almost a standard practice in most developing countries) in order to acquire rights to new exploration acreage. To ensure successful bidding at this initial stage, companies sometimes resort to the tactic of 'overbidding' and subsequent 'renegotiation' of terms and conditions. In Chapter 3, P. W. Hawley, A. D. Bramley and J. M. Castellani initiate an investigation into this practice. In a discussion which is full of insight and originality, the authors examine the background to the practice and the reasons for its existence, while canvassing support for an end to the tactic on account of its potentially harmful consequences for the interests of both industry and host governments.

The still-unfolding trends and patterns in transnational private-sector petroleum investment with its impending new geographical dimensions, coupled with the ongoing evolution in international oil and gas policies, hold significant implications for developing countries. Over the last decade oil and gas development policies in these countries have been designed to reflect prevailing trends in the international petroleum industry. This has been the case in particular with policies relating to direct involvement by the public sector in oil and gas operations through the medium of the state petroleum enterprise. The general tendency in recent years has been geared increasingly towards public-sector disengagement from direct involvement in the productive sectors of the economy. In view of this, and the prevailing worldwide trend towards the privatisation of public enterprises, it had been expected not so long ago that state petroleum companies, many of them in developing countries, would be earmarked for sweeping transformations.

But whereas some of these companies have gone through restructuring exercises and a few have been privatised, there are as yet no firm indications of any profound transformations either in their corporate identities or in their specified functions of representing the interests of the host state in oil and gas operations. What, therefore, does the future hold for state petroleum enterprises in the developing countries? Do current restructuring exercises aid in facilitating, or do they exclude altogether the possibility of a transfer to the private sector at some future date? In Chapter 4, George K. Ndi and Leon E. Moller cast some cautious reflections on the prospects for the privatisation of state petroleum enterprises in developing countries within the general context of the current global economic adjustment process and prevailing worldwide privatisation activity.

Still in relation to the developing countries, Chapters 8–11 set out to highlight specific national and regional experiences with regard to recent developments in the oil and gas sector. Sena Anthony (Chapter 8) appraises developments in the area of petroleum contracts and privatisation legislation in Nigeria, the leading African petroleum producer and exporter. In Chapter 9, Maria Kielmas explores issues of current relevance to the development of the oil and gas sectors in Latin America.

China remains a fascinating prospect for the international oil and gas industry. Following the opening up of acreage to international petroleum investment, that country could now be considered to be the most important of the still-centrally-planned economies where significant acreage and investment opportunities are either on offer or potentially on offer to international oil companies. David Peng (Chapter 6) presents an update on recent developments with regard to acreage licensing and foreign participation in the Chinese petroleum industry.

Still in the east, the Indonesian-inspired production sharing contract has over the years provided perhaps the most instructive and influential models for developing countries in the formulation of petroleum development policies. Its continuing influence on the form and substance of petroleum arrangements in some of these countries today remains indisputable. In Chapter 7, T. N. Machmud reviews the 25 years of the Indonesian oil industry's experience with the production-sharing agreement, examines the new generation of contracts, and considers the prospects for production sharing agreements over the next 25 years.

The past few years has also seen the emergence of a number of (newly) independent nations on the world scene, many of which are coastal states with claims under international law to territorial jurisdiction over relevant coastal and maritime areas. Many of these are around the regions bordering on the Baltic Sea, Caspian Sea, Black Sea, Adriatic Sea, and Red Sea. In the light of these developments, it is expected that offshore petroleum development in these regions will increasingly involve issues affecting the delimitation of offshore resource jurisdiction. Delimitation concepts have themselves undergone a radical transformation over the past 20 years. In Chapter 10, Jeremy P. Carver examines the basic concepts, methods and process, and discusses recent cases/arbitration, and intergovernmental agreements relating to the delimitation of offshore resource jurisdiction – i.e. the law of offshore petroleum development.

In view of its scope and complexity (the diversity of players, interests and attitudes involved) transnational investment projects inevitably give rise to divergent views and conflicting objectives between the providers and recipients of capital investment. Such conflict could in turn spawn an open dispute. This is particularly the case in the petroleum industry where vital interests are usually perceived to be at stake. In response to the need for the impartial adjudication of disputes if and when they do arise, a considerable number of institutional mechanisms for the international arbitration of investment disputes have come into being over the years. In Chapter 11, Stephen R. Bond examines institutional arbitration under the auspices of the Paris-based International Chamber of Commerce (ICC) from the point of view of negotiating international investment dispute settlement in the petroleum industry.

The focus of Part II is on recent developments in the oil and gas sectors in the ex-socialist societies in transition: Russia, the CIS republics and Eastern Europe. Notwithstanding the recent decline in production, Russia and the new CIS republics are still the world's largest producers of hydrocarbon resources. The region has huge reserves, massive acreage and attractive investment opportunities potentially on offer to the international oil and gas industry. In addition to oil, there are also known to be enormous reserves of natural gas, the production of which already provides the basis for a flourishing commercial venture between the region and Western Europe. The mechanics of this regional trade in natural gas from the former Soviet Union constitutes the subject matter of Jochen Alsleben's discourse in Chapter 22.

Russia and the CIS republics in particular require large-scale investment of capital to bring the oil and gas industry up to modern international standards. The challenges, difficulties, and risks involved are quite substantial; but so too are the investment opportunities and the promise of potential rewards. Andrei A. Konoplyanik (Chapter 12), Mark Moody-Stuart (Chapter 13), and Alfred J. Boulos (Chapter 14) assess these challenges and opportunities. In these chapters, the authors examine the investment requirements, analyse the commercial and the legal aspects of foreign investment in the oil and gas sectors in Russia and the CIS, and canvass the need for a sustained investment commitment in the region from the international petroleum industry.

The admission, entry and establishment of international oil and gas companies in Russia, the CIS republics and Eastern Europe requires stable economic, political and social institutions, without which the perception of commercial and political risk factors associated with long-term investment in the region will tend to discourage the inflow of much needed investment into the oil and gas sector. As of now, the consensus seems to be that such stability does not exist (see, with specific reference to Russia, Chapter 12) notwithstanding the adoption in many of these countries of democratic institutions and new economic, legal and social models. The introduction of these models has been fraught with particular difficulties and problems. In

Chapters 19 and 20, Doran Doeh evaluates the ongoing experiences of the oil and gas industries in the ex-centrally planned economies of Eastern Europe with the transition process, and with new legal and commercial concepts in a market environment.

The transformation of economic and other institutional structures lies at the heart of the efforts to attract overseas investment into the ex-socialist societies. On the other hand, these societies are said to be under intense pressure to import Western economic and social models – as well as Western legal concepts – as part of the transition. Hence questions have been raised as to whether these imported models – many of which are often quite abstract from the economic realities and social conditions prevailing in the region – can provide a satisfactory basis for the contractual and legal stability which is required for the commitment of high-risk and large-scale investment from foreign sources. T. Wälde (Chapter 16) addresses this question in relation to the preparation of oil and gas legislation in Russia.

How are the transition economies in the meantime coping with the new challenges of running the domestic oil and gas industry in an international market environment? Greater efficiency through private-sector ownership and management, and the restructuring or corporatisation of state energy enterprises, now pervades policy as to the future direction of the oil and gas industry. In Chapter 17, Jonathan Price examines the restructuring of the petroleum industry in Russia. In the area of foreign capital involvement in the development of the oil and gas resources of the transition economies, Reinhold Heus (Chapter 15) evaluates the prospects for international energy investment on the basis of a commercial partnership between the international petroleum industry and the transition societies of Russia and Central Asia. In this chapter, the author canvasses mutual understanding as the proper foundation for the formation of such a partnership while focusing on the cultural and structural perspectives of international energy investment in the region.

Other countries of the CIS and Central Asia have responded to the new challenges of the international market place and the global competition for oil and gas investment funds by enacting (through oil and gas, commercial and foreign investment legislation) investor-friendly investment conditions and legal framework governing overseas investment for the development of hydrocarbon resources. Martin Friedrich (Chapter 21) examines recent developments in the area of petroleum investment, policies and legislation in one of the leading petroleum producers, CIS, the Republic of Kazakhstan.

Despite its appeal to the international petroleum industry and its fashionable geology, Russia struggles still to overcome the technological and investment obstacles blocking the revival of its oil and gas industry. In the mean time, if the decline in its oil production and prevailing trends in energy supply and consumption were to persist, the forecast is that the country could become an importer of both crude oil and refined products within the next decade (see Chapter 12). The implications of this for the international petroleum industry could be far-reaching. How would the oil markets respond to such a scenario? Would OPEC be back once more in the 'driver's seat'? And what in turn would be the implications of this for producing countries and for the industry as a whole. Such questions illustrate quite clearly the significance of Russia and the CIS within the unfolding paradigm of the international energy industry of the future.

The evolution of investment conditions in the petroleum industry has been most vividly exemplified by the coming into being since 1992 alone of a number of national legislative acts and international instruments applying either to petroleum development or the transnational investment process in general. Some of these agreements (and protocols) set out to create international law obligations between the providers and recipients of foreign investment. Others, such as the World Bank's Legal Framework for the Treatment of Foreign Investment and the European Energy Charter, amount to 'soft law' instruments setting out investment guidelines and codes of conduct, the purpose of which is to secure a more stable environment for transnational investment relations in a rapidly changing economic and political landscape. A selection of some of the most pertinent of these national and international law instruments provide an appendix to the book. These include The World Bank's Legal Framework for the Treatment of Foreign Investment; the European Energy Charter (Text and Basic Agreement); the Oil and Gas Law of Russia (Revised Draft, 1993); the 1992 Subsoil Law of Russia; the Petroleum Law of Kazakhstan (draft); and 1992 Kazakhstan Code on Subsurface Resources and Crude Mineral Processing.

While no effort has been spared to ensure that the issues under discussion are kept up to date, it is yet possible that events (particularly as they unfold in Russia) may have overtaken us in some respects by the time this book finally comes into print. Even so, the vigorous and highly innovative analysis which the contributors have brought to bear on the examination and appraisal of key concepts and important practical issues should ensure for the book a continuing relevance as a key source of reference on international energy law and policies. From our point of view, many of the issues examined in the book will continue to exert a strong influence on the rapidly changing scene in the international petroleum industry for quite some time to come.

Part I

International Framework

Chapter 1

International Petroleum Investment and Policies: Green, Privatising, and Moving Eastward?

Thomas W. Wälde and George K. Ndi

1.1 INTRODUCTION

International oil and gas development policies have undergone a profound transformation over the last decade. The tendency on the part of host countries, faced with having to formulate and implement resource development policies in a highly competitive international environment marked by the scarcity of investment funds for exploration and development, has been more towards investment promotion and protection. New liberalisation measures continue to replace previously restrictive attitudes towards inward foreign investment.[1] This change in official attitudes has been brought about by prevailing economic conditions – fall in natural resources and commodity prices,[2] contraction in the volume of capital funds available for investment in exploration and development, and much greater selectivity on the part of transnational resource companies with regard to project identification and prioritisation. In this new climate, investment/enabling conditions have tended to assume a much greater importance and significance than ever before as criteria for the allocation of investment funds and technological resources.

Investment promotion and protection, in addition to the environment (environmental impacts of energy development, both global and localised), are

---

1.   Cf. T. Wälde, 'Investment Policies in the International Petroleum Industry: Responses to the Current Crisis', in N. Beredjick and T. Wälde (eds), *Petroleum Investment Policies in Developing Countries* (1988), 7; and K. I. F. Khan, 'Petroleum Taxation and Contracts in the Third World: A Law and Policy Perspective', *Journal of World Trade Law*, **22**, 1 (1988), 67. For similar developments in the mining sector, see T. Wälde, 'Third World Mineral Investment Policies in the Late 1980s: From Restriction Back to Business', in D. Gulley and P. Duby (eds), *The Changing World Metals Industries* (1988), 121.

2.   For an analysis of the effect of falling prices on the availability of investment capital and the corresponding influence on investment conditions, see A. Kemp, 'Petroleum Exploration and Contract Terms in Developing Countries After the Oil Price Collapse', *Natural Resources Forum*, **13** (1989), 161; and J-M. Martin, 'From the Erosion of Crude Oil Prices to a Re-Organisation of the Oil Industry', ibid., 149.

thus the currently dominant themes in the formulation of national oil and gas policies. The stark realities of the ecological consequences of unsustainable economic and industrial development practices have led to the rapid growth of national and international environmental policies and law-making. There is likewise a readily discernible trend involving the increasing fusion of natural resources development policies with environmental protection objectives. Over the past decade, the environmental protection component in petroleum and mineral development agreements has thus come to assume an increasing importance and significance.

Issues relating to state sovereignty/permanent sovereignty over natural resources (PSNR), and other such *leitmotifs* of the new international economic order era, on the other hand, now appear to be much less of the essence – even if questions of ownership and control over hydrocarbon resources, fuelled in part by economic nationalism, continue to retain a political and legal relevance in countries such as Russia, the CIS and the newly emergent regions. The once perennial and controversial international law themes of foreign investment protection and the limits of permissibility of the exercise of the sovereign prerogatives/public powers of the state within the framework of negotiated contractual arrangements for the development of petroleum resources now appear – for the moment at least – to have receded into the background.

In the developing countries, the design and implementation of resource development policies have come to be imbued with a new political realism driven by prevailing economic circumstances and by the ultimate realisation on the part of these countries of the limits of managerial competence attaching to public-sector involvement. This realism now dictates a hands-off approach underlined by public-sector disengagement from direct participation in petroleum development activity, the liberalisation of investment regimes, and a general improvement in investment conditions.[3]

A notable feature of emerging patterns in international oil and gas investment is the impending movement of such investment to the east. Transnational resource companies are increasingly seeking new investment opportunities in the transition economies of Russia, Eastern Europe, and the newly emergent societies of Central Asia. A similar trend can be discerned in relation to still frontier regions such as China, Papua New Guinea, and Vietnam. This process seems to involve a relocation of capital resources away from traditional oil provinces as well an expansion in the scope of transnational resource companies' operations. The maturity – and incipient decline in production – of the industrialised oil regions such as the United Kingdom's North Sea sector and the United States (excepting Alaskan production), has tended rather to accelerate the tendency for multinational companies to move into the newly accessible regions of the East in search of new oil and gas opportunities and new reserves.

However, the conditions surrounding the admission, entry and establishment of these companies in the 'new' countries remain clouded with much

___

3.   Cf. T. Wälde, 'Recent Developments in Negotiating International Petroleum Agreements', *Petroleum Economist (Special Supplement: International Energy Law)*, July 1992, 1.

uncertainty – in view mainly of the economic, legal and political circumstances prevailing in the region. As such, the ongoing associations of international oil and gas investment with the region has itself become the subject of economic and legal contentions. Similar uncertainty surrounds the entry and establishment of transnational oil companies in many developing countries today. Many of these countries, as is the case in Africa, are currently undergoing severe economic difficulties and political upheaval as largely tentative attempts at economic restructuring and democratic transition continue to falter.

These developments continuously occupy the attentions of advisers and strategists within the corporate structures of transnational resource companies. Part of their response so far has been mainly to employ political risk minimisation/management techniques, including the contractual stabilisation of essential economic, fiscal, legal and other relevant operational conditions.[4] It remains to be seen whether a similar model of contractual risk management will emerge in Russia and the transition societies of the CIS and Eastern Europe where confusion and uncertainty over legal regimes governing petroleum development (as well as negotiating and contracting authority) currently dominate the discussion on the long-term security of inward investment. The question which arises is that of whether or not the practice of contractually stabilising investment conditions could in future withstand pressures for change and renegotiation which could be brought on by evolving economic conditions, or new political and policy imperatives.[5]

These worldwide developments hold significant implications for the conceptual development and continuing evolution of the practice of international energy law. It is for this reason that the present chapter sets out to identify and to analyse the major issues currently at the forefront of developments in international oil and gas investment and policies.

Current trends in international petroleum investment and policies may be

4. Usually, part of the political risk management strategy would be to have the agreement formalised and institutionalised in the form of an investment contract. The rationale for the 'contract' form technique turns on the premise that the consensual and negotiated basis of the agreement should render any subsequent measures by the state aimed at its unilateral alteration, amendment or termination unlawful and a breach of contract – on the basis of the principles of sanctity of contract and *pacta sunt servanda*. Based on this perception, most companies would appear to have a preference for the investment contract form as opposed to legislated or administrative instruments (licences, permits, etc.) as the form of legal arrangement for the development of hydrocarbon resources when investing in politically unstable regions. For a discussion of this strategy, cf. T. Wälde and G. Ndi, 'Fiscal Regime Stability and Issues of State Sovereignty in Mineral Investment Negotiations', in J. Otto (ed.), *Mineral Taxation, London: Mining Journal Books, (forthcoming), Chap. 4.*

Other forms of political risk management will usually include political risk insurance, spreading the risk through joint venturing and project finance arrangements (thus involving as many parties as possible/advisable in the venture), and warding off the risk through economic, financial or political persuasion and leverage (e.g. use of bilateral investment treaties). Cf. H. Zakariya, 'Political Risk Insurance in Petroleum Development', in N. Beredjick and T. Wälde (eds), *Petroleum Investment Policies in Developing Countries* (1988), 205; J. Kinna, 'Investing in Developing Countries, Minimisation of Political Risks', *Journal of Energy and Natural Resources Law*, 1 (1983), 89; see also I. Shihata, 'MIGA and the Standard Applicable to Foreign Investments', *ICSID Rev.-FILJ* (1986), 327.

5. Cf. Wälde and Ndi, *supra*, note 4.

viewed within the overall context of the following issues which presently influence the character and pattern of such investments:

- worldwide evolution in investment policies and a re-defining of the role of the state in petroleum development strategy;
- evolution of contractual practice – with an increasing tendency towards contractual flexibility and stabilisation – and a general worldwide improvement in investment conditions;[6]
- the introduction in many countries of new and more liberal investment and petroleum legislation;
- the restructuring and rationalisation of state petroleum enterprises with a view to commercialisation, corporatisation or privatisation;[7]
- the declining role of *'permanent sovereignty over natural resources'* and the *'new international economic order'*;
- emerging new geographical dimensions in investment opportunities and in the pattern of transnational investment by multinational oil companies, which has led to the increasing importance and significance of the producing regions of Russia, the CIS, and other emerging nations in the international petroleum industry;
- the new dimension brought to the formulation of petroleum development policies by heightened international awareness of the environmental impacts of energy development, the rapid growth in international environmental law and policies over the past two decades, and in national regulatory responses in this area.

These are some of the issues currently shaping transnational investment in the petroleum sector which this chapter proposes to examine. Our discussion shall be extending further to an analysis of the implications of these developments for the developing countries in terms of inward foreign investment into the petroleum sector. The paper will also include some reflections on the development *versus* environment debate. It will likewise consider the implications of current trends for the international petroleum industry of the future.

1.2 CURRENT THEMES IN INTERNATIONAL PETROLEUM DEVELOPMENT POLICIES: Re-alignment of Institutional Structures

The very turbulent years of the 1970s in the international petroleum industry were characterised by a strong tendency towards growing self-assertiveness on

---

6.   For an analysis of these contractual developments in the petroleum sector, see H. Le Leuch, 'Contractual Flexibility in New Petroleum Contracts', in N. Beredjick and T. Wälde, *Petroleum Development Policies in Developing Countries* (1988), 81; and K. I. F. Khan, *supra*, note 1.

7.   Cf. T. Wälde, 'Restructuring and Privatisation', *Utilities Policy* (Oct. 1991), 412–17; G. Ndi and L. Moller, Chapter 4, *infra*. On the subject of privatisation generally, see A. Walters, 'Liberalisation and Privatisation: An Overview', in S. El Naggar (ed.), *Privatization and Structural Adjustment in the Arab Countries* (1989), IMF Washington D.C.

the part of developing countries aspiring to full political and economic sovereignty and control over the decision-making process in the development of their natural resources.[8] The period from 1980 onwards, on the other hand, may be said to be the time when concepts such PSNR either declined in importance, or have otherwise acquired a relatively more flexible character which serves to promote rather than restrict private-sector involvement in the development of petroleum resources. The change in official attitudes towards the role of overseas investment in the natural resources sector – often perceived to be the embodiment of the national patrimony and the key to economic and political self-determination – is very much mirrored by current developments in the areas of investment legislation and contractual practice with regard to investment promotion and protection in the oil and gas sectors.

In essence, these developments (which are of particular relevance to the international petroleum industry) are illustrative of the transition which is currently still taking place in the economic and legal regulation of the transnational investment process. In the section which follows we examine some of the major issues which currently underpin this transition from active state participation and previously restrictive attitudes towards overseas private sector involvement in the development of national petroleum resources to less restrictive, investor-friendly investment regimes worldwide.

1.2.1 Re-defining the role of the state in petroleum development activities

One consequence of the restrictive policies of the 1960s/'70s was the emergence of veritably innovative contractual arrangements which were designed specifically to accommodate and promote new political and economic imperatives which dictated mandatory public-sector participation in the development of national hydrocarbon resources. These policies and their attendant contractual forms also set out to promote and to facilitate state control over petroleum operations – in a manner perceived then to be in advancement of the national and public interests considerations inherent in development of indigenous natural resources. State participation through production sharing arrangements or joint ventures with designated state petroleum enterprises and similar contractual arrangements – designed with the intention of limiting the private company's control and management powers – thus became the norm.[9] Remnants of the pre-independence concession agreements were in most cases swept away as the new contractual arrangements took hold.

---

8. See T. Wälde, *supra*, note 3. Resource endowment was seen at that time by many developing countries 'as an important lever to gain economic power and private investment was excluded, restricted and constrained'.

9. Other new forms of contract arrangements for the development of oil and gas resources included management, service or work contracts which in principle – if perhaps much less so in practice – gave the host state control over policy-making with regard to production. Many of the new contract arrangements were also designed with the intention of maximising oil revenues for the host state.

The new regime which emerged in the post-concession period was thus characterised by extensive state involvement which was effected through regulatory controls and mandatory participation requirements – the latter two functions being exercised by the energy (or petroleum/mining) ministry and by the state petroleum enterprise respectively.

In practice, the implementation of the concepts of control and sovereignty over natural resources in many cases took on a highly centralised and bureaucratic character, with actual monitoring and supervision rapidly being replaced by extensive and sometimes quite complex administrative and regulatory mechanisms and procedures.[10] As a result, the implementation of public sector participation and involvement quickly acquired a definitively 'civil service' approach.[11] This in turn meant extensive financial obligations for the private investor or contractor. Such obligations included the provision of capital funds towards the financing of mandatory equity participation for the state entity partner; numerous administrative/regulatory approvals, authorisations and procedures to comply with; and, quite often, a very significant element of uncertainty as regards the future behavioural patterns of state conduct – i.e. the possibility of the unilateral alteration, amendment or termination of negotiated terms and other relevant investment conditions.[12]

Today, however, the situation has either largely changed or is changing in many countries with regard to the character, degree and magnitude of state involvement in the development of petroleum resources. The transformation in policies relating to oil and gas development has been more towards public sector disengagement, de-bureaucratisation of the commercial functions of state petroleum enterprises, and the rationalisation of essential administrative and regulatory procedures. Motivating these trends is the highly competitive international environment for investment funds, which in turn has spawned an increasing worldwide tendency towards commercial and fiscal deregulation. The objective, and current emphasis, of oil and gas development policies is thus much less on mandatory equity participation – which has tended to become less pervasive – nor on other forms of state involvement, which of late have become much less intrusive and much more rationalised. Core decision-making functions seem increasingly to be passing to the companies, and the latter appear to be gaining more leeway. This hands-off approach has received ample

10. This could be explained in part by the absence of local technical and professional monitoring expertise.

11. T. Wälde, *supra*, note 3, p. 2.

12. This element of uncertainty constitutes the – by now familiar – political or non-commercial risks factor in transnational petroleum operations. Increasingly, as the international petroleum industry moves into the frontier areas of Central Asia and the ex-socialist countries, the political risk element is bound to become ever more significant in terms of business strategy – i.e. the selection and prioritisation of investment projects based on political risk assessment. The main elements of such risk will generally include restrictions imposed on remittances, civil disorder and warfare, but more particularly the risk of expropriation, unilateral fiscal changes, and – increasingly – ensuing environmental restrictions. Cf. on political risk assessment in the petroleum industry, Gebelein, Pearson and Silberg, 'Assessing Political Risk to Foreign Oil Investment Ventures', in *Economics and Evaluation Symposium, Society of Petroleum Engineers* (Feb. 1977). For an analysis of various approaches to political risk management employed by the international petroleum and mining industries, see Wälde and Ndi, *supra*, note 4.

reflection in the provisions of a new generation of the familiar forms of contractual arrangements of the 1970s, albeit now much adapted to the present conditions and prevailing circumstances.

The increasing consistency in the practice of states in this area is also indicative of the significant shift in bargaining power within the framework of host state/resource company dynamics: more in favour of the companies, except perhaps in instances where the 'bonanza' type petroleum deposit/ discovery or investment opportunity tends to give the host country a much greater leverage in the bargaining process. In our view, the negotiation and conclusion of the petroleum exploration and development agreements of the 1990s are likely to continue to be influenced by these bargaining dynamics – as long as depressed economic conditions and other underlying factors continue to generate intense competition for the limited investment funds available for international petroleum development.

1.2.2 State petroleum enterprises: restructuring with a view to commercialisation/privatisation?

State petroleum enterprises (SPEs) have traditionally provided the principal vehicle for public sector involvement and participation in the development of hydrocarbon resources. Fostered by the oil nationalisations and mandatory state equity participation requirements which became the principal indicators of control, ownership and the PSNR concept in the 1970s, SPEs were able to acquire immense power and highly commanding positions. Such power would often be coupled with a privileged status created and fostered by special laws and regulations. As designated representative of the national interest SPEs were thus able to obtain participation in joint ventures, production sharing agreements and other forms of participation arrangements on a privileged 'carry-through' basis or other equally favourable terms. Hence the SPE became conceived both as a partner for the private investor party in petroleum development operations and as a national bulwark against foreign penetration – a somewhat incongruous role, but one which nonetheless made sense in actual practice as it allowed the state to limit, restrict, exclude or expand the scope of private sector involvement as it saw fit.

In the role of a bulwark against penetration by foreign economic interests, SPEs became the chief symbols of the restrictive practices towards foreign investment which became the principal derivative of the national sovereignty/ PSNR concept of the 1970s.

As a result, therefore, of the increasing tendency towards public sector participation which was then very much in vogue, strong and powerful SPEs emerged. Many of these were in the developing countries where ownership of – and control over – natural resources (as conceptualised in the PSNR principle) was at that time not only fashionable, but had also become something of a political crusade in the search for economic self-determination and the new international economic order. Among these companies, the most prominent were Aramco, EGPC, Ecopetrol, INOC, KUFPEC, NIOC, NNPC, ONGC, PDVSA, Pemex, Pertamina, Petrobrás, Petroecuador, Petronas, Petroperú,

Sonangol, Sonatrach, TPC, and YPF.

The advent of OPEC in 1960 was also closely associated with the concept of national ownership and sovereign control over the exploitation of hydrocarbon resources.

Today, however, new economic exigencies have mostly taken precedence over issues of sovereignty and political control. The close associations of SPEs with the internal political process and their largely quasi-commercial, 'civil service/functionary' approach to fulfilling their designated roles of representatives of the national interest in the petroleum sector meant that such enterprises could hardly have survived – structurally intact and with their legal status unaffected – the severe economic conditions and political re-orientations which ensued in the late 1980s and intensified following the collapse of communism and centralized economic planning. Commercially successful SPEs have been few and far between, and these have mostly been those with diversified corporate structures which enjoyed a considerable degree of managerial autonomy.[13] More typically, such enterprises invariably focused their attention on traditional supervisory and administrative functions. These functions had become increasingly obsolete in the changed economic climate and unfolding political landscape of the late 1980s to early 1990s. The restructuring of state petroleum enterprises had thus become an inescapable necessity: the only questions were that of when and how. Several options presented themselves as to the ultimate goal and objective of such restructuring: commercialisation, corporatisation, or privatisation.

The drive towards the privatisation of public enterprises, first set in motion in the United Kingdom in the early and mid-1980s with the transfer to the private sector of state-owned energy enterprises and other public utilities, has thus gained ground internationally over the past few years. In Latin America, Argentina has led the way in the privatisation drive for transferring petroleum enterprises to the private sector.[14] Bolivia, Peru, Chile and Mexico have all embarked on restructuring, with the underlying policy objective being to make SPEs much more competitive, more commercially focused and accountable, less politically-oriented, and generally to put them on a par with private companies in the field in terms of business focus, commercial autonomy, efficiency and productivity.

The general tendency has been more in favour of corporate reorganisation and restructuring, or some form of partial privatisation, as opposed to the complete transfer of ownership to the private sector. Key SPEs such as Aramco, NNPC, ONGC, Pemex, Pertamina, Petrobrás, Petronas, and Sonangol – to name but a few – have thus so far escaped the rigours of full-

---

13. We could perhaps name here Ecopetrol, Pemex, Petrobrás and Petronas.

14. Developments with regard to privatisation in the petroleum sector in Argentina have been closely monitored and chronicled by commentators. See, on the privatisation of the Argentinean State oil and gas companies, S. Albarracin, (petroleum – gas – privatisation and deregulation/open access to transportation networks), in *Journal of Energy and Natural Resources Law*, **9** (*Recent Developments: Argentina*) (1991), 301–4; cf. M. Dabinovic and S. Albarracin, in ibid., **10**, 1 (*Recent Developments: Argentina*) (1992), 118–20; S. Albarracin, ibid., **11**, 1 (*Recent Developments: Argentina*) (1993), 49; and R. Maciel, 'Argentina: Privatisation of Natural Gas Industry' (Notes and Comments), in ibid., **10**, 4 (1992), 371.

scale privatisation. Current restructuring and commercialisation policies sometimes appear to suggest that these are transitional or interim measures – but they fail to point decisively towards some form of privatisation in the future.

Internationally there is a mixed pattern emerging. As in Argentina, complete or partial privatisation of SPEs is now being considered in Peru and in Ecuador. On the other hand, reorganisation at NNPC and at Sonangol has been limited to corporate restructuring. Other forms of rationalisation have included the divestiture of equity interests (NNPC in Nigeria) or the leasing by the SPE of unutilised or underutilised exploration and development rights to private sector operators. The latter option has been applied, for example, to undeveloped YPF properties in Argentina (and in the mining sector, to Comibol properties in Bolivia). Another approach, not quite unfamiliar in the petroleum industry, has been to encourage the formation of joint ventures between the SPE and private companies for the development of new properties or the rehabilitation of old and inefficiently managed ones.

The scope of privatisation policies in the petroleum sector in developing countries appears in many cases to have been severely circumscribed by practical constraints as well as certain political impediments. The insufficiency of – or restricted access to – domestic financial resources, coupled with the absence in most cases of an adequately functioning capital market capable of handling the complex task of transferring assets to private-sector ownership, poses considerable economic and practical obstacles to the smooth implementation of privatisation programmes. For this reason, the option of the public offer of shares has so far had only limited appeal in several developing countries.[15]

It would thus appear that the economic feasibility of the implementation of national privatisation programmes in most developing countries would tend to depend on the infusion of considerable amounts of overseas private-sector capital resources. From a domestic political viewpoint, however, such a proposition could well generate much controversy: notwithstanding the current promotion of overseas private-sector involvement in natural resources development under various national investment regimes worldwide, in some cases remnants of internal political opposition and resistance to foreign involvement – driven as much by established economic interests as by genuine economic nationalism – remain to be overcome. Hence privatisation has thus become a politically contentious and sensitive issue and the subject of intense national debate in some countries.

In those countries with a strong political, cultural and legal traditions much in favour of public-sector participation in the development of national petroleum resources, the likelihood of popular opposition to the sale of SPEs to overseas private investors is bound to constitute a key consideration for the

---

15. Even in cases where this option has been tried out, such as with Petrobrás in Brazil, State control over the enterprise through the retention of a considerable percentage of shares and equity ownership has nonetheless been maintained as a means of filling the gap which complete privatisation would have left due to the insufficiency in domestic private capital resources required for the purpose.

government in formulating decisions as to the scope and extent of intended privatisation measures. Also to be taken into account are the significant adverse implications which privatisation may have on the continued employment of SPE staff and functionaries,[16] some of whom would have acquired their positions largely as a result of political patronage. For these various reasons, the association of privatisation programmes with foreign capital would tend to be viewed with much anxiety, suspicion and hostility by certain sections of the national public. These would be concerned as much with the threat to their personal economic security as with the impending loss of national ownership and control over natural resources, universally perceived to be a key sector of the national economy. These factors inevitably lead to an acute politicisation of the privatisation debate. The result would be that the final decision as to whether or not to privatise – and if so, to what extent – would often tend to be equally influenced by non-economic pressures and judgments as by rational commercial factors and economic criteria.

These obstacles and difficulties raise critical questions for the long-term future of current restructuring and privatisation measures in the petroleum sector in developing countries and in the transition societies (Russia, the CIS, Eastern Europe and other ex-socialist countries). This in turn raises vital questions for the long-term security of inward overseas investment into the petroleum sector in these countries. Current resource development policies tend to be driven more by economic necessity – and perhaps also by the spirit of competition which dictates a desire to conform to prevailing contractual practices and what is currently fashionable – as opposed to any real ideological or political convictions. Given this, a change in relevant economic conditions/ circumstances could well lead to pressures for a re-examination and re-appraisal of established terms and conditions governing natural resources investment agreements.

What therefore does the future hold for current privatisation policies? The distant horizon, as far as we can see it, appears to be rather dim and nebulous. Would a re-politicisation of the national ownership and control/sovereignty debate lead to the re-emergence of the highly controversial issue regarding the limits of permissibility attaching to unilateral state actions aimed at varying the negotiated and established terms and conditions of foreign investment agreements? In our view, given the current legal and political uncertainties surrounding the entry and establishment of overseas private investment in the petroleum sector in developing countries and in the ex-socialist countries, such a prognosis is not totally unlikely. This view seems to be somewhat reinforced by the prevailing confusion surrounding the precise status of legal norms and principles of international law purporting to regulate transnational investment in the natural resources sector.

In view of the practical difficulties and political sensitivities which often surrounds the issue of privatisation in developing countries, it would seem that a rather gradual and evolutionary approach to the process of transferring the

16. A possible solution could be the adoption of voucher programmes to enable and to facilitate employee shareholding in the privatised enterprise.

ownership of SPEs to the private sector is to be cautioned. Ultimate success in the implementation of such programmes will depend on wide-ranging consultations with all interest groups, as well as on the political will on the part of governments to carry through privatisation measures in the face of often rigid opposition.

The current re-alignment by host countries of institutional structures in the petroleum sector has been closely associated with similar developments in the area of governing legislation. The focus of our attention in the sections which follow shall be on these developments. Our analysis will be extending further to an examination of prevailing contractual practices with regard to investment promotion and protection in the petroleum sector worldwide.

1.3 INTERNATIONAL PETROLEUM LEGISLATION AND CONTRACTS: Current Trends

Investment legislation, as well as petroleum laws and contracts, have provided the principal framework for the implementation of changes which have taken place in investment policies in the petroleum sector over the last decade. Many of these changes are mirrored in overall enabling conditions, and in the general or specific legislative instruments and contractual arrangements which provide the legal framework for investment conditions.

1.3.1 Changes in governing legislation

The real magnitude of the change in investment policies which has taken place over the past decade may be discerned from the prevailing tendency on the part of most countries to adopt liberal, investor-friendly investment codes. Fiscal incentives and guarantees of stability in project regimes, very often designed with the natural resources and manufacturing sectors in mind, constitute the key elements of new investment legislation which have been adopted in countries as far afield as Africa, Asia, and Latin America.[17] This has been accompanied in many instances by a review of petroleum codes, model contracts and the introduction of new incentives and elements of flexibility with a view to attracting overseas investment. In Latin America, for example, the Andean Group Commission has replaced its formerly restrictive enactments such as the Andean Pact Decision 24 of 1976 with new measures

---

17. See excepts from the report of the UN Secretary General, cited in E. Paasivirta, *Participation of States in International Contracts and Arbitral Settlement of Disputes* (1990), pp. 25–6; cf. *International Direct Investment and the New Economic Environment*, OECD (1989), p. 38 *et seq.*; T. Wälde, 'Third World Mineral Development in Crisis: The Impact of Worldwide Recession on Legal Instruments Governing Third World Mineral Development', *Journal of World Trade Law*, **19** (1985), 3; and Pollio and Riemenschneider, 'The Coming Third World Investment Revival', *Harvard Business Review*, **66**, 2 (1988), 114.

encouraging foreign investment. These measures are now part of the new Common Foreign Investment and Technology Licensing Code of May 1987.

This new attitude has been accompanied, and sometimes preceded, by national legislation affecting inward foreign investment.[18] Bolivia has undertaken a modernisation of its petroleum and mining codes, with the new Hydrocarbons Law of November 1990 setting out to eliminate some of the monopoly powers of the SPE. The country has also promulgated a new investment code, and has introduced a new taxation regime which contemplates giving guarantees of long-term stability in the fiscal and regulatory regime of specific resource development projects involving foreign investors. New liberal investment codes have been adopted in Argentina,[19] Chile, Colombia, and Ecuador (Decree 415 of 13 January 1993). In the Caribbean, similar developments have taken place in Trinidad and Tobago.

In Africa, new and more liberal investment legislation or petroleum laws have been enacted in Egypt (new Foreign Investment Law 230), Zambia, Burundi, Côte d'Ivoire, Mauritania, Nigeria,[20] Zaire, Sudan, Ghana, and Liberia. In the late 1980s similar legislation and codes in Algeria, Angola, Benin, Cameroon,[21] Congo, Gabon, and Namibia. In Tanzania, the new National Investment Protection Policy Act offers protection against the nationalisation of private property. In the Asian region, new liberal investment codes and policies have been adopted in Indonesia, China,[22] the Philippines, Malaysia,[23] Mongolia (where the new Petroleum Law of March 1991 contains incentives to attract foreign investment for exploration and development), in

---

18. Some restrictive tendencies can still be identified. In Brazil, for example, the 1988 Constitution contains provisions restricting involvement by foreign companies in petroleum exploration and production, with such rights remaining the prerogative of the SPE, Petrobras: cf. C. Andrade, 'Some Key Aspects of the Brazilian Legal Framework on Energy and Natural Resources', *Journal of Energy and Natural Resources Law*, 7 (1989), 231; and W. Wood, 'Legal Aspects of Foreign Investment in the Oil and Gas Exploration in Brazil', ibid., 265.

In Mexico where constitutional provisions contain similar restrictions on foreign oil investment, petroleum exploration and production activities remain mainly within the jurisdiction of Pemex, the SPE monopoly.

19. Cf. E. Cardenas and T. Dabinovic, 'Argentina: Oil Legislation – New Requirements for Registration', *Journal of Energy and Natural Resources Law*, 9, 1 (*Recent Developments*) (1991), 67. For developments on the policy front, see J. Norman, 'Argentina: Oil and Gas – Deregulation', ibid., 8, 2 (*Recent Developments*) (1990), 143; and L. Erize, 'Argentina's Exploration Plan: The Return of Exploration Permits and Exploitation Concessions', ibid., 10, 3 (1992), 233.

20. For a discussion of new oil and gas investment policies in Nigeria designed with the objective of attracting inward foreign investment into the sector, see M. Kassim-Momodu, *Journal of Energy & Natural Resources Law*, 8 (*Recent Developments: Nigeria*) (1990), 149. Cf. S. Anthony, Chapter 8, *infra*.

21. Cf. G. Ndi, 'The Contractual and Legal Framework for Petroleum Exploration and Production in Cameroon', *Journal of Energy and Natural Resources Law*, 10, 3 (1992), 267.

22. For an analysis of recent developments in the offshore petroleum sector in China, see Chapter 6, *infra*. Cf. D. Peng, 'China's Offshore Oil Policy and Legislation', *Journal of Energy and Natural Resources Law*, 11, 1 (1993), 36. An amendment to the 1990 Chinese-Foreign Joint Venture Act now includes guarantees providing against the nationalisation of foreign-owned property or investment.

23. Cf. G. Tianwah, *Doing Business in Malaysia* (1990), pp. 59–72, for an analysis of the 1986 Promotion of Foreign Investment Act of Malaysia.

Laos in 1989,[24] and in Papua New Guinea. Laos and Vietnam now offer guarantees to foreign investors against the nationalisation of assets. Recent developments regarding investment and petroleum legislation in Russia, the CIS and Eastern Europe are examined under section 1.4 below.

1.3.2 Promotion and protection of private investment as the dominant principle in petroleum licensing and development: contractual practice

Notwithstanding the profound transformation in official attitudes towards foreign investment over the last decade, no new contractual forms have emerged in the petroleum sector. Hybrid versions of the old and familiar forms of agreements have continued to be employed flexibly to accommodate new investment conditions, investment incentives and more dynamic fiscal arrangements. The international competition in the promotion of national investment opportunities has been mirrored by the growing consistency of contractual practice in the petroleum sector worldwide, a practice which is now more inclined towards an improvement in contract terms and conditions for petroleum investment.[25] The general tendency in contractual practice has thus been to employ the contract form as a mechanism for facilitating the improvement in investment conditions. This objective is achieved through the granting of investment incentives, the creation of investor-friendly investment regimes and – in developing countries – the stabilisation of essential investment conditions.

The change in official attitudes is thus oriented more towards investment promotion and protection, an issue which now dominates the formulation of petroleum development policies worldwide. Issues of investment promotion and protection also seem increasing to take precedence over the objectives of national ownership, state participation and control over the development of hydrocarbon resources within the framework of contractual relations.[26]

1.4 THE EASTERN FRONTIER

1.4.1 The trend eastward: risks and reward?

Following the profound economic, political and ideological transformations

---

24. For an appraisal of recent economic and legal reforms in Laos directed at the liberalisation of investment policies and their impact on the natural resources sector, see G. Ndi, 'Mineral Investment Conditions in Lao PDR', *Professional Paper, Mining Journal Research Services*, London (1993).

25. See, for a discussion of contractual developments in the petroleum sector from the perspective of a specific national regime, W. Müller and J. Stern, 'The Evolution of Petroleum Contracts in Argentina: Issues of Foreign Investor's Legal Protection', *Journal of Energy and Natural Resources Law*, 7 (1989), 189.

26. Cf. T. Wälde, 'Investment Policies and Investment Promotion in the Mineral Industries', in *ICSID Rev.-FILJ*, 6 (1991), 94.

which have taken place in the former USSR and the ex-socialist countries as a result of the *perestroika* and *glasnost* policies of the late 1980s, the transition societies potentially have on offer some of the most attractive geological prospects and major investment opportunities for the international petroleum industry. These opportunities – whether they be in the form of energy joint ventures, the acquisition of development rights to new acreage, the acquisition of stock capital and the re-capitalisation of existing energy enterprises, or the modernisation/rehabilitation of old projects – are today considered in the industry to be among the most appealing worldwide in view mainly of the fashionable geology. Russia, Kazakhstan, Azerbaijan and (to a lesser extent) the southern CIS republics of Tajikistan, Turkmenistan and Uzbekistan offer the best prospects in terms of reserves and geological potential (the whole area covered by the former USSR is known to account for one-third of total world oil reserves). In addition to oil resources, the largest proved recoverable reserves (about 44.8 billion of oil equivalent), and the largest potential resources of natural gas in the world are also known to be in the territory of Russia and the CIS.[27] In the former centrally planned economies of Eastern Europe, Albania, Bulgaria and Roma. ia have also been attracting the interest of international oil companies following the collapse of communism.[28]

In a bid to attract inward foreign investment into the petroleum sector, many of the ex-socialist countries have been enacting new investment legislation as well as petroleum laws outlining investor-friendly enabling conditions for the entry and establishment of overseas enterprises. A Subsoil Law, essentially in the nature of a framework law for mineral operations, was promulgated in Russia in 1992. Included in this law are regulations and guidelines for licensing and bidding procedures. An Oil and Gas Law is expected later in 1994. In Kazakhstan several pieces of legislation have been enacted in the area of foreign investment, petroleum development and commercial/economic activity in general.[29] These include a Foreign Investment Law, a Concessions Law, and an Enterprise Law (all passed in 1991), and the Code on Subsoil Resources and the Processing of Mineral Raw Materials, promulgated in 1992. In Poland, new petroleum legislation encouraging inward foreign investment into the sector reached the statute books in March 1991.[30] These developments on the legislative front have extended to other CIS and Eastern European countries. It is mainly on the basis of these legal foundations that a number of discussions and negotiations have ensued between these countries and international oil companies.

The question then is whether there is indeed an impending movement eastward of oil and gas investment in search of new opportunities in the ex-communist countries. So far only very few definitive (and – from the financial

27. See J. Alsleben, Chapter 22, *infra*; cf. A. Konoplyanik, Chapter 12.
28. For a discussion of petroleum and mineral investment trends in the former centrally planned economies, see T. Wälde, *supra*, note 3, pp. 7–8. Cf. D. Doeh, Chapters 19 and 20, *infra*.
29. See M. Friedrich, Chapter 21, *infra*.
30. In Poland, the political tug-of-war between the executive and the legislature remains one of the main obstacles to foreign investment. For an analysis of recent developments in the mining sector in Poland, see A. Lipinski and J. Otto, 'Polish Mineral Legislation and Policies in Transition', *Journal of Energy and Natural Resources Law*, **11**, 1 (1993), 17.

point of view – relatively modest) agreements have been signed for the development of petroleum resources in the region.[31] Hence foreign private investment into the petroleum industry of the region has remained relatively insignificant both by international oil industry standards and in relation to the scope and magnitude of the investment prospects involved.

The reasons for the delay in concluding tangible agreements in the petroleum sector in the transition societies are many. These include, *inter alia*, the following:

- Political uncertainty: political problems and instability underlined by the failed coup in Russia in August 1991; the difficulties involved in the transition to democracy in many of the republics in the CIS and Eastern Europe; increasing regional and ethnic self-assertiveness leading to power struggles between central authorities and autonomous ethnic regions ('republics'), and between the Russian executive and legislature; ethnic conflicts and border disputes (for example, between Azerbaijan and Armenia: Nagorno-Karabakh conflict). These factors all pose problems to the long-term stability of contractual relations in the petroleum sector. A considerable degree of political and nationalist opposition from conservative forces and other vested economic interest groups to both the reform process and to foreign involvement in various economic sectors adds to the prevailing uncertainty. Exacerbating these tensions further is the ever-increasing friction between 'progressive westernising technocrats' who advocate full-scale reforms and rapid economic transformation to a free-market model involving the privatisation of various economic institutions in the oil and gas sector, and the nationalist 'oil generals' who strongly advocate a state monopoly in the sector.
- Contractual and legal problems: uncertainty lingers over questions such as title and ownership, negotiating and licensing authority, and the interpretation of certain legal concepts – e.g. the meaning of a joint venture; other difficulties which have been encountered (particularly in Russia) include attempts to draft a legal framework for oil and gas operations which has led to the long-running 'form and substance' debate on future oil and gas legislation, licensing procedures and forms of contractual arrangements.[32]
- Economic factors: the absence of developed capital and products markets, inadequate infrastructure, and currency exchange and transfer restrictions and regulations; these factors raise problems and difficulties for inward

---

31. e.g. 'White Nights', Canadian Fracmaster, 4MS/Shell (offshore Sakhalin Island), and Elf (Russia and Kazakhstan). The exception here seems to be Kazakhstan, where both British Gas and Chevron (Tengiz project), have both signed tangible deals. Substantial Western involvement in Russia has been mainly in the form of advisory/consulting services on the development of a legal framework, the restructuring of energy enterprises, and financing of energy ventures.

32. Cf. A. Jones, 'Energy and Developing Law in the Russian Federation (Letter from Siberia)', *Petroleum Economist (Special Supplement: International Energy Law)*, July 1992, 9.

foreign investment, particularly with regard to raising overseas finance for oil and gas projects in the region.[33]

Environmental issues also pose a problem for the development of the oil industry in the transition societies. In view of the severe environmental problems currently facing the petroleum industry in these countries, there is some measure of uncertainty as to who will eventually bear the costs of the cleaning up and of environmental rehabilitation programmes. This question applies equally to newly privatised ventures and to joint ventures for the rehabilitation of old projects.

All of these problems impact significantly on the entry and establishment of foreign oil companies in the region, both in terms of the rapidity, timing and scope of overseas involvement in the natural resources sector. The largely political nature of some of the problems has led some financiers to advocate a political risk insurance scheme under the European Energy Charter.[34]

Privatisation constitutes a special issue for the ex-centrally planned economies in transition. The restructuring and/or privatisation of, or the formation of joint ventures with state energy enterprises such as Rosneftegaz, GazProm, Kazakhstanmunaygaz (or with the mainly Russian/Siberian production associations) provides immense scope for the economic reform process and for the involvement of overseas capital in the development of the petroleum resources of the region. Full-scale privatisation of such enterprises, however, could well turn out to be an exercise fraught with immense political difficulties. There is bound to be a considerable measure of opposition from the 'oil generals' who run the production associations and from other nationalist groups to any large-scale transfer of the assets of public sector energy enterprises to the private sector, particularly if this involves foreign ownership and control. Restructuring and corporatisation appear thus to be the only feasible options.

The admission, entry and establishment of foreign capital in the petroleum sector in the ex-socialist countries is therefore currently taking place in circumstances the complexity of which is matched in scope only by the constantly changing scenarios. The diversity and disparity of the players, interests and attitudes involved renders agreement on oil and gas investment projects much more difficult than would normally be the case. In Russia, for example, sponsorship by Western oil companies of advisory projects on the development of a legal framework for the oil and gas sector has led to nationalist-inspired suspicions of all other forms of Western involvement.[35]

---

33. For a discussion on some of the problems associated with project finance in Eastern Europe generally, see F. Chronnell, 'Project Finance: The Way Forward in Eastern Europe', *Petroleum Economist (Special Supplement: International Energy Law)*, July 1992, 44–9.

34. Cf. *Petroleum Economist* (Feb. 1993), 40.

35. In general there has also been some criticism regarding the importation of foreign legal and regulatory models into the Russian petroleum sector. According to the critics, the virtual transplantation of these models has often proceeded without taking into full account the peculiar circumstances of the country – its history, political and legal attitudes, its culture, and its social institutions and prevailing economic infrastructure. Cf. T. Wälde, Chapter 16, *infra*.

1.4.2 Eastern prospects: rather risks than rewards?

These difficulties and problems have in turn given rise to a great deal of uncertainty on the part of Western investors who are contemplating committing funds to the region. This uncertainty has not been lessened by the growing concern over the long-term security of investments. The cancellation by Azerbaijan of a number of petroleum contracts to the value of US$ 100 million in June 1993 can only further heighten these anxieties and concerns.

The promise of substantial potential gains, however, remains a major attraction to transnational resource companies intending to invest in the transition economies. Even so the stimulus to large-scale investment from overseas remains to be found for many of these countries.

Does the prevailing instability of political and economic institutions in transition imply – *a priori* and *a fortiori* – the application of the concept of contract stabilisation to petroleum agreements concluded in the region? In our view, it is most likely that as the initial deals are made and concrete agreements begin to emerge we are likely to see an increasing tendency towards some form of contract stabilisation of essential investment conditions. Much less certain is the likely impact of expected opposition to such specific commitments and guarantees of non-intervention by the state to vary negotiated terms and established investment conditions.

1.5 ENVIRONMENTAL CONSIDERATIONS IN PETROLEUM DEVELOPMENT: Current Trends in Law and Policy

The process of extraction, transportation, refining and consumption of energy and hydrocarbon substances is now widely acknowledged to involve significant adverse environmental impacts. The nature and scale of such impacts will obviously vary with the character and scope of the particular activities or operations in question. Hence whereas the extractive process will more generally be associated with localised impacts, downstream activities involving the use of pipelines, tankers, refineries, and other installations will on the other hand tend to pose environmental risks of a transnational character. Whatever the category of environmental risks involved, hydrocarbons – whether as a matter of substance or perception – have traditionally tended to be viewed very much with misgivings in the environment/(sustainable) development debate.

Over the last decade, ecological concerns have thus become increasingly focused on the localised and global environmental impacts of the development and consumption of hydrocarbon substances: marine/offshore pollution resulting from pipeline leakages, tanker accidents, blow-outs, etc.; transnational and global environmental risks and impacts arising from the transportation, processing and burning of hydrocarbons (including coal and other fossil fuels, and from the flaring of associated gas); the emission of noxious gases and substances (CO_2, sulphur compounds, and nitrogenous gases); global warming and the greenhouse effect; and adverse effects of acid precipitation on vegetation (defoliation).

The localised environmental impacts of oil pollution on marine life, fisheries, agriculture, natural heritage, socio-economic and cultural impacts on local and national communities, and the generally adverse impact on other environmental resources can thus be far-reaching. Such impacts will often upset with lasting effect the ecological balance or natural equilibria of the affected milieu, as well as the socio-economic equilibrium of local communities.

Some of these impacts have been and are still being experienced worldwide with varying degrees of severity. Many have originated largely as a result of the formalistic and somewhat cosmetic role to which environmental considerations have been assigned in the past within the framework of the implementation of petroleum development policies. This was particularly the case in the developing countries, where – in the absence of adequate environmental policies or proper monitoring procedures – investment, production, and other economic priorities were generally seen to take precedence over environmental considerations. It is also now emerging that in the ex-socialist countries of the former Soviet Union and Eastern Europe, the development of petroleum resources in the past would seemed to have seriously overtaxed with lasting effect local environmental resources.

Environmental awareness increased rapidly in the 1980s following the worsening ecological situation worldwide – in particular drought and desertification in Africa, tropical deforestation, marine pollution incidents, and industrial (Bhopal) and nuclear (Chernobyl) accidents. Added to these the coming to light of new scientific findings bringing to public attention new environmental phenomena such as global warming and the depletion of ozone layer ensured for environmental issues a global constituency, political legitimacy and an administrative and legal platform – all driven by a strong undercurrent of public opinion. Environmental protection thus became the dominant issue affecting all sectors of economic activity in the 1980s, the petroleum industry being no exception.

These concerns have led increasingly to the initiation of environmental protection policies, laws and regulations at both the national and international level, with the guiding principles in the natural resources sector being variously or conjointly those of mitigation, remedial action, prevention, reversal of prevailing tendencies toward degradation, and a proactive rather than reactive approach to environmental protection. These various approaches have now been conceptualised into legal/environmental principles such as those of sustainable development, inter- and intra-generational equity, global commons, the precautionary principle, environmental security, etc. – many of which apply to the petroleum sector. Our discussion in the sections which follow shortly will focus attention on two main areas: international environmental law and policies, and national regulatory responses with respect to environmental regulation in the petroleum sector.[36]

---

36. For an analysis of environmental issues and policies in developing countries with specific reference to the mining sector, see T. Wälde, 'Environmental Policies towards Mining in Developing Countries', *Journal of Energy and Natural Resources Law*, **10** (1992), 327; and A. Warhurst, 'Environmental Management in Mining and Mineral Processing in Developing Countries', *Natural Resources Forum* (1992), 39–49. Cf. Mining and Environment ('Berlin')

1.5.1 The growth of international environmental law and policies

Reaction to ecological concerns have led to the rapid growth of a body of principles – contained in declarations, international agreements and conventions – of what has now become known as *international environmental law*. The legal embodiment of this body of principles takes two main forms: so-called 'soft law' (legally unenforceable declarations, guidelines, and principles) and 'hard law' (legally binding conventions and treaties).

International environmental regulation of offshore petroleum activities and the transnational movement of petroleum products, however, often tend to pre-date the relatively recent increase in public awareness over environmental issues. We may cite here regional and international legal instruments: the 1975 Paris Convention for the Prevention of Pollution from Land Based Sources, for example, seeks to regulate the level of oil contained in water discharged from North Sea oil installations, as well as pollution caused by the disposal of oil-contaminated cuttings from exploration and appraisal wells. Following a recent review, the levels of permitted oil content from the latter source, and from new development wells drilled with oil-based mud, has now been set at less than 1 per cent from 1 January 1994 – a target which must be achieved by all other wells as from 1 January 1997.

The International Convention for the Prevention of Pollution from Ships (MARPOL Convention) of 1973 covers offshore installations as well as oil tankers. This convention requires that both platforms and tankers be equipped with oil discharge monitoring and control systems for measuring and recording the oil content of effluent and other discharges. Such systems or instruments should be capable of automatically stopping discharge into the sea if the oil content exceeds permitted levels. The regulation of tanker safety in relation to oil pollution, on the other hand, is covered mainly by a number of International Maritime Organisation (IMO) maritime safety conventions.

Most international conventions relating to oil pollution are specifically concerned with the question of liability and compensation. This is the case, for example, of the Offshore Pollution Liability Agreement (OPOL) which covers direct loss or damage resulting from pollution caused by crude oil or natural gas liquids escaping from offshore exploration and production facilities located within the territorial jurisdiction of member states.[37]

Perhaps by far the most significant international instrument on the environmental regulation of oil pollution is the third UN Law of the Sea Convention (UNCLOS) of 1982, Article 194 (3-c) of which requires states individually or jointly to take measures aimed at minimising marine pollution. The article stipulates as follows:

Pollution from installations and devices used in exploration or exploitation of the natural resources of the seabed and subsoil, in particular measures for preventing accidents and dealing with emergencies, ensuring the safety of operations at sea, and regulating the design, construction, equipment, operation and manning of such installations or devices.[38]

Under Article 208 of UNCLOS, the responsibility for the regulation of seabed activities, including the development of petroleum resources and associated environmental issues in maritime areas under national jurisdiction falls to the coastal state. These states, in fulfilment of this responsibility, shall adopt laws and regulations – which in no case shall be less effective than international rules – for activities subject to national regulation. Coastal states are also required under the Convention to strive for the regional harmonisation of national policies in this area.[39,40]

These international environmental protection initiatives have not only given rise to the development of international environmental law as a specialised subject of international law. They have also been the principal impetus to the intensification of national environmental law-making at the level of the municipal legal system, an issue to which we shall now turn our attention.

1.5.2 National regulatory responses

Environmental awareness has led increasingly to the convergence of resource development policies and environmental protection objectives in recent years. Environmental impact assessments and other forms of environmental audits

38. See also Article 145 of the Convention which urges States to adopt appropriate rules, regulations and procedures for, *inter alia*: ... the prevention, reduction and control of pollution and other hazards to the marine environment, including the coastline, and of interference with the ecological balance of the marine environment, particular attention being paid to the need for protection from harmful effects of such activities as drilling, dredging, excavation, disposal of waste, construction and operation or maintenance of installations, pipelines and other devices related to such activities; Cf. Article 209 of the Convention.

39. The need for the regional harmonisation of policies with regard to the environmental regulation of natural resources development offshore has led to the signing of a number of regional conventions. These include the 1974 Helsinki Convention on the Baltic Sea; the 1976 Barcelona Convention for the Mediterranean; the 1978 Kuwait Convention for the Gulf Region (including the Protocol Concerning Marine Pollution Resulting from Exploration and Exploitation of the Continental Shelf); the 1981 Abidjan Convention covering the West African coast; and the 1981 Lima Convention for the South-East Pacific, all of which precede the 1982 UNCLOS. Subsequent to UNCLOS, the following regional conventions have been concluded: the 1982 Jeddah Convention applying to the Red Sea; the 1983 Cartagena Convention for the Caribbean Basin; and the 1986 Noumea Convention covering the South Pacific.

40. There has also been an increasing tendency towards North–South regional cooperation in the area of natural resources development and the protection of the environment. Such cooperation has led to an increasing number of multilateral conventions in this area. These are often aimed at a comprehensive, integrated, and intersectoral approach to fostering the objective of the protection of regional and global environmental resources. For an analysis of one such endeavour, see G. Ndi, 'EEC/ACP: Cooperation Towards Sustainable Development in the African ACPs', *Environmental Policy and Law*, **23**, 1 (Feb. 1993), 18.

and feasibility studies now form a prerequisite for the inception of petroleum development projects worldwide.[41] Environmental protection at the national level with regard to petroleum operations will tend to take the form of various regulatory instrument – general laws or specific environmental legislation; environmental regulations specifically designed for petroleum operations; environmental provisions in petroleum legislation; and environmental obligations contained in petroleum agreements.

Implementation measures and devices will generally range from periodic monitoring and assessment, the designation of 'safety' or 'security' zones around installations and platforms, and health and safety measures. Complementing these traditional command/control approaches to regulation will be other alternative measures aimed at encouraging environmental protection initiatives and higher levels of compliance from operators in the petroleum sector. These will normally include economic and fiscal incentives, and noncompliance disincentives.

Issues relating to compliance and enforcement lie at the heart of the implementation of environmental policies in the petroleum sector. Without adequate and proper monitoring and control, environmental protection initiatives tend to assume a formal but inconspicuous presence within the contractual, legal or regulatory framework. Effective monitoring and enforcement would require relevant expertise, administrative efficiency, political will, and professional as well as personal integrity and motivation on the part of the monitors. The absence of these policy components (as has mostly been the case in many developing countries and the transition societies of Russia, the CIS and Eastern Europe), could seriously compromise the effectiveness of national initiatives aimed at promoting environmentally sound and sustainable practices in the petroleum sector. In the absence of effective monitoring higher levels of noncompliance would without doubt ensue. Effectiveness in implementation and compliance can sometimes be fostered by external economic, financial and political leverage and pressures which may be exerted on the host government by donor organisations, financiers,[42] environmental pressure groups and NGOs. However, there is always the danger of a backlash if such pressures are perceived in the host country to be external dictates amounting to undue interference in domestic affairs. Criticism of externally generated pressures in the area of environmental protection has quite often focused attention on the possibly pervasive effects (or encroachment) of such pressures on national sovereignty.

Before concluding this section, it is worth drawing attention to the important issue of abandonment – i.e. the decommissioning of offshore petroleum instal-

41. The environmental obligations of petroleum companies will usually include the submission of independent environmental impact statements, comprehensive environmental management programmes, environmental bonds and guarantees to cover liability and the costs of remedial action or operations to repair or minimise oil pollution damage, the carrying out of environmental audits, the restoration of depleted petroleum acreage and the decommissioning of installations and other support facilities.

42. A good example to cite here would be 'green conditionalities' and other environmental protection safeguards attached to development finance, particularly in relation to the inception of mining – as well as oil and gas – development projects.

lations and platforms following the cessation of exploration, appraisal or production activities. This issue, which hitherto has been mostly limited to discussion within academic circles, is already assuming a practical relevance in some of the mature oil provinces such as the North Sea.[43] International law, as contained in Article 60(3) of UNCLOS and the IMO Guidelines and Standards of 1989, requires that there be either the complete or partial removal of off-shore installations following the termination of the search for or production of hydrocarbons.[44]

These international instruments are underpinned by policy considerations regarding the protection of the marine environment, the safety of navigation and shipping, and the protection of fisheries. National regimes regulating abandonment issues have already been developed in many of the industrialised countries including Australia, Canada, Germany, the Netherlands, Norway, the United Kingdom, and the United States.[45] The coming to maturity and incipient decline in production of oil and gas fields around the world will increasing raise questions of decommissioning and abandonment. It is therefore expected that abandonment issues will progressively acquire an increasing significance and prominence under national regulatory regimes and in international environmental law.

As with abandonment, the general tendency towards the adoption of international environmental standards in the oil and gas industries likewise has significant cost implications in terms of the introduction of appropriate technologies. At the downstream end of the industry, the application of pollution control standards through product specification could also entail a profound change in current consumption patterns. Increasingly, corporate policies and practices will tend to lay greater emphasis not only on the unobtrusiveness of exploration and production operations (making these as inconspicuous as possible when operating in populated areas), but also on local community involvement and participation in the design and implementation of environmental protection safeguards. Ultimately, the long-term accomplishment of environmental policy objectives in the oil and gas sector will depend on effective cooperation between the four principal set of actors: transnational resource companies, national governments, local communities, and NGOs.

---

43. This aspect of the protection of the marine environment with respect to petroleum operations has been given extensive coverage in a number of recent monographs. The principal ones among these are a series of articles appraising national abandonment regimes in the special issue of the *Journal of Energy and Natural Resources Law*, **10**, 1 (1992). For an analysis of comparative and international law aspects, as well as issues relating to compliance with, and enforcement of abandonment obligations, see various papers contained in *Topic 3, Energy & Resources Law '92, IBA-SERL Washington Conference Papers* (1992), 305–86. See also R. Higgins, 'Abandonment of Energy Sites and Structures: Relevant International Law', *Journal of Energy and Natural Resources Law*, **11**, 1 (1993), 6.

44. A considerable degree of confusion and uncertainty lingers as to the requirement for either *complete* or *partial* removal. The distinction between the two methods of decommissioning has significant practical, financial and costs implications. Whereas Article 5.5 of the 1958 Geneva Convention on the Continental Shelf requires '*entire*' removal, both Article 60(3) of UNCLOS and the guidelines set by IMO envisage the possibility of *partial* removal only – hence the confusion. It remains largely unclear as to which of these provisions can be said to be representative of customary international law. For a discussion of both the 1958 Convention and UNCLOS provisions dealing with the issue of abandonment, see R. Higgins, *supra*, note 43, pp. 7–10.

45. Cf. Special issue of the *Journal of Energy and Natural Resources Law*, **10**, 2 (1992).

1.6 IMPLICATIONS OF CURRENT TRENDS IN INTERNATIONAL PETROLEUM INVESTMENT FOR THE DEVELOPING COUNTRIES

The prospect of the opening up of Russia and the CIS to international petroleum investment, with the massive potential in exploration acreage and investment opportunities involved, has without doubt ushered in a new era of even more intense competition for scarce capital and technological resources required for the development of petroleum resources.[46] Developments in Russia and the CIS are thus influencing and, as far as we can see, will continue to dictate the pace and pattern of international oil and gas investment for quite some time to come. The range of investment opportunities either available or potentially on offer in Russia and the CIS – new acreage licensing, rehabilitation of old projects, joint ventures, and privatisation – is likely to take up much of the limited pool of investment capital and risk/project finance funds available internationally. The consequence of this will be that financing for petroleum exploration and development projects in developing countries will become ever more difficult to secure, notwithstanding that individual national geological prospects and investment conditions on offer will have to compete on their own merit.

Presented with a wide range of choices, transnational resource companies are more likely than ever to be applying far more rigorous selection and prioritisation criteria for the allocation of investment funds internationally. Such criteria will most likely include but are not limited to the following: geological prospects and potential, investment (contractual, legal, fiscal and other operational) conditions, and the level of technical, political and commercial risks associated with a given project or country.

How will the developing countries respond to this unfolding situation? Will it lead to the intensification of the restructuring and privatisation drive for key SPEs as a means of attracting inward foreign investment and loan capital for petroleum development? And are we likely to see an emerging new dimension to South–South international economic relations in which developing country SPEs increasingly expand their petroleum exploration and production activities into other developing countries? Indications are that the latter is already well underway with a growing number of SPEs increasingly embarking on overseas ventures in the upstream sector in other developing countries. It is also quite likely that in some cases (as in Argentina following the privatisation of public sector energy enterprises), indigenous private oil and gas companies could emerge. Which ever option or combination of options is chosen, the expected intensification of the competition for scarce investment funds implies that in future the promotion of national investment opportunities is by no means going to be an easily accomplished task.

There is also the issue of environmental regulation. What form will it take in developing countries? This group of countries are known to be unreceptive to

---

46. Cf. 'The Competition for Capital Intensifies', *Petroleum Intelligence Weekly* (Extra Edition: Special Supplement Issue), 15 March 1993, p. 1.

the idea of the globalisation of responsibility for current – but delayed – environmental impacts of past industrial activities which took place in the developed countries. They would rather that Western countries – known both for advocating environmental protection policies and for the highest energy-intensity consumption and intensity of environmental use *per capita* in the world today – should be paying for the environmental programmes desired. The developing countries likewise do not seem to be much persuaded by the advocacy of stringent environmental safeguards. The implementation of such safeguards would inevitably place limits on the drive towards economic development and industrialisation, the achievement of which is perceived by developing countries to be the key to genuine economic and political sovereignty.

The resolution of the conflict between environmental protection and economic/industrial development (the environment *versus* development debate) entails the search for compromise solutions. The principle of sustainable development has already gone some way towards accommodating the environmental component into economic, natural resources and industrial development strategy. In the upstream petroleum sector, a comparable concept to the principles of sustainability and optimal stewardship may be found in the condition requiring 'good oilfield practice' which usually accompanies the granting of production rights. A further principle developed at the UNCED 'Earth Summit' held in Rio de Janeiro in June 1992,[47] that of *common but differentiated responsibility* for current but delayed environmental impacts, also appears to have been the result of a compromise measure, the objective of which is to assign to developing countries a lesser responsibility and burden for the mitigation of environmental phenomena such as global warming and the depletion of the ozone layer.

With specific reference to petroleum development activities, the implementation of environmental protection measures in developing countries will tend to depend on the willingness of the particular country in question to trade environmental objectives against economic (petroleum) development goals. It will tend to depend likewise on the costs and benefits (financial, social, or environmental) involved in the control and minimisation of environmental damage through the incorporation of environmental criteria into petroleum development policies. Already, the steady growth of environmental policies and legislation in developing countries points ineluctably towards a much greater future role for environmental protection objectives in the design and implementation of petroleum development policies – without which the long-term future of reserves and of other natural resources and heritage could be seriously compromised by the unsustainable and environmentally damaging practices of unregulated operators. Inevitably, the articulation and implementation of environmental policies in the petroleum sector will tend to settle for those solutions which offer the highest environmental benefits for relatively little costs or investment.

In our view, three main issues will continue to shape the evolution of the

47. The texts of the UNCED documents are published in *International Law Materials*, 31, 4 (1992), 814.

petroleum industry in developing countries in the foreseeable future: these are the issues of restructuring and privatisation (already well underway in one form or another in many developing and some of the ex-socialist countries); the environment; and changing patterns in international petroleum investment brought about by the gradual opening up of Russia, the CIS and Eastern Europe to the international petroleum industry. There can be no doubt that each of these issues has global implications which in turn will continue to impact strongly and directly on the petroleum sector in developing countries for some time to come.

1.7 CONCLUDING REMARKS

The global prospects for international petroleum investment are as exhilarating as they are challenging. The ex-socialist countries, and to a certain extent large areas of the developing countries (Africa in particular) which remain either unexplored or poorly explored in the sense that modern exploration techniques and concepts are yet to be applied with any degree of consistency, present both opportunities and difficulties. Opportunities for petroleum investment are also opening up in still socialist countries such as China, Cuba, Mongolia and Vietnam.

The magnitude of the investment commitments and entrepreneurial resources required are considerable. The difficulties to be overcome, and the risks involved, are quite substantial: political, commercial, technological, cultural, and environmental. How will the international petroleum industry respond to these opportunities and challenges, many of which are not totally unfamiliar to the industry?[48] Will current political uncertainties and instability in many of these transition societies be viewed by the industry simply as a political risk factors *per se* and thus an impediment to investment, or as a precursor to democratic progress and ensuing political stability? As the current situation unfolds, there can be no doubt but that the international petroleum industry is clearly entering a new and critical phase in its ongoing evolution, but not one which is entirely devoid of excitement and the promise of potential rewards.

On the domestic front, the growing demands for the involvement of local communities in the inception and development stages of natural resources projects signals a new dimension to the PSNR concept. In countries as far afield as Australia, Brazil, Colombia, Ecuador, Peru, Nigeria, Papua New Guinea, and Thailand, local communities are increasingly advocating local involvement (or are already exerting some measure of influence) regarding the formulation of petroleum or mining development policies. Particular areas which have been targeted by these communities include the distribution of benefits and environmental issues (ecological and socio-cultural impacts).[49] In

48. See 'New Realities Challenge International Oil and Gas', *Petroleum Intelligence Weekly* (Extra Edition: Special Supplement Issue), 15 March 1993, 1– 2.

49. The socio-cultural impacts of natural resources development on local communities in developing countries are discussed in K. Tumsah, Mineral Operations in the Developing Countries: A Socio-economic and Legal Analysis of its Impact on the Communities, LL.M Dissertation, Centre for Petroleum and Mineral Law and Policy, University of Dundee (1992).

Russia and the CIS, competition between central and regional authorities over the direction of petroleum development policies has become so intense that it frequently overshadows other policy issues. Dealing with such delicate matters of domestic politics will in future require a great deal of tact and skillful negotiations on the part of transnational resource companies.

As the petroleum industry prepares to enter this new phase (and into the twenty-first century), international regulation of the industry, and of the transnational investment process in general, is becoming ever more of a necessity. This is in view mainly of the prevailing uncertainty and confusion surrounding the precise status of the norms and principles of international law which purport to govern transnational economic relations. Recent contributions to efforts at international regulation include the European Energy Charter, the objective of which is to promote private sector investment in the oil and gas industries of the ex-socialist countries,[50] and the World Bank's Legal Framework for the Treatment of Foreign Investment.[51]

The growing consistency in the practice of states with regard to investment promotion and protection signals the unsatisfactory outcome of previously restrictive attitudes. There is, however, always a danger of 'overshooting' with respect to the investment promotion and protection issue, with the result that agreements could increasingly be concluded under investment conditions which could not be sustained over the long term. If such a scenario were to unfold, the agreements of today could in future be perceived in some quarters as the 'bad deals' of yesterday, thus rapidly setting in motion once more unilateral state actions aimed at altering negotiated terms and established investment conditions. Hence, as the international petroleum industry moves into its farthest outposts, it is necessary for the long-term stability of essential investment conditions that a framework of uniform and widely accepted principles governing foreign investment protection in general should be evolved. Within the context of such a framework, it is equally essential that overseas investment in the oil and gas industries should be seen to have a role to play in the economic, industrial and social development of host countries – in accordance with the underlying principles of mutual benefit and economic equality on which such investments are grounded.

50. The Charter, when signed, will create international law obligations for Russia and the other CIS States with regard to private sector investment by overseas companies for the development of the natural resources of these countries. See Annex II, *infra* for the full text of the Charter.

51. The 'Guidelines', which cover four main areas – the admission, treatment, and expropriation of foreign investment, and the settlement of investment disputes – are also intended to assist in the progressive development of international law in this area. See Annex I, *infra* for the full text of the Guidelines.

Chapter 2

Structuring Legal Relationships in Oil and Gas Exploration and Development in 'Frontier' Countries

Sheila Slocum Hollis and John W. Berresford

2.1 INTRODUCTION

We live at an extraordinarily vibrant and challenging moment in international oil and gas law. Communism has fallen and free-market principles have triumphed in formerly 'Second'- and 'Third-World' countries. This turn of history has opened vast geological prospects which call like a siren to the 'First' World's petroleum business to discover (or rediscover) and assess formerly sequestered frontier areas.

'Frontier' countries usually need the capital and expertise of foreign petroleum companies. Only with them can a frontier country earn revenues from petroleum exports to finance its own development and meet its own domestic energy needs. At the same time, international oil companies and smaller entrepreneurial operations face relatively unpromising vistas in their home countries. Their economies are stubbornly in a low-growth mode, their largest domestic fields have been mostly exploited, and environmental restrictions may severely limit new domestic exploration and production. Both their need for a *raison d'être* and their stockholders drive them abroad to search for more lucrative opportunities.

Yet the very forces which propel the business into frontier countries may blind the careless to the dangers there. The laws of risk and reward, of profit and loss, and of human nature operate the world over as inexorably as the law of gravity. On every investment, wherever made there must be a potential rate of return commensurate with the risk. Profit-driven enterprise must protect its capital sunk into new projects from loss; although a perfect record of success is unattainable, over time there must be more wins than losses.

In this chapter, we report how international petroleum companies are maximising profit opportunities and minimising risk of loss today in frontier countries, and especially in the largest of them, Russia.

2.2 THE FRONTIERS

There are really two frontiers. There is, of course, the 'geological' frontier – subsoil to be explored and tested for petroleum resources. Locating and developing promising fields in this type of frontier country is usually difficult and complicated. It requires large amounts of capital, equipment, and technical and managerial skills, as well as inordinate amounts of flexibility and perseverance. And even the best exploration may still result in a non-commercial discovery or a dry hole.

But there is also another frontier, the political and legal, the primary focus of this chapter, equally important and potentially far more vexing. These frontier countries confront the oil and gas business with a combination of legal risks that challenge even the most aggressive exploration and production company.[1]

The 'old' exclusionary ways may be discredited there, but new ones have not been charted (much less travelled). Often, frontier governments simply forbade all foreign investment until recently. In communist countries 'home grown' capital simply did not exist; the very idea was heresy. Petroleum resources were objects of national pride, not to be sold, but to be used as a weapon in a geopolitical struggle. Both colonial history and the Marxist ideology to which it gave birth taught that no good could come from promoting foreign investment in 'the system'. Many frontier governments' only history of dealing with foreign businesses was one of a few unique agreements made in a legal vacuum.

Commonly, there were also hostile taxation, restrictions on the repatriation of profits and equipment, and corruption at many levels. When politics, personnel or moods in a frontier government changed, so often did laws or agreements, unilaterally. Larger political changes could endanger not only capital and equipment, but also personnel.

The exploration and production decisions of the typical frontier government were driven by the gigantism of dictators[2] and techniques to boost short-term production in ways that often destroyed the country's resources in the long term. Decisions about investment and pricing were often made without regard to their full cost or real profit. Indeed, no information about cost or profit *existed* because they were unimportant to the government's goal – keeping production high enough to supply a vast military complex and to heat the population 'for free'. In recent years, physical infrastructure in many countries, if it existed at all, became outdated and deteriorated, including both drilling rigs and pipelines.

Political frontier countries are only beginning to wake up from this nightmare. The obvious tools for self-improvement – capital, skills, and

---

1.   Geological and political frontiers are not mutually exclusive, of course. Some countries offer both, and consequently a relatively high-risk profile, to the petroleum exploration and production company.

2.   Most of the vast industrial projects begun by frontier governments were never 'profitable' by any standard. According to one observer, the government's major motivation in them was 'to keep the masses occupied, to give them something to do, while reducing them to a subsistence existence in which the human spirit ceased to exist.' R. Kaplan, 'Balkan Ghosts: A Journey Through History', (1993), 102–3.

equipment – are seldom at hand. Business infrastructure, such as telecommunications, accounting, and banking, is often primitive and unpredictable.[3]

Developed legal systems and an independent judiciary to enforce contracts and protect private property are rare. There is nothing comparable to centuries of caselaw to support even a basic legal concept like property.

For example, when you buy land, what does ownership mean? How do you establish your ownership? Often, there is nothing like our Recorder of Deeds offices, literally nowhere to establish title or record a mortgage. In the absence of a reliable recordation system, how can you be sure that the people who sold it to you owned it in the first place? How do they establish their ownership? And, if it can be owned, is it subject to government-run privatisation that will nullify any private transactions made today? Are you liable for pre-existing toxic wastes (which, if they exist, are unrecorded because there was no environmental watchdog)?

Free market ideas may still be somewhat suspect, if not unreal, in countries that have known only central control superimposed on a pre-industrial society. Governments (often several claiming the same authority) issue laws that often cannot be reliably understood, reconciled, or enforced.

Bureaucracies may be risk-averse and set in non-business-oriented patterns;  even newly 'privatised' governmental operations are little better. In the absence of antitrust enforcement (which all frontier countries lack), a newly 'privatised' company which used to be part of the bureaucracy is freed from whatever public or political control there once was, and can combine the worst of two worlds, an unregulated profit-maximising monopoly accountable to no one.

This is the psychological and historical reality of many frontier countries. Any western business could be forgiven for hesitating to plunge into such difficulties.

But wars, as Churchill said, are not won by evacuations. Risks must be confronted and overcome. Those who overcome them will own 'The Prize' of the twenty-first century.[4]

You can, too, see bright torches if you turn from the background of history to the foreground of recent events. The triumph of Boris Yeltsin and his economic reform programme over the Parliament in the popular vote this past April, the opening of even Vietnam to foreign investment and local entrepreneurship, and the emergence of a civil society seemingly from its grave in the Czech Republic, Hungary, and Poland, are testaments to the

---

3.   The primary function of most banks in frontier countries was to sort paper money. In many frontier countries, there are no wire transfers, checking accounts, letters of credit, signature guarantees, deposit insurance or regulation, and no concept of fiduciary duty. In one frontier country in Eastern Europe, the largest denomination of currency is worth about five dollars, and there is a saying that in order to buy a car you need a truck – to carry the cash.

4.   Daniel Yergin, in his Pulitzer Prize winning book *The Prize: The Epic Quest for Oil, Money, and Power*, states that 'petroleum remains the motivating force of industrial society and the lifeblood of the civilization that it helped create. It is still the basis for the world's biggest business, one that embodies the extremes of risk and reward, as well as the interplay and conflict ... between private business and the nation-state. It also remains ... an essential element in national power, a major factor in world economies, a critical focus for war and conflict, and a decisive force in international affairs. (D. Yergin, *The Prize* (1992), pp. 779–81.

eternal vitality of market motivations and human hope. In Bulgaria, one of the closest Soviet 'satellites', government statistics (drawn from the old state-run industries) show continual decline but, according to one resident, every family is running a small business out of its kitchen.

The eventual outcome is in sight, and the intellectual battle is over. Frontier governments will ultimately welcome foreign capital, technology, skills, teaching, and outsiders. Only with this influx will they build the foundations for a prosperous life for their citizens and eventual membership in the 'first' world.

In the oil and gas arena in particular, a frontier government has two related principal motives: first, to begin (or revive) domestic production so the country is self-sufficient in energy and can sell any surplus to foreigners for 'hard currency' (dollars, deutschmarks, and yen); and, second, to obtain a revenue stream from petroleum development as soon as possible through royalties, bonuses, production payments, or otherwise.

This chapter will examine the major issues, pitfalls, and new ideas in drafting and negotiating basic international petroleum agreements. We will point out the available tools for minimising the major risks. Careful negotiation aided by skilled counsel, prescient drafting of legal instruments, and insurance in many forms are irreplaceable. While they cannot remove all risks, they can reduce them to the point where investment in frontier countries is prudent. Without these protections, however, no company should expose a significant amount of its assets to risk inherent in a frontier country.

More important for the future, basic agreements can also create mechanisms for dealing with the problems that are likely to arise in an evolving new venture, and they can start a relationship between the international petroleum exploration and development company and its frontier partners that foster mutual respect, commitment, compromise, and profit.

Examples of frontier countries that may be of great interest include Russia and the other Russian Federation members, Vietnam, Sudan, Guatemala, Columbia, China, Indonesia, Somalia and Laos. Of course, each of these has its own unique geological, political, legal, economic and other 'make or break' risks. This chapter will describe the problems, and some of the solutions, that they all have in common. We will also emphasise Russia because it is considered by many to be the most plentiful in resources, has the most fluid political and legal frontiers, and demonstrates the gamut of business opportunities and legal and political dangers that await the unwary.

2.2.1 Russia

Russia's oil and gas complex collapsed with the fall in world petroleum prices in the late 1980s.[5] Oil output has been dropping ever since – last year, to a level 25 per cent below that of 1987. By mid-1993, 30,000 oil wells had been shut in. There is even talk of the country, which was once the world's largest exporter

---

5.   See D. Remnick, *Lenin's Tomb* (1993), 24, 199.

of oil, having to import it in the near future. Meanwhile, the government maintains prices for oil and gas at a fraction of world market prices. this makes for domestic tranquility but waste.[6] Much of the world's CO_2 emissions are reportedly a result of the release of natural gas from broken, faulty pipelines throughout the country, and some estimate that 25–30 per cent of all natural gas product is simply lost through leakage.

Last year, to revive the country's production, President Yeltsin adopted a plan which he believed would, over three years, unleash the petroleum industry from the old state monopoly he inherited from the Soviet era. Initially the government would act through its existing wholly owned subsidiaries; later, it would invest in new ones as part of a decentralisation plan. Complementing Yelsin's efforts, reformers in the Parliament attempted to enact an Oil and Gas Law.[7] This Law was supposed to enhance the existing Law on Underground Resources to encourage foreign investment, and to make that statute more specific about oil and gas issues.

Yelsin's and the reformers' general goal is to privatise Soviet-era production entities; to create a comprehensive and rational licensing system for the country's oil and gas, such as through a government body resembling U.S. New Deal regulatory agencies or state public-utility commissions; to have that body license exploration, development, and export of oil and gas to private parties; and to enact a tax regime for petroleum that would stimulate long-term investment.

To date, Yeltsin and his allies have been thoroughly stymied by the conservatives. The Parliament, the recently 'privatised' government corpora tion Rosneft, production associations, and the bureaucracy have fought liberalisation, privatisation, market pricing and predictability.[8]

Since Yeltsin's victory at the polls in April, the long-term outlook has brightened; the conservatives seem to have been routed and they and the military seem to have accepted the voters' verdict. Few concrete results can be expected, however, until a new legislature is installed and passes a reformist Oil and Gas Law (mid-1994 at the earliest, realistically). Informally, we are advised that significant progress is being made.

During all these political struggles in Moscow, much authority has been ceded to regional and local government units. Russia contains a total of 88 political subdivisions (not counting municipalities), each of which can tolerably claim authority to legislate concerning, and to tax, petroleum-related activities. Some officials there have become very sophisticated about the worldwide

---

6. A Russian acquaintance of one of the authors reports that because natural gas for home heating is still basically free, and the material used in bookbindings from the last years of the Soviet Union produce unpleasant odours in enclosed spaces, he routinely keeps his library windows open and the heat on full blast throughout the Russian winter.

7. See, e.g. M. Kh. Gazeyev, 'Conceptional Provisions of the Draft of the Law on Oil and Gas of the Russian Federation', E.I. Gostilovich and I.I. Kondratenko, 'The Law on Oil and Gas', 10 November, 1992, Papers presented at the University of Houston Law Center Conference on Russian Petroleum Legislation.

8. Unresponsive government and bureaucracy in Russia pre-date communism. See N. Gogol, *Dead Souls*, (1961), 159–73.

competition by all frontier countries for investment by foreign companies and are seeking inducements for foreign company investment.

Aside from the triumph of Yeltsin and the reformers, the greatest reason for long-term optimism is the significance of petroleum to the country. Russia's reserves of oil may be larger than many 'oil-rich' nations, and its gas reserves appear many times larger still. It is one of the world's last great oil and gas frontiers, and may be *the* last great geological frontier. The development of these reserves is the fastest way for Russia to earn desperately needed hard currency and, in the longer term, the key to its full membership in the world economic system.[9]

It may be unwise, however, for foreign petroleum investors to move before the Russian legal framework is clearer than it is today. Unresolved, for example, is whether foreign companies may do such basic things as own land or a long leasehold interest in it. Details of repatriation of profits and participation in privatisation remain uncertain. Foreign companies that moved to the blandishments of eager advisors earlier have reportedly regretted it. The troubled operations of the White Nights venture in Siberia earlier this year have been only the most publicised sign of the risks of premature investment.

Fortunately, there is time to wait; the overwhelming majority of Russia's oil and gas are unclaimed by foreign investors.

2.2.2 Kazakhstan and the Asian Republics

In the face of uncertainties in Russia, many international petroleum companies have turned to its neighbours, the other former members of the Soviet Union, and are investing in Kazakhstan, Kirgizstan, Tadzhikistan, Turkmenistan and Uzbekistan. Certainly, at the present moment they offer a more inviting prospect to the foreign investor. These Asian nations have resources that offer attractive alternatives to Russia's; and they are generally not burdened with Russia's political problems, its history of hostility to private enterprise, or its hold over central bureaucracy.

These countries quickly enacted laws concerning corporations, foreign investment, repatriation, and taxation that in many cases are more enticing than Russia's. In the field of currency reform, one, Kirgizstan, has already broken away from the ruble and is establishing its own currency regime.

The most popular of the former USSR Republics is Kazakhstan, whose government has proved far more welcoming to foreign investment than Russia's. A 1992 study of a hypothetical oil field in Russia, and Kazakhstan showed annual post-tax returns on investment of 10 per cent and 32 per cent, respectively (and 25 per cent for the United States). The striking advantage of Kazakhstan was due largely to its simpler legal system, including a comprehensible approval process and lower petroleum taxes.[10] Chevron, for

---

9.   The other obvious available means for Russia to obtain large amounts of hard currency quickly are to sell nuclear weapons to other countries.

10.   These legal measures were produced largely through the pressure of Kazakhstan's President, Nursultan Nazarbayev.

example, became involved in Kazakhstan five years ago and is now exporting oil.

Kazakhstan and the other identified countries really resemble Arab countries more than they do Russia. Compared to the Russians, they are short on hidebound, multi-layered political establishments. Their people do not expect permanent employment, free energy, and nurturing by an all-powerful state. Thus, doing a deal is simpler and free from a great deal of political baggage. From their recent history, they also appear to have governments and peoples that are willing to allow foreigners in on hospitable terms to develop their resources, untraumatised by any resentment at 'selling the family silver'.[11]

2.3 BASIC LEGAL ARRANGEMENTS FOR PETROLEUM VENTURES IN HOST COUNTRIES

2.3.1 Procedure for choosing the foreign company

Once a system is in place and awards of leases are no longer undertaken on an *ad hoc,* case-by-case basis, host governments usually award petroleum exploration and development contracts through a competitive bidding system. The winner is usually the company that promises the greatest revenue flow to the host government. Upon being chosen, the winner generally pays an initial bonus to the awarding government.

Because bidding requires competition among bidders if it is to benefit the host government, it is not used much in countries where few bids can be expected due to political risk, uninviting geography, or a small chance of a 'commercial' discovery (one that is big enough to make production profitable). In such situations, private negotiations between the host government and foreign companies are used.

Awards based solely on financial criteria do not allow room for other factors that can weigh heavily with host governments. A host government may also want to consider which foreign company will best serve its needs for employment of its citizens, association with its domestic petroleum companies, use of locally manufactured equipment or other materials, and sales of produced petroleum in the host country at low prices. Or, the host government may give a preference in bidding to, or impose a set-aside for, local investors or production associations which lack the capital and other resources of foreign companies.

After picking one of the foreign companies as the winner, the host government conducts detailed negotiations with the winning bidder about many major structural aspects of the venture that were not covered in the bidding. (During the bidding process, too, negotiations can occur as a practical matter by the government asking the foreign company to explain or amplify

---

11. To be sure, these countries have their share of problems – for example, the recent rebellion and emergency evacuations in nearby Azerbaijan.

parts of its bid. Libya, for example, conducts negotiations throughout the bidding process.)

Topics to be covered include the type of contract in which the agreement between the host government and the foreign company will be embodied; the specific territory to be explored and/or developed; ownership of geologic data developed during exploration; the foreign company's right to take petroleum and money out of the host country ('repatriation'); security for the foreign company against major political change in the host country; the duration of the contract; all sorts of payments to the host government (bonuses, taxes, etc.); 'discovery' and 'appraisal' clauses and the foreign company's right to 'relinquishment'; the work programme; dispute resolution; the extent of the host government's participation in the venture; training and use of host country personnel; ownership of equipment used in the venture; and environmental matters.

These negotiations conclude in the execution of a 'basic agreement' setting forth those details. These basic agreements often call for the negotiation of a subsequent 'operating' agreement to spell out more day-to-day details of how the venture will be conducted; and for the creation of a corporation under the laws of the host government through which the foreign company will conduct the venture.

Russia

In Russia as in some other frontier countries, a mixture of bidding and negotiation is now used. Bidding is often used to narrow the field to a few contestants, like a trial heat; then negotiations with the foreign companies that submitted the best bids are used to 'bid them up' against each other.

Deals made under the former regime of negotiation came under a cloud when the Russian Federation's Underground Resources Law was enacted, which prohibits negotiations. Whether the Law is retroactive is still unclear.

Russia's law and politics have been so confusing in the last few years that it has been difficult for foreign companies to know who 'the government' is that they are supposed to be bidding to or negotiating with. Which part of the federal government in Moscow? A ministry, a committee, or the Parliament itself? Or do you start with a provincial government? Or do you bypass the government (initially, at least) and start with the private sector (which may know more about which governmental body to approach)? But the distinction between 'government' and 'business' is often blurry because until recently everything was government.

One theory is to involve all of them, if not to join the venture, at least to review and approve of it. This reduces the risk of missing a key player, but of course involves a lot of unnecessary parties who have little to offer but will want something in return for their approval. Another approach is to go to the Parliament; this took one foreign company a full year but may prove worth the effort in enabling it to by-pass lower echelons. Yet a third approach is to conclude an agreement with one level of government quickly and then try to present the others with a *fait accompli* – a dangerous course in a society where bureaucratic turf protection is an art form.

2.3.2 Forms of arrangement between host governments and foreign companies

Once the foreign company is chosen, negotiations for a basic agreement occur between it and the host government about details of the venture that were not spelled out in the bidding or negotiation process. These negotiations usually begin with fitting the venture into one of several basic forms of arrangement.

In the nineteenth century, international petroleum contracts took one form, 'concessions', in which host governments granted to foreign corporations the right to explore, produce, and market petroleum as they wished. In some cases, the foreigners were granted almost governmental authority over huge territories in the host countries. The host government received payment in the form of a rent, royalty, tax, or fee, which was always in the form of cash or gold (not petroleum) and was often considerable. This payment, however, did not vary with the speed, size, cost, or results of the venture; all these risks and rewards were on the foreign company.

Starting in the 1930s, host countries wanted more control over their resources than the early concessions allowed. Most of them enacted petroleum statutes – many are still on the books – that grant to the government absolute dominion and control over petroleum, minerals, and everything else under the earth's surface. Additional legislation often delegates the authority to negotiate agreements about petroleum exploration and development to a government ministry or government-owned 'corporation'. The government, or the ministry or corporation, has the exclusive right to exploit the petroleum resources within its borders. Until recently, host countries were unwilling to diminish this absolute control. Examples of such laws are the Russian Federation's Law on Underground Resources, enacted in 1992 by the old Soviet-era Parliament; Article 33 of Indonesia's 1945 Constitution and its 1960 Oil Law; and Article 27 of Mexico's 1917 Constitution.

Under these laws, there were four basic forms of contractual arrangements: modern concessions, production-sharing contracts, service contracts, and risk-service contracts. All of them give the host country more involvement and control than the traditional concession, but each makes a slightly different allocation of authority, risk, and revenue between the state and the foreign company.

Modern concessions

In the modern concession, the host government usually acts through its energy ministry or state-owned corporation. Through one of these arms, the government still makes a basic grant of authority to the foreign company, but imposes numerous terms and conditions. Typically, the government approves and then supervises the foreign company's development plan, budget, and work programme. These conditions involve the host government in the foreign company's activities to such a large degree that what results is really a kind of partnership between the two. In essence, the host government and the foreign company agree that they will jointly explore for petroleum and, if the exploration proves fruitful, they will jointly produce it.

The foreign company assumes the risks of both a dry hole and political instability. The parties agree that if petroleum is found, they will create a new legal entity that will produce the petroleum. Any petroleum that is found will be owned by the new entity, not by the host country. The entity's profits will be distributed according to each party's participation in it. Sometimes the host government's profits will be in the form of cash, sometimes in the form of produced petroleum (which it can, of course, sell and convert into cash).

Production-sharing contracts

Production-sharing contracts, first used in Indonesia in 1966, allow the host government to exercise still more control over the foreign company than the modern concession. They leave in the govern's hands the exclusive right to exploration and production.

The host government merely hires the foreign company to perform certain services (exploration and production), typically laying down many conditions on the foreign company's work. The foreign company, being a mere hired hand rather than a partner, is in less of a position to control operations than it is in a concession arrangement. In Indonesia, for example, the state-owned oil and gas company Pertamina requires the foreign company to submit for approval a work plan including budgets, employment plans, and numerous performance schedules.

Typically, the foreign company must also spend a specified amount on seismic tests and exploration drilling; and all the equipment that the foreign company uses in the venture becomes the property of the host government. The foreign company is also required to pay the host government a cash 'discovery bonus' upon the discovery of a commercial petroleum reservoir. This bonus is not as onerous on the foreign company as it may sound, because it is payable only when it is reasonably certain that the venture will produce revenue.

The foreign company's compensation for being a hired hand is a stated percentage of whatever petroleum is eventually produced. Payment in the form of petroleum spares the host government the burden of paying hard currency, which is typically in short supply in host governments' treasuries. The foreign company sells its percentage share of the produced petroleum and thus makes money. The cash flow from these sales, of course, must be enough to compensate it for the costs of its exploration and development activities, its equipment, the discovery bonus, and a risk premium reflecting the venture's overall risk.

Some production-sharing contracts reduce the foreign company's risk by providing that all revenue from sales of produced petroleum will go to the foreign company until it has recovered its exploration and development costs, including equipment and overhead. Some host countries, including Nigeria, limit such costs to 'reasonable' amounts, such as by defining overhead as a percentage of actual operating costs. Only after the foreign company's authorised costs have been recovered are revenues divided between it and the host government according to the previously agreed percentages. Even in such relatively generous arrangements, however, the foreign company receives no revenue in the event of a dry hole and, in the mean time, it runs the risk of political instability.

Service contracts

Service contracts are a variation of casting the foreign company as the hired hand of the host government. The foreign company is retained to perform specific services or limited technical assistance to the host government. For its limited services, the foreign company receives a fixed fee, often in the form of set amount of petroleum.

Because of its limited nature, service contracts are used mostly for lower-risk production activities, not for higher-risk exploration. Foreign companies are shy of them because of the low-risk, low-reward ratio, especially the lack of rights to a percentage of the produced petroleum.

Risk-service contracts

Risk-service contracts allow the foreign company only to explore a specific area in the host country and evaluate its discovery potential. The foreign company pays all the expenses of its exploration at its own risk; it receives no payment unless a commercial discovery is made and production results. In that event, the foreign company receives payment for its services (and its initial risk). It may choose to receive its fee in the form of petroleum but, as with service contracts, the foreign company has no rights to exploit any reservoir it found.

Risk-service contracts are popular with Latin American governments, such as Mexico, which prefer to maintain total control over production.

Russia

Despite Russia's problems described above, adventurous members of the international petroleum and financial communities are making petroleum deals and extending credit. In June, the *New York Times* reported that Mobil and six other international companies had signed agreements to develop fields in the Caspian Sea. The World Bank pledged its largest credit facility ever – $610 million – for the repair and improvement of oil fields and equipment in western Siberia. The Export–Import Bank and the International Finance Corporation have made similar moves. Commercial banks, mainly in Europe, are also said to be willing to lend. It is doubtful, however, that many foreign companies will risk significant capital in Russia until its legal and political framework becomes more full and stable. The records of Russian authorities are filled with documents 'registering' ventures that have not yet come to life as functioning businesses.

Most Russian deals are announced as 'joint ventures', a general term of unclear legal significance under Russian law. Most of them appear to be production-sharing arrangements, with modern concessions being the second most common. Occidental Petroleum has exported oil from Western Siberia as part of production-sharing agreement in which it is providing technology to a Russian production association; Occidental receives 50 per cent of the produced petroleum. Enron Corporation and Gazprom, the Russian government's gas company, have an arrangement which contemplates Enron exporting natural gas for sale in Europe. Many Russian ventures call for the first step to be exploration, or a seismic or economic feasibility study, at the end of which the parties will make a go-no-go decision about a more substantial production venture.

Some ventures take account of Russia's falling production by giving the foreign company a percentage of the increased production (or of the production above a stated 'worst case' scenario of decline). The foreign companies in the White Nights venture, for example, plan to split 'enhanced production' 50–50.

One foreign company, Elf Acquitaine has entered into a production-sharing contract that calls for both exploration and production, and has noted that by undertaking the relatively risky step of exploration (which it didn't think was all that risky, given Russia's reserves), it was able to win favourable provisions for the production stage. Specifically, it will be able to control production without local partners (while splitting the produced petroleum with the government). According to press sources, the company

would have a 30-year production period during which the state would receive 12.5 per cent of the oil as a royalty, and Elf would get 55 per cent to recover its expenses. The remaining oil would be split on a sliding scale, with the Russian government initially getting 60 percent of the remainder and eventually getting 85 percent.[12]

Russian Oil Minister Shafranik is said to favour such production contracts.

Foreign companies in Russian petroleum ventures avoid qualifying themselves to do business in Russia; generally, they form a subsidiary, which is a new legal entity under Russian law, to perform the activities called for. It is the new Russian-domiciled entity that will hold any licences, operate in Russia, and receive compensation from the venture. There are, predictably, many forms of business entity under present Russian law. The advantages and disadvantages of each are beyond the scope of this article, but practitioners will be unsurprised to learn that the pluses and minuses of each form involve liability (both financial and environmental), taxation, ease of formation and licensure, and ease of assignment (both to affiliates and, as security, to sources of financing).[13]

2.4 LEGAL ISSUES IN NEGOTIATING BASIC AGREEMENTS

A choice of form of the international petroleum venture merely sets some of the bounds for negotiation, within which the parties exercise their strengths over a number of issues.

---

12. 'In an Oil Rush to the East, Elf Plays Pied Piper', *New York Times*, 27 June, 1993, at F-7, referencing *Petroleum Intelligence Weekly*.

13. For unusually comprehensive reviews of Russian corporate forms for petroleum ventures, see 'Evaluating Western Siberian Oil, Gas Opportunities – Deals', *Oil and Gas Journal*, 22 February 1993, 66; and Elena Kirilova, 'Current Developments in Russian Natural Resources Law' Paper presented at 24th Biennial Conference of the International Bar Association, 20–5 September, 1992.

2.4.1 The parties' basic bargaining positions

The host government has economic and other motives. Like any seller, it wants to sell, but only at a profit-maximising price. Its short- and long-term profit-maximising interests may conflict. In the short term, it wants the greatest possible revenue, which it can achieve by relinquishing all rights for the largest immediate cash flow from foreign companies. But in the long term it will realise more by retaining control over its natural resources (which are often a large part of its national wealth), and by participating in any exploration and production venture as a full-fledged, profit-entitled partner of the foreign petroleum company.

The host government's non-economic motives are also to keep control of its resources, lest its people see it as a sell-out of a national treasure to foreigners. Usually, it also wants to gain as much as it can for its people in terms of employment, training in petroleum skills, and use of local businesses. Finally, it wants the foreign company to be as committed as possible to the host country and to petroleum development in it.

The foreign company, for its part, wants the ability to back out if what it finds in the host country is small or unattractive compared with other opportunities that exist at the end of its exploration. But, if a commercial reservoir is found, it wants a large reward, probably in the form of long and exclusive production rights to as much of the produced petroleum as it can bargain for. Only with such secure, long-term rights will the foreign company feel safe into the twenty first century. So, in the best of all possible worlds, the foreign company wants the maximum long-term opportunities with minimal commitment (and risk) of capital, equipment, talent and time now.

Focusing on the parties' relative bargaining power, the host country's is least (and the foreign company's is greatest) in the pre-exploration stage, when it is uncertain whether the host country actually has anything to sell (commercial petroleum deposits). At this stage the foreign company will be best able to negotiate contract terms that compensate it for its high level of risk. Once commercial petroleum is found, both the company's risk and its bargaining power decrease substantially.[14]

Russia

Russia has potentially huge unproven reserves, especially of gas; many observers think that the chances of coming up with a 'dry hole' (the major risk at the exploration stage) there is minor. This and the country's slow pace of change so far have made the Russians hard bargainers. The leverage that foreign companies have on the other hand is Russia's inability to develop its resources alone. This is particularly true of Russia's offshore deposits, which its existing technology cannot reach.

---

14. After successful exploration, the foreign company's main risk is a fall in the world market price of petroleum.

2.4.2 Data concerning geologic assessment

Knowledge is power, and data concerning the geology of an area is obviously valuable at the pre-exploration stages (bidding, negotiating, and planning). The more data a foreign company has, the more realistic and prudent its bid or negotiating position can be. Likewise, data that is developed during exploration is valuable because it shows whether reserves exist in commercial quantities. Unfortunately, the data that a host government has in the early stages is often too sketchy to be of real value in determining whether reserves exist that are worth exploring, much less developing.

Some host governments consider such data as they have (or can gather from others) to be their private property (or that of their energy ministries or state-owned companies). Such data is often sold to foreign companies for a 'data acquisition' fee – which is, in effect, a cost to the foreign company of bidding for a licence or contract. Some host governments also require bidders to submit and evaluate such data as they have developed on their own as part of their bids.

Host governments often impose severe restrictions on use of the data. Each foreign bidder-buyer must keep it confidential and may not re-sell it. Some host governments go further and prohibit foreign companies to trade or sell even their own data to others, and require that a foreign company obtain data only from the host government. The same restrictions on ownership, use, and sale often apply to the data that a foreign company develops during its exploration.

On the other hand, some host governments take a more open approach, fearing that too much secrecy or too high a price will discourage bidders and prevent the world at large from knowing the country's attractions. Recently, for example, South-east Asian countries have begun to collect geophysical data and make it widely available in the belief (correct, in the authors' opinion) that it will attract enough interest to outweigh the income foregone in the short term. In the same vein, Pertamina in Indonesia has begun to sell geological data to parties other than those who have been awarded production-sharing contracts. Some governments, when production is in the offing, also make available information about transportation, refining, and other aspects of their infrastructure.

Russia

Russia is in the relatively 'close to the vest' group of host countries. Under its Decree 540, the Russian government has begun to collect geophysical data and make it available, but only subject to payment of a 'data export' tax. As noted above, many Russian contracts call for the development of geological data as a first step.

2.4.3 Repatriation

A foreign company will bring into the host country two key elements of the business, people and equipment, that it will probably want to take out. And, if the exploration and development are fruitful and the foreign company receives compensation in the form of petroleum, it will want to take the petroleum out of the host country (and onto the world market for sale). Or, if its compensation is in the form of cash rather than petroleum (or if it sells some of its petroleum in the host country for consumption there), it will want to take the cash out of the host country for dividends and reinvestment. Any cash will probably be in the form of the host country's currency. Such currency is typically not convertible into hard currencies. Yet shareholders expect dividends, and other host governments require payments, in hard currencies.

All these matters, and especially the financial ones, come under the rubric of 'repatriation'. On the way to satisfactory repatriation, the foreign company can face many problems short of the 'nightmare scenario' of total expropriation of its property and imprisonment of its people. Minor hiccups can include procuring entry visas, residence and work permits, and exit visas for employees (and their families); import and export of their personal possessions; taxation of employees' incomes (including interest, dividends and other income they earn in the US during their residency in the host country); maintenance of bank accounts in dollars; seizure of equipment; onerous conditions imposed on the export of petroleum; the conversion of the local currency into hard currency; and the repatriation of cash.[15]

BP
Russia
2008

Generally, problems arise when a host government faces a financial crisis and desperately needs to maximise its control over whatever is within its borders, when there is a change of government (even peaceful), and when a cynical host government decides to 'renegotiate' the basic agreement.[16] To be sure, a foreign company can want to renegotiate, too, either to increase its investment or to account for any other unexpected development on its side. Any renegotiation can lead to a sequence of tit-for-tat manoeuvres and amendments by both parties.

To some extent, these problems can be addressed in the basic exploration and development contract between the foreign company and the host government. Many host countries will negotiate general clauses that protect the investment, property, and personnel of the foreign company. The greater the specificity that can be won at the bargaining table, the more protection the foreign company will have when a problem arises later. Contract provisions may restate any laws that the host country has on these subjects, or may grant

15. Additional matters of the same type for which the foreign company may simply have to make provision on its own and at its own expense are the physical safety of employees from common crime; their housing in company-rented and company-furnished compounds; where few foreigners speak the local language, services to buy food and other daily necessities; financial services such as US banks typically provide, including fund transfers to US bank accounts; automobile accident liability (which may be strict and, as a practical matter, requires local drivers to assume the risk); health care; clean air and water; social activities; counselling on public appearance and activities (especially alcohol consumption) that differ from American ways; and plans for a quick exit in case local politics turns violent or a nearby frontier country's strife spreads to the frontier country (as has happened recently in Azerbaijan and Armenia).

16. See, for example, the current renegotiation by the new government of Azerbaijan of its arrangement with Western oil companies to develop fields in the Caspian Sea. Reportedly, the new government wants to increase its share of profits from 71 per cent to 85 per cent.

additional rights. Some countries, such as the People's Republic of China, will agree in principle in a contract that they are emphatically committed to protecting foreign investments, but will also reserve the right to seize oil and profits, subject only to governmental notice. In such cases, this additional risk should be reflected in the compensation that the foreign company will receive if all goes well.

Russia

Petroleum sales within Russia are largely profitless because the ruble is still inconvertible as a practical matter and the government has set energy prices at a fraction of world market prices.

There are a variety of treaties and Russian laws that provide some comfort to the foreign company regarding repatriation from Russia. Russia has signed the European Energy Charter, a multi-lateral treaty in which signatories pledge themselves generally to free trade and open-border principles in international energy dealings. (A detailed agreement remains to be completed, however – not to mention enforcement.) The Russian Law on Foreign Investments allows foreign companies to repatriate profits earned in hard currencies, but not those earned in rubles. Another Russian law allows enterprises that are 30 per cent or more owned by non-Russians to export oil with no licensing restrictions, a privilege not granted to other companies as a matter of course. But in July 1993 the Russian government forbade the export of any oil by joint ventures; and earlier in the year a law was in draft limiting petroleum joint ventures to exporting one third of their output. In sum, there are contradictory currents, at least on financial and petroleum repatriation, in Russia; and the slight experience of foreign companies has been troublesome. On other matters (equipment and personnel), not enough time has passed for a history to be built up.

2.4.4 Political risk

This is the 'nightmare scenario', the violent overthrow of the government of the host country and its replacement by another government that does not feel bound by the former government's commitments. Total losses have occurred within living memory in Somalia, Iran, Vietnam, and Guatemala. Another political risk in petroleum exploration is that while the government you have been dealing with stays in power, it loses control over the territory you are exploring. This occurs most often through war; it can also occur offshore through a settlement between sovereign governments or a neighbouring government's forceful assertion of power over border waters.

This risk must be assessed realistically by any company that has passed the business threshold of deciding that a country possesses sufficient petroleum reserves to warrant investment for exploration or development. Knowledge of a country's history, especially border disputes with its neighbours, of a government's popularity, of possible insurgent movements, and of all nearby countries' laws about territorial waters, is essential.

For development projects which may last more than twenty years, the long-term view must be taken. A foreign company may sadly, but wisely, decide to pass up a great petroleum opportunity because of the instability of the host country's government. Political risks which are relatively minor but still need careful study, concern the host country's economy and currency; if either collapses and the foreign company is dependent on it, the result may be little different from expropriation.

International petroleum companies probably have more experience with this kind of risk than any other international enterprises. They constantly research conditions in the countries in which they are considering investment. When their consideration becomes serious, they make visits to witness first-hand the domestic climate. Visits always include the capital and, often equally important, the local governments in outlying areas where exploration, development, and transportation will occur.

A foreign company can take a few unilateral steps that will reduce its political risk somewhat. It can reduce its exposure by bringing other companies into the venture to share some of its stake (which, of course, reduces its reward, too).[17]

Or, to reduce the risk of a new host government's imposing huge new liabilities on a foreign company, the company can create a subsidiary for each discrete venture, into which it dribbles capital and tangible assets on an as-needed basis. The separate subsidiary serves mainly to shield the assets of the foreign company in its home country (the United States, for example) from liability to the host government for retroactive taxes, damages, and other penalties. If a venture goes sour and the host government sues for sums allegedly owed by the foreign company, the company's home assets will probably be safe if it did business in the host country through an asset-poor subsidiary. (Of course, the host government can circumvent an asset-poor subsidiary at the outset by requiring a guarantee from the parent company.)

Other ways to reduce risk include negotiating with the host government for a quick payback on the foreign company's investment to limit its exposure in the later years of a venture; and for the host country to waive its sovereign immunity, thus making it amenable to lawsuits. In the latter case, the contract may provide for adjudication of disputes (including expropriation) by foreign courts or arbitration.[18] Also, the foreign company can also seek risk *compensation*, if not risk *reduction*, by negotiating for a return that reflects a high risk premium.[19]

The final protection is insurance that shifts political risk to a third party (at a price, of course) and spares the foreign company the time and expense of seeking redress from the host government. 'Political risk' coverage can insure against disputes that arise under contracts or international law, and can

17. Such consortia were popular in the early decades of the petroleum business, both to spread risk and to limit production. The latter motive is fundamentally contrary to modern antitrust laws, and careful counselling in forming consortia is needed to avoid such troubles.

18. See the discussion below in section 2.4.9 concerning dispute resolution.

19. It should be made clear to the frontier government that the less political risk it poses, the lower the risk premium the company will require, and the more of the venture's profits will be available for allocation to the frontier government.

guarantee indemnification if sovereign immunity or a political crisis results in total loss.

There are basically four sources of political risk insurance. First, the capital-exporting countries of the Organization for Economic Cooperation and Development (North America, Europe, Japan, Australia and New Zealand) have offered political risk insurance to encourage investment in host countries. Some developed countries have created their own insurance programmes to encourage their own exports of equipment going to host countries.

Second, in 1969, the United States government chartered the Overseas Private Investment Corporation (OPIC), which provides risk insurance to individuals, partnerships, and corporations in foreign countries. The basic conditions for OPIC coverage are: (1) insured businesses must be domiciled in the US and owned at least 50 per cent by US citizens, or domiciled elsewhere and owned at least 95 per cent by US corporations; (2) the insured venture must have positive economic trade benefits for the US; (3) the venture must have been approved by the host government and must contribute to its social and economic development; and (4) the venture must be a new one or an expansion of the old one. OPIC coverage is not available for petroleum projects in countries that belong to OPEC.

Third, the World Bank has developed the Multilateral Investment Guarantee Agency ('MIGA'), the only international insurer against political risks, which pledges the efforts of the World Bank and its International Finance Corporation to encourage host governments to protect foreign investment in their petroleum projects. Even 'jawboning' efforts by the World Bank and the IFC can be powerful with host countries that have other relationships with them.

Finally, in 1991, the European Economic Community, the European Investment Bank, and 39 countries formed the European Bank for Recovery and Development ('EBRD') to provide economic, political, technical, and environmental assistance to Eastern Europe. Like the World Bank's MIGA, the EBRD programme is one of encouragement to host governments rather than payment to foreign companies. EBRD's influence is like the World Bank's; it makes loans to, and equity investments in, projects in Eastern European countries to encourage their legal, regulatory and technological reforms and the privatisation of their industry. EBRD has a major role to play in making Eastern European countries self-sufficient in energy; and its displeasure would give pause to any host government contemplating the expropriation of a foreign corporation's property.

Russia

In Russia, nightmare scenarios have been easy to imagine; a coup in Moscow, Bosnian-style civil war in a petroleum-producing region. The risk of a coup has receded sharply since the April referendum that vindicated Yeltsin and the reformers. A more realistic scenario today is a cut-off of all exports (including those from foreign joint ventures) because slumping production leaves only enough to heat the country. Exactly this was announced for the month of July 1993.

There may be some comfort in the Russian Law on Foreign Investments, which guarantees that nationalisation will occur only in 'exceptional circumstances' and by decision of the Supreme Soviet. As with repatriation, not enough experience has been built up to estimate the seriousness of such legal protections.

On the insurance front, in mid-1993 OPIC issued its first loan guarantee in Russia, for $50 million (along with $100 million political risk insurance), to a petroleum joint venture in which Conoco has a 50 per cent share. And over this summer the World Bank has pledged huge loans to Russia that were mentioned above.

2.4.5 Duration

International petroleum contracts always specify the length of exploration and any development, and this gives the host government significant leverage over the foreign company's performance.

Contracts typically provide for at least an exploratory period and a development period. Risks are highest in the exploratory period, when the existence of a reservoir and its quantity and quality are unknown. In the development period (if there is one), these risks have proved illusory and commercial viability is relatively assured.

Host governments often gain further leverage over foreign companies by further dividing the exploratory period into several small phases, one for each area to be explored, and the development period into several task-based phases. Normally, exploratory periods are short, although a few extensions may be applied for and are usually granted for good cause.

If exploration of a territory ends in a disappointing but still commercial find, the host government is usually allowed to forbid the foreign company from exploring the neighbouring areas, thus prohibiting it from going where 'the grass is greener'. For its part, the foreign company is sometimes granted 'rights of relinquishment' at the end of its exploration, which permit it to stop activities in the marginally commercial areas. For example, Indonesian production sharing contracts allow a foreign company to back out of an undesirable territory so long as certain work has been performed and advance notice is given to the government.

The latter arrangements serve the interests of both parties, allowing the foreign company to concentrate on 'the glittering prizes' while allowing the host government to find other companies that want to explore and develop the other ones. This encourages the fastest development of the country's total resources.[20]

---

20. To prevent *de facto* relinquishment without the frontier government's approval, governments often forbid any foreign company to assign its rights without the prior permission of the government, or without offering the rights back to the government. Such prohibitions are similar to rights of first refusal in American business agreements; they allow the party who stays in the venture to have some control over the choice of a substitute partner.

Russia

Russian licences that are granted under the Underground Resources Law, and ones that would be granted under most drafts of the Oil and Gas Law, are 5 years for exploration and 20 years for production, with vague provisions for extensions and renewals.

2.4.6 Payments to host governments

From beginning to end of an international petroleum venture, there is a constant stream of payments from the foreign company to the host government. In some payments, the host country acts in its governmental capacity as a tax collector; in others, it is the owner-licensor of the land and petroleum that is the object of the venture.

These payments generally take four forms and can be stated in roughly chronological order as bonuses, duties, royalties, and taxes. To an extent that we are unaccustomed in the United States and Europe, even the taxes paid to host governments are negotiable. Any prudent cash flow analysis by a foreign company will view these exactions, however they are labelled, as different parts of the same thing – value flowing from it to the host government in exchange for value given.

Bonuses

Host governments often require the foreign company to pay 'bonuses' of fixed amounts of hard currency upon the happening of certain crucial events. Bonuses are typically due upon the foreign company being chosen over other bidders, the execution of the basic agreement, the discovery of petroleum, and the commencement of production. With the decline of world market oil prices in recent years, host governments have demanded fewer bonuses, and lesser sums in payment. Where they are still required, foreign companies may often negotiate their payment in pieces after discovery or the beginning of production; if a discovery proves less than originally believed or if problems develop in production, and a venture is scuttled, the foreign company can thus limit its losses.

Duties

Host countries, like others, levy fees ('duties') on the import and export of personal property, including equipment and petroleum. Often, host countries will agree to forego import duties (and any value added tax) on equipment that the foreign company imports for petroleum exploration and development if it agrees that the equipment will eventually become the property of the government (or its corporate subsidiary).

Royalties

Host governments' principal form of compensation for the valuable rights they give to foreign companies is royalties, a fee imposed on each unit of produced petroleum. The governments prefer to calculate royalties based on the amount of petroleum at the well-head, which leaves on the foreign company the risks (and rewards) of refinement, transportation, and sales. Host governments also prefer the option to receive payment in currency (usually hard) or in kind (a specified fraction of produced petroleum). Thailand's Petroleum Act of 1971 introduced a novel system of flexible royalties, with royalties set depending on production – a small percentage for small production, larger percentages for larger production. This wisely matches the willingness of foreign companies to pay more if they get more.

Taxation

The power to tax is the power to destroy, as a great judge once said; many foreign companies have experienced taxation as a kind of creeping expropriation. Specifying and understanding the impact on a venture of the tax laws of both the host country and the foreign company's home country is essential. It should be done as early as possible, and in no event later than the opening of contractual negotiations with the host government.

The plain fact is that most host countries' tax regimes are extremely new, and therefore full of gaps and uncertain in application. Often the host country has little day-to-day experience with profit-driven business activity. In truly communist countries, there was no such thing, even at a conceptual level, as property, income (not to mention different incomes for federal, state, and city purposes), profits, business expense, depreciation and appreciation, or even value. No accounting profession with generally accepted accounting principles exists in most host countries.

Host countries' stated tax rates are generally high by American standards.[21] They tend to have inherited expensive social-welfare schemes from the past, to be desperate for revenue, and to view foreigners as cash-rich. All these factors incline them to see taxation as a tempting means of short-term financing. Making matters even worse, central taxing authorities in some host countries often lack control over regional and provincial governments, which like to wield their own free hands. Host governments at all levels are often unused to the risk-reward calculations that are standard operating procedure for foreign companies.

Needless to say, the uncertain and potentially heavy liabilities that arise from such a frame of mind pose a major risk to the foreign company. A sudden and unexpected tax can turn a marginally viable venture into a gusher of red ink. Petroleum companies are especially tempting targets for taxation if they are viewed as taking out of the host country part of its national wealth.

In taxation as in other areas, however, the very fluidity of the situation in host countries creates great opportunities for foreign companies. Tax breaks and reductions can often be negotiated with the host government to a degree almost unheard of in the United States; in some cases, complete and self-contained tax systems can be agreed to in place of the country's normally

---

21. It bears remembering that even by developed countries' standards the United States is a low tax country.

applicable laws. Provisions, if they do not already exist in the host country's tax laws, should include tax holidays[22] and credits or deductions for bonus and royalty payments to the host government (and for tax payments made to regional and local governments); or a guaranty by the host government that taxes will not increase during the life of the venture.

Tax basis must also be studied, and can sometimes be negotiated, with host governments. If a tax or other payment is based on the price of produced petroleum, is the 'price' the world market price, or the host country's domestic price (which is often kept low for political reasons)?

Study of US tax laws is equally important. Because in many instances income taxes paid to a foreign government may be credited or deducted against US income taxes, it obviously behooves a foreign company to classify as 'income tax' (or as otherwise deductible) as many of the host government's taxes as can be fairly so characterised. Also, if a host country's taxation method is radically different from US taxation (for example, if it is based on an artificial petroleum price rather than a market one), it may be disregarded by US authorities. This can result in catastrophic double taxation. A foreign company should attempt to negotiate with the host government to provide that market values will be used in all valuations for tax purposes.

It is also prudent to negotiate up front the value to be placed on the assets that the foreign company will commit to the venture. Equipment may present few conceptual problems, but the valuation of such intangibles as employee services, knowhow, patents, and copyrights may confront the host government with form of 'property' which it did not recognise until recently. Legal protection for intangible and intellectual property may be non-existent even on the statute books of the host country.

Protection may be negotiated with the host government, though it may be difficult to enforce. For the next few years, it may be unrealistic to expect an appreciation of intellectual property rights from governments and peoples that until recently could not conceive of owning land and buildings. Asian frontier countries, especially, are notorious for being slow to accept intellectual property; only after years of complaints did the Bush administration impose penalties on the most notorious infringers. Foreign companies that import their own intellectual property may simply have to do so at their own risk; and should review any indemnifications they gave in contracts with manufacturers of machinery in their home countries.

Russia

Russia has a 32 per cent corporate profits tax, and some petroleum ventures are tax exempt for two years; both are fairly standard, or slightly better than average, for host countries.

But with inexhaustible creativity, the country is developing an ever-changing, crazy quilt system for taxation on oil and gas activities which has

---

22. Many frontier country's laws boast tax holidays for the first two or three years of a venture. These, however, are like the sleeves out of the proverbial vest if they last only for the venture's developmental phase – when it will produce no revenue to be taxed.

been the single most maddening aspect of the petroleum business there. One executive of an energy company recently added up all the taxes that were on the books of Russia's federal, regional and local governments, and concluded that for a hypothetical venture by his company they exceeded one hundred per cent of its assets and income. The White Nights venture began in 1990 expecting to pay a total of four taxes; earlier this year, it calculated that there were a dozen.

The single most controversial tax measure of the Russian government in petroleum has been a tax enacted in July 1992 on the export of petroleum, of 21 ECUs per metric ton. This amounted to $7 per barrel in August 1992, and has increased as the ruble has fallen. This was a disastrous surprise to the business plans of all existing ventures, and caused several to suspend operations. The government almost immediately promised broad exemptions, granting a blanket exemption to ventures that were formed before 1992 and that have more than 30 per cent foreign ownership. It also promised to consider individual waivers for other ventures. But the exemption lasts only until a venture recoups certain costs, and the government is not considering repealing the tax. This experience suggests strongly that foreign companies should negotiate acceptable caps on taxation in their agreements in Russia, and should be prepared for brinkmanship if the caps are exceeded due to unstoppable domestic political forces.

2.4.7 Payments by host governments

The cash flow is not necessarily one-way in all international petroleum ventures. Sometimes the host governments will make payments to the foreign company.

The problem for the host government is that the only means of payment that it has in abundance, its own currency, is often unconvertible into hard currency, which is the form in which stockholders expect dividends. Host governments' currencies, even if they are convertible, are also prone to extreme fluctuations over years and decades. In an economically marginal venture, hyperinflation of the host government's currency can be devastating.

The mot common solutions to this dilemma are letters of credit in hard currency with a reputable bank in a neutral country (which temporarily frees the host government from needing access to hard currency), payment in petroleum or gas produced by the venture, and payment in dollars or some other hard currency. Since the values of petroleum and the dollar fluctuate, contracts often provide for floors and ceilings of their valuation, for use of a 'basket' of currencies, or for renegotiation in the event of significant and unforeseen changes.

Host governments are usually conscientious about making their payments when due; they know that nonpayment will become known through industry grapevines and the world press, damaging their appeal to foreign investors. Nevertheless, foreign companies should assure themselves that any waiver of sovereign immunity and any political risk insurance they obtain applies to non-payment of contractual obligations by the host government.

2.4.8 Discovery and appraisal clauses

Most host governments require foreign companies to notify them immediately upon the discovery of petroleum, especially when that event triggers a bonus payment to the government. Promptly afterwards, the foreign company is often required to give a formal appraisal of the commercial viability ('commerciality') of the find.

Sometimes the host government will want to participate jointly in the appraisal out of concern that the foreign company will underplay a find that is viable but not spectacular. The host government will want its rights to participation set forth in the basic agreement.

One way to avoid disputes is to define 'commerciality' in the basic agreement. It is difficult to define success at an embryonic stage of any venture, but a good faith attempt can allay the host government's understandable anxiety while preserving for autonomy and flexibility for the foreign company.

Host governments also often insist that the basic agreement provide for appraisals to be completed within a set (and short) time, failing which the government may award the find to another company. If the time period is reasonable, the foreign company should have no reason to object in principle to such 'use it or lose it' provisions.

2.4.9 Dispute resolution

It is only prudent to erect some boundaries and procedures in the basic agreement for resolving internal disputes between the host government and the foreign company. Disputes arise even in carefully planned new business ventures, and outright breaches may occur under crushing political or economic pressures.

Foreign companies often put too much trust in written contracts. Indeed, people in host countries often have notions about contracts that are fundamentally different from ours. They may see them rather the way we see greeting cards, as statements of a present frame of mind rather than as a set of solemn promises to do things in the future. Of course, inaccurate translations or distortions in meaning may only exacerbate the understanding gap.

How shall disputes be settled? The foreign company's home laws and courts (e.g., American ones) are usually unacceptable to the host government because they are unknown and thought to be slanted in favour of the foreign company. The foreign company may not want its own laws and courts to apply, either, because the host country seldom has assets there (especially if, as often occurs, the host country deals with the foreign company through a corporation that was created especially for the venture and has few assets anywhere).

On the other hand, the host country's commercial laws and court system may be in their infancy, may be susceptible to political and popular pressure,[23]

23. American lawyers who believe their own country to be free of such flaws should remember federal courts' diversity of citizenship jurisdiction, which was created in 1789 to avoid the prejudice of state courts in favour of their friends and neighbours; and the specialised federal Claims Court, which since 1855 has heard suits against the United States government.

may render judgments only in the host country's unconvertible currency, and may lack collection mechanisms in any event. It is, however, not unknown for production-sharing and service contracts, as well as joint venture agreements, to be governed by the law of the host country, especially if it has accumulated some history of commercial activity.

Parties often agree that the laws and courts of, or arbitrators in, a neutral third country shall govern their disputes. Often also, internal dispute resolution mechanisms are placed in the basic contract, calling for escalation of problems through each party's hierarchy, with litigation as a last resort.

Finally, to create a *res* against which judgments can be collected, each party may agree to obtain letters of credit in a hard currency from a bank in a neutral country.

Russia

Russia lacks a well-defined commercial law and a court system that would satisfy most foreign businessmen. Therefore, wherever possible they negotiate for their agreements to be interpreted by the laws of, and disputes to be heard by the courts or arbitrators in, a country that has an established body of commercial law and was neutral in the Cold War. Switzerland and Sweden are the most popular choices.

A technique to nip internal disputes in the bud that is sometimes employed in Russian ventures is to employ Bulgarians as consultants to the venture. More westernised than the Russians, but with long historical and cultural ties to Russia, they are thought to represent a cultural middle that can bridge some misunderstandings between Western and Russian parties. For several years, Taiwanese have been employed in US–PRC ventures for the same reason.

2.4.10 Host government participation

Many a host government is deeply interested in participating fully in the development of any petroleum discovered during exploration. Aside from allowing it to 'watch the hen house', participation normally allows it an increased share of revenues from the venture.

A host government may act by itself or through its energy ministry or state-owned petroleum corporation. Participation is most easily achieved through production sharing and service contracts, or through the formation of a joint venture with the foreign company in which the host government has equity participation. Even in modern concessions and contracts which exclude host governments from an equity participation, they often insist on an option to participate somehow in petroleum development.

State equity participation occurs today in two ways, through 'carried interest' and 'working interest'. Both allow the host government to avoid any capital investment initially while enabling it to exercise considerable control over any production and, more generally, over its petroleum resources.

In carried interest, the foreign company pays the host country's share of exploration costs; in the event of a commercial discovery, the host country reimburses the foreign company (usually through assigning it rights to produced petroleum in an amount equal to the host government's share of the exploration costs). In a working interest programme, the host government has no role in exploration, but upon the discovery of a commercial reservoir, the government may become a partner in production, bearing its proportionate share of the production costs (again, frequently through assigning part of its share of the petroleum produced by the venture).

Involving a host government in a petroleum venture can be crucial to its success. Indeed, a successful American entrepreneur told one of the authors that he only became successful in a certain host country when he gave its government and citizens interests of over 50 per cent of his ventures.

Assuming a long-term view by the foreign company and the fundamental honesty of the host government, it should be possible to structure host government participation in almost any international petroleum venture. The authors personally favour what they call 'value added' participation. It is a fair generalisation that in the long run, each participant in a business venture receives compensation that reflects the value that it adds to the venture. From the point of view of the host government, if it simply 'rents the country', such as by allowing access to its petroleum resources for a fee, it will probably wind up with the traditional low return earned by the typical landlord. In the mean time, it will have sold its nonrenewable resources and, probably, will have spent its fee on living expenses. It will be poorer for the venture. (Sometimes this 'value added' principle is deliberately obscured, as when a weak host government is granted a disproportionate share to gain a critical concession. But in these cases the stronger foreign companies usually recoup their excess contribution during the life of the venture through interest rates, service costs, or some other mechanism.)

To receive more, the host government must add more value to the venture. But how can it do that? In the typical case, it does not have significant manufacturing capacity, specific technical or management organisation, a large skilled work-force, or financial resources. It may, however, offer, aside from its natural resources, favourable tax laws, open markets, or political predictability and stability. Of more use to the long-term success of the venture can be a country's dedication to the training and education of its people and its willingness to work for the long term rather than the immediate payoff. In the latter regard, willingness to sacrifice today to enable the next generation to have a more abundant life is crucial.

Finding a value in the host country which it can add to a venture gives it a larger 'piece of the action' and, therefore, an incentive to want the venture to succeed. This can be the ultimate protection of the foreign company's investment – aside from working to benefit the citizens of the host country.

Petroleum ventures can also be structured to involve host governments in ways that minimise unpleasant surprises for the foreign company (surprises such as are discussed above in 'Repatriation' and Political risk'). The basic idea is to make the venture unfold in a way that calls for each party to make a sequence of small performances. Ideally, each sequenced performance builds on the previous one, is necessary before the next one can occur, and adds value to the venture. What results is a series of 'tit-for-tat' increments by the parties; over time, the host government feels involved in the venture, has a stake in its success, and is less likely to walk away from it, to impose burdens and penalties on it, or to see it generally as a scheme by rapacious foreigners. This, too, can be a built-in protection of the foreign company's investment, not to mention the means for securing for the host government and its citizens the maximum benefits offered by the project. This is really a form of 'stakeholder management', a process with which all large American companies have been familiar for years.

Here again, Russia's very lack of legal structure and business history may help rather than hurt. The country's present fluidity may make it an ideal prospect for 'value added' and 'tit-for-tat' ventures.

2.4.11 Training and use of local personnel

Closely intertwined with the issue of host government participation is the training and use of local personnel. The host government obviously wants to boost employment among its population, especially in well-paying jobs, and to increase its national pool of technological skills and relationships with foreign businesses. Especially in Asia, governments often require (by statute or contract) that foreign companies give hiring preferences or fill quotas for the host government's local citizens. (Host governments often also impose requirements that foreign companies purchase set amounts or kinds of supplies and services from local businesses and contractors.)

In theory, a foreign company should have no objection to this. Certainly, a far-sighted company will share the host government's desire for a fully employed, highly paid, and highly skilled work-force; in host countries, the oil drillers of today are the oil consumers of tomorrow (when, for example, their standard of living rises enough for them to buy cars).[24] However, in a world where projects compete for foreign companies' capital by basis points, the foreign company is understandably wary of running a trade school rather than a petroleum venture. Again, contractual clauses can provide some relief by specifying skill-requirements for host country personnel and quality standards for its goods and services. And in negotiations, if the host government insists on unacceptably high 'quotas', negotiators for the foreign company can point out other countries' less onerous standards and the fact that capital is fluid and will seek the most welcoming environment.

Russia

Two difficult aspects of doing business in Russia today are a legal requirement that Russian employees of joint ventures be paid the same salaries as their American counterparts (which are astronomical by Russian standards), and a

---

24. Henry Ford, who in 1913 raised the wages of his factory workers to the unheard of sum of five dollars a day, may have realised that he was helping to turn his workers into middle-class buyers of his cars. D. Halberstam, *The Reckoning* (1986), 84–5.

prohibition on paying Russian employees in dollars (the government is committed to an all-ruble economy). Also, given the sad state of Russia's social infrastructure, your Russian partners may well want you to import more than drilling equipment. They may want you to build such secondary petroleum facilities as pipelines and refineries; [25] and to train the venture's Russian workers in skills such as new exploration and development techniques, production in shallow or heavy oil zones, reactivating shut-in wells, and water injection; or more general disciplines such as business administration, finance, procurement, management, and marketing.

They may also want you to build schools, hospitals, playgrounds, and other amenities. The first reaction may be to object that you are a businessman, not a town planner. The answer is that in Russia today the two are often inseparable. In truth, the same requests were made by Alaskans when their pipeline was planned, and were agreed to (at a price) by the developers from the 'Lower Forty-Eight'.

2.4.12 Ownership of equipment

A host government may require that all equipment and other technology imported into the country become its property. This may arise from its wish, as with local employees and subcontractors, to increase the national wealth; or it may be a quiet way to encourage purchases from local manufacturers. Whatever the motivation, this will understandably strike the foreign company as pure confiscation, and particularly penal if the venture ends before its expected term. It also acts as a discouragement from importing expensive high technology, thus impairing the output of the entire venture.

About the only bargaining leverage that the foreign company may have over the host government, other than outright refusal to accede to such demands, is to point out their futility. Sophisticated machinery requires constant maintenance and spare parts, which are available only from abroad and require hard currency. However, such demands may give an advantage in the bidding process to the foreign company that is technically sophisticated, vertically integrated, large, and willing to commit substantial resources to its venture in the host country. Such a company is best able to make quick repairs, including by flying skilled personnel and spare parts across the world on short notice. Saving time in this way can be crucial to the profitability of the venture, which can be effectively shut down by a small technical problem.

Russia

The state of Russian oil equipment is, in general, sorry. On the oil fields, it is common to see broken, mistreated, or obsolete equipment in massive quantities. Repairing it is often out of the question. One Russian joint venture, accordingly, involves import of arctic grade pipe, stanchions, and

---

25. Sometimes, the location of these facilities can as a practical matter determine how much production is for domestic use, and how much for export.

central processing equipment. Such imports, and loss of ownership of imported equipment, are probably an unavoidable feature of Russian petroleum ventures for a long time. Given the difficulty of exporting such equipment today due to the country's transportation facilities and export duties, the value of equipment should be viewed as a sunk cost and compensation for it should be built into the compensation that a foreign company will derive from a venture. This will, of course, limit the attraction of relatively speculative opportunities.

2.4.13 Environmental issues

Global environmental awareness and calls for global solutions to environmental problems have radically altered the practices of host countries. Petroleum and gas operations are no exception. Host governments no longer view pollution as an unavoidable by-product of industrialisatiion; instead, they want to improve on the West's history by taking environmental protection seriously from the start. Chernobyl, Bhopal, and Exxon Valdez have made clear the short-term costs of high technology that is incautiously inserted into a frontier environment. This is one area where public opinion counts strongly, too. For example, it is widely believed in many former Soviet satellite countries that radiation clouds from Chernobyl passed over them, despite all the scientific evidence that the only clouds that escaped the old USSR passed over Scandinavia. These beliefs were one of the fatal losses of credibility that undermined the satellite regimes in 1989.

Aside from wanting to avoid pollution, host countries have begun to view their environmental resources as national assets whose value should be preserved. Many governments have enacted strong environmental protection laws. Because these same countries often lack technical expertise, however, responsibility in petroleum ventures for reducing pollutants from refineries and offshore operations, and for preventing discharges into surface and ground waters, falls largely on the foreign company.

Host countries often require foreign companies to submit an environmental management plan before beginning operations. In Indonesia, for example, there is comprehensive environmental legislation whose petroleum provisions require the foreign company to enter into a partnership agreement with Pertamina. The foreign company must comply with all of Pertamina's environmental regulations, which range from preventing the flow of crude oil into water sources to requiring pollution prevention equipment on offshore drilling installations. If Indonesian environmental laws are violated, the government may imprison the individual violators, revoke the foreign company's licenses, impose fines, and require the foreign company to compensate any victims.

In other host countries, environmental laws contain only basic requirements that the environment not be compromised. Even here, though, much is expected of the foreign company; and as global concerns rise and environmental regulations multiply, foreign companies will need to improve their management programmes.

Host countries will no longer allow access to their resources on a foreign company's promise to undertake any clean-up at its own expense. Foreign companies will need to be pro-active and forward thinking in order to effect work programmes that prevent, contain, and minimise any damage. Most important of all is the development of an internal company philosophy that reflects concern and sensitivity to environmental protection, no matter in what part of the world operations occur. A sincere and professional commitment to the ecology is clearly demanded by the times.

Russia

The Soviet Union left a dreadful legacy of pollution, of which Chernobyl is only the most famous example. (The air in Russia's cities, for example, is so polluted that visitors there will see few joggers.) In the oil and gas sector, regions around production sites are visibly uninhabitable by contemporary Western standards (although, to be fair, Pittsburgh and London were no better within living memory).

Inattentiveness to the ecology damaged petroleum resources, too. For example, the Soviet government used drilling rigs that were so heavy that they forced drilling fluid into oil formations and polluted them. Pollution was also spread over the countryside by pipeline leaks. Government-set petroleum prices were so low that the leaking oil had little value. There was no incentive to fix the leaks and 'rational' producers simply pumped more oil and let the leaks seep into the soil.

Until recently, environmental issues in Russia were an afterthought in petroleum agreements. Russia's law On Protection of the Environment was a general statement without regulations. In agreements, the parties usually added a general pledge to be careful in the basic agreement and let it do at that.

This began changing in early 1993, however. In fact, some ventures have found their plans, after all the normal approvals, stymied by angry local citizens who, like their American counterparts, know how to use local zoning boards and lawsuits to tie construction projects up in knots for years. Once the Ministry of Ecology issues detailed regulations and enforces them, foreigners may expect their experiences to begin approaching their American ones.

A crucial issue to be addressed in any contract or negotiation with the government is responsibility for cleaning up the environmental problems left from the Soviet era. As a practical matter, the foreign company may be required to do so (who else can?), but it should be compensated through a larger share of profits or production, or recovery of expenses.

2.5 CONCLUSION

In the next ten years, what happens in frontier countries will fundamentally change the face of the worldwide petroleum business. Investors face huge opportunities, including participation in the political, economic and social rebirth of many nations.

The frontier countries, too, are poised for staggering changes. Their elites, which have controlled everything from exploration to prices at the pump, will face competition at every level (and are uniquely positioned to succeed at it). Their populations, used to state control, will ride the roller coaster of the marketplace and experience Western 'civilisation'.

Petroleum laws and contracts in these countries are still a mostly blank piece of paper. But we hope we have made clear that smart petroleum companies will want to help in the writing of both. They have not had such an opportunity in the United States, for example, since the dawn of the century.

Laws and contracts are as important to petroleum development as seismic tests and drilling equipment. They, too, are tools for exploration and channels through which capital flows in and oil and gas flows out. Skilled lawyering, with tactical wits and strategic vision, is needed as much as field engineering. Companies that thus venture wisely stand to make exponential financial gains for themselves, and equally grand ones for their stockholders and home countries, for today's frontier countries, and for their newly liberated peoples.

Chapter 3

Competitive Bidding Tactics for New Exploration Concessions

P. W. Hawley, A. D. Bramley, and J. M. Castellani

3.1 ABSTRACT

In some (mostly developing) countries, oil companies compete for new exploration agreements by bidding the key economic parameters. Companies are faced with a trade-off between profitability of potential discoveries and probability of winning the bid.

We believe that an increasing number of companies are making generous offers in order to win bids, in the expectation of being able to renegotiate economic terms if they make a discovery. This tactic is hard to recognise and may have a good chance of success, due to the strength of the oil company's bargaining position upon discovery. However, the tactic damages the performance of the E&P industry in developing countries – for governments and companies alike.

The means of combating 'tactical overbidding' rests largely with governments and national oil companies in making better contracts and taking a cautious approach to the evaluation of bids. Reputable companies can contribute to the process by emphasising that their bids are formulated in good faith and based on sound commercial considerations.

3.2 BACKGROUND

Countries such as Angola, Ecuador, Nigeria, and India select oil companies for new exploration agreements on the basis of formal bidding rounds, for which one important criterion is the economic terms proposed by the companies. Most commonly, these involve production sharing agreements where profit oil-sharing ratios are the key biddable variables in setting economic terms. Other economic variables might be depreciation rates, cost oil limits, investment 'uplifts' and the like.

Faced with a decision of how high a share of profit oil they can propose, foreign oil companies (FOC) clearly must consider the trade off of profitability on prospective discoveries versus their chances of winning the bid and obtaining rights to the exploration acreage (we have referred throughout to 'Foreign Oil Companies', since this reflects almost all contract situations in developing countries). Our contention is that some companies have focussed increasingly on first gaining the exploration agreement and then working out the profitability later via a renegotiation. We will refer to this phenomenon as 'tactical overbidding renegotiation'.

Carried to an extreme, this might entail bidding terms based only on very optimistic future conditions: high oil prices, large discoveries and low development and operating costs.

By the time a discovery is made, the company may be in a good position to request and achieve renegotiation of the key economic terms, if this rosy scenario has not actually evolved. We will argue that the company will believe – probably correctly – that the developing country's need for income from the prospective field is greater than the discoverer's needs, and thus the probability of being able to renegotiate terms to achieve a reasonable return on development capital (if not exploration costs as well) is good.

Tactical overbidding/renegotiation is an area of economic behaviour which is particularly relevant for exploration contracts in the petroleum industry. It is an area which has not been well examined in the existing economic literature on contracts and, as far as we are aware, has not been discussed in any previous industry forum.

The conclusions we draw warrant concern by both government and companies who are involved in bidding for exploration rights. Tactical overbidding/renegotiating threatens to reduce profitability and increase risks for all parties involved in the exploration business, except for successful overbidders/renegotiators themselves. The extent to which this damage can be avoided depends on how far both governments and companies are prepared to take measures necessary to combat the phenomenon.

3.3 TACTICAL OVERBIDDING/RENEGOTIATING: Evidence and Rationale

3.3.1 Evidence

The evidence for the existence of tactical overbidding/renegotiation is not easy to present openly. For understandable reasons of commercial sensitivity, neither companies nor governments are willing to openly identify and describe specific case histories. However, most officials – from both companies and governments – acknowledge that they at least strongly suspect that the tactic is used by some companies.

Our own views, as consultants who have worked over many years with both companies and governments in bidding rounds, are similar. It is almost impossible to present hard, incontestable evidence, but soft 'circumstantial' evidence leads us to believe that tactical overbidding/renegotiation does exist, and that furthermore it is damaging for the industry.

Discussions with a range of experienced observers indicate that certain specific companies are commonly identified as overbidders/renegotiators. This in itself is some evidence for the existence of the phenomenon.

3.3.2 Rationale

First, the process of bidding for contract award and the uncertain nature of the exploration business create an environment within which tactical overbidding/renegotiation can flourish.

The choice of bidding rather than negotiation may itself influence companies towards overbidding/renegotiation. The bidding process tends to focus companies' perceptions on the trade-off between contract profitability and the probability of winning the bid. Any tactic which offers the possibility of 'having the cake and eating it' becomes attractive.

Tactical overbidding/renegotiation is hard to recognise at any stage, due to the uncertain nature of the exploration business. High levels of uncertainty (on price, cost, prospectivity at the bidding stage) means that a wide range of bids is the norm rather than the exception. It is hard for any observer to be sure that a bid has been made unrealistically generous. This problem can be particularly acute for the National Oil Company (NOC) of a developing country, where limited resources are available to evaluate bids.

This inherent uncertainty persists even after the discovery has been made (see Figures 3.1 and 3.2). Even when a post-discovery renegotiation is in progress, there is no unique and independently verifiable way to assess whether the company's potential returns are adequate.

Having won the bid, the FOC is in an excellent position to strengthen its position, in preparation for a future renegotiation. This strengthening can be achieved by granting technical and economic assistance, political lobbying and many other means.

Renegotiation on discovery is to a certain extent a justifiable fact of life in the business, since the development of a contract which covers all economic

Figure 3.1 Illustrative exploration/development schedule

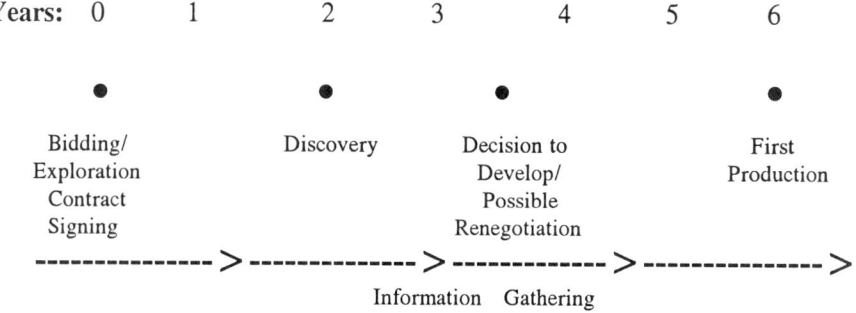

Figure 3.2 Levels of uncertainty in the exploration/development process

Stage: Uncertainty	Contract Signing	Decision to Develop	First Production
Oil Price	+ + +	+ +	+
Exploration Cost	+ + +	0	0
Development Cost	+ + +	+	0
Field Size	+ + +	+ +	+

Levels of Uncertainty: (0) = None; (+) = Low; (+ +) = Medium; and (+ + +) = High

and technical eventualities – what an economist would describe as a 'complete state of contract' – is generally impossible. There are many precedents for justifiable renegotiation of economic terms to adjust a company's profitability. These adjustments allow for changes such as lower prices or smaller than expected reserves. They are perfectly valid and have no relationship to tactical bidding.

Second, there may well be a negotiating advantage to the FOC at the time of discovery.

At first sight, any incentive to renegotiate terms in discovery may seem to lie with the host government/NOC rather than with the FOC. By the time a discovery has been made the FOC will have invested heavily in exploration costs. Thus exposed, it may seem that the FOC is in danger of losing out to competitor companies who are prepared to develop the discovery under production sharing terms which give an adequate return on development costs alone. There are many references in the general literature[1] of contract economics to this situation, where contracts have to protect the exposure of the party who makes the early investment. And indeed most exploration contracts give strong guarantees of the FOC's development rights for this very reason.

However, in practice the balance of negotiating power following an exploration success is significantly shifted toward the FOC:

- The most important effect is related to the fact that the FOC may be much more willing than the government to delay field development. The FOC still has not made its development investment and may well have alternative investment opportunities in other countries. In contrast, the host government – especially in a low income developing country – may badly need tax revenue. The government's development options are, of course,

1.   Rogerson, W. P., 'Efficient Reliance and Damage Measures for Breach of Contract', *Rand Journal of Economics*, **15** (1984), 39–53.

effectively limited by its country. In essence, the FOC's opportunity cost of capital may be significantly lower than the government's.

- If the government/NOC refuses to negotiate on economic terms, it will be faced with the need to 'sell' the development to a new FOC. This may be difficult, since the withdrawal of the existing FOC may give a strong signal to new FOCs that the development is not viable and discourage their participation.
- Any new FOC participant is inevitably at a disadvantage to the existing FOC, in terms of information and understanding of the discovery. This means that riskiness for the new FOC is higher and their expected rewards lower than for the existing FOC. Thus, there is an in-built tendency for the new FOC to demand somewhat more generous economic terms, all other factors being equal.

3.4 OVERBIDDING IS A DAMAGING TACTIC FOR THE E&P INDUSTRY

The adoption by oil companies of a bidding strategy based upon an anticipation of renegotiation is inefficient both for the governments and for the oil industry as a whole. It will cause reserves to be inefficiently developed – denying access to acreage by reputable companies; increasing the cost of negotiation; destroying trust between oil companies and governments and making genuinely justifiable renegotiation more difficult.

3.4.1 Inefficient resources development

Some companies may react to competitors using tactical overbidding/renegotiation by adopting similar methods. More cautious, but nevertheless capable companies will decline to adopt this tactic and will lose out. Their resources will therefore be utilised in less prospective areas and the efficiency of the worldwide industry will be reduced. Companies who do choose to follow their overbidding/renegotiating competitors risk damaging the effectiveness of exploration contracts for the entire industry, including themselves. The situation is similar to the unhappy outcome in the 'prisoners' dilemma', where decisions taken by individuals to protect their own position lead to worsening of the position of the group as a whole.

3.4.2 Costs of renegotiations

Renegotiating is a time consuming and expensive process which will draw heavily upon the resources of the FOC and the NOC/government, and generate costly project delays. The cost of unnecessary renegotiation will be damaging for all the parties, especially for resource limited NOCs in developing countries. Renegotiations will unnecessarily shift their scarce resources from a better alternative use. Potentially long delays in the development of the field caused by the renegotiation process will reduce the project value available for both parties, leading to a clear 'lose/lose' situation.

3.4.3 Distrust between government and oil companies

If governments come to believe that tactical overbidding/renegotiation is used by some companies, they will tend to be more cautious in their relations with all companies. This distrust will lead to less cooperative and therefore less effective negotiations and operations. The effect of unreliability of contracts has been studied in detail in the literature. Some economists[2,3] have emphasised the difficulty of writing efficient contracts as an important factor explaining vertical integration. In the exploration business, unreliable contracts could induce NOCs to be less reliant on foreign participation in the development of their national resource. This tendency, even if slight, is in no-one's interest.

3.4.4 Increased difficulty of genuine renegotiations

By stressing the high cost of unnecessary renegotiation we do not want to condemn all renegotiations. There will always be marginal discoveries which a company would not have anticipated in its original bid. For such a discovery, with a viable pre-tax economics, it is often both in the company's interest to adjust economic terms to allow development.

If a government suspects some oil companies of using tactical overbidding/ renegotiation, it will tend to distrust any claim for renegotiation. This attitude tends to be heightened because the FOC inevitably has better information and understanding of the field than the NOC. This may lead to unnecessary abandonment of marginal but economic fields, or at least to a costly and lengthy renegotiation process.

In summary, tactical overbidding/renegotiation reduces the overall efficiency of international E&P activities in countries where economic terms are biddable. This inefficiency hurts both companies and governments. If they are not identified, the companies using these unfair tactics become 'free riders' of the game, by securing an advantage with little added cost to themselves.

3.5 ALTERNATIVES FOR GOVERNMENT IN DEALING WITH TACTICAL OVER-BIDDING

Most of the damage caused by tactical overbidding/renegotiation is borne by governments. It is in their interests to develop methods to discourage this behaviour and they are in a better position to do so than are the oil companies. Several options exist.

2.   Klein, B., Crawford, R., and Alchian, A., 'Vertical Integration, Appropriable Rents and the Competitive Contracting Process', *Journal of Law and Economics*, **21** (1978), 297–326.
3.   Kornhauser, L. A., 'Reliance, Reputation, and Breach of Contract', *Journal of Law and Economics*, **26** (1983), 691–706.

3.5.1 Improve the government's bargaining position

One of the most effective and direct methods of discouraging tactical overbidding/renegotiation is to weaken the FOC's negotiating position by including in the contract a right for the government to take back discoveries which have not been developed within a reasonable time. The effect is to add greatly to the risk of renegotiation for the FOC. An example is the Angolan Offshore Production Sharing Agreement, where there is a 3- to 5-year time limit (depending on the water depth) between discovery and first production.

3.5.2 Improve contract fiscal efficiency

Using the profitability of a project as a basis for production sharing provides a way to approximate a 'complete state contingent contract'. Such a system is based on FOC profitability. Having agreed to a contract which covers a wide range of economic outcomes, it is then more difficult for the FOC to justify renegotiation after discovery.

3.5.3 Reputation

'Reputation' can be a potent force in influencing contracting parties to stick to agreements.[4] It is up to government/NOCs to take account of the past record of FOCs in evaluating their bids. However, 'reputation' can only be useful in curbing overbidding/renegotiation if such behaviour becomes public. This may be problematic because of the absence of clear-cut, direct evidence of the phenomenon.

3.5.4 Change basis of competition

One obvious way to block tactical overbidding/renegotiation is for countries using biddable economic terms to shift to a standard fiscal regime for all operators, such as exists in most developed countries. The government might attempt to capture economic rents by awarding contracts against bids for cash bonus payments. This regime would be similar to the system employed to allocate leases for the US Gulf Coast area. A serious problem in implementing this kind of regime more generally would be FOCs' perception of high political risks in developing countries. FOCs will be unwilling to make significant up-front payments if they believe their future returns are jeopardised by political risks.

Using negotiation instead of bidding may also reduce the problem. However, in most cases, the need to promote strong competition by attracting the investment of numerous bidders must remain paramount. This is especially true for new exploration areas.

4. Williamson, O., *Markets and Hierarchies: Analysis and Anti-Trust Implications*, New York: Free Press, 1975.

3.5.5 Improve NOC/government skills

Our own experience and discussions with industry has led us to believe that tactical overbidding/renegotiation happens most often in new exploration areas in developing countries. This may be partly explained by the technical and resource limitations of NOCs/governments in developing countries. Their abilities to combat overbidding can be greatly enhanced by an in-depth training in the fiscal and technical aspects of E&P, and in economic aspects of the business (price forecasting, international E&P trends etc.).

3.5.6 NOC equity participation

An equity participation by the NOC throughout the project's life may have the effect of reducing, or even removing, the disadvantage of having less information than the FOC. An NOC with equity participation will be better able to judge the genuineness of any request for renegotiation and may well be better placed to seek new foreign partners. Both these factors will improve the bargaining position of the NOC and therefore discourage the tactic of overbidding/renegotiation. Set against these potential advantages are, of course, the problems which many NOCs would face in funding genuine equity involvement.

3.6 ALTERNATIVES FOR COMPANIES

Although the most direct means of combating tactical overbidding/renegotiation lie with governments, there are several ways in which companies can help the situation.

3.6.1 Cultivate reputation for reliability

Companies can develop and demonstrate to governments their record in bidding in good faith and avoiding later renegotiations. As reliable companies develop good reputations, the actions of tactical overbidders/renegotiators will become easier to spot.

3.6.2 'Educate' governments

Companies can attempt to 'educate' the governments/NOCs with whom they deal to make informed commercial judgments on bids they receive. It may, of course, be difficult to give direct help in the form of training or technical assistance. A more subtle approach might be for a company to present its own bid with clarification of its expectation of field sizes, oil prices and development costs. If the government/NOC is encouraged to think in these terms, the anomalies underlying an overgenerous bid will become clearer.

3.7 AFTERWORD

The selection of oil companies for new exploration ventures is a highly complex subject involving many uncertainties. Bidding on a 'renegotiate after discovery' tactic is just one of many factors. Compared, however, to issues such as forecasting the probable presence of reservoir and source rocks, future oil prices, development and operating costs and even political risks, bidding strategies of oil companies in developing countries has received very little open and formal discussion. We would suggest that the subject is certainly worthy of further debate among companies and governments involved in bidding for production sharing agreements. The potential rewards for successfully countering tactical overbidding/renegotiating are a reduction of risks for the international industry and for developing countries, a corresponding increase in oil income.

Chapter 4

Restructuring or Privatisation? –
State Petroleum Enterprises and the Global Economic Adjustment Process

George K. Ndi and Leon E. Moller

4.1 INTRODUCTION

The prevailing tide of restructuring and privatisation of public enterprises which in many ways symbolises the worldwide economic liberalisation policies of the mid- to late-1980s has been sustained into the 1990s and as yet shows no signs of abating – even if popular enthusiasm for the process appears somewhat to be waning. A recent study conducted for the United Nations records some 3,106 privatisation exercises worldwide between 1980 and June 1992 – of which 1,336 had been completed, with 217 in the process of implementation, 1,336 planned and the status of the remaining 9 still unresolved.[1] This compares with an estimated 575 acts of expropriation of foreign property or investments worldwide over the period between 1960 and 1991. And whereas there were 1,508 privatisation exercises either planned, in progress or already completed between the period 1987–92, there was not a single recorded act of expropriation during this period[2] – a clear indication thus of the expanding role of the private sector in national economies worldwide.

The study further highlights the key role being played by the developing countries and the newly-industrialised nations in the privatisation process. Over the period covered, Africa, Asia, the Middle East, Eastern Europe and Latin America accounted for just over 85 per cent of worldwide privatisation projects either completed, in the process of implementation, or planned. Recently the ex-socialist countries in transition have also been actively seeking the transfer of public sector enterprises to the private sector following the collapse of the centralised system of economic planning. Undoubtedly, there is

---

1. Minor, M. S., *Privatization: A Worldwide Summary*, Report prepared for the Transnational Corporations and Management Division of the United Nations, Edinburg, Texas (Oct. 1992).
2. Minor, M. S., *Expropriation: Worldwide Trends, 1986–1991*, Report prepared for the Transnational Corporations and Management Division of the United Nations, Edinburg, Texas (July 1992).

still ample scope to sustain the worldwide privatisation process for quite some time to come – in view mainly of the extensive prospects potentially on offer to private sector management in some of the ex-socialist societies in transition (Russia and Central Asia), the Indian sub-continent, and the still-communist countries such as China, Mongolia and Vietnam. There is likewise some indication to the effect that in certain regions of the world such as Africa and Eastern Europe – as well as in certain key economic sectors – the process of transferring state-owned assets to private sector ownership and management is yet to reach its full potential or run its entire course.

In addition to privatisation activity, the ongoing restructuring of public enterprises worldwide offers a fuller picture of the magnitude and extent to which economic liberalisation policies are currently being pursued in the quest to attract overseas investment. Restructuring and privatisation policies may thus be viewed against the general background of the worldwide evolution in investment conditions towards the promotion of inward foreign investment.

From our point of view, however, a far more remarkable feature of current privatisation policies is the relatively little impact which the process seems so far to be having on the petroleum sector. While a number of countries have embarked on the restructuring of public sector enterprises and institutions involved in oil and gas operations, the privatisation culture is yet to permeate to any significant degree such enterprises – particularly in the major oil producing regions such as, for example, the Middle East. A possible exception is Latin America where the privatisation of State Petroleum Enterprises (SPEs) has taken place in Argentina and is planned in Peru. We do not, however, discern any definite trend or significant moves towards the privatisation of SPEs in other oil-producing regions such as Africa, the Far East, Russia or the CIS where many SPEs have so far remained immune to the prevailing tendency in favour of the privatisation of public enterprises.

The relative paucity of privatisation activity in the petroleum sector is all the more remarkable in view of the fact that in many countries a large number of privatisation exercises have either been scheduled or completed. These, however, have mainly been in sectors such as manufacturing, services and – to a lesser extent – agriculture.

Even so a recent report from the World Bank concludes that privatisation has been an inherent part of efforts aimed at the rationalisation of SPEs in over 80 countries. So far such efforts do not seem to have translated into actual privatisation practice, being mostly limited to corporate restructuring and commercialisation.

It is against the general background of global economic restructuring, involving in particular the evolution of investment conditions and worldwide privatisation activity, that this chapter proposes to examine the prospects for the restructuring and privatisation of SPEs in developing countries. The chapter advances some sobering reflections on the possible privatisation of SPEs in these countries within the general context of the current global economic adjustment process, and argues that the prospects may be somewhat less promising than had previously been expected or anticipated.

4.2 MAIN ISSUES

In oil-producing countries (excepting the major oil producers of the Middle East), the restructuring – and to a limited extent privatisation – of SPEs has over the past few years increasingly been seen as the means of addressing the now widely acknowledged shortcomings of previously interventionist command/control approach to state regulation of the productive sectors of the economy. This approach, through its failure to delineate clearly the boundary between state and economy, had in the past favoured a much more direct and active state or public sector participation in – *inter alia* – petroleum operations. Hence the advent of SPEs as the ubiquitous legacy of the nationalisation policies of the 1970s.

This chapter proposes to examine recent developments in the petroleum industry within the general context of the current privatisation process. It will examine the reasons (political, economic and social) for the paucity of privatisation exercises affecting key SPEs. It will also examine the reasons for restructuring seemingly being the preferred alternative to the privatisation of SPEs. The chapter's approach and focus will be conceptual as well as practical, highlighting the various approaches, options and obstacles to current restructuring and privatisation programmes aimed at SPEs in developing countries. It will thus seek to analyse the economic, legal, technical and policy aspects of the formulation and implementation of restructuring and privatisation programmes while building on the theme of institutional change and policy transformation (or perhaps transition) in the petroleum sector in developing countries.

The discussion of these issues will take place within the context of the current state of debate over the restructuring and privatisation of SPEs in developing countries. But it will go further by elucidating and illustrating the role and impact of restructuring and privatisation within the overall policy framework of public sector disengagement from direct participation or active involvement in the productive sectors of the economy. It will analyse the role and function of restructuring/privatisation as a mechanism for fostering the expansion of domestic private sector and in attracting inward foreign investment, and thus as a vehicle for promoting sustained and institutionalised growth in the oil and gas sectors beyond the expected realisation of efficiency gains. Finally, the chapter will come up with conclusions which will be aimed at clarifying the overall implications of current restructuring and privatisation programmes for the future of the oil and gas sectors in developing countries, and for the international petroleum industry as a whole. In particular it will examine the implications for the evolving structure of the world oil industry and future patterns of ownership and control. As part of this conclusion, we shall be asking the question whether these policies and the trends which they engender may now be considered as irreversible, even assuming the inevitability of changes in the prevailing economic conditions which currently drive and influence such trends.

The chapter will be set against the background of developments which are currently still taking place with regard to the restructuring, commercialisation and privatisation of SPEs in developing countries while examining the likely impact of similar developments in the ex-socialist countries on trends in the former.

4.3 RESTRUCTURING AND PRIVATISATION OF SPEs

4.3.1 Background

Restructuring and/or privatisation of SPEs is the currently dominant theme at the forefront of policies designed either to scale down or to rationalise public-sector involvement in petroleum sector development in the developing countries. Countries with what may appear to be promising oil and gas sectors now generally seek the restructuring, reorientation, and in some cases privatisation of public sector institutions as a means of improving efficiency in petroleum operations and attracting much needed private-sector investment for exploration and development. Privatisation, in particular, may be regarded as an alternative form of investment promotion to the traditional methods of exploration acreage licensing and the granting of development rights to petroleum properties; it may likewise be viewed as complementing such traditional methods of investment promotion.

In many developing countries, the restructuring or privatisation of relevant energy sector public institutions is now seen to be a panacea for the shortcomings of public monopolies: inefficiency, lack of proper business focus (with management often pursuing goals other than profit maximisation), undue or improper government interference, bureaucratic controls and procedures, and the political orientations of managers[3] – all with attendant adverse effects on productivity and the conduct of operations.

The current debate on the privatisation of SPEs in developing countries has to be seen against the background of the emergence and growth of these enterprises as powerful and important – if only (from a commercial perspective) less than successful – players on the domestic economic and political scene. Hence current restructuring or privatisation policies affecting SPEs may be viewed as much from an economic as from a political perspective.

On the economic front, the principal drawbacks of the public sector management model included the drain on public resources motivated by the 'civil service' approach which had very quickly become the principal hallmark of SPE management. Hence poor financial management and lack of commercial orientation became the chief consequences of the 'civil service' approach. Added to this was the establishment of a costly corporate structure which is frequently overstaffed, marked by inefficiency, and supported by mineral rents derived mainly from the SPEs domestic monopoly (or privileged position) in the petroleum sector.

---

3.   Wälde, T. W., 'Restructuring and Privatisation: Viable Strategies for State Enterprises in Developing Countries', *Proceedings of the Workshop on Global Management in the Oil and Gas Industries*, Montreal, CETAI (1991), 61–6.

Following on the heels of these shortcomings came the obsolescence of centralised planning as a macroeconomic management model. This ultimately led to the realisation of the limits of managerial competence attaching to state enterprise culture.

All of these shortcomings rendered economically unjustifiable the continuation of the corporate practices and management style of SPEs, even if plausible arguments could be found in support of their traditional role and function as custodians of the interests of the state in the petroleum sector.

From a political viewpoint, the role played by the decline in importance – and significance – of concepts such as *'permanent sovereignty over natural resources'* and the *'new international economic order'* during the latter part of the 1980s in weakening the foundations of state enterprise culture remains to be fully ascertained. The continuing relevance of these ideological models in an environment characterised by the intense competition for international investment funds has for some time now been open to question.

Even so it is possible that for ideological reasons, developing country governments may suffer from a certain psychological discomfort from the privatisation of SPEs and some are wary of the long-term implications. This is particularly so if the SPE in question is seen to have been a success in terms of assuring national ownership and control, even if not entirely so from a purely commercial perspective. Where, on the other hand, the enterprise is judged by national authorities to have a fair chance of commercial success if allowed to remain in the public sector, then insistence by external sources on restructuring and privatisation as part of overall macroeconomic prescriptions or other loan conditionalities could lead to complications. Restructuring or privatisation under these circumstances could be perceived by national governments to be tinged with a shade of doctrinal bias. This in turn can lead to frictions between the national authorities and the international donor community, with attendant adverse implications for the inception and implementation of restructuring and privatisation programmes.

The whole question of restructuring and privatisation activity in the petroleum sector in developing countries has thus to be viewed against this somewhat conflicting background – i.e. commercial pressures *versus* ideological uncertainty.

4.3.2 Overview of current restructuring and privatisation programmes affecting SPEs in developing countries

The overall policy objective of restructuring and privatisation has been to imbue SPEs with business autonomy and a commercial focus, thus rendering them more accountable, less politicised and more competitive within the domestic and international petroleum industry.

Privatisation options for SPEs will generally include the public offering of shares, the private sale of shares, the sale of assets, a management/employee buy-out, or the more limited forms of a management contract or the leasing of rights to acreage held by the SPE. In practice a combination of two or more of these methods will often be employed. The proposed privatisation of the

Peruvian SPE Petroperú, for example, plans to make use of all of these methods.

Some form of management/employee or citizen participation in privatisation programmes (financed in part or wholly by the issue of special nominally priced vouchers, as has been the case with privatisation exercises in other sectors in both Czechoslovakia and Russia) is becoming a regular practice. The rationale which is sometimes given for this requirement is the desire to ensure an equitable income distribution post-privatisation. However, a much more practical and plausible explanation for this would appear to be the necessity to dilute domestic opposition to the sale.

Of the restructuring or privatisation programmes so far completed or planned in the petroleum sector, three cases stand out for consideration:

- the privatisation of the state oil and gas monopoly in Argentina;
- the planned privatisation of the Peruvian SPE Petroperú;
- the restructuring and partial privatisation of public sector enterprises in thepetroleum sector in Nigeria.

Argentina has led the way in the privatisation of SPEs in Latin America with the state-owned oil and gas enterprises Gas del Estado (GdE) and Yacimientos Petroliferos Fiscales (YPF). The sell-off of GdE has now been completed. The first stage in the privatisation of YPF was completed in June 1993, almost six months ahead of schedule. Domestic private-sector enterprises were strongly represented in these privatisation exercises, which affected both the upstream and downstream sectors. The process itself is widely regarded to have been a success. The scale of the exercise, the transparency of procedures involved and its efficient administration have in particular received wide acclaim. Even so the process has not been entirely free from political difficulties – and the exercise is still to be completed for YPF. It is also worth noting that although partly privatised, YPF still retains it quasi-monopoly status in the oil and gas sector in Argentina.

Other SPE privatisation programmes which are planned in Latin America include that for Petroperú. The plan focuses initially on the sale, leasing or sub-contracting of downstream assets such a service stations, transportation facilities, oilwell service companies, and idle capacity in operating refineries. It is likely some of these will be sold either to management or employees. Limited sell-offs are also possible for Colombia's Ecopetrol and Petroecuador of Ecuador. But if and when these occur, both are expected to retain their core holdings.

In Nigeria, the focus of policy reform in the petroleum sector has been on commercialisation and a formal (legislative) commitment to privatisation which is yet to translate fully into practice. At the forefront of this commitment is the Commercialisation and Privatisation Act of 1990 which outlines the plan for the complete or partial privatisation of 98 public-sector enterprises, and for the complete or partial commercialisation of 35 others.

The policy envisaged for public-sector enterprises involved in oil and gas operations in Nigeria is that of restructuring, commercialisation and partial privatisation. The downstream sector represents the furthest limits of the privatisation policy in the petroleum industry. So far only *partial* privatisation has taken place in the sector. This includes the sale of equity interest in state-owned marketing companies (Unipetrol, African Petroleum, and the National Oil and Chemical Company) to private sector investors. The government, however, continues to retain 40 per cent equity interest in these companies.

In the upstream sector, the flagship of public sector involvement in the petroleum sector, the Nigerian National Petroleum Corporation (NNPC), has so far been earmarked only for commercialisation (defined by the Act of 1990 as the reorganisation of wholly or partly state-owned enterprises with the objective of transforming them into viable, efficient, profit-making commercial ventures capable of competing internationally and without government subvention). The government continues to retain full ownership of the corporation as well as general regulatory powers over its operations.

The government's continued ownership of NNPC – and the continuing presence of public-sector involvement in the downstream sector in Nigeria – provides a clear illustration of the limits of current privatisation policies as applied to the petroleum sector. The fact that the Nigerian petroleum sector is widely perceived to be the leader in the restructuring and privatisation process in the African petroleum industry only serves to reinforce this view. Even more so is the fact that other African SPEs (Sonatrach – Algeria; Sonangol – Angola; SNH – Cameroon; HydroCongo – Congo; EGPC – Egypt; Libya's NOC; and ETAP – Tunisia) have largely escaped unscathed the full rigour of the restructuring and privatisation process. In Gabon the authorities decided in 1987 to suspend the activities of the SPE, PetroGab, and to transfer its interests and operations to the government. It is still not clear if the options of restructuring or privatisation were ever given full and adequate consideration.

Closer examination of prevailing trends in the oil and gas sectors in developing countries therefore brings us to the conclusion that while a policy transformation may be underway, the scope and magnitude of institutional change may be far less profound than had originally been expected. Current policies in the petroleum sector regarding SPEs are without doubt driven by a new economic pragmatism. Nonetheless, the indications are that such policies may also be influenced to a significant degree by strategic considerations regarding national ownership and control. It has been said that improved conditions for the oil and gas industry are the result of macroeconomic reform policies rather than of any specific measures to ease investment conditions.[4] We on our part do not discern any clear pattern which is indicative of an emerging worldwide trend towards a profound institutional transformation involving the privatisation of SPEs. In this respect, we would agree that the privatisation of oil and gas enterprises in Argentina and the planned privatisation of similar enterprises in Peru may be regarded as being 'very much the exception'.[5]

4. Kielmas, M., 'Latin America: Reform and Privatisations Transform Investment Scene', *Petroleum Economist* (June 1993), 18.

5. See Note 4, *supra*.

4.3.3 Worldwide prospects

The greatest potential for restructuring and privatisation in the petroleum sector lies in the ex-communist countries in transition – Russia, the CIS and Eastern Europe. In Russia, Western experts and advisers have been playing a key role in the restructuring of the country's oil industry. With regard to the transition to private-sector ownership and management, however, the overall lessons emerging from privatisation exercises conducted for other economic sectors in the region do not seem to offer much optimism for privatisation in the oil and gas sectors. Having run into a host of problems including technical difficulties, political obstacles and uncertain outcomes, the indications are that the privatisation process in the ex-centrally planned economies is rapidly losing the ardent support which it enjoyed locally not so long ago. It is now common knowledge that popular enthusiasm over economic reforms and the transition process as a whole has waned considerably over the past two years in the ex-socialist countries.

The process itself has been characterised in many instances by much ambiguity. In countries such as Czechoslovakia, Hungary and many of the CIS Republics, for example, the state continues to retain title to (or a significant share of the assets of) 'privatised' enterprises. In Russia, on the other hand, the process appears to be in some difficulty as regards foreign participation – in view of the fact that the authorities seem to be either unable or unwilling to guarantee property ownership and the protection of property rights. Compounding these difficulties further has been the sheer magnitude and complexity of the restructuring programme which has included whole economic sectors and industries.

Political opposition to the privatisation of the oil and gas industries, fuelled in some cases as (in Russia) by economic nationalism, is likely to draw comfort and fortitude from the perceived failure of similar programmes in other sectors – much more so in view of the considerable social costs which such programmes are seen to have inflicted on society. Irrespective of the fall of communism, opposition to the privatisation of Russia's oil and gas enterprises (production associations) is likely to be accentuated by historical and social factors and by long-standing political and legal traditions. It is thus unlikely that either economic pragmatism or the commercial necessity of privatisation in the sector will be matched by political legitimacy, social acceptance or a even whole-hearted commitment from the authorities. The complicated institutional set-up of the Russian petroleum industry, with no clear delineation of authority and responsibilities between the various operating and regulatory bodies, can only constitute a further impediment to privatisation.

While privatisation on a small scale has taken place in the downstream sector in some Eastern European countries, the indications are that a similar more extensive exercise involving oil and gas enterprises in the major petroleum producing countries of Russia and the CIS does not appear – for the time being at least – to be a seriously considered option. Current restructuring programmes in the sector do not point in that direction. So far 'privatisation' in these countries has largely followed the 'Yugoslav model' of corporatisation and the offer of shares to management and/or employees. It would thus seem that the full potential for (overseas) private-sector participation in the oil and gas sectors of the ex-socialist countries in transition (including Russia and the CIS) will mainly take the form of acquisition of rights to exploration and production acreage, or of licences and permits for marketing and distribution.

Western European prospects appear to offer much more promise. Following the privatisation of UK energy utilities and the sale of the remaining government shares in BP by the Thatcher government in the latter part of the 1980s, other Western European countries have since adopted similar programmes. The Spanish SPE Repsol is now partly privatised. The French SPE Elf Aquitaine is scheduled for privatisation, even though President François Mitterand is reported to be opposed to the sale. The prospects for other SPEs such as Italy's ENI and the Norwegian giant Statoil are still very uncertain even though privatisation has been proposed or hinted at. In the case of ENI, the move towards privatisation appears to have stalled following allegations of corruption at the company and the arrest of five of its chairmen in March of 1993. Company executives at the time stressed that these developments were unlikely to slow down progress towards privatisation. Independent commentators seemed to think otherwise.[6]

The global outlook for the privatisation of SPEs reveals a mixed and somewhat erratic pattern. The indications, however, are strongly in favour of continued state ownership of restructured SPEs or the partial ownership of partly-privatised enterprises.

4.4 KEY CONCEPTS UNDERLYING THE PRIVATISATION OF SPEs

At the end of the 1970s, public-sector enterprises had come to dominate the economies of most developing countries. Bolstered by the wave of nationalisations which ensued in the 1970s – between 1970 and 1975 alone there were 336 recorded acts of expropriation of foreign-owned property, many of them in the petroleum sector[7] – SPEs came to command powerful and important positions within the national socio-economic and political framework.

The nationalisations of the 1970s were inspired and driven by clearly defined political/ideological concepts: national ownership, control and sovereignty over natural resources – with the SPE as the most commonly used instrument for achieving these objectives. The current process of restructuring and privatisation, on the other hand, seems to have been necessitated more by economic exigencies. This has been the case in particular in the developing countries where the process has not been matched with the same amount of ideological zeal which inspired the privatisation exercises of the Thatcher era in the United Kingdom.

6. See, for example, *Petroleum Economist* (April 1993), 28.
7. Minor, M. S. (July 1992), 8.

The role played by ideological factors in the current process has thus not been quite evident. With the exception of the collapse of communism which may be regarded as a factor within the overall global economic and political context, current restructuring and privatisation exercises in developing countries may be viewed from an ideological perspective only in so far as they can be considered to be the antithesis of the nationalisations of the 1970s.

The current reorganisation and privatisation process forms a component part of macroeconomic restructuring and in some cases structural adjustment programmes. Thus the attainment of the stated economic goals and objectives of efficiency, improved productivity and profitability constitute the key issues on which the restructuring and privatisation of SPEs are predicated. Also at the centre of the current economic exigencies driving restructuring and privatisation activity is the debt crisis. Hence the restructuring of public debt with possible recourse to debt-equity swaps has been a feature of recent privatisation exercises conducted in Argentina, Chile and the Philippines.

For governments in developing countries privatisation creates an ideological predicament as well as practical difficulties. Both these aspects relate to the desired objective of exercising national control over natural resources. Beyond an economic justification, concepts comparable to those of the *new international economic order* and *permanent sovereignty over natural resources* have not been found to give force to the current restructuring and privatisation process. The collapse of communism and centralised economic planning of itself does not seem to have spawned an ideological foundation or a heart-warming theme for the process. There have certainly been no catching policy manifestoes or ringing political proclamations – beyond an association of the process with general economic and (in some cases) political restructuring. Managerial autonomy as an inherent feature of restructuring and privatisation, on the other hand, creates a difficulty for developing country governments in their search to reconcile the twin objectives of maintaining national control over operations and the achievement of desired efficiency gains.

As a concept, privatisation raises the question as to whether the process, if implemented, can be progressive both in terms of efficiency gains and income distribution changes – i.e. how far can the convergence between efficiency and equity be achieved through privatisation as a neoclassical prescription to remedy the various shortcomings of the public sector management model? It has been said, for example, that 'anyone sympathetic with the importance of equitable distribution has an interest in pushing [selected] neoclassical prescriptions towards the convergence of efficiency and equity'.[8] While restructuring and privatisation in the oil and gas sector, as with other neoclassical prescriptions, may have the potential of promoting equitable outcomes and enhancing efficiency gains in the period following the reorganisation, there is still no guarantee that this will happen in actual practice.

The proceeds from the privatisation exercise without doubt provide the government with an opportunity to either increase social spending or to reduce

8.   Ascher, W., 'On the Convergence of Efficiency and Equity Via Neoclassical Prescriptions', Journal of Interamerican Studies and World Affairs, **31**, 1 & 2 (1989), 49, p. 50.

taxes. Depending on the manner in which such either of these policy options are implemented, this could contribute towards the achievement of some measure of income distribution. Even so the emergence of a domestic private sector in the petroleum industry could well lead to the economic empowerment of new sections of society with attendant inequalities in economic status, thus accentuating social divisions. On the efficiency side, in the absence of effective competition and proper regulation privatised enterprises would reap monopoly profits at the expense of consumers. Irrespective of these possible drawbacks, however, the potential for promoting efficiency and equity seems to weigh more in favour of a privatised enterprise which (at the very least) is not subject to government subsidies at taxpayers' expense.

Restructuring and privatisation continue to be the key concepts in macroeconomic reforms and adjustment policies worldwide, and in particular in the developing countries and ex-socialist societies in transition. Whether or not the process will ultimately lead to genuine structural changes remains open to question. It has thus been observed that while as a concept privatisation could be expected to lead to far-reaching economic and social transformations, the mere transfer of title is unlikely to achieve such an effect.[9] On the evidence of current trends, it would seem unlikely that any such transformations will be forthcoming in the oil and gas sectors through the medium of privatisation.

4.5 BENEFITS, PROBLEMS AND OBSTACLES TO PRIVATISATION

There are undoubtedly some benefits to be derived from the successful restructuring or privatisation of an SPE. Increased competition, greater efficiency, commercial focus and orientation, access to private sector capital resources and a general freshness of approach to management and the conduct of operations are just some of the principal derivatives of restructuring or privatisation. These factors form the basis for achieving enhanced performance and improved productivity for the restructured SPE or privatised enterprise. The privatisation theory postulates that greater exposure to competitive market forces – assuming that the enterprise loses its domestic monopoly pole position following the restructuring or privatisation exercise – should ensure that management pursues with a much greater vigour productivity and profitability goals as well as other performance incentives. Operating in a commercial environment devoid of political interference (and with the clearly defined financial interests of shareholders as the principal consideration) management will also be more inclined towards exercise stricter controls over cost accounting and expenditure programmes, thus increasing the mineral rent.

Following from this line of argument, such gains should not necessarily be limited to the company. The domestic economy as a whole also stands to benefit from a successful restructuring or privatisation exercise. Apart from the

9. Frydman, R. and Rapaczynski, A., 'Privatization in Eastern Europe: Is the State Withering Away?', *Finance and Development* (June 1993), 10.

immediate financial gains accruing to the national treasury from the sale of public assets, improved efficiency in performance and profitability implies greater fiscal benefits through the tax levy on a higher mineral rent. Invariably, privatisation offers greater scope for much higher fiscal revenues accruing to the state than are likely to be obtainable in a monopolistic public enterprise situation. From an economic and financial viewpoint, therefore, the domestic economy should benefit more from a privately run petroleum enterprise spurred on by competitive market forces towards the attainment of efficiency gains than from a monopolistic SPE which is more likely to generate less and consume internally much more of the mineral rent.[10] In addition to the earning potential of the enterprise under private sector management, considerable benefits to the national economy may also be derived from the dynamic impact of economic stimulation and the spawning of a domestic entrepreneurial culture from the restructuring or privatisation exercise. This would be the case in particular if market liberalisation forms a component part of the macroeconomic restructuring process, thus increasing domestic competition.

But as desirable as these benefits may be, there are nonetheless considerable difficulties and obstacles to be overcome on the road to the restructuring and/ or privatisation of SPEs. Such difficulties and obstacles explain in part the cautious approach which has so far been applied to the transition to complete privatisation in some countries.

In most cases the more immediate problem is likely to be that arising from the absence of appropriate transition mechanisms: local capital and domestic capital markets. Other constraints, such as the lack of an adequate policy framework, can lead to difficulties of implementation and hence to policies which may not be technically viable. Another problem concerns the proper (or acceptable) method for the valuation of assets – i.e. which standard to apply in trying to determine a reference value: current replacement value?; physical inspection as a means of determining actual productive value?; or estimates of remaining (productive) life-time of the asset. Difficulties regarding property and assets valuation for SPEs will often be compounded by the absence of a functioning domestic stock market, and hence a market value, to serve as a point of reference. The complexity of the valuation exercise is no less diminished by the fact that the actual value of assets may have been distorted by years of inadequate or non-exposure to market forces, outstanding liabilities, or the distorting effect of historical valuations which do not reflect the erosion of equity over time. A simple reference to book value or the balance sheets of the enterprise may therefore not be representative of the true value of the assets of the enterprise. This could result in either an overvaluation or undercapitalisation of the enterprise. A general impression that the enterprise had been undercapitalised prior to privatisation, as occurred recently in some East European countries, could in turn lead to the government being accused of offering national assets as 'gifts' to foreigners. Many of these difficulties are

---

10. Wälde, T. W. (1991).

largely of a technical nature and have already been widely discussed in the general literature on privatisation in developing countries.[11]

The absence of adequate domestic capital entails reliance on outside sources for financing the transfer of enterprises to the private sector. But considerable hostility to foreign ownership of perceived key sectors ('commanding heights') of the economy is known to constitute an enduring impediment to large-scale privatisation of prominent enterprises in some developing countries. This is particularly the case where the enterprise – such as an SPE – has attended the status of a national icon or is seen to be a symbol of the 'struggle' against domination by foreign economic interests. The overall economic objectives of the state could therefore go well beyond market-oriented performance and include issues such as national ownership and control of strategic or vital sectors of the economy. The natural resources industries readily springs to mind here as one such sector.

The restructuring or privatisation of an SPE thus raises questions and difficulties of both a political and social nature. SPEs are viewed as strategic institutions promoting the objective of national ownership and control over core industries. Viewed from this perspective, foreign participation in the SPE privatisation process is bound to be regarded in some quarters very much with apprehension and foreboding. For this reason privatisation in the oil and gas sectors in developing countries has remained a decidedly mundane theme far removed from the spontaneous excitement associated with the oil industry nationalisations of the 1970s. The only exceptions appear to be the sporadic eruptions of national passion generated in some countries in opposition to overseas involvement. In Argentina, for instance, the privatisation of the gas utility GdE generated considerable political controversy even though the domestic private sector was strongly represented. It is also for reasons of national ownership and control that in some countries the option of restructuring (Nigeria – NNPC) or partial privatisation involving an expansion of the capital base of the SPE (Brazil – Petrobrás) has been chosen as an alternative to full privatisation in the petroleum sector. The restructuring and privatisation of SPEs therefore raise problems of a political and social nature.

The restructuring and privatisation of SPEs is taking place within the context of economic conditions which readily provide commercial justification for the process. From an institutional viewpoint, there is nonetheless a perceived absence of authentic identification of existing institutional structures in the sector with the transition process. Inevitably, this gives rise to social tensions. The adverse effects which restructuring or privatisation may have for employment, for example, lends to the exercise a socio-political dimension. The close association of the restructuring and privatisation process with macroeconomic reforms and structural adjustment programmes has also led

11. See, for example, E. Hinzen, 'Privatisation of Enterprises in ACP Countries', *The Courier (ACP-EC)*, No. 139 (May–June 1993), Suppl. 1-4; see also Moller, L. E., The Unfolding of State Petroleum Corporations in Developing Countries, Centre for Petroleum and Mineral Law and Policy, LL.M Thesis, Dundee University Library (1993).

to the identification of the former with the social costs of implementing such programmes.

Some of these programmes are frequently regarded as being external impositions or macroeconomic prescriptions from the outside ('conditionalities'). Where restructuring and privatisation have been perceived to be driven by pressure exerted on the government by international financial institutions, the process has not been received whole-heartedly by reforming countries. As a result, there arises the basic problem of having to transform structures and institutions (some of which have grown used to functioning on the basis of deeply entrenched practices and procedures not easily amenable to change) with policies which may sometimes be considered as being alien and not home-grown.

Arguments in favour of much improved post-restructuring/-privatisation performance is often interpreted by SPE employees and by opponents of the process to mean cost-cutting which could entail staff and payroll reductions; hence cost-efficiency and efficiency gains are vaguely understood as meaning jobless growth. Under these circumstances the voice of political opposition is most likely to be endowed with a social relevance, if not perceived moral convictions.

From a cultural perspective, the frictions which are bound to be generated by the clash between the entrepreneurial orientations of a new business cultural and the bureaucratic, quasi-commercial, 'civil service' approach of the old public management model also poses some problems for the enterprise in the post-restructuring/-privatisation period. It is likewise not completely certain if restructuring is going to lead to greater efficiency. Greater accountability, for instance, may lead to more bureaucracy and longer procedures – with attendant delays in the decision-making process.

To sum up, the restructuring and privatisation process in general entails economic and infrastructural obstacles, possible political pitfalls, legal hurdles, and most probably some post-reorganisation difficulties. Most of these problems are likely to be accentuated when the restructuring or privatisation exercise involves an SPE. To add to these obstacles is the apparent ideological predicament of developing countries. The latter are seemingly having to face the prospect of the losing of control and sovereignty – however symbolic – over natural resources. In most circumstances, it will require political will and commitment – and where possible some degree of national consensus as to the desirability and form of the intended reorganisation – to be able to overcome these difficulties.

4.6 CONCLUDING REMARKS

Do current SPE restructuring programmes point ineluctably towards some form of privatisation in the future? The progression from restructuring to privatisation, far from being a logical step in the current reorganisation exercises being pursued in many developing countries with respect to SPEs, will tend to depend on a number of factors. These include the impact which the prospects for investment on offer to the international petroleum industry in Russia, the CIS and Eastern Europe will continue to have on the international competition for oil and gas investment funds and the extent to which the developing countries are prepared to go to secure such funds. Aversion to full-scale privatisation of developing country SPEs may in some cases be tempered by the need to attract private sector investment for exploration and development.

In the developing countries, the most likely candidates for some form of privatisation in the near future are once again likely to come from Latin America. Peru's Petroperú and Bolivia's Yacimientos Petroliferos Fiscales Bolivianos (YPFB) are in line for the next phase of SPE privatisations. The indications are that the oil and gas sectors in Brazil and Venezuela could in the near future also be opened up to greater participation and involvement from the private sector. However, uncertainty still surrounds the form or the extent of the proposed role of the private sector in the petroleum industry in these countries. There are as yet no firm indications of any moves towards the future privatisation of Brazil's Petrobrás or Venezuela's Petróleos de Venezuela. In general the prospects for Latin America look somewhat uncertain: in both Brazil and Mexico, for example, SPEs still continue to retain their constitutional monopolies over oil and gas operations.

The privatisation of SPEs in other developing countries such as those in Africa does not at the moment appear to be an option under consideration. Increased private sector involvement in these countries will therefore continue to take the traditional form of acreage licensing and the leasing of undeveloped SPE oil and gas properties. While the need for economic rationalisation points inexorably towards continued restructuring of SPEs in developing countries, privatisation – as far as we can see – does not for the time being appear to be the inevitable consequence of the current transition process. This notwith-standing, private-sector expansion in both the upstream and downstream sectors of the petroleum industry in many developing countries is likely to continue unabated and independently of the actual privatisation of public-sector enterprises involved in exploration, development or marketing/distribution – except for those countries where such enterprises continue to retain a monopoly over some or all of these activities.

It is also doubtful whether the restructuring or privatisation process is likely to have a profound impact on the existing structure of the international petroleum industry in the same manner as the profound transformations which were wrought by the nationalisations of the 1970s. Increasingly, restructured SPEs (Braspetro in Angola; NNPC in Ghana; Sapet Development Corporation, a subsidiary of the China National Petroleum Corporation, in Peru) or privatised oil and gas enterprises will embark on overseas ventures away from their traditional domestic jurisdiction. Even so the overall impact of this on the structure of the international petroleum industry – beyond any significant moves in the direction of vertical integration with a view to downstream operations overseas – is bound to be minimal.

Of much greater significance will be the impact of SPE restructuring or privatisation on the domestic economy. The structural impact on the national economies of restructuring or privatising countries is likely to be profound. But how will the newly commercialised and budding private sector petroleum enterprises cope with the pressures of domestic competition after having been for so long under the protective umbrella of public sector monopoly? Such competition is bound to intensify in the downstream sector, which in many developing countries has been one of the most inefficient. The long-term survival of the restructured or privatised enterprises will thus depend on how much competition and efficiency they can bring to their operations under competitive market conditions.

Finally, the advent of restructured SPEs or privatised petroleum enterprises constitutes a significant and important element of current policies promoting public sector disengagement from direct participation in the productive sectors of the economies of developing countries. Privatisation, as in Argentina, signifies the birth of a new domestic private sector with potential benefits for the domestic oil and gas sector and for the national economy as a whole. Overall, however, the magnitude and impact of privatisation on domestic economies appears to have fallen far short of the initial expectations of all involved – the private sector investor community, governments and commentators. The way forward for governments of countries considering the privatisation of SPEs would henceforth be to appraise the progress made on other projects and in other countries, and to anticipate and devise compromise solutions to some of the conflicting ideological and practical challenges which privatisation is likely to pose.

Chapter 5

International Petroleum Licensing, Exploration Activity and Fiscal Terms

Susan Hodgshon

5.1 INTRODUCTION

The general perception of current international E&P activity and the outlook for it in the short and medium term is pessimistic. It appears to be conventional wisdom that companies have overstretched themselves in international exploration over the past decade, that the results have not justified the investment and that, with significant exceptions, international exploration over the coming years will decline. Such exceptions include CIS investment and the effects of US companies allocating greater resources overseas as domestic exploration activity comes close to collapse. Incidentally, the effects of these two exceptions are contradictory, the one draining resources from the major oil companies, the others increasing further the numbers of companies operating overseas.

It is still too early to tell whether the Jeremiahs will be proved right. There is as yet no clear trend: exploratory wells drilled in the years since 1987 have fluctuated within a narrow band and the number of wells drilled over the first six months of 1992 is on target for the year to at least equal 1991 figures. But it is certainly true that less oil and gas has been found in the past decade than in any other recent decade. Figures 5.1, 5.2 and 5.3 illustrate this very clearly.

It is this lack of success that leads to permission for the future of exploratory activity.

Against this background of uncertainty about the future and apparently disappointing exploration results in the past, three main questions stand out for consideration. These are:

- Where are companies active in obtaining acreage?
- Where are companies drilling exploration wells?
- Is there any correlation between exploration activity and fiscal terms?

Figure 5.1. Offshore exploration 1987–1991 – NFWs drilled/oil discovered (excluding China, Iran and Iraq)

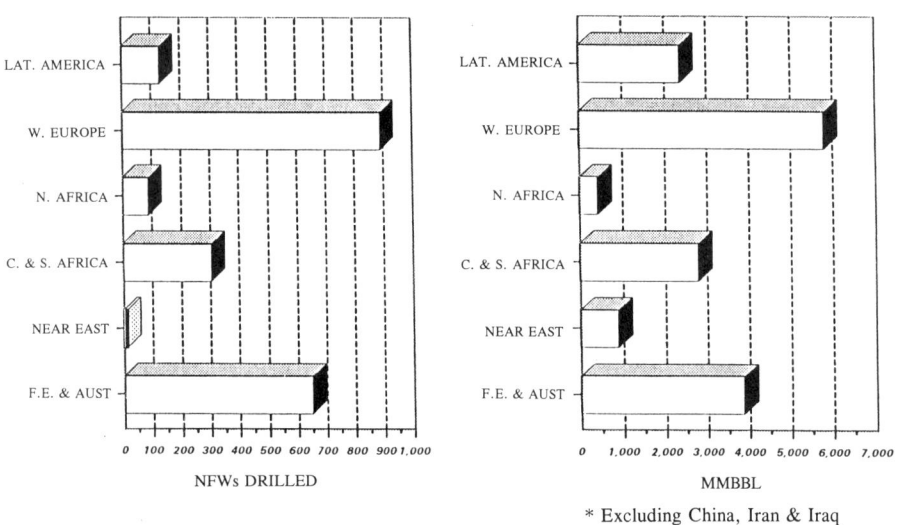

* Excluding China, Iran & Iraq

Figure 5.2 Offshore exploration 1987–1991 – NFWs drilled/oil discovered (Norway, Nigeria, Angola, Malaysia and Indonesia)

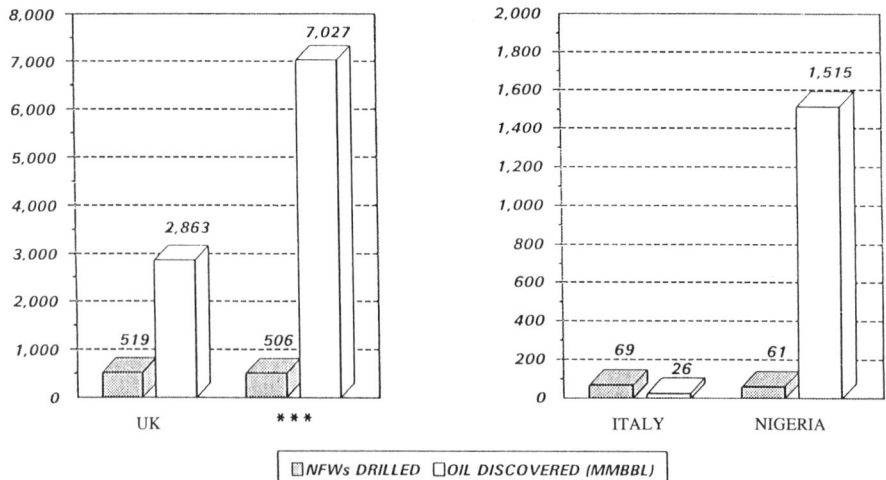

*** Norway, Nigeria, Angola, Malaysia & Indonesia

Figure 5.3. Onshore exploration 1987–1991 – NFWs drilled/oil discovered

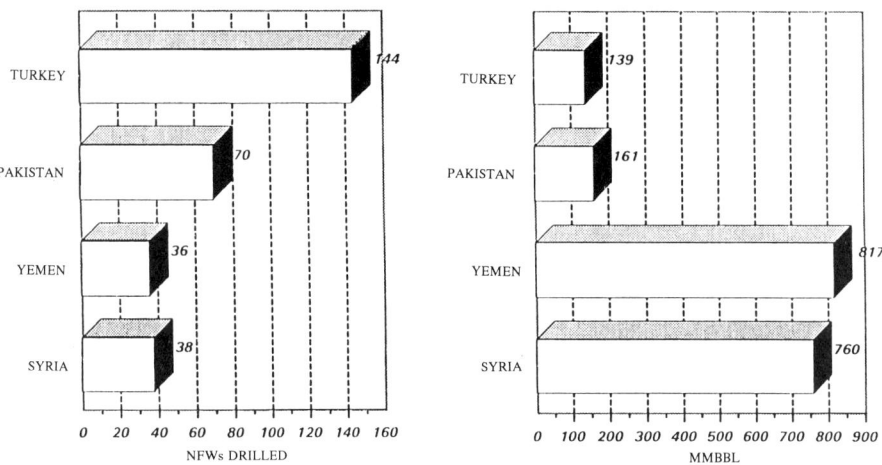

5.2 LICENSING ACTIVITY

A review of recent exploration licensing activity shows that both the number of licences awarded and the number of countries in which awards are made have remained remarkably consistent over the past five years. The number of countries with awards is constant at around 50 in any one year. The number of awards has also varied little – being around 500 in any year in which a UK licensing round is concluded, and 100–150 less in any other year.

A regional breakdown of recent exploration awards also reveals a consistent pattern, with Europe and the Far East being the most active region (see Table 5.1).

Table 5.1 Exploration licence awards by region, 1990–91

Region	Exploration licence awards (%)	
	1990	1991
Europe	38	48
Far East	27	26
Latin America	17	14
Africa	12	9
Near East	6	3

Figure 5.4 Exploration licence awards – 1986–1990

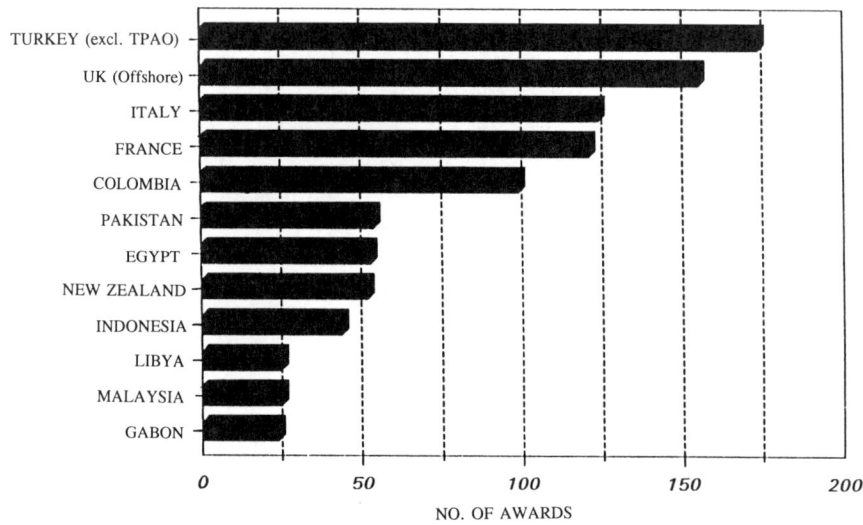

Figure 5.5 Exploration licence awards

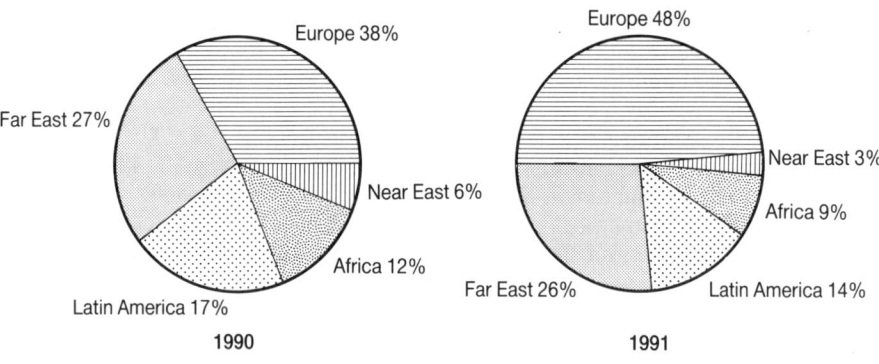

Closer look at the countries involved in licensing reveals an even more remarkable concentration of activity than the regional totals suggest. Of the 53 countries in which exploration licences were awarded in 1991, the top 10 countries account for nearly two-thirds, and the top five for over half. A similar story can be told of 1990 (see Table 5.2).

Table 5.2 Exploration licence awards: percentage of total, 1990–91

| | Exploration Licence awards (% of total) | |
	1990	1991
Top 5 countries	52	51
Top 10 countries	69	64
Rest of world	31	36

Figure 5.6 Exploration licence awards (percentage of total)

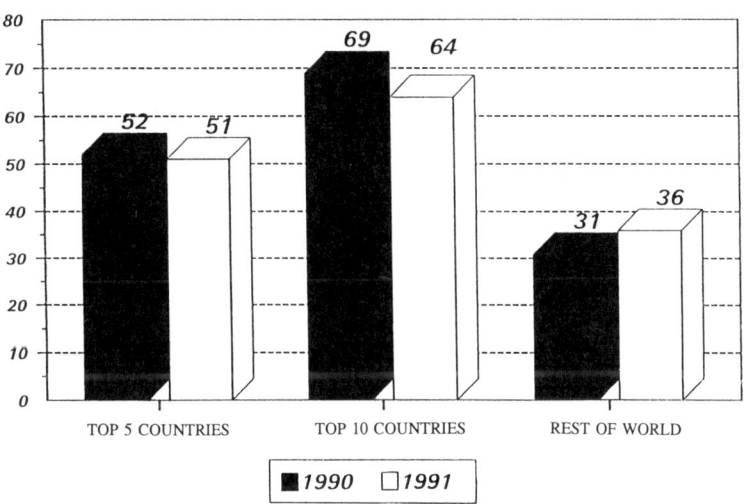

As a final piece of the jigsaw in this concentration of activity, it is interesting to look at the five most active countries over the past two years (see Table 5.3).

Table 5.3 Exploration licence awards: top five countries 1990–91

	1990	1991
1	Australia	United Kingdom
2	Netherlands	Australia
3	Turkey*	Colombia
4	Colombia	Turkey
5	Italy	Italy

There is virtually no change in the composition of the top five and at least three of the countries – Netherlands, Italy and Turkey – are not those that might be expected to be top of the list if a straw poll were taken of international exploration hotspots. If we look at the most active countries over a longer time-frame, the five years from 1986 to 1990, the same pattern emerges. Turkey, France and Italy are in the top five over the period, while Pakistan and New Zealand appear in the top 10.

So, while the answer to whether there is a decline in current international exploration licensing activity is 'no' it is qualified by the fact that such activity is concentrated in countries, many of which are among the less geologically prospective in the world.

5.3 EXPLORATION ACTIVITY

It could be argued that the fact that the less prospective – especially European – countries have been successful in their licensing efforts simply reflects the fact that they are low-cost environments with a highly developed infrastructure and low work commitments. That is true – up to a point.

But if we look at the acid test of a successful policy – the number of New Field Wildcats drilled – we see that more NFWs have been drilled over the past five years in the less prospective regions than in the more prospective ones.

Overall, there is no evidence of any trend towards declining exploratory activity. On a regional basis, there is a slight downwards trend in evidence in Latin America, due mainly to a steady decline in Brazil and Colombia. In other regions, apart from the Near East, there have been only minor fluctuations in activity. The Near East has seen a consistent increase in activity, particularly in Oman and Yemen, for very different reasons. In Yemen, the drilling has been prompted by enthusiasm over prospects while in Oman, the dominant company Shell is trying to stem a steady decline in reserves.

Looking separately at onshore, although Latin America is the most active region, the Far East and Europe are not far behind in NFW drilling. But these two regions perform poorly -and Europe dismally – in terms of oil discovered.

Offshore there is more correlation between the level of activity and the results achieved. The Near East, where onshore or offshore, will *always* be a wild card. But although Europe and the Far East are the most active regions, they are not the most successful. And if Norway were taken out of the equation, the European success rate would be significantly lower.

The same story can be seen in the level of NFW drilling for individual countries. In the five years 1987 to 1991, more NFWs were drilled onshore Pakistan than onshore Syria, Yemen, Libya or Algeria. There were more drilled offshore Italy than offshore Nigeria, Gabon or Egypt. More drilled onshore France or Turkey than onshore Egypt or Oman. Finally, there were more NFWs drilled offshore UK than offshore Indonesia, Malaysia, Nigeria, Angola and Norway combined. But again, as the details show, effort is not mentioned by results.

It is clear, then, that factors other than geological prospectivity are at work in promoting a successful licensing and exploration environment.

5.4 FISCAL TERMS

A number of non-technical factors attract companies to invest in exploration in any country. They include:

- regular licensing;
- a rapid and efficient negotiations process;
- entry costs (signature bonuses/data purchase costs);
- work commitments;
- the level and operation of state participation;
- appropriate fiscal terms.

Of these factors, the most important is the fiscal terms. Active countries like Pakistan may have a difficult negotiations process and significant state participation provisions. Turkey makes no attempt to publicise its terms at all. But the one factor common to all consistently active exploration environments is that they have moderate fiscal terms. In many cases the terms are highly attractive.

It is beyond the scope of this chapter to examine fiscal terms in detail. However, there is an enormous range in fiscal terms worldwide – from countries such as the UK at the one extreme of the scale where government take is commonly under 40 per cent to Malaysia at the other, with government take averaging over 85 per cent.

It is not surprising that the countries with the largest government take are also those that are highly prospective geologically – countries such as Malaysia, Indonesia, Nigeria and Yemen. It is common for countries, where major discoveries have focused company attention on them as an exploration hot-spot, to move rapidly to stiffen their terms to reflect their prospectivity. Recent

Figure 5.7 Average government take (percentage of pretax profits)

Attractive	Moderate	Moderate – Severe	Severe
(<50%)	(51–70%)	(71–80%	(>80%)
UK	Netherlands	Norway	Indonesia
France	Turkey	Angola	Malaysia
Italy		Gabon	Nigeria
Pakistan		Colombia	Syria
Argentina		Algeria	Yemen
Australia		Egypt	

examples of such a trend include Yemen after Hunt's Alif discovery, Gabon after the Rabi Kounga find, Vietnam (with no major find yet to its name, but still 'flavour of the month' among the oil companies). Even Colombia, which has in the past decade retained a relatively moderate and consistent fiscal regime, has recently started turning the screw on its terms. And, as long as the perception of their high prospectivity among companies remains, it seems that not only will they accept severe fiscal terms, but they will queue up to have such terms inflicted on them.

However, although companies are keen enough to toughen their fiscal terms when companies queue at their doors, they are slower to relax them when the queue shortens. Often they will wait until companies which are long established in their country start to pull out, and licensing and, subsequently, exploration activity drops disproportionately in relation to international trends. Countries where that process has either begun or is now beginning include Egypt, Syria, Gabon and Colombia. In all these countries the recent trends of licensing activity and/or production is significantly down over the past few years. All, except Colombia, have severe fiscal terms, and Colombia, as mentioned, is now increasing the severity of its terms.

At the other end of the scale, countries with moderate or even low prospectivity can maintain investment if they provide highly attractive fiscal terms. It is no coincidence that all the less prospective countries which maintain a consistently active licensing policy have attractive fiscal regimes, a wide spread of active companies and, almost as important as the first two factors, very broad ring fence provisions. By this we mean that companies with existing production can offset their continued exploration expenditure against taxes due on profits. This helps create a virtuous circle of continued investment, especially when the fiscal regime is so constructed that continued exploration investment can, in many cases, be offset against a high marginal tax rate. The UK is the prime example of this phenomenon.

5.5 OUTLOOK

To return to the beginning of our discourse, if the Jeremiahs are right and international exploratory activity is really due for a significant cyclical downturn, who will be the winners and who the losers?

The winners will undoubtedly continue to be those countries where companies feel they can make major discoveries. But if the perception of their prospectivity declines, the exodus of companies may be rapid. The losers in the short term will be those countries that fail to respond to their declining prospectivity by overhauling their fiscal terms radically and creating a moderate and consistent regime. Countries that do take such steps – as Argentina has in the past two years – should be able to halt and reverse the exodus of companies, or even attract an inflow where there was none before. This will be reinforced by the increasing number of smaller companies investing overseas.

And what are the prospects for those countries which, as we have tried to show, are the hidden success story of the 1980s – the less prospective countries which have already done everything they can to create favourable investment conditions? Can they perform the same trick in the 1990s? The answer, unfortunately, is likely to be 'no' for those countries where perception of their prospectivity is so low that even the most attractive fiscal terms cannot reverse the decline in activity. New Zealand is one recent example of such a country, onshore UK and Australia are two others. But those countries with a moderate prospectivity profile, e.g. UK, Netherlands, Italy, Pakistan, Argentina, a stable environment, attractive fiscal terms and a wide spread of active companies, are well placed to continue to attract a disproportionate share of an albeit diminishing cake.

Chapter 6

China's Petroleum Industry
Oil and Gas Development Policy and Legislation

David D. Peng

6.1 INTRODUCTION

China was one of the first countries in the world to discover hydrocarbons, yet it was not regarded as one of the world's major oil producers until 1978 when its annual output of crude oil topped 100 million tons. Since then, especially after 1979 when the country started offshore oil exploration with foreign oil companies as partners, China's oil regime has been a constant topic for discussion in the international oil arena. At the beginning, offshore oil exploration in China caught the attention of the energy world. Then the onshore oil activities in Northwest China, the so-called 'largest untapped oil bearing region in the world' were and are still in the limelight.

But what are the prospects for foreign investors in their oil ventures in China in the 1990s? And what are the latest developments in China's oil regime? In an attempt to find out the answers, this chapter discusses the development of China's oil policies and legislation in respect of oil exploitation both onshore and offshore China.

6.2 INVESTMENT POLICIES

Since the founding of the PRC, remarkable achievements have been made in China's oil exploitation – especially in the onshore sector. However, given the fact that about 80 per cent of China's sedimentary basins remain totally unexplored, there is certainly a long way to go for China's oil industry. Again, although over the last 10 years, by producing more than 100 million tons of crude oil per annum, China has managed to uphold its place in the forefront of world's major oil producers, yet in term of oil per capita, China is not only far behind many oil-producing countries but also far from satisfying the needs of the rapid growth of its economy and of its people's livelihood.

To solve these problems, China has been adopting a general policy which stresses both oil exploration and conservation. As far as exploration is concerned, China is attaching considerable importance to offshore and Northwest areas, both of which seem to have promising prospects but with difficult access. In the past, when exploring the Northeast and the East onshore areas, China could make do with the simple drilling equipment which was cheap and available at the time. It could also compensate its lack of capital by putting in a huge number of workers including the transfer of a whole division of its army into a team of oilmen for the so-called 'great battle of oil'.

Due to the capital and technology-intensive nature and hazardous condition of the exploration offshore and in the Northwest, it is almost impossible for China to use the same tactics and go all the way along on its own. Therefore, China seems to have decided to opt for a strategy of opening up more of its untapped areas for foreign participation.

6.2.1 Onshore Northwest

The PRC began its onshore exploration in Southwest and Northwest China in the early 1950s. However, as few drilling technology and exploration techniques were available and due to the lack of basic research in geology, no major development of China's oil industry was made during that period. From 1958 onward, China's oil exploration was mainly carried out in the Northeast and the Bohai Bay Basins where a number of large oilfields, e.g. the Daqing (the largest in China), Shengli (2nd largest) and Liaohe (3rd largest) etc. were found and developed.

In the early 1980s, when production from these major oilfields began to decline, China shifted the stress of its onshore exploration back to the Northwest and to other parts of the country. While this effort did not bear encouraging results in other areas of China, big discoveries were found in the Northwest, especially in the Tarim Basin.[1] This has aroused great interest among some major oil companies and large independents. For example, most of the foreign companies participating in China's offshore exploration programme have sent geological missions to the area to assess its petroleum potential. It is said that the British Petroleum has formed a consortium of companies to petition the Chinese Government to open the exploration in Northwest China to foreign participation.[2]

In spite of the growing interest shown by foreign oil companies, China did not open up to foreign exploration its prospective Northwest basins until February 1993,[3] more than ten years after China opened its offshore areas for

1. While Lloyd's List (28 May 1991) reported that the estimated reserves in the Tarim Basin alone is 10bn barrels of oil and 8.3tn cu m of natural gas, a later report from *Beijing Review* (18–24 Nov. 1991) put the estimated figure of oil reserves that have been found in the same Basin at 30bn tons.
2. K. Woodard and B. Vernor, 'Petroleum Exploration Update', *Oil and Gas Law and Taxation Review* [1988/89], 6.
3. Notification of Call for Tender by China National Oil and Gas Corporation dated 17 February 1993.

foreign cooperation. There can be many reasons for treating the two sectors differently but the following factors may be of some relevance.

Persistence of 'self-reliance' policy

In the late 1950s, due to the differences in ideology and politics between China and the then Soviet Union, hundreds of contracts were unilaterally terminated by the Soviets causing great difficulties and losses to China's economy. Since then, self-reliance has always been one of China's long-term policies, though it may have its ups and downs at times. In 1970 when Taiwan was in a joint development project with Japan and South Korea in the East China Sea, China accused the Taiwan regime of 'selling out the sovereignty and resources of our country' and in 1974 Li Qiang, the then foreign trade minister, said that China 'will never try to attract foreign capital or exploit domestic or foreign natural resources in conjunction with other countries'.[4] Both of these episodes took place at a time when the self-reliance policy was zealously pursued.

After the downfall of the Gang of Four in 1976, China adopted an open-door policy which was much preferred both at home and abroad. Even during that period, there was for some time a heated debate on whether China's offshore exploitation with foreign companies constituted an act of selling out the sovereignty and resources of the country. Given the result of opening up offshore for foreign cooperation remained to be seen and the fact that some old guards in the oil industry believed that China can develop all the onshore areas itself, the opening up of the Northwest has been considerably delayed.

Avoidance of possible ethnic conflict

Of the four Northwest basins (Tarim, Chaidam, Junggar and Turpan), three are located in the Xinjiang Uygur Autonomous Region which occupies about one-sixth of the area of China and has a large population of Uygur nationality. Since 1884 in the Qing Dynasty (1644–1911), Xinjiang has been an integral part of China. On 1 October 1955 it was given the current status as an autonomous region and has since enjoyed a weaker control from the central government compared with most of the provinces in China. The relationship of the Uygur nationality and Han Chinese in the region is said to be reasonably good and cordial in spite of what was rumoured to be a small-scale ethnic unrest during the period of Sino-Soviet conflict in the 1960s and the 1970s.

Compared with its neighbouring autonomous region of Tibet, there should be no real danger of ethnic conflict in Xinjiang. In the issue of Tibet, China has always accused some people in the West of supporting the exiled Dalai Lama and of stirring up troubles in Tibet. That is why for some periods foreigners were prohibited from visiting Lhasa, the capital city of Tibet Autonomous Region. In the case of Xinjiang, although there is no such person who has such religious influence to Xinjiang as Dalai Lama to Tibet, the ethnic influence of the Uygur nationality is always there. As such and due to the strategic

---

4.   Paul C. Yuan, 'China's Offshore Oil Development Policy and Legislation', *International Journal of Estuarine and Coastal Law*, **3**, 2 (1988).

importance of the Xinjiang region, it is understandable that China would not open in haste its Northwest for foreign participation and submit one of its least developed areas for a large intrusion of expatriate personnel and a possible invasion of western ideology.

Inputs of domestic capital

Admittedly, due to the lack of income in tax revenues and in foreign currencies, China's oil exploration has always been undercapitalised. However, China has never overlooked the importance of developing its oil industry. On the contrary, it has been doing what it can to keep things moving especially in respect of the exploration of new resources. In 1986, the investment capital in the oil industry was said to be $2.95 billions in terms of local currency. A year later, it jumped to $4.97 billions and in 1988 it increased to $5.4 billions approximately.[5] While some of the money was used in upgrading the existing oilfields, most of it was spent on the exploration of new resources including that in the Northwest and the offshore areas. It is said that in the last few years, China has spent each year an equivalent of more than $1 billions in local currency on the oil exploration and development in Xinjiang.[6]

Having invested so heavily in the region, China would expect to recoup or be near to recouping its investment very soon. However, due to the lack of world-class discoveries so far and the difficulty in oilfield development and crude oil transportation in the future, it may take another decade or two for China to see any sight of recovery of its investment should China do it all alone by itself. As China's eighth Five-Year Plan (1991–95) has set a target for the oil industry to bring the annual output of crude oil in 1995 up to 145 millions,[7] the most sensible way of achieving this seems to be the opening up of more onshore areas for foreign cooperation.

6.2.2 Offshore China

The first offshore seismic survey that China conducted is said to have taken place in 1965 in the area of Bohai.[8] This was followed by a further survey in 1968 under the auspices of the United Nations. Based on the data of these surveys, China undertook during the 1970s some self-financed drilling programmes in the Bohai Sea and the South China Sea. Due to the high cost of offshore drilling and the lack of offshore expertise, China decided in 1978 to solicit the participation of foreign oil companies.[9]

Hence began the 1979 seismic and geophysical surveys in cooperation with foreign companies over 420,000 km in the South China Sea and the southern part of the Yellow Sea. Since then there have been three offshore bidding rounds involving most of the major oil companies and large independents.

5. *Supra*, Note 2.
6. *People's Daily*, Overseas edn (6 Aug. 1991).
7. Excerpts of the Eighth Five-Year Plan, *Beijing Review* (13–19 May 1991), 11.
8. *People's Daily*, Overseas edn (15 Aug. 1990).
9. *The P. R. China Perspectives*, Arthur Andersen & Co. (Aug. 1984).

China's offshore investment policy has been developed throughout these years and brought about better terms for foreign companies in each new bidding round.

Companies participating in the First Round in 1982 and those which entered into bilateral petroleum contracts before 1982 may still remember how tough the Chinese were during negotiations. In addition to bearing all exploration expenses and risks, foreign companies were also obliged to transfer to China advanced technology, use Chinese supply and services whenever possible and pay a 50 per cent income tax on top of a 12.5 per cent royalty. Even the question of the appointment of an arbitrator could delay the signing of contracts.[10]

In November 1984, CNOOC called for the Second Bidding Round but, due to mixed First Round drilling results and the slump in oil prices, only eight contracts were signed under the bidding procedures.[11] In the light of the eroding of foreign investment, CNOOC adjusted its policy and modified in 1988 the exploration clauses and fiscal terms of its Second Round Model Contracts to reduce the investment risks shouldered by foreign companies and to provide them with more latitude in the petroleum operations. These adjustments and modifications which were later incorporated into the Model Contract of the Third Round Bidding on 3 January 1989 include:

- *More phases in the contracts or agreements*
  The exploration period (normally 7 years) could be divided into three phases. After the completion of each phase, foreign oil companies could chose to go into the next one or simply terminate the contract. Similarly, companies which signed the optional geological study or survey agreements could also have two phases (2 or 3 years each) and decide after each phase whether to go any further.

- *Waiver of royalty for small oil/gas fields*
  According to the Regulations for Payment of Royalty for the Exploitation of Offshore Petroleum Resources issued by the Ministry of Finance, with effect from 1 January 1989, there will be no royalty for an oil field with annual production of less than 1 billion tons of oil or a gas field with annual output of less than 2 billion cubic metres of gas. Royalty for bigger oil/gas fields will be levied on the incremental basis as shown in Table 6.1.

- *Payment of signature fee by instalment*
  The standard signature fee of US$1 million payable by those who entered into the third round contracts could be paid in three installments. The first instalment being one quarter (i.e. US$250,000) to be paid on signature; the second being another quarter to be paid when deciding to drill an exploration well and the third, i.e. the remaining half a million, to be paid when the development plan is approved.

---

10. R. O. Jackson, 'China's Oil Difficulties', *Petroleum Review* (June 1982), 18.
11. Another 14 bilateral petroleum contracts were signed outside of the formal bidding round, perhaps, on similar terms.

Table 6.1 Royalty rates for the offshore oil and gas sector

Oil production		Gas production	
Million tons	Royalty %	Billion cm/year	Royalty %
0.0–1.0	0	0.0–2.0	0
1.0–1.5	4	2.0–3.5	1
1.5–2.0	6	3.5–5.0	2
2.0–3.0	8	5.0+	3
3.0–4.0	10		
4.0+	12.5		

- *Reduction of cost of Chinese personnel*
  The costs of qualified Chinese personnel involved in petroleum operations should be 30 per cent lower than their counterparts in other southeast Asian countries and the number of Chinese representatives working in the Joint Management Committees can be reduced to the possible minimum.

- *Lenient policy for personnel training and technology transfer*
  Foreign oil companies' obligation to undertake training of Chinese personnel and transfer of technology under the contracts will not need to commence until a field development agreement is reached.

These changes were all significant moves to improve the investment environment for foreign oil companies. However, 'a more efficient and progressive CNOOC is not enough for foreign companies'.[12] There was still a cool response to the Third Bidding Round which by the end of 1990 produced only 2 petroleum contracts through competitive bids. Although there were a further 3 petroleum contracts and 5 geophysical survey/study agreements signed outside the bidding procedures, only 5 foreign oil companies were involved in all these 10 contracts and agreements.

On 9 April 1991 China promulgated a new income tax law[13] which, with effect from 1 July 1991, set a new tax rate for all foreign investment enterprises and foreign enterprises, including foreign oil companies, at a flat 30 per cent plus a 3 per cent local surtax. The detailed rules for the implementation of this new tax law further provided other preferential tax treatment to foreign oil companies in China.[14]

Encouraged by such an improvement in the tax regime and also in recognition of the fact that foreign companies were no longer as interested as they were in other offshore areas, CNOOC accelerated its long-fought campaign for the opening up of the East China Sea for foreign cooperation

12. Per Bruce Vernor, 'China's Sinking Surplus', *China Business Review* (Mar.–Apr. 1990).
13. The Income Tax Law concerning Enterprises with Foreign Investment and Foreign Enterprises.
14. See Section 6.3.2 below for details.

which had not been successful due to the lack of political developments on talks to resolve the dispute between China and Japan over the Diaoyu (Senkaku) Islands which lie in the middle of the East China Sea. Although historical evidence of usage and geographical arguments appear to favour China,[15] Japan has never given up its claim of sovereignty to these Islands. To put aside the sensitive issue of territorial dispute, CNOOC, through its Vice President Chen Bingqian, dropped hints by saying that '[W]hen a suitable joint venture project comes forward from the Japanese, we shall recommend go ahead to the (Chinese) government.'[16] The Japanese, however, did not seem to be interested in a joint development with the Chinese and did not respond to such an offer. The opening up of the East China Sea was once again delayed and the situation looked as gloomy as it could be.

On 25 February 1992 the Standing Committee of the National People's Congress, the Parliament, of China enacted the Law of the Territorial Sea and the Adjacent Zone of the People's Republic of China which declares China's sovereignty over the Diaoyu, the Nansha (Spratly), and the XiSha (Paracel) Islands etc.[17] This new law has, in a sense, paved the way for the opening up of the East China Sea and CNOOC lost no time in announcing, on 30 June 1992, the beginning of the long-awaited Fourth Round Offshore Bidding. The area up for bid comprised acreage totalling 72,800 km in part of the East China Sea which 'might contain one of the most prolific oil and gas reservoirs of the world, possibly compared favourably with the Persian Gulf'.[18]

Despite the disappointing exploration results of the past in other parts of offshore China, 53 foreign oil companics, including Exxon, Shell and BP, responded to the notification showing interest in participating in the bid.[19] Whether or not many of these companies purchase the data packages and eventually come up with bids will have a great impact on the future of China's offshore oil industry. Conversely, how China's offshore investment policy and legislation are being developed may have some bearing on whether foreign oil companies will venture into the East China Sea, particularly when oil prices are not so encouraging and other opportunities are available to them in the Commonwealth of Independent States and other parts of Asia.

6.3 PETROLEUM LEGISLATION

The framework of China's petroleum legislation is the Regulations of the People's Republic of China on the Exploitation of Offshore Petroleum Resources in Cooperation with Foreign Enterprises which were promulgated on 30 January 1982 (to be referred to as 'the 1982 Regulations'). The 1982

---

15. Jeanette Greenfield, *China and the Law of the Sea, Air and Environment*, p. 129.
16. 'Much Needed Boost for China Offshore Industry', *Lloyd's List* (19 Oct. 1991).
17. The Law of the Territorial Sea and the Adjacent Zone of the PRC, Article 2.
18. Report of the Committee for Coordination of Joint Prospecting for Mineral Resources in Asian Offshore Areas of the Economic Commission for Asia and the Fast East, Sixth Session 10, UN Doc. E/CN.11/:239 (1969).
19. *Petroleum Intelligence Weekly* (17 Aug. 1992), 7.

Regulations are being supplemented from time to time[20] by relevant rules and provisions of general laws or by model contracts, and by other separate rules and regulations which are wholly related to oil and gas activities. The following section discusses four aspects of China's petroleum legislation which might be of some interest to foreign investors.

6.3.1 Registration and licensing

Under Section 3 of the Mineral Resources Law of the PRC which was enacted by the NPC on 19 March 1986, China proclaims that the state owns all the petroleum resources under the land mass, the internal seas, the territorial sea, the continental shelf and the sea areas with the maritime resources under the jurisdiction of the PRC.

To exercise this right of ownership, the state established a system of registration for petroleum exploration and production activities in China. Under this system, domestic enterprises must file an application for registration with and obtain a licence from the Ministry of Energy[21] prior to the commencement of the exploration in an area or the development of an oil/gas field. For a Sino-foreign equity joint venture or contractual joint venture for petroleum exploration and production, preliminary approvals of the registration and administration authority must be sought before signing contracts with foreign partners. After the contract is signed and approval granted, the Chinese state-owned company must go through the formality of filing for registration and administration with the Ministry of Energy.[22]

Foreign companies participating in offshore exploitation activities are further required to establish branches or subsidiaries or representative offices in China[23] and must fulfil registration formalities in accordance with the Notice concerning Registration of Foreign Companies Involved in Cooperative Developments and Contracting Projects in China (to be referred to as the Registration Notice).[24]

According to the Registration Notice, all foreign companies having contracts with CNOOC must apply for registration with the State Administration of Industry and Commerce (to be referred to as the SAIC) in Beijing. The application includes the completing and filing of a form and the submission of a certificate pertaining to applicants' legal status and credibility and a copy of the contract with CNOOC and the relevant approvals. A registration fee is normally charged for each application on the basis of

---

20. It is believed that further to the opening up of more onshore areas for foreign cooperation, similar regulations governing onshore activities are to be issued very soon.

21. It is believed that, after the elimination of the Ministry of Energy at the latest NPC, the Economic and Trade Office under the State Council will take over the responsibility as competent authority.

22. Article 20 of the Provisional Rules on the Registration and Administration of the Exploitation of Oil and Natural Gas issued by the then Ministry of Petroleum on 24 December 1987.

23. The 1982 Regulations, Article 14.

24. Promulgated by the State Administration for Industry and Commerce on 12 March 1983.

registered capital, from 0.05 per cent to 0.1 per cent, but not exceeding RMB (Chinese currency) 30,000 (approximately £3,000) in total. As a preferential treatment, foreign oil companies are charged with a discounted registration fee of RMB 2,000 during the exploration period in consideration of their bearing the sole risks. When commercial production commences, however, foreign oil companies must re-register and are subject to the normal fee as mentioned above. Once the application is approved by the SAIC, a business licence will be issued to the applicant.

Foreign oil companies' contractors or subcontractors are also subject to the registration requirement so far as their contracts or services are performed in China. Their application for registration is normally filed with local bureau of the SAIC, but if their contracts or services are performed simultaneously in several localities, they must apply to the SAIC in Beijing for registration. The application process consists of the completing and filing a form, submitting a letter of introduction from a subsidiary of CNOOC and a copy of the project contract. Once the application is approved, the contractor or subcontractor is issued with a registration certificate which is only valid for the duration of a specific contract. This registration on contract basis is inconvenient to foreign contractors and subcontractors which frequently win contracts in China. But perhaps, for the protection of domestic contractors and suppliers, China does not really mean to provide too much convenience to foreign competitors. One way of getting around this system is to set up a more permanent entity, in joint venture with a CNOOC subsidiary for example, in China if additional contracts are attractive and worth bidding for.

6.3.2 Taxation regime

Before the economic reform of the early 1980s, there was very little tax legislation in China.[25] There were indeed very few taxes being levied and the state's revenue came mainly from the profits handed over by the state-run industry and commerce. Since 1980, especially after the 2nd Phase of the tax reform (the so-called turning the levying of profits to that of taxes), China has imposed a variety of taxes of which the following are perhaps most relevant to the offshore oil industry.

Consolidated Industrial and Commercial Tax

This is a turnover tax levied on foreign related enterprises and individuals engaged in industrial production, import of foreign goods, transportation, communication and service trade etc. The current rate for foreign oil companies engaged in offshore oil exploitation is 5 per cent of the annual production and the rate for offshore suppliers or contractors is 3 per cent of the contract price plus 1 per cent of local surtax on the tax payable.[26]

---

25. In *The Completed Collection of the Laws of the P.R.C. Commonly in Use* (Legal Press, Beijing, 1988), none of the tax laws collected was promulgated before 1980.
26. It is believed that this formula will be adopted in the onshore sector.

It should be noted that in accordance with the Rules on the Levy and Exemption of Customs Duties and Consolidated Industrial and Commercial Tax on Imports and Exports for the Chinese-Foreign Cooperative Exploitation of Offshore Petroleum, no consolidated industrial and commercial tax is levied on foreign oil companies' imported goods which are listed in the annex of the Rules and used directly for oil/gas exploration and production. The measurement of the exemption by way of a list which is not exhaustive has given rise to many arguments, for some of the goods used directly for exploration may happen to be outside the list. If the objective of the Rules is to encourage petroleum exploitation, it will be more sensible to exempt all goods, whether listed or not, used directly for exploitation. This is especially the case since, under the same Rules, the importation of the goods has to be verified and approved by CNOOC.

Income Tax

Branches or subsidiaries of foreign oil companies and their foreign contractors must pay income tax on their income derived from production, business operation and other sources within the boundary of the PRC. The rate applicable at the moment is 30 per cent plus a 3 per cent local surtax on taxable income.[27] Starting from 1 July 1991, exploration expenditure of foreign oil companies may be offset, by instalment of not less than one year, against their income of a developed oil or gas field. Foreign oil companies which have stopped operations and withdrawn establishment in China because of failure to discover commercial oil or gas can register with the tax authority for their exploration costs incurred. If they enter into new contracts within ten years after the termination of their previous contracts, their registered exploration costs may be carried forward and offset from the income of their new contract areas.[28]

Individuals (both Chinese and foreign nationals with the exception of certain groups of people) are subject to income tax according to their duration of residence in China and the sources of their income. For those working for foreign enterprises or for enterprises with foreign investment in China or foreigners employed (e.g. by contractors) in the offshore oil sector, their income from the sources in China (whether received from a foreign employer or not) is taxable. For those who live in China for no fewer than 365 days within a tax year, their income from both inside and outside China is taxable. The current individual income tax is levied on a successive incremental basis according to the difference in monthly income. There are four tiers of rates at the moment with the lowest at 5 per cent for the part of income between RMB 801 to 1,500 and the highest at 45 per cent for the part beyond RMB12,000. However, starting from August 1987, foreigners working in the offshore oil sector may enjoy a 50 per cent reduction of the above tax rate on their wages.

27. The Income Tax Law for Foreign Investment Enterprises and Foreign Enterprises, Article 5.
28. The Detailed Rules for the Implementation of Income Tax Law for Foreign Investment Enterprises and Foreign Enterprises, Article 48.

6.3.3 Environmental protection

In the last 43 years of development of China's onshore oil industry, there has been little evidence that enough attention has been paid to the issue of environment protection. However, there is something to be said for China's offshore oil exploitation regarding the protection of the environment.

First, at the beginning of the offshore oil exploration, China included in its Offshore Regulations an article concerning the protection of the maritime environment. It calls for all operators and subcontractors to comply with both the relevant laws of the PRC and the international practice regarding the protection of fishery resources and natural resources and the prevention of pollution to the air, seas, rivers, lakes and land.

Second, in the Marine Protection Law of 1982, China devotes a full chapter[29] to the prevention of marine environmental damage from offshore oil exploration and development. In that chapter, there are eight sections covering the submission of a marine impact report, the protection of fishery resources, the recovery of oil residues and waste oil, the ban on the discharge of oil and oily mixtures into the sea, the prevention of seepage, leakage and the installation of pollution prevention facilities and equipment etc.

Third, for the purpose of implementing the Marine Protection Law mentioned above, China promulgated the Offshore Environmental Regulations which, in addition to spelling out detailed requirements applicable to enterprises, institutions, operators and individuals engaged in China's offshore oil exploration and development, confers power to the National Bureau of Oceanography as the competent authority in charge of environmental protection in offshore oil activities.

Finally, in all the offshore petroleum contracts entered into, there are always articles and clauses requiring the operators to strictly abide by the laws, decrees and regulations on environmental protection and to use their best endeavour to prevent pollution damage to the atmosphere, oceans, river, lakes, harbours and land. It also requires the operators to make prior contacts with the appropriate authorities of the Chinese government when carrying out petroleum operations in any fixed fishing net casting area and/or aquatic area.

It should, however, be pointed out that although the issue of environmental protection has been better addressed by the offshore oil sector, there is still a lack of awareness for potential dangers to the environment among not only the people in the field but also the legislators. A typical example is the failure in petroleum legislation to impose an obligation on the oilfield/gasfield operator to remove or partly remove abandoned or disused offshore installations. On the contrary, the Offshore Regulations stipulate that once the foreign contractors' (normally operators being included) investment has been compensated as provided for, the ownership of all assets purchased or built by the foreign contractors to carry out the petroleum contract should transfer to CNOOC.[30] While acquiring some assets for the benefit of China, this

29. Chapter 3.
30. The 1982 Regulations, Section 22.

provision has actually created an ambiguity as regards who should be responsible for the removal and residual liability of the offshore installations when abandoned or disused, the former owners (i.e. foreign contractors) or the present and future owners?

Similarly, in the model contracts used in the past, although abandonment costs 'shall be paid by the Parties in proportion to their participating interests in the development of [the] oilfield and/or gasfield [to be abandoned]',[31] it is not clear whether liabilities, especially residual liability towards offshore installation, would cease upon the payment of the abandonment costs. Worse still, the same model contract further provides that if the Contractor (foreign oil companies) decides to abandon the field while CNOOC chooses to carry on with the production, 'all of the Contractor's rights and obligations under the Contract in respect of the said Field, including but not limited to the responsibilities for payment of abandonment costs in respect of such Field, shall be terminated automatically'[32] from the date on which the Contractor receives CNOOC's written confirmation that CNOOC would go ahead itself. Does this mean that the Contractor shall no longer be liable for abandonment costs and residual liabilities incurred from thereon? If so, it will cost China dear when it comes to the implementation of the Guideline and Standards of the International Maritime Organization for the Removal of Offshore Installations and Structures on the Continental Shelf and in the Exclusive Economic Zone.[33]

6.3.4 Disputes settlement

Generally speaking, there are four methods of settling disputes arising from foreign trade and economic contracts in China, namely consultation, conciliation, arbitration and litigation. Although all these methods except litigation may be utilised under Section 27 of the Offshore Regulations, China's offshore oil industry has opted only for the practice of consultation and arbitration in disputes settlement.

According to the relevant provisions of the Third Round Model Contract, the parties shall endeavour to settle amicably through consultation any dispute arising in connection with the performance or interpretation of the contracts. Should such effort bring about no settlement within 90 days after the dispute arises, either party may refer the matter to arbitration.[34]

The Model Contract further provides that if agreed by the parties, any dispute referred to arbitration shall be decided by the China International Economic and Trade Arbitration Commission in accordance with the arbitration proceeding rules thereof. If, however, the parties fail to agree upon the arbitration arrangement mentioned above, an *ad hoc* arbitration tribunal shall be set up to conduct arbitration in accordance with the arbitration rules of the United Nations Commission on International Trade

---

31. The Third Round Model Contract, Article 4.6.2.1.
32. Article 4.6.2.2.
33. IMO Resolution A. 672 (16) as adopted on 19 October 1989.
34. The Third Bidding Round Model Contract, Article 26.2.

Law ('UNCITRAL') of 1976.[35] The *ad hoc* tribunal shall consist of three arbitrators. The parties shall each appoint an arbitrator and the two so appointed shall designate a third arbitrator. If one of the parties does not appoint its arbitrator within 60 days after the first appointment, or if the two arbitrators once appointed fail to appoint the third within 60 days after the appointment of the second arbitrator, the relevant appointment shall be made by the Arbitration Institute of the Stockholm Chamber of Commerce, Sweden.[36]

By such a provision as '[a]ny award of the arbitration shall be final and binding upon the parties' and because Chinese courts do not accept and hear disputes over foreign economic and trade contracts which already contain arbitration provisions, the Chinese petroleum contracts rule out the possibility of settling disputes through lawsuits in a Chinese court.

Although the arbitration provisions discussed above have not been tested in practice,[37] they have for the most part shown the willingness of CNOOC in accepting and utilising international arbitration practice. This can be regarded as an encouraging progress of China's petroleum legislation.

In the early days of China's offshore oil exploitation in cooperation with foreign enterprises, the question of applicable law was frequently raised but never resolved. The 1982 Regulations have no appropriate provision as to what applicable law governs petroleum contracts in China. What it merely says is that 'all activities for the cooperative exploitation of offshore petroleum resources within the scope of these Regulations shall be subject to the laws and decrees of the People's Republic of China and relevant provisions of the State...'.[38] It was not clear from such a wording whether or not the petroleum contracts which create the offshore activities should also be governed by the laws of the PRC. This ambiguity was perhaps the deliberate act of the Chinese legislators as there was at the time no proper Chinese laws for them to refer to. This resulted in some peculiar clauses on applicable law in the early round of petroleum contracts. One such clauses reads '[I]n the implementation of this contract in the People's Republic of China, the Operator, Contractors, Subcontractors, their foreign employees and other engaged by them shall be subject to and shall comply with the applicable laws, decree, rule, and regulations of the People's Republic of China...'. Again no mention is made as to whether or not the validity and interpretation of the contract itself should be governed by the laws of the PRC.

On 21 March 1985 China promulgated the Foreign Economic Contract Law which applies to all foreign economic or trade contracts except for international transport contracts. Under Section 5 of this law, it is stipulated that 'the parties of a contract may choose an applicable law for the handling of

---

35. But where the UNCITRAL Rules are in conflict with the arbitration provisions of the petroleum contracts, the latter shall prevail.

36. China's preference of the Stockholm Chamber of Commerce in matter of arbitration is once again shown through such a provision.

37. There are so far no disputes arising from China's petroleum contracts that have been referred to arbitration.

38. The Offshore Regulations, Section 3.

disputes arising from the contract. Where the parties have not chosen an applicable law, the law that is most closely related to the contract shall be applicable.' This was the first time that the free choice of law appeared as a principle in a Chinese law. Such a move must have been welcomed by foreign investors who are interested in the China market but somewhat put off by the uncertainty or lack of development in Chinese laws. Unfortunately, this provision does not apply to the petroleum contracts, for the same law further provides that 'the contracts of Sino-foreign equity joint ventures, of Sino-foreign contractual joint ventures for exploration and development of natural resources which are performed within the territory of the People's Republic of China shall be governed by the laws of the People's Republic of China. In case no relevant stipulation is provided in the laws of the People's Republic of China, international practice may apply.'[39]

Here the law has provided a clear answer to the question of applicable law and has brought about changes to the model clauses. Starting from the second round of bidding, China's offshore model contracts provide that 'the validity, interpretation and implementation of the contract shall be governed by the laws of the People's Republic of China. Failing a relevant provision of the laws of the People's Republic of China for the interpretation or implementation of the contract, the principles of the applicable laws widely used in petroleum resources countries acceptable to the parties shall be applicable.' It should be noted that the 'international practice' mentioned in the Foreign Economic Contract Law is here paraphrased as 'the principles of the applicable laws widely used in petroleum resources countries' which one would presume must have included some Middle East or Far East oil producing countries. Moreover, with the wording of 'acceptable to the parties', the application of some international practice may in fact be hindered by the intention of the parties concerned.

6.4 CONCLUSION

In the absence of a developed legal system,[40] China's petroleum investment policy has been improved through the years and some basic rules and principles of the legislation have been established to meet the needs of the development of China's oil industry. Although both the policy and the legislation are far from perfect and indeed there are many other problems to be resolved in addition to those that have been briefly touched upon in this chapter,[41] the overall investment environment is much better than what it was in the past. Against this background, foreign oil companies interested in offshore oil ventures in China in the 1990s may have less uncertainty to worry about.[42] However, they

---

39. Section 3.

40. There is for the time being no Company Law nor Petroleum Law in China.

41. e.g. Under Article 30 of the 1982 Regulations, detailed rules for the implementation of the Regulations should be formulated by the Ministry of Petroleum. It has been 10 years since the promulgation and the Ministry of Petroleum no longer exists, but there is still no sight of the detailed rules. Or is there a need for them now?

42. Even if there is any change in government policies etc., it is probably changing for the better.

do need to worry about the existence of commercial oil or gas in the blocks that they are bidding for. But that is mainly a question to be answered by geologists and geophysicists.

Chapter 7

The Production Sharing Contract in Indonesia[1]

T. N. Machmud

7.1 INTRODUCTION

It was in January 1967, over 25 years ago, that the government of Indonesia approved the first Production Sharing Contract for an Offshore Block North West of Java. It so happened that this particular contract was the forerunner of the contract ARCO has been operating under since 1967. This event marked a new era in the history of the Indonesia oil industry. Up to that time the oil industry in Indonesia had been dominated by three international oil companies: Shell, Caltex and Stanvac. These companies, after the Second World War and after the Republic of Indonesia had gained independence from Dutch colonial rule, had repossessed their old petroleum concession areas on Java, Sumatra and Kalimantan, destroyed during the war, and had turned them again into viable and profitable oil and gas producing ventures, rebuilding refineries and infrastructure in the process.

To these major companies, the new production sharing concepts, embodied in the PS Contract signed by a small independent (IIAPCO – Independent Indonesian American Petroleum Company) in August 1966 and which was the forerunner of ARCO's PS Contract as mentioned earlier, were an unwelcome development, and were contrary to the very principles under which the majors operated, primarily the principle to own and manage their own assets and operations without what they considered undue interference by the host government.

To the learned practitioners of the legal profession, the first PSC also appeared as a rather incomplete legal document, barely describing the basic principles on which it was based and leaving a great deal of uncertainty as to how possible disagreements on implementation would be resolved. The reason

---

1.   Paper presented at the 'LAWASIA' International Energy Conference, Kuala Lumpur, Malaysia, 18–22 October 1992.

was simple: it was indeed an unfinished product. I know because I was one of the lawyers working on that contract.

The then President Director of PERTAMINA, Dr Ibnu Sutowo, the creator of the PS concept, decided the time had come to execute the document and that any incompleteness or imperfections could be dealt with by side letters and *addenda.*

Whatever its perceived shortcomings at the time of its conception, we all know that today, more than 25 years later, production sharing has become an accepted pattern for Petroleum Exploration and Exploitation Agreements between host governments and private oil companies, not only in Indonesia but in many developing countries around the world, accepted even by major oil companies, which initially turned the concept down as unacceptable and against the very principles they had so staunchly defended.

In hindsight, it is easier to understand what made the PS concept a success in Indonesia and a blue print for other countries to follow even if at the time it appeared revolutionary and highly experimental.

The basic concept of production sharing is that the petroleum resource is owned and controlled by the host country, that all cost and risk of exploration and production are borne by the contractor who, if successful, will be allowed to take freely and lift his share of petroleum, based on cost recovery and a preset percentage of profit oil.

In the case of Indonesia, it took the government more than 17 years after independence, and nearly as many years after the majors had reclaimed their concessions, to create the legislation and the legal instrument that would satisfy the principles laid down in its constitution, which states that:

Article 33

Section 2: Branches of production important to the State that govern the lives of the majority of the people, have to be controlled by the State'.

Section 3: Land, water and the natural riches contained therein are controlled by the State and are used for the greater welfare of the people.

In Indonesia this control is expressed in the ownership of the oil and gas and the ownership of the facilities by the state oil company and in the management clause, which grants the state oil company PERTAMINA the right to manage the operations.

The fact that the PS concept satisfied the national aspirations of the host country, has made it to stand up to time, even if the economic terms changed over time. This fact was coupled with the understanding on the part of the host government that the economic terms must remain attractive to the foreign investor for continued exploration efforts. We might also say that what appeared to be legal shortcomings of the first PSC – its briefness and the lack of detailed provisions – has also proven to be its strength, since it provided flexibility to adapt its implementation to changing conditions.

7.2 THE SECOND- AND THIRD-GENERATION PSCs IN INDONESIA

In Indonesia, we now speak of third-generation PSCs, after the government of Indonesia offered new incentives packages in 1988 to encourage exploration for oil in its eastern provinces and in remote, so-called frontier areas. The second generation came along in 1976 which changed the economic terms in the host country's favour, when a sudden upward movement in oil prices was perceived to result in excessive profits to the contractor under the then existing terms.

We should summarise at this point the changes in economic terms imposed by the Indonesian government on the PSCs, both existing and new, during the last 25 years. The use of 'imposed' here is not meant as an absolute term. The totality of changes in terms were the result of negotiations between the host government and the oil companies. This was necessarily the case with the changes negotiated in 1976 with the oil companies operating under existing PSCs which had a validity of over 20 years left under the original terms. As is well known, Indonesian PSCs feature a 30-years validity period. The basic terms of the *first-generation contracts*, starting from 1966, featured a cost recovery cap of 40 per cent of total annual revenue. The remaining 60 per cent both for oil and gas was shared 65%–35% between PERTAMINA and the contractor, while PERTAMINA was liable for all contractor's taxes, including its Indonesian income tax. The contractor, however, was required to supply 25 per cent out of its share to the domestic market at a price of US$ 0.20/bbl. The bottom line guaranteed an approximate 49 per cent government take out of annual production.

However, developments in the world market, starting with the 1973 oil crisis which caused oil prices to escalate dramatically, made the government realised that 65%/35% split allowed the companies far greater profits than foreseen in the 1960s. In addition, expectations at that time were that oil prices would continue to escalate and might reach US$ 50–US$ 60/bbl within the decade. A change in equity split was, therefore, negotiated based on the principle that 'windfall profits' caused by price escalation over the base price of US$ 5/bbl, were to be split 85/15 in favour of the government.

Subsequently a new IRS ruling in 1975 disallowing tax credits for Indonesian corporate taxes paid by PERTAMINA on behalf of US oil companies necessitated another change in PSC terms. After renegotiation of the terms, the modifications of the PSC can be summarised as follows:

1. income taxes are paid directly by the oil company;
2. no cap on cost recovery;
3. depreciation of capital expenditures over 7 years' double declining balance;
4. a new split of profit oil, which was determined in such a way as to allow contractor takes of 15 per cent for oil and 30 per cent for gas after tax;
5. incentives for discovery of new fields, in the form of a conditional 20 per cent investment credit and full market price for the Domestic Market Obligation (DMO) over the first 5 calendar years of production.

These new terms were applied both to the old PSCs and the new *second-generation PSCs* signed after 1976.

The new terms, which allowed for a high front end recovery of investments, proved to be still attractive to foreign investors, who continued to apply for new areas under the new terms. In the late 1980s, however, the need for further modifications made itself felt. The government was concerned about decreasing oil prices and increased production cost, which with no cap on cost recovery resulted in a lower government take. The oil companies were dissatisfied by the criteria applied by PERTAMINA on allowing incentives on new field developments, and many of the earlier PSCs were reaching a stage in which large capital investments would not be justified unless an extension of the contract would be guaranteed. These three concerns, coupled with the government's desire to stimulate development of its petroleum reserves in its eastern provinces, brought the parties back to the negotiating table.

The new or *third-generation contracts* which resulted from these negotiations addressed the following issues:

1. *first tranche petroleum*, or 20 per cent of production to be split between PERTAMINA and contractor, before the recovery of operating cost; this guaranteed PERTAMINA a minimum share out of production, from the very start of production when costs still equal or exceed gross production proceeds;
2. *improved contractor share for frontier areas* of 25 per cent after tax up to 50,000 bbl/day produced, and of 20 per cent up to 150,000 bbl/day produced;
3. improved incentives for new fields, such as unconditional investment credits and higher DMO prices (from US$ 0.20 to 10 per cent of export price);
4. deregulation in the area of procurement of materials and services, which allowed more efficient operations.

The new terms were announced in two stages by PERTAMINA, on 31 August 1988 and 22 February 1989, in the so-called 1988 and 1989 incentive packages. PERTAMINA subsequently started negotiations with companies interested in extending their existing contracts for an additional 20-year term, offering to apply the new incentives upon signing of the extension immediately, which meant a second substantial change in the existing contracts for the remaining 7–10 years of the original contract period. We may note here that as opposed to the practice in Malaysia, Indonesia did not make use of the contract extension to impose participation by the state oil company for a substantial percentage, although the contract provides an opportunity to do so.

For such participation by PERTAMINA a different kind of contract is being used, specifically the Joint Operating Agreement/Joint Operating Body (JOA/JOB) in which PERTAMINA is a 50 per cent interest holder in the contract, the Loan Agreement and the Technical Assistance Agreement used by PERTAMINA to develop acreage under its control. However, these kinds of cooperative agreements are mostly used for areas with low risks or with already existing production.

It is appropriate to mention here that in September 1992 the government of Indonesia announced a new incentive package (the August 1992 incentive package). Again these new incentives were intended to stimulate exploration for and exploitation of oil and gas resources in remote and high risk areas. Of particular interest is the fact that these new incentives in the form of investment credits are equally applicable to oil and gas development.

7.3 THE NEW PACKAGE

The new package covers:

1. depreciation of capital cost for gas fields is set at 50 per cent of the asset's useful life, both for fields with reserves of more than 7 years and for fields with reserves of less than 7 years;
2. investment credits, both for new oil and gas fields, are raised for pre-tertiary rocks or fields in deep water to 110 per cent and 125 per cent respectively;
3. equity splits for gas for new contracts are improved in favour of the contractor from 70%/30% to 65%/36% for conventional areas and to 60%/40% for frontier areas; for areas with a water depth of 1500m the split for existing contracts is changed to 60%/40% and for new contracts in frontier areas to 55%/45%;
4. equity splits for oil from fields in frontier areas will be a fixed 80%/20% for new contracts while for oil from deep water areas the split has become 75%/25% for existing and new contracts;
5. the price of DMO for new fields has been raised from 10 per cent to 15 per cent of the export price for extended and new contracts.

For the future of the petroleum industry, especially in the developing countries, it appears that production sharing has not yet outgrown its usefulness. Earlier optimism, that in 20–30 years the national oil companies might have developed sufficient technical expertise and financial strength to be able to take over the production areas, has proven to be less than realistic. In Indonesia, more than a few of the original PSCs have been extended under the new terms, even before their official expiration dates in the late 1990s.

In 1990, ARCO extended its Offshore Northwest Java PS Contract, signed in 1966, which was to expire in January 1997, for an additional term of 20 years. For that privilege, it was to pay a signature bonus and agree to additional minimum expenditures and further relinquishments of acreage. On the other hand, it gained application of the new incentive packages on new fields as of the date of signature or roughly 7 years over the life of the old PSC. This was important to the company to eliminate the uncertainties over the new field incentives, which under the new terms were granted regardless of the government share in the additional production yielded by the new discovery.

Does this mean that the Indonesian PSC in its present format already adequately covers the relationship between the host governments and the foreign investor?

This holds probably true for the development of petroleum reserves both in the existing contract areas and the frontier areas in east Indonesia, for which the new contract format provides its special incentives as discussed above.

However, new needs have arisen that need to be addressed, by the development of large gas reserves which are not suitable for export but can be used to satisfy the domestic market for electrification and industrial uses.

A new pattern is now developing as a result of the finding of sufficient gas reserves in the Java sea, both west and east, by ARCO and its co-venturers, which has been earmarked by the government to satisfy the growing energy needs of the populous island of Java.

7.4 NEW CONTRACTUAL ARRANGEMENTS FOR GAS DEVELOPMENT

The existing PSC was written for the development of crude oil rather than gas and gas was treated as a by-product, although a different profit split of 70/30 was established for gas, as against 85/15 for oil. ARCO's associated gas that was not suitable for export as LPG or LNG had to be delivered to PERTAMINA for domestic sale through PERTAMINA's pipeline at the nominal price of US$ 0.20 MMBTU, a price which remained unchanged over the years. The reason for the nominal price was that gas was considered to be a by-product which would otherwise have been flared. In other words, the 20 cents, albeit little, was still 20 cents more than the contractors had coming in case of flaring.

Understandably this price did not provide an incentive to explore for gas or develop gas fields already discovered. It took an electricity crisis coupled with the discovery of a large gas field offshore East Java in the Kangean Block, the so-called Pagerungan Field, by ARCO and its co-venturer BP, to bring home to the government of Indonesia the realisation that true commercial terms were needed to make the development of gas for the domestic market economical to the producer.

In the first place, there was need for a realistic gas price. Pricing was not left to the seller and the buyer, which happened to be all state companies: PERTAMINA, the State Electricity Company (PLN), the State Gas Company (PGN), and a State Petrochemical Plant (Petrokimia), but was to be determined by the government – i.e. the Minister of Mines and Energy.

Second, the need for payment arrangements that would guarantee timely payment in foreign currency to the producer over the life of the supply period (20 years) to justify the large investment needed.

The PSC, even in its newer version, does not adequately regulate the relationship of the national oil company and the contractor in their role of supplier and joint seller of gas to domestic energy companies, which are also state-owned entities. As a consequence, the PS contractor and PERTAMINA had to devise a document – called a supply agreement – containing terms and conditions for supply of gas to PERTAMINA and a sales contract as between PERTAMINA and the domestic consumer, its terms being back to back with those of the supply agreement. Although this arrangement is rather cumbersome, it is workable. It is also necessary because the PS contractor can not deal directly with the local gas buyer, as its *raison d'être* is that of a contractor to PERTAMINA.

Since the trail was laid in east Java, now a similar arrangement is being put in place to develop new gas from the ONWJ Block to provide gas to the west Java market. These are trail blazing arrangements which took a long time to materialise because new ground had to be broken, given the absence of arrangements in the PS contract.

Again, the inadequacies of the PSC have not stopped the oil industry in Indonesia from developing new arrangements acceptable to both the government and foreign oil companies; such arrangements will continue to be developed for areas other oil and gas. Geothermal energy is already being developed. Other areas of endeavour will eventually need to be thought through and be dealt with.

7.5 THE NEXT 25 YEARS

What do we see for the future of production sharing in Indonesia? We could say that the first 25 years were the hard part.

In the first place, both PERTAMINA and the companies that have extended their old PSCs for an additional term of 20 years starting in 1997 and beyond have expressed their confidence that the PSCs will be adequate, acceptable and workable for the next 25 years.

This is also a vote of confidence and trust that both parties have lived up to their commitments and are willing to negotiate and come to mutually acceptable solution, if difficulties arise. It is a vote of confidence to a now more mature PERTAMINA that we will work it out, if we run into roadblocks, and we all know we will.

Does this mean that there are no problems associated with production sharing arrangements as they are administered in Indonesia today?

By definition this is not the case. The PSA has a built-in tension, between the desire by the host country to dominate and maintain control over its very important assets, and the need of the oil company to maximise net present value of its investments. This expresses itself from the government's side in a tendency to over-regulate, especially in areas of national sensitivity, like the participation of nationals in the workforce from labour to management positions, and the enforced use of national products and services.

Governments being governments, the means used to impose these legitimate goals on private industry often give rise to complaints by the latter of bureaucratic interference with the efficiency of its operations. On the other hand, the government may be justified in the assumption that unless sanctions are applied, private industry will tend to circumvent regulations that do not suit its immediate needs to the detriment of the government's long-term objectives.

The truth lies somewhere in the middle. Much to the government's credit, persuasion rather that force continues to be applied to come to an agreement on how to implement such policies in a mutually acceptable manner. The industry's voice through the IPA continues to be heard before formulating and implementing industry-wide regulations. If this cooperation can be further developed, it will serve to alleviate investors' concerns about loss of control over investment funds in times of scarcity of resources. If that can be achieved, the PSA will have a bright future in the years to come.

References

Abda'oe, F., *Petroleum and Petrochemicals: The Outlook for Indonesia*, March 1991.

Abda'oe, F., *Prospects and Constraints in Natural Gas Development: The Case of Indonesia*, August 1991.

Moch-Anwar, A. S., Suyanto, F. X. and Zahar, D., *The Model Production Sharing Contract: Its Development and Current Status*, 1989.

Chapter 8

Recent Developments in the Legal Structuring of Petroleum Investments in Nigeria

Sena Anthony

8.1 INTRODUCTION

Petroleum exploration commenced in Nigeria in 1908 but did not achieve a major level of activity until the 1960s when a number of international oil companies like Mobil Oil, Gulf and Safrap (now Elf) decided to invest and operate in Nigeria. Oil was first discovered in significant commercial quantities in Nigeria in 1956 with a production level of 5,100 barrels of crude oil per day which, as a consequence of the increased level of activity mentioned above, quickly rose in the 1970s to about 2 million bb/d. The petroleum industry, therefore, from the 1970s became the key industry for the Nigerian economy, contributing from then onwards between 80 and 90 per cent of the annual foreign currency earnings of the country.

It is, therefore, not surprising that the Government of Nigeria has through legislation, policies and contracts executed, played a major role in the operations of the petroleum industry in Nigeria. This chapter examines the legal structures which have been used over the decades to operate, monitor and encourage investment in the Nigerian petroleum industry. The chapter further evaluates the effect of privatisation and commercialisation on the said industry.

8.2 UPSTREAM AND DOWNSTREAM SECTORS OF THE PETROLEUM INDUSTRY

The Nigerian petroleum industry, like all other petroleum industries worldwide, can be categorised into two sectors, namely:

1. the upstream sector (i.e. exploration and exploitation including transportation prior to refining or processing);
2. the downstream sector (i.e. processing of crude oil and/or natural gas into their derivatives, e.g. petroleum products like gas oil, diesel, motor spirit, liquefied petroleum gas and liquefied natural gas).

The above-mentioned distinction is necessary and needs to be borne in mind in our discourse, as in Nigeria the legal structure, fiscal regime and investment incentives of the upstream sector differ from those of the downstream sector. However, the principal legislation which governs the petroleum industry in Nigeria – i.e. the Petroleum Act Cap 350 Vol. XIX of the Laws of the Federation of Nigeria (1990) – regulates both upstream and downstream activities in the Nigerian petroleum industry. Consequently, oil-prospecting licences, oil-mining leases, as well as licences for the construction or operation of a refinery in Nigeria, are issued pursuant to the Petroleum Act.

This chapter therefore treats the issues to be discussed as it affects the upstream and downstream petroleum industry separately, commencing with the upstream sector.

8.3 PETROLEUM LEGISLATION IN NIGERIA

There are about nine major pieces of legislation including their ensuing regulations which govern the upstream petroleum industry in Nigeria. In addition to these, the industry is regulated by government orders, directives, circulars and policy statements issued from time to time.

The key legislation of the industry, however, is the Petroleum Act Cap 350 of the Laws of the Federation of Nigeria 1990 Vol. XIX, to which reference has already been made above. Section 1 of the Act vests in the Federal Government of Nigeria the entire ownership and control of all petroleum in, under or upon any lands within Nigeria, under the territorial waters of Nigeria or forming part of its continental shelf.

The Petroleum Act also regulates a plethora of issues e.g. oil exploration licences, oil prospecting licence, oil-mining leases, fees, rents and royalties payable to government for such licences and leases, safety of oil operations, sea transportation of crude oil, petroleum products, pipelines and storage of petroleum products. However, one of the milestones which the Petroleum Act also achieved was to lay down the basis for upstream joint venture arrangements as a vehicle for participation by the Federal Government with private investors in the petroleum industry in Nigeria. Paragraph 34 of Schedule 1 of the Petroleum Act empowered the Minister of Petroleum Resources – 'if he considers it to be in the public interest' – to impose on a licence or lease to which the Act applies terms and conditions as to the 'participation by the Federal Government in the venture to which the licences or leases relate on terms to be negotiated between the Minister and the applicant for the licence and lease'.

The joint venture arrangement did not however commence until after 1971 when Nigeria joined the Organisation of Petroleum Exporting Countries (OPEC), which had in 1968 passed a Resolution calling on each member country to achieve public sector participation in the oil industry operating within its territory and prescribing a minimum level of participation for member states.

8.4 GOVERNMENT PARTICIPATION IN THE OIL INDUSTRY

In the 1960s the petroleum industry in Nigeria was completely controlled by foreign investors. The 1970s therefore witnessed the era of the commencement and development of government's participation in the Nigerian petroleum industry. The Federal Government of Nigeria commenced participation in the Nigerian oil industry in the early 1970s in three different ways:

1. the acquisition of Participating Interest through its National Oil Corporation in certain oil producing companies and the creation of un-incorporated joint ventures with these companies;
2. the use of service contractors or production sharing arrangements to develop concessions vested by government in the National Oil Corporation;
3. the creation of a National Oil Company which, *inter alia*, manages government's investments in the unincorporated Petroleum Joint Ventures and executes direct petroleum activities.

8.5 THE UPSTREAM JOINT VENTURE ARRANGEMENTS

By 1 April 1973, the government of Nigeria had acquired an undivided 35 per cent participation interest in all oil-producing companies then in Nigeria which had attained a commercial production level defined as 10,000 barrels per day.

The proportion of government's participating interest in the oil-producing companies increased at various periods after 1973. The terms and conditions of these joint venture arrangements are provided in each case in the participation agreement and joint operating agreement which relate to the particular venture. The participating agreements were executed with the respective affected petroleum producing companies over a period of time in the 1970s and 1980s. The participating agreement sets out the terms and conditions of government's undivided percentage interest in the Joint Venture Operation and assets of the company. These are:

1. the oil mining leases held by the company;
2. the fixed and moveable assets of the company in Nigeria including development, production and transportation, storage, delivery and export operation and associated assets such as offices, houses and welfare facilities;
3. the working capital applicable to the joint operations of the oil prospecting licences and oil mining leases.

The joint operating agreements were however for various reasons not executed until 1991. The salient features of these joint operating agreements are as follows:

1. The parties share the cost of petroleum operations in the proportion of their participating interest.
2. Each party has the right to lift and separately dispose of its participating interest share of available production of crude oil subject to payments of PPT and royalty due.

3. One party is designated the operator who conducts the operations in accordance with the joint operating agreement (JOA) between the partners.
4. The operator has freedom of action in specified matters and up to certain limits beyond which it must seek the approval of the joint venture partners.
5. The operator prepares and proposes programmes of work and budgets of expenditure for the prior approval of the joint venture partners.
6. Technical matters are discussed in technical committees and policy decisions are taken at Operating Committees on which the parties are represented in accordance with their proportionate participating interest.
7. Three schedules to the JOA, namely Uniform Accounting Procedure, Uniform Project Implementation Procedure and Uniform Nomination, Ship Scheduling and Lifting Procedure, are to be strictly complied with.

8.6 OTHER UPSTREAM PETROLEUM ARRANGEMENTS

In addition to the upstream joint venture arrangements described above, other upstream petroleum arrangements were introduced in the 1970s and 1980s to enable government – through its National Oil Corporation – to participate in petroleum industry operations. These are the production sharing contract and the service contract. These arrangements enabled the government of Nigeria to participate in the industry without having to bear the heavy front-end burdens of an investor in the industry. The National Oil Corporation was the holder of the oil prospecting licence or lease, as the case may be, in these arrangements, while the foreign contractors provided the technical expertise and the finance. Only one production sharing contract was executed within the period under discussion and it was with Ashland Oil Company. The salient features of the said agreement are as follows:

1. The foreign company bears all the risk and cost of exploration, development and operation.
2. The concession belongs to the Nigerian government.
3. The foreign company is given a share of oil produced to meet its capital investment operating costs and fiscal obligations.
4. The remaining oil produced (i.e. profit oil) is divided between the company and the government in a contractually agreed ratio.
5. The initial contract term is 20 years, renewable for a further period of 5 years. However, should the contractor decide to terminate the contract before spending the minimum amount agreed on petroleum operations, an amount equal to the unexpended portion of the amount should be paid to government.
6. The contract automatically terminates if no commercial discovery is made within a period of 5 years.
7. In order to promote technology transfer, the contract obliges the foreign company to recruit and train Nigerians.

The service contract has elements which are similar to those of the production sharing contract (PSC) described above – in that the contractor provides all the funds and bears all risks for exploration, development and production activities. However, the service contract differs from the PSC in that the primary term of the contract otherwise known as the exploration period is for a period of 5 years consisting of an initial term of three years renewable for an additional 2 years. Other salient features include the following:

1. The contract automatically terminates if no commercial oil discovery is made within the exploration period.
2. Each service contract relates to a single block or contract area unlike the PSC which could cover more that one Oil Prospecting Licence (OPL) area.
3. The contractor does not have title to the crude oil produced.
4. If a commercial discovery is made, NNPC and the contractor will meet to agree on terms which will enable the contractor to recover its costs.

In 1979 eight service contracts were signed with three oil companies in Nigeria, namely Agip Energy, Elf Aquitaine and Nigus Petroleum Oil Company. The Agip 'Energy Contract' is at present the only surviving one. Apart from the joint venture participation arrangements for upstream petroleum investments described above, the government of Nigeria also commenced direct participation in petroleum activities for the first time. This was through the Nigerian National Oil Corporation (NNOC) which was established in 1971, and – later – through the successor of the NNOC, the Nigerian National Petroleum Corporation (NNPC), established in 1977.

By the 1980s, therefore, upstream petroleum producing activities without government participation became minimal (albeit legally possible) in the form of concession contracts. Under the concession, the oil companies obtained concessions over some specified area of the country. The company bears the risks and costs of exploration as well as the development and operating costs. Such company has title to all the crude oil produced. It pays royalty, petroleum profit tax, and tax concession rentals to government. Prior to the emergence of the joint venture arrangements, companies operated under the concession arrangement. The government no longer grants such concessions. There are, however, indigenous independent operators who operate entirely on their own without any form of participation arrangement with the government or the NNPC. Dubri Petroleum Oil Company is one of such independent indigenous companies.

8.7 THE FISCAL REGIME

Upstream petroleum producers operate under a fiscal regime that is unique to the upstream petroleum industry in Nigeria. The principal legislation in this respect is the Petroleum Profits Tax Act of 1959 Cap 354 of the Laws of the Federation of Nigeria 1990 (PPTA) which imposes tax on the profits from petroleum production and makes provisions for the assessment and collection thereof. Section 19.1 of the PPTA provides that the assessable tax for any accounting period of a company shall be an amount equal to 85 per cent of its chargeable profits. However, it is pertinent to note that where a company has not yet commenced sale or bulk disposal of chargeable oil under a programme of continuous production, its assessable tax for any accounting period during which is has not fully amortised all pre-production capitalised expenditure due is 65.75 per cent subject to a limit of five years. Upstream petroleum producers also have to pay royalty to the Federal Government of Nigeria computed as a certain percentage of the official selling price of petroleum produced.

Current royalty rates are as follows:

1. 20 per cent for land and swamp areas;
2. 18.5 per cent for territorial waters and continental shelf up to 100 meters water depth;
3. 16.3 per cent for territorial waters and continental shelf beyond 100 meters water depth.

Finally, it is pertinent to mention that all companies operating in Nigeria are normally subject to the operations of the Companies Income Tax Act 1971 Cap 60 Laws of the Federation of Nigeria 1990 (CITA). The profits of oil-producing companies whose petroleum operations are taxable under the PPTA (as mentioned above) are however exempted from payment of tax under CITA. Section 19(h) of CITA provides as follows:

The profits of any company engaged in petroleum operation, within the meaning of section 2 of the Petroleum Profits Tax Act shall, in so far as those profits are derived from such operations and liable to tax under that Act, be exempt from the tax imposed under this Act.

8.8 PRIVATISATION, COMMERCIALISATION AND THE UPSTREAM INDUSTRY

By the later half of the 1980s, the wind of privatisation and commercialisation was sweeping through the world. Commercialisation and privatisation arrived in Nigeria in the form of the Privatisation and Commercialisation Act 1989 Cap 369 Vol XXI of the Laws of the Federation of Nigeria 1990. The Act defined privatisation as the relinquishment of part or all of the equity and other interests held by the Federal Military Government or its agency in enterprises whether wholly or partly owned by the Federal Government. Commercialisation, on the other hand, is defined by the same piece of legislation as the 're-organisation of enterprises wholly or partly owned by the Federal Government in which such commercialised enterprises shall operate as profit-making commercial ventures and without subvention from the Federal Government'.

The Privatisation and Commercialisation Act provided the scope and legal framework for the privatisation and commercialisation programme in Nigeria. It listed 25 enterprises for partial privatisation, 73 for full privatisation, 24 for partial commercialisation and 11 for full commercialisation. A Technical Committee on Privatisation and Commercialisation (TCPC) was established to provide the appropriate administrative machinery for the planning, control and monitoring of the programme.

Privatisation is effected by the sale of all shares of the affected enterprise on the Nigerian capital market by public issue. Commercialisation, on the other hand, is effected by the retention by government of full ownership of the affected enterprises but empowering such enterprises 'to operate as purely commercial enterprises' which, subject to the general regulatory power of the Federal Government, may:

1. fix rates, prices and charges for goods and services provided;
2. capitalise assets;
3. borrow money and issue debenture stocks;
4. sue and be sued in its corporate name.

In order to give effect to commercialisation in the NNPC, an extensive strategic planning project was undertaken by the NNPC. The project focused on certain key issues – efficiency, profitability and prudent management – which had to be addressed before commercialisation. The planning project thereafter proffered suggestions on how to change NNPC into an integrated commercial international oil company, fully capable of operating and funding its future development on an autonomous basis.

The process of commercialisation commenced in NNPC in 1988 and is still going on. It has so far resulted in the re-organisation of the structure of NNPC into a headquarters having several directorates (at present six) with eight fully owned subsidiaries reporting to the Group Managing Director. According to the Privatisation and Commercialisation statute the aim of such re-organisation was to create an organisation that would be 'efficient', 'thoroughly viable' and 'would be able to fulfil its commercialisation objectives, compete internationally and successfully face any challenges'.

A tripartite Profitability Agreement between the government of Nigeria, the NNPC and the Technical Committee on Privatisation and Commercialisation was negotiated and should soon be executed, its objective being to define economic criteria and milestones for monitoring the commercialisation of NNPC. Pursuant to the re-organisation of NNPC, the management of government's investment in the upstream petroleum joint ventures was placed under one of the six NNPC Headquarters Directorate known as the National Petroleum Investment Management Services (NAPIMS). NNPC's direct upstream activities were placed under two fully owned NNPC subsidiaries, i.e. International Data Services Limited (IDSL) in respect of seismic activities and the interpretation of seismic data produced by NNPC or other Nigerian foreign companies, and the Nigerian Petroleum Development Company (NPDC) in respect of exploration and exploitation activities. Both companies have witnessed considerable successes since their incorporation, with IDSL winning seismic processing contracts both in Nigeria and internationally in Ghana. NPDC on the other hand had discovered oil in commercial quantity in 1990 in one of the blocks that was directly allocated to it.

In respect of upstream joint venture arrangements, pursuant to the spirit of commercialisation and the need for the petroleum investors participating in these arrangements to realise adequate profits to attract further investments, incentives were given to these investors. These incentives formed the basis for the conclusion of a number of Memoranda of Understanding (MOU). The MOUs are understandings reached between the Federal Government of Nigeria and each of the oil-producing companies on incentives for encouraging investments in exploration and upstream development activities, the objective being to enhance crude oil exports. The first of these MOUs were signed in 1986 with the aim of guaranteeing to the oil companies a certain minimum profit margin irrespective of market conditions after tax and royalty had been paid. This objective was achieved by modifying – through incentives – the calculation of official selling prices of petroleum products upon which a revised government take is based.[1] The 1986 MOU was revised in 1991 with the effect of increasing the minimum profit margin to US$2.30 per barrel.

The July 1991 MOU also introduced the 'reserve addition bonus' for companies adding to petroleum reserves, through exploration activities, above their production level in a given year. The bonus is given to a company if in any one year the additions to oil and condensate ultimate recovery exceeds the production for that year as a result of increased exploration activities undertaken by the beneficiary. The modalities of calculating the bonus are outlined in the MOU and the bonus is given by way of an offset against Petroleum Profit Tax for that year.

In consideration for the MOU incentives, the oil-producing companies undertook to increase their work programme and lift certain volumes of NNPC's equity oil which the NNPC was unable to dispose of. In return, they were to share the profits derived from the marketing of such oil on an equal basis with NNPC.

8.9 INVESTMENTS IN NATURAL GAS

The system of giving incentives to investors in the upstream petroleum sector of the Nigerian petroleum industry has been very successful, leading to a substantial increase in the level of petroleum exploration and exploitation activities in the country. However, in respect of upstream investment in natural gas, such activities have until now been minimal. Although Nigeria has vast natural gas reserves (currently estimated at 2800 billion cubic metres, with about 50 per cent associated and 50 per cent non-associated gas) none of these reserves was discovered as a direct consequence of deliberate activity by any of the oil companies in search of natural gas.

The reason for this is obvious. The domestic consumption of natural gas is low, estimated at about 350 million standard cubic feet per annum. On the other hand, downstream projects for gas utilisation are expensive and require high front-end capital investment. Consequently, considerable amounts of gas are still being flared despite regulatory efforts by government to reduce or eradicate gas flaring through legislation. Among these are the Associated Gas Re-injection (continued flaring of Gas) Regulation of 1985.[2]

Before 1990, the fiscal regime for the upstream production of natural gas was

1. The minimum profit margin under the January 1986 MOU was US$2 per barrel.
2. Cf. Cap 26 Vol. 1 of the 1990 Laws of the Federation of Nigeria.

the same as that of crude oil described above. However, based on the spirit of commercialisation and realising the need to encourage investment in the exploration and production of natural gas, a Natural Gas Pricing Policy and Incentives for the Development of the Natural Gas Industry was announced in 1990.

This fixed a minimum price of 5.24 MSCF with effect from 1 January 1990, with provisions for annual adjustments. It also outlined the fiscal package for Gas production, which:

1. reduced the applicable tax rate under the Petroleum Profits Tax Act from 85 per cent to 40 per cent as in the Companies Tax Act;
2. fixed a capital allowance at the rate of 20 per cent per annum in the first 4 years, 19 per cent in the fifth year and the remaining 1 per cent in books;
3. fixed Royalty payable as 7 per cent onshore and 5 per cent offshore.

The policy also announced the fiscal regime for gas to be supplied to the LNG project as follows:

1. applicable tax rate under the PPTA to be 45 per cent;
2. capital allowance to be 33 per cent per annum in the first three years while 1 per cent remained in the books;
3. investment tax credit of 10 per cent with royalty remaining the same as in other upstream gas investments, to which reference has been made above.

8.10 NEW PETROLEUM ALLOCATIONS

In order to increase the crude oil reserves of Nigeria – and also consistent with the principles of commercialisation – in 1990 the Government placed a total of 136 blocks on open tender in an exercise which was the largest undertaken since 1960. In fact, pursuant to Government Notice No. 311 of 1972 which vested all areas not covered by oil mining leases, oil prospecting licences or oil exploration licences in NNOC, no new oil exploration licence, oil prospecting licence and oil mining lease had been granted since 1972. Following the revocation of this notice in 1990 and the tender exercise mentioned above, in May 1991 some of the acreage was allocated to existing and new multinational oil companies as well as indigenous petroleum companies. Among those who benefitted from this exercise were British Petroleum/Statoil, Dupont, Mobil, Agip and Exxon. Each of the new allotees is expected to enter into a PSC with NNPC. In April 1993 two new PSCs were executed with Shell Petroleum Development Company and Elf Petroleum Ltd, respectively, in respect of the new acreage. The new PSCs differ materially – in content but not in form – from the Ashland PSC described above. The major differences occur in terms of duration, modalities of recovering costs, and the sharing of profits. Furthermore, since the acreage covered by the new PSCs are in frontier areas, new incentives were also given which included an Investment Tax Credit of 50 per cent and a reduced tax liability of 50 per cent. Similar PSCs are expected to be executed soon with the other allotees who are covered by the PSAs. A significant point which should also be noted is that as a consequence of the allotment exercise the number of indigenous companies in the upstream sector increased considerably.

8.11 INVESTMENTS IN THE DOWNSTREAM PETROLEUM SECTOR

The downstream petroleum sector in Nigeria consists mainly of investments in refineries, petrochemicals plants, petroleum trading companies, product pipelines, depots and marketing companies for the trading and distribution of petroleum products. Government's investment in the downstream sector consists mainly of the four petroleum refineries with a combined refining capacity of 445,000 barrels per day, two petrochemicals plants, 3,000 km of a national network of product pipelines, and about 17 petroleum storage depots spread across the country. Private investors dominate the downstream petroleum sector by their numerical strength in the area of road transportation and distribution of petroleum products through marketing outlets. This, however, was not always the case. Prior to 1978 only foreign petroleum companies marketed and distributed petroleum products in Nigeria. Such companies still exist as major petroleum marketers although some of them are now owned fully or partly by the government of Nigeria. These include Shell (now known as National Oil), Total, Texaco, British Petroleum (now known as African Petroleum) and Esso (now known as Unipetrol). Agip and Elf incorporated marketing companies later which joined the above-mentioned majors. Each major marketing company has over 100 petroleum outlets which are spread all over Nigeria. The independent marketers' scheme was introduced in 1980 to achieve among other things the participation of Nigerians in the marketing of petroleum products. In line with the spirit of commercialisation and privatisation, this scheme has been nurtured by government and expanded rapidly to the extent that there are now over 700 active independent marketers in Nigeria trading in about 40 per cent of the petroleum products sold in petrol stations in the country.

It is, however, pertinent to note that private investors were not allowed to own, operate or construct a refinery or petrochemicals plant in Nigeria as a matter of government policy. The existing investments by government were managed by NNPC and its subsidiaries. By 1988 the government of Nigeria also had equity interests in three major marketing companies, namely: Unipetrol Nigeria Limited (100 per cent equity interest), African Petroleum Limited (80 per cent equity interest), and National Oil and Chemical Company Limited (60 per cent equity interest).

Following the Commercialisation and Privatisation Act (TCPC), the above-mentioned marketing companies were privatised. The government's equity interest was reduced to 40 per cent in each of the companies. The equity interests divested by government were sold to private investors in conformity with the Privatisation and Commercialisation Act.

It is clear from the above, therefore, that government prior to 1993 had taken major steps to encourage the active participation of private investors in the distribution of petroleum within the downstream petroleum industry.

However, in April 1993 more fundamental and far reaching changes were announced through the Investment Policy on the Downstream Petroleum Sector. The most fundamental of these changes was the reversal of government's policy on private ownership of refineries and petrochemicals plants which by virtue of the policy can now be owned 100 per cent by private investors. The downstream petroleum policy also contained incentives to encourage investment in the downstream petroleum sector. These covered:

- 'Security of tenure of investments. In this regard, the assumptions on which investments are based would be guaranteed if adversely affected by new Government regulations and policies.
- Generous tax holidays.
- Guaranteed export earnings including permission to operate offshore escrow accounts to facilitate the servicing of project loans.
- Competitive pricing of feedstock.
- Attractive and flexible capital allowance.
- Relaxation of restriction on importation of intermediate feedstock for downstream industries.
- Guaranteed crude oil supply at normal international prices for export oriented refineries.'

The priority areas of investment identified by the policy included methanol, MTBE, fertiliser and LNG plants, petrochemicals plants and petroleum refineries.

As regards liquified natural gas, it is pertinent to point out that as far back as 1988, Government through NNPC had together with foreign affiliates of the local oil-producing companies (Shell, Elf and Agip) incorporated Nigeria LNG Limited. The shareholding of the new LNG company was in the following proportion: NNPC (60 per cent), Shell (20 per cent), Elf (10 per cent) and Agip (10 per cent). Shell was appointed the Technical Adviser to the project which is conceived to construct and operate a 4.5 million metric tons LNG plant for the sale of LNG to Europe and the USA. The Nigerian upstream petroleum producing joint ventures involving NNPC with companies such as Shell, Elf and Agip have executed a gas supply agreement for the supply of natural gas to the LNG plant.

In view of the magnitude of the investment and in furtherance of government's desire to develop downstream investments in natural gas, far-reaching incentives which had never been granted to other projects in Nigeria were granted to the Nigeria LNG Company and its shareholders by virtue of a piece of legislation known as the 'Nigeria LNG Fiscal Incentives Guarantees and Assurances Decree' of 1990.

The Downstream Investment Policy has just been announced. Modalities for its detailed development are not yet known. It is, however, clear from the principles enunciated in the policy that far-reaching steps have been taken to attract private sector investments into the downstream petroleum industry.

8.12 CONCLUSION

Commercialisation has brought far-reaching changes to the petroleum industry, opening up the industry – under innovative legal arrangements – to private sector investors who can now invest in areas that had hitherto been the preserve of government. In announcing the Downstream Petroleum Policy, government gave its reasons for the incentives given to private investors as follows:

1. in appreciation of the qualitative contributions of private entrepreneurs to the efficient utilisation of productive factors;
2. government's limited financial resources;
3. the need to encourage the abundant potential of the downstream sector of the oil and gas industry.

These reasons also apply to the upstream sector and are indeed common reasons for the commercialisation of the petroleum industry in countries where similar developments have taken place. The process of commercialisation and privatisation in the petroleum industry in Nigeria has so far been a very successful one. However, commercialisation and privatisation is a continuous process, and most of the changes effected still need to be incorporated in relevant legislation, and be put into practice. To a large extent, therefore, the story of commercialisation and privatisation has only just begun and still continues to unfold.

Chapter 9

Oil Investment in Latin America

Maria Kielmas

9.1 INTRODUCTION

One of the most unexpected side-effects of the collapse of communism in Eastern Europe and the Soviet Union in the late 1980s has been the emergence in the early 1990s of Latin America as a favoured target for foreign investors. Latin American enterprises, especially the state-owned oil companies, have become welcome borrowers on the international financial markets. In 1991 the region became a net recipient of capital for the first time since the 1982 debt crisis. The inward flow of capital to Latin America in 1992 was US$57 billion. The reasons for this turnaround are various and linked both to macroeconomic reforms undertaken by Latin American governments and the failed attempts at equivalent reforms in many of the former communist countries. An upturn in private-sector investment in the Latin American oil industry has developed simultaneously. This has been also the result of a process of elimination – most Latin American countries now offer internationally recognised investment guarantees which are unavailable in regions such as the former Soviet republics – and a product of the Latin American governments', in varying degrees, opening up a state-dominated oil sector to private investment. The real imponderable is: how sustainable are the reforms in a world economy and a world oil market which offer diminishing returns for over-extended and over-geared oil companies, what kind of political obstacles lie ahead in a region where all oil contracts essentially are still a political matter and how quickly will the competition from the former Soviet republics catch up?

The discovery of two major oil fields of over one billion barrels recoverable oil reserves in Colombia, Caño Limón and Cusiana, in the space of less than a decade, has attracted much private-sector investment in oil exploration in the sub-Andean sedimentary basins at a time when international oil prices, in real terms are, are at the same level as in the late 1960s or, in more recent terms, equivalent to the low reached during the price drop of 1986. Yet the fiscal terms on offer to private-sector investors in most Latin American countries, with the exception of Argentina, are some of the most conservative in the world. The region did not follow the pattern adopted by governments in the Far East, Middle East and Africa in easing up on fiscal terms during the mid-1980s oil-price fall in order to promote exploration and development. Indeed, the tax burden, notably in Colombia, has risen. In further contrast to other parts of the world in the mid- to late-1980s, the Latin American oil industry became more, rather than less, statist. In Peru the government of former President Alan García, nationalised assets belonging to the US oil company Belco, now part of the Enron Corporation. In 1988 the Brazilian government changed the country's constitution which established a monopoly for the state oil company, Petrobrás, in all sectors of the oil and gas industry.

The 1980s did produce a counter-trend in the overall investment climate in Latin America, namely the adoption of internationally recognised investment guarantees. Nearly all countries have signed investment guarantee accords, either on a bilateral basis or through the World Bank's Multilateral Investment Guarantee Agency (MIGA). The Calvo Doctrine, formulated in the nineteenth century by the Argentine jurist, Carlos Calvo, which stipulated that disputes involving a foreign entity should be adjudicated in the state concerned, is being eroded. The overall business environment, one which encourages private-sector investment and provides for a 'sanctity of contract' is proving to be a bigger magnet for individual investors than just a change in fiscal terms.

However, the economic reforms which were adopted by governments in the wake of the 1982 debt crisis highlighted the financial precariousness of the state oil sector, which had suffered from decades of mismanagement, political interference and embezzlement. In Argentina, the government of President Carlos Saúl Menem opted to privatise the state oil and gas companies, respectively, Yacimientos Petroliferos Fiscales (YPF) and Gas del Estado (GdE). Privatisation of Peru's Petroperú and Bolivia's Yacimientos Petroliferos Fiscales Bolivianos (YPFB) are being planned. In Brazil, senior managers from Petrobrás have been lobbying for an end to the state oil monopoly and there have been calls for a greater private sector role in the Venezuelan oil sector. Only in Mexico does the state remain the unchallenged controller of the oil and gas industry, through Pemex, although financial problems have forced Pemex to restructure its organisation and shed staff and ancillary holdings. But the problem of financing the state sector remains crucial to its survival. If private-sector direct investment is proscribed or curtailed, then the state companies have to fund ever more exotic, and more expensive, forms of finance. Pemex, Petróleos de Venezuela (PDVSA) and Petrobrás have been some of the largest issuers of bonds on the international markets with Mexican, Brazilian and Argentine private-sector companies following closely behind. In all, Latin American borrowers since 1989 have issued more than US$25 billion in eurobonds. Warning bells about a burgeoning private sector debt began in early 1993,[1] followed by international bankers saying the same in mid-1993 and criticising the lack of transparency in the intended uses of the funds raised, in the accounts of both state and private-sector borrowers.[2]

1. *Latoil* (Jan. 1993).
2. *Financial Times* (5 July 1993).

On the basis of the view that the days of high commodity prices and commodity cartels are over, and that oil-producing countries must diversify their economies in order to grow, the days of the state oil company could be limited, since governments will be obliged to divert funds formerly intended for oil investment into other parts of the economy. But this view must be counter-balanced by a growing protectionism in the industrialised world, of which the clearest example for Latin America is the European Community's policy on restricting banana imports from south and central America, in favour of EC producers in the Spanish and Portuguese offshore territories such as the Canaries and Madeira, coupled with preferential treatment accorded to mostly former French and British colonies in Africa, the Caribbean and the Pacific (ACP) under the Lomé conventions. A reluctance on the part of the industrialised world to allow developing countries to trade may in future be matched by an even greater political reluctance on the part of major-oil producing countries, such as Mexico and Venezuela, to allow foreign investment in their oil sectors, irrespective of the financial consequences. Equally, the growing influence of non-governmental organisations (NGOs) from the industrialised world in matters concerning the environment and indigenous land rights in Latin America and their targeting of the oil industry, is proving counter-productive and has prompted a backlash from many political sectors in the region, including the military, who complain of an unwarranted outside interference in their affairs.

The result has been the creation of a different form of nationalism which, combined with the high poverty levels in the region and self-financing insurgencies, which in turn have targeted the oil industry, will provide a risky and complicated counter-balance to ongoing economic reform. But Latin America's over-riding advantage as an oil investment target is that the kind of political turmoil, and trial and error democratisation, the region has experienced over the last half century is still a future peril which still has to be faced by countries in the Middle East, Africa, the former Soviet republics and, for all its economic achievements, even the Far East. From being the world oil industry's Cinderella, dogged by expropriations and revolutions, Latin America's oil history could provide an insight to the future elsewhere.

9.2 NATIONALISATION AND THE STATE OIL COMPANIES

The debate about the state's role in the oil sector has continued in Latin America for the greater part of this century. The reasons for the creation of state oil companies were various: the inherited Iberian tradition of the crown controlling natural resources and commerce in strategic commodities, a necessity on the part of the newly independent republics to establish political institutions, a reaction to nineteenth- and early-twentieth-century economic liberalism during which foreign oil companies first developed commercial oil production, to provide a source of funding for the military establishment, and the need for heads of state to assert themselves against the power of the foreign investors and new domestic interest groups such as oil industry labour unions.

The belief that sovereignty over natural resources would ensure economic development and national self-sufficiency was regarded as a universal tenet among many fashionable commentators during the 1970s when the Organisation of Oil Producing Countries (OPEC) was a real power in the oil market and high commodity prices fuelled much debt-led growth in developing countries. Even in the industrialised countries state intervention was regarded as an imperative both in the natural resources sector and in the provision of welfare services.

The real costs of such statist policies in both the northern and the southern hemispheres was never really calculated. The state companies were created as political institutions and employment agencies from the outset, not as profit centres. The economies of countries such as Venezuela and Mexico became distorted from an over-dependence on oil revenues while investment in small scale industry, which would provide much-needed employment, was sacrificed in favour of developing state oil companies, on the official excuse that they were necessary to compete with the multinational majors. But the geographical diversification of resources and cost control, the basis of the oil majors' financial power, was never part of the state oil company's make-up. Brazil's Petrobrás made undoubted progress in developing deep water oil technology but the costs to the Brazilian economy as a whole of such an expensive exercise have never been calculated. Economic development throughout this period was stymied by the lack of an adequate private oil sector in Latin American countries. Although Argentina has the largest national private sector in oil, the reality was that these companies were little more than highly paid service providers to the state, rather than risk-takers. Although by the late 1980s and early 1990s the pendulum has swung back to favour the private sector, the preservation of state oil companies as such remains a matter of internal power politics because of the scale of revenues the oil sector handles and the vested interests – such as the military and the unions – which these revenues finance.

Volatile oil prices in the 1980s and the debt crisis put an end to ambitions for a state-led oil industry although the period of change will be longer in some countries than others. The debt crisis has brought about a fundamental change and a redefinition of the role of the state in the economy. In the Mexican case this has introduced a transformation from a highly regulated and a protected economy towards an open and market-oriented one. According to the OECD,[3] the roots of the debt crisis were so deep-seated that it took more than six years of painful adjustments and comprehensive reforms (many of which are still in the process of being implemented) for the new process to start paying off. Only towards the end of the 1980s did real output return to the levels attained in 1981. Similarly inflation fell below pre-crisis levels only after eight years. The reasons for this were a decade of heavy government spending, four decades of protectionist trade policies and increasing government intervention which had left a legacy of macroeconomic imbalances such as persistently high fiscal deficits, loss-making public enterprises, rampant inflation, chronic deficits in trades in goods and services and an export sector heavily dependent on oil.

3.   OECD Economic survey on Mexico, 1992.

But none of these reforms has affected the fundamental monopoly of Pemex. The government of President Carlos Salinas de Gotari has, however, imposed budgetary control and a restructuring of Pemex although to date there is little evidence, outside of the official propaganda machine, that the state company is more efficient. Events were propelled in April 1992 by an explosion in the sewers of Guadalajara, Mexico's second city, which killed 204 people and destroyed homes and businesses in the city's La Reforma district. Blame for the disaster was pinned on Pemex, although the company denied liability from the outset. The result was an order from President Salinas to speed up a reorganisation of the company which had been underway for over one and half years. The new corporation created four new subsidiaries, Pemex Exploration and Production, Pemex Refining, Pemex Gas and Basic Petrochemicals and Pemex Secondary Petrochemicals. There is a fifth subsidiary, Pemex International (PMI), which handles crude exports and trade in natural gas, retaining the role it had played since its creation in 1989. Each of the operating companies are independent business units with separate boards of directors and their own staff and support functions. The result, according to foreign bankers who negotiate with Pemex, has been an increase in bureaucracy and even more delay in decision-making.

The role of the private sector in Mexico's oil industry remains insignificant and restricted to drilling service contracts. Although these are now offered in competitive bidding rounds the result is that they are awarded to former Pemex associates.[4] The role of the state in the oil sector did not form part of the North American Free Trade Agreement (NAFTA) prompting much speculation that, once Nafta is ratified, the oil sector will be opened. The NAFTA pact's real relevance for future private-sector oil investment in Mexico, whenever that is allowed, will be in the Mexican government's first recognition, albeit modest, of the concept of international arbitration. The three countries, Mexico, USA and Canada, agreed to make use of the General Agreement for Trade and Tariffs (GATT) in dispute settlement. Although the timing of a future NAFTA agreement looked precarious in June 1993 following a US court ruling which ordered the US Trade Representative to prepare an environmental impact assessment of NAFTA, there has been little evidence that opening up of the oil sector has ever been on President Salinas' political agenda. Salinas was elected in 1988 on a bare majority and with his Partido Revolucionario Institutional (PRI) at only a very slight majority in the Chamber of Deputies. This meant that he had two objectives during his term of office: the reform of the economy and the protection of the PRI-dominated system, which had lasted in Mexico for over six decades, from challenges both from the left and the right.[5] Since Pemex occupies the position of the national icon, it is likely that the PRI party would not be able to survive its dismantling. Nevertheless, after the Guadalajara disaster the government started a softening-up process which targeted the state sector as a whole,[6] detailing the losses of the state sector in

4. *Latoil* (Feb. 1993).
5. Morris. S., 'Political Reformism in Mexico: Salinas on the Brink', *Journal of Interamerican Studies and World Affairs* (Summer 1992).
6. *Latoil* (May 1992).

contrast to the efforts of the private sector. For good measure later in the year, the government introduced new school text books which downplayed earlier demonisation of the Porfiriato, the turn-of-century dictatorship of President Porfirio Diaz when foreign trade boomed, and attenuated the previously heroic descriptions of the 1938 oil nationalisation under President Lazaro Cárdenas. But the financing of Pemex investments will be a more determinant factor in its future (see below).

Venezuela nationalised its oil industry almost 40 years after Mexico during the first presidency of Carlos Andrés Pérez (1974–79). During his second term as president up to his suspension in May 1993 for alleged embezzlement of public funds Pérez presided over an increase in government influence over PDVSA and a small opening to private-sector investment. The latter change meant that private-sector companies, national and foreign, could invest in what were deemed 'strategic associations' – a euphemism for high-cost, high-risk investment in the development of heavy oil reserves and the processing of synthetic crudes – and in the reactivation of marginal oil fields which had been abandoned as uneconomic by the state company. The proviso was that PDVSA remains the majority partner in all of the ventures, as stipulated under Article 5 of the 1976 Nationalisation Law. There is no other form of petroleum legislation in Venezuela. The government's propaganda machine elevated this very small move in the direction of liberalising the oil industry as a great achievement, a view not shared by the private oil sector. Two bidding rounds for the field reactivation programme attracted much attention at first but interest began to fall away as potential investors realised that the projects on offer were not suitable for project financing. Venezuela was offering a service contract where all oil production was to be sold to the state company. This meant that there were no assets in the form of equity holdings in oil fields, which could act as security for financiers. The only way in which prospective investors could fund the venture would be through cash flow or through borrowing on the strength of their own balance sheet. The first casualties of this process have been companies which form the nascent private oil sector in Venezuela.

Venezuela's highest profile project, the Cristobal Colón LNG project which seeks to develop and process gas from four fields in the Caribbean north of the Paria peninsula, has moved ahead slowly since it was first conceived in the late 1970s. A joint venture partnership between PDVSA subsidiary Lagoven, and Shell, Mitsubishi and Exxon was formed in June 1990 with a view to starting operations in 1997. Negotiations between the partners and the government stalled on subjects such as taxation and the provision of international arbitration until March 1993 when a preliminary agreement was reached to begin a US$200 million pilot scheme. The partners had agreed on international arbitration but not on tax. This project, together with another agreement between Conoco and Maraven, concerning heavy oil development, was presented to the congress for its approval just as the alleged embezzlement case against Pérez culminated in the president's suspension and the campaign for the December 1993 presidential elections began. There has been an assumption that Venezuela's political classes will not oppose the approval of these projects but that a further opening of the oil sector, is by no means certain.

When Carlos Andrés Pérez took office in February 1989 he introduced two fierce austerity programmes which received plaudits from foreign creditors and investors but whose social costs were enormous in a country where half of the population lives below the poverty line. Unlike the Mexican reforms where President Carlos Salinas de Gotari launched a simultaneous and high-profile social spending programme called Programa Nacional de Solidaridad (Pronasol), Pérez underestimated both the social cost and the eventual backlash which culminated in two attempted military coups in February and in November 1992. A debate underway at the same time concerned the future financing of PDVSA as Pérez cut back the state company's US$51 billion, five-year planned investment programme to just over US$40 billion by mid-1993. Pérez also put to an end two years of conflict between PDVSA and the energy ministry by ousting the independent Andrés Sosa Pietri as PDVSA chief and replacing him with the former education minister, Gustavo Roosen. Sosa Pietri believed that OPEC quotas restricted the development of Venezuela's oil reserves base and that PDVSA should exploit its advantages in finding new markets rather than cutting oil production to defend prices. Such a notion has been at odds with Venezuela's oil policy as an OPEC founder although it had support among some members of the then opposition Copei party. But economic reform, especially since the fall of Pérez, has to be demonstrated as successful before another step is taken. Thus investment policy in the mid-1990s in Venezuela will depend on the success or otherwise of the field re-activation rounds and the financing of high-cost, high-risk heavy oil projects. Any setbacks in the programmes under way, even under a market-friendly president, will stall rather than encourage further opening. A debate over the relative merits of investing in the oil sector and of opening up to private-sector investors in order to free funds to provide venture capital for small industries, which would help create employment, has yet to begin in Venezuela.

In Brazil, the reduction of Petrobrás' monopoly has been urged by the company's own management, largely because the company cannot sustain its role as both an innovator at the frontiers of deep-water technology as well as a provider of fuel subsidies. Petrobrás imports 650,000 b/d of Brazil's 1.2 million b/d needs at world prices but sells refined products at prices dictated by the National Department of Fuels (DNC) at an average of 30 per cent below the world price. The DNC is supposed to compensate Petrobrás for its losses but this has always been a slow process. At December 1992 the DNC owed Petrobrás US$3.2 billion. Petrobrás has pleaded repeatedly for a rise in domestic fuel prices but governments have eschewed this measure for fear of its inflationary impact. Following the removal from office of President Fernando Collor de Mello in September 1992, his replacement, President Itamar Franco, raised telephone prices and was scheduled to raise electricity tariffs but had no plans to raise fuel prices. The result has been that Petrobrás has either canceled or delayed investment plans. The long-standing ambition of expanding national oil production to 1 million b/d is unlikely to be achieved this century. The company's future is also hampered by its vast workforce of 53,000 which is represented by over a dozen labour unions.

Petrobrás management has signalled its willingness to forego its monopoly in areas such as crude refining and marketing but has equivocated on the subject of gas development. By the early 1990s plans of over 40 years' standing to construct a 1,800 km gas pipeline between Bolivia and Brazil materialised as far as the signing in February 1993 at head of state level of an initial accord covering both the route and gas prices. With an evident view towards exploiting the energy industry of the future, Petrobrás reached provisional gas distribution agreements with provincial gas companies. This prompted a reaction from the Brazilian private sector, which is based mostly around São Paulo and is the ultimate buyer of Bolivian gas, which also wanted to participate in what it deemed will be a profitable project. But for the project to receive funding from the multilateral lenders two conditions had to be fulfilled: both Bolivia and Brazil have to restore relations with the international financial community and the private sector should have management control over the gas pipeline project. The antagonism which has arisen between the Brazilian state and private sectors over who will have ultimate control of the pipeline project is only going to be resolved after a review of the 1988 constitution (scheduled for October 1993), and of the government's monopoly over oil and gas.

9.3 FINANCING THE STATE SECTOR

With direct private-sector investment either proscribed or limited to marginal projects, state oil companies in Mexico, Venezuela and Brazil have become regular borrowers on the international markets both in terms of bond issues and receivables-linked loans. Colombia's state oil company, Ecopetrol, will become a significant player in the international bond market in order to finance its half share of the US$5.9 billion Cusiana oil field development, where it is in partnership with foreign companies. As long as the economic reform process in the region continues, Latin American lenders are likely to remain welcome in the financial markets. But the state oil company borrowers may become a different matter because the oil sector is always subject to political manipulation. Pemex, PDVSA and Petrobrás have issued bonds or contracted receivables loans for periods which extend into the terms of the next president or two. The risk for the lenders is that future governments will honour earlier obligations.

These companies have been tapping the international markets partly because interest rates are low in comparison with their home markets. Investors are offered big gains in return for the risks they take. Many of the investors have been institutional buyers in the Far East who have never invested in the region before. A Petrobrás note floated in May 1992 was priced at 4.4 per cent above the London interbank borrowing rate (Libor) compared with 2.5 per cent above Libor during the worst time of economic crisis during the late 1970s and early 1980s. Brazil has not completed a Brady debt rescheduling but international lending has become a major source of finance. The result is that Brazil's foreign debt has inflated from US$115 billion in 1989 to US$136.8

billion in 1993.[7] In March 1993 Pemex let it be known that it hopes to raise over US$500 million in oil receivables financing as well as to float US$525 million of bonds in the international market. PDVSA issued US$1 billion in bonds after the suspension of President Carlos Andrés Pérez and his replacement by Ramón Velàsquez.

Derivatives financing, such as oil receivables loans, have become popular capital markets instrument. Bankers believe that they have reduced their overall risk to the lender since the loan agreement stipulates a price for the commodity. The lenders are accepting the risk that the company will continue to produce and deliver the commodity, while its export revenues can be captured offshore. The belief is that over the short and medium term at least, governments will not redirect oil revenues into the national budget but will continue to service the loans. It also pre-supposes that the companies will produce oil in much the same volumes as at present. In the case of Mexico, whose officially declared figure for oil reserves has never been independently scrutinised and is thus thought by many analysts as over-exaggerated, the risk is that Pemex may not be able to sustain its oil production levels. Lenders are also beginning to question the lack of transparency in state oil company accounts and the quality of information they receive. If the state companies are to continue to borrow in the international markets, they may be forced into more disclosure. This in turn may trigger questions, and later political controversy, at home over how they are run and for whose benefit. Whether this process in turn leads to a further dismantling of the role of the state in oil is open to question and depends on the outcome of oil and gas privatisation in the region.

9.4 PRIVATISATION

Argentina was the first Latin American country to create a state oil company in 1936 and the first to privatise state oil and gas interests: Gas del Estado in December 1992 and YPF in June 1993. In the case of YPF, it was never a state monopoly and after privatisation has not ceased to be an agency of the state. This leaves Argentine oil policy in a state of flux which may be manipulated by future governments. YPF was created in 1910 under the presidency of Roque Sàenz Peña and in the face of opposition from politicians representing the landed elite. According to Solberg,[8] these argued that free market capitalism was the key to Argentina's prosperity. Private enterprise and foreign investment would bring results as spectacular as those seen in the agricultural sector and that the government should stay out. Sàenz Peña was an advocate of the free market but his antipathy to the US Standard Oil, which was the principal foreign oil investor at the time, persuaded him to establish the state

7.   Lagniappe Letter (28 May 1993).
8.   Solberg. C. E., 'YPF: The formative years of Latin America's pioneer State oil company, 1922–39', in J. D. Wirth (ed.), *Latin American Oil Companies and the Politics of Energy*, University of Nebraska Press (1985).

company. Anti-US sentiment in other countries such as Ecuador at around the same time allowed European companies such as Shell to expand their interests. There are arguments which state that much the same process is underway at present. European oil companies, whether state-owned, part-privatised or entirely private sector, have been quite blatant in exploiting anti-US sentiment in Latin America. The kind of political and financial support which European governments provide for their national oil and gas companies is not matched in the US. During the privatisation of GdE special care had to be taken to ensure fair competition and that US companies would be among the winning participants.

The role of YPF was strengthened between 1922 and 1930 during the period when General Enrique Mosconi, a determined military administrator, was its director-general. Mosconi's efforts were aimed at fighting the influence of Standard Oil, which held a concession in Northern Argentina's Salta province and extending into Bolivia. The ruling oligarchy in Salta province preferred to deal with the US company rather than with Mosconi. Eventually Mosconi, though he detested the foreign oil companies, was pragmatic enough to realise that some of their money was useful, and so cut back on his ambitions to control all parts of the oil industry. The result was a confusing compromise between state, domestic private-sector companies and foreign capital. The domestic private sector worked largely in a service role for YPF where it received fees far in excess of the world average. This created a comfortable national oil cartel sinking ever deeper into debt and failing to attract foreign investor interest because of the lack of investment guarantees or events such as the nationalisation of exploration concessions by Radical Party governments in the 1960s. The first democratically elected government after the military dictatorships of the 1970s and early 1980s, led by the Radical Party's President Raúl Alfonsín, attempted to attract foreign investors into the upstream oil sector through its 'Houston Plan', but the legal and fiscal terms on offer were too punitive for most of the international industry to consider and the offer failed. The subsequent Peronist Party government of President Carlos Saúl Menem adopted a two-pronged oil policy – the dismantling of the state oil and gas companies, and the introduction of the most attractive oil exploration terms on the continent through the 'Plan Argentina'.

The privatisations began through sales of assets such as oil and gas fields, moving on to sales of refineries, tankers and various plant and equipment. Gas del Estado was broken up into two transportation and eight distribution companies, all of which were privatised in a competitive bidding process. The assets sales generated considerable controversy as nearly 70 per cent of the disposals were bought by local companies and firms such as Pérez Companc, Sociedad General de Plata, Pluspetrol, Bridas – most of them part of family-owned and controlled industrial and financial conglomerates run similarly to their Italian counterparts. Expansion and acquisitions are financed usually through debt rather than equity in order to avoid dilution of family holdings and the disclosure of corporate information. Critics have called these acquisitions the creation of a 'new oligarchy' which will take over the control of the Argentine oil sector in the place of the state.

Although the 1992 Gas Act (which enabled the privatisation) was mired in political controversy as it ploughed through the Argentine congress, the final sales of the gas companies was exemplary and for the first time in Argentina, anti-monopoly measures were introduced – transportation companies were not allowed to buy a controlling stake in distribution companies and vice versa – to compensate for the lack of anti-trust legislation in the country. Gas prices remain fixed by the government until no later than July 1994 when a completely deregulated market comes into force. But one of the major problems tackled during the GdE privatisation was how to circumvent YPF's dominance of the gas market – it controls 65 per cent of gas reserves – so that the transportation and distribution companies were not exposed to YPF pricing. One idea mooted was to draw up five-year supply contracts between the gas producers and the purchasers in order to ensure a smooth transition to a deregulated market. The government was not convinced from the outset that there was a serious matter of monopoly power to be tackled, but eventually it allowed itself to be convinced. YPF stalled for as long as possible, signing gas contracts with the transportation companies only at the eleventh hour and then only managed to include a restriction on YPF pricing for over two years after the privatisation. This period expires at the beginning of the next president's term of office in 1995 and could again throw open the whole question of a deregulated gas market.

YPF itself was part-privatised in June 1993, some six months earlier than originally planned. President Menem's aim in bringing forward the sale was to curry favour among the electorate prior to October 1993 congressional elections, after which he hoped to introduce a constitutional reform which would enable his own re-election in 1995. Because of the need to demonstrate a success to the electorate, proceeds from the privatisations were used to bale out the indebted state pension system, which owed US$7.5 billion compared with obligations of US$16 billion. This in turn was to ease the transition towards private pension funds. YPF's quasi-monopoly status in the country – it produces half of the total oil as well as controlling 65 per cent of gas reserves – convinced international investors to buy. But even after the sale and the pension fund payments, the federal government and provincial governments between them still own 31 per cent of the company, leaving it open to considerable manipulation by future governments although a future re-nationalisation tends to be discounted. The company's earnings over the longer term are far from ensured since it hopes to expand in the domestic downstream market where it already faces severe competition from the foreign oil majors.

In Peru the government of President Alberto Fujimori considered a similar privatisation of state Petroperú but rejected the idea, opting instead to sell off its assets piecemeal some time before 1994. The reason was assumed to be that the sales receipts would be higher if an asset stripping exercise were to be mounted than a flotation. The price of Petroperú would have to be significantly discounted in order to sell on the international stock exchanges at a time when shares in more European state oil companies were expected to come to the market. Another government agency, Perupetro, is to be created to replace Petroperú in its role of administering contracts with private sector companies, a plan criticised by many former stalwarts of Petroperú as introducing much legal confusion into the country's foreign oil investment policy. In Bolivia the government of Gonzalo Sánchez de Lozada which was elected in June 1993 has a populist policy – necessary in order to counter oil workers' union opposition – of selling the entire stock of state-owned Yacimientos Petroliferos Fiscales Bolivianos (YPFB) and investing 51 per cent of the receipts in a social fund. The fund would be able to contract loans on its own account for necessary infrastructure projects and poverty alleviation, rather than tapping state resources. Then at some indeterminate time in the future, the fund would also be privatised, through distributing its shares to all Bolivian citizens. Just as the timing of the economic reforms in different Latin American countries coincided, so their pre-occupation with social programmes to alleviate poverty has also coincided. But there have been warnings[9] that such measures, whether or not they are effective in their outcomes, could bring back the old 1970s spectre of fiscal indiscipline.

The government of President Sixto Durán Ballén in Ecuador produced a draft oil law and new regulations for the state oil company, Petroecuador. In a World Bank-ordained policy similar to Peru's, the state company is to be reduced to a state agency for administering contracts with private sector companies while its operational subsidiaries will be cut down and part-privatised.

9.5 BOOSTING OIL EXPLORATION

An undoubted success over the last decade has been the way in which oil exploration in Latin America has had two boom periods, one in the early 1980s and one in the early 1990s. The former materialised as a result of changes in legal and fiscal terms introduced by mostly the Andean country governments in the late 1970s or early 1980s. These changes were a halfway house between a total state monopoly and allowing a form of risk or service contract with private- sector investors in the hope of taking advantage of high oil prices of the time. Colombia was the exception in that although the oil contracts had changed from a concession licence to an association contract in the late 1960s, there had been no nationalisations of foreign oil interests since the industry began. Exploration work during the early 1980s laid the groundwork for discoveries such as Caño Limón and Cusiana in Colombia. Oil companies which had survived the mid-1980s oil price drop and subsequent corporate restructurings were able in the early 1990s to take another look at the region, now made popular by the big discoveries. But for exploration to continue longer than the mid-1990s, Latin American governments will be obliged to change their terms. Exploration success in Colombia in particular has mesmerised some oil companies into thinking, or persuading their share-holders to believe, that the discovery of multi-billion barrel oil fields is likely to be the norm rather than the exception, thus prompting a negative reaction when a smaller discovery is made.

9. *Latin Finance* (March 1993).

Exploration interest in Latin America is mainly focussed on the sub-Andean sedimentary basins which extend along the eastern foothills of the Andes and their adjacent plains between the Caribbean coast and Tierra del Fuego. These basins run parallel with the trend of the Andes mountains between Colombia and Bolivia, while in Argentina the basin trend cuts across the mountains. The area is believed to hold some of the richest untapped oil reservoirs in the world. Some basins have only been lightly explored while others remain untouched. Proven oil reserves in the sub-Andean trend alone are about 100 billion barrels oil and oil equivalent gas. Giant fields have been found all along the trend from Loma de la Lata in Argentina (600 million barrels), Shushufindi in Ecuador (900 million barrels) and Caño Limón and Cusiana in Colombia (both 1.5 billion barrels). Most of the commercial oil production in these basins started in the 1930s with sporadic exploration and development efforts up to the 1970s. The greatest reserves were found in Venezuela but oil nationalisation in 1976 removed these from any private-sector involvement. The discovery of the Sacha and Shushufindi oil fields in the Ecuadorian jungle, known as the Oriente, in the early 1970s, gave a major boost to exploration. In the late 1970s the Colombian government eased the terms of its existing association contract which governed oil exploration, starting a process which culminated in the discovery of Caño Limón in the mid-1980s by Occidental Petroleum. This discovery shifted the focus of exploration interest in Colombia from the Magdalaena Valley, both the traditional economic artery of Colombia and until then its main oil-producing region, to the eastern Andean foothills and plains.

The Cusiana prospect, just south of Caño Limón, was identified in the late 1960s by geologists from Ecopetrol and drilled in the mid-1970s. Some oil was discovered by Ecopetrol with its Taramena well but the company did not have the funds to proceed further. The area was opened up to foreign investors and subsequently taken up by Dallas-based Triton Energy whose team of geologists, led by Jim Edwards, worked up the Cusiana prospects and spent four years trying to find other oil companies to invest in the licence. The Cusiana discovery well was eventually drilled in 1991 after British Petroleum and Total farmed into the licence in the late 1980s.

Exploration interest in Ecuador and Peru, which peaked with high oil prices in the early-1980s, fell back through a combination of the oil price drop in the mid-1980s and statist policies adopted by the former governments of Rodrigo Borja in Ecuador and Alan García in Peru, the latter culminating in the nationalisation of foreign oil company assets. Peru has still to recover from this setback in terms of international confidence which the García nationalisations inflicted. Under petroleum legislation passed during the preceding presidency of Fernando Belaúnde Terry, oil companies were obliged to reinvest 41 per cent of their net profits in further exploration. Confusion which arose from the interpretation of the law and the precise meaning of net profits opened up oil contracts to a massive political scrutiny culminating in the nationalisations. Peru is believed to have the richest unexplored oil prospects in the whole of the sub-Andean area after Venezuela but the legal confusion which arose in new petroleum legislation proposed by President Alberto Fujimori has done little to improve matters. Political turmoil resulting from the presidential coup mounted by Fujimori in April 1992, when the congress and the judiciary were dismissed, has had little effect on oil company interest. This was blunted instead by vacillation over contract approvals both within the government and the energy ministry.

The real attraction of oil exploration in the sub-Andean basins has been for small independent oil companies. In general fields are small enough and accessible enough to offer a relatively economic development programme which is sufficient to boost asset values and cash flow of the small company. For the larger companies and the international majors the opposite is the case. Under their 1990s corporate strategy, larger oil companies are seeking big developments, such as the Cusiana fields, or billion barrel fields in places such as the West African deep water offshore, and they are selling their interests in smaller fields. But in contrast to the 1970s and 1980s, many of the majors are carrying much heavier debt loads while oil prices are unlikely to rise for the remainder of the decade, unless there is a major political disruption such as the overthrow of the government of Saudi Arabia. Given their concentration on high-cost, high-risk and supposedly high-reward developments while having to service their debts, all in a low price environment the question is: is oil exploration providing just diminishing returns and should companies concentrate on boosting existing production? Industry opinion on high-cost developments has been divided into two camps: that the financial implications of these projects are still unappreciated by the oil companies and that by the end of the 1990s their financial health will be considerably weaker, and the optimistic view is that the targeting of high-risk high cost investments is the only way for the oil companies to move forwards. The alternative is developing existing oil fields in return for an equity stake. International companies have been suggesting discreetly to the governments of Venezuela and Mexico that this could be their future role whenever foreign investment in the oil sector, in return for equity participations, will be permitted in both countries. But this is the kind of operation where competition from the former Soviet states will be significant.

The opening of the former Soviet Union to foreign investors has provided the industry with an enormous oil province full of fields which require re-activation. Oil exploration in the former Soviet states is not an imperative. The same will apply eventually to Iraq, in the event of UN sanctions against the country being lifted since that country has signalled it will allow foreign companies to return. On the assumption that eventually an internationally acceptable legal and accounting framework will be developed for the former Soviet states, including a solution to the whole issue of private property, companies will be able to redevelop these fields at a relatively low cost compared with the exploration expenditure necessary to find similar accumulations. If the future legal framework provides for guaranteed equity holdings by the foreign investors, then a stabilised former Soviet Union could, in theory, mop up much of the world's oil investment dollars, to the detriment of oil exploration elsewhere, especially South America. But this is likely to be stymied by political processes in the former Soviet republics which bear a remarkable similarity to events decades ago in Latin America, especially the progressive involvement of the military in the oil sector. The parallels with Argentina and Brazil in the 1940s are unmistakable. When combined with the increasing distaste for foreign speculators felt by the Russian population, and the Russian government's excessive taxation of oil profits, it is not impossible to imagine that Russia and its neighbours will need many decades of political trial and error process, including nationalisations just as in Latin America, before some form of co-existence with foreign oil investors is reached.

9.6 SECURITY ISSUES

Latin America's insurgency movements, especially in Colombia and Peru, are arguably the best documented in the world. Up to the early 1980s they were no threat to international oil investors. Foreign oil companies and insurgents in Central and South America reached a *modus vivendi* whereby if the oil companies provided the insurgents with necessities such as food, medicines and even prostitutes, but never money, the insurgents would not attack oil installations and give oil field personnel safe passage through the areas they controlled. National armed forces, therefore, were unnecessary for oil field security. The view was that the foreign investors would still be necessary for the country if and when the rebels achieved power. The insurgencies were motivated through various, usually leftist, ideologies and founded on a principle of correcting social injustices as they saw them. The whole picture changed once these movements found a way of financing their operations through kidnapping, extortion and drugs dealing. The result has been the commercialisation of terror. The original reasons for the insurgencies arising in the first place, social injustices and weak governments, still remain but these have become irrelevant to the maintenance of a business which for the Colombian rebels turns over US$350 million annually. The rebels have hired highly paid consultants to help them plan their attacks on the oil industry while they recruit in poor rural and urban areas with a mixture of intimidation and indoctrination. The last half decade has witnessed a shift in the rebels' activity from the poor areas of Colombia to the wealthy ones. Colombia has a long history of political violence. The largest and oldest Latin American insurgency, Fuerzas Armadas Revolucionarias Colombianas (FARC), has some 6,000 operatives under arms and has never shown signs of wishing to demobilise. The rebel groups have tended to overlap in their activities with other groups such as peasants' and ranchers' self-defence organisations as well as paramilitary groups and the drugs trade. This change dates from the mid-1980s in Colombia when the Ejército de Liberación Nacional (ELN), a leftist rebel group whose stated ideology is to drive out foreign oil companies, kidnapped technicians from the construction site of the Caño Limón oil pipeline to the Caribbean oil terminal at Coveñas. The engineers were finally released after US$5 million in ransoms was paid. The evolution of this process has been well documented in Latin America though it is by no means unique to the region. Similar self-financing insurgencies cause problems for oil operators in Asia, Africa and the

Middle East. Latin American governments have attempted through a mixture of negotiation and repression to tackle the insurgency threat. The crackdown on the maoist Sendero Luminoso rebels in Peru and the capture of its leader, Abimael Guzmán in 1992, has resulted in a demythologising of the organisation and its supposed strengths. Sendero remains active in the Peruvian countryside although the government claims it has successfully neutralised it in urban areas. An offensive launched in May 1992 by the Colombian armed forces against the insurgents culminated in the worst killing seen in the country for 30 years. The government has claimed that it is succeeding in crushing the rebels through the military offensive. At the same time it is offering a rehabilitation programme to the rebels which is aimed at persuading them to demobilise. The offer has not been welcomed whole-heartedly by the latter. In the late 1980s the Unión Patriótica demobilised only to see 1,000 or more of its members killed by paramilitary death squads. But since 1991 the M-19, which for a period joined in the government of Colombian President Cesar Gaviria, the bulk of the Esperanza, Paz y Libertad (EPL) and the indian insurgency, Quintin Lame, have demobilised. Through-out 1993 there were tentative suggestions that a significant proportion of the ELN, calling itself Corriente Renovadora Socialista (CRS) was ready to negotiate about demobilisation.

But whatever the outcome of such negotiations, there will always be vast areas in Colombia and Peru where the government has no control, or indeed ever had, and where the power vacuum is filled by insurgents or some affiliate of the drugs gangs. But though they have moved their operations to wealthier areas, their victims remain overwhelmingly the poor populations of each country rather than foreign oil executives. The foreign companies have sufficient resources to organise security whose costs are generally about 1 to 2 per cent of total company outlay in the country concerned. Events in the Middle East, where political crises have spawned urban insurgencies, will place the Latin America problems in an entirely different light throughout the remainder of the 1990s. Although the debate about the origins, the effects, the ideology or otherwise of the rebels in Latin America has been stifled periodically through censorship, democratisation and the return to elected government has allowed it to take place. It has reduced the 'superman' image of the rebels and forced the government into some concessions on political reform, the 1991 constitution in Colombia being one example. There is no equivalent democratisation process in the Middle East, and in Africa only tentative and faltering steps have been taken in this direction.

9.7 CONCLUSION

The politicisation of the oil industry throughout Latin American history has meant that every political change has brought with it a new oil policy. The late 1980s and early 1990s witnessed governments changing their entire economic culture from a Napoleonic-type corporate state to the adoption in part of Anglo-Saxon liberal capitalism. The changes so far have succeeded because they have been to the advantage of local business interests, such as the family-owned industrial and financial conglomerates. These have been welcomed as clients for foreign financiers, especially in their acquisitions of oil operations in Argentina and Peru. This process bears a remarkable similarity to the way in which private- sector conglomerates in southern Europe expanded during the run-up to the 1992 Single European market and as economies of the southern European countries expanded on the back of EC structural loans. The introduction of a free market in North America, if and when the legislatures of the US, Canada and Mexico all ratify the treaty their heads of state signed in 1992, will bring in competition to Mexico from more efficient and better financed US corporations, to the detriment of the Mexican industrial sector which could lose market share. Unlike the EC, the NAFTA has no provisions for transfer of funds from the rich north to the developing south. The reaction in Mexico will be one of two things: pressure on the government to introduce greater protectionism or pressure on the government to open up exclusive preserves of state such as the oil industry to private-sector investors so that local industry, rather than the foreigners, will be the first to benefit. It is unlikely that pressure from foreigners will persuade any Mexican government to open up its oil sector. The southern cone countries of Argentina, Brazil, Paraguay and Uruguay are planning to reduce tariff barriers between their own markets under the Mercosur (southern cone market) plan, which is scheduled to start in 1995. Cross-border trade in crude and refined products will be liberalised, once more putting domestic companies in competition with international companies whose sales operations are more efficient. By the middle of the 1990s the over-geared domestic oil sector may find itself forced to dispose of the very oil and gas assets which it acquired in the late 1980s, in order to meet its debt obligations, or because of its inability to finance further operations.

Structural changes and market liberalisation in European economies inflicted pain and bankruptcy on European businesses, although this was very publicly prefaced by declarations that somehow the process had been an economic miracle. There are too many parallels between the continental European economies of the early 1980s and those of Latin America in the early 1990s for the pitfalls not to be evident: e.g. madcap acquisitions and inflated expectations. The sustainability of Latin America's economic reforms, and the welcome accorded to private-sector oil investors, will in part depend on if and how the local private sector copes with increased competition and a business downturn. At the other end of the political and social spectrum, governments are facing increasing demands for social spending. In rural areas the agricultural industry is in crisis which in large part has been caused by low world commodity prices and lack of access to world markets. Funds are needed to encourage local industries, halt a migration to over-crowded city slums or a diversion into the drugs trade. There are three sources for the funds: taxation, privatisation receipts or funds originally budgeted for a state oil company's investment programme but later diverted into social spending. The oil sector will be at the receiving end of all three eventualities. Immediate political developments are crucial. The ambitions of Presidents Alberto Fujimori of

Peru and Carlos Saúl Menem of Argentina to be re-elected, and to change their countries' constitutions for that purpose, could have dire long-term political consequences. Commentators in both countries have said that the process is not the same as re-electing the president of Switzerland. The region's experiences with eternal presidencies has been so bad that it is not for nothing that only the Dominican Republic allows direct re-election. Events over 1992 and 1993 in Venezuela, Peru, Brazil, Guatemala and Chile showed that there is still a very tentative balance between democracy and a restless military behind the scenes. Attempts by any head of state to remain in power beyond his mandate, with or without the support of the military, through changing the constitution could tip the balance back to dictatorships. Although the oil industry and dictatorships in Latin America have coexisted profitably in the past, if an authoritarian head of state such as Fujimori changes the constitution to help himself, then the government will change existing oil contracts all the faster. The same argument has been put forward against Menem's ambitions for re-election in Argentina. The achievements of economic reform in Latin America have been remarkable but they have to stay in place for oil industry investment to continue and develop. Even though they have been far-reaching, the risk of a reversal has not disappeared.

Chapter 10

The Law of Offshore Petroleum Development
Basic Concepts and Main Issues

Jeremy P. Carver

10.1 CONCEPTS

Concepts of offshore delimitation have undergone a radical transformation during the past twenty years and require a brief introduction. The first and basic concept was that of *high seas* in which all nations were free to navigate without interference from any coastal state. The state had full sovereignty out to a limited margin of three miles: a marine league, or the distance a cannon-shot might be expected to reach. In the 1940s, the first clear sightings of a more expansionist policy were seen: not in the famous Truman Proclamation of 1945;[1] but in a series of agreements and declarations made, primarily, by the United Kingdom in the Caribbean and with Venezuela in the Gulf of Paria.[2] Thus was born the legal regime of *continental shelf*.

Over the next decade, coastal states started to appropriate to themselves ever larger areas of sea-bed in the hope of petroleum wealth. To introduce some order into this latter-day Yukon, the first Conference on the Law of the Sea was convened in Geneva, and gave rise to four important Conventions,[3] which to a considerable extent constitute the body of hard law on which we still rely in this area. Not everything could be agreed in Geneva; and one particular omission was an agreed width of territorial sea. The powerful maritime nations held out against the desire of many to increase the permitted width to 12 nautical miles. Today, with both the UK and US declaring their own 12 miles

---

1. *AJ*, 40 (1946), suppl., p. 47 and the UN Publication, *Laws and Regulations on the Regime of the High Seas* (vol. i, 1951), p. 38. In the latter volume there will be found, on pp. 3–44 and 299–305, proclamations of many other States at that time.
2. UK (Trinidad and Tobago)/Venezuela Agreement of 1942, relating to the Gulf of Paria, Law of Nations Treaty Series vol. 205, p. 122; S.R. & O (1942), vol. 1, p. 919.
3. See Official Records of the UN Conference on the Law of the Sea of 1958, UN Doc A/CONF 13; United Nations Treaty Series, 516, p. 205; United Nations Treaty Series 40 p. 82; United Nations Treaty Series 499, p. 311; United Nations Treaty Series 599, p. 285.

limits,[4] no-one doubts the extent or legal content of the *territorial sea* regime.[5]

Beyond this, Geneva established a *further* margin of up to 12 nautical miles, potentially to be known as the *contiguous zone*.[6] The coastal state had no sovereignty in this area; but could declare certain limited jurisdictional rights for the purpose of control of customs and immigration and similar matters.

Co-extensive with this, and stretching much further was the better known *continental shelf*. Originally, this was a geomorphological phenomenon, of particular interest to petroleum prospectors because the 'shelf' was an accessible extension of the landmass beneath the sea.[7] The original justification for rights in this area was that it was merely the 'natural prolongation' of the state's landmass beneath the sea. As such, its width varied from a few hundred metres to hundreds of kilometres. Even neighbours found that nature had been capricious in the distribution of the shelf along their respective coasts. Thus Argentina's shelf stretched far out into the Atlantic, whereas Chile's coastline dropped steeply into the abyssal depths. It was for this reason that Chile made a claim on 23 June 1947 to an extended territorial sea up to 200 nautical miles from its coasts.[8]

Geneva tried at least to confine the shelf to a maximum depth of 200 metres.[9] More important, it sought to clarify exactly what rights the coastal state could exercise over the sea-bed.[10] It had no sovereignty, only certain defined rights. But these rights belonged to the state without the need to claim them:[11] otherwise, we would have seen a mad scramble reminiscent of the California land claims. In its shelf area, the state had the exclusive right to explore for and exploit the non-living resources of the sea-bed. This primarily means petroleum.

The major difficulty – in Geneva, throughout the Third United Nations Conference on the Law of the Sea which extended from 1973 to 1982 (UNCLOS III), and still today – is the failure to agree on how to delimit the continental shelf (and, indeed, any of the other maritime areas) between

4.   For the UK see the Territorial Sea Act 1987, which entered into force on 1 October 1987. The baselines from which the 12 nautical miles are measured are set down in the Territorial Waters Order in Council 1964 (and the amended Schedule of 1979, following new surveys of the Outer Hebrides).

5.   Article 3 of the 1982 Convention on the Law of the Sea provides that: 'Every State has the right to establish the location of its territorial sea up to a limit not exceeding 12 nautical miles, measured from boundaries determined in accordance with the Convention.' For the US see Proclamation of the President on 27 December 1988. 'The Territorial sea of the United States henceforth extends to 12 nautical miles from the baselines of the United States determined in accordance with international law.'

6.   Article 33 of the 1982 Convention on the Law of the Sea, op. cit.

7.   Article 1 of the 1958 Geneva Convention on the Continental Shelf defines it as 'the seabed and subsoil of the submarine areas adjacent to the coast but outside the area of the territorial sea, to a depth of 200 metres, or, beyond that limit, to where the depth of the superjacent waters admits of the exploitation of the natural resources of the said areas.'

8.   *ILQ*, vol. 2. (1948), pp. 135–7; *The Law of the Sea: National Claims to Maritime Jurisdiction*, UN Publications E.91.v.15, p. 29.

9.   See note 7, *supra*.

10.   Art. 2, 1958 Geneva Convention on the Continental Shelf.

11.   The International Court of Justice described this concept as existing *ipso facto* and *ab initio* in the North Sea Continental Shelf cases, *ICJ Rep.* (1969), 22; 41 *ILR*, 51.

neighbours, whether opposite or adjacent. Geneva sought to lay down a preference for *equidistance* as a principle of delimitation.[12] This holds that you start from a line every point of which lies equidistant from the closest points of the states' respective coasts. But there were strong opponents; and it was no accident that these tended to be states who had more to gain from favouring another way of dividing the sea-bed. The debate continued without resolution throughout the nine years of UNCLOS III; and it remains unclarified by the text of the 1982 Treaty.[13]

UNCLOS III, however, did serve to resolve a number of other difficult law-of-the-sea issues. One led to the establishment of a fifth maritime regime, namely: the EEZ or *exclusive economic zone*.[14] This deals only with the water column and its *living* resources; and thus has limited appeal to those instructed in oil and gas exploration. Nevertheless, it is a fertile source of controversy over delimitation problems; and we can expect to hear much more about it – whether or not in the context of continental shelf disputes.[15]

10.2 METHODS OF DELIMITATION

It may be helpful to explain one or two other methods of delimitation, as favoured by many, but far from all. Even equidistance is far from easy; because you need to agree on the base-points from which equidistance is to be measured. This puts the spotlight on the state's baselines from which their territorial seas are measured. In what circumstances can an island, rock or low tide elevation off the coast be treated as if it is part of the coast? When the United Kingdom, eventually, declared a 12-mile sea,[16] it had the result of including *as new base-points* several low tide elevations, among them Happisburgh Sands on the Norfolk coast. Thus UK waters at this point were extended, not 12 miles, but 21 miles, radically altering the status of the gas field which straddles the new outer limit.

Sometimes, you hear people talk about 'strict' equidistance, in distinction from some modified form. The term is misleading. There is no one way of constructing an equidistance line: its course is affected by many factors and assumptions. In many cases, any equidistance method would produce a complex line, particularly off a serrated coastline; and such a line defies practical policing and maintenance. Thus, nearly all maritime boundaries established by agreement based on equidistance are not 'strict' equidistance lines, but rationalisations of such lines, adjusted to reflect the range of factors prevailing between the contracting states.

Ranged against the supporters of equidistance are the protagonists for

---

12. Art. 6 of the 1958 Geneva Convention on the Continental Shelf.

13. Art. 83 of the 1982 UN Convention on the Law of the Sea prescribes an equitable solution, as a method of delimiting the continental shelf between states, but does not mention 'equidistance'.

14. See Part V, Arts. 55–75 of the 1982 UN Convention on the Law of the Sea.

15. *Tunisia/Libyan case concerning the Continental Shelf, ICJ Rep.* (1982) p. 3; 67 *ILR*, 4 – see dissenting opinion of Judge Oda.

16. Note 4, *supra*.

equitable principles.[17] As any law student knows, the phrase has no defined content. It simply means: what is fair. But it is, of course, a lawyer's paradise: because it can mean exactly what one says it means, and thus encourages endless debate and disputation. Recognising this, the International Court as long ago as 1969 tried to define a number of particular concepts. The attempt failed. These concepts too were deployed selectively in ways in which the Court never intended, fuelling further disputes. Moreover, even the parties to those *North Sea Cases*[18] (Denmark, Germany and the Netherlands) decided to ignore the judgment and to adopt their own agreed delimitation which bore little relation to the principles which the Court had tried to set out.

Among these principles are 'proportionality'. This is not a rule; but more of a factor, which suggests that there should be some relationship between the lengths of the respective coastlines and the areas of shelf.[19] There is 'natural prolongation' itself: the implication that nature has shaped the shelf as a sort of echo of the land territory.[20] But is the shelf the 3-dimensional (geomorphological) extension of the land, or the 2-dimensional (geographical) reflection of the coastline? In one case before the International Court, Libya contended that its shelf had been defined by the movements of the African and European tectonic plates 175 million years ago.[21]

There are economic factors: either of need (for example, relative populations)[22] or of resource (a sharing of mineral wealth opposed by the integrity of the known deposit).[23] History also plays a part: most obviously in the location (and, perhaps, direction) of the last part of the land boundary between adjacent states;[24] but also in the traditional uses to which peoples have subjected sea and sea-bed areas over hundreds, or even thousands, of years.[25]

Many of these factors have been argued at considerable length in a variety of cases which have come before the Court in The Hague or international tribunals pursuant to agreements to arbitrate. Few have had much influence in the decision, or indeed in the general understanding of how to resolve similar such disputes elsewhere. Thus, rather than try to illustrate the topic by trying to analyse the decision of a handful of judgments or awards in recent delimitation cases, it may be more helpful to explore the author's own conclusions, and to illustrate these by reference to the, still, hypothetical offshore international boundaries between Scotland and England. Had the UK April 1992 General

17. This approach was suggested in the *Tunisia/Libya* case, op. cit. note 15. See separate opinion of Judge Gros.

18. *North Sea Continental Shelf* cases (Federal Republic of Germany/Denmark and Federal Republic of Germany/The Netherlands), *ICJ Reports* 1969, p. 3; 41 *ILR* 29.

19. *North Sea* cases, op. cit., para.98 of Judgment; whereas the tribunal in the Western Approaches case looked more at the converse, i.e. disproportion.

20. See the *Tunisia/Libya* case, op. cit., *ICJ Report* 1982, p. 29; 67 *ILR* 22; see also the *Western Approaches* case (France/UK) 54 *ILR* 6; see also Jaenicke, 'The Delimitations of the Continental Shelf on the Basis of the Natural Prolongation Concept', *Proceedings of the Law of the Sea Institute, 15th Annual Conference* (1981); see also *New Directions in the Law of the Sea*, VIII 283.

21. *Tunisia/Libya* case, op. cit.

22. *Anglo-Norwegian Fisheries* case, *ICJ Reports*, 1951, pp. 116–206 at p. 128.

23. *North Sea* cases, op. cit., para.97 of Judgment.

24. *North Sea* cases, op. cit., para.96 of Judgment.

25. *Tunisia/Libya* case, op. cit., 67 *ILR* at p. 5.

Election had a different result, these might have become a live issue; and they could become so in the future.

10.3 DELIMITATION – HOW IT SHOULD BE DONE

The starting point for all delimitations is that there is no one definitive answer which will meet all the relevant circumstances, and do justice to all the applicable rules of law. For every principle espoused by one side, the other can assert another just as convincing; for every method of delimitation proposed by one, others with different results can be suggested with equal justification. We start, therefore, with a rather different proposition, which is the need for agreement. The neighbouring states should – if at all possible – reach an agreement over the course of their common boundary. This is not only because the International Court has laid down that parties must genuinely have striven to negotiate a solution before referring their dispute to the Court.[26] A freely-agreed line must be in both the long- and short-term interests of both countries and their peoples.

Once the need for agreement is accepted, we find that we are approaching the problem in a different way. Instead of casting around among old decisions reached in other situations, and among the writers (and there are many) of learned volumes and articles, we are forced to look at the area in issue, and at the actual characteristics which inform the discussion. Instead of devising arguments with which to try to convince a third-part decision-maker, we need to concentrate on proposals which will satisfy a far more demanding audience, namely: the other party in the negotiations. There may be a variety of relevant circumstances; and it must be acknowledged from the outset that what is relevant for one may not be for the other. We may find ourselves in a balancing exercise; juggling the relative weight of contrasting factors. But none, either individually or in combination, really leads to a boundary. To find the boundary, you have to start with a construction. This should be a neutral construction; and the best that has so far been proposed is based on equidistance. To start from this is not to espouse it as a principle. It is simply the most obviously fair method of delimitation between either opposite or adjacent states *in the absence of any other factors whatsoever*. Equidistance alone may produce a hopelessly *in*equitable result; but it cannot be faulted as a touchstone against which account may be taken of the factors which the parties consider to be relevant.

One circumstance which is clearly relevant for a delimitation is the presence of islands, particularly small islands whose influence on an equidistance can be totally disproportionate to the land territory of the island.[27] Sometimes, an island is a part of a state's total territory. On the other hand, it can be the entirety of the state's territory. Malta, whose delimitation case with Libya went to the International Court of Justice[28] ten years ago, is such a state. For most

26. *Fisheries Jurisdiction* case (United Kingdom/Iceland) 55 *ILR*, 149.
27. *Western Approaches* case, op. cit.
28. *Libya/Malta Continental Shelf* case, *ICJ Report*, 1983, p. 13; 70 *ILR*, 527.

practical proposes, the tiny Venezuelan island of Aves can also be treated as an island state: to the considerable confusion of the continental shelf delimitations in the Caribbean north of Colombia and Venezuela.[29]

A solution for small islands which seems to have passed the test of time is to be observed in the Arabian Gulf. In 1968, a number of agreements were made between states bordering the Gulf. These resolved an added complication that ownership of many islands, despite being virtually uninhabitable, was disputed between the states concerned. Thus, Saudi Arabia and Iran agreed to divide, one to each, the adjacent islands of Arabiya and Farsiya, and to draw their boundary in such a way as to give to each island a sea and seabed of no more than 12 miles (with a straight median line drawn between their coasts).[30] An enclave solution was also adopted for the small island of Dayyinah, halfway between Abu Dhabi and Qatar, which has been recognised as owned by Abu Dhabi. Based on the fact that both Abu Dhabi and Qatar claimed a territorial sea of only 3 miles, the continental shelf boundary is drawn so as to leave a 3 mile sea around Dayyinah. The seabed nearby has been subjected to a joint regime, which has worked effectively for some 20 years as the Bunduq Field.[31]

Figure 10.1 illustrates these two solutions at the points marked (A) and (B). It also shows the other boundaries which have been agreed: Iran–Oman,[32] Iran–Bahrain,[33] Iran–Dubai (UAE),[34] Iran–Qatar[35] and Bahrain–Saudi Arabia.[36] There have been other agreed boundaries not shown. One such concerns the island of Abu Musa, which was the subject of a complex multi-party dispute 20 years ago, now largely resolved: on the basis of a 12-mile enclave of territorial sea around the island.[37] Between Qatar and Bahrain, one sees perhaps the latest delimitation dispute to be referred to the International Court. Although confined to two parties only, the issues raised are complex and no easy solution can be expected.[38]

29. See, for example Boundary delimitations Treaty between the Republic of Venezuela and the Kingdom of The Netherlands (31 March 1978), Law of the Sea: Maritime Boundary Agreements (1970–84), p.139, UN Publications E. 87 V. 12.

30. International Boundary Studies, Series A 'Limits in the Seas', No. 24: Continental Shelf Boundary: Iran–Saudi Arabia, US Dept. of State, 6 July 1970.

31. Agreement on settlement of maritime boundary lines and sovereign rights over islands between Qatar and Abu Dhabi. Signed on 30 March 1969. Date of entry into force: 10 May 1970 at p.82.

32. International Boundary Studies, Series A 'Limits in the Seas' No. 67: Continental Shelf Boundary: Iran–Oman; US Department of State, 1 January 1976.

33. International Boundary Studies, Series A 'Limits in the Seas' No. 58: Continental Shelf Boundary: Bahrain–Iran; US Department of State, 13 September 1974.

34. International Boundary Studies, Series A 'Limits in the Seas' No. 63; Continental Shelf Boundary: Iran–United Arab Emirates (Dubai), US Department of State, 30 September 1975.

35. Agreement concerning the boundary line dividing the continental shelf between Iran and Qatar, 20 September 1969. Date of entry into force 10 May 1970. *The Law of the Sea: Maritime Boundary Agreements* (1942–67), UN Publications E.91.V.11 at p. 84.

36. International Boundary Studies, Series A 'Limits in the Seas' No. 12; Continental Shelf Boundary: Bahrain–Saudi Arabia', 10 March 1970.

37. 'Documents on the Understanding Concerning the Island of Abu Musa', *Middle East Economic Survey*, Supplement to **15**, 28 (5 May 1972).

38. An application instituting proceedings on Maritime Delimitations and Territorial Questions between Qatar and Bahrain before the International Court of Justice was filed in the Registry of the Court on 8 July 1991.

Fig. 10.1 Map of the Arabian Gulf showing agreed maritime boundaries (source: ICJ)

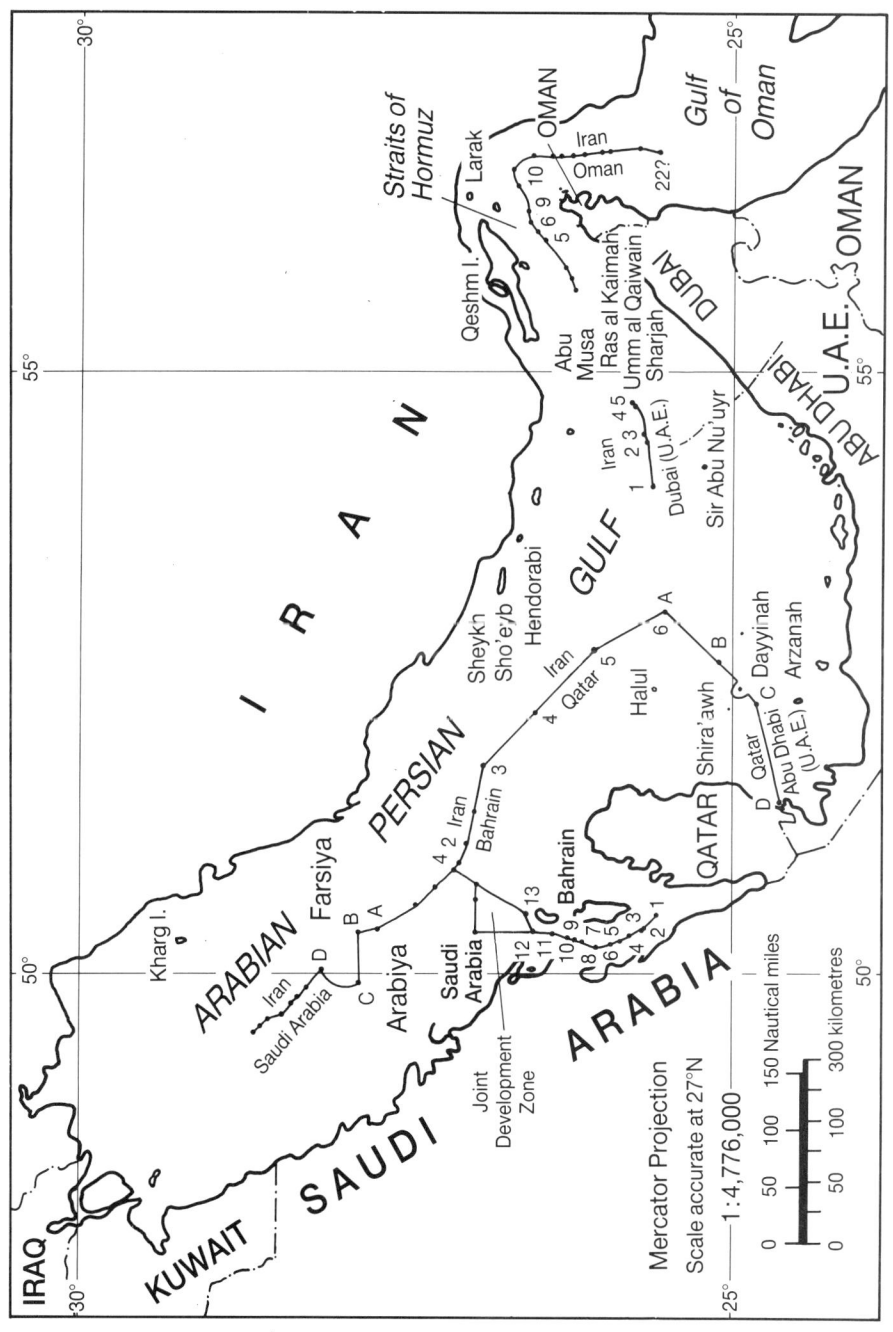

What should also be noted about most of these Gulf boundaries is that they have been agreed largely on the basis of equidistance lines. None is a 'strict' equidistance construction; but they are approximations, or rationalisations, dictated often by the need to allow exploration for oil and gas, and for their exploitation when found.

We find the same phenomenon in the North Sea, where the sea-bed has been delimited by agreement between all the coastal states. Even in front of a concave coastline, where one state – Germany – found itself squeezed between two small states – Denmark and the Netherlands – the solution agreed between the three started from equidistance, heavily adjusted to favour Germany, which nature appeared to have disadvantaged.[39]

Between the United Kingdom and its opposite neighbours, equidistance was the preferred starting point.[40] Difficulties lay in deciding the base-points from which to measure equidistance.[41] Baselines were amended again after the UK adoption of a 12 mile territorial sea (see note 4 *supra*) to take account of low-tide elevations within the 12 mile range. Even after this phase had been resolved, and the delimitation defined and precisely delimited on Admiralty charts, oil companies started to report problems. They found that when they positioned their platforms, which had to be done with a high degree of precision, the readings from the satellite belied the boundary which had been agreed as the median line in the enclosed sea. So far as I am aware, there is no point on the agreed delimited boundaries constructed as a median line running north–south in the North Sea which *is* in fact on the median line. Through inevitable distortion in the charts, the boundaries have been established on the western (i.e. *UK*) side – in places, significantly – of a true median line.

This is not the only time that the United Kingdom has lost areas of continental shelf through technical error. In the *Western Approaches* case,[42] between France and the United Kingdom, the Tribunal engaged an expert to delimit the boundary which the award defined. Unfortunately, the expertise led to error, causing the UK to seek a correction. A further round of pleading and argument failed to resolve the issue to the UK's satisfaction; and there was nothing that it could do to recover areas which the Tribunal had (in its view) clearly awarded to the UK.[43]

39. *North Sea* cases, op. cit., paras 83–98 of Judgment.
40. See Agreement between the United Kingdom and Norway on the delimitation of the continental shelf between the two countries (10 March 1965), *New Directions in the Law of the Sea*, I, 120–2; also United Kingdom/Denmark Agreement (3 March 1966); ibid. 125–6; and United Kingdom/Netherlands (6 October 1965), id. 126–8; United Kingdom/Federal Republic of Germany (25 November 1971) *The Law of the Sea, Maritime Boundary Agreements*, p. 81 (UN Publications E.87.V.12).
41. UK baselines were redrawn after it enacted the provisions of the United Nations Convention in the Territorial Sea and the Contiguous Zone (1958) into domestic legislation; particularly by the use of straight-line baselines and low-tide elevations as a starting point for baselines: see the Territorial Waters Order in Council, 1964, and the amended Schedule of 1979, following new surveys of the Outer Hebrides.
42. See Note 20, *supra*.
43. For the text of the UK application to have the Judgment reviewed, see the 14 March 1978 decision of the Court of Arbitration, *New Directions in the Law of the Sea*, VIII, 389. There is a commentary in J. R. V. Prescott, *The Maritime Political Boundaries of the World*, Methuen 1985.

The southern North Sea has seen a new rash of agreements after Belgium and France found a way to resolve differences over the treatment of certain low tide elevations off their respective coasts. Two Belgium shoals appear on most international charts as dry at normal tides; but a French shoal was not shown save on a French chart. The solution was to give limited effect to the French shoal. This paved the way for a triangle of agreements between Belgium, France and the United Kingdom (see Figure 10.2).[44] It should be added that Belgium has yet to agree its maritime boundaries with Netherlands; but the problem concerns only base-points, not method of delimitation. All states bordering the North Sea accept that equidistance is the most appropriate method, or, at least, starting point.

10.4 ANGLO-SCOTTISH OFFSHORE BOUNDARIES?

Although commentators have recently stressed the complexity of the issues involved, they are more simple in reality. To start with, it needs to be appreciated that we are here discussing the dissolution of the Union. A great many matters wholly unrelated to offshore boundaries have to be discussed and resolved to achieve this. Continental shelf delimitation takes its place in the long agenda. As on many of these matters, there is no certain solution: everything is for negotiation; and the negotiation will be dominated, on all issues, by political considerations. It is pointless to speculate how these might operate: they will be a product of the circumstances which have led to the talks; and those conditions plainly do not prevail today.

But suppose that the will to find a fair solution existed on both sides: with an unselfish mutual desire to apply the most rational objective principles – what then might be the result?

In the North Sea, there have been two main contenders (see Figure 10.3). These are the administrative and jurisdictional boundary set down in the Continental Shelf (Jurisdiction) Order of 1968. This was a straight line of parallel at latitude 55 degrees 50 minutes. But save for the fact that it has been a working administrative boundary, there is no legal justification for it to constitute an *international* boundary. No regional practice exists in the North Sea for adopting parallels as boundaries. It may make administrative sense for all the main oil fields in the northern sector of the UK's continental shelf to be treated as within the same area; but that is quite different from saying that the continental shelf should be so divided for all purposes.

The traditional approach to the problem would be to see what an equidistance line would do. As the figure shows, it has the effect of placing

---

44. (1) The twin Agreements between Belgium and France concerning the delimitation of the territorial sea and the continental shelf, respectively, signed together on 8 October 1990: UN Law of the Sea Bulletin No. 19 (Oct 1991), pp. 27–30; (2) the Agreement between Belgium and the United Kingdom relating to the delimitation of the continental shelf between the two countries, signed on 29 May 1991: UK White Paper Belgium No. 1 (1991), Con. 1735; (3) the Agreement between France and the United Kingdom on the completion of the Shelf Boundary in the Southern North Sea, signed on 25 July 1991.

Figure 10.2 Map of waters between the Straits of Dover and latitutde 53° North to illudtrate recent boundary agreements in the Southern North Sea (source: 41 *ICLQ*, 1992, p. 420)

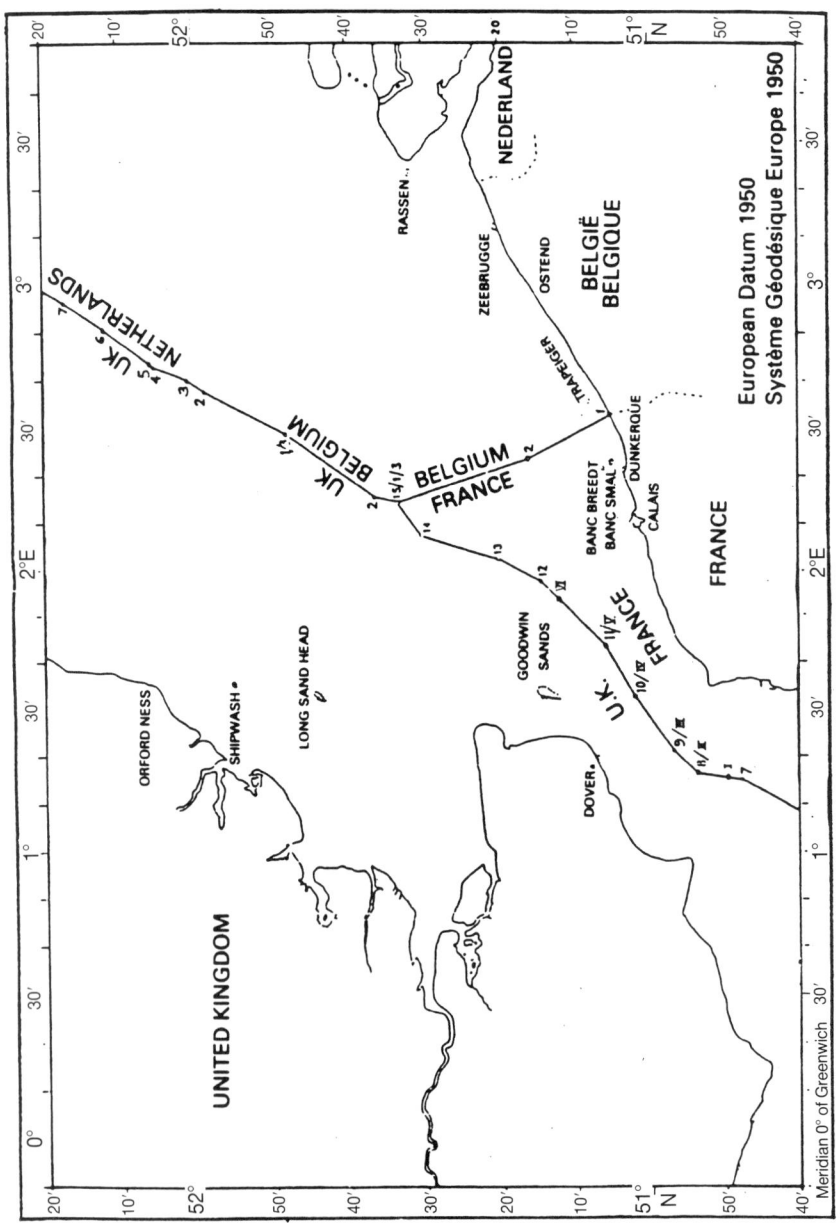

Figure 10.3 Oilfields and possible maritime boundaries between England and Scotland (source: IBRU – International Boundaries Research Unit)

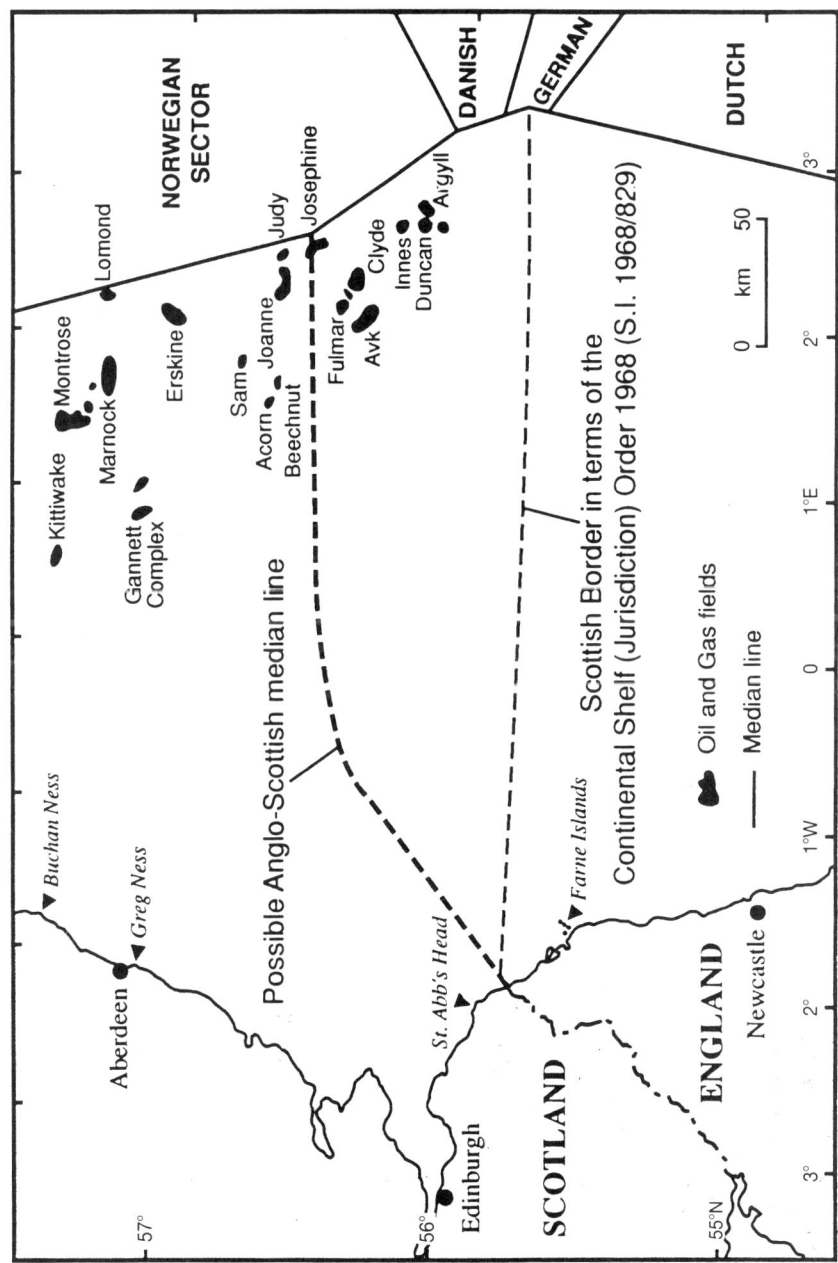

in the English sector seven oil fields. Together these are estimated to contain reserves of 121 million tonnes, possible 10 per cent or even more of the total UK oil reserves. These reserves, and the integrity of the various fields for exploitation purposes, are of course 'relevant circumstances'. So too are the relative populations of the emerging states; the lengths of their coastlines; anomalous geographical features, such as the Farne Islands which have a significant effect on construction of any line by measurement from the coast. We should bear in mind too that there may be a quite separate issue for resolution as a condition precedent to *any* offshore delimitation; namely, the location of the terminus of the new land boundary. There have been rumours that the people of Berwick might wish to join a new Scotland.

All of these questions have to be addressed and resolved before a new offshore boundary can be established. If the will is there, a delimitation can be agreed; but it would be a rash person indeed who could today prophesy what the course of that line would be.

To the north, everything depends on the status of the Orkney and Shetland Islands. Will they remain with Westminster? Join with Scotland? Or assert independence?

On the western (Atlantic) side, a major question is what happens to Northern Ireland or to the Isle of Man. There will be some sea boundary between Scotland and England; and this too suffers from a continuing uncertainty over the exact course of the land boundary as it reaches the Solway Firth. To the north of all these, the focus is on Rockall: that minute, steep-sided rock, visited only by sea-birds and the periodic hardy naval officer to inspect the fruit of Britain's last imperial act. The fact that, in claiming it, the Westminster government of the day declared it to be a part of Scotland may be indicative; but there is no certainty in that. Rockall has constituted a bone of contention with Scotland's northern neighbours: Iceland, Denmark and Norway; but agreement has at last been reached with Ireland.[45]

10.5 CONCLUSION: WHAT WAY FORWARD?

It is worth offering, in conclusion, a quite different approach to resolving the undoubted difficulties in maritime delimitation. There are probably more unresolved continental shelf limits around the world than settled boundaries. Not all open areas require early resolution; but a number do. Some states badly need to invite oil companies to explore marginal areas; or need to settle fishing areas where traditional marine resources are under threat from overfishing. But it may be too great a step to expect states to agree on a precise delimitation. Recent years have seen a growing tendency to leave marginal areas unlimited, but confined within a zone which is subjected to a *joint* regime. Both states retain their claims; but, pending agreement, it is possible to allow exploration,

45. Agreement between the Government of the United Kingdom of Great Britain and Northern Ireland and the Government of the Republic of Ireland concerning the delimitation of areas of the Continental Shelf between the two countries, 7 November 1988. Entry into force: 11 January 1990. (*The Law of the Sea, Maritime Boundary Agreements* (1985–91) p. 6, UN Publication E.92. V.2).

exploitation or fishing. Figure 10.4 illustrates six such joint zones. These are not the only joint solutions that have been attempted. Problems, of course, arise with any joint regime, but this is surely a more constructive area for research than the *minutiae* of hard cases sent to arbitration or the International Court of Justice and now ended.

Figure 10.4 Six joint Economic Development Zones (source: IBRU – International Boundaries Research Unit, 3 January 1992)

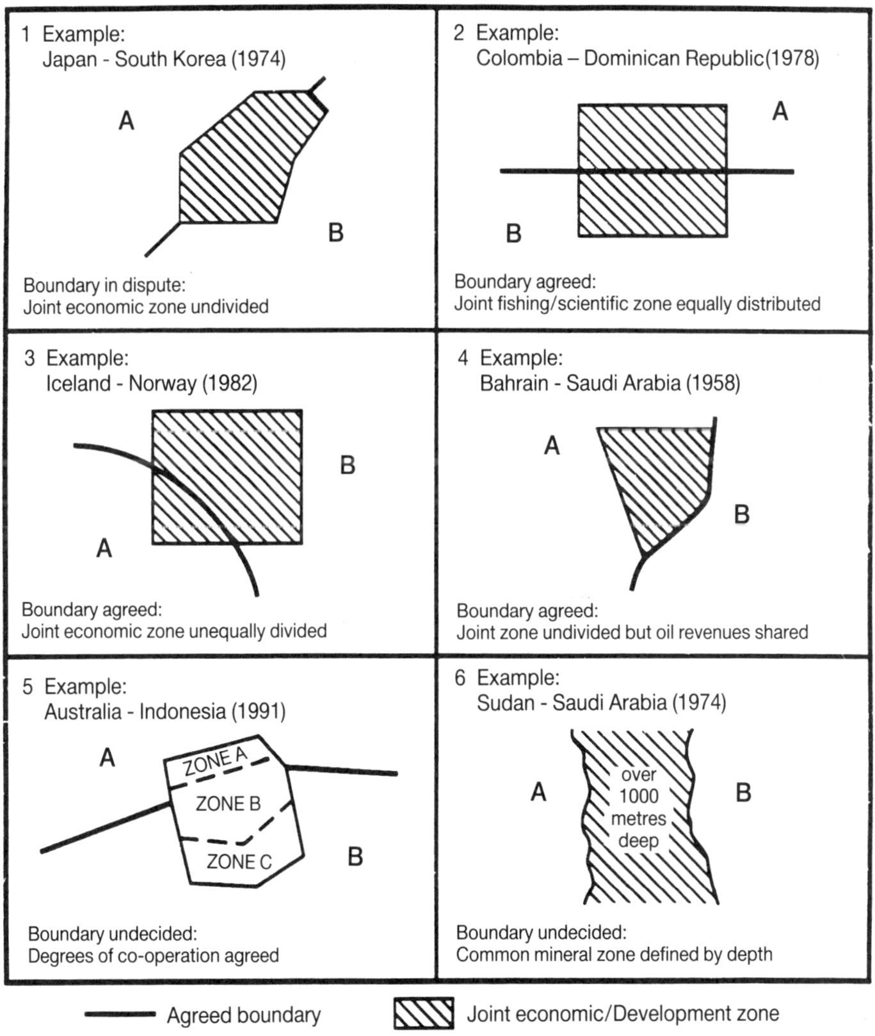
1 Example:
Japan - South Korea (1974)
A
B
Boundary in dispute:
Joint economic zone undivided
2 Example:
Colombia – Dominican Republic(1978)
A
B
Boundary agreed:
Joint fishing/scientific zone equally distributed
3 Example:
Iceland - Norway (1982)
B
A
Boundary agreed:
Joint economic zone unequally divided
4 Example:
Bahrain - Saudi Arabia (1958)
A
B
Boundary agreed:
Joint zone undivided but oil revenues shared
5 Example:
Australia - Indonesia (1991)
A
ZONE A
ZONE B
ZONE C
B
Boundary undecided:
Degrees of co-operation agreed
6 Example:
Sudan - Saudi Arabia (1974)
A
over
1000
metres
deep
B
Boundary undecided:
Common mineral zone defined by depth
Agreed boundary
Joint economic/Development zone

Chapter 11

Negotiating Dispute Settlement in the International Petroleum Industry:
The International Chamber of Commerce

Stephen R. Bond

11.1 INTRODUCTION

This chapter is based on two studies of arbitration clauses in cases submitted to the ICC's International Court of Arbitration. The earlier (and apparently first systematic) analysis of cases concerned those submitted in 1987.[1] Because the results of the first study lead to certain conclusions that could influence not only the practical aspects of drafting an arbitration clause but also certain developments in international arbitration itself, it was decided to conduct the second study (based on cases submitted in 1989) and to compare the results.[2] As will be noted, the results of both studies seem to concur.

The subject of 'how to draft an arbitration clause' is one about which much has been written.[3] Numerous articles analyse the essential ingredients for an arbitral clause and sometimes conclude with the presentation of the 'miracle clause', that will solve almost every problem inherent in an arbitration. However, there are several difficulties in putting these miraculous clauses into practice.

1.   The results of this first study were published in Bond, 'How to Draft an Arbitration Clause', *J. Int'l Arb.*, **6** (1989) 66.
2.   This second study was published in 1 ICC International Court of Arbitration Bulletin, No. 2, at 14 (1990). Special acknowledgement is given to Mr F. Mantilla Serrano, attorney-at-law, for his able assistance in the 1989 survey, which was done as part of the international internship program of the International Court of Arbitration.
3.   W. Craig, W. Park and J. Paulsson, *International Chamber of Commerce Arbitration*, 2nd edn (1990). Ulmer, 'Drafting the International Arbitration Clause', *Int'l Law.* **20**, 4 (1986), 1335; Redfern, Drafting the Arbitration Clause/Forum Selection, unpublished speech to the American Bar Association, National Institute Seminar on Resolution of International Commercial Disputes (1987).

First, too often, as has been said, the dispute resolution clause is done as an afterthought and without very much thought. Preparation and study of the matter is essential.

Second, the other party may have very different ideas as to what constitutes an ideal clause. The relative bargaining strength of the parties comes into play and the negotiator must know what is essential to his interests and what can safely be given up.

Third, the all-purpose clause may not, in fact, be suitable for all situations. For example, it is all very well to provide clearly in the ideal arbitration clause for payment of interest, but if a party ever has to execute upon an award based on such a clause in Saudi Arabia or certain other countries, the mention of interest may render the entire arbitration clause and award invalid. So too, it is generally preferable to indicate in the arbitration clause the place of arbitration. However, if that place is in a particularly unstable country so that there is a chance that when a dispute arises it might not be possible, for political or security reasons, to hold the arbitration in the place designated, the result may be to render the clause unworkable and to forfeit the ability to arbitrate.

Still, the fact remains that because of the consensual nature of arbitration and the various requirements for the validity of the arbitral clause, if it is desired that arbitration be the method of dispute resolution between a party and a business partner, there will have to be an arbitral clause. It is also true that many of the difficulties that most often complicate and delay an arbitral proceeding and the possible enforcement of an arbitral award can be removed or diminished by a well-drafted arbitration clause.

Moreover, the more effective the arbitral clause that is negotiated, the less likely it is that it will ever be used. This is because an ineffective dispute resolution clause will be less of a deterrent to a party that is considering a breach of contract. Thus, even business people who wish to deal with lawyers as little as possible have a major interest in involving an attorney in the negotiation of the dispute settlement provision unless those businesspeople wish to prove, once again, the old adage that arbitration is a procedure that has too few lawyers in the beginning (when the clause is drafted) and too many in the end (when an arbitration is actually under way).

This chapter will present some thoughts as to elements which should be considered in drafting and negotiating an arbitration clause. In addition, so that the article will be as pragmatic as possible, arbitration clauses contained in the 237 arbitration cases submitted to the ICC's International Court of Arbitration in 1987 and in the 215 submitted in 1989 have been analysed. (Note: these cases do not represent the total number of Requests for Arbitration in these two years but only those disputes which were actually submitted to the ICC International Court of Arbitration in order to set in motion the proceedings.) From these clauses, some practical lessons can be learned as to what elements the parties themselves consider important and where improvements in the drafting of arbitration clauses might most usefully be suggested.

11.2 DO YOU NEED AN ARBITRATION CLAUSE?

This is not the place to write at length of the advantages of arbitration over litigation for international commercial dispute resolution. Suffice it to note that, as a general matter, arbitration continues to be more rapid and less expensive than litigation, even if the growing complexity of international commercial transactions and the increasing use of litigation-style tactics in arbitration have somewhat mitigated, though not eliminated, these advantages.

The confidentiality of arbitral proceedings, neutrality of the forum and the independence and expertise of the arbitrators attract users to arbitration. Of course, arbitral awards are also generally more enforceable in a foreign country than are national court decisions.

If a party wishes these advantages, must it put an arbitration clause into its contract or can that sometimes difficult and disagreeable negotiation wait until a dispute actually breaks out?

Experience makes clear that if a party wishes to have arbitration, an arbitration clause must be incorporated into the contract or otherwise become part of the written agreement establishing the commercial relationship between that party and its business partner.

Of the cases submitted to the ICC Court, only four in 1987 and six in 1989 resulted from a *compromis*, that is, an agreement to submit an already-existing dispute to arbitration. The other cases arose from clauses compromissoires, that is, an arbitration clause agreeing to submit future disputes to arbitration.[4] The reasons are obvious. Once a dispute arises, in most instances the parties can no longer agree on anything, including how to resolve their dispute. Rather, each rushes to the national court where it believes it is most advantaged. Any previous oral agreement to go to arbitration is virtually worthless, if only because to benefit from the New York Convention on the Recognition and Enforcement of Foreign Arbitral Awards an arbitration clause must be in writing. Thus, as has sometimes been said, an oral agreement is not worth the paper it is written on.

11.3 THE ARBITRATION CLAUSE IN GENERAL: THE GOOD, THE BAD AND THE UGLY

An arbitration clause need not be lengthy or complicated, but if it is to be effective it must be clear. Ambiguity is the worst enemy to be imagined, for it may either render an arbitration clause ineffective or, at the least, create complications that cost both time and money and thus defeat some of the very reasons that lead the parties to select arbitration.

Frederic Eisemann, for many years the Secretary General of the ICC Court, called these unfortunate clauses 'pathological' and such clauses are found every

---

4. A recent and important development in this area is the decision by the Cairo Court of Appeal (Egypt) of 13 June 1990, according to which a *clause compromissoire* is valid for international arbitrations situated in Egypt even if it does not contain the names of arbitrators.

year at the ICC.[5] For example, the ICC Court is continually faced with clauses which misidentify the ICC Court, most often by referring to the ICC 'of Zurich' or 'Geneva.' There were 16 such clauses (7 per cent of the total) in 1987 and 12 such clauses (6 per cent of the total) in 1989. It can be seen as flattering that the ICC is considered to be as neutral, trustworthy and respected as Switzerland, but there is, in fact, only one International Chamber of Commerce in the world and it is headquartered in Paris. This seemingly harmless error can crate serious difficulties. In one case the claimant actually commenced an *ad hoc* arbitration before the Zurich Chamber of Commerce before agreeing to the defendant's view that the clause in fact was intended to be for ICC arbitration. In another case, the defendant vigorously contested the competence of the ICC, asserting that the clause was intended to mean an arbitration following the Rules of the Zurich Chamber of Commerce.

Yet another of the 1987 clauses referred to 'arbitration in Seoul, Republic of Korea, before the Korean Commercial Arbitration Tribunal in accordance with the Rules of Conciliation and Arbitration of the International Chamber of Commerce'. The parties could not agree which arbitral institution was meant and after several actions before Korean courts, the arbitral tribunal appointed by ICC had to issue a partial award on the point. Even a clause mentioning 'the official Chamber of Commerce in Paris, France' may create uncertainty as it did in one case, the International Chamber of Commerce not being the only 'Chamber of Commerce' in Paris.[6]

One classic arbitral clause illustrates that clarity is far more important than eloquence. It read 'English law arbitration, if any London according ICC Rules'. UK courts held this to be a valid arbitration agreement providing for the arbitration of any dispute in London in accordance with ICC Rules with English law governing the contract.[7] The court even held that this clause constituted an 'exclusion agreement', excluding any appeal to the courts, a subject which will be discussed below. Yet another example along these lines reads: 'Arbitration – Place Paris, rules according to International Chamber of Commerce'.

11.4 ELEMENTS OF AN ARBITRATION CLAUSE

11.4.1 Ad hoc or institutional arbitration

While this question can itself be the subject of entire seminars, it is a fundamental choice which must be made before going any further as the

5. See B. Davis, 'Pathological Clauses: What Frederic Eisemann Still Sees', *Arb. Int'l*, 7 (1991), 365.

6. '*Société Asland v. Société European Energy Corporation*', *Revue de l'arbitrage*, IGI Paris (1990), at 521, note by Pluyette at 353. The French Court held that the parties had manifestly chosen the ICC which is the recognized arbitration centre in Paris for resolving international disputes.

7. See '*Arab-African Energy Corp. Ltd. v. Olieprodukten Nederland B.V.* (Q.B. Com. Ct.)', *Lloyds Rep.*, 2 (1983), 419.

decision on this point affects everything else in the arbitration clause. The present author's view, based on his experience both with the ICC and as a private attorney, is that in international arbitration the arbitration clause should provide for institutional arbitration. This choice necessitates the payment of an administrative charge, but with a good institution there is value for the money. For example, with the ICC the users have an arbitration system tested by over 7,000 cases, with an experienced International Secretariat and special features, such as scrutiny of draft arbitral awards by the ICC court, that result in an overwhelming number of ICC awards being honoured voluntarily by the parties and the balance overwhelmingly upheld by national tribunals. For these reasons, the majority of international contracts that provide for arbitration provide for it to be carried out under the auspices of the ICC Rules.[8] (Certain advocates of *ad hoc* arbitration apparently prefer it in part for the reason – which is often whispered about but almost never mentioned in writing – that, as arbitrators, they hope to benefit from the rather elevated fees that arbitrators generally command in *ad hoc* as opposed to ICC arbitration, for example.)

It appears that to shift from an *ad hoc* arbitration clause to one specifying an arbitral institution is extremely difficult once a dispute has broken out. Accordingly, wisdom and prudence, two watchwords of good attorneys, mandate an effort to incorporate institutional arbitration into the clause. Then, after a dispute arises, if for any reason it subsequently appears desirable for the parties actually to resort to *ad hoc* arbitration, experience indicates that the parties can often reach agreement to do this.

A note of caution, however, is raised by ICC Case 3383.[9] Here, the parties commenced arbitration based on an ICC clause. They then decided to shift to *ad hoc* arbitration, using the same arbitral tribunal, and drafted a *compromis* which, *inter alia*, required that an award be issued within three months of its date, which term could be extended four times. Defendant then challenged the legality of this arrangement under its domestic law and refused to agree to any extension. The arbitral tribunal declared that its mandate had expired. The claimant thereafter tried to recommence ICC arbitration but the ICC's sole arbitrator held that the *compromis* had superseded the original ICC clause and that, consequently, there was no longer a valid arbitration clause between the parties giving competence to the ICC.

11.4.2 The standard arbitration clause

The choice of an institution naturally presents the parties with the standard or model arbitration clause advocated by the chosen institution. The ICC, for example, has the following model clause:

All disputes arising in connection with the present contract shall be finally settled under the Rules of Conciliation and Arbitration of the International Chamber of Commerce by one or more arbitrators appointed in accordance with the said Rules.

8. Ulmer, *supra* note 3, at 1336.
9. ICC Case 3383; *Y.B. Com. Arb.*, **7** (1983), 119.

It is short, simple, but contains what has been called the three 'key expressions' for any effective arbitral clause:[10] 'All disputes in connection finally settled.' How often is this standard clause actually used? Of 1987's 237 arbitration clauses, the standard clause, word-for-word, was used exactly once. Of 1989's 215 clauses, it was used thrice.

Does this mean that the standard clause is valueless? Not at all. It is a basic clause, intended to create an enforceable agreement to arbitrate. However, many parties wish to add elements to it. In fact, the publication containing the amended ICC Arbitration Rules in force from 1 January 1988 itself notes, following the standard clause, that:

Parties are reminded that it may be desirable for them to stipulate in the arbitration clause itself the law governing the contract, the number of arbitrators and the place and language of the arbitration.

Thus, the standard ICC clause, with perhaps minor variations of wording, was used in 47 arbitration clauses (20 per cent) in 1987 and in 21 arbitration clauses (10 per cent) in 1989, generally with the addition of the place of arbitration.

Let us return to the standard ICC clause, which has certainly withstood the test of time,[11] to examine some of its basic elements.

Scope of the clause: 'in connection with'

The standard ICC clause refers to all disputes 'in connection with' the contract. Many of the arbitration clauses submitted to the ICC refer to disputes 'arising out of or related' to the contract, disputes 'arising under' the contract, disputes 'related directly and or indirectly to the performance' of the contract, etc.

These various phrases may all appear to have roughly the same meaning. However, a line of legal analysis has developed that draws a sharp distinction between a so-called 'narrow' arbitration clause and a 'broad' arbitration clause. A 'broad' arbitration clause is more clearly 'separable' from the contract in which it is contained so that even when there is an allegation that the contract itself is null and void because, for example, it was induced by fraud, the 'broad' arbitration clause permits the arbitral tribunal to retain jurisdiction in order to determine its own competence.

In one US case a Federal District Court found that the phrase 'arising hereunder' was 'relatively narrow as arbitration clauses go' and the relevant arbitration was considered by this Court to be restricted solely to 'disputes and controversies relating to the interpretation of the contract and matters of performance'.[12] Under such an interpretation, matters relating to fraud in the inducement, for example, could not be examined by the arbitral tribunal.

In a more recent US case, a Federal District Court, relying on the case just

---

10. Craig, Park and Paulsson, *supra* note 2, at 111.
11. The ICC's Commission on International Arbitration created a Working Group to examine whether the clause should be modified. In its final report, approved by the Commission on 22 October 1991, the Working Group recommended maintaining the standard clause in its present form except for the deletion of the words 'Conciliation and'.
12. *Mediterranean Enterprises, Inc. v. Sangyong Corp.*, 708 F and 1958 (9th Cir., 1983).

cited, concluded that the phrase 'in connection with this Agreement' in an ICC clause should be 'somewhat narrowly read' and excluded one of the nine categories of disputes between the parties. This holding was reversed on appeal, with the Court of Appeals stating that 'the ICC's recommended clause must be construed to encompass a broad scope of arbitration issues. It embraces every dispute between the parties having a significant relationship to the contract regardless of the label attached to the dispute.'[13]

This language and the surrounding reasoning clearly demonstrate the advantages of utilising the key phrases of the ICC clause as well as referring arbitration to a widely used arbitration institution which is well-known by judges in national courts. Thus, parties should be extremely careful not to narrow inadvertently the scope of the arbitration clause by restricting the clause simply to disputes 'arising under' the contract or 'related to execution or performance' of the contract.

'Finally settled' and 'the International Chamber of Commerce'

These points are considered below.

'Which version of the ICC Rules is applicable?'

This question was especially pertinent several years ago because as of 1 January 1988, amended ICC Rules came into force. At that time, in my capacity as Secretary General of the ICC Court, I issued a cover-letter to the amended Rules in which it was written that:

The amended ICC Rules of Arbitration will govern arbitrations which commence on or after 1 January 1988. Parties may also agree to have the amended Rules govern arbitrations initiated prior thereto. Where the parties had provided in an arbitration clause agreed to by them prior to 1 January 1988, to apply the ICC Arbitration Rules then in force, such agreement will be respected regardless of when the arbitration is commenced.

During 1987 some ten arbitration clauses specifically dealt with this question. Two of the clauses referred to the ICC Rules 'then in force', presumably meaning at the time of the submission of the dispute to the ICC. The other six clauses provided for the ICC Rules 'as modified from time to time' or 'as amended', thus also accepting any future version of the Rules. Only three clauses in 1989 dealt with this question, two of which referred to the ICC Rules 'then in force'.

It should be noted that when the ICC Rules were last modified, in 1975, the question of which version of the Rules applied very rarely went to the arbitrators and, so far I am aware, went before national courts a mere handful of times. This has also been the ICC's experience with the 1988 Rules. Indeed, a great many Terms of Reference have specifically stated that the 1988 Rules

---

13. *J. J. Ryan & Sons, Inc. v. Rhône Poulenc Fibers, S.A.; Rodia A.G.: Sodetal, S.A. Rhône Poulenc. S.A.* 863 F 2d 315 (4th Cir. 1988). See also *'Tennessee Imports Inc. v. Pier Paulo Filippi and Prix Italia S.R.L.:* US District Court for the Middle District of Tennessee (19 Aug. 1990)', *Int'l Arb. Rep.*, 5, 9 (1990) at 9.

govern the case even though the arbitration commenced prior to 1 January 1988.

11.4.3 The place of arbitration

The importance of the place of arbitration cannot be overestimated. Its legislation determines the likelihood and extent of involvement of national courts in the conduct of the arbitration (either for judicial 'assistance' or 'interference'), the likelihood of enforceability of the arbitral award (depending on the international conventions to which the situs state is a party), and the extent and nature of any mandatory procedural rules to which the parties will have to adhere in the conduct of the arbitration. Such factors are of far greater importance than the touristic attractions of any particular place that sometimes appear to be the decisive factor in making this decision.

Parties generally appear to be aware of the importance of the situs, at least if one can judge by the fact that in 1987 some 136 arbitration clauses (57 per cent) specified the city or country in which any arbitration held pursuant to the clause would take place. In 1989 the figures were even higher: 146 clauses (68 per cent). This mention of situs is, along with the choice of applicable law, the element most often added to the basic ICC arbitration clause.

The choice of the place of arbitration may literally determine the outcome of the case. In one ICC arbitration[14] between a Finnish corporation and an Australian corporation, London was selected as the place of arbitration in the arbitration clause. The case involved royalty payments allegedly not made and the purported cancellation of the relevant agreement in 1976. In 1982 the licensor initiated arbitration. The arbitrator found that, because the arbitration was taking place in England, the statute of limitations contained in the English Limitation Act had to be applied. Even assuming that Finnish law was applicable and Finnish law had no comparable statute of limitations, the arbitrator applied the relevant English 6-year statute of limitations and barred all claims arising prior to 1976, which effectively meant all claims. (A subsequent amendment to the law exempts from the scope of the Limitation Act international arbitrations in England when neither party is English.)

Another case involved a contract between American and Iranian parties that had been drafted before the Iranian Revolution in which Iran had been fixed as the situs of the arbitration. The US Court[15] refused to accept a request by the Iranian claimant to shift the situs of the arbitration to the United States. The request was made because Iran is not a party to the New York convention and any award rendered in Iran would not have been recognised in the US, which acceded to the Convention subject to the 'reciprocity reservation'. The Court stated that it had:

no statutory or equitable mandate that allows us to redraft the agreement premised on the convenience of the parties ex post. There is neither doctrine nor policy that supplies

---

14. No. 4491, published in *J. Int'l Arb.*, **2**, 75 (1985).
15. *National Iranian Oil Co. v. Ashland*, 817 F.2d 326 (5th Cir. 1987).

(the Iranian party) a polestar with which to circumnavigate the plain language of its forum selection clause and thereby avoid its initial, unequivocal and contractually chosen course.

This is the appropriate place to add a special comment related to the choice of a place of arbitration. In 57 (24 per cent) of the arbitration clauses submitted to the ICC in 1987 and in 56 (26 per cent) of the arbitration clauses in 1989, reference was made not simply to the ICC, but to the ICC 'in' Paris or 'of' Paris or 'de' Paris. As discussed above, this is, in fact, unnecessary as there is only one 'International Chamber of Commerce' in the world. Understandably, however, many parties feel more comfortable with this additional clarification. (Indeed, in one relatively recent ICC case, the arbitrator's award on jurisdiction had to deal with a defendant's allegation that the arbitration clause was not intended to refer to ICC arbitration precisely because it did not specify 'in Paris' and because there were, the defendant alleged, 'a large number of international chambers of commerce in the world'. The arbitral tribunal quite correctly dismissed this line of reasoning.)

Parties should be aware, however, that reference to the ICC 'of' Paris or 'in' Paris will be interpreted by the ICC Court of Arbitration as an indication of the intended place of arbitration, unless another situs is clearly indicated in the clause (as does often happen). A breakdown of the figures for 1989 shows that out of those 56 cases where reference was made to the ICC and 'Paris', 33 of the clauses contained also a specific designation of an arbitration situs.

The 'rule of interpretation' noted above was thus applied in 11 per cent of cases in 1989. It is also utilised when an arbitration clause mistakenly refers to the ICC 'of' Geneva, or 'in' Zurich or any other place. After all, as there is only one ICC, such a reference to another city can, logically, have no other meaning. This position of the ICC Court has been given solid support in several ICC awards and decisions of national courts.[16]

11.4.4 Applicable law

While the choice of the law to be applied by the arbitrators to determine the substantive issues before them is not an element necessary for the validity of an arbitration clause, it is certainly desirable for the parties to agree upon the applicable law in the arbitration clause if at all possible. Failure to do so is a significant factor in increasing the time and cost of an arbitration. Moreover, the decision of the arbitral tribunal on the matter (for it is an issue to be decided by the arbitrators, even if institutional arbitration is used) may bring an unpleasant surprise to one of the parties. Finally, where an institution is to select the chairman or sole arbitrator, as a practical matter it is far easier to

---

16. See Case No. 3460, and accompanying comment reported in *Journal du droit International* (1981) at 939. In the *Tennessee Imports v. Pier Paulo Filippi* case, *supra* note 13, a US District Court interpreted a dispute resolution clause referring to 'the Arbitration Court of the Chamber of Commerce in Venice (Italy)' as being a reference to the ICC (International) Court of Arbitration with, implicitly, Venice as place of arbitration.

appoint the best possible person when it is known in what country's law the arbitrator should be most expert.

For these reasons, the element most often added to the contract, often directly in the arbitration clause itself, is that of the law applicable to the contract. Some 178 contracts (75 per cent) in 1987 and 146 contracts (66 per cent) in 1989 contained reference to a specific applicable law, either by naming the law of a particular country or of the country of one of the parties (e.g. 'law of seller's country'). The applicable law was included in the arbitration clause itself some 81 times in 1987 (111 times in 1989). Also of interest is the rarity of clauses which authorise the arbitral tribunal to resolve the dispute on the basis of equity, amiable composition, *ex aequo et bono*, or with the arbitrators acting as mediators. In 1987, only some nine clauses (3 per cent) incorporated any such basis for resolving the dispute. (Some other clauses specifically forbade amiable composition, although in ICC arbitration the arbitral tribunal may not act as amiable compositeur unless specifically authorised to do so by the parties.) Out of the eight 1989 clauses (4 per cent) providing for amiable composition, some specified that a national law could be applied at the same time.

One contract between Yugoslav and Kenyan parties in a case submitted before the ICC Court in 1987 provided that any dispute should be settled 'on the basis of international law'. Another provided that disputes would be settled according to 'traditional Rules Covering International Contracts'. Yet another contract stated that 'General Principles of Law applicable in Western Europe' would apply. No clause in 1987 or in 1989 mentioned *lex mercatoria*.

While the object of this chapter is certainly not to examine the 'philosophy' of arbitration, the statistics just cited support the view that arbitration is generally not sought by the parties because they wish an 'extra-legal' resolution to their disputes. Rather, the parties appear to desire a resolution based on a specified, predictable legal regime. What the parties clearly do not want is such a legal regime being applied by the national court of the other party.

A few points to be borne in mind in deciding upon an applicable law will briefly be mentioned.

First, it is preferable that the legal system agreed upon be adequately developed in regard to the specific issues likely to arise in any eventual dispute. Second, the parties may wish to exclude the conflict of laws principles of the chosen law, either explicitly or by specifying the 'substantive law' of the particular country concerned. Third, be sure that the national law chosen permits the subject matter of the contract to be resolved by arbitration. The validity of a patent, antitrust matters, etc. often may not be resolved by arbitration, but only by the national courts.

11.4.5 Composition of the Arbitral Tribunal

The next element which should be given the most serious attention is that of the composition of the arbitral tribunal. How many arbitrators do the parties want? How should they be selected? Should they have any particular qualifications? No broad generalities can cover all the situations likely to arise.

Regarding the number of arbitrators, in 1987's arbitration clauses some 58–

24 per cent (in 1989, 62 clauses – 29 per cent) specified either one or three arbitrators. Of these 58, eleven (seven in 1989) specified one arbitrator and 47 clauses (55 in 1989) specified three. It is interesting to note that in some 83 of the 1987 cases where the arbitration clause did not determine the number of the arbitrators, the parties were able to reach agreement between themselves on the point prior to the ICC Court having to make a decision. This would indicate that, as a practical matter, it will often be possible to reach agreement on this element even after a dispute has developed. Consequently, it is less urgent to reach agreement on this point in negotiating the arbitration clause than on certain others.

In 1987, four of the arbitration clauses (two in 1989) specified one arbitrator if the parties could agree upon him, otherwise there would be three arbitrators. Although the statistics are too meagre on this point to draw general conclusions, these few clauses may provide an insight into a major concern of the parties, namely the need to have an arbitral tribunal in which the parties can have confidence. Confidence is engendered either by knowing and agreeing upon an individual or, if this cannot be done, by having a three-person tribunal, one of whom can be proposed by each party. Probably for these reasons the ICC's experience has been that parties from developing countries and socialist countries have a strong preference for three-person arbitral tribunals. Such parties seem to believe that, even though co-arbitrators must be independent of the party proposing them pursuant to the ICC Rules, a co-arbitrator of the same nationality can explain to his fellow arbitrators the legal, economic and business context within which that party operates.

Of course, three-person arbitral tribunals are more expensive and the arbitration tends to take longer, considerations that cannot be ignored when drafting the arbitration clause.

Arbitration clauses tend to include no mention of other elements relating to the arbitral panel. Only three clauses in 1987 specified the nationality of the chairman and in each instance he had to be Swiss. Only a single clause in 1987 set out professional qualifications, namely that the chairman should be 'fully educated and trained as a lawyer'.

In 1989, out of 13 clauses containing special requirements, 10 concerned the nationality either of the chairman or of all arbitrators. Some clauses gave positive indications such as 'the chairman shall be a Swiss professional judge'. Others excluded certain nationalities. In three different cases, it was provided that 'none of the arbitrators shall be nationals of either of the parties hereto'. (Confirming the analysis set out above, none of the three cases involved parties from socialist or developing countries.)

It may well be that ICC clauses are not typical in this regard because parties know that the quality of ICC arbitrators is excellent and the ICC Rules require that the chairman or sole arbitrator be from a country other than those of the parties. Thus, with regard to the selection of arbitrators, confidence in the arbitral institution may well have reduced the degree of detail parties would otherwise have put in an *ad hoc* arbitration clause, for example.

11.4.6 Language of the arbitration

Many parties mistakenly believe that the language in which the contract is written will automatically be the language of any arbitration arising out of that contract. It is true that the ICC Rules, for example, state in Article 15(3) that the arbitrator shall give 'due regard in particular to the language of the contract' in determining the language of the arbitration. It will, however, be for the arbitral tribunal to decide the question should the parties not have agreed on it.

As can well be imagined, simultaneous interpretation at hearings and translation of all documents into two or more languages are enormously expensive and time-consuming. If it is not possible to agree on a language in the arbitration clause then it would be desirable to try to agree either that costs for interpretation and translation are shared or else borne by the party requiring the interpretation or translation. However, not a single clause in 1987 or in 1989 contained such a provision, although some 32 clauses (13.5 per cent) in 1987 (and 40 clauses – 19 per cent – in 1989) did select a language. English was specified in 25 clauses (31 in 1989), French in six (four in 1989), French and/or English in one clause. (In 1989, one clause provided for French and Spanish, another for English and German.)

11.4.7 Waiver of appeal/'exclusion agreement'

A primary advantage of arbitration is that it is, in principle, essentially free from judicial involvement during the arbitration itself and an arbitral award is 'final' in the sense that it is intended to be free from judicial examination of its substance. Article 24 of the of the ICC Rules provides that 'the arbitral award shall be final' and the parties are deemed to waive their right to any appeal insofar as such waiver can validly be made. Despite this language, in 1987 some 49 arbitration clauses (21 per cent) and in 1989, 56 clauses (26 per cent) specifically provided, in essence, that the award issued is to be 'Final and binding upon the Parties who agree to waive all right of appeal thereon'.

Depending on the nationalities of the parties and the place of arbitration as well as the location of assets that may be needed to satisfy the award, a specific waiver of appeal in the arbitration clause could well be useful. For example, in England, the 1979 Arbitration Act that modified the 'case stated' system (which permitted arbitral awards to be brought before the English courts if errors in law were alleged) requires an 'exclusion agreement' between the parties if they desire to ensure the ouster of court jurisdiction to review the award.

As already noted, the English courts have interpreted an ICC arbitration clause itself as constituting such an exclusion agreement in the light of Article 24 of the Rules.[17] However, in Switzerland, while Chapter 12 of the *Loi federale sur le droit international privé* does permit non-Swiss parties to adopt

---

17. See *Arab-African Energy Corp. Ltd. v. Olienprodukten Nederland B.V.*, *supra*, note 7.

an exclusion agreement, recent decisions of the Swiss Tribunal Federale make it clear that an exclusion agreement must be explicit and that the reference to a set of arbitration rules such as those of the ICC would not constitute a valid exclusion agreement.[18]

11.4.8 Entry of judgment stipulation

In US arbitration clauses it is often provided that judgment may be entered upon the award in any court or competent jurisdiction. The model clause of the AAA contains language to this effect and it has been said that it is preferable to include such a phrase in clauses with US parties or where execution may be sought in the US. Some 31 clauses (13 per cent) in 1987 and 21 clauses (10 per cent) in 1989 had such a stipulation, and not always where US parties were involved. In one instance, the parties relied on a contractual penalty clause to ensure that the arbitral proceedings and the enforcement procedure would run smoothly. The clause provided that any party who refuses to go to arbitration or to enforce an award and by doing so forces the other party to bring the case before local courts shall be bound to pay to the other party a sum of 1,000,000 French Francs.

11.4.9 Other matters

Much could be said about the advantages of including various other elements in the arbitration clause where, according to circumstances, they could prove useful in facilitating a less expensive and time-consuming arbitration. However, in 1987 and 1989 these other elements were virtually never mentioned. This does not, of course, detract from their utility, but is probably a reflection of the practical difficulties of negotiating an overly detailed arbitration clause and of the fact that it takes the incentive and stimulation of an actual arbitration before most minds can adequately focus on such matters.

Nevertheless, for the sake of completeness there will be listed these other elements so that they may be borne in mind should the occasion arise where one or more of them might one day prove to be important in a particular arbitration. (The number of times each element was included in an arbitration clause in 1987 and 1989 is also noted.)

1. The applicable procedural law (1987 – one; 1989 – one).
2. Power of the arbitrator to adapt the contract (1987 – one, refusing any such power; 1989 – none).
3. Extent of discovery and cross-examination (1987 – one; 1989 – none).
4. Waiver of sovereign immunity (1987 and 1989 – none).
5. Accommodation for multiparty disputes (1987 – four; 1989 – two). Division of costs of arbitration between parties (1987 – two).

18. See S c. K Ltd., ATF 116 II 639, 1991, *ASA Bulletin*, 262; and D c. B and F, 1991, *ASA Bulletin*, 160.

6. Partial awards either forbidden or required (1987 and 1989 – none).
7. Technical expertise (1987 – none; 1982 — two).

11.5 CONCLUSION

The present chapter does not conclude with a presentation of the all-purpose, miraculous arbitration clause because there is no single clause that is appropriate in every case. A party cannot escape the need, each time an arbitration clause is negotiated, to undertake a rigorous analysis of the circumstances related to the particular transaction in order to produce an arbitration clause tailored to the situation at hand. In the long run, this effort will result in immeasurable savings of time and money.

Part II

The Trend Eastward: Russia, CIS and Eastern Europe

Chapter 12

The Russian Oil Industry and Foreign Investments:
Legal Aspects and the Problem of Business Risk

Andrei A. Konoplyanik

12.1 INTRODUCTION

The Russian energy sector and in particular the oil industry has been passing through some difficult times. The decline in energy production continues unabated. The total volume of primary energy production decreased in 1992 by 104.5 million tonnes of coal equivalent (mtce), or by 6 per cent as compared to 1991. Based on that figure, primary energy consumption in the country dropped by 47.8 mtce, or by 3.8 per cent while energy supplies to the former Soviet Union (FSU) diminished by 23 per cent.

The oil industry in Russia faces a very difficult situation. Oil and gas are among Russia's principal sources of wealth. Its potential reserves of hydrocarbons constitute over one-third of world reserves. These reserves could serve as a source of the country's economic prosperity and meet a considerable portion of the world's demand for oil and gas.

Over the past few decades Russia's oil and gas industry developed at a rapid rate, providing for the raw material requirements of the FSU and yielding a large part of hard currency earnings through the export of oil and gas. During the past few years the gas sector has developed relatively rapidly, but there has been a substantial decline in oil production. Thus, during 1986–91 production fell by more than 20 per cent. Oil production in 1992 was 62.3 million tonnes lower than in 1991. As compared to the record production of 1988, the 1992 level is 170 million tonnes lower. That is equivalent to US$ 20–22 billion of annual export losses. That, in turn, is equivalent to half of Russia's 1993 foreign debt repayment obligations (US$ 41.8 billion according to the Ministry of Foreign Economic Relations) if existing restructuring deferrals were not taken into account. (As a reminder, Russia's export earnings in 1992 were equivalent to US$ 44 billion, but the country was only able to pay lenders US$ 2.5 billion out of US$ 75.8 billion of the total foreign debt of the FSU.) That is why the problems of the oil industry have directly affected the macroeconomic situation in Russia including its foreign economic aspects.

In 1993 the situation in the oil industry is going to remain difficult. Oil and condensate production are anticipated at 350.6 million tonnes, which is 48.2

million or 12.1 per cent lower than in 1992. The total export volume is expected to be 38.3 million tonnes in 1993 or 27 per cent lower than in 1992.

12.2 THE CAUSES OF THE CRISIS IN OIL PRODUCTION AND REFINING

The major high yield deposits of the exploitable kind which form the basis of available resources have been depleted to a large extent (depletion rates are put at 60–90 per cent). Accordingly, production has dropped significantly. The fact that the depletion occurred at an inadmissibly rapid rate of 6–12 per cent of initial reserves also contributed to the fall in production. As the result of the intensive – and by no means efficient application of secondary recovery methods – the water cut of produced liquids went up sharply. This led to a large number of deposits being taken out of use and to an increase in the proportion of marginal reserves. In turn, the deterioration in the quality of the current 'residual' reserves means that much financial and technical resources will have to be expended to develop them.

The quality of new discoveries has also deteriorated sharply. No high-productive deposit has been discovered recently. The average daily production of new wells in the Tyumen Region (Russia's main oil province) fell from 138 tonnes per well in 1975 to 12–13 tonnes in 1992. Thus the financial, material and technical costs of producing 1 tonne per day from new wells has risen by a factor of 10 in 17 years.

There has been a drop in the financing of exploration. This fact, and the reduction in the quality of new reserves (here the 'knock-on effect' comes into play), resulted in a progressive reduction in the absolute growth of oil reserves. Thus, from 1989 onwards financing for geological work dropped by 30 per cent. Exploratory drilling was reduced by the same amount in Western Siberia, where the level of new field development is around 35 per cent of all finds. As a result, the growth in commercial reserves of that region fell one and half times. This having been said there are considerable potential oil resources in Russia – at present no more than 40 per cent of estimated reserves have been exploited and sufficient supplies will be available over the next 46 years.

The oil sector is in dire need of new technology and extraction and drilling equipment. Depreciation of most of the technical resources is put at over 50 per cent. Only 14 per cent of machines and equipment meet world standards, 70 per cent of the assets of drilling installations are outdated and in need of replacement, and a third of well repair units was taken out of production 5–7 years ago. At the same time the domestic industry satisfies only 40–80 per cent of the sector's requirements for the principal types of material and technical goods. After the collapse of the USSR the situation with respect to supplies of oil field equipment from CIS republics deteriorated. Being monopoly producers of many types of goods (Azerbaijan alone currently produces about 37 per cent of material and technical goods required for the oil industry), factories in the republics are inflating prices and cutting supplies of equipment to Russia.

Low domestic oil prices have made it impossible for oil production enterprises to finance themselves (this situation remains the same despite a series of increases in oil prices). At the same time a high rate of reserve depletion has created the need for an accelerated rate of compensation for the withdrawal of extraction capacities. This resulted in a sharp deterioration in the availability of material, technical, financial and hard currency resources to the sector. In 1992 alone the total volume of investment in the oil industry fell by 25–30 per cent (in comparison with 1991). At the same time the volume of budget appropriations (previously the main source of financing) fell by over 40 per cent. The sharp reduction in investment by the government, the shortage of hard currency resources available to enterprises and the severed economic relations with some republics of the FSU have led to a sharp decrease in supplies of oil field and drilling materials and equipment to a reduction in the volume of drilling. Thus, in order to maintain Russia's current level of oil production, new facilities must be installed providing for the extraction of 118 million tonnes a year. This will require the drilling of 62 million meters of borehole of development wells. In 1991 only 27.6 million meters were drilled (i.e. 2.2 times less than was required), and only 20.3 million meters (i.e. 3.1 times less) were drilled in 1992.

During the last few years oil and gas production enterprises have consistently suffered from shortages in the supply of material and technical resources which are needed to keep the wells producing. Moreover, equipment supplied by domestic factories is of low quality, leading to an unjustified increase in the volume of repair work. The number of idle wells has therefore increased sharply – as of 1 March 1992 the number of idle wells was over 25,000 (17.3 per cent of the total number of producing wells). Of these 12,400 were above the technically justifiable norm for shutdown. At the beginning of 1993 the corresponding figures were significantly higher: 31,900 (21.7 per cent) and 12,800. The average daily productive rate (minimum estimate) for idle wells is about 8 tonnes of oil. For that reason alone at least 30 million tonnes annually remain unextracted.

Owing to the shortage of efficient and environmentally safe equipment the problem of pollution in the sector has become particularly serious. This means that considerable material and financial resources are diverted to resolving problems which do not lead directly to an increase in oil production. The intensive increase in the extraction and refining of oil without an accompanying increase in the efficiency of raw material use resulted in the fact that upgrading has not changed substantially since the 1970s, and stands at present at around 65 per cent.

A significant depreciation of equipment (up to 70 per cent) and low technical standards of oil refining have led to a high energy consumption of the product, an irrational production structure and low quality of oil products within the total volume of one type of production. Unleaded gasolines and low-sulphur diesel fuels constitute around half of corresponding product's production, and the proportion of high-index lubricants is even smaller.

The haphazard deployment of refineries and a high average unit capacity of oil refineries have caused a surplus of refining capacity in some regions and a complete lack of it in others, leading to a considerable pressure on cargo traffic and to disruptions in the supply of oil products to consumers.

12.3 DEMAND-SIDE APPROACH TO SOLVING THE PROBLEMS

In the long term it is impossible to solve the problems of the fuel and energy complex without restructuring the whole system of energy utilisation and wider application of energy-saving technologies.

At the end of the 1980s the energy intensity of the USSR/Russian GNP was 2 times higher than in major West European countries and 1.5 times higher than in the USA. During 1990–92 the level of economic activity in Russia declined by 18-20 per cent but energy consumption stayed almost constant. That is why the energy intensity increased by another 16–18 per cent and significantly exceeded its all-time maximum of 1975. In 1992 the GNP energy intensity was 34 per cent higher than in 1988 – the year of maximum energy production.

It is estimated that 35–40 per cent of Russian energy production goes to meet excess consumption. This production alone costs Russian taxpayers approximately 1 trillion roubles annually. This is money which might have been saved. On the other hand, the excess energy produced could have been exported in return for much needed hard currency or the repayment of foreign debt.

It is well known that investments in energy conservation are 2–3 times more effective (from the macroeconomic point of view) than respective additional investments into energy production as a result of subsequent cost reduction for the consumer. That is why the maximum improvement in energy use efficiency is our strategy. But any major results of energy-conscious policies (from technological and structural energy savings) will not appear until later – in some 5–7 years. And during the first two years of initial investment requirements for energy conservation programmes may be as high as or even higher than the annual costs of normal energy expansion.

At present the primary short-term objective is to stabilise Russia's energy production and, first of all, to halt any further runaway slide of its oil production. If all of the above-mentioned trends persist, and given the current domestic demand for crude and refined products, the country may find itself having to import crude and/or refined products within the next few years.

12.4 FOREIGN PARTICIPATION: EXTERNAL FINANCING REQUIREMENTS

Today, foreign investments in the Russian oil sector among others may effectively contribute to the stabilisation of the oil industry.

Taking into consideration the specific importance of this sector for the entire Russian economy, the government adopted Decrees NN 368, 369, and 372 on 1 June 1992 which specify short- and medium-term (until 1997) requirements for external financing of oil production and refining amounting to $30 billion. That is only 1.4–1.5 times higher than the export price of the annual volume of Russian 'lost' oil production for the year 1988 – the year of maximum production.

Only one source of external financing existed for the USSR/Russian economy in the recent past. The source was foreign, almost completely governmental loans secured by sovereign (governmental) guarantees. These loans were then distributed by authorised governmental agencies among enterprises at 'no cost' to the latter. Currently, as Russia has been transforming to a market-oriented system of business management, the economic independence of the enterprises has increased significantly. But as the national oil supply can hardly meet the demand, this monopolistic form of providing external financing is no longer appropriate. One of the reasons for this is that the required amount of external financing (US$ 30 billion) can not be provided exclusively in the form of debt. In this case, more than 50 million tonnes of oil export would be additionally required each year from 1993 to 1998. But taking into account the current situation in the industry, that is impossible, even theoretically.

So it is necessary to look for new approaches other than debt financing to attract foreign financial and industrial capital, with emphasis on direct foreign investments. Moreover, we need to pay attention not only to State financing, but also to private investment, since at least 80 per cent of international financial flows comes from non-governmental sources. So the necessary change is quite clear: from governmental loans to direct private investments.

Unofficial expert assessments indicate that foreign investors are ready to invest as much as US$ 60–70 billion into the Russian oil industry. That is even higher than the short-term external financing requirements of this country.

Of course, one does not expect that these investment will flow speedily into the Russian economy immediately. There are some reasons for this.

At present, there is a high demand for investments on international financial markets. Therefore many firms and financial institutions which are interested in a stable business environment for their activities prefer to keep investing in traditional oil producing countries with proven stable legal and economic environment (i.e. the Middle East, South East Asia, or North America) rather than entering the new and risky Russian oil industry which not until recently was closed to foreign investors.

However, the Russian oil industry does have a tremendous appeal for foreign investors. Its principal attraction to potential oil and gas investors lies in its large resource base, production costs which compare favorably with those of many other countries, the high skills of its workers, and the conversion potential of the former defence industries to the production of oil and gas equipment.

Even so no major rechannelling of cash flows in favour of Russia can be expected until the country creates an investment climate which would be at least as favourable as that in the traditional oil and gas producing areas.

Western analysts believe, however, that for the time being there are many obstacles and uncertainties for oil and gas investment in Russia. Tables 12.1

Table 12.1 Obstacles and barriers for foreign investors in the Russian petroleum industry (opinion of Canadian experts)

1.	High political instability
2.	High (prohibitive) levels of taxation
3.	Export tariffs (1/3 of world market prices)
4. (a) (b)	Legal environment: Delays with issuing the law 'On Oil and Gas' The law 'On Subsurface' requires revisions: ● Direct negotiations are needed in addition to bids and auctions ● Settlement of disputes by international arbitration rather than exclusively by competent Russian authorities
5.	The negotiation process on new oil projects with participation of foreign capital is riddled with red tape
6.	No distinct division of authority among federal, regional and local governments, and the management of oil producing enterprises and associations
7.	Issues pertaining to the operation of oil and gas transportation systems need to be settled on an intergovernmental level.

and 12.2 summarise the respective opinions of US and Canadian analysts. These opinions can be accepted or questioned (regarding in particular the inconsistency of the Russian government's decisions with respect to the enactment of oil and gas legislation as observed by US analysts), but at least they represent a certain system of concepts that are entertained by (some in) the North American oil business community. But if we are to promote a practical and mutually beneficial interaction with Western industrial groups and financial institutions, we should learn to live with these opinions and, consequently, take into consideration what we perceive as uncomplimentary and/or erroneous pronouncements.

12.5 INVESTMENT CLIMATE: RECENT PAST

A few years ago none of these problems in the relationship with foreign investors existed. The explanation for this is as follows.

Until very recently, notably while the USSR was still a union with its mighty institutions of central government, federal agencies were in charge of establishing any contacts with foreign companies. Such agencies naturally preferred to go to a handful of major companies for investment. The orientation towards foreign companies located at the top tier of the industrial and financial hierarchy and possessing a formidable economic capability narrowed such cooperation down to a small number of multi-billion dollar 'superprojects' and an equally small number of credit lines obtained from the

Table 12.2 Outstanding issues for US businesses with respect to potential investments in the Russian oil and gas industry (opinion of the US oil and gas industry)

1.	The existing Russian laws and regulations applicable to foreign investments are not sufficiently developed yet:
	(a) many issues associated with the division of authority between federal and local governments remain uncertain;
	(b) no accurate information is available on who is authorised to execute contracts;
	(c) Although in general the Law 'On Subsurface' and the Procedure for Licensing the Use of Natural Resources refer to concessions, production sharing contracts, and other generally accepted international contracts, they fail to define their terms and conditions, including execution.

2.	Legal and financial guarantees (this issue is particularly important, owing to the long-term nature of investments in the development of oil and gas fields):
	(a) Russia's membership of the Multilateral Investment Guarantee Agency is yet to be approved by the Supreme Soviet;
	(b) Russia is not a member of the International Finance Corporation.

3.	Investment climate in general:
	(a) uncertain and unstable (taxation system, foreign trade environment, and currency controls);
	(b) Export tariffs:
	• its unexpected introduction in January 1992 led several US–Rusian joint ventures to the verge of bankruptcy;
	• the Executive Order, passed by the Government in July 1992 granting exemption from the tariffs to joint ventures registered before 01/01/92, is not enforced, which creates uncertainty in companies.

4.	The activity of US companies is affected by the following recent governmental acts which contained 'serious violations of Russian laws':
	(a) Decrees of the Government of the Russian Federation:
	• #90 dated 12/30/91 'On Export and Import Licenses: Quotas on Goods (work and services) in the Territory of the Russian Federation in 1992' (as amended);
	• #91 dated 12/30/91 'On the Introduction of an Export Tariff on Specific Goods Exported from the Russian Federation' (increased export tariffs for enterprises with foreign capital investment;
	(b) Decrees of the President of the Russian Federation:
	• #629 dated 06/14/92 'On Partial Revisions to the Procedure for Mandatory Sale of Hard Currency Proceeds and the Collection of Export Duties ('contained violations of the current RF Law "On Foreign Investments" ');
	• #Decree dated 11/25/92 'On Measures to Expedite the Development of Oil and Gas Fields on the Continental Shelf of the Russian Federation' ('contained violations of the current RF Laws "On Foreign Investments" and "On the Subsurface" ').

governments of their home countries. That made it possible to keep such projects under the constant control of federal agencies. Also, such projects required, as a rule, appropriate governmental guarantees, which could only be obtained through governmental authorisations for particular investment projects, credit lines, and commercial deals.

Therefore, alongside the widely used intergovernmental financial agreements, virtually the only other type of interaction with foreign companies was the so-called 'diagonal' deals, whereby a contract is executed between the government of the host country and the foreign company in question, rather than between two companies – i.e. between economic entities of the same level.

Under such circumstances any developed and comprehensive system of legislation regulating foreign investment, trade and political issues became somewhat redundant – because cooperation with a small number of large companies could do without such laws, relying instead on governmental resolutions adopted on a case-by-case basis. Besides, no one generally questioned the legitimacy of direct contacts between the supreme governmental agencies of the USSR as the host country and major foreign monopolies with annual sales equivalent to the GNP of some small countries.

But as governmental agencies become decentralised, as an increasing number of enterprises and associations enter into direct relationships with foreign companies, and as the scope of cooperation with potential foreign investors grows as a result of the enlistment of small and medium-sized businesses from both sides, the above scheme of things (which is known as the 'system of individual legal restrictions') simply cease to work in view of the fact that the number of entities involved becomes too great.

In this situation the only legal regulatory medium for the relations between the host country, which owns the subsurface, and the prospective investors is a comprehensive system of economic laws. Such a system is only just beginning to emerge in Russia. According to V. Shumeiko, First Vice-Premier of the Russian Federation, the country will have to draft and enact at least 100 laws for such a system to emerge fully. Y. Shafranik, the Russian Minister for Fuel and Energy, believes that at least 50 laws are required for the privatisation process alone.

The existing legislative system does not include the necessary general and specific laws and regulations the objectives of which are to govern activities in the energy sector – and specifically the oil industry – in a market-oriented economy or in the process of transition thereto. For this reason we attach much importance to creating the necessary business and legal environment in the energy sector, particularly in the mining industries, which suffer from the largest number of legislative 'white spots'.

12.6 CURRENT LEGISLATIVE ACTIVITIES

At present our internal legislation already includes some fundamentals of a legal base which regulates relations between the owner of the subsurface and the investor, as well as other aspects of the use of the subsurface. In June and September 1992 the Supreme Soviet of Russia adopted the Law 'On the Subsurface' and 'The Procedure for Licensing the Use of Natural Resources', respectively. In October 1992 the Government of Russia approved the Regulation 'On the Procedure and Conditions for the Right to Use the Subsurface, Water Areas and Sections of the Seabed'. In November, pursuant to the October Decree by President Yeltsyn 'On the Introduction of an Excise Tax on the Users of Underground Resources in the Territory of the Russian

Table 12.3 Package of priority laws associated with activities in Russia's fuel and energy sector (drafted and/or scheduled to be drawn up)

A.	Special ('Internal') energy laws
(a)	'Horizontal' Laws (applicable to several sectors):
1.	On the Fundamental Energy Policy of the Russian Federation
2.	On Safety and Environmental Properties of Facilities of the Fuel and Energy Complex
3.	On the Integrated Power System of Russia
4.	On the Integrated Gas-Supply System of Russia
(b)	'Vertical' laws (governing a specific sector):
5.	On Energy Saving
6.	On Oil and Gas
7.	On the Power Industry
8.	On the Use of Nuclear Power
9.	On the Use of Unconventional Renwable Energy Sources
B.	Other relevant laws and legislation
10.	Law on Amendments to the Fiscal System of the Russian Federation with Respect to the Use of Energy Resources and the Operation of Energy Facilities
11.	Law on Concessions and Production Sharing Contracts.

Federation', the Russian Government adopted the Resolution 'On an Excise tax on Oil Produced in the Territory of the Russian Federation'. In February 1993 the Supreme Soviet of the Russian Federation approved the Regulations 'On the Off-Budget Fund for the Replenishment of Known Mineral Resources' and the Russian Government adopted the Resolution 'On Price Control in the Oil Industry'.

The Russian Ministry of Fuel and Energy, Russian Ministry of Science, and other agencies have developed a concept for Russia's new energy policy which was reviewed and approved by the Russian Government in September 1992. The concept contemplates the drafting of a package of priority laws to regulate operations in the energy sector. The procedure for the development of the said legislation, and the time-frame for the submittal thereof have been agreed upon by the leadership of the Supreme Soviet of the Russian Federation (see Table 12.3). For the energy sector as a whole the most important bill is that 'On the Fundamental Energy Policy of the Russian Federation', the first version of which should be ready in the near future.

To coordinate the drafting of the legislation outlined in Table 12.3, the Government of the Russian Federation, in concurrence with the Supreme Soviet of the Russian Federation, set up an Interdepartmental Coordinating Group headed by A. Samusev, Deputy Minister for Fuel and Energy of Russia. Working groups whose task is to prepare each of the other draft bills have also been set up.

Work is underway to draft the Laws 'On Oil and Gas', 'On Concessions and Production Sharing Agreements', 'On Amendments to the Fiscal System of the Russian Federation with Respect to the Use of Energy Resources and the Operation of Energy Facilities'. All of the above-mentioned are priority bills for the oil industry.

12.7 OIL AND GAS LAW

Soon the draft law 'On Oil and Gas', the main 'dedicated' law for the oil and gas industries, will be completed. When working on this draft law the special interdepartmental commission managed to avoid some errors made during the preparation of the law 'On the Subsurface'. Such errors included, for example, submission to the RF Supreme Soviet of two 'conflicting' versions prepared by the Russian Committee for Geology and the Ministry of Fuel and Energy respectively. The two versions were mutually exclusive in some respects. Attempts were made to reach agreement as to how to proceed on these versions at the early stage of discussions in the RF Supreme Soviet. But these attempts only resulted in confrontation between promoters of the two versions rather than a common desire to find a mutually acceptable wording to certain articles.

There seems to be no such confrontation this time despite the fact that three versions of the draft law 'On Oil and Gas' initially existed – as compared to the law 'On the Subsurface' which only had two.

The first version of the law 'On Oil and Gas' was prepared by the VNIIOENG Institute. It is called the 'Tishchenko version', by the name of the Study Group manager and Institute director.

The second version, called the 'Gas version' was prepared by the Ministry of Gas Industry experts who proposed separate laws for oil and for gas.

The third version, called the 'Gazeev-Hardy version' was the result of a joint effort of the group that included Russian experts headed by M. Gazeev, a department manager of the VNIIKTEP Institute, and a group of World Bank experts headed by G. Hardy III, a professor of law at the University of Houston (USA).

The above versions were discussed and reviewed by the Ministry of Fuel and Energy and other interested governmental organisations, by Russian and foreign experts and organisations, and by 'independent experts' at conferences and workshops including international forums. They were also discussed and reviewed by the RF Supreme Soviet Commission headed by G. Kalistratov, Deputy Chairman of the RF Supreme Soviet Committee for Industry and Power Engineering. Based on the experience of passing the draft law 'On the Subsurface' through the RF Supreme Soviet, it was understood that a uniform 'trade-off' version of the draft Law 'On Oil and Gas' should be prepared for submittal to the Supreme Soviet. To this end, a Commission headed by the above-mentioned A. Samusev was created. This commission, together with a special sub-commission – a Working Group of experts headed by A. Perchik, a professor of law at the State Academy of Oil and Gas – was assigned the task of preparing such a version.

The 'trade-off' version of the law known as the 'Perchik version' is now under independent expert examination and review in order to prepare the draft law 'On Oil and Gas' for submission to the RF Supreme Soviet.

12.8 THE EUROPEAN ENERGY CHARTER

In December 1991, Russia – together with 48 other nations and two inter-governmental organisations drawn from three continents – signed the European Energy Charter which became the first international agreement signed by the republics of the former USSR as independent sovereign states. Currently, active negotiations are under way on a package of binding legal documents supplementary to the Charter. This package, which is known as the Basic Agreement, as opposed to the Charter *per se* (a purely political declaration by the signatories) will comprise: (1) a multilateral 'horizontal' commercial, political, investment, economic, and legal agreement; and (2) 'vertical' Protocols on cooperation in selected energy sectors – among which the Protocol on Hydrocarbons is the most significant.

In our law-making activities we assume that relations with all states and companies should be built on principles stated in the European Energy Charter and its supplementary binding documents. Pursuant to these documents, a common energy, economic, and legal framework for the whole industrially developed part of the world will be created – 50 European, North American, Pacific Rim and CIS states are negotiating the package comprising the Charter. Here uniform conditions will be created for all participants with respect to access to energy resources, markets, transportation facilities (including transit privileges), technologies, capital markets, etc. Such a system would provide a balance of interests for the host countries and potential investors both in terms of investment regimes and of commercial and political issues.[1]

We believe that the development of our internal 'energy' legislation is closely linked to the negotiations in Brussels since in our opinion the problem of creating the necessary economic/legal environment in the Russian energy sector includes three distinct aspects, each of which complements the other. These are:

1. creating within the domestic legal system a series of special 'energy' laws reflecting the distinctive features of the energy sector – including the mining sector – as an object of legal regulation (some of such legislative acts were mentioned above; currently, a package of 11 basic legislative acts related to activities in the energy sector is being developed, of which 9 are designed for 'internal' use in the power industry – Table 12.3).
2. development of a diversified general legislative system, with the energy industries as one of the subjects for regulation (e.g. tax and concession laws – see Table 12.3).
3. development of a system of bilateral and multilateral international

---

1. European Energy Charter: First Anniversary Signature, *Finvest (Financial Newsletter)*, **51** (1992).

Table 12.4 Minimum rates of return acceptable to United States investors (as measured by some American companies)

United States		Western Europe		USSR/CIS/Russia	
		Political risk	1%	Political risk	$\gg$ 3%
		Geographical risk	2%	Geographical risk	$\gg$ 3%
		Currency risk	2%	Currency risk	$\gg$ 3%
Commercial risk	4–5%	Commercial risk	4–5%	Commercial risk	$\gg$ 6%
Financing risk	2–3%	Financing risk	2–3%	Financing risk	$\gg$ 3%
Investment risk	2–3%	Investment risk	2–3%	Investment risk	$\gg$ 3%
Long-term inflation	4–5%	Long-term inflation	4–5%	Long-term inflation	$\gg$ 4%
Real ROR	3–4%	Real ROR	3–4%	Real ROR	$\gg$ 3–4%
Minimum acceptable ROR	15–20%		20–25%		$\gg$ 25%

US Treasury Bills (7-day maturity)	
Long-term inflation	4.5%
Real ROR	3–4%
Minimum acceptable ROR:	7–9%

contractual and legal acts facilitating integration of our national economy into the world economy and into the system of international economic relations (e.g. international agreements on mutual protection of investments, on avoidance of double taxation, etc. The package of legally binding documents supplementing the European Energy Charter also belongs here – see Table 12.4).

In our view, the development of an efficient and balanced package of legally binding documents as a supplement to the European Energy Charter and their ratification by the Parliaments of the negotiating parties will undoubtedly help to stabilise the business environment in the Russian energy industry and make it less risky.

12.9 INVESTMENT RISKS: CURRENT SITUATION

According to both Western and domestic experts, the current situation in Russia is still characterised by a high risk for potential investors. Western estimates of risk for foreign investment in the USSR/Russia/CIS countries have already been analysed elsewhere.[2,3] These estimates dictate that minimum rates of return which would satisfy US investors should be 25–40 per cent higher in Russia than in Western Europe and from 2/3 to 3/4 times higher than

2. A. Konoplyanik, 'Foreign Investments: Risk Ranges', *Finvest (Financial Newsletter)*, **9** (1991), 12.

3. A. Konoplyanik, 'The Less Risk, the Better', *Energy: Economics, Technology and Ecology*, **3** (1992), 23–6.

Table 12.5 Business climate in Russia: estimated risks (rated from 'best' (1) to 'worst' (10)

Risks in 1992 and 1992	July 20	Oct. 20	Jan. 20
Social and political	6.485	6.57	6.74
Domestic economic	6.70	6.85	6.65
Foreign economic	4.125	5.20	5.45
Weighted average	5.812	6.21	6.28

Source: 'UNIVERS' Independent Information Agency (*Izvestiya,* 16 Jan. 1993, pp. 1, 4; and 30 Jan. 1993, pp. 1, 4).

in the US, thus reflecting the perception by some US companies of the relative risk of investing in the region (see Table 12.4).

A similar picture with respect to risks typical for the business climate in Russia is presented by 'UNIVERS', an independent Russia information agency. According to their data, quantitative estimates of risk lie in the range between its mean and worst possible values for each of the three assessed risk categories – socio-political, internal economic, and foreign economic. Developments that occurred in the second half of last year and in the beginning of the current year caused an insignificant increase (4 per cent) in socio-political risks and a noticeable (1/3) increase in foreign economic risks. As a result, the weighted average estimate of risk involved in the Russian business climate has gone up 8 per cent over 6 months (see Table 12.5).

Nonetheless, despite repeated statements to the effect that oil business in Russia is highly risky, many foreign companies spare no effort to secure, in one form or another, a place in the Russian oil industry. In a manner of speaking they are trying to establish a sort of stepping stone for the future large-scale expansion of their businesses in the country in case its legal and economic environment evolves in an investor-friendly direction. Hence, about four dozen joint ventures that are operating or being established in the Russian oil industry seem to be forward-based emissaries of Western investors on the Russian oil market. The objective of this task force is to participate in formulating the rules of the game, 'show flag (presence)' in the Russian oil industry and also to 'track from the inside' changes which are taking place in the Russian balance of economic forces.

Direct investments made by foreign companies into the development of Russian oil fields are insignificant and only slightly exceed US$ 150 million, according to estimates made by the Main Administration on Coordination of Foreign Economic Activities of Fuel and Energy Complex under the Ministry of Fuel and Energy. These investments, however, are very noticeable, particularly in Western Siberia. The data presented in Table 12.6 confirm this fact by showing that one quarter of Russian oil fields and 40 per cent of Tyumen oil fields will reach production and maturity between 1992 and the

Table 12.6 Planned foreign content in the development of Russian oil fields, 1992–2000

	Planned total number of fields to be put into production 1992–2000	Proved recoverable oil reserves (A/B/C1), (million tonnes)
Russia's total	551	5.132
Of which the Tyumen region (% of Russia's total)	183 (33%)	4,061 (79%)
Fields put into production with foreign participation (planned)		
Russia's total (% of total)	143 (26%)	1,205 (23%)
Of which the Tyumen region (% of total) % of Russia's total	70 (38%) (48%)	739 (18%) (61%)

Source: 'State Program of Russia to Stabilise Operations in the Oil and Gas Industry in 1992–1995 and Through 2000: (Part 1)', Ministry of Fuel and Energy of the Russian Federation, Moscow, May 1992, Annex #10.

year 2000. Many of these will be brought into production with the participation of foreign companies. Western companies are also taking part in activities associated with the development of proved recoverable oil reserves (Categories A + B + C1), which amount to one-fourth of Russian fields and about one-fifth of the Tyumen fields to be developed by the end of the century. More than half of the Russian fields to be brought into production (with the assistance of foreign companies) between 1992 and the year 2000, and 3/5 of Russian oil reserves, are located in the Tyumen Region.

So this is not a matter of involving more foreign companies in the oil industry in Russia (their number is already high enough, as shown in Table 12.6), but rather of a better environment for the existing interaction between Russian oil producers and foreign companies, and of more benefits for Russia from foreign capital investment in the petroleum sector.

Chapter 13

Foreign Investment in Russia:
Obstacles and Opportunities[1]

Mark Moody-Stuart

The potential of Russia is not in doubt in Western energy circles. This chapter is intended as an overview of recent developments with regard to foreign investment in Russia, the focus being on some specific points of the Russian oil industry which are of particular interest to the international energy industry. Among these we would point to the:

- abundance of untapped oil and gas fields;
- capable – and confident – oil industry;
- well-educated population.

For projects in Russia, difficult climatic and geographical conditions, and huge distances from the major markets, are the norm. It is a tribute to the Russian oil industry that it became the world's largest producer of oil and gas. In partnership with Western technology and experience, it can consolidate its leading position. We are not aware of any oil or gas project that would be beyond the combined reach of Russian and international industry expertise. Nor do we doubt that the finance and technology is available – for the right projects. The question is, structuring the project so that it is 'right': in other words, so that each partner can benefit in line with its contribution to the project's success.

Defining the role of each partner is essential. The local industry can provide not just the oil and gas reserves, manpower and infrastructure; we are also sure that there is abundant additional scope for the further development of Russian and CIS-based manufacturing industry in, for example, drilling equipment, and pumping and compression equipment. A case in point is the gas turbines from Nikolayev that are powering compressors on the gas trunklines from Siberia.

We see the most significant contribution of the international energy industry as supplying the management skills and technological expertise that are essential if a mega-project is to work in Western economic terms. This means ensuring that all the individual elements are linked in the optimal fashion, so that the final product is better – a lot better – than the sum of the parts. The

---

1. From an Address initially presented to the Second Annual Russian Oil Conference held at the Hilton Hotel, London, 12 February 1993.

international partners would also bear the geological, technical and business risks that are inherent in any major new oil and gas development project.

The third element is finance. The international industry participants in a major energy project would be likely to supply perhaps a quarter to a third of the project finance in the form of equity. Western commercial banks would be doubtful participants without clear support of the EBRD or the World Bank. Such finance would be unlikely to be forthcoming to international oil companies lacking a proven track record of comparable project developments.

The progress that has already been made in the Russian oil and gas sector must be readily acknowledged. One is also pleased to hear of the future intentions. For the potential Western investor, however, some important issues still remain insufficiently resolved:

1. settlement of internal division of responsibilities;
2. a stable legal and fiscal framework for foreign investment;
3. decisions on what Russia wants from foreign oil companies;
4. only difficult and costly fields are on offer;
5. reserve estimates are not based on economic criteria;
6. implementation of environmental and operational standards.

Let us examine some of these points in more detail.

The first three are related. They add up to a clear organisational, legal and economic framework within which oil companies can assess and plan specific projects. To Western eyes, the Russian oil industry appears complex. It is clear that a number of individuals have power and influence: for example, the head of a major, production association controls oil production and much of the infrastructure of an area having the size and population of the UK – and he is one among several! It is not always so clear who has the ultimate authority to speak for various sectors, and to negotiate and sign agreements.

The process of evolution from a centrally directed economic system is not easy. Clearly, there has been progress towards a legal and fiscal framework for Western investment. We should remember that it can take five years to pass a piece of EC legislation, so we can hardly expect an entire new Russian structure to appear overnight. Nevertheless, the lack of a clear framework is still the greatest single obstacle to Western oil company investment.

The next problem is that as yet there is no clear understanding of the sorts of contractual arrangements that might be offered to Western oil companies. Many oil majors are used to working in a wide range of contractual contexts, depending on which country they are negotiating with. Given a framework – whatever its nature – that is stable, one can start to assess individual projects. Until it exists, and has been tested in practice, attempts to evaluate individual projects must be based on so many assumptions that the results may be of little real value.

If one took account of all the taxes, royalties and levies that are proposed at the levels suggested (see Table 13.1) any project would be hopelessly uneconomic and investors would all be wasting their time in Russia. The fact that so many are there means that they must hope that reason will prevail. Many are relying on individual projects finding some special exemption from

Table 13.1 Taxes, royalties and levies on oil exportation

Royalty	16%
Excise tax	18%
Replacement of reserves tax	10%
Income tax	32%
Mandatory exchange finance charge	2%
Dividend withholding taxes	up to 15%
plus $5 per barrel export duty	

some or all of these levies, based on some accident of history or timing of venture formation. It is our belief that this can never be enough for significant investment to take place – there must be a clear general policy, applicable to all ventures, with manifest legislative support to ensure stability.

We still seem to be some distance away from such conditions. This is illustrated by a recent and well-attended meeting in Western Siberia, held to launch a bidding round. Participants were struck by the large number of impositions and restrictions, many of which were not yet clearly defined. There seemed to be an assumption that industry would find the fields on offer so attractive that they would tolerate almost any terms. Bad news. It is in no-one's interest to have bidding rounds before terms and biddable items are clearly defined. Worse, however, is the underlying uncertainty regarding the stability of any term or condition, even if it is clearly defined, in the absence of a workable oil and gas law. Perhaps because of this uncertainty, there is a noticeable preoccupation with short-term revenues, aggravated by an ever-shifting balance of influence between the various levels of public administration.

From a technical viewpoint, it would appear to us that only difficult and costly opportunities are on offer. This is not unreasonable; why otherwise should the Russian industry look for partners? But if a project does involve additional technical resources and risk, the development terms need to take account of this, with the potential rewards – in discounted future money – correspondingly greater than the initial investment. This is not always the case.

One reason behind the differences of views on particular projects lies in a differing perception of certain terms. One such is 'reserves'. The Russian view is that there is a known amount of oil in place; a set recovery factor is applied; and the resulting volume of oil should therefore be produced. Western industry regards reserves as a moving target, dependent on economics, reservoir behaviour and improvements in technology. A Western oilman would regard the Russian view as over-optimistic, leading to uneconomic projects, particularly when data quality is poor. The Russian oilman would certainly regard the Western approach as 'taking the cream', leaving behind oil that is physically recoverable. Hence the need to understand each other's viewpoints, in order to avoid suspicion.

Another misunderstood term is 'feasibility study' – to us, just that. This would be followed first by basic and then more detailed development plans, as new information leads to a more complete (or less incomplete) picture of the extent and structure of the reservoir and its behaviour. Then come economic assessments and discussions and agreements with bankers before the project gets the final, formal commitment. The project will almost certainly start modestly and grow with experience and confidence. To our Russian colleagues, used to a planned economy where projects go straight from feasibility study to investment decision, this process seems as drawn-out and unnecessary as some of their procedures appear to us.

Our next point is the importance to Western companies of being able to maintain their established standards in such areas as operations, safety and environmental protection wherever they operate in the world. They would be unwilling to become involved in projects where there is a dubious environmental legacy from previous, possibly unrecorded, activities. That could be tantamount to signing an environmental blank cheque.

We would expect a 'level playing field' in terms of equal performance requirements for all operators, whatever their origins. In the interests of both efficient use of resources and benefit to the environment, legislative efforts should be concentrated on bringing the worst performers up to an acceptable standard, rather than on demanding that the best increase their standards still further. Better still, the aim should be policies and targets, rather than rigid prescriptions, so that resources can be focused on areas where the greatest environmental benefits can be achieved.

None of these issues we have touched on is insuperable; but each is significant. Many projects have been floated in the CIS, but it is probably fair to say that two in particular – Tengiz (Chevron), along the northern coast of the Caspian Sea in Kazakhstan, and offshore Sakhalin Island (now 4Ms/Shell) – are regarded by Western companies as a bellwether for Western investment. Both projects are being developed by strong teams combining wide international and local experience, project management skills, technological expertise and financial strength. If these players cannot make their projects fly, the confidence of other companies may be damaged.

One other area has also given rise to some misunderstandings. In our view, there is a clear distinction between project investment and contribution to community. Companies pay signature bonuses, taxes and royalties, from which governments allocate expenditure as they see fit, including to such community infrastructure as roads, housing, hospitals, schools and so on. Certainly, there may have to be some development along these lines as part of an energy project, but we would wish not to assume what is the rightful responsibility of governments in providing for the needs of their own communities. We fully accept that once a venture is established and is making profits, a good corporate citizen will contribute to the development of the community in which it operates. This is, however, very different from making community investments at the outset, which add to the costs of the project at a stage when its economic viability may still be far from secure.

Such contributions to the welfare of the communities in which we work are encouraged by Shell companies' *Statement of General Business Principles,* which guides our conduct worldwide. In this respect, as also in the areas of environmental responsibility, fair treatment of employees and avoidance of corrupt practices, we would abide by these principles in Russia as we do everywhere else.

This commitment extends to helping the authorities maintain a culture in which these principles may be upheld, and drawing their attention to practices that may inadvertently undermine their efforts.

One such practice relates to oil pricing. There has been, and as far as one can see the intention is to retain, a significant difference between the domestic and export prices of oil. This difference, together with the non-convertibility of the Rouble, is of course the major obstacle preventing Western upstream interest from extending to projects aimed at satisfying domestic demand. In addition, such price differences can also lead to corruption, because the gains for someone who can illegally switch volumes from one stream into the other are enormous. Such temptations, dangerous anywhere, are even greater in an economy in flux, where the traditional steady, respectable and respected livelihood of many people is under threat. The gains from one area are then diverted to distort and corrupt other areas of the system in turn. Many Russians have said that they believe that this is a major threat to rational economic development and normal commercial competition.

Another potential problem relates to the allocation of field developments. We fully support the authorities' efforts to ensure that the tender process is clearly understood and open – the 'level playing' field mentioned earlier in a different context. Short cuts and hidden agendas are no basis for a long-term relationship; they also threaten the resilience needed for the major projects that Western companies are pursuing. Any deviations from set procedures – even with the best of intentions – can open the process to abuse by those with contacts and connections, or who are prepared to exploit current short-term preoccupations and the concerns of local communities by making promises that will subsequently be forgotten.

The more reputable Western companies will not play these games, and will then be excluded, or will exclude themselves, from participation. Our wish is that the authorities and the people of the former Soviet Union will be successful in controlling these practices.

Can all the points that which have been raised in this chapter be resolved? Of course. Discussions and the exchange of views at gatherings, conferences and other fori continue to break down suspicions and replace them first with mutual understanding, and perhaps then with a shared perspective. Russian industry leaders with joint ventures in mind should also be encouraged to go and see for themselves how comparable projects elsewhere in the world have been structured and carried through, and how their endeavours have been to the mutual, long-term benefit of participants, communities and host governments alike.

Chapter 14

Oil Industry Perspective on Investment:
in the CIS/Russia[1]

Alfred J. Boulos

14.1 INTRODUCTION

The most intriguing aspect of the topic on 'Oil Industry Perspective on Investment in the CIS/Russia', following the fall of the USSR and its impact on energy ventures in the CIS is the fact that the swift fall of the USSR was not predicted by many experts before its actual dissolution in December 1991.

In the international oil industry, as recently as late summer 1991, the expectation was that the Soviet Oil Ministry would continue to dominate petroleum developments in all the Republics of the USSR, particularly following the unsuccessful coup of August 1991.

Yet several months later, all such expectations were abruptly ended with the demise of the USSR in December 1991. The oil industry had to go back to the drawing board to consider how oil deals could be entered into between oil companies and the Republics – separately – of the new Commonwealth of Independent States ('CIS'), composed of most of the Republics of the ex-USSR. In many respects, ex-Soviet Energy Ministry structure was transferred almost intact into the ministry structure of the Russian Republic. This was inevitable since 90 per cent of the energy reserves of the ex-USSR are located in the Russian Republic.

We thus start with this background of uncertainty and swift change in the former Soviet Union. It makes our task intriguing in trying to analyse the various themes and trends and their consequences following the demise of the ex-USSR in respect of energy joint ventures in the CIS.

To achieve this objective, we need in the first instance to understand the global nature of the international energy industry and to emphasise the fact that the energy industry has throughout this century faced and resolved many difficult problems. I do not view the problems and opportunities in the CIS as separate and in isolation from problems and opportunities confronting the international energy industry in its earliest days. In this emphasis on the historical perspective and the global nature of the industry, we can take

---

1. The views expressed in this chapter are those of the author and do not necessarily reflect the views of his company affiliation.

renewed hope in the ability of the industry to resolve problems and seize opportunities as it considers joint ventures in the CIS.

Thus, I would like to discuss the demise of the ex-USSR and the potential for energy ventures in the new CIS in terms of my global perspective and experiences in the oil industry for the past 30 years, as both a participant and commentator on the many changes we have experienced in the industry.

This emphasis on the global perspective and my experiences in dealing with the developments and changes of the oil industry will provide me with the opportunity to discuss several negotiations which I have conducted with host governments worldwide since the early 1960s. This would place the right perspective on problems and opportunities in the CIS.

The changes that have taken place recently in the former Soviet Union have been so profound that it is difficult to consider any other nation this century that has been so severely affected. In October 1991, for example, I presented a paper at a major international oil conference on energy ventures in the USSR by foreign energy companies. In preparing this present chapter, I have found that many facts and assumptions of last year have changed so much that they are no longer valid. Moreover, in this chapter I will use the term 'CIS', or Russia and the Republics, to indicate references to the former Soviet Union. Accordingly, many references to the ex-USSR now refer to the CIS or to Russia, which has over 90 per cent of all hydrocarbon resources, and from time to time as the text shall indicate, to the other Republics in the CIS, particularly those Republics with important energy resources.

14.2 OVERVIEW OF THE PRESENT SITUATION

14.2.1 The threshold question: should the energy industry invest in the CIS?

The threshold question for the energy industry in Russia and the other Republics of the CIS is whether there are now unique opportunities for energy joint ventures in the CIS or are the risks for such ventures too great to assume at this time?

When companies began a few years ago to discuss business arrangements with the ex-USSR, the government and industry were closely linked. Companies dealt with central ministries, the Republics and the local oil and gas organisations.

With the breakup of the former Soviet Union and the emergence of the CIS, a new mood of uncertainty has emerged in energy companies regarding energy joint ventures in Russia and other Republics. The main question now is whether energy investment in the Republics is prudent at this time in view of the present uncertainty.

To answer this question, we have to consider the other side of the equation. What can the CIS do to help promote energy investment from foreign firms? Initially, the same basic need that was faced by the old Soviet Union remains the same for the Republics: how to provide the optimum business climate possible to meet the investment needs of energy investors? This is the crux of the threshold question.

Let us start with an overview of the CIS at this time. The CIS has 90 separate administrative regions within its 11 member Republics. Forty of these are in the Russian Republic. The CIS has a population of 300 million, speaking 120 different languages. Many border disputes are unsettled. There is a continuing struggle to adapt to a form of market economy, a need to curtail high prices and remove shortages, a fear that another coup may be possible and a concern on the increased emphasis on ethnic and religious differences and a general unrest in the Republics, all of which indicate that the optimum business climate required for energy and other foreign investments may still be lacking. Yet, since the opening of the ex-USSR to foreign investment in 1986 and continuing today with the emergence of the CIS, foreign industry has considered opportunities for energy investment in the CIS to be among the most attractive worldwide.

In spite of this desire by the CIS to open the door to investments, there have been severe technical and conceptual problems. Although the CIS would like to encourage foreign investment as a development tool, the leadership has not succeeded as they would have hoped in creating economic and legal incentives that will encourage outsiders. Rather, the intended incentives send conflicting signals that have, so far, generated more anxiety than reassurance. None of the countries in Eastern Europe has produced more laws intended to encourage investment than has the CIS, yet the contemporary CIS environment presents greater uncertainty for foreign investors than any of the other formerly socialist countries.

At the heart of the Russian's and the other Republics of the CIS's effort to restructure its economic system lies a deep paradox. The country needs a fundamental overhaul of its economic, organisational, and managerial institutions. By any measure their capacity to make use of its labour and material resources is still in the transitional stage: labour productivity is low and declining; the level of technology commonly employed in production compares unfavourably with much of the developing world, and much less favourably with the developed countries; environmental despoliation and workplace health hazards are rampant; and the population's low standard of living needs to be improved. It is the severity of these problems that has hindered a consensus on how best to deal with them.

In addition, another area of difficulty is the natural suspicion and envy arising in the Republics from the emerging dominance of Russia. The Republics, having done away with the USSR, are not keen to accept domination from their largest equal Republic. There is a major task ahead for greater political and economic cooperation between Russia and the other Republics. This will be essential in the future for such relationships to develop into more positive and cooperative relationships.

A final aspect to consider is the lack of a history of economic freedom and private business development in energy and other sectors for most of this century. Added to this difficult history is the lack of any similar historical perspectives in business, even in the Czarist days before the 1917 Revolution.

The political freedom which the Republics now enjoy does not necessarily translate itself into the economic freedom and a true market economy which the Republics seek.

14.2.2 Risks and problems for the energy industry

As a result, the efforts of the energy investor and risk-taker in CIS energy investments who should be rewarded by an appropriate rate of return and a value enhancement of his investments are not a part of the culture of the Republics. They cannot easily accept in their dealings with energy companies that a reward is due the risk-taker. There is also an uncertainty as to whether the energy companies may be getting the better part of the bargain. So there is a long road to travel for economic freedom and a true market economy for foreign companies in their dealings in energy ventures in the CIS.

Another aspect to add to these problems is the tradition of bureaucracy and regulation in the Republics. For a people who have been born and bred in a system wherein the state provided almost all of the economic and social needs of life, the change into a free market system, and the encouragement of new business, has not been without considerable strain.

If we expect progress and an optimum climate for investment, foreign energy companies must do what they can to help in the transition. Here are opportunities for those with business, legal, financial and other experiences to share their knowledge and know-how with the enterprises and individuals of the Republics. Foreign energy and other business groups cannot expect that overnight the people of the Republics can readily adapt to free market economic traditions without the willingness of the foreign firms to provide intensive help and know-how. Basic concepts such as the function of a market system, the role of a business enterprise and the meaning of accounting and financial terms, are some of the areas for dialogue and understanding which must proceed further energy and other business ventures in the CIS.

For example, the Marxist system has never developed a natural profit motive. There has not been incentive for profit nor any concept of ownership interest that would lead to an overall purpose of efficiency. Moreover, there has not been a market system for measuring or assessing the fair market value of commodities or services. Concepts as basic as supply and demand have long been absent. Systems of inventory, marketing and financial decision-making – if they exist – are treated differently than in free market economies. Value of money is also a misunderstood concept – the Marxist system did not provide for a true value of currency or for real market value or input costs. These differences are merely suggestive of the wide gulf in business and economic experiences which still separate the ex-Soviet and free market economies.

From a political and economic viewpoint, therefore, the tasks ahead may be formidable but they are not unsurmountable. The fifteen Republics that have declared independence since the August 1991 coup and the December 1991 dissolution of the Union must move forward to end the continuing uncertainties. It will not be easy. The former Soviet bureaucracy has now split along republican lines. Republican parliaments have introduced legislation to cement their status as independent states. Republican economies are coming under control of local administrators and entrepreneurs. Taxes are being collected and foreign relations pursued with other nations. Republican institutions have emerged and consolidated.

In all of this change, notwithstanding, the energy industry continues to view the CIS as the most promising place for energy ventures available anywhere in the world. Russia remains the prize for the energy industry with its vast mineral resources and a huge population of over 150 million. The need for cooperation between Russia and the other Republics also remains an important consideration for the energy industry. A confrontation between Russia and the other Republics would give rise to worry and serious political risk. There is, at present, a disturbing scenario in respect of Russia and the other Republics – continued instability, continued lack of reform, the emergence of authoritarian controls, the development of inter-ethnic and inter-state conflicts – which, if unresolved, would shut the door for a long time to any meaningful energy joint ventures by the foreign oil industry in the CIS.

To add to the above political and economic uncertainties in Russia and the other Republics of the CIS, both within each Republic and in their relationships with each other, are the uncertainties of concluding energy ventures in today's investment climate. The problems in concluding deals – as, for example, the recently enacted export taxes, the proposed VAT and turnover taxes, the many jurisdictional layers of authorities and the continuing bureaucratic entanglements – give pause to energy companies as to whether the Republics, Russia in particular, are serious about wanting to enter into energy ventures with foreign companies at this time.

Thus, for example, the end of the USSR and the removal of the Soviet layer from the jurisdictional layers of authority have not ended the continuing jurisdictional disputes between the republican administrations, the provincial governments and the local production associations. In any deal, an energy company will need the agreement of all the jurisdictional entities. An energy company must maintain good relationships with all such jurisdictions in the Republics – as it does with host governments worldwide in its energy relationships – in order to ensure that the final energy venture agreement does not fail because of a lack of agreement by any of the jurisdictional entities.

Let us summarise some of the major risks and problems now facing energy investors in Russia and the Republics:

- Draft laws on oil ventures continue in various stages of the legislative process. A new Mineral Resources Law, enacted to come into force on 1 March 1992, continues the uncertainty of the applicability of legislative changes on energy investments.
- There remains no clear division between jurisdictional authorities in national and local governments with respect to oil and gas matters.
- Joint ventures with state production associations need to be reviewed in light of recent government legislation published in late December 1991, on privatisation law, on a privatisation programme and related matters.
- Uncertainty in Russia with respect to tax legislation – the Profits Tax of 1 January 1992 and the Income Tax Law to be effective 1 January 1993, the

Export Tax of 31 December 1991 – with no exceptions for foreign joint ventures – continues to restrict investments by the energy industry.

- Legislation with respect to export quotas and licensing requirements appears to be at variance with foreign joint venture exemptions granted in past decrees.
- The compulsory sale under Decree 335 of 30 December 1991 of 10 per cent of a joint venture's foreign currency export receipts to the Russian government in exchange for roubles, which presented many problems, has now been rescinded but may still be reinstated.

The above overview of the present situation indicates that there are uncertainties and continuing economic and political problems in the CIS. Yet, in spite of such scenario, there are many energy companies who believe that the energy investment potential in the Republics justifies the risks of energy investment. These companies know that there are risks but that there are also substantial rewards. Moreover, an in-depth analysis may suggest that risks may nevertheless be assumed under the circumstances to justify energy investment in regions with the highest hydrocarbon potential anywhere in the world. Let us now consider these contentions which would give rise to this optimistic appraisal and which would justify the investment decision to go forward in energy.

14.3 BACKGROUND OF THE ENERGY INDUSTRY IN THE CIS

14.3.1 Energy production profile in the CIS

The production profile of energy production and export in 1992 in the former Soviet federation shows the depressed state that the industry continues to face. Government spending in the energy sector was down nearly 1 billion roubles in 1990 and between 1 and 2 billion roubles in 1991.

Let us consider some of the statistics of energy production.

Exports of crude oil and refined products from the Republics of the former Soviet Union averaged about 2.1 MM bbl/d in 1991, down about 950,000 bbl/d or 30 per cent from 1990. Crude oil exports fell to 1.15 MM bbl/d from 2.1 MM bbl/d in 1990. Refined products exports were unchanged at 950,000 bbl/d.

The industrialised West now receives 70 per cent of CIS oil exports, up from little more than half in 1989. Russia says it will permit export of 20 per cent of its oil output, up from a previous 10 per cent. CIS oil output averaged 10.41 MM bbl/d in 1991, down 1.22 MM bbl/d or 8.6 per cent from 1990, and 2.41 MM bbl/d or 18.8 per cent from the peak of 12.82 MM bbl/d in 1988. Last year's production included 9.32 MM bbl/d in Russia, 500,000 bbl/d in Kazakhstan, 220,000 bbl/d in Azerbaijan and 70,000 bbl/d in other Republics. Output is projected to fall to 9.5 MM bbl/d in 1992, which would be the first decline below 10 MM bbl/d since 1975. Oil consumption in the Soviet

Republics is expected to fall this year to 7.7 MM bbl/d from 8.3 MM in 1991. Yet, shortly before production topped out in 1988, ex-Soviet oil experts predicted production would rise above 13 MM bbl/d in the 1990s.

To understand this sobering fact of continuing decline, we shall review the background of the oil industry of the Republics in relation to the economic structure of the former USSR since the 1917 Revolution. This is the starting point to understand the production declines which have resulted from state control and Marxist economic concepts and objectives of the ex-USSR.

For the past 70 years, as we have noted above, Republics of the CIS and foreign market economies have had profoundly different economic structures. In the CIS, an economic system based on Marxism and state control of the overall economy has produced a generation of economists, industrial leaders and government officials unfamiliar with the day-to-day experiences of the Western and foreign economic market system. Thus, concepts such as 'net profits', 'depreciation', 'royalties', 'private property', 'rates of return', 'net present value' and other economic market system terminologies have not been a vital part of the daily economic vocabulary of ex-Soviet managers due to the non-market nature of their economic activity. In our dialogue with the Republics, we must start with maximum efforts to create a basic understanding of the meaning of fundamental economic and other terms. It is essential to establish a foundation of common language as the basis for expressing our common interests.

Although the CIS has abundant petroleum reserves and oil production reached its peak of 12.82 MM bbl/d in 1988, production has now decreased and has continued to decrease throughout 1991. There are several reasons for such decrease:

- oil fields are depleting at faster rates of depletion than expected and some of their giant fields are in the final development stages;
- more sophisticated production equipment and technology are needed together with improvements in field management and secondary recovery;
- capital has been diverted to alleviate internal economic problems;
- equipment is outmoded with an unlikely possibility of timely replacement; and,
- technological advances used in the West are not available.

14.3.2 The need for foreign investment

Oil experts in the CIS have publicly stated that their oil industry is in need of a major reconstruction. The specifics of the structural crisis in their oil industry, as they themselves have explained, include the following factors:

- a need to deal with market prices in a non-market economy;
- an underdeveloped infrastructure in all aspects of the petroleum industry – E&P, refining, transportation, pipelines and marketing; and
- the neglect of petroleum investment due to an extensive emphasis on nuclear power.

In addition, the structural crisis in the oil industry continues to be influenced by the current severe downturn in the economies of the Republics. This has resulted in even less state capital investment in the oil industry. Yet, oil and gas is still the key industry. It continues to provide the principal source of funds and foreign exchange to the budget of several Republics, contributing as much as 70 per cent of the net revenues of the Russian budget. Thus, for the CIS, revitalising the petroleum industry is of utmost importance.

Let us consider further aspects of the former Soviet oil industry:

- As production declines, pressure is placed on balancing the need for hard currency, or exports, versus internal demand for petroleum. So far, declines in domestic demand resulting from economic slowdowns have allowed exports to share in a smaller percentage of the overall production decline.
- If domestic demand increases, or production declines outstrip current estimates, the ability to generate hard currency would be significantly restricted. Until the production decline is arrested, exports and hard currency revenues will suffer.
- The Republics of the CIS have now reached a point where it is essential to generate hard currency. Hard currency is the key to acquiring foreign-manufactured products and technology. The capital that traditionally would have gone toward exploration and production has been diverted to help alleviate other serious economic problems. This sets the stage for foreign investment.

There are other issues regarding uncertainty in the energy industry. There have been problems with the proclaimed sovereignty of Republics creating areas of conflict with various regional and administrative bodies. There have also been new and different approaches to the system of taxation, the system of payments for equipment and land and the system of penalties for environmental pollution. The oil industry is also faced with other serious problems.

It is thus clear that the oil industry will now require substantial investment. In view of the economic crisis facing the CIS, they alone cannot provide their oil industry with the large capital investments required to meet the need for modernisation and increased efficiency. What is now needed is a substantial increase in foreign energy ventures in the CIS.

14.3.3 Views of the energy industry in the CIS

The views of energy leaders from Russia and the Republics have been positive and constructive. They have established an attitude of cooperation and an expectation that investment will increase in the future. This was stated by the Deputy Minister of the then Soviet Oil and Gas Ministry, Vagit Alekperov, at a seminar in Houston, Texas, in June, 1991. His comments were reported as follows:

The Soviet Oil and Gas Ministry hopes to increase the number of joint-venture oil agreements signed this year, stressing that obstacles that once kept investors away are being removed. Mr. Alekperov said the Soviet ministry was working to reduce the legal, financial and tax problems that Western companies face. (*The New York Times*, 25 June 1991, p. C4)

The above attitude has not changed since the breakup of the ex-Soviet Union. Many of the same Soviet oil leaders continue in Russia and the Republics in similar responsible posts.

The above quotation is but one of many statements of energy officials who, at conferences and in public statements, declare openly that they are actively seeking to attract foreign investment in the Republics of the CIS. These attitudes make it most unlikely that the CIS oil industry in partnership with foreign energy companies would create unnecessary problems with energy investment in the decade of the 1990s. They are more likely to be constructive partners in energy ventures because they need the investments.

The CIS energy officials have spelled out the priority areas for investment. They are, for example, as follows:

- new methods of exploration, seismic surveys, data correlation and processing;
- new technologies for deeper exploratory drilling, for offshore drilling, for more efficient refining and for more sophisticated environmental protection equipment; and
- new technologies and investment in development of reserves in fields presently difficult to produce.

With respect to other priority areas, the protection of the environment is high in all the Republics. Throughout the country, intensive traffic in oil producing areas has created problems with respect to the sensitive eco-systems. The people and authorities now view the environment as a priority issue in the drilling, production, processing and transportation of oil.

Finally, we see from the above the acute needs of the oil industry in the CIS. The fall in production in 1991, as we have noted from the statistics, only confirms the difficulties of the industry. Such declines can only be prevented in the 1990s by much greater capital investment in production capacities. Problems have mounted in developing new oil regions. Several promising fields, such as the giant Tengiz field in Kazakhstan, have not gone into production for several reasons, including irregular shipment deliveries and delays by construction organisations. In other fields, oil flow is less than expected because of planning errors. A critical situation prevails in providing material and technical resources for enterprises of the oil-producing industry.

14.3.4 Views of the CIS regarding energy joint ventures

We conclude with a story that we believe sets forth some of the positive views which prevail in the CIS in respect of energy joint ventures in the 1990s in the CIS.

It is an excerpt from a talk by a senior deputy minister of the ex-USSR Ministry of Oil and Gas at a Houston, Texas, conference in June 1991, which we have previously referenced. In his talk, the deputy minister stated that the foreign energy industry should have confidence in its energy investments. He said that whatever may be the political structure of the nation in the future – nevertheless he believed that energy investments by foreign energy companies would be secure. He explained why by reference to an old Russian proverb as follows:

Do not cut off the branch of the tree on which you are sitting.

My opinion is that this proverb sums up the importance that the CIS will give to energy investments. They need the energy industry and the energy industry needs them. Both parties will no doubt, I believe, go the extra mile to do whatever needs to be done to ensure success in energy investments in the CIS.

This attitude – which I believe is prevalent in Russia and the Republics and in companies seeking energy investment in the CIS – leads me to my opinion that energy joint ventures, though not without problems, shall ultimately be successful in the 1990s. Moreover, I believe that the 1990s will be an important channel of increased oil activity, development and expansion in the CIS because of foreign energy participation. I believe further that the CIS energy industry and its foreign partners will be important producers worldwide of oil and gas in the new oil regime of the 1990s.

In May 1991, two ex-Soviet reformers, Messrs. Primakov and Yavlinsky, in a well-publicised letter requesting foreign aid, stated the following:

Joint cooperation between the leading industrial powers and the Soviet Union aimed at economic stabilisation and the creation of a market economy inside the Soviet Union will create a reliable base for the promotion of positive changes which are underway in today's world. (*The New York Times*, 30 May 1991, p. A12)

The above letter sets the tone that it is both desirable and necessary – from the CIS point of view – for energy ventures to succeed in the CIS.

A recent example in support of the positive and constructive intentions of the CIS to cooperate in energy joint ventures may be evidenced by the production sharing contract signed in Russia in February 1992, by Elf Aquitaine. The agreement is tangible evidence that attractive energy investment deals are available in Russia. Both Elf and Russia indicate that they are pleased with their energy deal. This deal was the first pure exploration and production risk agreement concluded in Russia since the industry was nationalised in 1920. Under previous arrangements, about a dozen or more joint ventures have been concluded, but mostly as service contracts to develop producing fields. *Petroleum Intelligence Weekly* described the Elf deal as follows:

Terms of the Elf deal haven't been announced but Elf President Le Floch told PIW in a wide-ranging interview last year that the firm would not enter the upstream of Russia ... without equity and a good financial return. (*Petroleum Intelligence Weekly*, 10 February 1992, p.3)

This positive attitude to make deals continues to emerge frequently in statements from energy officials in the CIS. In Russia, for example, oil and gas affairs are controlled by the Russian Ministry for Fuel and Energy, and its Russian National Oil and Gas Corporation, called 'Rosneftegaz'. The

President of 'Rosneftegaz', Mr Lev Churilov, the former USSR Minister of Oil and Gas, has emphasised such positive attitudes. He has promised in recent statements that his organisation will be efficient, able to make decisions as rapidly as possible and be fully responsive to the foreign energy industry. These statements further indicate a continuing of a positive business climate for energy joint ventures in the CIS.

Finally, in considering positive influences, we should consider recent commentary regarding the emergence of a rule of law in the CIS. The rule of law emphasis in the CIS would give added support to the expectation of foreign investors that there will be stability of contract in all energy ventures. This is essential for energy companies.

The CIS is aware that energy companies expect guarantees that their investments will be protected and agreements honoured. I believe that the CIS will guarantee investments and honour contracts because the concept of adhering to contracts is in keeping with traditions of jurisprudence and the rule of law in the Republics of the CIS. Certainly, international economic consequences from failure to abide by contracts may always be a deterrent to non-performance. I am persuaded, however, that adherence to a stability of doctrine is based on a fundamental national tradition in the CIS based on a rule of law in that a contract has to be honoured. They have said so themselves – contracts are to be honoured even if no direct reference is made to a rule of law. I believe, further, that this tradition of adherence to a stability of contracts doctrine will continue to prevail in the CIS.

Let us review recent commentary regarding the emergence of a rule of law jurisprudence in the CIS. In a talk presented at the Association of the Bar of the City of New York entitled 'Transforming the Soviet Union into a Rule of Law Democracy: A Report from the Front Lines' by Alexander M. Yakovlev, a distinguished ex-Soviet legal expert, a member of Parliament – the Congress of Peoples Deputies of the USSR – and a member of the Committee on Legislation of the Supreme Soviet, described the building of a rule of law as follows:

I believe the task of building a State based on the rule of law is quite realistic.... Currently, building the State based on the rule of law is going on in three areas: reform of the political system, major changes in economic relations and radical revision of the judicial system.

If there is anything standing above every official in the land, the President of the USSR included, it must be the rule of law – the idea of law is constant and supreme. (*The Record of the Association of the Bar of the City of New York*, Vol. 46, March 1991, pp. 130, 131, 133)

Moreover, I have been impressed by a recent statement of another legal expert on the rule of law tradition in the CIS. The most distinguished Western legal commentator on law in the ex-USSR, Professor John N. Hazard, of Columbia University, who was the first US lawyer to be officially received in the USSR in the 1930s, recently wrote with respect to the attempted coup in August 1991, as follows:

Whatever the explanation, the desire for freedom had been nurtured, and Gorbachev senses his people's readiness to support a rule of law society; as the new CIS pursues its policies, one senses that a fresh breath is being taken, especially among those who make and administer the law. ('Soviet Law Takes a Fresh Breath', *The Harriman Institute Forum*, Vol. 5, No. 6, February 1992, p. 13)

Whether or not the rule of law emerges clearly in the future in the jurisprudence of the CIS, certainly the above commentary of Professors Hazard and Yakovlev shows an awareness of the importance of seeking a rule of law for the country. While there may be differing attitudes regarding the rule of law in the CIS, it is an important point to emphasise for a foreign energy company. Such emphasis on building the rule of law as part of the tradition of honouring contracts are positive aspects which would help to provide stability to energy joint ventures in the CIS.

The above discussion shows some of the positive views of the CIS in respect of issues between the CIS and energy companies in energy ventures. The issues do not admit to easy solutions. Yet, it is to be hoped that the above positive views and developments will help considerably in negotiations between the parties. I believe that such negotiations, if conducted with effort, patience, determination and goodwill by both parties should lead to workable and equitable joint venture agreements between energy companies and the CIS. This certainly will be the path to increased energy joint ventures for the mutual benefit of both parties and the beginnings of a new regime for international oil in this decade of the 1990s.

14.4 ATTITUDES OF THE FOREIGN ENERGY INDUSTRY

14.4.1 Opportunities for energy joint ventures in the CIS

Although at the beginning of 1992, following the tumultuous events of August and December 1991 in the ex-USSR, the energy industry was undoubtedly more cautious in its energy investment in Russia and the other Republics, there remain important reasons why the industry would like to invest in energy joint ventures in the CIS. Let us consider the incentives for the energy industry. For the industry, the opening up of the CIS to joint ventures and investments presents special opportunities to gain access to substantial crude oil and gas reserves, unexpected as recently as three years ago. I personally remember in 1989 a seminar discussion I had with senior oil experts. Most of the experts believed that the possibility of foreign oil investments in the former USSR was too remote to consider seriously. There were doubts as to whether the Soviets were serious in their intentions or whether oil companies would be prepared to undertake the investments and risks which would be required. My opinion is that such uncertainties from both sides are doubts of the past. There is now a pragmatic attitude that foreign energy investments in Russia and the Republics are both necessary and possible.

The attitudes of the energy industry are that the opportunities to acquire rights to substantial oil reserves have rarely been greater than now. Among non-OPEC countries, CIS has the largest remaining oil reserves – twice the remaining reserves of the US – and CIS estimates may even be too low. The potential for finding new oil and gas is greater in the CIS than in most other areas of the world. The industry has always known of the vast hydrocarbon reserves in the ex-Soviet Union. There are significant oil and gas fields classified as giants, having 100 MM/bbl or 600 bcf of proved reserves. It is only in the last several years that the possibility of becoming a partner in exploring and producing such immense reserves has transformed into a reality.

Further attitudes can be seen in respect of specific opportunities that now appear available to oil companies. They may:

- acquire stock capital of Russian and Republic companies that have rights to exploit some of the world's richest oil fields;
- acquire rights to develop new oil and gas fields;
- acquire rights to help increase production in fields that currently have low oil output;
- set up joint ventures to develop the complex technology required to process hydrocarbon resources and to utilise useful by-products; and
- finally, participate in the modernisation and development of all phases of the petroleum industry.

14.4.2 Expectations of the energy industry in petroleum agreements

In the negotiation process, there are contractual and fiscal issues, which are important to the foreign energy industry in concluding a petroleum agreement with host governments worldwide. These same issues are equally important in joint ventures in the CIS. These may be summed up as follows:

- reasonable petroleum legislation and fiscal framework governing oil and gas exploration and production so that the objectives of both the CIS and the energy companies are met fairly and equitably;
- access to production and reserves for a company's worldwide operations;
- sufficient and prompt cost recovery arrangements;
- reasonable rate of return commensurate with the level of the investment commitment and technical, economic and political risks;
- right to freely export petroleum in international market transactions;
- repatriation of earnings without restrictions;
- rouble convertibility at realistic market rates;
- degree of control over operations within the framework of the work commitments in the petroleum agreement and in the conservation, safety and environmental regulations both of the Republics and the world community;
- impartiality and self-executing procedures in dispute resolution provisions;
- the financial commitments required and the sharing with the Republics, whenever feasible, of capital and risk burdens; and
- of special importance, the 'stability' of the agreement, and the Russian and other Republics' policies and attitudes with respect to foreign investors.

From an energy industry viewpoint, the above points are the foundation for a successful petroleum agreement in the CIS, as they are worldwide, and the basis on which investments may be made in exploration, production and other oil-related agreements. Agreements on the above points would lead to successful energy joint ventures in the CIS by the energy companies. Such success would result in greater productivity for the CIS energy industry which would thus become a major player in the global oil industry in the new oil regime of the 1990s and into the next century.

14.5 TYPES OF AGREEMENTS IN ENERGY JOINT VENTURES BETWEEN THE CIS AND ENERGY COMPANIES

We now deal with a difficult problem in energy joint ventures between the CIS and energy companies. The problem is to decide on the type of energy joint venture agreement to be used by the parties. The basic problem is one of communication. Each party must understand the frame of reference and the background of the other party in discussing the venture agreement. They have each had different experiences – one, from a state-directed economy, based generally on meeting quotas and providing for supply and demand patterns of production and consumption without reference to profitability; the other, a competitor in a market economy concerned with maximising revenues and minimising costs to achieve an acceptable rate of return and the creation of wealth and value to the company.

Let me explain further the importance of mutual understanding, particularly in respect of the meaning of a 'joint venture.'

At a recent seminar of ex-Soviet and energy industry representatives, several discussions took place relating to meanings of oil and gas terms such as a 'joint venture'. There was confusion as to the meaning of a 'joint venture'. To oil industry representatives, joint venture meant a 'joint adventure' – that is, a form of partnership or cooperative agreement between two or more companies with the purpose of achieving a specific undertaking, i.e. the exploration and production of oil or gas. There are rights to joint control, sharing of profits and losses, mutual contributions, mutual rights and obligations and provisions for such matters as dissolution and default. The parties also agree on a joint accounting procedure. The joint venture is not a separate type of agreement; usually the 'joint venture' is not incorporated, nor does it create a new entity. Each joint venture company retains its own identity and assumes its rights and obligations under the joint venture agreement. The reason for so many joint ventures in the energy industry is that the very high costs of capital and expenditures make it almost impossible for companies to undertake energy ventures on their own. To some ex-Soviet representatives, however, 'joint venture' meant a joint enterprise or joint stock company in which equity would be owned in specific percentages by two or more companies. It would be a separate entity. I cite the above discussions as an example of the importance of understanding what the other party means in the use of specific terms. In this case, each party would understand the term 'joint venture' entirely differently from the other party.

14.5.1 Procedures to initiate joint ventures in the CIS

Prior to reviewing the types of agreements in energy joint ventures between energy companies and the CIS, it would be important to understand the procedures under which a joint venture would be initiated in the CIS. The procedures are basically the same in all the Republics of the CIS.

1. The initial step is for a Republic energy enterprise – usually the local exploration and production company – and a foreign company to enter into a Protocol of Intent. This will generally provide for a preliminary feasibility study of a cooperation project and the expected results of the cooperation project. This Protocol of Intent is negotiated with the advice and participation of the governmental or industry entity which will have jurisdiction in respect of the cooperative project. In view of the many changes now taking place in the CIS, it would be important to include all entities which may have jurisdiction at the time of negotiations.
2. Thereupon, a Feasibility Study, elaborate and detailed, which in all Republics of the CIS is regarded as a most important document in the approval process, will be undertaken to review and discuss the scope of the project. At the same time, basic documents relating to the draft agreement and draft charter of the energy joint venture will also be reviewed. In addition, concurrent discussions would also be held with Republic and local environmental and other authorities. Approvals must thereupon be obtained from the appropriate environmental authorities in the Republic and local jurisdiction, before the project is submitted to the mining supervisory bodies and others granting approvals. Finally, when all agreements are completed, the appropriate authority issues a decree authorising the energy joint venture; the documents and agreements will be submitted for registration with the appropriate jurisdictions.
3. Approvals also shall have to be considered in respect of the energy joint venture. No clear procedures can be spelled out at this time regarding appropriate jurisdictional authorities. Suffice it to say herein that approvals for any oil and gas joint venture should be obtained for production associations, provincial governments, Republic governments and any other authority so as to ensure compliance as best as possible with all jurisdictional entities.
4. With respect to terms of development of an energy joint venture, these will be stipulated in the special decree and in the licence to explore and to exploit issued by the respective supervisory jurisdictional authorities.

   A wide range of ministerial, provincial and governmental instructions also apply to oil and gas development. The Republic partner can render further exploration and exploitation services to the joint venture. As a rule, blocks of reserves open for bidding have already been explored well enough to be divided into separate sites for development. The Republic partner's abundant primary geological and geophysical data may be converted into Western format and be transferred to the foreign partner or to the joint venture on a commercial or other basis. The governmental mining supervisory body issues the non-transferrable right to exploit under certain terms and conditions within the parameters of the government decree. This licence is issued either for a fixed or undetermined period. Joint ventures can acquire it, provided that they are registered under the law.

5. All the above comments are only suggestive of procedures that a foreign partner may need to consider in respect of a Soviet oil joint venture. These are not hard and fast rules. They may be subject to even further change. These are intended to provide an overview of the kind of procedures which should be considered in respect of an energy joint venture. Moreover, it should be noted that the success of conducting feasibility studies and negotiating energy agreements requires patience and time – sometimes as long as two years – to conclude.

6. There is no legislation in Russia or the other Republics relating specifically to foreign investment in oil and gas projects. Essential legislation – such as a petroleum and mining law and a foreign investment law – has not as yet been adopted although there are university study groups and other consultants who are reviewing and proposing legislation for enactment in the Republics of the CIS.

7. The lack of relevant legislation has not deterred energy companies from entering into negotiations with the Republics with respect to energy joint ventures. This trend may have a positive effect. Those negotiations leading to contracts will have an effect on future petroleum and investment law and can only lead to a more realistic basis on which such laws will be ultimately enacted.

14.5.2 Review of specific energy joint venture agreements

Let us now consider the type of energy joint agreement to be entered into between the parties. So far, the Republics have not designated any specific type of petroleum agreement as the appropriate structure for a joint venture. In fact, the ex-Soviets have entered into discussions with energy companies on the basis of joint stock associations, production sharing contracts, risk service contracts, and may even be willing to consider a traditional tax-royalty contract as a basis of a joint venture.

It appears that the Russian and other Republics in the CIS are flexible at this time to varying forms of petroleum agreements. They have been presented with our tax-royalty agreements, production sharing contracts (PSC) and service contracts. They appear to be seriously interested in PSC and in the long run the PSC may emerge as the most likely form of agreement.

Let us now consider each type of agreement as well as the Russian Joint Venture Association model.

Tax/royalty agreement

This system applies a royalty to gross revenue, and a tax to the revenue remaining after deduction of royalty and costs. The tax/royalty system is one of the oldest yet still widely used agreements. It is estimated that the tax/royalty agreement is in effect in countries with about 50 per cent of total worldwide production. Companies generally favour the equity attributes of this type of agreement. Governments also favour certain features – such as a high royalty which assures revenues from the first year of production and guaranteed stream of revenue that is not dependent upon the contractor's profitability.

Taxes and royalties are 'up front' fiscal issues that generally commence the negotiations. A reasonable rate of tax and royalty acceptable to both parties needs to be negotiated. As to the comparative importance of each to the companies, it is generally accepted that companies prefer taxes rather than royalty for government take. An obligation to pay a rate of tax on realised profits is less burdensome to an oil company than an obligation to pay a royalty before any profits are earned. A tax/royalty agreement with both a high royalty and high tax may offer no flexibility and can discourage development of the marginal field. By marginal field, at today's prices, I am referring to fields in areas lacking the infrastructure necessary to be developed at low cost.

I need to indicate here, however, a risk for companies in tax/royalty agreements where the tax rate is set by legislation and is not specifically set out in the contract. Under these arrangements, a host government may change the tax terms by legislation – thereby altering fundamental contractual terms for the company.

To have a clearer picture, let us now consider an example of tax/royalty contract fiscal terms now in use in a country where many oil companies operate.

As is shown in Table 14.1, the major features of the contract are a fixed 15 per cent royalty and a 55 per cent income tax. Depreciation of tangible investments for tax purposes is taken over 5 years. All other expenditures can be expensed in the current period. The result of these provisions is a relatively low maximum rate of government take from an additional barrel of production. Such terms provide the oil company with an effective incentive to find and develop large prospects even if the risk involved is relatively high.

Production sharing contract

Under the PSC, the company is considered a contractor to the government. The government, acting on its own behalf or in conjunction with its state company, owns the hydrocarbons and all facilities. The contractor takes a percentage of the production to recover costs and a profit split with the host government from production of oil.

Table 14.1 Tax/royalty agreement terms

Royalty:	15% of revenue
Income tax:	55% of taxable income
Depreciation:	
Operating cost	1 Year
Royalty	1 Year
Intangible capital	1 Year
Tangible capital	5 Years

Table 14.2 Cost recovery and profit-sharing terms

Cost recovery terms	
Cost recovery limit	If production is greater than 30,000 barrels per day (bpd), 50% is the cost recovery; otherwise, 40% if production is less than 30,000 bpd
Amortisation: all costs 1 year	
Excess cost recovery	Shared as profit oil
Profit sharing terms	
Royalty	10% of 0–30,000 bpd 20% of over 30,000 bpd
Income tax	56.25% of taxable income
Production bonus	$1 million at initial production $2 million at 20,000 bpd $3 million at 30,000 bpd
Contractor Profit Share (After-Tax):	0–20,000 bpd 27% 20–30,000 bpd 20% 30,000 to more bpd 15%
Domestic market penalty	10% discount on price for up to 15% of contractor's crude, based on a pro rata formula for total crude produced

Let us now consider an example of a PSC now in use in a country where many major oil companies are now operating.

As Table 14.2 shows, under cost recovery, all expenditures are eligible for recovery in the year that they are incurred. But cost recovery is limited to 40 per cent of the first 30,000 bpd and 50 per cent of all production above that level. This enables the company to recover costs rapidly. Cost recovery that is not claimed is shared between the company and the government as profit oil.

But, the profit sharing shows another side of the PSC. The two-tiered royalty is combined with a 56 per cent income tax rate to create a system in which the government can claim over 90 per cent of oil revenue. As is the case with many other production sharing contracts, oil must be sold in the domestic market at a discount from the market price. Production bonuses are required at first production as well as at the threshold production levels shown here.

From the review, it can be seen that, all other things being equal, the tax/royalty agreements are generally considered preferable for energy companies when compared to the PSCs. This of course depends on the specific terms and conditions of each contract. Nevertheless, PSC sometimes are structured so as to limit the upside potential for a company. This may present a real problem for countries that are attempting to develop high-cost or high-risk resources without sufficient other incentives to the companies.

Risk service agreement

The 'risk service agreement', sometimes called the 'service agreement', is basically a variation of the PSC. Under this variation, the company may be paid in cash or in kind at a fixed fee for its services rendered to the host government. It is not used in many countries and is often intended to emphasise the ownership of natural resources by the government. The role of the energy company is labelled as a contractor whose only involvement is to be paid in cash or crude oil for its efforts. Yet, as above reviewed, there are enough aspects of the risk service agreement in respect of relationships with host governments to include it as a joint venture international petroleum agreement. These are often not attractive to oil companies because they generally do not let the company share in the upside potential in production.

While there are variations, almost all of these contracts are 'risk' (the company supplies risk capital) and rarely service agreements. If a discovery is made, the company finances the development. Thereafter, the state entity often has the right to take over the operation. Exploration costs are reimbursed from production (usually without interest) and production costs are also reimbursed (usually with interest) from production. The company has the right to buy a portion of the production at world market prices that is equal to its payment, i.e. if its fee is $10 million per year, the company may buy and export an equivalent amount of crude oil using world prices. Often, however, this right of purchase and export only applies so long as the state entity can buy crude on the international market. If it cannot, the company cannot export. Taxes are paid by contractor from his earnings. The risk service contract shares the usual elements of duration, work obligations and other similar terms with tax/royalty and PSCs.

Joint venture association in the CIS

Let us now consider what we know of the Republic models for a joint venture and what they understand to be the meaning of 'joint venture'.

1. Although it may be expected in due time that there will be petroleum legislation and probably model oil contracts, the joint venture concept in the Republics is probably best understood to mean a joint venture association with a state-owned enterprise and the foreign energy company in which each would hold a percentage interest in the enterprise through its ownership of equity.
2. The joint venture association, based on the knowledge we have of relevant laws and decrees, provides for many complex features and is different from the energy industry's past agreements with other host governments. As an overview, let us consider some of the features applicable to joint venture associations between a state entity and a foreign energy company, as follows:
   (a) A joint venture establishment ('JV') would provide for investment in the equity of a joint stock company by a Soviet enterprise and the foreign company, including possible loans to the JV by the foreign company.
   (b) The JV assets would be invested in petroleum operations, say exploration and production, which if successful, will result in development and production of hydrocarbons.

    (c) The JV will generate JV revenue through sales of hydrocarbons and will deduct costs and expenses to calculate a new profit.

    (d) Thereupon the JV would continue to conduct all operations in accordance with procedures applicable to JV associations.

3. The above overview is intended only as a 'pro forma' discussion of the main features of a JV association. There are other more complex features to the JV association which need not be discussed here. Suffice it to say that extensive negotiations could be expected if the Russians and other republics choose the JV association as the preferred energy venture type of agreement with the oil industry.

Criteria for judging energy venture agreements between energy companies and host governments

Each of the types of contracts outlined above, if used in energy joint ventures in the CIS, involves different levels of net benefits between the host government and the oil company under various outcomes defined by reserve discoveries, oil field development, operating costs and oil prices in world markets. Clearly, under all circumstances, both parties would expect an equitable share of returns. This should be the result even though there will be inevitable trade-offs and concessions in the course of negotiations. In any event, whichever of the above types of contracts are used, the ultimate criteria for judging an agreement in the CIS will be the willingness of the parties to recognise their common objectives which will provide an equitable share of returns to both foreign energy companies and Republic partners in the appropriate contractual framework. Moreover, I believe, that both parties – the CIS and the energy companies – with patience and goodwill, will be able to implement these complex agreements for their mutual benefit. This will enable the CIS energy industry to plan its part as a major player in the new oil regime which will emerge in the 1990s and into the next century.

14.6 CHALLENGES AND OPPORTUNITIES IN ENERGY JOINT VENTURES IN THE CIS

With the above equation of needs of the CIS Republics and energy companies' ability to satisfy them, why isn't everyone rushing to sign petroleum agreements? We already know of some of the difficulties. The significant challenges may not be technical, nor a question of oil deposits, but may be predominately cultural and commercial in nature. These are fundamentally different challenges for energy companies who are now faced with new and complex issues in the new CIS.

14.6.1 Key challenges and opportunities

The key challenges and opportunities which energy companies and the CIS will face together are the following:

- A determination has to be made with respect to the decision-making authorities – whether the Republic, the local authorities, the producer associations or all the above collectively. A determination is further necessary with respect to which authority shall clarify the meaning of ambiguous and overlapping legislation on oil and gas joint ventures. This is a critical issue for the energy industry.
- As we noted, the tax and fiscal system in the CIS Republics is changing frequently and needs stability. More frequently than not, a new decree or law is passed addressing some facet of foreign investment or ownership rights. Many of these are authorised but have yet to be published or detailed to allow their implementation. They tend therefore to create uncertainty.
- Convertibility of the rouble and export rights are two oil industry challenges in any investment. Most petroleum initiatives are requesting the right to export 100 per cent or a majority of production. This mainly is in response to rouble non-convertibility and below market product prices for domestic sales. Ultimately, domestic market prices must change, as domestic demand will require an increasing portion of these crude volumes. However, to support energy industry investment, assuming domestic sales, Republic domestic prices must reflect free market demand and the rouble must become a freely convertible currency. Otherwise, there would be no incentive for foreign energy companies to invest in the CIS unless they can freely export their production for hard currency.
- Questions still remain concerning ownership of the reserves. Clear ownership rights for oil and gas must be established. If clear ownership rights can be established, this will eliminate a major concern of the oil industry.
- The establishment of ownership rights will further develop options for alternate corporate structures, such as production sharing agreements and concession agreements, versus the traditional joint venture association. These structures eliminate many concerns that energy companies and financial institutions have with joint ventures: management control, profit repatriation, asset ownership, and other concerns. Moreover, the Russians and other Republics of the CIS now appear to favour competitive bidding, and probably production sharing contracts, in place of the traditional joint venture association, as the basis for foreign energy investment.
- Management control is appropriately perceived by energy companies as a make or break issue. To benefit fully from energy company participation, the CIS must initially allow the energy companies the right to management control of joint venture investments. Companies cannot isolate technology transfer from their business and management practices. This decision is supported by the need to manage field development on an economic feasibility basis rather than the quota-driven operating practice. It would also provide for safety, environmental and management practices in accordance with oil industry worldwide standards.

14.6.2 Commercial and fiscal challenges

There are other challenges and opportunities which must be addressed by energy companies, their home governments and the CIS in their investment decisions other than the above commercial and project challenges. These concern the overall operation. These must also be managed. The following may be critical to success:

- The CIS Republics and the host governments of energy companies should negotiate tax and trade agreements to eliminate tax and trade barriers to foreign investment.
- Commercial banks, host government agencies and venture funds have been cautious regarding significant CIS investments. If energy companies are willing to negotiate and address the challenges highlighted herein, they will need the support and help of international financial institutions and their respective governments to support these energy investments.
- In negotiations in the CIS, managements, shareholders and all stakeholders of energy companies should be kept fully apprised of the progress, the problems and the need for patience. Much support from all participants will be needed to deal with many problems over the next several years in CIS joint venture operations.
- One hopeful sign is membership in the International Monetary Fund ('IMF'). Without membership in the IMF and other international financial institutions, the CIS Republics stand little chance of stabilising their economies. The CIS needs IMF support to provide balance of payments support, provide technical and financial assistance, provide a stabilisation fund for the rouble to become convertible and provide favourable structures for increased private investment.

Finally, we note that all of the above challenges will require significant efforts, in both capital and manpower, for energy investments to succeed. It is a task that many energy companies and the CIS will continue to undertake because there are rewards and mutual benefits for both parties in energy investments in the CIS.

14.7 VIEWPOINTS AND CONCLUSIONS

14.7.1 Viewpoints

1. While we have noted above the complexities of energy company investment in joint ventures in the Republics, we need to emphasise again that the importance and benefits of oil exploration, development and production for the oil industry in the Republics are self-evident both for the industry and the Republics. There is an urgent need for energy investment in the region; and, in my opinion, petroleum investments will be the most important and pressing areas for private investment. There are many reasons for urgent oil and gas investment in the CIS. Its economy is in transition, there is a decline in production activity, there are changes in patterns of economic distribution and there are increasing economic uncertainties. What shall be the response of the energy industry?

2. I do not want either to underestimate or overestimate the scope of the problems for the energy industry in the Republics; the petroleum industry is still in a state of flux and it is not possible to predict the future. Here are some dimensions to those problems:
   (a) the jurisdictional uncertainties in the CIS make it difficult, sometimes impossible, to know who to deal with or to know which entity has jurisdiction;
   (b) all the relevant petroleum and tax laws may not be in place and the appropriate and relevant laws may not be known for certain;
   (c) the transition from state control to a market economy and from sovereign-to-sovereign dealings to sovereign-to-private investment company dealings still needs time for full development; and
   (d) the lack of a convertible currency is a continuing impediment to concluding business deals.
3. From my experiences, I am of the opinion that much benefit can be achieved for both energy companies and the CIS in energy joint ventures. Such benefits will accrue to both parties for many reasons, including the following:
   (a) there has been a consistent decline in oil and gas production levels throughout the Republics;
   (b) energy companies can provide state-of-the-art technology and equipment to find new petroleum and develop already discovered petroleum fields;
   (c) business know-how in a competitive energy market, capital investment, environmental protection and safety practices are available from oil companies; and
   (d) technical advances that have been made in the West need to be implemented in the CIS – high-quality seismic technology, latest well-logging and drilling equipment, new rig capabilities, sophisticated computer applications, advances in deep water drilling and production and innovative geological technology. These are available in joint ventures with the oil industry.
4. However, this is a two-way street. The CIS also has the right to expect from the energy companies a constructive and positive attitude. The energy companies must be willing to be creative in adapting their oil practices to needs of the CIS oil and gas industry and must be understanding of the ex-Soviet oil industry absence from the world's oil market economies for many years. The energy companies shall also need to have the confidence and the determination that a petroleum agreement will always be possible based on fair dealings and a recognition of a mutuality of interests between the parties.
5. From the energy industry viewpoint, the opening up of the CIS promises opportunities for becoming a partner in some of the richest oil and gas deposits worldwide, opportunities which seemed remote only several years ago. Here are some of the reasons:
   (a) in some areas of the region, for example, in Russia, oil and gas production rank among the highest worldwide;

(b) proved reserves in some areas of the CIS are among the world's highest and maybe even higher because not all reserve numbers are published; opportunities for the oil industry have rarely been so attractive as the potential for discovery and development of significant quantities of hydrocarbons; and

(c) there are vast unexplored and under-explored areas, numerous basins and structures, and a significant number of oil and gas fields classified as giants, having 100 MM bbl or 600 bcf of proved reserves.

6. We have mentioned political risks in relation to the August 1991 attempted coup and the uncertainties following the break-up of the Soviet Union in December 1991. Political risks are an important factor. Although the industry has successfully survived expropriations, abrogation of contracts, revolution and dramatic changes in political ideology worldwide, in the Republics political stability will be important for attracting private investment. Most energy companies are prepared to accept political risk, if the prospects of political stability are favourable and the potential reward is sufficiently attractive. Notwithstanding the August 1991 attempted coup and December 1991 dissolution of the USSR, and other possible political problems in the future, the best case scenario may be that the mutual interests and inter-dependence of the Republics, which has the oil, and the foreign energy companies, who have the resources and the skills to find, develop and produce it, would bring a certain degree of stability to their relationship. These overriding considerations should maintain a certain security in investment, even though there shall be uncertainties and caution as a result of the August 1991 attempted coup and the December 1991 USSR dissolution.

7. I strongly espouse the importance of a partnership and a doctrine of mutuality of interests for future petroleum joint ventures in this area. The history of past misunderstandings should be buried in the past. The former emotional words of the past such as capitalism and socialism; the belief in the past that no exploration nor exploitation of natural resources by foreigners should be allowed; the expectation in the past that interests of each party are inevitably in conflict; and the view of the past that the parties position themselves to extract the last ounce of benefit for their special interest goals and that the ultimate relationship is that of suspicion of each other should be, in my opinion, ghosts and relics of the past no longer sustainable anywhere in today's energy world. I hope that we shall now enter into a new order of relationships – a recognition of a mutuality of interests. This would be a cornerstone for oil progress for the Republics in the 1990s and a removal of any constraints on energy investment in the CIS in the 1990s.

8. Since the Republics of the CIS now lack specific rules applicable to oil and gas ventures, both parties will have an obligation to undertake a careful negotiation of the terms of the petroleum agreement in order to be certain that all rights and obligations are provided in respect of the parties. Such negotiation may be time- consuming and may result in delays in concluding an agreement. There is, therefore, a need for the Republics of the CIS and

the energy industry to review laws and regulations applicable to joint venture petroleum agreements which will open the doors to foreign investment. This is where we in the energy industry must help. We must provide our input in considerable measure so that we can jointly structure reasonable and comprehensive agreements for the mutual benefit of both parties.

14.7.2 Conclusions

1. My conclusions are that the opportunities for energy joint ventures in oil and gas exploration, development and production and other petroleum activities in the CIS are significant and will continue to be promising. Notwithstanding serious problems, I conclude that opportunities shall be significant and promising in the Republics for the following reasons:

- There are already patterns of success for companies in both energy and non-energy industries in concluding joint venture agreements, protocols and feasibility studies.
- Success in concluding agreements results from many factors including determination, patience and understanding the rules of the game.
- There is a view, either expressed or implied, that oil and gas investments in the Republics may be uniquely treated among other investments because of its special role in generating hard currency, reducing the balance of payments and increasing the wealth of the country. According to this view, energy investment might be expected to be 'insulated' from whatever political and economic difficulties might otherwise evolve in respect of other industries;
- The recourse to adversarial proceedings, whether in litigation or arbitration to resolve disputes, is anathema to the culture and experiences of the CIS; this augurs well for negotiations – even if not easy – as the primary and best means of resolving disputes;
- There is a further expectation of contract stability in dealings with the Republics – their tradition in that they share a common culture with the Western community, their desire to provide a rule of law foundation as a basis for restructuring their economies, their tradition in honouring their deals, their tradition of enterprise in expanding into market economies and their tradition of maintaining relationships based on trust.
- There is a continuing awareness of problems and desire to resolve them in order to promote business with the foreign energy companies.

2. We conclude further with a hopeful and optimistic commentary, entitled 'Russian Renaissance', by Alexei Izyumov, an economist and analyst at The Soviet Academy of Sciences and a fellow of the Freedom Forum Media Studies at Columbia University. He wrote, in part, as follows:

New and powerful currents are growing and in the near distance future they will help propel that crisis-ridden country towards the progress and prosperity its people have for so long deserved. First is an entrepreneurial revival ... Hand in hand with the resurgence of the private initiative goes a spiritual revival ... The third hopeful trend is the generational change – the pivotal role of the younger generation as the main player in CIS politics.

Russia and the Republics will have in due time the basic structures of a market democracy largely in place. And it is then that the great renaissance will start to gather momentum. (A. Izyumov, 'Russian Renaissance', *Washington Post*, 1 December 1991, p. 14)

3.   Finally, I am also confident – notwithstanding the attempted August 1991 coup and the December 1991 USSR dissolution and other potential political uncertainties – that there are unique opportunities for energy joint ventures in the CIS, because this is a special time in history when both the oil industry and the CIS need each other. All parties need each other to maximise opportunities in energy exploration, development and production and other petroleum activities. The CIS needs to revitalise and enhance their economies and the oil industry needs to discover and develop new and substantial oil and gas resources.

There are great hopes for success for energy joint ventures in the CIS in the 1990s. Our belief is that such energy joint ventures will be successful for the mutual benefit of both the CIS and the energy industry. We believe further that the partnership of the CIS and the energy industry will emerge as an important part of the new international oil regime of the 1990s.

Chapter 15

Outlook for the Energy Sector of Russia and Central Asia:
Structural and Cultural Perspectives

Reinhold Heus

15.1 INTRODUCTION

Since the opening up of the former Soviet Union in the late 1980s, significant international finance for many energy projects have yet to be mobilised. What has caused these delays? Could it be that there are powerful barriers to the development of the CIS energy sector?

This chapter proposes to approach this issue from the perspective of the author's personal observations and experience in Russia and Central Asia over the past 3 1/2 years. In particular it is the aim of the chapter to address some of the structural and cultural factors which influence the development of the CIS energy sector.

15.2 MUTUAL DISCOVERY

On the author's first visit to Moscow in January 1990, there was a great sense of adventure. Satisfying of curiosity was top priority for both sides. The assumption that good business would inevitably follow was taken for granted. Great expectations were cultivated on both sides, unrealistic perhaps in hindsight, but understandable in those early years.

But much has changed since then. The initial feelings of excitement have abated, and curiosity has gradually been replaced by a sense of wariness and frustration. The love affair is over and it is only now that both parties are taking a serious look at each other in the cold light of morning, the morning of a period of real mutual discovery. Some may not like what they see and will reconsider their initial commitment. Others will remain convinced that they cannot afford not to be part of the CIS and will attempt to get their feet on the shifting ground. But these attempts will not succeed if the process of mutual discovery is only scratching the surface. It is more than ever necessary to look beyond the facade of position-taking, and come to understand the real long-term interests of both sides. Only this type of mutual discovery will eventually lead to lasting solutions.

15.3 INTERNATIONAL FINANCE: A PANACEA?

There are numerous problems which are continuing to beset the CIS energy sector. Few major projects have been making any serious progress to date and some large foreign corporations are seriously reviewing their position in certain 'test-case' projects. Over the past years many announcements for transfers of large international funds have made the headlines, but the reality is that relatively small amounts of foreign funds have actually gone into the development of the CIS energy sector.

Many believe that if only the money would really be made available for equipment supplies and modernisation and extension of the infrastructure, all would be well in the end. As a financier I certainly do not wish to belittle the importance of money, but in my view the development of the CIS energy sector is too important to be left to international financiers. The vast problems of the CIS energy sector cannot simply be reduced to a problem of finance.

Of course the timing has not been very good: unlike the 1980s when plentiful capital was chasing few good projects, the opening up of the CIS unfortunately coincided with global recession. A rapidly increasing number of projects is pursuing a limited international pool of available finance.We should not delude ourselves: the current shortage of available international funds is not the real cause of the current frustration, nor will increased availability of cash be the main key to long-term solutions. But if money is not a panacea, in which direction should one explore for real long-term solutions?

Other factors have to change to make sure that whatever funds flow into the CIS will lead to positive results for both sides. So far even practical matters common at the start of any project such as agreeing the minimum requirements for international finance have proved to be a tedious and frustrating experience for those involved. At the surface level seemingly unbridgeable negotiating positions are being taken which point to deep-rooted differences that go beyond a mere inadequate understanding of basic business concepts.

It is not an issue of bridging the knowledge gap: persistent attempts in the past years to persuade the Russians from various angles to adopt a PSC regime, a contractual arrangement common to other frontier regions, have so far proved to be unsuccessful.

To think that this failure is due to incompetent salesmanship or problems in communication is to mislead oneself.

15.4 RELUCTANT BRIDE?

Entrenched in day-to-day problems it is easy to lose sight of the long-term nature of profound social change. It may take us well into the next century before we can witness an acceptable degree of integration of the CIS into the world economy. The integration of the CIS energy sector into the world energy sector will certainly not be quicker.

This process of integration poses many unique challenges to both sides. But the fundamental challenge is not financial, technological or infrastructural in nature, it is social; it is a challenge about the integration of people.

It can be said that both the willingness and ability to change one's thinking and ways of doing things in a short space of time is in general limited. Furthermore, and particularly in the case of the CIS, the willingness to change is influenced by the attitudes and perceived intentions of the foreign parties.

Like in a marriage of individuals, the success of a marriage between the CIS and the international energy sector is heavily dependent on the willingness on both sides to look after each other's long-term interest.

The courtship in the past few years has not been all too successful, as one party (the bride?) is still unconvinced about the long-term intentions of the other party (the groom?). In addition the long and wide experience of the groom has given him a false sense of comfort. Surely having successfully wooed many partners in other areas, the success formula will work with this older, albeit very rich girl, who seems desperate to get married? But the other party is not comfortable to be cast into a role of bride, and on top of that having more wealth makes her naturally suspicious and a rather reluctant partner to seduce. So she sends out conflicting signals, apparently ready to get married, but none of the sophisticated suitors has been able to get her into church.

Both the success of a courtship and the subsequent partnership are dependent upon the willingness of both parties to change. A cosmetic adjustment of behaviour will not do. Only honest self-examination of intentions and beliefs could lead to the change that is required.

15.5 JUST ANOTHER FRONTIER PLAY?

Three years ago the former USSR was widely considered as the new frontier play. The vanguard for international energy financing would without any doubt rapidly shift from previously fashionable frontier areas such as South East Asia to this new area of great wealth and further unknown riches, the new 'Wild East'.

Of course in comparison with previous frontier regions this new frontier play was much bigger in size, but in general it was agreed that the CIS challenge would primarily be different in scale, not in quality. It was tacitly understood that the experience gained in the past decades in other areas could without too much modification successfully meet the formidable challenges of the CIS.

Few beliefs have proved to be more wrong. The present frustration is to a large extent rooted in this mistaken assumption. It is only now that many have started to realise that the challenges are not only different in scale but of a quite different nature than anywhere else.

Russia and Central Asia are not just another, bigger frontier play. It is not a question of more of the same. The CIS and its energy sector pose many incomparable structural and cultural barriers for which previous experience in other regions is a very poor guide. To succeed in these areas one has to appreciate much better its unique features, and become much more aware of the hidden structural and cultural barriers. To transfer experience successfully, the challenge in the CIS must be comparable to those of previous frontier regions. The current frustration indicates that the challenges posed by Russia and Central Asian countries are much less comparable to those in other oil regions than was previously assumed.

One has to understand the key forces that determine the relative uniqueness of these challenges in order to make any judgements about the possible development of the energy sector in Russia and Central Asia.

15.6 RELATIVE UNIQUENESS OF THE CIS ENERGY SECTOR

The relative uniqueness of the CIS energy sector is in our view based upon the interaction of three factors: first, the specific nature and history of the CIS oil industry; second, the fact that the former USSR is a society with cultural and structural features of both the East and the West; and the third factor is the legacy of an autocratic decision-making structure.

In the final analysis it is the combined interaction of these three factors that produces the unique challenges of the energy sectors of Russia and Central Asia. Unless both sides share a better understanding of these challenges, wrong solutions and inadequate models will be developed.

15.7 TEACHER OR PUPIL?

Running the largest oil industry in the world for many decades without any foreign assistance is one thing, but more importantly, unlike any other frontier region the former USSR had discovered most of their oil and gas reserves all on their own. This is a key reason why there is a quite different sense of reserve ownership and a greater sensitivity regarding their development by foreign entities than in the oil-producing countries where energy reserves were discovered either by the foreign parties or with the assistance of foreign parties. In the latter regions it was implicitly understood that foreign parties will be given the right to develop reserves that they have helped to develop. One cannot expect a similar sense of implicit obligation to develop in Russia or Central Asia.

Without a full appreciation of the critical differences of this situation compared with other frontier regions, one will not understand the reluctance to proceed rapidly on matters such as PSC agreements.

In other frontier regions the foreigners found a clean slate and offered to explore for oil and gas. The local people were prepared to accept this teacher–pupil relationship on the condition that they would receive new oil wealth. This model worked quite well, and if it took two parties to tango, then in many frontier regions eventually the tango was and still is danced very well. However, in Russia and Central Asia for well over 70 years they have been proudly dancing another dance. And it is quite awkward to observe two skilled dancers trying to dance together, each with a different dance in mind.

The limits of transferring international experience are very tangible here. The specific pupil–teacher relationship, successful in other frontier regions, will not work in Russia and Central Asia. Both sides perhaps will have to learn a new dance which suits both parties. The West will have to instil a new sense of curiosity and humility by starting to admit its limitations in dealing effectively with challenges in Russia and Central Asia.

This will mean that in the case of the development of the CIS energy sector both sides will have to adopt the role of teacher and pupil at the same time.

15.8 CULTURAL PERSPECTIVES

This brings us to the second factor. The frustration currently experienced between foreign corporations and CIS counterparts is often attributed to a lack of knowledge or understanding on the part of the CIS counterpart. 'If only we could find ways to make it better understood' – is a common reflection. But more explanation is not going to improve things as it is not a problem of understanding. Unless new solutions address the real underlying concerns and reflect an attitude aimed at protecting the other side's long-term interests, they will not find any real acceptance nor will they be implemented.

It is easily forgotten that the CIS countries are historically a result of European and Asian cultural influences. One could easily make the mistake to infer from the apparent intellectual compatibility with the West that there will be an underlying emotional and social compatibility or even similarity. A look at history explains why emotionally there is more compatibility with Mediterranean cultures than with those of the north of Europe. But more importantly when one considers the implementation of economic development models, one has to realise that the social structures and processes in Russia and Central Asia resemble to varying degrees those of Oriental cultures, where a stronger group consciousness exists.

From this it can be seen that many of the proposed solutions or models coming from the West, although intellectually supported, encounter simultaneously emotional and social rejection, to stronger and lesser degrees. On the other hand, Asian models of political aristocracy and economic liberalism, although having much less intellectual appeal, might meet social and emotional receptiveness particularly in the Central Asian republics. Now both sides start to realise that there are considerable cultural and social barriers, which if not properly understood will perpetuate the frustration. The consequence is that solutions and models that have worked well in the East or the West will have only limited relevance to the challenges in the CIS.

15.9 STRUCTURAL BARRIERS

The degree of incompatibility of the CIS energy sector to other frontier regions is further increased by structural barriers. The legacy of a command system combined with the aforementioned Euro-Asiatic cultural origins have produced a decision-making structure that is both unstable and opaque. There exists little transparency nor any stability, both vertically between central and regional authorities, and horizontally between industrial and political powers. Quite a number of projects have run into considerable difficulties because there has been a mechanism for developing an internal consensus about the degree of decentralisation of authority and separation of industrial and political powers.

To come to a consensus about the separation of authority structures both vertically and horizontally will be one of the most formidable challenges to the Russian and Central Asian societies. Without the development of a robust consensus on the nature of the decision-making structures, stability and transparency will not improve, and the process of integration into the world economy will be hampered.

But as said earlier, the process of social change can take decades, and change of attitudes will be slow. Analysing the cultural constraints mentioned before, one can only speculate about how the decision-making structures may evolve. Oriental cultures are characterised by a higher group focus ('other-awareness') than Occidental cultures, and they tend to generate more overlap in political and industrial power (hence less transparency) than Western cultures (in particular the Anglo-Saxon variety). The basis of the latter is a more strongly developed 'individualistic consciousness' which provides a more fertile basis for more transparent decision-making structures, i.e. they will allow for greater separation of powers.

Our prognosis is that in the very long run the authority and decision-making processes in Russia or the CIS at large will become more transparent than most in the East, but will have the inclination to remain more opaque than those in Europe and the USA.

15.10 FROM THE OUTSIDE LOOKING IN

If we want solutions to be adopted and implemented we have to consider the long-term interests of both parties. If both sides are prepared to take care for at least 50 per cent of the interests of the other side then progress can be made.

But how best to look after the long-term interests of both sides?

A useful insight is provided by looking at the perspective from which both sides see the economic development of the CIS. The dominant perspective of most foreign companies is one 'from the outside looking in'. In this view Russia and Central Asia are seen as markets – almost passive receivers of foreign expertise, finance, products etc., and simultaneously exporters of primarily natural resources. But this 'outside-in' perspective whereby the foreign party is the groom and the CIS the wealthy but reluctant bride serves in the long term only the interests of one side and is therefore inadequate.

This 'outside-in' perspective needs to be complemented by an 'inside-looking-out' perspective, whereby the internationalisation of the Russian and Central Asian industries is taken as the starting point, exploiting the advantages of labour costs and currency exchange rate. If in the next 25 years Russia will not have developed various small or large multinational corporations in the energy sector or other industries, its integration into the world economic system will be quite limited.

15.11 FROM THE INSIDE LOOKING OUT

In the long run Russia and Central Asia can domestically become stronger if they develop early on an international perspective. The development of many of the Asian tigers (Singapore, Hong Kong, Taiwan and South Korea) and the NIC's (Thailand, Malaysia and Indonesia) and recently China, is to a different degree dependent on exploiting labour cost and a favourable currency exchange rate plus developing a strong international network. They did not develop themselves by focusing inward, but by looking and moving outward into the international arena.

It is quite understandable that most foreign companies have no particular reason to wish Russia a dismal outlook, but equally there is no particular incentive for foreigners to assist Russia in becoming a strong industrial nation. It is primarily in the interest of the Russians to want to develop a strong industrial nation. From a short-term perspective, it is much more attractive for foreigners to treat Russia and the Central Asian nations as markets for their products, and to help these countries to export more of their natural resources.

However, any foreign company which does not to some extent adopt an 'inside-out-perspective' in developing business in Russia, which is not aiming to sit alongside the Russian counterpart and share at least 50 per cent of their ambition and problems, will quickly be found out and distrusted – and will sooner, rather than later, discover that things do not move as expected.

For Russia and Central Asia not to want to develop multinational (state or private) oil corporations in the coming decades would be very surprising. So foreign investors should at least be aware that their proposals are likely to receive much more support if such proposals also reflect an 'inside-out' perspective.

15.12 OUTLOOK: DOMESTIC FOCUS OR INTERNATIONAL ORIENTATION?

Therefore, coming back to the theme of this chapter, in addressing the outlook of the Russian Energy Sector, it is not enough to consider only the domestic aspects. It is crucial to evaluate the various options of internationalisation. Will it be internationalisation models like those of OPEC nations (such as the downstream integration model of KPC), or will it follow instead internationalisation models of European state enterprises, with a bias towards upstream expansion overseas? Or will it be like the international expansion of the Anglo-Saxon oil enterprises?

Whatever internationalisation model will be adopted, assistance is required in areas such as international finance, management and selection of joint venture partners abroad. Could the latter mean that it is the international energy community who perhaps will be cast in the role of bride, and the Russian or Central Asian side as perhaps hesitant groom?

At present there is often serious role confusion. And this is a reflection of false assumptions and incomplete perspectives. To make any progress both parties have to look beyond surface behaviour, behind the positions that are taken, to consider their underlying interests. If both sides were prepared to exchange posturing for real negotiations on substance, if they were prepared to assume the role of both teacher and pupil, of bride or groom, and forego an exclusive focus on one of the archetypical roles, things might improve. No exclusive monopoly on one role or perspective will work.

The outlook for the CIS Energy Sector is a two-way street. Only if a combined domestic and international perspective is taken as a starting point for project proposals, partnerships or models for development, will the long-term requirements of both sides be satisfied.

Only by approaching the development of the countries of the former Soviet Union from this two-fold perspective and by making sure that both sides fully understand each other's long-term interests is real progress possible.

Chapter 16

Oil and Gas Legislation in Russia
From Texas to Siberia – Is a Russian Model Emerging?

Thomas W. Wälde

16.1 BACKGROUND

A Moscow workshop organised in October 1992 by the European Community for the Russian Ministry of Fuel and Energy through the Centre for Petroleum and Mineral Law and Policy (University of Dundee) and the Institute for International Energy Law (University of Leiden) brought a European dimension to the on-going debate on Russian petroleum legislation. European experts from the two academic institutions, the British OfGas regulator, from Treuhand (Germany), the Netherlands, Spain and Italy (ENI) reviewed and discussed with Russian specialists from the Moscow Ministries, Gazprom, the Russian oil industry associations and the Komi region the main issues underlying the current debate.

It may be recalled that for approximately two years an advisory project by the University of Houston, supported, mainly, by US oil companies, had been advising the Russians. A World Bank team got involved subsequently, both by providing funding to the Houston project and by providing input on the substance of draft legislation; the prospect of a large World Bank energy loan project and its conditionalities provide the background for these advisory services. There has also been some activity by the European Bank for Reconstruction and Development (EBRD) on questions of environmental regulation. European oil companies also contributed expertise on Russian legal concepts and petroleum law. A 'Law on Subsoil' – essentially a framework law for mineral exploitation – and a regulation/guidelines for licensing/bidding of mineral resources were enacted in 1992. What is now at issue is the formulation and enactment of a definite oil and gas law which is meant to regulate:

- title and ownership;
- licensing and negotiating authority, rules, procedures and criteria for licensing, in particular bidding and negotiations;
- taxation, including investment guarantees and incentives (in particular retention/repatriation of foreign exchange);
- relations between central governments, the various ethnically characterised 'republics', autonomous regions and regional authorities of the Russian Federation, with respect to title (who owns?), licensing (who licenses and

negotiates?), taxation (who taxes) and revenue distribution (who gets what part of the revenues?);

- regulation of gas extraction, transportation and distribution;
- role and structure of state ownership/regulation in the energy sector – which government authority should own which productive assets in what way?
- environmental regulation, enforcement procedures and enforcement mechanisms.

As of October 1992, three drafts were available to deal with the issue: the main 'Ministry draft', to an extent based on very complex and detailed drafts prepared by the foreign advisers (Houston/World Bank – others); the VNIIOENG-draft, prepared by a Russian research institute on oil technology, a draft prepared by GAZPROM reflecting the gas monopoly's perspectives. Other complete or partial drafts may or may not be in the process of draft, drafting or being promoted to members of the Supreme Soviet (there is some unclear reference to a draft law on concessions). There is apparently now a plan to merge these drafts, or some of them, into a compromise draft to be prepared by members of the Gubkin-Institute, a reputed petroleum and minerals technology and economics institute. At first sight, the relative dearth of lawyers involved seems surprising – less so if one takes into account the fact that lawyers, who have not played an important role in the former Soviet Union, exist only in small numbers. There is also a tradition of decision-making on economic policy and planning by engineers. It may be useful to view this still unclear situation against the broader background of Russian history which produces the main attitudes now struggling with each other.

16.2 POLITICAL ATTITUDES IN RUSSIA: Westernising Technocrats *versus* Nationalist Oil Generals

Russian history over the last five centuries is characterised very much by the conflict between the 'Westernisers' (engineers, technocrats, economists advocating the adoption of the methods of the West) and Russian nationalists ('Slavophiles') advocating rather closure and insulation from external influences not suitable and perhaps even pernicious for the very fabric of Russian society and life. This tension very much pervades today's discussion. Westernisers, largely academic researchers in their forties and thirties (of which Russia seems to have produced millions), have been made to believe – with perhaps quite some encouragement from many of their enthusiastic, and politically often quite naive Western advisers – that simple adoption of Western models, largely along the Anglo-Saxon model (not reality) of free market, privatised industries and copycat approaches to mainly US legislative models would generate a dramatic upturn of the Russian economy within a very short time-span. These expectations have failed – as they had to – and the reformers are now facing the backlash from Russian nationalists, Communist, ex-Communist or whatever their political and economic creed. Expectations which were exaggerated are resulting in failures seen as dismal – and this failed expectation may be of more importance in the debate than the substantive matter of the policies at issue.

Western advisers more often than not were fired rather by enthusiasm and naïveté – Americans in particular seem to need a spiritual crusade in each decade – than by the more sobering experience one could have developed out of the thirty-year-long attempts at economic development in the still so denominated 'Third World'. Articles, notes and private memoranda circulated by American lawyers over the last two years are full of the sense of great excitement over the chance of remaking the former 'Empire of Evil' into the 'American Way of Life and Business'.

It is indeed difficult to find a real-life model for the transition challenges in the former Soviet Union: on one hand, the analogy to developing countries may be said to be misleading; Russians, in particular Muscovites, are among the world's best educated people – though an analogy with the often very high state of education for the elites at the dawn of decolonisation may strike some observers experienced in the culture of the Third World. There is a distinctly 'European' look, feel, consciousness and attitude in Russians who resent strongly any analogies to developing countries, in particular to former client countries of the USSR. On the other hand, when it comes to the everyday life of capitalism, there is an other-worldly colour to the private beliefs and the personal culture of most educated Russians which is in stark contrast to the business culture in almost all (in particular the successful Asian) developing countries. Culturally speaking, Russia is much closer to Europe than even many of Europe's former colonies; in terms of a commercial frame of mind, the Third World often would seem to offer a much more propitious environment for capitalist-led growth.

Russia is as much an Asian as a European country. For quite a while, the attraction of US society, perhaps the most remote, had generated quite a following among the Russians. As they settle into their long and deep crisis and as market miracles do not seem to work, they may discover their Asian side as well. Positioned between the capitalist mixed economies of Germany, Austria and Scandinavia on one side, the fiercely competitive, but highly disciplined and successful Japanese economy and the authoritarian, but in its way successful Chinese model on the other side, it is likely that the Russians will look more closely at these neighbours to pick up policies and move away from the more exotic brands of Western capitalism. The Japanese government, for example, has quite a record of protecting its energy industries in the infancy stages before releasing them into a more competitive world. This example may have quite some meaning for Russia where the academic recipe of total opening to foreign competition would probably leave the domestic industry in complete collapse – as has been happening in Eastern Germany over the last two years.

When it comes to the oil and gas industries, these tensions and mis-apprehensions are further exacerbated by the antagonism between Westernis-ing technocrats who have moved from Moscow research institutes to the Russian government on one side, and the roughnecks steeped in Siberian oil, slush and ice who manage the oil and gas operations on the other. While the old house of Russian oil was not perfect, it did work in its own strange ways;

what the westernising technocrats are accused of having done is to destroy an imperfect old order without creating a better new order. We feel it is imperative to view the current debate on Russian oil and gas law against this background which is steeped deeply in Russian history, psychology and self-perception.

16.3 THE DEBATE ON OIL AND GAS LAW: Towards a 'Russian Solution'?

There is no doubt that the two years of Western advice have focused attention on how to formulate the most suitable policies for the Russian oil and gas sector; in addition, quite some knowledge – though often quite academic and idealistic – on international oil and gas law, tax and licensing practice has entered Russia. A major problem, in our view, has been the heavy emphasis of the Houston Group on a detailed, specific, all-embracing oil and gas law. This may be the current model in Texas where a century of oil and gas industry and decades of regulation by the Texas Railroad Commission has built up a perfectly workable legal system meant to maintain an oil industry threatened by gradual decline. Experience with successful petroleum investment in 'starter' countries – e.g. Saudi Arabia and the Gulf (which have no real oil and gas law), Indonesia, China, Angola, but also Norway and the UK – indicates that it may be premature to enact very detailed and specific legislation before the time is ripe, e.g. before enough understanding of the oil industry has been absorbed by the local culture (politics, government, industry, academics, practitioners). Indeed, an immature political culture is unlikely to be able to absorb or generate a proper comprehensive regulatory regime for such a vast and sensitive industry. Focusing the discussion on numerous detailed issue is likely to create more suspicions, generate more debate, heat up more political antagonism than is good for such a vulnerable industry.

It is no doubt for such and similar reasons that a very successful way of handling the oil industry, in particular foreign investors, has been by an approach focused on individual transactions, i.e. by focusing on how to create a sufficient legal basis for investment projects on a mainly contractual basis. A short law of empowerment combined with gradually evolving model agreements has proved to be a way to success in probably most of the countries which have achieved major growth in oil and gas production around the world. This essential wisdom – quite unrelated to the rather terminological and philosophical issue as to whether Russia is a 'developing country' or not – was disregarded when the Houston Group carried Texas oil and gas law in its mental backpack when tackling the most momentous challenge of petroleum legislation in this decade. It might indeed have been better to reflect for some time on what mechanisms have proved to work best in difficult countries and to listen to what there was in terms of legal and policy tradition in Russia, perhaps to look out for societies more similar than the Texas model, before embarking on a massive process of drafting and seeking to import alien models to Russia. In fact, it may well be argued that the emphasis on detailed and specific all-embracing solutions has kept Russia away from what would have been the best precedent for a workable petroleum law model: the completion of successful negotiations with major international oil companies based on *ad hoc* agreements. An *ad hoc* solution is usually easier – politically, negotiation-wise – than the design of a comprehensive oil and gas law meant for the next decades. A successful *ad hoc* solution, in addition, provides a live example of how to structure a successful and workable regime. By not focusing on a pioneer deal to set example for others, but on a grandiose over-all scheme, the westernising technocrats and their foreign advisers may actually, and inadvertently, have delayed significant foreign investment when and if it was economically and politically feasible. This – and much less the nationalist-inspired suspicions of Russians against the funding of the Houston project by oil companies – seems, with the benefit of hindsight, to be one of the major flaws of past advisory assistance.

The debate in the October 1992 EC workshop in Moscow on oil and gas legislation indicated this significant shift in Russian attitudes: the representative of the Russian Ministry of Energy and Fuel highlighted the need to look for a 'European model', closer to the Russian situation and less alien; the concluding statement by the director of the VNIIOENG institute went further by regretting the absence of European advisers in the early stages, the unsuitability of much of the foreign models reflected in the current drafts and highlighted the perhaps evident recognition that Russia was a unique situation, that foreign models were only useful to a very limited extent and that Russia had to find a 'Russian solution' to its oil and gas policies. Subsequent statements by senior politicians in Russia emphasise the growing criticism of Anglo-Saxon academic models – both European countries with internationally competitive state companies (e.g. France, Italy and Austria) and Asian countries (Japan and China) are cited as more relevant examples to look at.

16.4 SPECIFIC ISSUES OF THE OIL AND GAS LEGISLATION DEBATE

16.4.1 Framework law or detailed legislation?

Different from the Texas approach to Russian oil and gas law, the European experts emphasised in the discussion with their Russian counterparts the advantages of having a short framework law complemented by model licences/contracts. International experience (including the UK) demonstrates the advantages of developing legislation gradually based on the practical experiences with workable model agreements or licences. The emphasis on a framework law may also be compatible with the civil law tradition of Russia, and most of the European legal systems to which Russians feel closest.

16.4.2 Separate gas law?

The Russian state gas company – having suffered much less a decline than the oil industry – advocates strongly a separate gas law. This advocacy embraces a separate, and most probably unitary Russian gas monopoly, from production to distribution and export. The view of most specialists outside Gazprom was that a monopoly at the extraction stage is not advisable. The European situation demonstrates that in the infancy stages of an industry gas transportation monopolies may be helpful to mobilise finance for long-term investment. As the industry matures, greater competition is usually possible – measures such as third-party access, practiced in the UK and advocated by the EC Commission – indicate the greater maturity of a gas industry ready for liberalisation.

Any monopoly needs to be counterbalanced by regulation, for protecting consumers from abuse of market power and for bringing about greater efficiency by direct intervention, by structural reform and by economic incentives. The British regulator, Sir James McKinnon, presented to the Russian side the UK model illustrated by a gradually diminishing gas monopoly faced by an energetic regulator.

16.4.3 Environmental regulation

Allegedly, up to 10 per cent or more of Russian oil production is lost by leakage in production and transportation. Better conservation, as well as energy efficiency, is accordingly both an environmentally and economically sound objective. There is no doubt that better environmental regulation is required. The problem is, naturally, enforcement in a situation of deterioration of organisational order and authority. Environmental regulation has two directions: first, the thorny issue of how to enact and even more so enforce regulation against existing producers struggling with supplies, absence of capital and direction; second, there could easily be a tendency to impose unrealistic standards on foreign newcomers – it is generally easier to impose exacting standards on foreign investors than to settle the much larger risks posed by existing producers and transporters. Ultimately, it seems doubtful that an improved environmental regime can truly work before the structure of the oil industry has completed its transition towards a workable system.

16.4.4 Licensing, bidding and negotiation

The probably central issue at the moment is the question of title, ownership, licensing and negotiating authority. Ultimately, it is quite irrelevant who owns title to the underground mineral resource – the US model of land-ownership encompassing subsurface minerals being internationally an exception and probably likely to cause confusion in today's Russia. What is essential is that there is a clearly defined and legally fully recognised party who can grant a valid right to an oil company to explore and to extract oil and gas. Internationally, assigning the ownership of subsurface minerals to the state is usually and probably the easiest way to settle the title/ownership issue and to set up a clear licensing and negotiating authority. Discussion on ownership *per se* – central government, the ethnic republic and autonomous regions or the regional governments or local production associations – is likely, in the Russian context, to complicate matters further and delay significant investment. The consensus among all European experts was that it would be better to focus all efforts on settlement of the licensing authority. The two years spent on detailed drafting of ultimately secondary issues solvable by contract negotiations may have delayed significantly substantial foreign investment. Indeed, one should now be worried about the window of opportunity for foreign investment being closed under the impact of the nationalist passion aroused by the economic situation in general and the debate on the oil and gas legislation process in particular.

It is, however, understandable that both the Moscow drafters and their foreign advisers have not found a solution – the basic problem is political and centres around the conflicting claims by both Moscow authorities (Geology Commission *versus* Ministry of Energy), regional authorities and production associations. The distinction between framework law and regulation, mineral licensing and direct ownership and operations characteristic for market economies is, naturally, not deeply appreciated in the current Russian debate. The new drafts have moved towards a concept of joint licensing which, if the joint licensing authorities are able to come to unified decisions, may indeed be a suitable mechanism.

In the end, these are constitutional issues requiring an overall political settlement for which an oil and gas law itself may not be the proper place. If the Russian Federation sets up the structures of a truly federal state, precedent and example would tend to locate much of the licensing authority (perhaps excepting the offshore areas) towards the regional authorities. Federal tasks would then typically be income taxation and perhaps some coordination through export regulation. However, given the centralist tendencies of Moscow governments since time immemorial, such decentralisation may be difficult for the Moscow authorities to embrace. In addition, would they tend to exacerbate – or perhaps to curb? – the centrifugal tendencies visible not only in the former USSR, but even in the Russian Federation? In principle, it should be possible to set up at least a temporary joint licensing process involving both central and regional authorities, with smaller projects perhaps being much more under regional jurisdiction, without that the constitutional issue needs immediate solution.

There is a strong Russian tendency – at least evidenced by the central Moscow-based authorities – for very rigidly circumscribed bidding procedures. 'Objective', quasi-mathematical bidding concepts seem to have a strong appeal to the academic technocrats in Moscow. Not perhaps unlike the concepts of a planned economy, it provides the appearance – much less so a reality – of automatised selection of what is good for society. An 'auction' system – basically assignment of licences to the highest cash bidder – and a 'contest' system, based on a more qualitative assessment of a number of selection criteria – are envisaged to give force to the overall imposition of a bidding system by the 1992 subsoil law. This preference for bidding procedures may reflect the political and professional objective of the central authorities for control over *ad hoc* negotiations by and in the oil and gas regions.

The European experts were much less enthusiastic about rigid bidding procedures. Strictly regulated competitive bidding can discourage many qualified investors, add considerable delays, while still being subject to numerous political and biased influences. In an initial period, the objective was rather to get investment projects moving than to have a perfect system of licensing. Accordingly, the preference was rather for a less formal system of inviting offers for identified blocks and prospects.

16.4.5 Discrimination: in favour or against foreigners and Russians?

The issue of discrimination wakes up most of the dormant concerns about foreign penetration into Mother Russia: it is hard to ignore the fact that foreign investment requires some basic discrimination in favour of foreign companies – tax stability, foreign exchange repatriation, independent arbitration and respect for contractual engagements. This unavoidable discrimination in favour of foreign investors, necessary as it may be, feeds and provokes anxieties and resentment with the budding Russian companies who fear that in a competitive environment they will anyway be gobbled up by the international oil companies. A much deeper exploration of the discrimination issue is required. It will demonstrate that to attract foreign capital to high-risk areas, certain guarantees are indeed necessary. On the other hand, there may well be arguments for discrimination as well in favour of Russian companies. The evolution of the Norwegian, Italian, French and Japanese oil industry demonstrates that there are strong, for some convincing, arguments to provide a privileged access to oil and gas production to national companies, and indeed to force or induce foreign companies to get access to national reserves through the channel of national companies.

The issue of discrimination also plays an important role with respect to licensing: foreign companies in all likelihood require a standard international regime, adapted to the Russian environment (most probably production-sharing agreements with the usual accoutrements of such investment arrangements). Russian companies in the process of being born need some kind of standardised and rather simplified licensing process to confirm and to regularise their access to oil and gas resources, without intensive negotiation, basically some form of legal recognition of the *de facto* title their Communist precursors already enjoyed under the Soviet system.

16.4.6 Taxation

The issue of taxation in Russia has two dimensions. First, there is the familiar, but in Russia currently exacerbated tension between the central government in need of foreign exchange and the national oil industry; taxing the oil industry (domestic or prospective foreign investors in the future) is a natural remedy for a government strapped of cash. Price differentials between regulated domestic prices and world market prices expressed on the basis of the rouble/$ exchange rate create a potential for windfall profits, mainly by traders. Taxing these windfall profits by way of an export tax seems morally, politically and commercially legitimate. As a result, the domestic oil industry is starved of cash-flow, foreign exchange to purchase equipment and capital to undertake major rehabilitation or new projects; foreign investors, both those who already operate (e.g. 'White Nights') or those who contemplate major investment are wary because of the utter unpredictability of revenues. Second, there is a need for a stable and reasonable tax regime for foreign investors, with an added requirement to compensate pioneer investors for the political and commercial risks assumed. The central authorities seem to be moving towards a tax regime characterised by royalties, income taxes and the special profits tax (windfall profits, return-based oil tax) familiar from a number of developing countries and conceptualised in the 1970s by academic resource economists.

The European experts expressed considerable scepticism if a comprehensive oil tax regime should be legislated at this moment. The economic and fiscal environment for Russia's oil industry is far too clouded, and too much influenced by sudden U-turns of tax and economic policy and the tug-and-pull between the oil industry, the government and the regional authorities for a normal long-term oriented tax regime to evolve effectively. Windfall profit taxes can be good for political consumption and have a basis in the economic theory of mineral rents, but they may not be too suitable in such a volatile situation when the issue is that of how to encourage investment into high-risk situations. Accordingly, the recommendation was to leave major fiscal variables open to negotiation and to ensure that a contractually safeguarded fiscal regime for foreign investors evolves. In addition, there is the clear risk that the politically and publicly popular battle against 'oil speculators' could degenerate into overtaxation and thereby the destruction of one of Russia's most vital industries.

16.4.7 Role of the state in the oil and gas industries

Russian debate focuses very much on how the state and a future Russian oil and gas industry should interact. On one hand, advocates of state monopolies for oil and for gas would prefer a respective single state monopoly (one in oil and one in gas) covering Russia, much under the control of the previous state managers of the industry, perhaps even with regulatory and licensing powers. Westernised technocrats, on the other hand, seem to prefer privatisation (and it is not clear if what is meant is only a transformation to corporate status or the full sale of assets and shares to domestic and foreign investors) of many integrated oil or gas companies in different shapes and forms to create a competitive industry structure, with licensing and regulatory powers left with the Ministry of Energy and Fuel.

There seems to be a shift from the exclusive emphasis on privatisation *as soon as possible* to the quest for establishing a viable and effective system of state enterprises first; this, indeed, seems to be the gist of the advice given by a UK/Japanese/US advisory group to Rosneftegas. Indeed, Italian and French experiences indicate that state enterprises can be commercially viable and strong actors in the world oil industry provided they are given commercial autonomy, are subject to performance accountability and have to compete internationally. It is then rather 'corporatisation' than full-scale privatisation which should be undertaken at the moment. Here, advocates of a central solution would tend to see Rosneftegas become the one and only Russian state oil company, while actual tendencies towards setting up several integrated oil and gas companies (Lukoil; Yuganskneftegas; etc. seem to indicate rather the emergence of several main players. The dilemma of the Russian government is then how to exercise public ownership in these emerging oil and gas companies.

First, the question has to be resolved which government agency (Ministry of Energy/Fuel; Ministry for State Property; regional authorities; managers/employees) would hold shares and be entitled to exercise the control element inherent in share ownership. It is not easy to come to a systematic discussion and solution of these policy issues, since a number of actors – notably the State Property Committee, but also regional authorities (Komi Republic) reportedly have already started to set-up new oil companies or transform existing operations into oil companies on their own initiative.

Once the question of ownership and exercise of public shares were resolved, the next question is that of whether or not specific regulations and procedures (e.g. parliamentary scrutiny; inter-governmental coordination; standardisation of rules on executive, managerial and employee appointment contracts; financial accountability; commercial autonomy) should apply to public enterprises. Lastly, but perhaps most importantly, the Russian government's need to restructure the current oil and gas industry into viable individual entities, with probably one or several holding companies interposed between the political process and the commercial operations. Real, and probably partial, privatisation can and should only occur once these essential decisions have been taken and proven to be workable. European experts emphasised the usefulness of 'Golden Share' methods whereby the state retains some dominant influence irrespective of its share percentage as well as 'transition agreements' whereby public concerns and public service obligations of the state companies are stipulated to govern a transition period from full state-ownership to partial or full privatisation.

16.4.8 Pipelines

Control over and the ownership and usage rules for gas and oil pipelines will remain an essential factor of Russian oil and gas policies for a long time to come. All possible policies are under debate in Russia, with the entities currently controlling the pipeline network – including the central government – clearly in favour of retaining this important control lever in view of the decentralising or even centrifugal tendencies of the industry. European models under discussion are the mechanism of third-party access advocated by the EC Commission, the regulation of gas pipelines and usage terms by an independent gas regulator and the breaking-off of pipeline networks from integrated oil and gas companies for conversion into separate oil and gas transportation enterprises. The legal freedom to construct new pipelines was raised as an important lever to create a more competitive system.

16.5 CONCLUSION

The complex debates on Russian oil and gas policies, as evidenced by the petroleum law discussion, reflect the interests and attitudes of numerous players with often divergent interests, including domestic and foreign entities and their spokesmen. The ground under this debate is continuously shifting and it would seem pretentious to claim any power to forecast the ultimate outcome. Questions specific to foreign investment (licensing authority; taxation; non-discrimination; investment guarantees) are tied up with domestic issues (licensing for existing operations; re-capitalising and restructuring the Russian oil industry; emphasis on rapidly productive state monopolies or on a competitive industry perhaps more productive in the longer term). Foreign investment itself is fraught with the quite usual tensions: Need for capital, technology and modern business culture *versus* repugnance against letting foreign powers take over Russia's vital industry.

The Russian government, as other CIS-states, is now very much involved in negotiations under the European Energy Charter for its subsidiary protocols. If signed and ratified, these will create international law obligations for the CIS-states. Will these obligations in actual practice be complied with? Looking at the negotiations, one is struck by the fact that the negotiations are carried out by central Ministry (energy/foreign affairs) technocrats which are opposed strongly by both regional authorities and the leaders of the oil industry. Is the negotiation of international law obligations a strategy by the Ministry technocrats to impose their policies on a recalcitrant industry – and will this strategy ultimately work? As we all know, the oil industry needs a stable legal and institutional framework – but it is not very likely to arrive soon in Russia.

Chapter 17

The Restructuring of the Russian Oil Industry

Jonathan Price

17.1 INTRODUCTION

It is perhaps necessary in introducing this topic to give a little explanation as to how Daiwa Securities, which is known throughout the financial world for its activity in stock exchanges and capital markets, became involved in the Russian oil and gas business.

In 1989 Daiwa Europe, the European regional head office established an Energy Group staffed by experienced staff recruited from oil companies. The aim of the group was to arrange mergers and acquisitions in the oil and gas industry and to offer strategic advice to governments and to oil and gas companies. This group has been particularly successful in developing its business in the former Soviet Union and other emerging countries in Asia and was incorporated with the Central and East Europe group and the privatisation group in 1992 to form the Emerging Regions and Sectors Division.

17.2 STRUCTURE OF THE RUSSIAN OIL INDUSTRY

For the fifteen months commencing October 1991 the central co-ordinating body of the Russian oil industry was the Russian National Oil and Gas Corporation, Rosneftegas. Rosneftegas was created by the metamorphosis of the Soviet Oil and Gas Ministry into a private corporation which was approved by a Russian government decision in October 1991. It occupied the premises of the Ministry on the prime site overlooking the Kremlin across the Moscow river and employed almost all the former Ministry's civil servants.

As a child of the Ministry which had for decades ruled the industry with a rod of iron, Rosneftegas was considered by many outside Russia as a hangover from the old system and inherently bad. One did not have to look far for evidence that such a judgment was too simplistic. Rosneftegas was of course very concerned that the industry should not fragment, as its President and Board believed, in my view correctly, that an immediate breakup would precipitate a very steep decline in production, but this view did not mean that Rosneftegas wanted to maintain a stranglehold on the entire industry.

It is noteworthy that Rosneftegas was established on an explicitly democratic basis. The President, Lev Tchurilov, was elected on a free ballot against two other strong candidates, one of whom had been Deputy Soviet Oil and Gas Minister at the same time when Tchurilov was Minister. More significantly, the oil and gas production associations, which constitute the body of the industry, were not obliged to be members of Rosneftegas and indeed several prominent production associations did not join.

By mid 1992 the real power in the industry had started to drift away from Moscow, in favour of the production associations and their general directors – the famous 'oil generals'. To the extent that power remained in Moscow, it was wielded by the Ministry of Fuel and Energy, although the Ministry was handicapped by a lack of experienced oil personnel and for the first half of 1992 by having as Minister a man not well regarded by the oil generals.

In 1992 therefore the structure of the industry had the Ministry at the top representing the state; Rosneftegas beneath the Ministry acting as day-to-day central co-ordinator for the industry and continuing many of statistical, reporting and administrative functions formerly carried out by the Soviet Ministry. In the field, the oil and gas production units, the NGDU's were grouped on a regional basis together with many types of service and 'social' unit into production associations, employing up to 100,000 people each. Over 90 per cent of these associations were members of Rosneftegas, the main exception being the members of Lukoil, a rival body comprising one production association and two refineries in Western Siberia.

The Russian oil refineries were not generally members of Rosneftegas, as that part of the industry was grouped under a very similar body called Rosnefteprodukt.

17.3 ROLE OF INTERNATIONAL ADVISERS

Soon after the establishment of Rosneftegas, its President and Board decided that in order to play a decisive role in the restructuring of the industry in the transition to a market economy, which they were determined to do, they needed expert advice. They accordingly organised a competitive tender among investment banks and in January 1992 appointed Daiwa Europe and Bankers Trust as joint advisers.

The appointment had two phases, each planned to last six months. The first phase was the preparation of a report advising Rosneftegas on the overall structure of the industry.

The task for the advisers was not clearly defined by Rosneftegas, as the Board had only the vaguest idea of what it was trying to do. It amounted in fact to the creation of a vision of how the industry should look in the future and a plan for its implementation.

The second phase of the appointment was the implementation of the plan.

17.4 DIFFICULTIES FACED BY THE INDUSTRY

In 1992 the Russian oil industry was faced with a series of pressing problems, both internal and external. Lack of capital investment in equipment and infrastructure was exacerbating a production decline, while a reduction in exploration drilling and the development of new fields meant that the rate of decline could only accelerate. Uncontrolled inflation in the cost of inputs such as equipment, combined with a strictly controlled domestic price and restrictions on exports meant that refineries and production associations quickly built up mountainous inter-company debts. This problem alone threatened at one stage to bring production to an almost complete stop. The decline in central authority meant that supplies could not be assured, even at the inflated prices.

In addition to these physical problems, Rosneftegas and the production associations were struggling with philosophical or rather psychological difficulties. There is very little consensus within the industry or within the government as to whether the industry should be privatised and if so, when, or indeed what privatisation should mean. The oil generals are forced to wrestle with unfamiliar concepts such as privatisation when all their available time is taken up fire-fighting serious practical problems. The generals are in any case ill equipped to deal with these new issues as they are unused to thinking in conceptual rather than practical terms. They are also in many cases unused to dealing with foreigners and as a result meetings with Western bankers can easily turn into a dialogue of the deaf unless the bankers take great care to express themselves as clearly as possible.

This unfamiliarity can often extend to outright suspicion of foreigners, whom they believe to be out to cheat them of their hard earned cash. Business is seen as a zero sum game and win-win negotiating is one of the most difficult concepts to convey.

17.5 WESTERN 'SOLUTIONS'

Against this background it is easy to see why glib Western recipes for change such as: instant price liberalisation; anti-trust breakup of production associations; bankruptcy as a means of restructuring; transfer of ownership of oil reserves to lowest level; taxation of profit rather than revenue; abolition of Rosneftegas and introduction of massive foreign investment, have been seen as recipes for Western domination of the Russian oil industry, rather than its survival.

Foreign investment in particular has been seen as something of a Trojan horse even when well intentioned.

17.6 RUSSIAN 'SOLUTIONS'

The preliminary Russian 'solutions' to the problems received an equally cold reaction from foreigners: delayed price liberalisation; maintenance of quotas for production and export; continuing of state order system; establishment of a limited number of vertically integrated holding companies; and the prevention of competition and bankruptcy of production associations.

17.7 CONCLUSIONS OF ADVISERS

Faced with a unique situation in the field of strategic advice and the lack of an obvious starting point, Daiwa decided to develop a framework within which to analyse the vision of the future. The framework was based on a recognition of the fact that the future of the industry was a combination of internal factors – essentially the structure of the industry; and external factors – the policy environment in which it operates.

Operating within this framework are eight instruments, or levers of change available for the government to use. On the external, policy side these are: oil and gas legislation; taxation; contracts; and pricing. On the internal, industry structure side, they are: private ownership; market structures; competition; and demarcation of responsibilities. (The last of these refers to the fact that oil production associations currently undertake all sorts of non-business functions such as schooling, agriculture, etc.)

The framework and the levers of change can be best appreciated in the following chart.

Figure 17.1 Key Objectives of the Interim Report

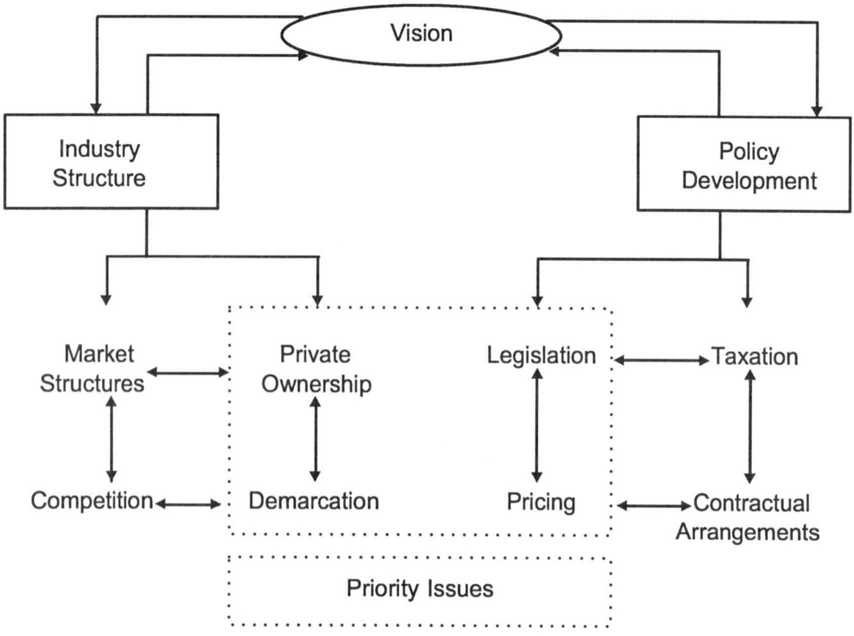

Having thus analysed the situation the industry was in, it was possible to define a list of objectives for both investment policy and industry structure. In their simplest form, the policy objectives were defined as:

1. creation of an attractive business framework (for Russian production associations themselves as much as for foreigners);
2. adequate legal protection;
3. competitive financial returns for investors;
4. flexible contractual arrangements.

For industry structure:

1. creation of proper market mechanisms;
2. development of a variety of organisational forms;
3. promotion of private ownership to stimulate motivation and improve accountability.

The report concluded among other things that a small number of production associations could be privatised as soon as possible on a pilot basis. This recommendation was accepted and acted on and the two international advisers were each allocated two associations to corporatise and privatise before the end of 1992, one in Western Siberia and one in the Volga/Urals basin.

17.8 RECENT EVENTS

Another key conclusion of the report from Daiwa's point of view, although resisted by our American co-advisers, was that a centralised body such as Rosneftegas should continue to play a major role in the industry at least for a transitional period. We did not feel that a complete free-for-all survival of the fittest was a practical proposition in the short term, unless one was prepared to countenance severe energy shortages for consumers.

Since the report was submitted, the Russian government has acted to re-establish its authority over the industry and regularise the privatisation process which was in danger of developing into a rape of national assets. Rosneftegas is at the time of writing once more metamorphosing, this time into Rosneft, which will be the state holding company for its portion of the shares of the oil production associations (in most cases 38 per cent). The remainder of the shares are being distributed to employees and local residents with a small proportion being sold for privatisation vouchers. The state's holding is expressly stated by the decree establishing Rosneft and ordering the privatisation to be for a transitional period of three years, without saying what will happen at that time.

It is significant that there is no restriction on foreign ownership of shares contained in the decree. This leaves open the theoretical possibility that foreign investors could buy shares from workers or local citizens immediately or from Rosneft in three years' time.

17.9 OUTSTANDING ISSUES

Despite the fact that much progress has been made and many of the report's detailed conclusions have been implemented (some as a result of the report, others merely coincidentally) many difficult issues remain outstanding. One of the most intractable is the tension between the Russian Federal government and the regional governments, whether of oblasts or of autonomous republics. This tension is manifesting itself in arguments over the allocation of shares; for example in one autonomous republic, the parliament is demanding that they receive half of the state's share allocation from the local production association, leaving Rosneft with only 19 per cent.

A similar tension exists between the production associations themselves and their local governments. The latter are in many cases demanding substantial rights over the business of the production associations which they perceive to be their only chance of escaping bankruptcy. The former of course have no intention of allowing their industry to be run by local bureaucrats who know nothing of oil, particularly as they have only recently escaped from the control of the central bureaucracy.

Finally there exists considerable tension over the question of the domestic price of oil and of oil products. The producers need a liberalisation as soon as possible if they are to become independent oil companies, but the consumers, whether state companies or other state bodies such as Agrokom cannot even afford the current prices. It will be interesting to see how the Prime Minister, who (at the time of writing) is reputed to be very pro industry, but whose background is in energy, deals with this question. The advisers for their part urged as swift a liberalisation as possible, but without much confidence that their advice on that point would be heeded.

Chapter 18

Environmental Protection Legislation in Russia's Oil and Gas Industry

Nicholas A. Robinson

18.1 INTRODUCTION

There has never been a period of such profound redefinition, in a relatively peaceful if nonetheless stressful way, as the Russian Federation confronts today. While local authorities continue to compete with Moscow's central government, and while in Moscow the Supreme Soviet still functions under the 1977 Constitution as the popularly elected presidency of Boris Yeltsin builds a new governing system, the accretion of daily decisions is assembling the structure of the new Russian state. Amidst this gradual but profound revolution, the production of natural resources haltingly continues, and it too faces a challenge of redefinition.

The sphere of producing oil and natural gas faces redefinition induced by the urgent need to modernise the production and distribution infrastructure. New equipment and the retraining of management and workers is needed to avoid wastage, achieve efficient production levels, and integrate sales into the international market. These objectives cannot be realised unless at the same time world standards for environmental protection are established and attained. Again, retooling of all levels of operations and retraining of personnel is needed to make this goal a reality.

The demand for environmental protection is a social and political one. Many Russians would say it is a moral demand. Those who look only at economic or technical needs of Russia's oil and gas industry will make a colossal blunder if they ignore the environmental dimension. Local and regional authorities feel the political pressure to assure the public that environmental protection will advance together with new economic measures.

An opinion poll, conducted in June 1993 in 12 Russian regions by the Russian Academy of Sciences Institute on Sociology, showed that even in this period of hyperinflation most Russians stated that their greatest fears were inflation (69.7 per cent), the growing crime rate (49 per cent), and environmental pollution (30.7 per cent).[1] Russian media regularly report

---

1.   British Broadcasting System, World Service (English Broadcast, 0738 Greenwich Meantime, 24 July 1993).

environmental news, and green political groups, such as the Socio-Ecological Union, have active chapters throughout Russia. Moreover, although Vice President Alexander Rutskoi and his supporters disagreed profoundly with President Yeltsin and his supporters, they espoused rather similar demands for protection of Russia's nature, *'Priroda'*.

Given this constant public pressure on Russian policy-makers to restore environmentally damaged areas, to maintain ecological systems and avert new contamination, it is important to survey what any new environmental protection legislation might require for production in the Russian Federation. Proposals for conservation and environmental protection ('C & EP') legislation have been made by the University of Houston Law Center (UHLC),[2] by the World Bank, and others. The possible scope for new Russian environmental legislation is outlined here. Where the word 'conservation' is used, it is in its narrow sense of avoiding waste; where 'environmental protection' is used, the meaning is broader, encompassing all ecological and nature protection activities.

Preparation of any proposed 'Petroleum Conservation and Environmental Protection Act', such as that of the University of Houston Law Center in collaboration with the Ministry of Fuel and Energy and the State Committee on Fuel and Energy of the Russian Federation, will also need to consult additional Russian ministries in Moscow. There must be consultations with the Ministry of Ecology and Natural Resources. This Ministry, headed by Victor I. Danilov-Danilien, has relevant sectors on Environmental Impact, Minerals and Geology (Prof. Juri M. Arsky) and on Protected Territories where oil and gas development would be prohibited (Prof. Nikita F. Glazovinski) and on Environmental Law (formerly headed by Prof. Oleg S. Kolbasov). In addition, separate state committees exist for Hunting and Fishing, the Arctic Region, Ecological Emergencies and Sanitary Control. All these other authorities have jurisdiction over aspects of oil and gas development, as do regional or autonomous republic and local authorities within the constituent geographic areas of the Russian Federation.

18.2 THE LEGAL BACKGROUND

Before evaluating possible C & EP legislation, it will be useful to put the proposed law into its legal contexts. The first context is the prevailing pattern of oil and gas law as it developed in United States of America. Because oil was first produced in large scale in the USA, the American legal approach has had a significant influence on the content of oil and gas law internationally. For instance, the UHLC drafting groups drew on these prevailing patterns of regulation, especially as to conservation of oil and gas and efficient production and operations. The second context is the current state of Russian law reform

---

2. The University of Houston Law Center undertook drafting model laws for the Russian Ministry of Fuel under Minister Lapoukin, submitting a draft on 6 March 1992. The European Bank for Reconstruction and Development provided financial support for parts of this project.

and the allocation of competence in the Russian Federation among ministries and between federal and regional or local authorities. The third is the fact that many private and governmental interests are simultaneously at work assisting Russia as to oil and gas matters, and since any C & EP legislation affects those endeavours, and vice versa, they should be kept in mind.

18.2.1 Evolution of oil and gas law in the USA

Oil and gas production began in 1859 with the drilling of the first well in the United States. Since then, elaborate private law contracts, leases, and interests have been developed to provide a basis for worldwide petroleum production and commerce. Two sets of governmental regulations have emerged as well: (1) conservation regimes and (2) environmental protection regimes.

In the early twentieth century, state governments in the USA were authorised to 'prevent waste' of oil and gas from production methods. At Common Law, a property owner could 'capture' oil and gas from under his land and become its owner. In production, oil could be lost through gushers spilling oil into the ground or through drawing down a subterranean pool in such a way as to leave other oil in the reservoir which the owner of the land above it could not recover ('economic waste'). To 'conserve' oil for maximum production, and protect the correlative rights of other property owners to capture their fair share of oil underlying their land, laws developed to protect such rights by imposing 'conservation regulations' restricting the spacing and location of wells and limiting the production levels.

States established commissions, or other governmental authorities, to promulgate rules for oil and gas conservation, and to administer such rules. Oil fields were unitised to permit allocation of fair shares and market demand prorating. Rules were set for maximum efficient rates of recovery, for compensating non-participating real property interests, for commencing and ceasing operations, and related matters.

These controls on private property were transformed into comparable rules to be followed in the private leasing of governmental public lands and off-shore areas. The Outer Continental Shelf Lands Act[3] governs leases for exploration and production of oil on the outer continent shelf to oil companies through competitive bidding. Leases cover exploration and production.

The second major area of regulation covers environmental protection. Oil and gas exploration and production are subject to the National Environmental Policy Act's rules for Environmental Impact Assessment (EIA) at the federal level,[4] and half the states have EIA laws as well for state operations. Environmental laws also govern exploration and production in wetlands, in or near natural wildlife habitats, and regulate operations to prevent air and water pollution, and to manage solid and hazardous wastes. Restoration of environmental conditions in well fields is required after production ceases.

The *Exxon Valdez* accident in Alaska resulted in enactment of new federal

---

3. US Code, vol. 42, sections 131 *et seq.*
4. US Code, vol. 42, sections 4321 *et seq.* and Part 1500, Code of Federal Regulations, vol. 40.

legislation. Congress adopted The Oil Pollution Act of 1990, to create an Oil Spill Liability Trust Fund, with a system of fines and penalties.

18.2.2 The contemporary Russian legal context

The Russian Federation is redefining the allocation of competence between Federation central authority and the constituent republic or regional authorities. Establishment of a recent treaty among constituent republics which had declared their sovereignty is a significant step towards completing the draft of a new Constitution which will define each level's competence.

The Russian Federation's Supreme Soviet has enacted a Land Use Code (1991), a Law on Local Self-Government (1991) a Law on the Protection of the Ambient Environment (19 December 1991, No. 2060-1), and a Law on Natural Resources (21 February 1992). The allocation of competence to autonomous republics, krays and oblasts, autonomous areas (autonomous okrugs and oblasts), and to municipalities and rayons is generally provided in these laws, but may be redefined further in the new Constitution.

In general, local control is provided over whether to develop a natural resources and how to do so. As a matter of policy, protection of life and health is to be given precedence, and a scientific balance for the rational development of natural resources, while ensuring healthy and favourable ecological conditions, is encouraged. The Federal government has broad authority to 'coordinate the activities of ministries, departments and other institutions and organisations on the Territory of the Russian Federation in the Field of the protection of the ambient natural environment' (Article 6, Environmental Protection Law of 19 December 1991). The Ministry of Ecology and Natural Resources has 'control' authority over the use and protection of 'lands, mineral wealth, surface and ground waters, air, forests, flora and fauna, natural resources, the continental shelf and marine economic zone' (Article 7, ibid.). The Ministry has power to establish rules and monitor conditions, and 'restrict or suspend enterprise activities and objectives, regardless of their status and forms of property, if their operation results in violation' of environmental rules. The Ministry's decisions are binding on all juridical entities.

Republics within the Russian Federation can establish their own policies, plan for protection of the environment, issue permits for the use of land, minerals, waters, forests and flora and fauna, and generally exercise state ecological control. Localities can prohibit construction of ecologically harmful activity, issue use permits, establish and protect nature sanctuaries, and exercise powers allocated under the Law on Local Self-Government. The adoption of the Federal Treaty[5] is the basic act confirming the often co-equal powers of local authorities with Moscow. The Russian Constitution will incorporate the terms of this treaty. This allocation of governmental competence also now encompasses separate roles for private enterprises and non-governmental organisations. The Environmental Protection Law of 19

5.   O Federativnom Dogovore, *Vedomosti RF*, No. 17, Item 898 (1992).

December 1991 (Article 13) for instance, gives public ecological societies the right to function, demonstrate, participate in EIA and 'to demand the allocation of timely, authentic, and complete information on pollution of the ambient environment or nature protection'. They can also demand initiation of EIA ('state ecological examinations'). Private enterprises, whether shareholding companies (*aktsionernoe obshchestro*) or joint ventures, may obtain rights to the use of resources, but the natural resources belong to the people. Since land is a state property, the use of land is not 'private property' in a western sense of absolute title (e.g. at English Common Law, fee simple). Rather, it is a usufruct as in a civil law context (*ius utendi et fruendi*). Private enterprises can obtain the use of land for natural resource development where land is located and which authority has competence to allocate its use is often difficult to ascertain.

In addition to these new laws, many ministries at the federal or local level have issued their own decrees and regulations relevant to oil and gas issues. Thus, the State Gas Concern ('Gasprom') has temporary regulations for the evaluation of environmental impact in feasibility studies, construction of new facilities and reconstruction or expansion of existing facilities for development of hydrocarbon facilities (effective 1 June 1992).

In the past, oil and gas extraction was a governmental activity. The production authority in the USSR was given full powers over the area of its extraction. There is no tradition of needing to develop rules regarding waste or conservation (unitisation was unnecessary). Measures for maximising efficiency in production and transport and storage of oil and gas are largely absent from Russian practice. No competing economic oil and gas interest existed. While substantial oil and gas was wasted, no countervailing interests had the right to identify and stop the waste, or encourage a regulated flow. Since independent environmental controls over pollution were very weak before 1990, and the stronger legal controls since then have not yet been fully implemented, there is no experience with environmental protection measures in Russian oil and gas activities. With the advent of democratically elected local legislatures, the newly installed Peoples Deputies to Local Soviets have complained about pollution and used their authority to prevent new or expanded activities which pollute.

18.2.3 Various oil and gas study initiatives

In addition to such C & EP legislation as proposed by the UHLC Project, the World Bank is commissioning the preparation of an EIA for the Russian Petroleum Critical Imports Loan, on behalf of the State Committee of Fuel and Power and the Ministry of Ecology and Natural Resources. The study is to focus on the West Siberia oil and gas fields. The results of this study would be useful in evaluating the type of legal provisions which the C & EP legislation could contain. The Terms of Reference for the World Bank's Environmental Assessment (pursuant to the World Bank's Operational Directive 4.01 on Environmental Assessment), cover the following topics:

- Introduction
  - A. Brief history of Russian oil and gas development
  - B. Description of West Siberia oil and gas field
  - C. Economic considerations of the West Siberia field
  - D. Environmental and social issues relating to oil and gas development in West Siberia.

- Policy, Legal and Administrative Framework
  - A. Russian environmental policy for EA
  - B. Russian environmental legislation regarding EA
  - C. Environmental institutions regarding EA

- Project Description
  - A. Location
  - B. Objectives
  - C. Proposed activities

- Baseline Information
  - A. Physical characteristics of the project area
  - B. Biological characteristics of the project area
  - C. Socioeconomic characteristics of the project area

- Environmental and Social Project Impacts (positive and negative)
  - A. Physical
  - B. Biological
  - C. Socioeconomic

- Analysis of Alternatives
  - A. Development of new fields
  - B. New drilling in existing fields
  - C. Others
  - D. No project

- Proposed Mitigation Measures (Mitigation Plan)
  - A. Environmental protection standards
  - B. Environmental training and management
  - C. Enforcement of environmental regulations
  - D. Proposed environmental studies to be included in the project
    1. Type of studies
    2. Location of proposed studies
    3. Recommended institutions to conduct study
    4. Estimates of study costs

- Proposed Environmental Supervision and Monitoring Plan

- Extent of Participation by Affected Populations

The scope of discussion is to be as follows:

To a degree, it is important to discuss some issues which are commonly associated with oil and gas development projects in the summary even if these issues are not likely to be a serious problem with the proposed project. For instance, deforestation is commonly associated with hydrocarbon development projects. Even if deforestation were found to not be a likely issue with the proposed project, the summary should note that it would not be a serious project impact. Since the summary may be the only environmental document that will be presented to them, the summary must provide a clear picture of both the important environmental and social issues which could present serious problems and provide an equally clear picture of which issues are not likely to cause serious negative impacts.

An interdisciplinary team of Russian environmental experts has undertaken to prepare the EIA. This study has informally educated leading ecological and environmental protection citizen organisations about the environmental protection aspects of oil and gas production. Such concerns, therefore, are likely to be raised when any C & EP law is submitted to the Russian Parliament.

18.3 GENERAL CONSIDERATIONS FOR CONSERVATION AND ENVIRONMENTAL PROTECTION ACT

There are broad comments that can be made regarding the style of any C & EP legislation. These observations are as follows:

18.3.1 Style

First, much C & EP legislation in Europe or the USA is more detailed than is traditional in Russian legislation. A set of fundamental principles should be added at the outset, to clarify the policy of the law and guide a reader in interpreting the statute. Such Fundamentals (*oznovy*) would strengthen the normative force of any statute, or structure the systems that the Republics and oblasts in the Russian Federation will enact.

It is not customary in Russian legislative drafting to provide a title or definitions. The objectives appear usually as preambular policy introducing the statute or as Fundamental Principles. Definitions are usually not used, although Russian legislation would be clearer and more effective if definitions were included. Many of the definitions here, however, are not needed (as 'Act', or 'Conservation') or are clear enough without definition ('natural gas" or 'gas' or 'oil') and the actual definition does not seem to make a significant difference to the subsequent text. Other definitions are substantive in nature and could usefully be elaborated in the body of the law ('MER' or 'Waste'). The several definitions in Chapters G and H could be incorporated into the texts.

On balance, to conform with Russian legislative style it is appropriate to incorporate all these definitions into the body of the statute rather than include them in a separate section.

18.3.2 Environmental impact assessment (EIA)

Second, C & EP legislation should include EIA provisions to conform more fully to standard practices,[6] *and* to apply to the exploration *and* production *and* cessation of production aspects of petroleum generation. Definition of these stages should be provided.

---

6. Such as required by the European Community Directive on EIA, 85/337/EEC.

18.3.3 Hazardous chemical management

Third, provision should be made for hazardous chemical management. In many regimes including the environmental laws in the USA, oil is separately regulated from other hazardous substances in order to provide regular and consistent controls for the entire oil industry. The Russian Federation has not yet enacted any laws on hazardous substances and waste. In order to eliminate uncertainty about liability and to encourage investment in modernising and expanding the Russian oil and gas industry, it would be useful to establish a management regime for oil and gas related substances. The regime could cover the following elements:

1. There are no waste storage, treatment or disposal facilities in Russia. Separate regimes, or best management practices systems, should be established for each waste associated with petroleum production. These methods will vary from region to region depending on latitude, hydrologic conditions, etc. Improper waste practices, especially in already polluted areas or in remote areas, can present long-term threats to health and the environment. Unless such regimes are established, local authorities may resist new or upgraded production operations, or may adopt their own rules.

2. With regard to drilling wastes, provision should be made to incorporate leak minimisation into facility design and maintenance, e.g. requiring oil sumps from rainwater drains; methods for handling spent drilling muds, especially oil based muds or water muds with oil additives. If salt contents are high, disposal should avoid altering soils or vegetation. Mud pits should be lined with impermeable membranes.

3. With regard to production wastes, water should be treated to remove oils and solids. Reinjection may be the only economically viable option in many areas.

4. Types of wastes and possible methods of disposal include the following:

Related wastes	Treatment options
Sludge	Burial; incineration; land application
Liquid	Biological; chemical, mechanical treatment.
Process water; washwater	Biological treatment; incineration (if oil content high); chemical treatment; injection; treat/recycle.
Gases	Scrubber unit; catalytic burner; injection.
Produced water	Downhole disposal; treat and discharge; water flooding.
Filters	Incineration; treatment and land fill.

Oil-contaminated soils	Incinerate; stabilise and bury; land farming.
Water base muds/cuttings	Recycling muds; injection; solidification and burial; stabilisation and/or washing for use as road fill; land spreading.
Oil base muds/cuttings	Recycle muds; reinjection; solidification and burial; stabilisation; land farming; incineration for use as road fill or burial.
Spent treatment fluids	Reinjection of water-based material; recycle or incinerate oil-based material.
Unused drilling chemicals	Chemically neutralise and bury; solidify and bury.
Waste lubricants	Recycle, fuel; incinerate.
Domestic refuse	(Petruciable wastes) incineration; land fill; composing; injection.
Industrial refuse (inorganic)	Recycle; incinerate; burial.
Squeeze/fracturing fluids	Recycle; injection; burial.
Tank and plant sludges	Recycle for increased recovery (refinery); reinjection; incinerate; or solidify; stabilise and bury.

Regime for used or waste oils could approximate the European Community's Directives on the Disposal of Waste Oils.[7] To adhere to EC Directives, Russian Law should require collection and reuse of such oil, and prohibit its discharge into waters, drainage systems, or soils. A permit system, presumably under the purview of the Ministry of Ecology and Natural Resources, for disposal or reuse or burning of waste oils, would be required. While these Directives apply primarily to waste lubricating oils or used oils from refineries, they illustrate the standard of environmental protection which Russian petroleum law should use as a guide.

7.   75/437/EEC and 87/101/EEC.

18.4 SPECIFIC ISSUES FOR CONSIDERATION IN C & EP LEGISLATION

18.4.1 Competent authority

The C & EP law can encompass licensing, conservation and environmental protection roles. It may be sensible to combine licensing and oil and gas production conservation authorities in one agency. It is doubtful whether environmental protection can be consolidated (since Russian law already provides otherwise), or should be. Comparative environmental law experience in most nations reveals a consensus not to combine these roles, since to do so compromises the independent judgment of the environmental officials. The prior Soviet Union practice was to combine production and environmental control groups together, and invariably in order to fulfil production plans the environmental controls were ignored or rejected in favour or maximising production.

The 'single-window' for licensing of exploration and production is a useful measure to streamline Russian practices. To be such a 'single-window' in actuality, the already adopted Russian Law on Natural Resources licensing provisions could be revised to consolidate licensing for oil and gas in the Federal Competent Authority. Environmental regulatory tasks should be removed from the Competent Authority's responsibilities.

In providing legislation for 'Confidentiality of Certain Licenses Information', while absolutely necessary to protect competitive positions and proprietary information, the legislation should not restrict access to ecological baseline data.

Similarly, defining dispute settlements, such as those 'Disputes Between The Authority and Licensees', can allow for the international arbitration of exploration plans or production plans. Other disputes are to be decided by 'Arbitrazh'. In either event, it is probably not appropriate to submit environmental protection disputes to either dispute resolution processes.

In providing for 'Administrative Orders' and 'Adoption of Rules', legislation should expressly provide for the publication of such document in adequate numbers to provide copies to all other authorities, to the licensee and other enterprises, and to all citizens, ecological and other groups. These printed copies should also be posted for the general public to read. Unless the law requires such printing and dissemination, Russian practice has been not to do so. The success of the law will depend on these seemingly simple requirements. It will not be enough to rely on newspaper publication, or a single office copy on file for the public to inspect.

18.4.2 Exploration and production plans'

The provision of a system for Exploration Plans and Development and Production Plans is a useful system to ensure that petroleum resources are prudently developed. The Plan should be required to provide specific means for complying with all environmental protection rules, not just those 'delegated to the Competent Authority'. Potentially, the Plan provides a mechanism for consolidating compliance with all applicable local, regional and federal environmental requirements in one document. This provides an economy of procedure. One EIA can be provided per plan, and the presence of one master plan for use by all authorities should be an extremely valuable and efficient innovation.

The EIA process provided for Exploration Drilling under Production Licence has rather short time periods. There is no process for public notice and hearings. Presumably, this procedure should follow whatever standard process for EIA procedures is adopted by the Ministry of Ecology and Natural Resources. Since the Exploration Licence is non-exclusive (Article 6 of the Licence Law), it is the Production Licence under which the Exploration Drilling is allowed. No use of a Production Licence to drill may proceed without EIA. To make the EIA effective, the data used in Exploration Plans should be studied and expanded upon for the Exploration Drilling and the full Production Plan. This effectively provides for a tiering of EIA in three phases. This is now implicit in the text, and perhaps could be made explicit.

There is no provision for minimising the adverse environmental effects during exploration of transportation, roads, airstrips, site clearance, borrow sites, temporary base camps, water supplies and wastes, in connection with the exploration plan and drilling. Provision for exploratory well abandonment for dry holes and site restoration might be made (compare Article 21 on 'well abandonment').

18.4.3 Operational requirements

The conservation operations should be well defined to avoid waste. Emergency preparedness could be expanded to include fires, spills, explosions, civil disorder, weather episodes, natural catastrophes (earthquakes, floods), and medical emergencies. Local fire protection and hospital authorities should be referenced and included in emergency planning.

18.4.4 Environment and safety

The requirement to produce baseline data on site contamination for an Exploration Plan, or a Development and Production Plan could be identified as a desirable or necessary component of the EIA. The limitation of liability for past site conditions will be difficult to establish in practice unless a detailed site report is assembled.

Environmental management provisions should be included. In the training requirements, some provision could be included to assure that environmental personnel will meet the examination standards to be established by the Ministry of Ecology and Natural Resources.

In any provisions on EIA, requirements should be made for EIA to list *zapovedniki*, *zakhazniki*, and national parks and other legally protected natural areas. Moreover, this 'baseline' data is very different than the reference to baseline data which is a contamination site study. Perhaps different terms should be used.

In general, the EIA provisions should correspond with those to be developed by the Ministry of Ecology and Natural Resources. Reference to cumulative impact should be included, as this is not usually understood to be subsumed in 'indirect' impacts. The EIA provisions can provide for a scoping process, although reference is made to the appropriate extent of planned activity being the guide for the EIA. This misapprehends 'scoping' which is a consultative process of gathering possibly affected and interested authorities and persons together to decide which issues should be studied in depth and which are adequately understood with less study. Scoping helps avoid unnecessary study, thereby saving costs and promoting efficiency in the EIA procedure.

18.4.5 Oil spill preparedness plans and fund

Useful provisions comparable to laws now in place in the USA or in international practice should be included for oil spill and response. Each licensee should be required to make payments, in hard currency, to the emergency fund. Each licensee should also be required to establish a reserve fund for financing emergency its own response efforts.

The responsibility for actual clean-up activity could be based in the Competent Authority. This is a remedial activity requiring some expertise, and is not the same as an environmental regulatory duty of the Ministry of Ecology and Natural Resources. Since the USA has an off-shore Oil Spill Emergency Fund for the Bering Sea area, it is useful for Russia to have a comparable level of protection in this shared area. Russia already cooperates in the Helsinki Convention for Protection of the Baltic Sea.

18.5 ADDITIONAL POSSIBLE QUESTIONS

Any C & EP legislation should also consider a range of related questions. Four relatively obvious ones are the following:

1. Does this statute intend to require Licensees to perform environmental audits?
2. Should this statute require restoration of disturbed areas?
3. Should the Transportation Treaty require (a) use of transboundary EIA (UNECE Espoo Convention), and (b) include an international law dispute resolution clause?
4. Should the C & EP law contain a more focused set of special phased-implementation provisions for the transition period during which the competent authority is established and the new conservation and environmental authority is established and the new conservation and environmental protection rules are developed and applied? Russia's existing Producer Associations are not structured like an international petroleum

enterprise, have no environmental policies, staffs or budgets, and are ill-equipped to understand and observe the provisions of this draft C & EP law.

18.6 ADDITIONAL POSSIBLE CONSULTANTS

The European Bank for Reconstruction and Development may wish to obtain other reactions to the draft C & EP law from within Russia. The Bank's environmental mandate is served at least by ensuring that the Russian Ministry of Ecology and Natural Resources is consulted. The following other interested entities could be considered for consultations.

It is preferable in a federal system to allow each level of government to apply its appropriate environmental protection expertise, as an exercise of the principle of subsidiarity. It is problematic whether a sound administrative system can combine both environmental protection and petroleum production regulation in the same authority, as the C & EP Act proposes. It is also doubtful that the same authority could (or should) exercise *all* environmental protection competency. Environmental issues involve different disciplines, different constituencies and different recourse systems from those involved in regulating the production of oil and gas. For example, local residents clearly have a role to play in environmental matters, but are not specialists in the contract or management issues of petroleum production; recourse for determining whether a foreign investor has complied with standards for oil or gas production, accounting and management could be referred to international arbitration to settle disputes, but recourse for determining whether waters have been contaminated or whether a nature refuge (*zapovedniki* or *zakhazniki*) has been injured is appropriately handled under Russian administrative or judicial processes.

Since the Russian Federation is the largest country in the world (17,000,000 sq. km) with 21 republics, 10 autonomous regions or districts, 6 territories, 49 regions, 3,220 cities and towns, 1,837 rural communities, 23,197 villages, containing more than 100 cultural nationalities among its 150,000,000 people, it is unrealistic to try to consolidate all environmental protection in one 'complete authority'. As a practical matter, a more pluralistic approach is required.

Chapter 19

Oil and Gas in Central and Eastern Europe[1,2]

Doran Doeh

19.1 INTRODUCTION

In Russia, they have an unusual story about the creation of the world. They say that God had a lot of precious stones, metals and minerals of all kinds left over when he finished. He needed a vast space in which to place them, so he buried them in Siberia. Then he covered the whole area with snow, so that no one should find them.

Like the snow in the Russian story, a lot of confusion covers this subject. It concerns an enormous geographical area and a wide range of activities. There is relatively little law specifically governing oil and gas in this region. However, legal problems of a general kind are among the foremost concerns of those involved in oil and gas activity there. Many of these raise fundamental issues such as the very nature of the state, the extent of its powers and authority and even the extent to which law can be distinguished from political policy. Lawyers find themselves among the foremost of professionals consulted by those in business and in politics who seek strategies for dealing with these fundamental problems. A practising lawyer must reconsider at a very basic level, the nature of law and of legal systems, the reasons why people obey the laws and comply with their legal obligations and how these can be enforced.

The object of this chapter will therefore be to present a lawyer's view of developments rather than to concentrate on specific legal questions. It will focus first on some general observations, followed by brief country reports.

---

1. This chapter does not contain definitive advice. It should not therefore be used as a basis for giving definitive advice without checking the primary sources.

2. The phrase 'Central Europe' is used here to refer to the former Soviet bloc outside the former Soviet Union. It does not include Germany and Austria, although a traditional definition would do so. The term 'Eastern Europe' is used to include the whole of the former USSR. This includes Siberia and the Central Asian Republics.

19.2 OVERVIEW

19.2.1 Regional interdependence

One of the most striking things about the area as a whole is the degree to which it was – and remains to a significant extent – dependent on supplies of petroleum from the former Soviet Union. The two main reasons are the nature of the existing transportation infrastructure and (decreasingly, however, outside of Russia itself) Russian price subsidies.

Transportation

Oil, including both crude oil and refined products is easily transportable where good transportation exists – by ship, by river barge, by road tanker, as well as by pipeline. However in Central and Eastern Europe the modes of transport alternative to pipelines are in many places not practicable. The road network is very poor. This presents particularly serious difficulties in the huge land-mass of the former Soviet Union and those Central European countries without sea ports. To make things worse for certain countries, access to the Adriatic Sea has been disrupted by the civil war in the former Yugoslavia. Those countries with access to the Baltic Sea have found it easiest to diversify their sources of oil.

The desire of Central and Eastern European countries to reduce dependence on Russia would be understandable even if only political reasons were driving it. However, the sharp drop in Russian oil production in recent years has also meant that less Russian oil is available for sale on preferential terms outside Russia. The need to improve the oil transportation infrastructure is therefore of great importance, but for the time being the existing oil pipeline network in and from the former Soviet Union remains an important – and in some places, critical – source of oil supply. Pipeline transportation is even more essential for gas. Methane, which is of primary importance for domestic and industrial use, is too volatile to be readily transported over land by means other than pipeline. It can be converted into liquid natural gas (LNG) by cooling but this is only practicable if there is access to the sea and it is expensive.

The gas pipeline network extends all the way from Siberia to Western Europe. Gas from Russia is supplied to Germany, Austria, France and Italy, a supply which is likely to increase since, by some estimates, Russia holds over 35 per cent of the world's known gas reserves.

To minimise the scope for disruption, Soviet planners kept the route of the main gas pipeline away from countries they regarded as potentially troublesome, such as Poland. The gas main pipeline goes from a gathering point in Ukraine through the former Czechoslovakia. The Soviets never imagined that an independent Ukraine could cause problems for the Russian heartland. This happened just a few months ago when the Russians refused the Ukrainians supplies because the latter declined to pay higher prices. The Ukrainians decided to divert supplies from the system, and deliveries to the West were reduced. The matter was resolved very quickly, but relations between Russia and the Ukraine remain troubled. There is now talk of an alternative pipeline to run through Belarus and Poland.

As with oil, the countries of Central Europe are seeking to become less dependent on Russian gas, but this will not be easy to achieve until pipeline infrastructure is in place which can bring in gas from the North Sea or North Africa.

For both oil and gas there is, as yet, no long-term regional agreement on transport charges and delivery rates. Neither is there a legal regime that establishes how private entities can have access to the pipeline systems. The vital pipeline networks throughout the Central and Eastern European region lack a basic legal framework to regulate their function.

Russian subsidies

Another important point is the extent to which Russian oil and gas was, and is, very heavily subsidised. By keeping energy prices low within the former Comecon area, Russia was able to keep all other domestic prices low – but at the cost of grossly distorting its own economy. In late 1991, the Russian oil price was approximately 70 roubles a tonne or 10 US cents a barrel at the then prevailing exchange rate. Since then the official price was raised to R2,000, then R4,000 and R8,000 and more but the Rouble has been rapidly inflating and Russian domestic prices are still controlled. In February 1993 oil was trading on the Moscow Oil Exchange (which is mainly influenced by official prices within Russia) at less than US$5 a barrel rouble equivalent.

The problem for the countries in the region is that they became dependent on low Russian prices. If the price of oil rises, the price of virtually everything else has to rise to a greater or lesser extent – with highly inflationary consequences. Despite these difficulties, the countries of Central Europe are already well advanced in the process of paying world prices for oil as a part of their political effort to emancipate themselves from the Russians. For the countries of the former USSR the problem is much greater because their economies are very interdependent: the Soviet Union was organised to operate as one centrally planned country. There is now an element of barter in the relationship between these countries. However, as Russian production has declined, the levels of domestic supplies to Russia itself and hard currency exports – at world market prices – have been maintained. The other countries of the former Soviet Union have had to bear the brunt of cuts in supplies.

19.2.2 Industrial organisation

In Central and Eastern Europe the oil and gas industry is organised very differently than in the West.

The activities of the oil industry in the West are generally divided, as a matter of convenience (and, in some cases, in order to minimise anti-trust problems), between upstream operations (exploration and production, transportation, and wholesale marketing) and downstream operations (refining into products, product transportation and consumer marketing).

In the West it is common for all of these activities to be gathered under one corporate roof in an integrated oil company. Certainly the biggest Western oil companies are integrated. This is not to say that there are not some very successful specialist companies who deal exclusively with one or other phase of upstream or downstream activity. The advantage of the integrated companies is their flexibility over the long term – they can adapt themselves to focus on those activities which are particularly profitable during any given period of time.

In the command economies which formerly prevailed in Central and Eastern Europe, markets – and the flexibility to follow their fluctuations – were irrelevant. The state set production targets and the logic of its centralised ministries dictated that specialisation was most appropriate for achieving these. Hence exploration enterprises were established separately from production enterprises, and in either case each enterprise had only a local focus. Refineries were also separately established. Only pipeline systems and export marketing tended truly to be organised on a national basis.

In some countries, the ministry served as a holding company for these enterprises and has now been converted into a state oil company. However, this is a change of form rather than substance, and the degree of specialisation which prevails in the constituent parts of the national petroleum industry is now regarded as undesirable in most countries of the region. Efforts are therefore being made either to seek closer integration or to sell off marketable assets to international companies who can rationalise them.

19.2.3 The political dimension

Everywhere in the world petroleum excites political sensitivities. It is both a scarce resource and a basic economic necessity. It produces enormous revenues and yet employs relatively few people. In those countries which have petroleum reserves, they all regarded them as part of their national inheritance and tend to be suspicious of those who obtain – or wish to obtain – rights to exploit these resources.

As a result, it is usual to find a high level of government interest, particularly in the upstream industry. This can manifest itself in different forms – state ownership of petroleum resources, establishment of national oil companies and – inevitably – substantial government 'take', either in money or in kind.

The high level of government interest also tends to lead, in one way or another, to a certain degree of long-term instability in the legal regimes governing petroleum exploration and production activity. For an example of this we need to look no further than the UK, where the rate of government take was raised very dramatically in the mid-1970s at the same time as a national oil corporation was established which acquired rights to 51 per cent of oil production. The oil companies have never completely forgiven the British government for this, complaining that it was effectively nationalisation by the back door.

The behaviour of the British government was, however, mild compared with those of the Middle East where virtually all petroleum assets were actually nationalised.

Through bitter experience over the past 25 years, oil companies have had to learn to work in legal environments all over the world which reflect the consequences of political change. In making investment decisions nowadays they always have to take political risk into account and balance it against the opportunities. The opportunities in certain parts of Central and Eastern Europe attract them notwithstanding the high political – and legal – risks.

19.2.4 The historical dimension

In dealing with Central and, more especially, Eastern Europe it is important to appreciate the scale and distances involved. The former Soviet Union occupies one-sixth of the world's land surface. A large portion of Western Europe would fit inside Kazakhstan alone. This enormous region was, until recently, ruled by an iron grip exercised from Moscow. The Communist Party constituted an unofficial parallel government throughout Central and Eastern Europe. Although the Communists maintained legal forms to cloak their ruthlessness and brutality, ultimate authority lay in the Party's Politburo and not in national or republican governments. The removal of the Party from power has meant that the methods through which these countries were governed – cruel, but effective in their own way – have disappeared.

However, the political and legal mechanisms needed to reconcile disparate interests and resolve disputes in a democratic society are to a large extent undeveloped. Competing claims by different ethnic and regional, as well as political, groups are proving seriously problematic in many areas. Older patterns with deep historic roots are reasserting themselves.

Certain of these older patterns are based on the historic contours of the great empires that ruled this area. Their spheres of influence are important if we are to understand the legal and cultural history of the states in the region. The map at the end of the chapter shows the limits of the Austro-Hungarian and German Empires in the late nineteenth century and the European border of the Russian empire. By that time the Turkish Empire, which had formerly occupied much of south-eastern Europe, had already receded. The German-speaking peoples have a strong tradition of respect for law. This has been abused – particularly during the Nazi period – but is nonetheless of considerable importance. As a consequence, in many of the countries of the former Austro-Hungarian and German Empires (i.e. Poland, the Czech Republic, the Slovak Republic, Hungary) there are well established code-based legal systems. These countries are having problems modernising their laws, but the basic legal infrastructure exists. The significance of this inheritance is not, however, only in the nature and existence of the laws themselves but in the attitudes of the population to compliance with the law.

Poland is an interesting example. From the late eighteenth century to 1918, Poland was divided between Prussia (East Prussia, Silesia, Pomerania) – which was itself subsequently incorporated in to the German empire – Austria (Upper Vistula/Cracow Region) and Tsarist Russia (Eastern Poland). The preponderant exterial cultural influence was German and Austrian rather than Russian. When formed in 1918, Poland based its legal system on the systems existing in Germany and Austria, and not on the legal system used in Russia which was, of course, by then in the throes of Bolshevik revolution. After the Second

World War, the established Polish system continued to be used within Poland's redrawn borders, although it had a Communist overlay imposed on it which the present administration has been in the process of removing for the last few years.

In contrast, those areas once ruled by the Turks (i.e. Serbia, Bosnia-Herzegovina, Macedonia, Albania, Bulgaria and most of Romania), do not have as strong a legal heritage to draw on. On achieving independence from the Sultanate in the nineteenth and early twentieth century[3] they did adopt legal systems that were essentially based on those of continental Western Europe. However, such systems never became firmly established; political instability and frequent wars in the region continued right up to the creation of Communist states in 1945, and indeed are rearing their ugly features once more now that Communist control has weakened. The long decline of the Ottoman Empire, the ensuing conflicts in the region, and the harsh control of the people by Communist governments, has created in the Balkans a culture in which respect for the law has never become a tradition.

The Russian inheritance is that of a powerful autocratic state ruled by the Tsars, and subsequently by the Communists, in an absolutist manner. Although law is respected, this arises more from a sense of fear of official wrath rather than experiences of reliance on it as a medium for ordering civil and commercial affairs.

The traditional Russian attitude towards law may be characterised, to an extent, by the practice of issuing secret laws, which continued up until the Bolshevik revolution and was maintained by the Communist regime afterwards. Indeed, there can be no assurance that in parts of the former Soviet Union this practice is not continuing.

The fact that any government could contemplate ruling through secret laws reveals a great deal about the regard for law in the society that it governs. In the West, laws are promulgated so that the public can understand and comply with them. Clearly, this cannot be the case with a secret law. Secret laws are for officials to know and understand and for them to apply to the wretched subject, whose role is that of victim rather than citizen. This is the very essence of the police state which was one of the more sophisticated developments of the old Tsarist Regime and which was vastly enhanced and improved by the Bolsheviks, and later exported first to Nazi Germany and then to the Soviet satellite states in Central Europe.

Although the police state has come to an end in all the former Soviet bloc countries, the damage that it has done to the social and legal fabric remains, especially in the former Soviet Union itself. There are difficulties instilling regard for the rule of law and a general suspicion of legal rationalism.

However, the situation in Russia is changing rapidly towards one in which law is playing a more significant role. The combination of unresolved political conflicts with a strong underlying desire to avoid internal violence is leading to a greater emphasis on legal methods of dispute resolution.

Unfortunately, in Central and Eastern Europe the most interesting areas from an oilman's point of view – those where large accumulations of oil or gas are to be found – lie in those countries which are heirs to the Russian and Turkish empires.

3. Serbia 1812, Romania 1878, Bulgaria 1908 (autonomy in 1878), and Albania, 1912.

19.2.5 The legal situation today

In addition to having to come to terms with legal cultural problems, lawyers – and their clients – have to cope with the confusion created by the flood of new legislation. This can be particularly problematic in Russia and some other countries of the former Soviet Union which lack a well-practised legal system in their recent past on which to base this new legislation. Even under the old Soviet system, legislation often fell into a chaotic state of confusion and inaccessibility. Many of the legislative instruments issued from different sources are contradictory. Many are simply not enforced. The problem has been exaggerated by the weakness of central government control particularly in Russia.

The situation is a little different in many Central European countries because in most cases they have kept a substantial part of their old pre-war laws which emanate from the main stream of the continental civil law tradition. The Communists overlaid the old laws with new, ideologically inspired ones, but these additions are now being stripped away leaving laws that were adequate for the 1930s but are very out of date now. Many of the new laws being rushed in by Central European legislatures are often poorly drafted and little thought through – by admission of even some of the politicians responsible.

Another feature which causes concern both to lawyers and to prospective investors in Central and Eastern Europe is the weakness of the court systems.

In most of the formerly Communist Countries the majority of the people are not accustomed to litigate either to defend their rights or to resolve civil disputes. There is deep mistrust of the courts which have previously been controlled by the Communist Party and in many cases are still manned by the same judges as before. With the disintegration of the Communist Party, the courts were freed from the dictatorship of unwritten political orders and instructions. Nonetheless the Courts remain overloaded with work, underfinanced and with judges and staff who are underpaid, mistrusted and, in many cases, poorly trained and inexperienced.

Without a strengthened court system it is difficult to see how the inadequacies of the legislation can be dealt with. Many of the new laws passed are very brief by Western standards and amount to little more than statements of policy. Subordinate legislation, necessary to fill the gaps, is often lacking; even where there is such legislation it is frequently ambiguous. To resolve ambiguities, it is common for lawyers to refer question of law to the relevant minister and ask his advice as to the meaning of the law in question. Such written advice is regarded as proscribing the minister from taking an alternative approach and therefore to be relied upon. But what happens when the minister changes? One can readily appreciate the sense of unease which such a system instils in a Western lawyer and even in Western clients.

19.2.6 The approach of the oil companies

Attempting to create a stable legal environment

The experience of trying to establish a stable legal framework in an unstable legal environment is not a new one for oil companies. Throughout much of the world, they have sought to reach agreement with host governments or their state oil companies on all-embracing concession arrangements or production sharing contracts which provide within their four corners for all aspects of regulation and government take.

Production sharing is a particularly popular form. The production sharing contract will be between the oil company and either the host government or the national oil company, if there is one. The contract usually provides for the oil company to pay for all the costs required to produce the oil. Costs can be recovered from part of the oil produced and the remainder is shared between the oil company and the host government/national oil company in pre-agreed proportions. These proportions may vary, depending on when cost recovery is achieved and how prolific the oilfield is. From an oil company's point of view, one particular advantage of the production sharing contract is that it provides a substitute for taxation, with all the complex calculations and opportunity for unilateral change by government, which taxation usually entails.

In many parts of Central and Eastern Europe, unfortunately, although oil companies have been keen to follow this route by entering into contracts with the host governments or their national oil companies, the movement towards privatisation may make this approach unsuitable. In a privatised economy the state is more likely to want to exercise its powers through regulation and taxation and less likely – in the long term, at any rate – to wish to maintain the confusion between commercial and fiscal objectives which production sharing implies. Also, native entrepreneurs may object to having to compete with commercial interests maintained by the state. This may make it more difficult for oil companies to follow the production-sharing pattern in those countries most keen to progress towards real market economies. It would be ironic if the oil companies – who often regard themselves as the champions of free enterprise – should find that they have the most success in the least progressive states in the area.

If oil companies fail to establish a stable environment in a country, the effect may be felt most strongly in one of the most sensitive areas – taxation.

19.2.7 Taxation

One of the biggest problems the governments in this region have is collecting revenues. People are not used to paying taxes on a self-policing basis or to operating the sophisticated accounting systems needed to implement taxation regimes. The governments have very little means of investigating accounts. There is widespread tax evasion. In the Russian oil sector, which has officially controlled prices, there is inevitably temptation to avoid both price controls and taxation with disastrous results for the Russian government.

Apart from this, the fundamental problem facing all these regimes is that they lack satisfactory sources or methods of collection of revenues. Without proper accounting systems it is very difficult to tell what the underlying profit is. The lack of financial sophistication among both the managements of state enterprises, on the one hand, and those who have to prepare and apply tax legislation, on the other, makes it very difficult to establish a reliable revenue tax. Either they do not understand the concepts or the concepts cannot easily be applied to their enterprises. The consequence is a vicious circle in which a government short of money looks to the most obvious sources of revenue. In the case of oil there is a tendency to tax volumes of production or volumes of exports. Unfortunately this is very discouraging for the industry, in particular the Western petroleum industry which would like a tax on profits that limits their exposure if investment is unsuccessful.

19.3 COUNTRY REPORTS

19.3.1 Central Europe

Czech Republic, Slovak Republic, Poland and Hungary

The Czech and Slovak Republics, Poland and Hungary are in roughly similar positions. Oil and gas in the ground are owned by the state. Unfortunately except in southern and western Poland the amounts of oil and gas to be found in these countries are minimal. There are established regimes based on the mining laws under which petroleum exploration and production could proceed if any substantial reserves of oil and gas were to be found.

Under the Communist Regime most of the oil and gas for consumption in these countries came from Russia at highly subsidised prices. Since Russia has been trying to obtain world prices for its exported oil and gas, the governments of these countries have been forced to negotiate with the Russians while seeking alternative supplies on the world market. This is part of the process of adjustment to the market economy which they have accepted.

The Czechs and Slovaks have a good bargaining card because the oil and gas pipelines pass through their territory on the way to Western Europe, where the best market for Russian oil and gas lies. These pipelines are managed by a joint stock company whose shareholders are both the Czech and Slovak Republics.

There is refining capacity in these countries, some of which is being sold off to foreign companies. Oil companies are also establishing marketing outlets in the form of petrol stations.

Hungary has a state oil company MOL which is, in effect, the old ministry transformed. MOL has been endeavouring to privatise itself, so far without success.

Unfortunately, although these countries have the strongest legal traditions, they have only small reserves of oil and gas. Greater reserves are found further south, in the area of the former Turkish Empire. Fortunately from the point of view of the oil companies, although the legal traditions there are weaker, the key countries there have governments whose centralised approach to decision-making has enabled the companies to arrive at a *modus vivendi*.

Romania

Romania was the largest producer of oil in Central Europe before the Second World War. Romania has had a strong post-Communist government which, although not flavour-of-the month among human rights activists, has been able to establish a regime with which certain oil companies, at any rate, feel that they can do business. Most output of crude currently still comes from onshore fields in the south of the country and in the Carpathian Mountains. There are also two offshore fields currently operational in the Black Sea accounting for approximately 10 per cent of total production. Romania has established a national oil corporation, Rompetrol, and a number of oil companies – Canadian Occidental, Enterprise, Amoco and Royal Dutch/Shell – have entered into production sharing agreements with Rompetrol on terms which are recognisable to Western oilmen. These deals, delayed by several months until the Romanian Parliament passed enabling legislation, essentially provide for an initial five-year exploration period with production rights for 25 years in the event of a commercial find. Rompetrol would have a back-in right to acquire up to 20 per cent in any development. The companies have received substantial tax concessions and are free to export their share of production.

Bulgaria

In Bulgaria the government operates through the State Geological Committee, known as Comgeo, which is the equivalent of a state petroleum company. In the first licensing round (announced in April 1990) the terms were that Comgeo would have a carried interest during the exploration phase with an equity interest (with full voting rights) subject to negotiation during the production phase. At the production stage Comgeo would have the right to nominate a Bulgarian company to which its interest would be assigned. The production term is 25 years. It is interesting that in the case of Bulgaria the oil companies were happy to agree the first licensing round without any legislation in place which was either specific to the terms of the licensing round or general in relation to the regulation of the exploration and production activities involved in the petroleum industry.

Albania

In Albania, six foreign oil companies have recently signed contracts to explore for oil in five offshore blocks in the south west of the country. They plan to start drilling in the second half of 1993. Albania's production of oil has fallen dramatically over the last few years. The main cause apparently being outdated technology rather than depleted reserves. The Albanian government is currently working on establishing a legal infrastructure for oil and gas exploration and production to help attract interested foreign investors. Drawing on the experience of other Central European countries, it has created Albpetrol, a state oil company based in Fieri, close to the oil-producing fields. Like Romania and Bulgaria, there is a centralised post-Communist Government in Albania with which oil companies seem to be able to do business.

19.3.2 Eastern Europe

In the countries of the former USSR the situation is much more complicated. In those without their own oil reserves the situation is similar to those that I have sketched out in north Central Europe, except that having been under Russian tutelage for so long, they have no well-established legal regime. There are significant refining and shipping activities in the Baltic states, particularly in Latvia where Ventspils was, and remains, one of the main oil exporting ports of the former Soviet Union. However, the main areas in which petroleum reserves are found are Kazakhstan, Azerbaijan, Turkmenistan and Russia itself. A number of apparently ambitious deals have been announced in the area, but on closer examination many of them are only for feasibility studies. So far, relatively little Western money has actually been spent.

Kazakhstan

Kazakhstan appears to be the most successful of the former Soviet Republics in attracting petroleum investment.

Kazakhstan has relatively poor legal infrastructure. Whereas most countries in Central and Eastern Europe have passed a flood of new legislation, Kazakhstan has been more cautious. To some extent this is useful, as there is less confusion. However, the main advantage of Kazakhstan, compared with Russia, is that President Nazarbayev has remained in firm control. He has ensured that there is somebody to talk to and somebody to do a deal with, that timetables are kept and progress is orderly. These deals have been, or are being, individually negotiated, and there is no general pattern. Four major western oil companies have been particularly active in Kazakhstan.

The biggest project involving a foreign company is the Tengiz field, for which Chevron was negotiating since before the breakup of the Soviet Union. Tengiz was discovered in the 1970s, but serious technical problems have made production very difficult without Western technology. At one point, Chevron's prospects of success looked very poor, because the terms were regarded as too generous to Chevron at a time when nationalist passions were running high. However, a signature of a joint venture deal has been announced publicly and President Nazarbayez has issued a decree to provide a legislative basis on which it can proceed.

Indications are that Chevron will go ahead with its project – which involves investment of an estimated $20 billion over many years.

The Karachaganak project is also one where there is already a producing field. British Gas and the Italian company Agip are currently negotiating a $6 billion dollar development of the field. An agreement for a feasibility study has been signed. The negotiations are expected to be completed before this summer. British Gas has very kindly indicated what remains to be done before their project can be finalised. They expect there to be a full field development plan, a production sharing agreement, an operation of field facilities agreement, a gas and liquids transportation agreement and a gas and liquids sales agreement. They also require that appropriate Kazakh legislation be enacted which will in effect confirm the basis on which these agreements have been entered into. This is a good example of how a petroleum company can create a legal environment by agreement and with minimal legislative back-up.

The French company Elf have also taken a major interest in Kazakhstan. They have an exploration deal for the Tamir Field for 5 years which is extendable to 10 years and if they discover anything they will get a 30-year production licence.

Although, there is existing refining capacity in Kazakhstan it chiefly runs crude oil supplied from Russia. The Kazakhstan government has announced plans to establish several high-capacity oil refining complexes within the next few years to refine Kazakh production. It has already invited tenders for a new refinery at Mangistau on the East Caspian coast.

Potential investors have been encouraged by the situation in Kazakhstan and there is a great deal of interest in that republic. There are certain drawbacks, however. Kazakhstan is landlocked. The Caspian Sea, although highly productive of caviar, does not communicate with any other navigable body of water. The Caspian Pipeline Consortium, which includes Kazakhstan, Oman, Russia and Azerbaijan, intends to construct a new pipeline linking the major Kazakh oil fields via Grozny to Novorossiysk on the Black Sea.

There is also a potential ethnic problem, with Russians, who comprise nearly half the population, concentrated in certain areas and native Kazakhs concentrated in others. So far relations between the two communities have remained good, and President Nazarbayev has taken pains to allay fears on the part of the Russians.

Azerbaijan

In Azerbaijan, a number of deals in principle have been announced. The government of Azerbaijan has formed a state oil company SOCAR which has been negotiating deals with a Turkish company, with Pennzoil of the United States in partnership with Ramco, with a BP-Statoil consortium and with a consortium including Amoco and Unocal. The conflict between Azerbaijan and Armenia presents an uneasy background but appears not to have diminished oil company enthusiasm.

Turkmenistan

Some time ago Turkmenistan announced a licensing round managed by an American technical advisory firm, and there was a certain amount of interest. Only one award – to a consortium of little known companies – has been announced so far. However there have been indications that a new bidding round – involving the more interesting offshore acreage – will take place soon.

Russian Federation

Russia has enormous discovered reserves. It has neither the technology nor the equipment to develop them effectively. It is also short of capital. In theory, this should make it an ideal place for Western investment.

Unfortunately Russia is by far the most complicated place to work in of all the former Soviet republics. Politically it is characterised by a series of deep-seated conflicts between the President and the legislature, between the centre and the regions, and between ministries and the state enterprises. The attitude towards foreign investment in the petroleum industry is highly ambivalent.

In the Russian Federation, the more central the authorities the less power they seem to have. Responsibility for administration of the petroleum industry is divided at Federal level between different ministries. In addition each of the regional and local administrative authorities – which are numerous and overlapping – also claim authority over petroleum in their respective areas. Most significant is the position of the state enterprises which have been carrying on the industrial and commercial business of the state. Although owned by the state, state enterprises – particularly in the oil sector – are autonomous in practice and have to be dealt with as such. These state enterprises are divided by geographical area and function.

The situation in Russia has been described as 'political *matrioshka*'. A *matrioshka* doll is a typical Russian souvenir in which a large doll opens to reveal a small one which reveals a smaller one and so on until one reaches a very tiny one. Veterans of the current Russian business scene will recognise the aptness of this analogy.

To try to solve this problem in relation to minerals generally, the Federal government passed the Law on Sub-surface Resources in 1992 which provides for jurisdiction over petroleum and other minerals to be shared between the Federal government and the regions. Although this law is intended to be an umbrella law, and a specific petroleum law is to be promulgated, it does outline a system under which licences will be issued for up to 25 years. Even without a petroleum law, there appears to be, therefore, a basis on which licences may be issued. Unfortunately, however, it is not absolutely clear what 'shared jurisdiction' means and the regions have increasingly been contesting the authority of the Russian government. The result is that anyone seeking to explore for or develop petroleum reserves on a legally recognised basis has to deal with a plethora of authorities.

He will also have to deal with the state enterprises in areas with discovered reserves. It is important to understand the position of the state enterprises in relation to the ministries. In the former USSR, indeed throughout Central and Eastern Europe, the state enterprises were established to carry on locally managed operations, though ultimately answerable to the relevant ministry. They have their own management and their own staff; more importantly, they are the bodies which are almost literally sitting on petroleum assets. Without reaching agreement with the relevant state enterprise, a foreign oil company will not be able to obtain satisfactory access to those assets.

Under the old system, the state enterprises would be granted annual budgets, of which the managements would be at liberty to dispose as they saw fit provided they fulfilled the plans issued to them by the supervising ministry. The state would then tax or simply call up what might, very loosely, be called 'profit' – and require the enterprises to sell their production to the state at fixed prices. The system as such provided no incentive to managements to be efficient in Western terms. The measure of success was whether or not the enterprise concerned fulfilled its plan.

Because there were no market mechanisms by which enterprises could obtain equipment and materials which they did not produce, they had to negotiate with each other. As price was a relatively meaningless concept without a market, trade between the state enterprises amounted to a complex and unreliable form of barter, and in many cases it was simpler to produce the goods oneself. Furthermore, the state enterprises were in a better position to obtain goods for distribution to their workers than the workers were themselves. Consequently, the most successful enterprises built up large empires based on being as self-sufficient as practicable and retaining as much benefit for themselves and for their workers as possible. The director of a Siberian oil production enterprise, speaking at a conference in London last year, gave an example of this. He explained that out of 60,000 employees in his enterprise only 10,000 are engaged in producing oil. The remainder are involved in making equipment, building houses and roads and providing food and other necessities.

The collapse of the central planning system, and the disintegration of the former ministries previously responsible for administering it, has left the managements of the large state enterprises – temporarily at least – in positions of power and influence which they never enjoyed under the Communist system. It is this level of management, trained under the old system and having survived its collapse, which stands to lose or gain the most from both foreign investment and privatisation. Westerners wanting to do business with such an enterprise need to demonstrate that the enterprise as a whole will benefit from it – profit alone is not a sufficient motive. The risk to the management if things go wrong is enormous and Westerners have to build up a high level of trust and understanding with them before they really will do business. This has made it very difficult for Westerners to do business in the established areas like Western Siberia.

The situation in the oil industry is unsatisfactory from the Russian government's point of view. The Russian government's approach to this problem has been to try to corporatise and restructure the oil industry under the aegis of Rosneftegas. Rosneftegas is basically the old Oil Ministry transformed into a joint stock company. The advantages of corporatisation – which means converting the state enterprises into joint stock companies – is that the relative positions of the parties are made more transparent and the organisation of the enterprise can be dealt with more systematically, particularly if the transformation is coupled with the introduction of Western accounting and reporting systems.

Towards the end of 1992 the Russian government announced a plan whereby all the Russian oil industry enterprises would be corporatised and the resultant joint stock companies would in turn be controlled by holding companies. In line with the privatisation legislation it was envisaged that workers and managements in the enterprises would be given preference shares and opportunities to buy ordinary shares on a preferential basis. The state would, however, retain control for at least three years.

This programme of corporatisation of the oil industry has begun to be implemented. Rosneftegas has been turned into a holding company called Rosneft, and there are three other smaller holding companies called Lukoil, Yukos and Surgutneftegas. However, state control remains an important feature and the plan has not solved the problem of how adequate capital is to be made available for their operations.

The final problem in the set concerns the position of foreigners. The Russian domestic industry would like to be self-sustaining and independent as quickly as possible, while at the same time the government is trying to regain control.

Although the government would like to encourage foreign investment, it does not have the power to insist that foreign investment must be accomplished in the face of a reluctant industry. There are also the usual nationalistic fears about foreigners making off with the national heritage. The industry is understandably hesitant to welcome foreigners until their own position is settled. Their argument is that they do not need foreign skills and management – except in areas like finance and law which they think of as peripheral. However, they do need foreign capital. Unfortunately, the terms on which foreign capital is being offered currently are, on the whole, not very attractive to them because they would have to give up control.

Ironically it is in Western Siberia – the area that is most attractive to foreigners and where there are the highest volumes of discovered reserves – that the least progress has been made in Russia. The large international oil companies have spent a lot of time looking around there but have not made major investments.

There have been a few entrepreneurial ventures in Western Siberia, however. The Fracmaster project is reported to be successful, but the White Nights project appears to have a number of very serious problems.

The Siberian Oil Corporation project has been making steady progress. It is based on the idea of creating a private Russian integrated oil company with minority Western participation that will finance itself through access to Western capital markets. The company has recently announced that it has been granted its first licence under the new legislative regime. It is constructing a pipeline which will improve production of the Yuzhnoye field. The success of the company so far is in large part due to the enthusiasm of its Russian and Western backers for this unusual consent.

There have been a number of successful ventures elsewhere, particularly in Komi, where Gulf Canada and British Gas have a production project. An ambitious production project in Archangel by Conoco appears to be proceeding satisfactorily.

Another area of interest is the Russian Far East where a licensing round in Sakhalin has been held up because of differences between local and central government. Shell has now joined the Marathon/Mitsui/McDermott consortium and it is hoped that the problems can be solved.

In contrast to the oil industry in Russia, the gas industry has remained under central state control and has not encountered the structural difficulties crippling oil production. It is generally agreed that the gas industry in Russia functions nowadays much better than the oil industry and consequently the monopoly is likely to continue, even in corporatised form.

19.3.3 How can lawyers help?

The problematic legal situation in Central and Eastern Europe does not make lawyers redundant. If anything, lawyers are needed more than ever, to help structure the deals, to help make them work as well as possible from transactional point of view and to bring legal discipline to a disorderly situation. It is important that the lawyer should be regarded as part of the team from an early stage, not just somebody to consult when things go wrong or when the deal is ready to be put in the form of a written contract. Although the lawyer cannot promise to solve all the problems, the process of resolution through legal methods can be a highly constructive one which reduces both risks and misunderstandings.

Figure 19.1 The Austro-Hungarian and German Empires and the European Border of the Russian Empire (late Nineteenth Century).

Chapter 20

Legal and Tax Issues of Eastern European Oil and Gas Investment.

Doran Doeh

20.1 INTRODUCTION

The breadth of this topic is so vast that we can safely take advantage of it to concentrate on some of the things that are of the most interest. It is also important to focus on the broader issues which affect business generally in the former Soviet bloc countries, including petroleum investment. Russia will be included in our definition of Eastern Europe, and in view of its importance in the petroleum scene – and because the problems are particularly acute there – we will place quite a high degree of emphasis on it. We shall begin by looking at the rule of law, the national constitutions and the court systems, and we shall then consider certain specific problems, including ownership of property and privatisation, foreign investment, taking of security, insolvency and taxation.

20.2 THE RULE OF LAW

It is of the greatest importance to appreciate that the roots of many of the practical legal problems arising in Eastern Europe lie in areas of jurisprudence and political theory which are nowadays rarely addressed in the West outside academic institutions and political think-tanks. They raise fundamental issues such as the very nature of the state, the extent of its powers and authority and even the extent to which political policy can be distinguished from law. The practising lawyer must reconsider at a very basic level the nature of law and of legal systems, the reasons why people obey the laws and comply with their legal obligations and how these can be enforced. It is only by doing this that one can hope to protect business arrangements in the very unsettled situation prevailing throughout this area.

In the West questions of this kind are now seldom raised. At least where eighteenth-century liberal ideas of the separation of powers prevail, legislatures enact laws, the executive arm of the government implements them, and once they have attained constitutional legitimacy, they pass into the realm of lawyers and judges in which the political elements of the state are not supposed to interfere. One can argue that this is not always the case throughout the West, but on the whole there is little doubt that both relations among citizens and relations between citizens and government are subject to the rule of well-defined law.

In the formerly Communist countries, neither liberal ideas nor the rule of law were respected. The Communist Party acted as an unofficial parallel government for nearly 75 years in the former Soviet Union and for about 40 years in the other parts of Eastern Europe. The Communists cynically and contemptuously maintained legal forms to cloak their ruthlessness and brutality, but ultimate authority lay in the Party's Politburo and not in national or republican governments. So long as the Party was composed of an elite of professional revolutionaries, these methods were – in political terms – successful. When – as was probably inevitable – a new class of professional bureaucrats numbering many millions succeeded the revolutionaries, the difficulties of governing a huge land mass populated by a bewildering variety of national and ethnic groups reasserted themselves. Paradoxically, it was the strength of the 'bourgeois' notions of constitutional government and national identity which inspired all those who rose up to defeat the Communist regimes, from the days of the Solidarity movement in Poland until the abortive coup in Moscow in August 1991.

The significance of all this – particularly to investors – lies in the fact that however careful the lawyers may be in establishing the documentation for business arrangements, the role and approach to law in this area is such that only limited reliance can be placed on conformity with legal requirements. It is essential, therefore, that in structuring any transaction in this area the Western parties should have regard to the practical effectiveness of the documentation which they are preparing. One has to ask oneself, far more critically than in the West, who personally is going to sign the document, who will approve it, against whom it can be enforced, through what institutions or methods it can be enforced and who can repudiate it. Similar questions need to be asked about legislation, and we shall be returning to this in a moment.

Clients who have carried on business successfully in this area understand this. They establish their deals with the support of the key players. They accept legal uncertainty as part of the risks they run. Nonetheless, they want the best quality documentation they can get, so that they can at least demonstrate what has been agreed and have something to show if it is later called into question.

Even this very practical approach, however, understates the difficulties of working in a situation of high instability and relatively weak central government. This is currently problematic particularly in many – but not all – of the countries of the former USSR. In Kazakhstan, for example, where there is currently a relatively strong central government, oil companies have found it much easier to finalise deals than in the Russian Federation where the Federal government is beleaguered by attacks on its authority from all sides and at all levels.

The dismantling of the Communist network of control has not led to a satisfactory solution to problems which have troubled this part of the world since the last century, particularly in the area of the former Russian Empire. Whereas the Austro-Hungarian and German Empires had legal systems which commanded a certain degree of respect and were to a certain extent politically independent, this was never the case in Russia. Serfdom was not abolished until 1861, and even after that Russia was regarded as having one of the most authoritarian systems of government in the world. The practice of issuing secret laws in Russia continued right up to the Revolution and was maintained by the new regime afterwards. The fact that any government could contemplate ruling through secret laws reveals a great deal about the attitude towards law in the society it governs. The police state has also been one of Russia's greatest exports – first to Germany in the 1930s and then throughout Eastern Europe in the late 1940s and 1950s. It was said: 'If you want to be free, join the police. If you want to be completely free, join the secret police.'

Although the police state has come to an end in all the former Soviet bloc countries, the damage it has done to the social and legal fabric remains behind. The political and legal mechanisms needed to reconcile disparate interests and resolve disputes in a democratic society are to a large extent undeveloped. Competing claims by different authorities and the absence of established legal structures are proving seriously problematic.

20.3 CONSTITUTIONAL ISSUES

In the old days it was relatively simple. If a deal could be done at all, it was with the relevant ministry in Moscow, or in the appropriate national capital if you were dealing outside the USSR. The Communists had a reputation for being very tough in negotiations. However, once the contract was signed it was honoured to the letter. This was not because the Communists had respect for the sanctity of contracts, but rather because they had regard to their business reputation and, most importantly, they had the power to deliver. Anyone who has tried to do business in Eastern Europe in recent years has found a totally different situation.

This is particularly the case in Russia. There, the more central the authorities, the less power they seem to have. Responsibility for administration of the petroleum industry is divided at federal level between different ministries. In addition, each of the regional and local administrative authorities – which are numerous and overlapping – also claims authority over projects in its respective area and needs to be dealt with. Furthermore, and most importantly, the state enterprises who have been operating the indigenous petroleum industry, although owned by the state, in practice are autonomous and have to be dealt with as such. There are many of these and they are divided by geographical area and function – separate enterprises deal with exploration, production, transportation, refining, marketing. The power base of the state enterprises will be examined in more detail when discussing the ownership of property and privatisation.

The 'political *matryoshka*' situation which has already been described in Chapter 19 is probably at its most troublesome in the Russian Federation. It is better in some of the other countries of Eastern Europe where the integrity of the central state is generally respected, but one should not underestimate the problems arising from the rapidly evolving situation. Czechoslovakia has recently split up. Yugoslavia – although not a part of the Soviet bloc for many years – figures nightly on our television screens. By contrast – to use examples relating to the petroleum industry – in Bulgaria and Albania, there have been successful licensing rounds largely because the national government still retains – or is seen to retain – strong central control.

One of the problems a Westerner has in trying to evaluate the legal scene is the confusion created by there being so many different forms of legislation. Again, this can be particularly problematic in the Russian Federation. Legislative acts there can take any of the following forms:

- laws;
- resolutions on implementation of the legislation;
- presidential decrees;
- government decisions;
- governmental orders;
- instructions of ministries, committees, national banks and so on;
- ordinances of ministers, chairmen of committees and so on.

We shall not go into a detailed explanation of the differences but some instruments are more to be relied on then others. Many of the legislative instruments which issue from different sources are contradictory. Many are simply not enforced. As we saw earlier in relation to contracts, the personalities involved are very important. In relation to a decree, for example, it is important to see who signed it. The larger the body responsible for the issue of any piece of legislation, the broader is the consensus – and the greater the reliance that can be placed on it.

To add to the confusion, publication of laws adopted by the legislature is frequently delayed. In Russia, President Yeltsin often keeps a law in his office without signing it beyond the 10 days stipulated for publication, sometimes for several months. It is even rumoured that Yeltsin's political rivals actually hide legislation or steal it from his office to prevent it from receiving the Presidential assent.

The situation is a little different in many other Eastern European countries because in most cases they have kept a substantial part of their old pre-war laws which emanate from the mainstream of the continental civil law tradition. The Communists overlaid the old laws with new, ideologically inspired ones, but these additions are now being stripped away leaving laws that were adequate for the 1930s but are very out of date now. This has led to many new laws being rushed in, often poorly drafted and little thought through.

At a recent International Bar Association conference in Hungary, the President of Hungary, himself a lawyer, commented that his country was producing a high volume of legislation, but that the quality of much of it was low and the practice even worse. He explained that Hungary had little alternative in the circumstances and begged the foreign lawyers for their cooperation in helping to improve standards. Now, Hungary is one of the more developed and westernised of all the former Communist Bloc countries and a frank admission of this kind from the President of Hungary – which was echoed by representatives of a number of other countries present – gives one much pause for thought.

The constitutions under which the laws are passed are, of course, often inherited from the Communist period. Clearly there is paramount need for new constitutions commanding widespread public respect and capable of enforcement. In the Russian Federation, a wide variety of constitutions have been proposed and debated, but so far none has been adopted. The result is that the constitution inherited from the Soviet era is still in force. The continuing clash in Russia between the President and the legislature is now causing major concern. Until recently, it was suggested that President Yeltsin found that the obstructive and reactionary behaviour of many delegates of the Russian legislature acted as a convenient counterpoint to the reformist approach of the Gaidar government, which enjoyed the confidence of the international community. This situation is rapidly changing as the reforms begin to cause serious discomfort to much of the population and to arouse opposition from the industrial establishment.

There is, therefore, a growing clamour – both in Russia and from abroad – for constitutional reform that will do away with many of the more obvious contradictions and provide a more consistent approach to government. Whether and how such reform will take place, however, remains to be seen. The danger is that if it does not take place, strong government will be reimposed by another regime which has the same disregard for the rule of law and liberal ideas as its predecessors.

Although they are a little less dramatic, constitutional problems also abound in many other countries in the region. In Czechoslovakia a long standing constitutional battle between the two republics and the federal centre can only be resolved by the break up of the country. In Poland the President and the parliament have been at daggers drawn and much new legislation has fallen through the gap between the two.

20.4 THE COURTS

Another feature, which in our view requires the most urgent attention, is the court system. In the West, particularly in the English-speaking countries, the dispensation of high quality justice through open and free access to the courts has been one of the most important 'commodities' provided by government to the governed in return for their allegiance. Western lawyers nonetheless expect few of the commercial transactions they help to establish to end up in litigation before the courts. One of the principal reasons is that the laws are well understood, and there is a relatively high degree of certainty as to how they will be enforced by the courts. There is little point in disputing matters the resolution of which within the legal system is fairly clear.

Unlike their Western counterparts, the majority of the population in the former Communist countries are not accustomed to litigate, either in defence of their rights or to resolve civil disputes. For reasons explained earlier, there is deep mistrust of the courts, which had previously been controlled by the

Communist Party and in many cases are still manned by the same judges as before. With the disintegration of the Communist Party, the courts were freed from the dictatorship of 'unwritten' political orders and instructions. Nonetheless, the courts remain with judges who lack a real understanding of the importance of their role in the emergence of a new society.

Without a strengthened court system it is difficult to see how the inadequacies of the legislation can be dealt with. Many of the laws passed are very brief by Western standards and amount to little more than statements of policy. Subordinate legislation necessary to fill in the gaps is often lacking. The laws themselves and the subordinate legislation, where it exists, are frequently ambiguous.

Given the breakdown in society and the disintegration of strong central authority, the importance of the law and the courts should in theory increase – as the only medium through which many disputes and uncertainties can be amicably resolved. Limited steps have been taken to try to improve the situation. However, a great deal more effort will be required to establish the pre-eminence and prestige of the court system before the courts can play a proper role.

20.5 SPECIFIC PROBLEMS

We shall now focus our attention on some specific issues.

20.5.1 The ownership of property and privatisation

The most significant of these, in our view, concern the ownership of property and privatisation.

The situation in Russia has been described by the retiring Moscow bureau chief of the *Toronto Star* as 'frontier capitalism'. Violent crime is on the increase, corruption is rife, certain individuals are becoming enormously rich by Russian standards while the majority are becoming ever more impoverished. Similar things are happening in the other countries of Eastern Europe. In certain ways, this is reminiscent of the western United States in the last century, and talk about 'the wild East' is not amiss.

In our view, this wildness derives in part from certain features of the previous system. Where everything belongs to everybody, nothing belongs to anybody. In the absence of property rights, there were two ways of appropriating goods and land to one's own use – one was to get permission and the other was just to take it. While the Communist reign of terror prevailed, the latter was – to say the least – inadvisable. However, that period is now well over, people look much more to their own devices and there is relatively little control over them. They seek to assert claims to assets with which they are associated, and in a period of legal uncertainty possession amounts to a great deal.

Another feature of the system, which arises both from lack of personal property rights and the consequent absence of markets, is the concentration of power in the managements of the state enterprises. These are legal entities, in each case answerable to the relevant ministry, set up under the Communist regime to manage the state's business operations in all spheres of the economy.

Under the old system the state enterprises would be granted annual budgets, of which the managements would be more or less at liberty to dispose provided they fulfilled the plans issued to them by the supervising ministry in Moscow. The state would then tax or simply call up what might very loosely be called profit and require the enterprises to sell their production to the state at fixed prices. The system as such provided no incentive to managements to be efficient. The measure of success was whether or not the enterprise concerned fulfilled its plan.

Because there were no market mechanisms by which enterprises could obtain equipment and materials which they did not produce, they had to negotiate with each other. As price was a relatively meaningless concept without a marketplace, trade between the state enterprises amounted to a complex and unreliable form of barter, and in many cases it was simpler to produce the goods oneself. Nonetheless, in an economy without a marketplace, the state enterprises were in a better position to obtain goods for distribution to their workers than the workers were themselves. Consequently, successful enterprises built up large empires based on being as self-sufficient as possible and retaining as much benefit for themselves and for their workers as possible.

The collapse of the central planning system, and the disintegration, particularly in the former Soviet Union, of the former ministries previously responsible for administering it, has left the managements of the large state enterprises – temporarily at least – in positions of power and influence which they never enjoyed under the Communist regime. It is this level of management, trained under the old system and having survived its collapse, which stands to lose – or to gain – the most from both foreign investment, privatisation and competition.

Westerners wanting to do business with such enterprises need to demonstrate that the enterprise as a whole will benefit from it – profit alone is not a sufficient motive. The risk to the management if things go wrong is enormous and Westerners have to build up a high level of trust and understanding with them before they will really do business.

Obviously, in order to reform such a system it is necessary to get property into private ownership on a large scale and either to privatise the state enterprises or to reconstitute them on a basis which would enable them to behave like companies in the West in pursuing their business aims.

Most of the countries of Eastern Europe have passed laws permitting the ownership of private property. The actual transfer of property into private hands, however, raises many extremely difficult problems. As a result of this, differing rates of progress have been achieved in the various East European countries.

Throughout the region, governments have been seeking to 'corporatise' state enterprises, as an interim measure, to pave the way to privatisation. Under these programmes, all state enterprises over a certain size must turn themselves into joint stock companies. It is no doubt hoped that this will curtail the power and improve the efficiency of the state enterprises. Presumably, it is also hoped that if they are placed in a Western legal structure they will start to behave in a more businesslike manner.

It remains to be seen what effect this will have. Professionals in the West all know of cases where ailing groups have milked successful subsidiaries to meet group liabilities and conversely cases where management have grown fat at the expense of shareholders and creditors. The advantages of corporatisation in Western form can be that the relative positions of the parties are made more transparent and the organisation of the enterprise can be dealt with more systematically, particularly if coupled with the use of Western accounting and reporting systems. But corporatisation will only be successful if the state is prepared to walk away from its babies and let them sink or swim.

To protect the state's interests, many countries have established some form of entity to hold shares in the newly formed companies. In certain of the former Soviet states, this is the state committee for the management of property – Goskomimuchestevo in Russian, or GKI for short – set up by the republic's government. Similar bodies have been established in almost every country in the region. The idea is that state property will be vested in the committee and that the committee will, in the course of privatisation, be able to establish and give good title to property and to the acquirers thereof.

Part of the purpose in establishing these holding entities is to head off 'spontaneous' privatisation whereby the management and workers who operate a particular state enterprise affect the transfer of the operating assets to a private vehicle established and held by them. 'Spontaneous' privatisation has been a problem throughout Eastern Europe. Needless to say, the purpose of preventing it has not been wholly achieved, partly because the privatisation process has been far too slow to suit the more ambitious elements in the societies of these countries, but also because the political influence of many of these is such that neither state property committees nor state anti-monopoly committees are able to impede their progress.

In order to try to speed things up and overcome the public's disillusionment with the privatisation process, many countries in the region are attempting some kind of mass privatisation programme. Czechoslovakia is the most advanced with its voucher scheme already up and running. Poland's mass privatisation scheme now seems to be back on course after many problems and Russia's is just getting underway.

It should be noted that the Russian privatisation law originally provided that workers were to get 25 per cent of the capital of the enterprise in the form of preference shares, the management to get 5 per cent and together the workers and management to get options over a further 10 per cent, with the state retaining 60 per cent for sale to the public. This is roughly similar to the percentages applied by other countries in the region. It is reported – from Russia at any rate – that workers and managements in many industries feel their share is too small. Alternative schemes have been developed whereby workers and management can buy up to 51 per cent or get options over 20 per cent. Looked at from a Western point of view, the apportionment they already have looks extraordinarily generous for large capital intensive industries such as petroleum. The prospect of having to give away such a large portion of state assets may well inhibit privatisation in such cases, or the workers' and management's portion may have to be capped at a lower percentage. In some countries, however, questions do arise, particularly in respect of land, as to whether those who owned land under the pre-Communist regimes should want to be allowed to retake the land which once belonged to them. This has been a more serious question in the East European countries outside the former Soviet Union, which were only under Communist rule for the post-war period.

The issue in the countries who have invited land claims is who should be entitled to exercise their rights, because to go back to the immediate post-war period neglects the extent to which property was taken away, particularly from Jews, during the Nazi period which immediately preceded it. In Russia, this is not a serious question largely because the Russian Revolution took place so long ago. Furthermore, property was not widely distributed before the Revolution, and indeed one of the deceptions which Lenin practised on the people of Russia was to trick the masses of peasants into believing that they would be given land by the Communists if they supported them against the Whites.

Privatisation of land is a particularly sensitive subject. People are concerned that if their land is put up for sale, foreigners will buy it all and they will revert to their ancient status of landless peasants. In practice, this is unlikely, but it is difficult to calm the fears of people who have suffered traumatically over many decades.

20.5.2 Foreign investment

We may well ask how foreign investors fit into all this. Virtually all the regimes of Eastern Europe have passed laws for the protection of foreign investment. The fact that such laws are considered necessary is a comment on the uncertainty and suspicion on the part of the foreign investment community. These laws generally provide that foreigners are entitled to invest on equal terms with native people and that foreigners are to be protected against arbitrary changes in the law. Of course laws such as these can be changed arbitrarily and the fact that they have been passed is no real protection. They are, however, encouraging as statements of policy of the new regimes. Of more real concern to foreigners are rights to export production and to repatriate profits, on which the position is often less satisfactory. Of concern to the native population is the question of how they can possibly compete with foreign investors on equal terms.

Many of the new regimes have also passed wide-ranging anti-monopoly laws, of which they are extremely proud. These are regarded as both an invitation and a warning to foreign investors. They are an invitation in the sense that local monopolies will not be tolerated and that foreigners will have the opportunity to compete on equal terms, a warning in the sense that foreigners must not become too powerful.

An important element in the attraction of foreigners is the ability to set up corporate entities on terms reasonably familiar in the West. On the whole this has been done by imitating Western legislation.

20.5.3 Finance and taxation

We shall now briefly examine the laws which are essential for financings to take place. Throughout Eastern Europe, governments are passing laws to allow banks to take security over assets. This is essential to allow project financing to take place. However, taking of security is very much in its infancy in these countries and the practice needs to develop. For example, banks not only need security over assets, but to be assured of realising cash flow. One issue which has arisen is whether foreign banks should be permitted to take security, and in cases where they are not – or the position is unclear – local banks need to be engaged to front up transactions. More importantly almost, managements of local enterprises have very little idea of what taking security involves and a great deal of explanation may be required to achieve a satisfactory solution.

Coupled with this from a banker's point of view needs to be progress on insolvency laws. This is, of course, a complex matter and will take time. In Russia, President Yeltsin has issued a bankruptcy decree. The main purpose of it appears to be to force state enterprises to become more efficient through threat of being put into bankruptcy, rather than to protect creditors. In some of the other countries, there is pre-war legislation which can be revived, but it is not clear how appropriate it is to contemporary circumstances.

Taxation is an extremely difficult area. The former Communist societies do not have the habit of either paying or collecting taxes in the same orderly way as in many Western countries. Individuals were used to being paid net of tax and, because of the general oppressiveness of the system, never to question what they were given. Conversely because the state could take away levies from the state enterprises there was little point in taxing them, although there were forms of taxation and the motions were gone through. There is a saying in these countries – 'We pretend to work and you pretend to pay us.' They could say similarly, 'You pretend to tax us and we pretend to make profits.' Unfortunately, this does not apply to foreigners, and they are very vulnerable.

Under the command economy, it was, however, very difficult to assess what the profitability of state enterprises was, since this was not a measure of success. Accordingly, accounting practices were and still are largely incapable of indicating a state enterprise's profitability, and instead simply meet the requirements of the state budget. Accounting conventions are, obviously, very different from those in the West.

Personal income taxes are high and whereas a local person may shrug his or her shoulders and either pay or find ways of disguising his income, a Westerner feels much more exposed. There are withholding taxes, high levels of VAT, different forms of corporate income or profits tax, excise duties, import and export duties. In some countries, there are also requirements for mandatory conversions of foreign currency earnings.

We do not wish to dwell on particular tax problems because the situation is changing very rapidly and will, no doubt, continue to do so. However, we do want to mention the fundamental problem that all of these regimes have, which is that they have no obvious sources or methods of collection of revenues. Without proper accounting systems it is very difficult to tell what the underlying profit is. The lack of financial sophistication among the managements of state enterprises on the one hand and those who have to prepare and apply tax legislation on the other makes it very difficult for them to produce a reliable revenue tax. Either they do not understand the concepts or the concepts cannot easily be applied to their enterprises. The consequence is a vicious circle in which a government short of money looks to the most obviously sources of revenue, which are taxes on consumer spending – VAT – and on exports – export duties. These are regressive taxes which cause the most harm to the public in general and to the stronger industries which are capable of producing exports. This in turn produces general misery among the population and discourages investment in exporting industries, which in turn produces less revenue.

20.6 CONCLUSION

Now, having painted what must seem like a pretty dismal picture, we want to conclude by looking at the more positive aspects. The understanding of the problems by people both in the countries concerned and overseas is increasing very rapidly. There is no way back; and we believe that very few people want to go back to the police state, whatever they may say. All of these countries are searching for better solutions. Advice is being taken from some of the best people in the West. It is easy to be sceptical about this, but the good will and moral support of the Western world is important. It is something Russia is enjoying for the first time in centuries, and virtually none of the countries in Eastern Europe has ever had the present level of outside support. That support is also increasingly material. The fact is that many people are out there trying to do deals. As professionals, we will undoubtedly have to adapt our practices to the situation in the East, but the interplay of ideas and viewpoints is healthy and this, it is hoped, will lead to constructive progress.

Chapter 21

Petroleum Investment in Kazakhstan[1]

Martin Friedrich

21.1 INTRODUCTION

In December 1992 the Kazakh government held two promotional meetings for joint exploration and development projects in Kazakhstan. It was the first attempt of the Kazakh administration to seek actively to attract oil companies and investors by means of promotional seminars abroad. However, a number of petroleum contracts were already negotiated over the last couple of years. The following is a brief account of the difficulties encountered by both sides when negotiating a contract.

On 13 June 1992 the Kazakh Code on Subsoil Resources and the Processing of Minerals came into force. The law contains provisions concerning the ownership of mineral resources, the award of licences for the exploration and development of those resources, and the distribution of power between the central government and local authorities. However, there is no specific petroleum legislation as such in place in Kazakhstan[2] nor is the existing tax legislation terribly sophisticated. Petroleum operations are therefore subject to regulation under the generally applicable legislation. The main provisions governing economic activity are contained in the Foreign Investment Law of 17 January 1991, the related Concessions Law of December 1991, the Enterprise Law of 15 January 1991, the Tax Law of 14 February 1991 (as amended), and foreign exchange legislation.[3]

21.2 NEGOTIATION AND AWARD PROCEDURE

When applying for petroleum rights the first hurdle that has to be mastered is to identify the appropriate negotiation partner since the competence to enter

1. This chapter presents the terms and conditions applicable to oil operations in Kazakhstan as of early December 1992. An extract of the present chapter was published in *Oil and Gas Law and Taxation Review*, 4 (1992).
2. The Kazakh Oil and Gas Law is currently being drafted with the assistance of the World Bank. It has been reported that the law may be finalised as early as February 1993.
3. The Law 'On Currency Regulations' of 13 June 1991 which was in most aspects replaced by relevant sections of the Presidential Decree 'On the Organisation of Foreign Economic Activity' of 25 January 1992 although the 1991 las was not formally repealed.

Figure 21.1 Map of Kazakhstan

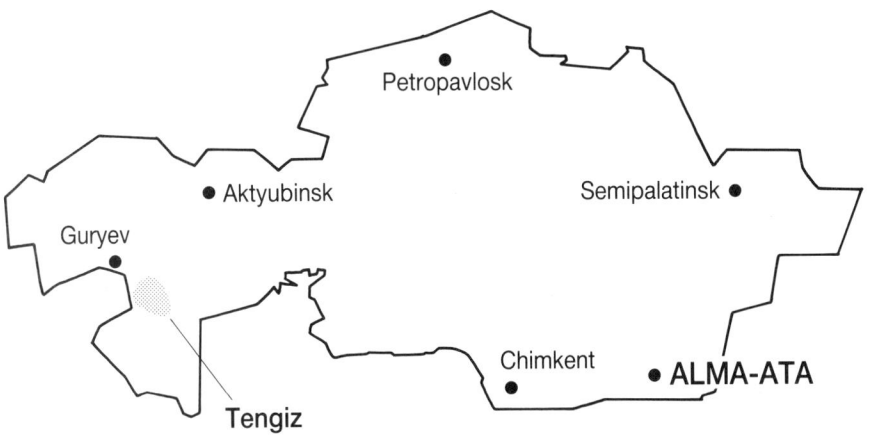

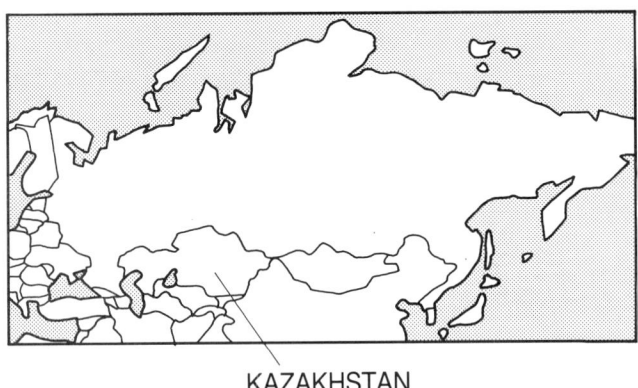

KAZAKHSTAN

into contracts with foreign companies has not been sufficiently defined. Kazakhstan has two ministries primarily responsible for petroleum operations. These are the Ministry of Geology and Protection of the Subsoil and the Ministry of Energy and Fuel Resources, others being the Ministry of Foreign Economic Relations, the Ministry of Industry and the Ministry of Ecology.[4]

4. On 7 February 1992 President Nazarbaev issued a Decree 'On the Implementation of Organisation and Activity of the Administrative State Bodies of the Republic of Kazakhstan under Conditions of Economic Reform' which reorganised and created ministries, state committees, and the Bank of Foreign Economic Activity.

Basically the Ministry of Geology is responsible for the administration of reconnaissance and exploration work while the Ministry of Energy takes over responsibility as soon as development and production operations commence. As a result of this division the Subsoil Law provides for local authorities, jointly with the Ministry of Geology and the Supreme Soviet, to be responsible for the award of contracts.

Which of the authorities must be approached depends also on the type of licence you wish to obtain. In Kazakhstan (as in Russia) companies wishing to carry out petroleum operations must obtain a number of principal rights and licences:

1. In accordance with business legislation[5] companies must register their activities and obtain a business certificate from the Executive Committee of the local Soviet of People's Deputies at the seat of business. The registration authority does not have the right of decision whether an entity will be permitted to conduct entrepreneurial activities or not. The only function of the registration process is to ensure that the constituent documents comply with the requirements laid down by the relevant legislation. After registration, certificates of registration shall be provided within one month. In addition to this registration any company with foreign participation must register[6] also with the following:
   (a) the Ministry of Finance;
   (b) the Ministry of Foreign Economic Relations; and
   (c) any other body authorised by legislation of Kazakhstan.
2. In accordance with the foreign investment legislation certain types of activities carried out by a foreign company require a concession.[7] This is basically a permit to carry out the said activity. Concessions are granted by the local branch of the State Committee of State Property only on the basis of competitive bidding and after an investigation into the financial reliability and the professional experience of the applicant has been carried out.[8] With the application the following documents will have to be submitted:
   (a) draft concession agreement between the foreign investor and the 'host party' which is the local division of the State Committee of State Property,
   (b) feasibility study;[9] and
   (c) evidence from financial institutions who are willing to act as guarantors for the project.

---

5. Law 'On Enterprises' of 13 February 1991 and the Law 'On Economic Activity and Entrepreneurship' of 15 January 1991.
6. Law 'On Foreign Investment' of 17 January 1991.
7. Preamble of the Law 'On Concessions' of December 1991.
8. Article 6(3), Law 'On Concessions'.
9. For the coverage of the feasibility study, especially with regard to environmental matters, see Friedrich Eicke: 'The Impact of Russian Environmental Regulation on Petroleum Operations', *Oil and Gas Law and Taxation Review* (1992). Although this article refers to feasibility studies prepared in the Russian context the conceptual approach of the Kazakh authorities appears to be analogous to that of the Russian administration.

The examination of these documents shall not take longer than one month.

3. The third main right that must be obtained is the actual petroleum right. However, since Kazakhstan has no specific petroleum legislation this right is awarded under the general subsoil resource legislation as set out in the June 1992 Code on Subsoil Resources and the Processing of Minerals. The code vests all rights to subsoil resources in the state which for certain resources awards production rights against the payment of tax and royalty and subject to the compliance with environmental, safety and other obligations.[10]

4. Finally, the right to use the surface in the licensed area must be obtained in accordance with the land legislation.

This being the principal concept President Nazarbaev has introduced another authority into the award process. On 8 June 1992 he issued a Decree establishing the National Foreign Investment Agency of Kazakhstan. Its remit is not exactly clear. Although the agency is financed by state funds, credits and loans it is also required to act in accordance with 'commercial principles'. This might indicate that the agency is taking on the role of both a promotional body as well as that of a commercial enterprise.

Despite all these efforts to establish a clear line of authority one cannot point to a single authority when asked for the award of petroleum rights. With regard to identified fields – whether developed or undeveloped – it is recommended to approach the production entity which holds the right to the discovery as well as the respective local authorities, and then follow up with contacts to the central authorities unless – of course – the project is regarded as being of 'national importance' as for example the Tengiz field.

For classic exploration and production projects it may be better to approach central authorities first while at the same time maintaining close contacts to the local branches of the Ministry of Geology.

When negotiating a petroleum agreement in Kazakhstan there are two different types available: Joint venture and production sharing. However, the joint venture concept is favoured by the Kazakh side, especially by entities on the local level. The reason is that they feel that within the framework of a joint venture they are able to obtain positions in the management and other levels of administration. In this context it must be recalled that traditionally the oil industry in the former Soviet Union has taken on a number of non-specific tasks like for example growing vegetables, running kindergartens, etc. It has been said that the relation between employees in the primary sector of business to those which work in the non-specific sector could be as high as 1:4.

With regard to joint ventures there may arise the problem that the Kazakh side must meet its cash obligations proportionate to its participating share. Since all entities are stripped of hard currency this is a problem that should not be underestimated at least up to a stage when the joint venture starts exporting against convertible currency. In the past some contracts have been signed in Kazakhstan which failed to address this problem. Although it will usually be

10. Article 5, Code 'On the Subsoil Resources and the Processing of Minerals'.

better in such an environment to oblige the foreign contractor to obtain sufficient funds for the development of the fields and then reimburse it from the Kazakh partner's share, this may not always appeal to small potential Western investors, especially those with no oil industry experience since it may be impossible for such companies to advance the necessary funds.

Therefore these contracts usually contain a provision providing for equal contributions for the financing of the project, based on the respective participating share of the partners. However, since the Kazakh side may seek to negotiate a high participating share in excess of 60 per cent it eventually inevitably causes a number of difficulties when it comes to paying up.

However, difficulties arising as a result of the specific problems experienced in the CIS may on the other hand be solved by means which are provided by the somewhat unusual conditions of these countries. A solution for one of the Kazakh joint venture partners was to 'lend' oil from one of its producing sister companies for a price which equalled the domestic market price. This price is much lower than the world market price, which at the time of the transaction was about \$4/bbl. It was agreed that as soon as the joint venture commenced production it would deliver the same amount back to its supplier.

For the time being the joint venture went on to export the obtained oil to the West and realised an obviously higher price on the open market. Although it had to pay the equivalent of \$4/bbl as a deposit to its oil supplier it could nevertheless use the difference between the domestic and the international market price to contribute towards its cash obligations.

An alternative approach in the form of an asset swap could have been suggested to the Kazakh partner by an oil company with existing assets elsewhere in the world. Such a solution would have the additional advantage to the Kazakh company to learn from the experience in other parts of the world and to gain a comparative commercial insight into developed concepts for the financing of such projects.

21.3 TRAPS IN THE LEGAL SYSTEM

Existing legislation promulgated in the era of the former Soviet Union may continue to be relevant to new projects. This can be illustrated with the following example. With the passing of the Subsoil Law in May 1992 the government issued an implementing resolution repealing the 1975 Subsoil Law. Although petroleum rights had been awarded before that date nobody cared to have a look at the 1975 law. In a case which could possibly have gone to arbitration this law would have been of importance. It required production entities which made no use of a discovery to return the block to a state committee. Thus, it prohibited producing companies to assign a field to another entity. However, this was exactly what producing entities did when assigning their rights to a joint venture under a contract with a foreign company.

Another example for the relevance of local legislation is the choice of law clause. In one case the partners agreed on Kazakh law as the governing law of the contract. At the time when the contract was signed the foreign investment legislation of January and June 1991 had not been passed which spells out the grounds on which a foreign investment contract may be revoked. Surprisingly enough the petroleum contract itself contained no provisions either. So one had to go back into Kazakh contract law. Although the contract law, which is of the late 1950s, was designed for the purposes of a communist society it contains one provision which allows the contract to be rescinded if one party does not comply with its obligations under a mutual contract. However, the provision is obviously too plain to cater suitably for the requirements of an investment contract.

21.4 FISCAL TERMS

The presently prevailing form of cooperation is a joint venture[11] although production sharing contracts have been signed with Chevron for the giant Tengiz field and with Elf for various development projects in the Aktyubinsk Oblast.

All terms relevant to the joint venture or production sharing contract are negotiated individually by the relevant regional organisations depending on the kind of project, e.g. development projects, enhanced oil recovery projects etc.

Fiscal terms given below are applicable to joint venture arrangements only. It is understood that in a production sharing contract other terms may be negotiated.

Royalties are payable at a negotiable rate, sometimes as high as 20 per cent. In December 1991 a profit tax with a general rate of 35 per cent was introduced. Joint ventures pay at a preferential rate of 30 per cent (if the foreign share exceeds 30 per cent) or at the general rate (if the foreign share is less than 30 per cent).[12]

Export tax is levied at 40 per cent on all hard currency revenues.

The following are deductible from the balance profit: rentals, dividends, the amount received from participation in a joint venture except from income received abroad and allocations to the construction, maintenance and repair of local highways.

No depreciation provisions have been reported as being established.

The state has the right to receive a fixed quota of the production. It also has a priority right to purchase all or part of the rest of the production, on terms to be agreed.[13]

11. In December 1992 a list of projects was presented at government-sponsored promotions in London and Houston, for which joint ventures were proposed by the Kazakh authorities.
12. Law 'On Taxation of Enterprises, Associations and Organisations' of 14 February 1991 (as amended).
13. Article 15, Law 'On Concessions'.

Figure 21.2 Republic of Kazakhstan fiscal regime – schematic representation (numbers in italics represent negative cash flow elements).

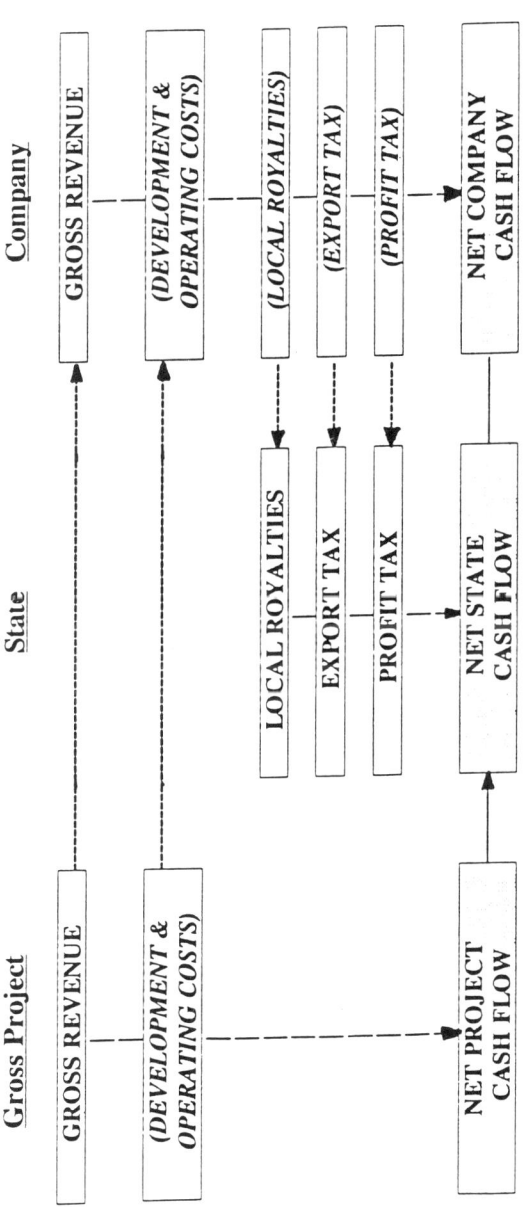

21.5 SUMMARY OF TERMS AND CONDITIONS[14]

21.5.1 Laws

On 13 June 1992 the Kazakh Code on Subsoil Resources and the Processing of Minerals came into force. The law contains specific provisions concerning the ownership of mineral resources, the award of licences for the exploration and development of those resources, and the distribution of power between the central government and local authorities. However, as such there is no specific petroleum legislation in place in Kazakhstan. Therefore petroleum operations are subject to regulation by generally applicable legislation. The main provisions governing economic activity are contained in the Foreign Investment Law of 17 January 1991, the related Concessions Law of December 1991, the Enterprise Law of 15 January 1991, the Tax Law of 14 February 1991 (as amended), and foreign exchange legislation.

21.5.2 Licensing authority

The competence to enter into contracts with foreign companies has not been sufficiently defined. However, the Subsoil Law provides for local authorities, jointly with the Committee of Geology and the Supreme Soviet, to be responsible for the award of contracts. In addition President Nazarbaev issued a Decree on 8 June 1992 establishing the National Foreign Investment Agency of Kazakhstan. Its remit is not exactly clear. Although the agency is financed by state funds, credits and loans it is also required to act in accordance with 'commercial principles'.

21.5.3 Contract type

The presently prevailing form of cooperation is a joint venture although production-sharing contracts have been signed with Chevron for the giant Tengiz field and with Elf for various development projects in the Aktyubinsk Oblast.

All terms relevant to the joint venture or production sharing contracts are negotiated individually by the relevant regional organisations depending on the kind of project, e.g. development projects, enhanced oil recovery projects etc.

21.5.4 National oil companies

None, as such. Each region has state organisations which negotiate agreements in their region.

---

14. For a detailed review, see Petroconsultants (UK) Ltd, *Acreage, Laws and Tax – CIS, Kazakhstan* (Vols 2 and 3).

21.5.5 State participation

None.

21.5.6 Licence terms

All terms relevant to the joint venture or production sharing contracts are negotiated individually by the relevant regional organisations depending on the kind of project, e.g. development projects, enhanced oil recovery projects, etc. However, certain terms are set out by existing legislation.

Under the law 'On Enterprises in Kazakhstan' certain activities may not be undertaken by enterprises without a licence. These activities include (*inter alia*) geological operations and the exploration of mineral deposits, forests and water resources (Article 4).

21.5.7 Fiscal terms

The terms given below are applicable to joint venture arrangements only. It is understood that in a production sharing contract other terms may be negotiated.

Royalty	Royalties are payable at a negotiable rate, sometimes as high as 20 per cent.
Taxation	In December 1991 a Profit Tax of 35 per cent was introduced. Joint ventures pay at a preferential rate of 30 per cent (if the foreign share exceeds 30 per cent) or 35 per cent (if the foreign share is less than 30 per cent).
	Export tax is levied at 40 per cent on all hard currency revenues.
Deductions and depreciations	The following are deductible from the balance profit: rentals, dividends,the amount received from participation in a joint venture except from income received abroad and allocations to the construction, maintenance and repair of local highways.
	No depreciation provisions have been reported as being established.
Development fund	Contributions to the Business Support and Development Fund must be made at a rate of 1 per cent of after tax profit.
Domestic supply obligation	The state has the right to receive a fixed quota of the production. It also has a priority right to purchase all or part of the rest of the production, on terms to be agreed.

21.5.8 Bonus and other payments

Payments law: 'On Concessions'	There are four types of payments the concessionaire will be liable for ● bonuses, ● rentals,

- production based payments (royalties), and
- income based payments (taxes).

Bonuses
The payments made in form of bonuses are non-recoverable as they have to be made before the commencement of investment activities. The amount to be paid will be agreed in the concession agreement.

Rentals
Rentals are independent of the income of the concessionaire. Their amount will be fixed by the local Soviets in accordance with the guidelines contained in the legislation. Local Soviets are free to introduce progressive rates of rentals or rentals only for a limited term (eg until the beginning of production) in order to provide the concessionaire with financial incentives.

Insurance
Under the Concessions Law the details concerning risk insurance will have to be agreed between the parties to the concession agreement. Social insurance for employees is regulated by legislation and/or in the case of foreign employees by the individual employment contracts.

21.5.9 Foreign exchange provisions

Provisions
In January 1992 the President of Kazakhstan issued the Decree 'On the Organisation of Foreign Economic Activity'. In most aspects the provisions of this decree replaced the relevant sections of the Law 'On Currency Regulations in the Kazakh SSR' of 13 June 1991.

Note: As the 1991 Law has not, however, been repealed it remains in force and foreign investors will have to keep its provisions in mind especially as far as they are not contradicted by the later decree. Furthermore, Article 1 of the Law provides an extensive list of definitions of the terms used by the legislator.

The decree of 25 January 1992 envisages that the State Bank:

(a)   fix an exchange rate for the rouble in 1992 to be used for the obligatory hard currency sales to the Republican Currency Fund and the Currency Funds of the Oblasts' Soviets;

(b)   set the marginal difference between the exchange rate applicable to purchase of currency and that applicable to sales of currency; and

(c)   set the limit on the amount of currency that may be purchased and exported.

Foreign currency sales
Foreign currency will only be sold to legal entities registered in Kazakhstan if required for the purpose of importing goods or services and to foreign investors for the purpose of remittance of profits. The exchange rate used for these sales shall be determined according to supply and demand on the currency markets.

According to the currency legislation this will be done through transactions on the Exchange market which may be performed by anyone through Kazvnesheconombank or any other bank licensed to conduct operations on the Exchange.

Note: As long as there is no separate currency for the Republic of Kazakhstan it seems unrealistic to expect these suggestions to be effective except for the conversion (on paper) of foreign currency.

Foreign currency transactions within Kazakhstan

All transactions in foreign currency between legal entities and physical persons for the purpose of remuneration for employment are prohibited. The existing consumer trade and services provided for foreign currency in Kazakhstan will, however, be maintained.

According to currency legislation both residents and non-residents shall be free to import foreign currency into Kazakhstan without limitation. Any such currency imported must, however, be put into a foreign currency account with Kazvnesheconombank or any other bank licensed to perform foreign currency transactions. Non-residents may conduct currency transactions only through Kazvnesheconombank.

Remittance

Under Kazakh law the remittance of profit from foreign investment activities in Kazakhstan is generally permitted. This has been expressly laid down in the investment legislation, the currency legislation, and the legislation governing foreign economic activity.

21.6 MAIN LEGISLATIVE SOURCES OF KAZAKHSTAN APPLICABLE TO PETROLEUM OPERATIONS

*I-K-1	The Law 'On Ownership in the Kazakh SSR' of 15 December 1990
*II-K-1	The Law 'On Free Economic Zones in the Kazakh Republic', 30 November 1991
II-K-2	The Law 'On the Land Reform in Kazakhstan' on 31 July 1991
II-K-3	Decree 'On the Improvement of Organisation and Activity of the Administrative State Bodies of the Republic of Kazakhstan in Conditions of Economic Reform' of 7 February 1992
II-K-4	Law 'On Destatisation and Privatisation'
II-K-5	Presidential Decree of 28 April 1992 'On Measures for the Activisation of the Decentralisation and Privatisation of Property in the Branches of Material Production', 28 April 1992
II-K-6	The Law 'On Mortgage', 23 December 1991
*III-K-1	The Law of the Kazakh SSR 'On the Main Principles of Foreign Economic Activity of the Kazakh SSR' of 17 January 1991
*III-K-2	The Law of the Kazakh SSR 'On Investment Activities in the Kazakh SSR' of 10 June 1991
*III-K-3	The Law 'On Partnerships and Shareholding Companies' of 21 June 1991
*III-K-4	The Law 'On Free Economic Activity and the Development of Entrepreneurship in the Kazakh SSR' of 15 January 1991
*III-K-5	The Law 'On Foreign Investments in the Kazakh SSR' of 17 January 1991
*III-K-6	The Law 'On Enterprises in Kazakhstan' of 13 February 1991
*IV-K-1	The Law 'On Concessions in the Republic of Kazakhstan' of December 1991

*V-K-1   The Code 'On Subsoil Resources and the Reprocessing of Minerals' of 30 May 1992

*VI-K-1   The Law 'On the Taxation of Enterprises, Associations and Organisations' of 14 February 1991, as amended by:

*VI-K-1A The Law 'On the Amendments to the Law of the Kazakh SSR' On Taxation of Enterprises and Organisations' of 24 December 1991VI-K-2The Kazakh Law 'On Value Added Tax' (with a few exceptions this law is absolutely identical to the Russian Law of 6 December 1991: VI-R-2)

*VI-K-3   The Law 'On the Fiscal System of the Kazakh SSR' of December 1991

VII-K-1   Presidential Decree 'On the Organisation of Foreign Economic Activity in the Republic of Kazakhstan for the Period of Stabilisation of Economy and Market Transformation' of 25 January 1992

VII-K-2   Law 'On Currency Regulations in the Kazakh SSR' of 13 June 1991 (N661-XII).

Chapter 22

Natural Gas from Russia/CIS for Europe

Jochen Alsleben

This chapter sets out to examine the development and current status of natural gas trade between the former Soviet Union and Europe, with the emphasis being on trade with Germany.

22.1 NATURAL GAS FROM THE FORMER SOVIET UNION

22.1.1 Sources of German gas supplies

As illustrated in Table 22.1 the former Soviet Union is one of the most important trading partners for natural gas supplies to the former West Germany, and as far as East Germany is concerned, natural gas from the former Soviet Union is the only notable foreign source of natural gas at present.

Table 22.1 Natural gas supplies in Germany

Source	Old Federal States		New Federal States		Germany	
	1990	1991 (tentative)	1990	1991 (tentative)	1990	1991 (tentative)
Domestic	24%	23%	26%	30%**	24%	23%
foreign	76%	77%	74%	70%	76%	77%
Netherlands	28%	33%	–	–	25%	29%
CIS	32%	29%	74%	70%	37%	34%
Norway	15%	14%	–	–	13%	13%
Denmark	1%	1%	–	–	1%	1%
Total supplies	100%	100%	100%	100%	100%	100%
(Mtoe)	(49.4)	(approx.53)	(6,8)	(approx.6)	(56.2)	(approx.58)

*Natural Gas and associated gas.

**including former West German supplies (approx. 6%).

Figure 22.1 World gas resources

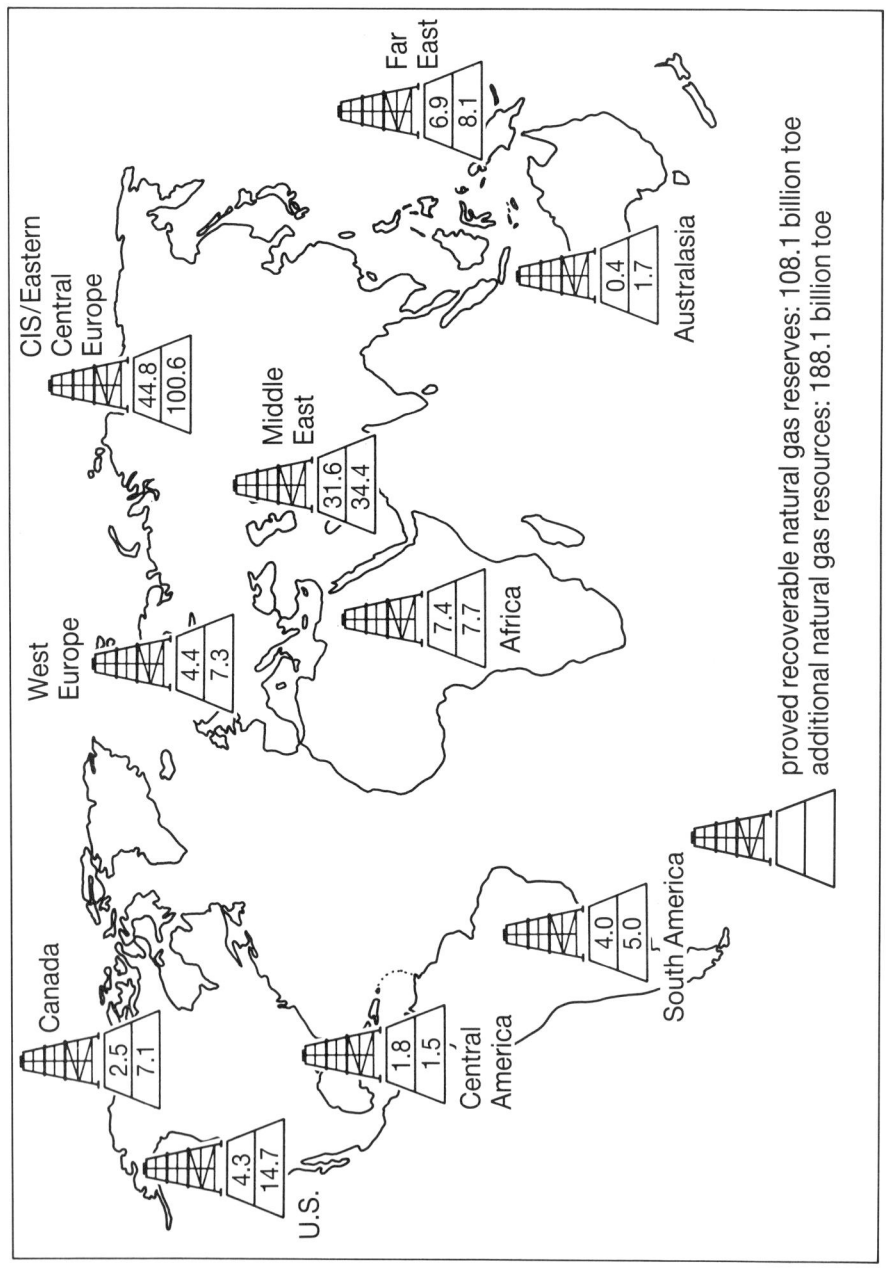

Figure 22.2 Energy production in the former Soviet Union/CIS

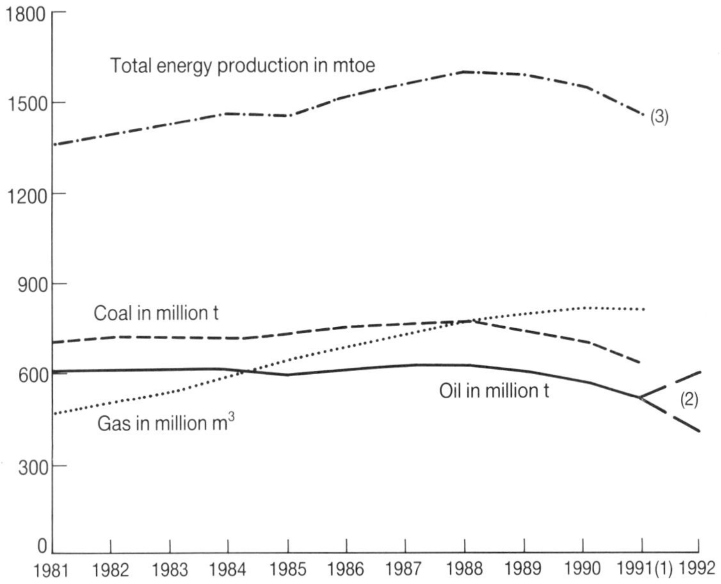

(1) C.I.S. = former Soviet Union exclusive of Baltic Republics and Georgia
(2) 460 million t forecast by Russia, 425 million t forecast by western Europe,
   410 million t forecast by Russian Oil Company
(3) estimate

22.1.2 The ex-USSR share of natural gas supplies

The former Soviet Union is also one of the most important gas trading partners in the world. As Figure 22.1 shows, it has:

- the largest proved recoverable natural gas reserves in the world, namely 44.8 billion tonnes of oil equivalent; and
- the largest potential resources (100.6 billion tonnes of oil equivalent).

Approximately 38 per cent of the world's proven recoverable reserves, are located within the territorial boundaries of the former Soviet Union. This is in line with the CIS's huge energy production as can be seen from Figure 22.2.

Figure 22.3 shows that the peak of natural gas production was reached in 1990 with 815 billion m[3], and that gas production then slightly decreased to 810 billion m[3].

Nearly 90 per cent of the natural gas produced in the Soviet Union (1973: 200 billion m[3], 1981: 435 billion m[3], 1991: 810 billion m[3]), is destined for domestic use. In spite of this the Commonwealth of Independent States is still the largest natural gas exporter in the world (Figure 22.4). Only approximately 12 per cent (1991: approx. 110 billion m[3]) of the natural gas produced by the CIS is exported. Approximately 50 per cent is used by Eastern Europe and 50 per cent by Western Europe.

Figure 22.3 Natural gas production in the former Soviet Union

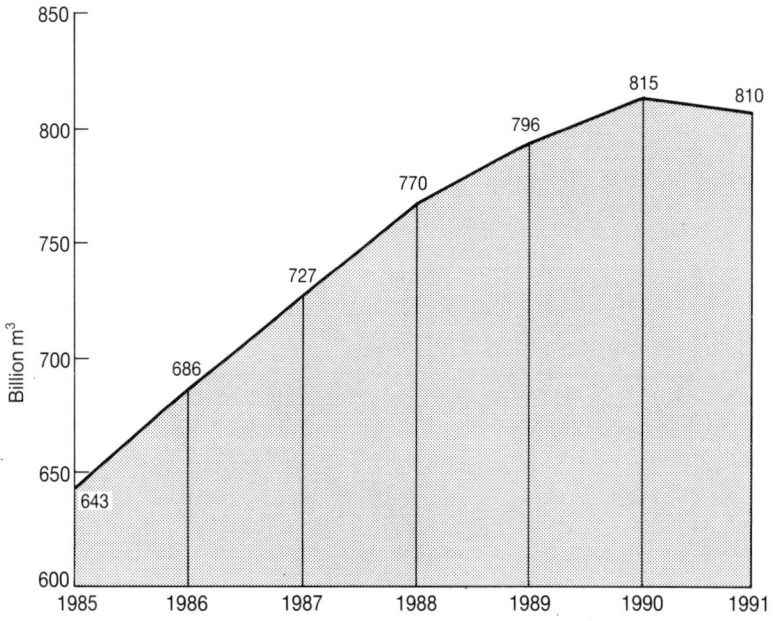

Figure 22.4 Natural gas exports of the former Soviet Union.

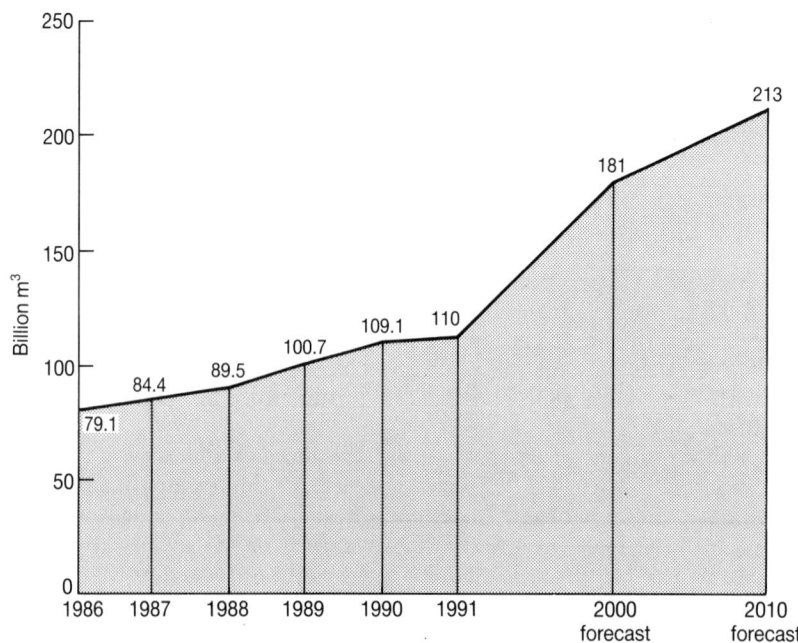

Figure 22.5 Gas supplies from the former Soviet Union

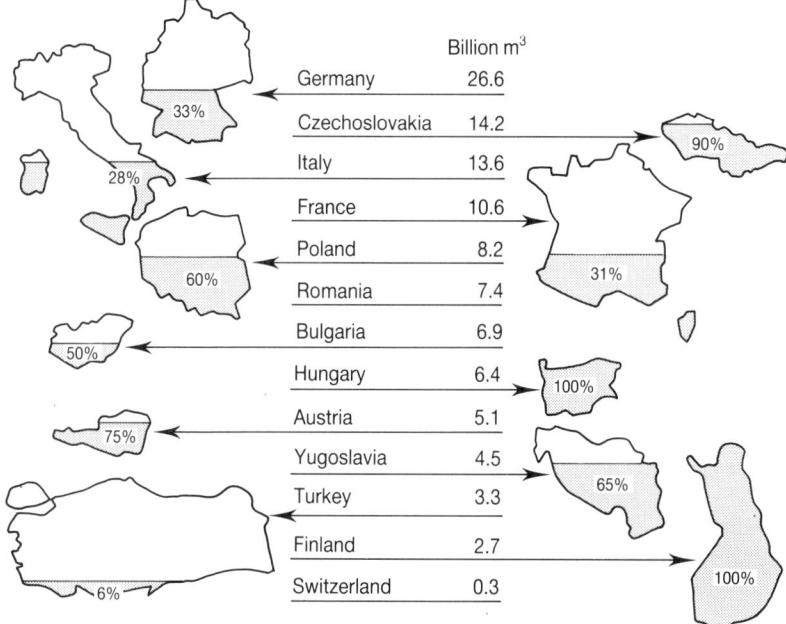

	Billion m³
Germany	26.6
Czechoslovakia	14.2
Italy	13.6
France	10.6
Poland	8.2
Romania	7.4
Bulgaria	6.9
Hungary	6.4
Austria	5.1
Yugoslavia	4.5
Turkey	3.3
Finland	2.7
Switzerland	0.3

Figure 22.5 gives a survey and comparison of the importing European countries.

22.1.3 The geographical origin of natural gas in the former Soviet Union

The largest and most productive natural gas fields are situated in the territory of the Russian Federation (Figure 22.6):

- the natural gas region of western Siberia: the most important natural gas producing region in the world, which accounts for approximately 60 per cent of all natural gas production in the CIS countries; the Medvesche, Yamburg (plateau ca. 250 Mrd. m[3]/a), Vyngapor and in particular the Urengoi fields (plateau ca. 300 Mrd. m[3]/a), currently make up this region;
- Orenburg;
- Baku;
- and in future also the Jamal peninsula.

At present most of the natural gas produced in Western Siberia comes from the Urengoi field, the proven recoverable reserves of which total approx. 8,000 billion m[3]. The last of the so called giant natural gas fields in West Siberia to go into production was Yamburg (1986). The reserves of Yamburg, a neighbouring field to Urengoi, are half those of Urengoi.

Figure 22.6 Gas from CIS for Europe

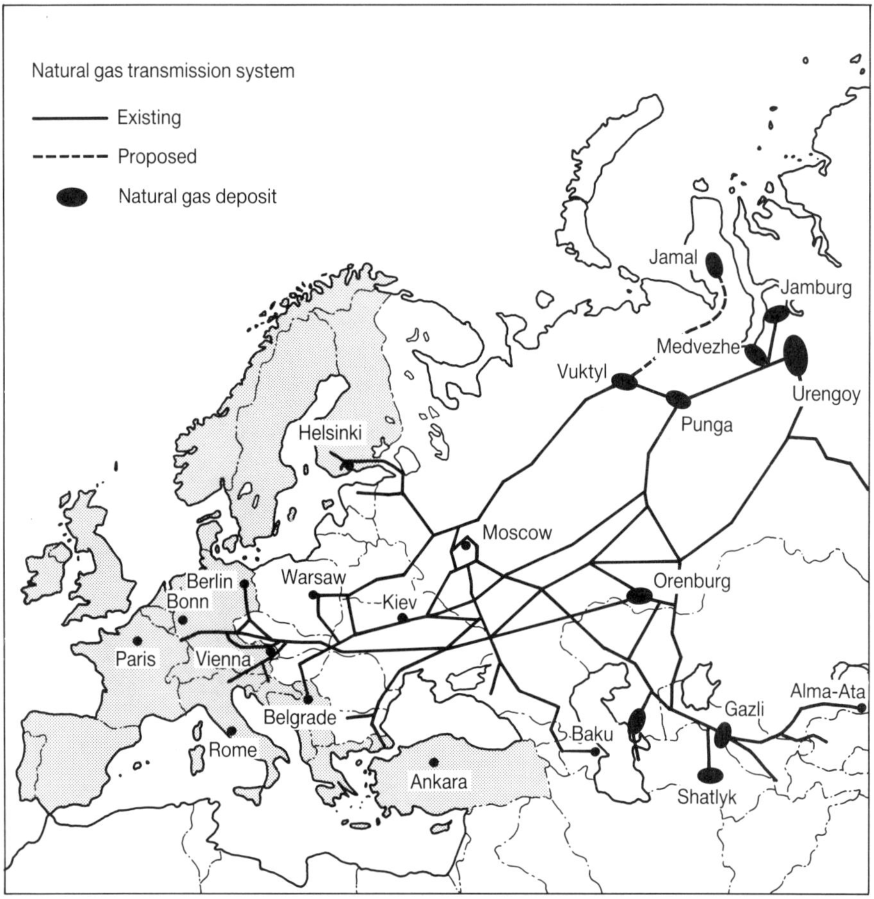

22.1.4 Transit lines of Russian gas to Germany

The natural gas produced in Urengoi is first transported through a 6-string pipeline system to the centre of the Russian Federation. From there part of the gas is then shipped to its western borders (Figure 22.7). The natural gas flows through the Ukraine to reach Czechoslovakia at Uzgorod/Velke Kapusany and then reaches Germany at the German–Czechoslovakian border at the delivery station near Waidhaus. There the Russian gas is fed into the Ruhrgas and MEGAL pipeline systems and then flows through three main strings to customers in Germany and France.

The natural gas bound for East Germany also flows through Czechoslovakia and reaches the German border at St Kateriny/Sayda.

Figure 22.7 Transit lines in the CSFR

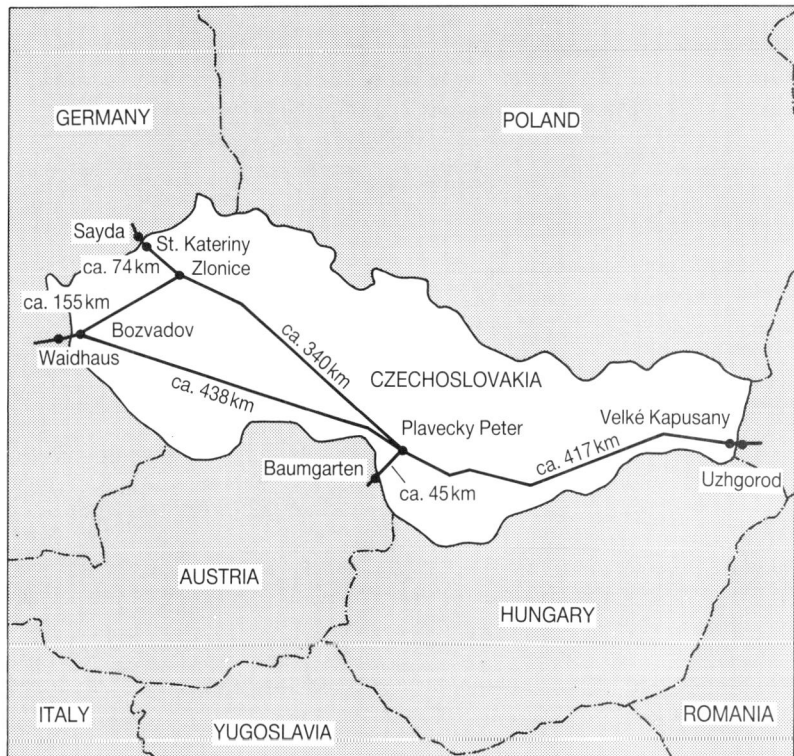

22.1.5 The current situation and prospects for the future

Western European natural gas production today accounts for some 45 per cent of all gas consumed in Western Europe. By the year 2005, this figure will probably fall to one-third, leaving a gap which will have to be made up by new imports commencing around the year 2000 and totalling some 70 billion m[3]/ year. Russian gas will therefore continue to play a major role in gas supplies for Germany as well as for Western and Eastern Europe.

This presupposes that the CIS countries continue to be reliable trading partners delivering natural gas at competitive prices and on conditions appropriate to the international market.

The CIS states have had severe problems with their energy production, especially with their gas and oil production, for some years now. While oil production fell from 620 million tonnes in 1990 to 515 million tonnes in 1991, gas production now seems to stagnate at the 1989 level. The trend towards declining rather than increasing production has also continued in 1992.

The main reason is the lack of capital and skilled personnel to rehabilitate the outdated plants and equipment. This lack of capital has become particularly acute since the production facilities are no longer state-financed but have to find their own funds.

The search for new deposits (the exploration and development of new oil and gas fields) will also be stepped up. The Russians now want to concentrate on the Siberian Yamal project, which, when completed, will provide another 20 to 40 million m[3] of natural gas for export, but not before 1997/98.

22.2 HISTORY OF CONTRACTUAL RELATIONS

22.2.1 Survey

In 1969, the first negotiations on the delivery of natural gas from the Soviet Union to West Germany took place between Ruhrgas AG and the Soviet foreign trade company V/O Sojuznefteexport (later to be called V/O Sojuzgazexport and now GVP Gazexport).

In 1970, the first supply agreement for an annual 3 billion m[3] of natural gas was signed; deliveries commenced in October 1973.

In 1972, a second agreement was signed increasing the annual quantities by 4 billion m.

In 1974, a third agreement for another annual 2.5 billion m was signed. Within a few years, three agreements now running to the end of the year 2008 had been signed, and an annual 9.5 billion m of gas had been contracted.

In 1975, a complicated agreement between the National Iranian Gas Company and the German Ruhrgas, the French Gaz de France and the Austrian ÖMV AG was signed for an annual quantity of approx. 13 billion m which was to be delivered to Western Europe across the Soviet–Iranian border from 1981 onwards. At the same time the three West European companies concluded an agreement with V/O Sojuzgazexport on the transit of these quantities through the Soviet Union. However, as a consequence of the Iranian Revolution in 1979 the National Iranian Gas Company was no longer prepared to implement this interesting agreement on the purchase of Iranian natural gas.

In 1980, Ruhrgas again started negotiations with Sojuzgazexport on the contracting of further quantities of natural gas.

In 1981, another agreement was signed which provided for natural gas to be supplied across the German border at Waidhaus from 1984 to the year 2008. In connection with this project, the Soviets also declared their willingness to make natural gas available for supplies to West Berlin.

In 1982, an agreement, significantly participating Ruhrgas, was signed by Sojuzgazexport for the delivery of an annual 380 million m[3] of natural gas for the supply of the Confederation of Switzerland via Waidhaus, deliveries of which commenced in 1988.

In 1983, an agreement was signed between Ruhrgas and Sojuzgazexport for the delivery of an annual 700 million m[3] of natural gas (1. Berlin Contract) across the border between Czechoslovakia and the former German Democratic Republic (East Germany). This gas was destined for the West Berlin market and commenced to flow in 1985. Ruhrgas signed an agreement on the transit of that natural gas through the former German Democratic Republic with former East German state-owned company Verbundnetze Energie (KVE). To move this gas KVE constructed and operated a separate 235 km natural gas pipeline system.

In 1986, an agreement between Ruhrgas and Sojuzgazexport was signed for the delivery of an annual 180 Mio. m[3] for the supply of a West Berlin power station (2. Berlin Contract), deliveries commencing in 1988.

22.2.2 Political background

All four big supply agreements made history with the slogan 'Natural Gas Pipeline Deal'. Each of the deals was accompanied by the delivery of large-diameter pipes and/or other equipment for the Soviet gas industry as well as by a loan, although implemented on the basis of legally independent agreements.

The Natural Gas Pipeline Deals unleashed hefty debates between the USA and Western Europe. In particular, the fourth natural gas agreement was signed in November 1981 despite resistance from the Americans. The Natural Gas Pipeline Deal became the largest East–West project in history and, by virtue of its sheer magnitude, also became a symbol of diverging European and American views on the new East–West policy of détente.

There are three main considerations which made the Gas Pipeline Deals so publicly known and successful.

Political reasons

When the first negotiations on the import of natural gas were held towards the end of the sixties, the Cold War between East and West was still in full swing. The new 'Ostpolitik' of the German government aimed at detente with all means available. One of these means which was hotly disputed by the politicians of the time was the build-up of economic relations in the energy sector, and in particular agreements on the delivery of natural gas from the former Soviet Union.

Economic reasons

For the Soviet Union, trading relations with West European energy industries were of prime importance as a main source of foreign exchange. The main goods imported by the Soviet Union were and still are pipes and other equipment for the gas industry.

Since the 1973/74 oil crisis there have been efforts throughout the world to substitute oil by gas. In Germany, for example, natural gas only covered 5 per cent of the entire energy consumption in 1970. In 1981, it had already risen to 16 per cent, and today it is almost at 18 per cent in former West Germany.

National security

The national security aspects did not prevent Western European countries from starting trade relations with the Soviet Union particularly with natural gas, because Western Europe's domestic supplies of gas are much larger than its domestic oil supplies.

22.3 CURRENT ISSUES IN NATURAL GAS RELATIONS: A New Marketing Strategy for Gazprom

For the last three years gas policy in CIS states has been made by the state-owned concern Gazprom, which fully replaced the former Soviet Ministry of Gas in 1989. After the reunification of the two German states in October 1990, Gazprom came up with a new concept aiming at penetrating the European natural gas market for the period from 1991 through the year 2000.

In September 1990, Gazprom created a joint venture company with Wintershall a 100 per cent subsidiary of the large chemical producer BASF. Gazprom now offers quantities of Russian gas to the main East German merchant company called Verbundnetz Gas through this joint venture called Wintershall Erdgas Handelshaus GmbH, but demands higher prices than any other Western European country pays for Russian gas. The strategy of Gazprom has led to a real gas to gas competition: Russian gas sold by Wintershall Erdgas Handelshaus now competes against Russian gas sold by Verbundnetz Gas.

Chapter 23

International Petroleum Exploration and Exploitation Agreements:
A comprehensive environmental appraisal

Zhiguo Gao*

23.1 INTRODUCTION

Petroleum exploration and exploitation have been carried out in many developing countries by international oil companies since the turn of this century. The legal and commercial relationship between petroleum-producing countries and foreign oil companies was defined and governed by what were called traditional oil concession agreements before the 1950s, and since then by what are known as modern petroleum contracts.

The development of international petroleum exploration and exploitation agreements has caught the attention of interested scholars. Although there has been in recent years some academic discussion of the new forms of contracts utilised by developing countries, recent legal studies seem to suffer from several common deficiencies. Among these is a narrow focus on the economic aspects of the contracts, specifically the financial and fiscal regimes, to the exclusion of socioeconomic aspects. From an environmental point of view, oil exploration is a potentially destructive process beginning with exploration and ending in extraction. But environmental concerns have generally been neglected by, not only the governments of producing countries and exploiting companies, but also nearly all writers and commentators. Hardly anyone has suggested that environmental protection and resources conservation also be part of the petroleum agreements.[1]

* Post-doctoral fellow currently at the East-West Center, Honolulu, the United States; J. S. D., Dalhousie University, Halifax, Canada, 1993. The author wishes to thank Prof. Thomas W. Waelde, Director, Center for Petroleum/Mineral Law & Policy, University of Dundee, for his encouragement and constructive comments in the course of preparing this paper. The assistance in editing this chapter by Mr John John Thomas at the East-West Centre is also gratefully acknowledged.

1. To this author's knowledge, Alfred J. Boulos is perhaps the only writer who has suggested that environmental conditions be also one of the objectives of the petroleum contract. See A.J. Boulos 'Mutuality of interests between company and government: myth and fact?' in Section

317

Unfortunately, this problem has not been well documented and consequently has received little attention from the world in general and the petroleum industry in particular.[2] So an important general question that has been ignored so far is how environmental management is dealt with in the contractual relationships between government and company. The specific questions raised here are these: (a) Have environmental conditions been made an integral part of petroleum agreements? (b) What trends are observable in petroleum agreements with respect to environmental management? (c) What are the problems with the existing environmental provisions in petroleum contractual arrangements? (d) Can basic environmental provisions be developed for consideration by producing states and incorporated into their model contracts? (e) How can environmental sustainability in petroleum production be promoted in practice? In this chapter an attempt is made to fill the gap by examining these issues behind the evolution of the environmental aspects of various legal arrangements for international petroleum exploration and exploitation.[3]

23.2 INTERNATIONAL PETROLEUM AGREEMENTS AND ENVIRONMENTAL PROTECTION

23.2.1 Environmental regulation of traditional concession contracts

During the first half of this century, the world community was first beset with global wars and then faced with such urgent tasks as decolonisation, reconstruction, and development. Environmental protection and resource conservation had not caught world attention. The petroleum industry and concessionary arrangements were no exception to this general lack of environmental awareness.

As for the environmental aspects of traditional concession agreements, a careful examination of the concession system confirms that many of the traditional oil concessions are silent. The 1901 D'Arcy concession,[4] the 1933

cont.
on Energy and National Resources Law (SERL) of International Bar Association (IBA) ed., *Energy Law '90: Changing Energy Markets: The Legal Consequences* (Proceedings of 9th Advanced Seminar on Petroleum, Mineral and Energy Resources Law, 22–7 April 1990, the Netherlands) (London: Graham & Trotman, 1990), pp. 12–13.

2.   For instance, a recent study by the United Nations Centre on Transnational Corporations (UNCTC) on world petroleum and mining agreements listed 13 factors to be taken into account in the formulation of exploration contracts for the 1980s, but environmental management was not mentioned in the checklist. See UNCTC, *Main Features and Trends in Petroleum and Mining Agreements*, UN Doc. ST/CTC/29, 1983, pp. 44–5.

3.   For a comprehensive discussion of this issue, the reader is referred to the author's thesis entitled 'International Offshore Petroleum Contracts: Towards the Compatibility of Energy Need and Sustainable Development', JSD dissertation, Dalhousie University, Halifax, Canada, July 1993.

4.   For the Agreement between the Government of His Imperial Majesty the Shah of Persia and William Knox D'Arcy, see Appendix to Annex 1419c, the League of Nations, *Official Journal*, XIII, 1932, pp. 2305–7.

Arabian American Oil Company (Aramco) concession and its 1939 supplemental agreement,[5] and the 1953 Abu Dhabi Marine Areas (ADMA) concession, as revised in 1966,[6] represent just a few examples of this majority group.

Environmental protection in some other concessions, if any, was only a barely relevant reference such as this: all petroleum operations must be conducted 'in workmanlike manner with reasonable precautions'.[7] But this phrase was used to require that petroleum exploration and production be carried out in a proper and unwasteful manner. It provided little environmental protection.

As an exception to this general trend, a few concessions in the early days did mention oil pollution. For instance, the 1925 Iraq Petroleum Company (IPC) concession included a clause under the subtitle 'Access of Water, *etc.*,' which reads:

The Company undertakes to take every reasonable precaution against the pollution of the elements in the vicinity of its installations. But the Government recognizes that in certain circumstances a pollution of the elements is inevitable by reason of the nature of the operations of the oil industry, and will not for the purpose of preventing this inconvenience ask the Company to undertake any measures which it could not be reasonably asked to undertake.[8]

Besides other legal defects, this provision contains a major deliberate loophole which speaks for itself: it recognises that oil pollution in certain circumstances is 'inevitable', so the company will not be asked to undertake any preventive measures. This is tantamount to authorising the concessionaire to go on to pollute under 'certain circumstances' which are not defined at all.

Generally, traditional concession agreements concluded in the first half of this century made no reference to environmental protection and management. Concerns for natural resources conservation and sustainable development were not expressed at all during this development period. This is hardly surprising, because at the time these agreements were developed environmental consciousness and thinking was in its infancy. Concerns for environmental protection and sustainable development have travelled very slowly into modern petroleum contracts, as will be demonstrated in the following section.

23.2.2 Environmental aspects of modern petroleum contracts

The third quarter of the century witnessed the decline of the old concession system and the steady emergence of new contractual arrangements. It is not

5. For the texts of the 1933 Aramco and its 1939 supplemental concessions, see Barrows Company, ed., *Middle East: Basic Oil Laws and Concession Contracts*, Vol. 1 (New York: The Petroleum Legislation Co., 1959), pp. Saudi Arabia A 1–17, A 21–9 (hereinafter *Middle East Contracts*).

6. For the text of the 1953 ADMA concession as revised in 1966, see Barrows Company, *Middle East Contracts, ibid.*, Supp. 28, 1970, pp. Abu Dhabi A 1–24.

7. Art. 2 of the Kuwait Oil Company concession, Barrows Company, *Middle East Contracts, ibid.*, Vol. 2, 1959, p. Kuwait A 1–11.

8. Art. 9 of IPC concession, Barrows Company, *Middle East Contracts, ibid.*, pp. Iraq A 1–37.

feasible to present here a detailed examination of the environmental provisions of all the petroleum arrangements in the developing world. For convenience of discussion, four developing countries have been selected as case studies of four principal categories of the modern petroleum contracts: the concession contract, the production-sharing contract, the risk service contract, and the hybrid contract.

A Thailand's modern concession contract

Thailand has little history of environmental protection and this is reflected in its petroleum concession system. It is perhaps one of the most lenient states regarding environmental regulation over international petroleum operations. Its original model contract of 1971 and all the individual concessions negotiated and concluded in the first 12 rounds before 1989 were silent on environmental protection, despite a brief reference in the 1971 Petroleum Act which reads in full:

In conducting petroleum operations, the concessionaire shall take appropriate measures in accordance with good petroleum industry practice to prevent pollution in any place by oil, mud or any other substance.

In the case where pollution of any place by oil, mud or any other substance results from the concessionaire's petroleum operations, the concessionaire shall take immediate action to combat such pollution.[9]

Failure to comply with this provision may result in a fine of up to Baht 100,000 (approximately US$3,900).[10]

This simple regulation has remained unimproved to date. The model contract was not revised until 1989 to include a simple addition to the existing structure of an insurance requirement, which reads:

As an assurance for obligation to prevent and make good such damages the concessionaire shall secure insurance coverage with an insurance company acceptable to the Government with coverage amount appropriate for its operations.[11]

This insurance programme is the only improvement on the concession system in nearly 20 years. The recent amendment has by and large failed to make adequate improvement over the existing provisions.

Thai contractual provisions on and practice of environmental protection show several weaknesses. The concession system provides little more than the traditional requirement of 'good petroleum industry practice' in terms of environmental protection. Neither precautionary and anticipatory approaches nor substantive preventive measures are required. Even the nominal penalty charge set by the Petroleum Act suggests a rather casual attitude toward environmental responsibility. Indeed, a couple of thousand dollars is not

9. Sec. 75 of Petroleum Act B.E. 2514 of 1971, *Gov't Gazette*, Vol. 88, Special Issue, 23 April 1971, p. 43; also reprinted in Barrows Company, ed., *Asia and Australasia: Basic Oil Laws and Concession Contracts*, Supp. 31 (New York: The Petroleum Legislation Co., 1973), pp. Thailand A 0–29 (hereinafter 'Asia Contracts').

10. *Ibid.*, sec. 108.

11. Clause 11 (2) of Ministerial Regulation No. 17 B.E. 2532 of 8 December 1989 (revised model concession contract), *Gov't Gazette*, Vol. 106, Part 227, Special Issue, 25 December 1989.

substantial enough to compel concessionaires to take their environmental obligations seriously, and it is absolutely insufficient for damage compensation caused by any kind of pollution accident. Some of the wording of environmental provisions is ambiguous, and few detailed or explicit standards have been spelled out to govern the actual environmental protection process. For instance, phrases such as 'in a way instructed by the Minister' leave considerable scope for debate about the manner of pollution control and the abandoning of rigs.

In addition to these inherent flaws in the contractual provisions, there are other unknowns to the concessionaire, such as whether existing environmental regulations will be applied to and enforced in the petroleum concession sector since no reference is made in either these regulations or in the petroleum legislation.[12] In short, international oil companies in Thailand have been operating under no real obligation to protect the environment. Some reconsideration of the basic contract structures is required if environmental resources are to be adequately protected.

B. Indonesia's production-sharing contract

Indonesia's production-sharing system has displayed little concern for the social and ecological impact of the extractive operation. Production-sharing contracts, both model and individual, do not have a separate article dealing with environmental protection. The issue is only briefly referred to in the general obligation clause for the contractor, which reads in full that the contractor.

Be responsible for the preparation and execution of the Work Program, which shall be implemented in a workmanlike manner and by appropriate scientific methods, and *contractor* shall take the necessary precautions for protection of navigation and fishing and shall prevent extensive pollution of the sea or rivers.[13]

This brief reference is the only environmental provision in Indonesia's production-sharing system. The environmental provision appears far from legally sound for several important reasons. First, its primary objective is obviously the 'execution of the Work Program'. Environmental protection is given only a subordinate position. Second, environmental obligations are not spelled out in operational terms. For instance, the phrase 'extensive pollution' is quite vague and open to many interpretations. Yet it appears that the contractor assumes no responsibility unless its operations have caused 'extensive pollution'. Third, the provision fails to specify either the environmental goals to be achieved or several important requirements such as specific preventive measures, clean-up and restoration operations, or

12. Bunnag, J., 'Thailand's mineral resources crisis: A legal practitioner's viewpoint', 10 *J. Energy & Nat. Res. L.* 169 (1992).

13. Sec. V, art. 1.2 (d) of the Draft Production-Sharing Contract of August 1976, Barrows Company, *Asia Contracts*, *supra* note 9, Supp. 52, 1977, pp. 1–55; Production-Sharing Contract dated 12 February 1979 between Pertamina and Citco Indonesian Petroleum Corp., *ibid.*, Supp. 70, 1981, pp. 50–93; and Production-Sharing Contract of 30 August 1985 between Pertamina and Sceptre Resources Bunyu,*ibid.*, Supp. 89, 1986, pp. 1–27.

insurance programmes. The wording of this provision sounds more like a policy suggestion than legal requirements. They are not sufficiently precise or strict enough to compel foreign companies to take their environmental obligations seriously.

In addition to these limitations, nowhere in the production-sharing contract is the national environmental legislation mentioned. The contract thus fails to refer production-sharing contractors explicitly to Indonesia's existing environmental regulations. In short, the broad terms of environmental reference are basically unenforceable because they contain no enabling definitions and regulations.

C. Brazil risk service contract

Latin America has the most lax environmental control regulations over the activities of transnational corporations in the world.[14] Brazil is certainly no exception to this general situation. The issue of environmental protection was conspicuously absent from Brazil's original model risk service contract of 1976 and the individual contracts concluded in the first bidding round, though they were drafted fully four or more years after the United Nations Conference on the Human Environment held at Stockholm in 1972. The subsequent model and individual contracts made a little progress by adding to existing provisions a brief paragraph which reads in part:

Such services must also be performed in such a way that will result in a minimum ecological disruption and shall cause no damage to the public and private property located along the shore. In case pollution is caused by *contractor's Operation,* contractor is obligated to carry out the clearing operations, without prejudice of its responsibility to third parties and to competent authorities.[15]

Despite periodic revisions of the risk service terms, this provision has not been improved in subsequent model contracts and stands as the only environmental provision in Brazil's risk service contract system.

The risk service contracts have undergone a process from zero to limited environmental regulation. But the environmental provision just mentioned is far from adequate: it is vague about the environmental goals to be achieved; it provides no specific targets or objective measures of contract fulfilment; its principal purpose appears to be definition of the clean-up obligation; and it requires neither precautionary nor preventive measures during the course of petroleum operations.

In view of these defects, it seems fair to say that the risk service contract has no effective provisions on environmental protection and that foreign contractors have operated under no specific environmental obligations except the clean-up responsibility. In the absence of legal provisions in either the

14. UNCTC, *Environmental Aspects of the Activities of Transnational Corporations: A Survey,* UN Doc. ST/CTC/55, 1985, p. 23.

15. Art 5 (5.1.9) of the Model Contract between Petroleo Brasilero S.A. (Petrobrás) and Private Contractors for Offshore Exploration/Exploitation of 1977, in Barrows Company, ed., *South America: Basic Oil Laws and Concession Contracts,* Supp. 51 (New York: The Petroleum Legislation Co., 1978), pp. 1–91.

petroleum laws or the risk service contract and of an effective government and active non-government organisations to scrutinise the foreign oil companies, 'environmental and social guidelines are simply ignored.'[16]

D. China's hybrid contract

Since approximately 1980, a new type of petroleum arrangement which mixes the various prototypes has been introduced. Today hybrid or compound contracts are in use in India, Jamaica, Liberia, Tanzania, and elsewhere. The best-known example of a deliberate combination of elements is perhaps the Chinese system introduced in 1982. Chronologically, the hybrid contract is the latest type of petroleum agreement to appear on the scene after modern petroleum arrangements have been developed over a period of 20 or 30 years. China is thus the beneficiary of not only the developments in modern international petroleum agreements but also the world environmental movement.

The Chinese legislation and the hybrid contract system have developed a substantial body of provisions on environmental protection. The hybrid contract contains several environmental stipulations whereby the contractor is obliged to (a) arrange an insurance programme including 'liability for pollution and expenses for cleaning up ... [and] expenses for killing blowouts';[17] (b) prepare and submit to the Joint Management Committee for review and approval the 'emergency procedures on safety and environmental protection' before petroleum operations commence;[18] (c) 'furnish CNOOC [China National Offshore Oil Corporation] in a timely manner with reports on safety, environmental protection and accidents' in the course of petroleum operations;[19] (d) avoid any disturbance to fishery resources; and (e) provide the Chinese environmental inspectors with all necessary facilities and assistance in carrying out their functions smoothly.[20] Finally, the article on environmental protection and safety requires the contractor comprehensively to

make its best efforts to prevent pollution and damage to the atmosphere, oceans, rivers, lakes, harbours and land ... [and] use all reasonable endeavour to eliminate promptly any pollution occurring in the performance of the Petroleum Operations and minimize its consequences.[21]

16. Thomson, K., and Dudley, N., 'Transnationals and oil in Amazonia', 19 *The Ecologist* 224 (1989); For a discussion on the energy crisis and the environment in Brazil, see T.F. Kelsey, Brazil, in D.R. Kelley ed., *The Energy Crisis and the Environment: An International Perspective* (New York: Praeger Publishers, 1977), pp. 189–217.

17. Art. 21 (21.3) of the Model Contract for Offshore Operations (Beijing, China: China National Offshore Oil Corporation, 1983), 85 p.; Model Contract for the Second Round of Bidding (Beijing, China National Offshore Oil Corporation, March 1985), 83 p.; and Model Contract for the Third Round of Bidding (Beijing, China: China National Offshore Oil Corporation, September 1988), 114 p.; Petroleum Contract dated Mat 28, 1985 between Hai Nan Petroleum Development Corporation and CSR/BHP/Basin/Base Resources, Barrow Company, *Asia Contracts, supra* note 9, Supp. 97, 1988, pp. 1–83 (hereinafter collectively referred to as the 'Model and Individual Contracts').

18. *Ibid.*, art. 7 (7.2.9) of the 1985 and 1988 Model Contracts. Please note this requirement was missing in the 1983 Model Contract.

19. Art. 8 (8.5.2) of the Model and Individual Contracts, *supra* note 17.

20. *Ibid.*, art. 24 (24.2 and 3).

21. *Ibid.*, art 24.

In addition to these contractual provisions, both the Offshore Petroleum Regulations and the contract contain reference clauses requiring that the petroleum operations be carried out in strict compliance with China's environmental protection laws and regulations.[22] The most important of these laws concerning offshore oil development are the Marine Environmental Protection Law of the People's Republic of China (MEPL) and the Regulations of the People's Republic of China concerning Environmental Protection in Offshore Oil Exploration and Exploitation (the Offshore Environmental Regulations).[23] The law and its supplementary regulations contain a series of important requirements for environmental protection, such as 'Environmental Impact Statement', 'emergency plans', discharges standards, resources protection measures, an Anti-pollution Record Book, and violation fines up to RMB ¥100,000 (approximately US$20,000) and even criminal liabilities against serious violations.[24]

It is clear that the hybrid contract has introduced a legal framework for environmental protection in oil exploration and exploitation which uses a more intensive regulatory approach. This system adopts performance- and technology-based controls, preventive and reactive measures, and civil and criminal liabilities. All the legal requirements are clearly spelled out in precise terms. It may be said that the Chinese hybrid contract has the most comprehensive environmental protection system among contractual arrangements in the developing world.

Unfortunately, these useful regulations have produced little immediate practical value because they have, for one reason or another, not been brought fully into play.

23.3 INTERNATIONAL PETROLEUM AGREEMENTS AND SUSTAINABLE DEVELOPMENT

In the mid-1980s, environmental concerns moved one step farther from environmental protection to sustainable use of all environmental resources, including the non-renewable energy of oil and gas. Entering the 1990s, the concept of sustainable development has received widespread support across the world, but the principle has not been picked up by the petroleum industry at either the national or international levels. There is a real danger that the

22. *Ibid*; art. 24 of the Regulations of the People's Republic of China on the Exploitation of Offshore Petroleum Resources in Cooperation with Foreign Enterprises, reprint in 21 *Int'l Legal Materials*, 132–36 (1982). Please note that before 1992 cooperation with foreign oil companies in China was only allowed in offshore areas.

23. *The Marine Environmental Protection Law of the People's Republic of China* (Beijing: Ocean Press, 1982) (hereinafter MEPL); and Regulations of the People's Republic of China Concerning Environmental Protection in Offshore Oil Exploration and Exploitation (Beijing: State Oceanic Administration, 1983) (hereinafter the Offshore Environmental Regulations), reprinted in L. Ross and M.A. Silk, *Environmental Law and Policy in the People's Republic of China* (Connecticut: Greenwood Press, Inc., 1987), pp. 313–19, 330–5.

24. *Ibid.*, arts 10–17, and 24 of MEPL, and arts 5–7, 10– 13, 15, 19 and 27 of the Offshore Environmental Regulations.

industry will regard sustainable development as just another vague principle which has to be given only token support.

Developing countries have traditionally preferred development to environment for historical, ideological, and economic reasons. Energy policies in most developing countries have given little attention to the issue of resource conservation. Conservation objectives, if any, must follow investment and production priorities. With respect to sustainable development, the awareness and knowledge of the issue is very low. There is little conscious effort to adopt measures conducive to sustainable development of natural resources.

This is precisely the case of the four countries examined in this study. Being energy-producing countries, they all have problems associated with dependency on petroleum as a major source of export earnings or tax revenue, or impractical insistence on self-sufficiency in oil or self-reliance in petroleum development. Although self-sufficiency in oil or self-reliance in petroleum development may be legitimate goals, total self-sufficiency and self-reliance often make neither economic nor environmental sense in today's interdependent world. To meet the rapidly increasing demand of domestic consumption, politically motivated production quotas, or export goals to maximise hard currency earnings, these countries have been depleting their resource deposits. With the help of international oil companies, petroleum resource countries engaged in a policy of rapid depletion, often at the expense of the environment. It seems that these countries are intent on using up whatever might be available without concern for the future.

It is hard to imagine that contractual arrangements with little commitment to environmental protection would have incorporated requirements for sustainable development. Indeed, the four contractual systems examined in this chapter are silent on sustainable development. Foreign companies have complied with no requirements whatsoever. In consequence, the environment and resources have generally been sacrificed for the sake of accumulating oil wealth.

Domestic resources of oil have dried up in many countries. The rise and decline of the giant Renqu oil field in China, which went on stream with an annual production of 10 million tons in 1976 and is now nearly depleted, in a period of only about 15 years, provides the best example of this depletion practice in developing producer countries.[25] As the fourth largest oil producer in the world, China will become a net importer of oil by the middle of this decade, perhaps even sooner, if substantial additional resources are not discovered and developed rapidly. The estimated recoverable reserves of oil and gas in China have a possible life of only about 20 years at the present rates of production and consumption.[26] If the present rates of depletion continue

25. X.H. Chen and Y.Z. Li, 'Warning Bells to the Big Oil Producer: Part I & II', *Outlook Weekly*, No. 35, 31 August 1992, p. 14 and No. 36, 7 September 1992, pp. 14–15; see also 'Discussion and Prospects of the Chinese Oil Industry', *ibid.*, No. 41, 12 October 1992, pp. 11–13 (in Chinese).

26. W.K.H. Kinzelbach, 'Energy and environment in China', in B. Glaeser ed., *Learning from China? Development and Environment in Third World Countries* (London: Allen & Unwin, 1987), p. 175.

unchanged, Indonesia will no longer be a member of the Organization of Petroleum Exporting Countries (OPEC) by the year 2010.[27] In Brazil the rush to realise the political goal of self-sufficiency in oil, so much sought after by the nation for well over half a century, has caused premature exhaustion of many oil fields and early depletion of reservoirs. Current production output can be sustained for only some 15 years.[28]

Oil and gas have been extracted without any regard to future development. Since the establishment of the modern petroleum industry at the beginning of this century, the consumption of fossil fuels has grown by a factor of 30.[29] This pace has accelerated in the past few decades. Between 1959 and 1979, worldwide fossil fuel use quadrupled.[30] Humankind expends, in one year, an amount of fossil fuel that it took nature roughly a million years to produce.[31] Global oil production will begin to decline sometime in the next 15–25 years.[32] From these facts, it is evident that the current pattern of petroleum production and consumption is not sustainable, as pointed out in a special energy report to the World Commission on Environment and Development (WCED):

Unfortunately, today's energy choices by governments, industries and individuals, and the narrow terms of reference within which those choices are made, results in overall energy patterns which, in the aggregate, are not sustainable; neither ecologically, nor economically.[33]

To sum up, international petroleum agreements are the product of a single-minded pursuit of narrow interests and profits. They are not designed for sustainable development but rather are aimed at rapid exploitation in the event of a commercial discovery. The need for sustainable development does not imply that the previous patterns of exploration and exploitation were inappropriate for their time. Rather, given the unbalanced relationship between resource development and rates of depletion, it suggests that current practices under the existing contractual systems are no longer sustainable.

27. Lecture by Mr Paul Cartrier, Deputy Director of Environmental Enforcement Agency of Indonesia, at the School for Resource and Environmental Studies, Dalhousie University, 21 October 1991; some even say that the country will become a net importer of oil by the year 2000. See also K. P. Livesley, 'The Timor Gap Treaty', IBA, Energy Law '90, supra note 1, p. 63.

28. Cited in International labor Office, Brazil and Peru: Social and Economic Effects of petroleum Development (Geneva: ILO, 1987), pp. 52–3.

29. MacNeill, J., 'Strategies for sustainable economic development', in Managing Planet Earth: Readings from Scientific American (New York: W. H. Freeman & Company, 1990), p. 109. The global energy consumption can be put in another way. The global energy consumption rose from 21 exajoules in 1900 to 318 exajoules in 1988 (an exajoule is 10^{18} joules, approximately one quadrillion British thermal units, or the heat that would be released by burning 170 million barrels of crude oil).

30. L. Brown, State of the World (New York: W.W. Norton, 1980), p. 11.

31. J.H. Gibbons, P.D. Blair and H.L. Gwin, 'Strategies for energy use', in Managing Planet Earth, supra note 29, p. 87.

32. Cf. Repetto, R., The Global Possible, Resources Development and the New Century (New Haven: Yale University Press, 1985), pp. 508–9.

33. Energy 2000: A Global Strategy for Sustainable Development (London: Zed Books Ltd, 1987), p. vii.

23.4 CURRENT STATE OF THE ENVIRONMENTAL/ SUSTAINABLE DEVELOPMENT PROVISIONS

The preceding review of four country studies is revealing. Environmental issues have not received enough attention from the representative oil and gas contracts. This finding also holds true for the petroleum agreements used in many other developing countries. A comprehensive survey of petroleum agreements in over a hundred developing countries by this author reveals that the agreements, by and large, have followed the pattern of a general principle of, or reference to, environmental protection. Systematic and substantive requirements are missing.[34] This is the common problem shared by many developing countries in their petroleum arrangements with international oil companies.

The findings of this chapter about inadequate environmental provisions of developing countries' petroleum agreements are further illustrated by the opinions of relevant international organisations. The report on Environmental Law Reform in the Seychelles, sponsored by the United Nations Development Program (UNDP), concludes, after a detailed examination of the country's model petroleum agreement, that its 'contractual framework includes limited provisions for the protection of the environment.'[35] The United Nations Centre on Transnational Corporations (UNCTC) observes in a report on alternative arrangements for petroleum development that in many developing countries' petroleum contracts 'the only explicit reference to environmental protection is a brief clause', such as:

Contractor shall ... carry out operations in such a manner as to cause minimum social and ecological disruption and use its best endeavours to cause no damage to public and private properties. If pollution results from contractor's operations, contractor shall promptly carry out cleaning operations to the satisfaction of the appropriate governmental authorities and the costs therefor shall not be chargeable as exploration, development or production costs.[36]

Based on the findings of this and other commissioned reports, the state of environmental management provisions in modern petroleum agreements can be summarized into the following points:

- There is in recent petroleum agreements a slowly increasing recognition of the issue of environmental protection, but most agreements have little more

---

34. It is not possible to examine here, country-by-country, the environmental provisions of all these petroleum agreements. Nevertheless, the reader is strongly encouraged to consult the following outstanding publication for a complete view of the environmental aspects of the world petroleum agreements. Barrows Company, ed., *Middle East; North Africa; South and Central Africa; Europe; Asia and Australasia; Central American and Caribbeans; and South America: Basic Oil Laws and Concession Contracts*, Vols 1–2 and various Supps (New York: The Petroleum Legislation Co., 1959–present).

35. G.H. De B. Romilly, *Environmental Law Reform in Seychelles: Marine Pollution Legislation* (Draft), sponsored by United Nations Development Program, August 1991, p. 86.

36. UNCTC, *Alternative Arrangements for Petroleum Development: A Guide for Gov't Policy-Makers and Negotiators*, UN Doc. ST?CTC/43, 1982, p. 43.

than conventional requirements on 'sound technical and engineering principles' or 'good international oil field practice'.

- Many countries still lack comprehensive and systematic environmental regulation and administrative capacity; this is particularly true in the petroleum sector.
- Developing countries have, to date, generally not required the submission of environmental impact assessments prior to exploration operations nor have they required appropriate rehabilitation or abandonment procedures after exploitation.
- A few contractual systems have devoted greater emphasis to environmental protection, but in many cases the environmental objectives of these provisions have not been adequately backed up by political and administrative constituencies.
- Sustainable development is, to date, a non-issue in the legal frameworks for international petroleum exploration and exploitation. Not a single contractual system has made even a general reference to the principle.

23.5 CRITIQUES OF EXISTING ENVIRONMENTAL PROVISIONS

It should be apparent from the preceding examination that modern petroleum agreements, no matter what their form or regulatory approach, have provided little environmental regulation of exploration and exploitation activities. Environmental regulations, if any, are supplementary to the principal operative articles. The reason for the lack of environmental protection clauses in petroleum contracts is simple: economic development outweighs environmental protection. Both parties to the contract view the environmental obligation as somehow in conflict with their own interests. The producing countries are afraid of scaring away potential investors by imposing strict environmental requirements. The investing companies consider the environmental obligation as an extra burden to exploration cost.

The inadequacies of the environmental aspects of the four representative contracts in this chapter are evident. In this section, some further legal analysis is carried out to offer more critiques of the existing contractual clauses. As observed, many oil and gas contracts have adopted the usual approach of a general reference to environmental obligation. In theory, such a principle indicates that investment and production must take priority over environmental objectives. In practice, a general reference leaves many questions unanswered. For instance, under the Thai concession, how would a concessionaire determine 'appropriate measures'? Does that term require anticipatory and proactive actions? Under the Indonesian production-sharing contracts, how can the term 'extensive pollution' be reasonably or quantitatively defined? Does the contractor assume any responsibility in the case of less 'extensive' pollution? If yes, to what extent? Under the Brazilian risk service contract, what happens if the liability for pollution or clean-up expenses is beyond the financial capacity of the service contractor? Disputes may well arise precisely from these delicate areas.

A second major limiting factor with the existing environmental provisions is that many of them, like Thailand's modern concession, Indonesia's production-sharing contract, and Brazil's risk service contract, tend to place greater emphasis on clean-up operations and insurance coverage. These requirements are obviously reactive rather than proactive with respect to environmental problems. Such a position has several problems. First, the emphasis on retroactive measures may be interpreted to mean that foreign contractors assume no environmental obligation until their operations have cause pollution or damage to the environment. Second, these provisions do not conform with the precautionary principle of international environmental law, which requires not only preventive actions but also proactive and anticipatory measures in environmental protection and resources conservation.[37] Third, it is not enough simply to hand over environmental responsibilities to the insurers, because insurance policies will no longer cover companies that have chosen to disregard anti-pollution measures.[38] Moreover, there is a tendency towards limitations on environmental liability policies with respect to coverage. Finally, the costs of reactive actions are much greater than those of proactive and anticipatory procedures and preventive measures. Indeed, pollution should be prevented, not compensated.

A third defect, as already observed in the case studies, is the supplementary character and generality of the contractual clauses. Environmental provisions are often a general goodwill principle added on to an existing clause such as conduct of operations. As such, the provisions emphasise the traditional concept of 'good oil-field practice' or 'sound technical and engineering principles', which really means minimum waste of the oil rather than environmental protection in the modern sense. Moreover, most environmental provisions are ill-drafted and vague. Under such general references, the environmental objectives to be achieved are unclear and the environmental obligations are not spelled out in measurable terms, which makes fulfilling these obligations difficult, if not logically impossible. In reality, environmental concerns are assigned a mere cosmetic role by both parties during the life of the contract. In the final analysis, the use of vague principles and general references is a rather casual way of addressing an important problem that is likely to cause multimillion-dollar liabilities as well as other ecological and social problems.

A fourth complication rests with double environmental standards. The developed and developing countries have different perspectives on environmental protection. In the energy sector, developed nations such as the United States exercise much stricter environmental control over the petroleum industry than do developing countries. The consequence of the double environmental legal standards is that transnational oil companies have been allowed to conduct exploration operations in developing countries which

37. For the precautionary principle in general, see J. Cameron and J. Abouchar, 'The precautionary principle: a fundamental principle of law and policy for the protection of the global environment', 14 *B.C. Int'l & Comp. L. Rev.* 1 (1991); E. Hey, The precautionary concept in environmental policy and law: institutionalizing caution, 4 *Geo. Int'l Env. L. Rev.* 303 (1992).
38. W.E. Sheeline, 'Pollution: who will pay?' 119 *Fortune* 12–16 (1989).

would be considered environmental unsound in developed nations. For example, pollution control expenditures reduced by more than 10 per cent the profits of big American oil companies in 1989,[39] whereas there is no compulsory environmental spending in most developing countries. Strict environmental regulation is one of the reasons for the American oil industry's switch to investment overseas over the past 10 years. Warnings have been issued that the refining industry will follow the oil producers abroad, partly to escape tough environmental regulations at home and to enjoy the less stringent requirements in developing countries.[40] Some European oil companies have given little attention to environmental procedures in developing countries compared with operations at home.

A fifth restriction is that environmental management is found to be inadequate in modern petroleum agreements, because the contracting parties consider the environment only after development objectives have been set, and they separate the environmental performance from the contract objectives. As a result, the existing structures are considered to be either incapable of or inappropriate for the tasks of environmental protection and resource conservation.

As a last point, modern petroleum arrangements have not taken into consideration the issue of sustainable development. Consequently, petroleum development, even under current systems, is not truly unsustainable in terms of modern resource protection: (a) contracts are designed with incentives for maximum production; (b) current development patterns authorised by these arrangements foreclose long-term opportunities; (c) the systems allow profits to be made regardless of resources depletion; (d) environmental resources have not been made an explicit part of these arrangements; and (e) no current system provides incentives or requirements for sustainable development.

Based on the foregoing review and analysis, we may arrive at the conclusion that environmental protection, if it exists at all, is generally found only in terms peripheral to the principal exploration and exploitation conditions, and sustainable development is neglected in the overall arrangements.

23.6 CORRECTIVE RECOMMENDATIONS

The relationship between environment and development is now in the process of reassessment. The world has begun to realise that the two are not mutually exclusive but interdependent. It is equally clear that the environment is also a scarce commodity of great value for both present and future generations: environmental protection is not a cost but an investment in the future. To achieve the goals of economic development, the environment must be saved. Unfortunately, current economic growth is obtained by overtaxing environmental resources; this is beyond doubt not only unsustainable but also self-destructive. It is for these reasons that environmental protection is suggested

39. 'Oil Companies: Split Profit', *The Economist*, 3 March 1990, p. 62.
40. 'Energy: in the Oildrums', *The Economist*', 18 April 1992, p. 75; also L.S. Howard, 'Risk management in Asia: only public ire spurs action on risk', 95 National Underwriter 9 (1991).

for consideration as an important new issue in petroleum arrangements. There is a clear and urgent need for actions to improve and correct the current contractual approach to environmental protection and sustainable development.

For many developing countries, it is advisable to incorporate well-designed environmental provisions into the model and individual contracts rather than to pass new and comprehensive environmental laws. Accordingly, the following corrective resolutions are recommended for consideration.

23.6.1 Environmental impact assessment

Environmental impact assessment is an effective tool in the service of environmental management. It is the most effective form of precautionary procedure which provides for detailed assessment of the expected direct and indirect environmental effects of the proposed operations, possible mitigation measures, and so on. Socioeconomic, physical, and biological effects may also be considered. Many countries, particularly industrialised nations and increasingly developing countries, have passed legislation requiring an assessment of the effects a project is likely to have on the environment before development begins.[41] Petroleum contracts should require at a minimum the submission of a separate EIA by recognised independent environmental experts before drilling operations begin.[42] The EIA serves a dual function: it informs the producing state of the potential effects on the environment of the proposed petroleum project, and it gives the contractor an opportunity to mitigate any likely environmental damages posed by the exploration. In view of the fact that petroleum exploration is a high-risk venture and foreign companies may be deterred by stringent requirements, it is more feasible for the producing states to postpone the requirement of a formal EIA until a commercial discovery has been made.[43]

23.6.2 Environmental management plan

A comprehensive environmental management plan may be required, and it should specify, among other things, the operator's capability and experience in environmental management, environmental personnel and their responsibilities in the internal organisation, emergency procedures and antipollution equipment, and environment training and technology transfer to the government or state oil company.

41. For instance, the European Community (EC) issued on 27 June 1985 a directive requiring Member Nations to assess the environmental effects of all major projects to be undertaken within their respective jurisdictions. For a comment, see L.L. Bono, 'The implementation of the EC directive on environmental impact assessments with the English planning system: a refinement of the NEPA process', 9 *Pace Env. L. Rev* 155–86 (1990).

42. For an example of environmental impact assessment, see 'Convention on environmental impact assessment in a transboundary context', 30 *I.L.M.* 800–15 (1991); particularly its Appendix II: Content of the Environmental Impact Assessment Documentation.

43. UNCTC, *Alternative Arrangements, supra* note 36, p. 43.

23.6.3 Environmental report

The contractor may be obliged to file at specified time intervals an environmental report on the environmental situation, pollution accidents, and the measures adopted to mitigate adverse effects.

23.6.4 Environmental liability assurance programmes

The governments of producing states should make the mandatory insurance programme or bank guarantees for environmental liabilities a necessary component of the environmental obligation. The insurance programme should provide adequate coverage for pollution liability, clean-up expenses, and, particularly, expense for killing blowouts.[44]

23.6.5 Rehabilitation/abandonment obligations

The issue of reclamation and abandonment has increasingly attracted the attention of the industry. Rehabilitation is intended to restore resource sites to a safe state or to some approximation of the previous natural state through such methods as refilling or replanting. In the case of offshore petroleum development, restoration of depleted areas poses essentially the same problem, but in a different form of abandonment of offshore platforms. The purpose of rehabilitation or abandonment is to minimise adverse effects on the environment.

Rehabilitation/abandonment is becoming a standard requirement.[45] The Maritime Safety Committee (MSC) of the International Maritime Organization (IMO) developed in 1988 'Guidelines and Standards for the Removal of Offshore Installations and Structures on the Continental Shelf and in the Exclusive Economic Zone' for adoption by individual member states.[46] Developing countries should be able to include an obligation based on these guidelines into their petroleum contracts. Since the obligation of rehabilitation or abandonment does not occur until the maturity of the field, which usually takes from 30 to 50 years after the agreement, it may be advisable for developing countries to incorporate into the contract a general clause on rehabilitation and abandonment. The details of the obligation can be worked out after commercial production has commenced.

44. Transnational oil corporations administer scores of contracts at a time, and insurance programme often receive inadequate attention. Moreover, many of the lawsuits concerning liability and indemnity clauses resulted from inadequate insurance coverage. CF. Hunt, C.D., 'Topic 4: new issues of offshore liability, indemnity, and insurance: Canada', IBA, *Energy Law '86* (New York: Matthew Bender, 1986), p. 283.

45. For instance, the Province of Ontario, Canada, passed a new legislation (Mining Act, RSO 1980 as amended by SO 1989) to require the total rehabilitation of all mining sites. For a discussion of the legislation, see H. Frawley, 'Environmental law developments affecting Ontario's mining industry', 2 *J. Env. L. & P.* 107–15 (1991).

46. See IMO, MSC/Circ. 490, 4 May 1988, pp. 1–2 and its Annex, pp. 1–6, reprinted in 4 *Int'l J. Est. & C.L.* 76–9 (1992). For a legal history and review of the guideline, see G.C. Kasoulides, 'Draft guidelines for the removal of offshore platforms', *ibid.*, pp. 71–6.

23.6.6 Environmental audit

As a relatively new form of environmental management, the environmental audit is being increasingly adopted in the developed nations. It serves as a kind of follow-up or monitoring procedure which facilitates the management control of environmental protection, evaluates the environmental performance, and ensures compliance with environmental obligations. An environmental audit is considered to be one of the most effective tools in managing environmental protection.[47] To be effective in environmental regulation, petroleum contracts should include an audit obligation to be fulfilled in either of the following ways: requiring the contractor to carry out internal environmental audits and report on the results if there are no national audit procedures and standards to follow; or allowing a competent government agency to arrange for an independent environmental audit to ensure that the environmental obligations are faithfully complied with. A successful environmental audit should do the following: (a) conduct a pre-audit analysis; (b) set objectives; (c) draw up audit documents; (d) determine areas to audit; (e) report; (f) implement changes; and (g) conduct a post-audit review.[48]

23.6.7 Sustainability provisions

It is possible to develop non-renewable resources such as oil and gas in a quasi-sustainable manner by limiting their rate of depletion to the rate of creation of renewable substitutes.[49] Quasi-sustainable development requires that any investment in the exploitation of a non-renewable resource be paired with a compensating investment in a renewable substitute, for example, oil extraction coupled with tree planting for wood alcohol. The idea is to divide the next receipts from the non-renewable resources into an income component for current consumption each year and a capital component for investment in renewable substitutes. Capital must be invested in a sustainable substitute in such a way that it produces, at the end of the life of the non-renewable resource, an annual sustainable yield equal to the income portion of the receipts from the non-renewable resource.[50] In this way, the development of nonrenewable resources is made 'sustainable', since the consumption reduced from the non-renewable resource is converted into sustainable consumption.

---

47. G. Vinten, 'The blossoming of the environmental audit', 91 *Industrial Magt. & Data Systems* 19 (1991); see also J.N. Philbrook, 'Environmental audits: determining the need at mining facilities', 43 *Mining Eng.* 207–9 (1991).

48. Vinten, *ibid.*, p. 25.

49. H.E. Daly, 'Toward some operational principles of sustainable development', 2 *Ecological Economies* 4 (1990).

50. The division of receipts from a non-renewable resource project into capital and income components was originally proposed by El Sarafy, see S. El Sarafy. 'The proper calculation of income for depletable natural resources', in Y.J., Ahmad, S. El Sarafy and E. Lutz, ed., *Environmental Accounting for Sustainable Development* (Washington, D.C.: The World Bank, 1989), pp. 10–18. For an account, see H.E. Daly and J.B. Cobb jr, *For the Common Good: Redirecting the Economy Toward Community, the Environment, and a Sustainable Future* (Boston: Beacon Press, 1989), pp. 73–4.

One application of the quasi-sustainable development principle might be the establishment of a 'Resource for the Future Fund' (RFF) which sets aside a specific percentage of royalty or rent paid by foreign companies for sustainable development, such as research and development of renewable substitutes, or saving for future use. RFF is one of the mechanisms that can transform non-renewable resources into renewable ones.

For the RFF provision in international petroleum exploration and exploitation agreements, something like the following may be suggested:

Article X: Resources for the Future Fund

The Concessionaire/Contractor shall pay to the Government of _____ $1 per barrel/the sum of _____ at specified production levels upon the establishment of commercial production for the purposes of a Resources for the Future Fund for petroleum sustainable development, including funding researches, studies, and development of renewable energy sources.

This payment shall be made within thirty days from the ending date of the year the commercial production has been established. Each subsequent contribution shall be made quarterly within fifteen days after the ending of each calendar quarter.

This provision is intended to serve as an illustration only. The specific formulation of such a clause, particularly the time, amount, method, and use of payment to the fund, can be negotiated between the contracting parties along the lines suggested in the preceding discussion.

23.7 SUMMARY AND CONCLUSION

The environment has not historically been a focus of world petroleum arrangements. Modern petroleum contracts are generally able to achieve and maintain a necessary balance of rights, interests, and benefits between the contracting parties, but they have failed in principle to provide adequate environmental regulation and, in their entirety, to address the issue of sustainable development. They are therefore inappropriate for the development of a unique non-renewable resource faced with possible depletion in the next few decades.

It is important to emphasise that petroleum exploration and exploitation can be neither equitable nor sustainable unless environmental considerations are taken into account. The traditional commercial relationship, which took care only of the interests of the contracting parties without regard to those of the world community and future generations, must be reconsidered. It must be recognised that important environmental and resource consequences arise from the developmental behaviour authorised by petroleum contracts. These consequences can be addressed effectively only by changes in that legal system and the resultant behaviour.

Environmental sustainability must be made an explicit and specific part of all investment arrangements. Through the proper use of contract terms that contain elements favouring sustainable development, economic and environmental interests can both be accommodated. The policy suggestion for a Resources for the Future Fund in petroleum agreements provides such an approach to integrate environmental sustainability into resource development.

The future direction for petroleum agreements is that they must recognise explicitly the inherent interdependence of commercial viability and sustainable development. Only under such a contractual system can energy development be made legally justifiable, politically acceptable, ecologically sustainable, environmentally sound, and economically viable.

Annexes

Annex 1

Legal Framework for the Treatment of Foreign Investment, Volume II (1992)
Report to the Development Committee and Guidelines on the Treatment of Foreign Direct Investment[*]

1992 The International Bank for Reconstruction and Development/The World Bank

[*]   Prepared by the General Counsel of the World Bank (the International Bank for Reconstruction and Development and the International Development Association), the International Finance Corporation and the Multilateral Investment Guarantee Agency and submitted to the Fall 1992 meeting of the Development Committee of the Boards of Governors of the International Monetary Fund and the World Bank which on 21 September 1992 discussed the Report and called the Guidelines to the attention of member countries.

CONTENTS

FOREWORD

For the first time, the world community found it appropriate last year to ask the World Bank Group through the Development Committee to prepare universal standards for the legal treatment of foreign direct investment. This task has now been completed and the Development Committee has agreed in its September 1992 meeting without reservation to call the guidelines prepared for this purpose to the attention of our member countries.

This publication includes the text of these guidelines and the detailed report which explains that text. It should be of great relevance to the continuous efforts in our member countries to improve investment climates and facilitate greater investment flows. The guidelines may also assist in the progressive development of international law in this important area.

Lewis T. Preston, President
World Bank Group
September 25, 1992

INTRODUCTORY NOTE

In April 1991, the Development Committee, which is a Joint Ministerial Committee of the Boards of Governors of the International Monetary Fund and the World Bank, requested the Multilateral Investment Guarantee Agency (MIGA) to prepare a 'legal framework' to promote foreign direct investment. Realizing that this was a matter of interest to all World Bank Group institutions, the President of these institutions assigned the project to a small working group consisting of their General Counsel and asked me to chair this group.**

The approach followed by the task force was described in a Progress Report submitted to the April 1992 meeting of the Development Committee and published in Volume I of the *Legal Framework for the Treatment of Foreign Investment*. The Report explained that the World Bank Group could not issue binding rules to govern the conduct of member States in this or other fields. A draft convention could of course have been prepared and opened for signature by interested countries. The working group however found it more advisable at the present stage to prepare a set of *guidelines* embodying commendable approaches which would not be legally binding as such but which could greatly influence the development of international law in this area in view of their preparation by organizations of universal membership after broad consultations and their eventual issuance by no less an authority than the Development Committee.

First drafts of the guidelines and of their accompanying explanatory report were circulated to the Executive Directors of the World Bank, IFC and MIGA in May 1992. Extensive consultations followed with the Executive Directors, as well as with other representatives of interested member countries, intergovernmental organizations, business groups and international legal associations. In the consultations, it became clear that certain clarifications and modifications were necessary or desirable. These were incorporated into the text but did not fundamentally change its basic balance. The resulting guidelines cover each of the four main areas usually dealt with in investment treaties, namely the admission, treatment, and expropriation of foreign investments and the settlement of disputes between governments and foreign investors. Although they are based on general trends distilled from detailed surveys of existing legal instruments (published in Volume I of the *Legal Framework for the Treatment of Foreign Investment*), the guidelines are formulated in such a manner as also to incorporate policies that the World Bank Group institutions have been advocating in recent years. This approach, aimed at progressively developing rather than merely codifying applicable rules in the field, has made possible the formulation of progressive standards which are open, fair and consistent both with emerging rules of customary international law and with commendable practices identified by the World Bank Group.

The guidelines and accompanying report were submitted to the Development Committee for consideration at its September 1992 meeting. The Committee reviewed the guidelines with interest and called them to the attention of member countries. In so doing, the Committee noted, in the words of the communiqué of its meeting, that the guidelines should 'serve as an important step in the progressive development of international practice in this area.'

** Original members of the working group included Ibrahim F.I. Shihata, Vice President and General Counsel, World Bank, José E. Camacho, Vice President and General Counsel, International Finance Corporation (IFC) and Luis Dodero, General Counsel, MIGA. In fact, the working group also included Daoud L. Khairallah, Deputy General Counsel, IFC and benefited from the assistance of the staff of the International Centre for Settlement of Investment Disputes (ICSID), in particular Antonio R. Parra, Legal Adviser, ICSID. Bertrand P. Marchais, Senior Counsel, MIGA, also contributed to the work of the group.

With the successful completion of this task, it gives me great pleasure to bring its product to the attention of a wider audience through this publication which was envisaged in the communiqué of the Development Committee.

Ibrahim F.I. Shihata
Vice President and General Counsel, World Bank
Secretary-General, ICSID
September 25, 1992

Report to the Development Committee on the Legal Framework for the Treatment of Foreign Investment

INTRODUCTORY REMARKS

1.   This report is prepared in response to the Development Committee's request, made in its Spring 1991 meeting at the initiative of France, for a report on 'an overall legal framework which would embody the essential legal principles so as to promote FDI.' It follows a progress report submitted to the Committee in its Spring 1992 meeting which described the approach to be followed and its rationale and outlined the scope of coverage of the proposed framework.

2.   The work reflected in this report differs from the task being undertaken since 1977 by the UN Centre on Transnational Corporations (UNCTC) in at least two respects. *First*, this report covers general principles suggested to guide governmental behavior toward foreign investors; it does not include rules of good conduct on the part of the foreign investors. A set of rules for the latter purpose was reflected in negotiated provisions of the UNCTC draft Code of Conduct, which is now being reviewed 'in the light of the changed international economic environment.'[1] As previously prepared, '[t]hese provisions shared the common goal of maximizing the contributions of [transnational] corporations to the economic and social development of the countries in which they operate and of minimizing their potential negative effects.'[2] They specifically relate to disclosure of information by foreign corporations, environmental and consumer protection, restrictive business practices, the avoidance of corrupt practices and transfer pricing, parent-affiliate relations as well as labor relations and working conditions. While the framework covered by this report avoids a repetition of these principles, the guidelines are meant to apply to *bona fide* private investments, where investors act in good faith and in full conformity with the laws and regulations of the host State.[3] They also provide that restrictions applicable to national investment on account of public order, public health and the protection of the environment will equally apply to foreign investment.[4] Furthermore, the proposed framework includes a recommendation for all States to take appropriate measures for the prevention and control of corrupt business practices and the promotion of accountability and transparency in dealings with foreign investors and to cooperate with other States in developing international procedures and mechanisms to this effect.[5]

---

1.   Report by the President of the Forty-sixth Session of the General Assembly, 23 July 1992.

2.   UNCTC, International Arrangements and Agreements Relating to Transnational Corporations: International Framework for Transnational Corporations – Report of the Secretary-General, U.N. Doc. E/C. 10/1992/8, para. 24 (Feb. 18 1992) (hereinafter UNCTC Report). In addition, in 1976 the members of OECD adopted Guidelines for Multinational Enterprises which laid down standards for the activities of such enterprises. See Annex 1 to Declaration of 21 June 1976 by Governments of OECD Member Countries on International Investment and Multinational Enterprises, in OECD, The OECD Declaration and Decisions on International Investment and Multinational Enterprises: Basic Texts 9 (1992).

3.   See Section 2 of Guideline I of the guidelines attached to this report. As indicated in the commentary on that section (at *infra*, para. 15), this principle is often reflected in existing multilateral instruments on the treatment of foreign investment, such as the Lomé IV Convention and the draft UNCTC Code of Conduct on Transnational Corporations.

4.   Section 5 of Guideline II.

5.   Section 8 of Guideline III.

3.   *Second*, this report does not aim at representing a codification of what are necessarily agreed upon, binding rules of international law. Rather, it attempts to reflect at this stage generally acceptable international standards which meet the objective stated in the Development Committee's request, i.e., the promotion of foreign direct investment. Fortunately, any gap that may exist between principles which are widely accepted as legally binding international law and the guidelines attached to this report is narrowing as a result of the changing realities and perceptions related to the policy environment for foreign investment in practically all developing countries and the intensified normative activity in this field in recent years, at both the regional and global levels. It is recognized, however, that some of the standards prepared here, though not the ultimate that the world community may aspire to, do reflect emerging, rather than settled, standards under contemporary international law and for this reason represent in several respects what is deemed to be desirable, rather than common practice. As they are meant to provide the elements of an *international* framework which may develop in the future into generally accepted standards, the guidelines should not also be read as the ultimate recommended policy for every country interested in attracting foreign investment. The conditions of a specific country may well require it to adopt a more liberal approach, which is justified by its circumstances, than what are deemed to be internationally acceptable standards at this stage.

4.   The attempt to formulate generally acceptable international standards to promote the flow of foreign investment is both timely and useful. It is *timely* because of the growing importance of private direct foreign investment in developing countries. Such flows have increased substantially, reaching in 1991 a level almost three times higher than that of 1986[6] and accounting at present for about ten percent of all private investment in the developing countries.[7] They also hold a significant potential for further growth in the 1990s, compared to the expected modest growth in official assistance and commercial lending.[8] This work is also timely because of the great transformation of economies in Eastern Europe, Central Asia and indeed many developing countries, from inward looking economies, based on public sector control and inspired by import substitution policies, into outward looking market economies, based on private sector development and open competition. In conjunction with this transformation, such events as nationalizations of foreign investments are becoming increasingly rare and, with changing patterns of foreign investment flows, traditional classifications of and distinctions between 'home' and 'host' countries have lost some of their significance, suggesting in turn a more balanced approach to foreign investment issues.[9]

5.   This transformation process and the general trend to attract foreign investment make it particularly *useful* to try to devise a general understanding of a desirable normative framework to guide future governmental conduct affecting foreign investment. In this, as in other fields, a sound legal framework, in terms of the availability of clear, stable and reasonable general rules as well as of honest and efficient mechanisms of implementation, enforcement and dispute settlement, is essential. Obviously, such a framework, necessary as it is, cannot be expected alone to cause a major shift in the conditions of investment markets or in investor attitudes towards such

6.   *IBRD Debt and International Finance Division, Financial Flows to Developing Countries: Current Developments*, March 1992 at 9.

7.   *IFC, Trends in Private Investment in Developing Countries*, 1992 edn at 2 (by Guy P. Pfeffermann and Andrea Madarassy).

8.   See IBRD, *Global Economic Prospects and the Developing Countries*, 38–39 and table 3.5 (1991).

9.   UNCTC Report, *supra* note 2, para. 7.

markets. Establishing a sound legal and regulatory framework must therefore be seen as one of many basic requirements which together can make a difference in investment decisions and behavior. Providing conditions of political stability, reducing macro-economic imbalances and economic uncertainties, lowering price distortions and improving the functioning of factor markets generally, strengthening financial institutions, improving physical infrastructure and government administration and ensuring the availability of trained, disciplined labor, including white collar and supervisory labor, and of relevant information, along with the presence of successfully operating foreign investors, are other essential requirements which allow an appropriate legal framework to produce the desired results, not only for the growth of foreign investment but for private sector development generally.[10] The need for international legal standards is increased by the quest for improved investment climates on a worldwide scale and the uncertainty surrounding international law rules in this field at present. As the latest UNCTC report indicated '[t]he question is no longer whether international norms should exist but whether the international framework as it exists today is sufficient or, indeed, adequate to ensure stable, reliable and mutually beneficial foreign investment relations in the new economic and political landscape.'[11]

6.   While the UNCTC continues its efforts to codify internationally agreed rules to govern the future behavior of foreign investors and their host countries, this report and the guidelines attached to it attempt to identify a set of principles which, it is hoped, are both acceptable in view of recent trends, and likely to enhance the prospects of investment flows to developing countries. Such recommended guidelines may thus guide further work on the subject at the national and international levels. To the extent that the practice of States conforms to these recommended guidelines in a consistent manner and reflects a general conviction of their binding character, the guidelines may then positively influence the development of customary international law in so far as they do not already reflect its rules. While the guidelines could serve these important purposes, they are clearly not intended to constitute part of World Bank loan conditionality or to assume for the Bank a legislative role which it does not have.

7.   The remaining parts of this report provide explanatory notes to the guidelines and are meant to facilitate their understanding and help in paving the way for their general acceptability. In reading these guidelines, it is of particular importance to bear in mind the following factors:

(i)   The guidelines address, and are meant to apply to all member States and indeed to the world community at large; they are not addressed only to developing countries or to a specific coherent regional group of countries.

(ii)   The guidelines address the conduct of States *vis à vis* foreign investors but not the conduct of foreign investors. The exclusion of the latter topic is not due to its lack of relevance or importance; it only reflects an understanding of the request made by the Development Committee and a desire to avoid repetition of the comprehensive work carried out by UNCTC, and earlier by the OECD, in this field.

10.   See Shihata, 'Factors Influencing the Flow of Foreign Investment and the Relevance of a Multilateral Guarantee Scheme', *The International Lawyer*, **21** (1987), 671; *MIGA and Foreign Investment* (1988); and 'Promotion of Foreign Direct Investment – A General Account, with Particular Reference to the Role of the World Bank Group', *ICSID Review – Foreign Investment Law Journal*, **6** (1991), 484. See also IFC, *supra* note 7, at 5–6; Mody and Srinavasan, *Trends and Determinants of Foreign Direct Investment: An Empirical Analysis of U.S. Investment Abroad* (World Bank Working Paper, Dec. 1991).

11.   UNCTC Report, *supra*, note 2, para. 34.

(iii) The guidelines, being prepared for a practical purpose and not as an academic exercise, are written with a sense of realism, bearing in mind existing legal instruments, complemented by desirable practices consistent with World Bank Group policies.

(iv) The guidelines are meant to present a general framework which complements, but cannot substitute for the broad array of international instruments consisting of bilateral investment treaties, regional conventions and other instruments of broader application issued by specialized organizations such as the ILO, GATT, OECD, EC and others, all with the view of securing stable investment conditions in the territories of their members. In this respect, the guidelines, if adopted, would be relevant to situations where such bilateral treaties and other instruments do not exist or are silent on matters provided for in the guidelines. Thus, while the guidelines represent another step in the overall international effort to improve investment conditions and in the continuous evolution of improved standards in this area, they provide a foundation on which other instruments, especially bilateral treaties, may further build.

(v) Last, but not least, the guidelines are meant to serve the purpose of promotion and encouragement of foreign investments, so that such investments may increase in volume and spread out to as many countries as possible, and so that their flows may be governed only by economic considerations and not be hampered by avoidable non-commercial factors.

SCOPE OF APPLICATION OF THE GUIDELINES

8. Guideline I of the guidelines delineates their intended scope and purpose. The guidelines may be applied by members of the World Bank Group and other States in their efforts to attract increased flows of private foreign investment. However, the guidelines would not by themselves have a binding or mandatory effect. This is made clear by the contrast that Section 1 of Guideline I draws between the guidelines and such binding instruments as pertinent bilateral and multilateral treaties. The guidelines would be subject to any such treaties and should facilitate the conclusion of more bilateral investment treaties. At the same time, the guidelines may play a useful role in complementing binding instruments in the field of foreign investment. As already indicated, the guidelines incorporate lessons gained from experience of the practices and policies that may be conducive to building an attractive investment climate.

9. A particular practical contribution that the guidelines may make would, as suggested in Section 1 of Guideline I, be to assist in the development of domestic legal rules on foreign investment. For the drafters of national laws on foreign investment, the provisions of the guidelines may, depending on the circumstances, needs and policies of the country concerned, be suggestive of desired provisions in the laws; or the guidelines may simply serve as a check-list of the types of matters that the laws might usefully address. In this context, the guidelines could also help in the coordination of technical assistance to countries in the formulation of investment laws on the basis of a minimum of broadly acceptable standards. More importantly, the guidelines may help in the progressive development of international principles and rules on foreign investment by arbitrators and scholars and may be reflected over time in the practice of States which do not already follow similar standards. The practical value of the guidelines in all these respects is enhanced by the fact that they also present general principles and current trends inferred from extensive comparative background studies of bilateral investment

treaties, multilateral treaties and other instruments pertaining to foreign investment, international arbitral awards and writings of international law experts, as well as national investment codes.[12] Thus, the guidelines, while not having a binding character as such, have a basis in existing legal instruments and may not be inconsistent with what some sources may consider to be settled international law. Their adoption is recommended however without prejudice to the different positions held by States and scholars on what international law may or may not require at this stage of its development.

10. The various potential contributions of the guidelines are nevertheless essentially legal in character, as envisaged in the Development Committee's request. Hence the guidelines are in large measure drafted in a normative manner (while using language that is as simple and clear as possible). This would not, of course, itself impart to the guidelines any legal force. As already emphasized, the guidelines are not intended to, nor could they, supersede by themselves such binding instruments as national laws or treaties. Instead, such legal force as the guidelines might eventually acquire would depend on their incorporation by States into domestic or international law in the ways described above.

11. The guidelines are meant to apply to *private foreign* investments. However, the broad general principles set out in the guidelines equally apply to investments made by foreign public entities such as foreign State enterprises or intergovernmental organizations. They also have obvious relevance to investments that are made by local nationals, and in that sense domestic, but with funds brought in from abroad.[13]

12. As they would be intended to assist in the encouragement of private foreign investment generally, the guidelines are purposely broad in scope. Thus while they may in several respects be particularly relevant to private foreign direct investment,[14] there is no reason to limit their application to such investment, to the exclusion of portfolio investment.

13. Indeed beyond specifying that they should be private and foreign, *the guidelines contain no restrictions as to the nature of the covered investments*. In this respect, the guidelines would be similar to most bilateral investment treaties and multilateral instruments which either adopt broad definitions of covered investments or do not qualify them at all.[15] Thus the guidelines would apply to indirect, as well as to direct, investments and to modern contractual and other new forms of investment where funds, equipment, technology and/or services are provided in a variety of continuously

12. These studies are reprinted in World Bank Group, *Legal Framework for the Treatment of Foreign Investment*, Vol. 1. They are the bases for the generalizations in the present report about bilateral investment treaties, multilateral instruments, national investment codes, and international arbitral awards and scholarly writings.

13. Compare Article 13(c) of the MIGA Convention which opens the possibility of equating local nationals to foreign investors eligible for the Agency's guarantee where the local nationals are investors transferring to the host country assets from abroad.

14. Paragraph 408 of the *IMF Balance of Payments Manual* (4th ed. 1977) defines direct investment as 'investment that is made to acquire a lasting interest in an enterprise operating in an economy other than that of the investor, the investor's purpose being to have an effective voice in the management of the enterprise.'

15. For example, many bilateral investment treaties define covered investments as including 'every kind of asset.' Under the MIGA Convention (art. 12), investments eligible for the Agency's guarantee potentially include virtually any 'medium- or long-term form of investment.' In the ICSID Convention (art. 25(1)), which like the guidelines takes the broadest approach, the term 'investment' is purposely undefined.

evolving ways, as long as the investor's return depends in whole or in part on the fortunes of the enterprise, as well as to traditional types of foreign investment such as equity contributions and concessions. The guidelines could in general also apply to investments made in local as well as foreign currencies and to investments made in kind as well as in monetary form. They similarly contain no restrictions as to the nature of the covered foreign investors themselves, which may be corporate entities as well as individuals.[16]

14. *State* and *nationals* are other terms frequently used in the guidelines. In foreign investment matters as in other fields, States generally act through their responsible agencies or other public entities. In addition, nationals of a State may include not only individuals who have the nationality of a State but also companies and similar bodies established there. To avoid any misunderstanding, Section 1 of Guideline I specifies that the guidelines are intended generally to cover the stance of a State (or any constituent subdivision or institution acting as the instrumentality or agency thereof) in respect of both individuals and juridical persons possessing the nationality of another State under the law of that State.[17]

15. The guidelines, seeking to set out a general framework for the treatment of foreign investors by their host States, cover each of the main areas in this respect, namely the admission of foreign investment, standards of treatment and transfer of capital and net revenues, expropriation and its compensation and the settlement of disputes. While, as earlier explained, rules regarding the conduct of foreign investors in their host States are not covered, the guidelines only envisage investments made and carried out in good faith and in complete compliance with local legal requirements. This fundamental assumption, which is often articulated in existing multilateral instruments on the treatment of foreign investment, is emphasized in Section 2 of Guideline I and is also reasonably reflected in Section 9 of Guideline IV.

16. Obvious differences distinguish the respective situations of foreign and local investors. Arrangements for the eventual repatriation of investment capital and returns, for example, are typically made with foreign investors only in mind. However, the situations of foreign and local investors may be similar to each other in many more respects. Experience indicates that, *to the extent the circumstances of foreign and local investors are thus essentially similar*, their equal treatment and hence competition on an equal footing, are important factors in creating a sound investment climate. The practice of granting foreign investors special privileges unwarranted by their particular circumstances may distort trade and competition and, in the final analysis, contribute little to the attraction of foreign investment. As is underscored by Section 3 of Guideline I, the guidelines are not intended to endorse the extension of such special privileges to foreign investors. This does not however derogate from the fact that in some respects the nature of the investment or of the investor as foreign may justify a different treatment as indicated above.

16. In potentially accommodating these various forms of investment and investors, the guidelines may be compared to the MIGA Convention (at arts 12 and 13) and MIGA's Operational Regulations (at paras 1.01–1.19).

17. Similarly, under the ICSID Convention (art. 25), States parties may include agencies and subdivisions of States, and nationals of States may include juridical as well as natural persons from States. (Under general international law, a dual national who has the nationalities of the host State and another State or States is considered a national of the host State unless it agrees to treat him differently.)

ADMISSION

17. Guideline II covers the question of the admission or entry of foreign investments into host countries. Like corresponding introductory provisions of most bilateral investment treaties and many multilateral instruments and national investment codes, Section 1 of Guideline II makes explicit the need for host countries to encourage foreign investment. In so doing, the Section calls attention to the fact that the encouragement of foreign investment may usefully be directed not only to contributions of capital but also to the transfers of the technology, knowledge and skills that frequently accompany foreign direct investment and add to its value for the efficiency and competitiveness of the host country.[18]

18. Section 2 of Guideline II gives practical expression to the general principle set forth in Section 1. In common with the provisions of many bilateral and multilateral investment treaties and national investment codes, Section 2 envisages that host countries will facilitate the admission and establishment of foreign investments. Particular reference is made in this connection to the need to avoid overregulation of and the erection of unnecessary bureaucratic obstacles to admission. In this respect, the guidelines may be compared to many modern national investment codes which seek to do away in principle with admission procedures and, where such procedures are necessary, to streamline them through such devices as 'one-stop shops' for investment approvals.[19]

19. Some regulations on admission exist however in all legal systems. Section 3 of Guideline II makes it clear that States maintain the right to make such regulations. In this respect, the guidelines are consistent with most bilateral and multilateral investment treaties which also recognize that the admission of foreign investment is ultimately a matter for each State to decide upon and regulate in the exercise of its sovereignty.[20]

20. However, Section 3 of Guideline II cautions against a restrictive approach and in particular against the inclusion in such regulations of certain performance requirements (such as minimum local ownership and staffing or export targets) as conditions of admission of foreign investment. As the Section explains, experience indicates that the imposition of such requirements may deter investments or encourage abuses. Reflecting this experience, performance requirements of these kinds are in fact becoming rare in national investment codes. Such codes increasingly take the approach of making admission a largely automatic process, confining exclusions or approval requirements to specified types of investment judged in need of such control.[21] Section 3 of Guideline II endorses this approach, while pointing out that the fact that a given investment requires no specific approval does not, of course, exempt it from the host State's laws and regulations which typically require registration and expect full compliance.

21. Sections 4 and 5 of Guideline II mention especially important types of exclusions that States may legitimately make under the liberal approach endorsed by Section 3. Thus States may open admission to investments without the need for prior approval but exclude from their territories foreign investments which threaten national security under

18. See Shihata, 'Factors Influencing the Flow of Foreign Investment and the Relevance of a Multilateral Guarantee Scheme', *supra*, note 10.
19. See e.g. Mahmassani, 'The Legal Framework for Investment in Poland', *ICSID Review – Foreign Investment Law Journal*, **3** (1988), 286, 297.
20. In their investment laws also, States uniformly reserve to themselves the ultimate decision on the admission of foreign investments.
21. See e.g. Pogany, 'Recent Developments Relating to Foreign Investment in Hungary', *ICSID Review – Foreign Investment Law Journal*, **6** (1991), 114.

clearly defined requirements or which belong to sectors reserved by the law of the State to its nationals on account of the State's economic development objectives or national interest requirements. Beyond this, there may be other exclusions of investments that would apply equally to national and foreign investments. Such exclusions would relate to investments which are contrary to *ordre public* (sometimes translated into English as 'public policy'), i.e. investments that violate fundamental values of society in the country concerned as defined in its laws and judicial practice, and investments that adversely affect the environment or public health. It is important to note, however, that exclusions of foreign investment are not meant to be applied lightly by the host State, but rather as limited exceptions after careful consideration. This point is recalled in Section 4 of Guideline II.

22. Investment codes also frequently reserve to nationals investments in sectors where it is considered that national interests demand such local control of the sectors concerned. As in some of the more recent codes, however, this latter type of restriction should be limited to sectors which are normally by nature of primarily local interest in any event. Section 4 of Guideline II recognizes that such limited restrictions may be inevitable; it does not suggest them as a rule but as an exception.

23. Assessments of local investment conditions invariably precede the decision of a serious investor actually to make an investment in a country. In order to attract foreign investments, States may find it useful actively to facilitate such assessments by prospective investors. Of special importance in this connection is the identification of relevant current local legal requirements and policies. Language and cultural differences can make this a particularly onerous undertaking for foreign investors. Their task in this respect may be partially eased by consolidating in one publication the main rules that will apply to foreign investors. Such an investment handbook may summarize the applicable rules, refer to all relevant laws and regulations and provide other information that intending investors typically require, whether or not they are reflected in an investment code.[22] Apart from the great interest of foreign investors in such a publication, it may provide a good occasion for host States also to assess the appropriateness of their foreign investment regimes. Some host States follow the approach of making available such handbooks or other summaries and Section 6 of Guideline II commends the practice.

TREATMENT

24. Guideline III covers both the general standards of the treatment to be accorded to foreign investors by their host States and particular aspects of such treatment, notably the transfer of investment capital and returns.

25. A standard of treatment is by definition a general criterion. It clearly could lose much of its value if it only applied to parts of the activities of foreign investors. In fact, bilateral investment treaties and multilateral instruments that lay down general standards of treatment appear never to restrict the scope of the standard in this way. Accordingly, Section 1 of Guideline III makes it clear that the level of treatment recommended would cover not only the establishment of an investment but also the various aspects of its operation and the activities reasonably ancillary to it including the

---

22. Compare Wälde, 'Investment Policies and Investment Promotion in the Mineral Industries', *ICSID Review – Foreign Investment Law Journal*, **6** (1991), 94, 112.

ultimate disposal of the investment.[23] In so doing, the Section recalls that the guidelines are meant to apply simultaneously to all States. It also emphasizes that the detailed standards provided for in the guidelines are subject to applicable bilateral treaties, multilateral conventions and other binding international instruments as well as to generally accepted rules of customary international law.

26. Most bilateral investment treaties and several multilateral instruments in the field prescribe an objective standard of 'fair and equitable' treatment to be accorded to foreign investors. Section 2 of Guideline III follows this example and relates the standard to the guidelines as a whole.

27. Most bilateral investment treaties also require that foreign investors be accorded treatment that, in addition to being fair and equitable, is as favorable as that accorded by States to their own nationals. Many multilateral instruments and national investment codes similarly provide for a supplementary standard of national treatment. One important aspect of this standard is that foreign investors should not lack the protection and security afforded to nationals, for example with respect to the safeguarding of their persons or property interests. Another important implication of the standard is that foreign investors should not, in comparison with nationals, be put at a competitive disadvantage in respect of access to the permits or authorizations necessary to conduct business operations in the country concerned. These factors are all taken into account in Section 3(a) of Guideline III, which elaborates on the principle of 'protection and security' and recommends that, in the application of this principle, foreign investors be granted treatment as favorable as that granted to nationals, provided, of course, that investors' interests and rights over their property, including intellectual property, are thereby fully protected in all its aspects of ownership, control and benefits and, more generally, that the treatment is also fair and equitable.

28. Section 3(a) of Guideline III recalls that foreigners may receive national treatment to the extent that the circumstances of the two groups are similar. As indicated earlier, obvious differences between the situations of foreigners and nationals may call for them to be treated differently in certain areas. Section 3(b) of Guideline III recommends that, where this is the case, the host State's rules should not discriminate among different foreign investors on the grounds of their respective nationalities. In this respect, the guidelines are similar to several multilateral instruments on investment formulated in both industrial and developing country fora and provide for the equivalent of a 'most favored nation clause' which is the formula typically used in the context of bilateral treaties.

29. At the same time, many bilateral investment treaties in particular allow for the drawing of distinctions in the treatment of foreign investors on the basis of membership in such treaty arrangements as customs unions and free trade areas. Section 4 of Guideline III acknowledges this common exception which, in the present context, can be viewed as another application of the principle that the guidelines are subject to applicable treaties. Consistent with the approach taken under the General Agreement on Tariffs and Trade (GATT), however, investors from third countries should not as a result be accorded less favorable treatment than that which they enjoyed prior to the formation of the customs union or comparable arrangement.

30. In addition to the general standards of treatment, the guidelines provide several concrete illustrations of treatment conducive to attracting foreign investment. These

---

23. It can in this connection be noted that the scope of some bilateral investment treaties is explicitly extended to cover activities associated with investments as well as investments themselves.

include the timely issuance of such authorizations as may be required for the smooth operation of investments. In this respect, the guidelines reflect the spirit of modern national investment codes the provisions of which typically seek to facilitate and expedite such authorizations.[24] Such codes sometimes still require foreign investors to recruit a minimum number of their personnel locally. However, this approach is increasingly being abandoned in favor of one emphasizing market freedom in hiring. While mentioning the normal practice of following certain procedures to establish the need for foreign personnel, Section 5(b) of Guideline III recommends a flexible approach as one more suited to stimulate foreign investment. It recognizes the importance of labor market flexibility in this and other areas, and emphasizes in particular the investor's freedom to fill top management positions regardless of nationality. Such flexibility will normally result in largely local hiring in any case because of the relatively higher cost of foreign personnel.

31. The transfer of funds abroad is another fundamental aspect of the treatment of foreign investment. Such funds include the salaries and savings of expatriate personnel, investment profits, amounts needed to service debts and other contractual obligations of the investment enterprise, as well as investment liquidation or sale proceeds. Minimization of restrictions on the transfer of such funds is a hallmark of existing instruments that is reflected in the guidelines. Thus many bilateral investment treaties envisage that foreign investors should be free to repatriate their net profits; like several multilateral instruments, Section 6(1) of Guideline III provides for the same freedom. Obviously, this freedom may be subject to exceptions provided for in binding international instruments such as the Articles of Agreement of the International Monetary Fund (IMF) (which prevail over these guidelines).[25] As in the case of several bilateral investment treaties and over a dozen national investment codes, comparable freedom of transfer is envisaged by Section 6(1) for salary and savings remittances of foreign personnel and for debt service and other contractual payments. Bilateral and multilateral investment instruments and national investment codes typically provide for similar freedom of transfer in respect of investment liquidation proceeds. In view of the large sums that such proceeds may involve, some bilateral investment treaties and national investment codes refer to the exception of effecting transfer of liquidation proceeds over limited periods (of up to five years) where this is dictated by the balance of payments positions of the countries concerned. Section 6(1) of Guideline III likewise refers to this exception only in the context of the repatriation of investment liquidation or sale proceeds, as a derogation from the rule of free transfer when necessitated by the lack of adequate foreign exchange in the central bank (or similar agency) at the time the request for transfer is made and, in all cases, subject to the payment of interest. Finally, Section 6(1) of the Guideline also refers to freedom of transfer of other amounts such as those to which an investor may be entitled as compensation for expropriation or under a judicial or arbitral decision.

32. Bilateral investment treaties and several multilateral instruments contain provisions designed to assure that amounts may be transferred in currencies usable to the investor. In this connection, Section 6(2) of Guideline III, in a manner similar to bilateral investment treaties, refers to currencies imported by the investors concerned (if

24. See text accompanying *supra*, note 19.
25. The latter exceptions include exchange restrictions in effect when a country became a member of the IMF and maintained as transitional arrangements and restrictions approved by the IMF. For details, see Silard, 'Exchange Controls and External Indebtedness; Are the Bretton Woods Concepts Still Workable? – A Perspective from the International Monetary Fund', *Houston Journal of International Law*, **7** (1984), 53.

the currencies remain convertible), currencies designated by the IMF as freely usable, or currencies accepted by the investors. Obviously, only the latter two methods will apply to investments which do not take the form of monetary contributions. Bilateral investment treaties also specify that transfers will be made at prevailing exchange rates. In this connection, some bilateral investment treaties refer to official rates of exchange, others to exchange rates determined in accordance with IMF regulations, and some to the market rate of exchange. In the context of foreign investments, the market rate may in general be likely to be a particularly reliable measure of the actual value of the local currency concerned. Accordingly, Section 6(2) of Guideline III, in recommending that transfers be authorized at exchange rates prevailing on the date of the transfer, refers to the market rate of exchange applicable to the transaction concerned.

33.   Section 6(3) of Guideline III also recommends the payment of interest on the local currency received by the banking authorities of the host State in respect of any delays in effecting the required transfers. Such interest would, in particular, compensate the investor for delays in the transfer of the local currency amount representing liquidation proceeds in the exceptional cases when, as foreseen by Section 6(1)(d) of Guideline III, such transfer may be made by installments. Comparable provisions on interest for transfer delays may be found in some but not all bilateral investment treaties.

34.   Under the applicable law, which will normally be the law of the host State, the investor might be entitled to compensation for loss due to events of international or civil strife, such as war or revolution. Section 6(4) of Guideline III recommends that the Guideline's provisions on transfer of capital should also apply to the transfer of any such compensation to which the investor may thus be entitled. In this respect, the guidelines may be compared to provisions of many bilateral investment treaties calling for such compensation to be freely transferable.

35.   If the investor so chooses, it is clearly normally in the best interests of the host State that investment returns and liquidation proceeds be reinvested there rather than repatriated.[26] Section 7 of Guideline III accordingly recommends that host States permit and facilitate such reinvestment. This does not in any way imply that the State should create obstacles to free transfer.

36.   After the provision of Section 8 of Guideline III on the need to prevent and control corrupt business practices (referred to in paragraph 2 above), Section 9 of this Guideline presents recommendations of 'best practice' with respect to the further area of tax exemptions and other fiscal incentives. The Section cautions against the granting by host States of such exemptions and incentives, a practice which is increasingly motivated by competition among host States. It will be recalled that these exemptions or incentives often represent unjustified sacrifices on the part of host States or serve as poor substitutes for appropriate overall policies affecting investments. Foreign investors may in fact be discouraged by the instability or unpredictability of a regime that incorporates tax holidays and the like followed by significant increases in tax rates to offset the initially foregone revenues of the host State. As Section 9 of Guideline III explains, reasonable and stable tax rates provide better incentives to investors. Where the host State decides that fiscal exemptions are nevertheless justified, Section 9 of Guideline III recommends that, in keeping with other parts of the guidelines, they be made available, for the types of activity to be encouraged, to foreign and national investors equally and with a minimum of bureaucratic discretion in the matter. On the other hand, Section 10

26.   Reinvestment of investment amounts is encouraged by, *inter alia*, the MIGA Convention (art. 12(c)(ii)) to avoid negative effects on the balance of payments of the host country.

of Guideline III mentions a number of measures[27] which some investors' countries take to assist investment flows to developing countries; in this respect, the Section recognizes the granting of fiscal incentives to investors by their home States as a possibly effective means of encouraging such flows.

EXPROPRIATION AND UNILATERAL ALTERATIONS OR TERMINATION OF CONTRACTS

37. Guideline IV covers the subject of expropriation of foreign investments. The Guideline also addresses the question of unilateral changes by host governments of contracts with foreign investors for non-commercial reasons, a subject which is often associated with and made subject to several of the same principles as those governing expropriation. These have been controversial subjects. The background studies on which the guidelines are partly based show that there is however significant consensus on most of the issues involved. Building on this consensus and best practice, the guidelines offer practical solutions to such issues and avoid the ideological approaches that have led to much of the controversy in the past.

38. Many national investment codes, virtually all bilateral investment treaties and most pertinent multilateral instruments contain provisions to the effect that host States may expropriate foreign investments only if the takings are done in accordance with applicable legal procedures, for a public purpose and against payment of compensation. These provisions are typically broad enough to encompass partial as well as total expropriations of foreign investments. The provisions in the bilateral investment treaties and multilateral instruments also often explicitly cover not only outright expropriations but also measures, such as excessive and repetitive tax or regulatory measures, that have a *de facto* confiscatory effect in that their combined effect results in depriving the investor in fact from his ownership, control or substantial benefits over his enterprise, even when each such measure taken separately does not have this effect (so-called 'creeping expropriations').[28] A further element that frequently appears in the bilateral investment treaties and multilateral instruments is that takings by the host State of foreign investments should not discriminate among investors on the basis of their nationalities. All of these elements are also supported by international arbitral awards and scholarly writings on the subject. Each element is incorporated into the definition of permissible expropriations in Section 1 of Guideline IV which, for the sake of clarity, adds that the required pursuit of a public purpose be in good faith.[29]

39. The point of significant disagreement over the conditions of permissible expropriations has concerned the measure of compensation for such expropriations. Most bilateral investment treaties and many western writers have adopted the well-known formula calling for 'prompt, adequate and effective' compensation. Many national laws (of both industrial and developing countries) and most multilateral instruments employ more general terms to describe the required compensation, such as 'just' or 'appropriate.' The two approaches are not, of course, mutually exclusive – for example, compensation that is prompt, adequate and effective may also be the most

27. See also the paper on Resource Flows to Developing Countries prepared by World Bank and IMF staff for submission to the Development Committee in September 1992.

28. See e.g. Dolzer, 'Indirect Expropriation of Alien Property', *ICSID Review – Foreign Investment Law Journal*, 1 (1986), 41.

29. A similar precision regarding good faith is included in a provision (para. 1.36) of MIGA's Operational Regulations on the expropriation risk.

appropriate. As pertinent international arbitral awards indicate, much depends in this area on the circumstances of the case at hand. With this in mind, the guidelines take a practical approach to the matter, employing first the all-embracing term – appropriate – for the recommended general standard on compensation in Section 1 of Guideline IV, and then specifically applying this in Section 2 to indicate, in the context of the taking of a specific investment by a State, that compensation will normally be deemed to be appropriate if it is 'adequate, effective and prompt.' Sections 36 of Guideline IV elaborate upon this recommendation by providing important practical details suggested by judicial and arbitral experience. Of particular value in this connection are the findings of international arbitral awards which provide details on the often vague general standards embodied in treaties, other international instruments and national legislation.

40.   Thus in line with many such awardsas well as significant numbers of bilateral investment treaties and multilateral instruments and some national investment codesSection 3 of Guideline IV explains that the level of compensation for such a taking will be deemed to be 'adequate' if it is based on the fair market value of the taken asset immediately before the taking occurred or the State's decision to take the asset became publicly known. Section 4 of the Guideline encourages agreements between States and foreign investors on how this value should be determined. Where the parties fail to reach such agreement, Section 5 of Guideline IV, again following international arbitral precedent, recommends that the fair market value may be assessed by determining the price that a willing buyer would normally pay to a willing seller of the investment, after taking into account all relevant circumstances such as the nature and duration of the investment. Throughout, reasonable criteria would be applied with a view to ascertaining the market value of the investment.

41.   While the guidelines would not and could hardly seek to impose rigid criteria or hard and fast rules in this respect, Section 6 of Guideline IV presents, on the basis of experience in international arbitrations in particular, different methods of valuation for different types of assets, as examples of appropriate ways of determining the market worth of an investment.[30]

42.   For a *going concern*, i.e. an enterprise consisting of income-producing assets and already in existence for a sufficient period of time to generate the data necessary for proving its profitability and the calculation, with reasonable certainty, of its income in future years (on the assumption that the taking did not occur), Section 6 of Guideline IV suggests that *discounted cash flow* may represent an acceptable method of valuation. This method values an income-producing asset by estimating the *net* cash flow which the asset could be realistically expected to generate over the course of its life, and then discounting that net cash flow by a factor that reflects the time value of money, expected inflation and the risk associated with the cash flow. This method is regarded as appropriate for valuing enterprises with a firmly established income-producing capacity because it recognizes that the economic value of such an enterprise to its owner is a function of the cash that the enterprise can be expected to produce in future. However, particular caution should be observed in applying this method as experience shows that investors tend to greatly exaggerate their claims of compensation for lost future

---

30. On the experience in international arbitrations in this respect, see in particular Friedland and Wong, 'Measuring Damages for the Deprivation of Income-Producing Assets', ICSID Case Studies, *ICSID Review – Foreign Investment Law Journal*, **6** (1991), 400.

profits.[31] Compensation under this method is not appropriate for speculative or indeterminate damage,[32] or for alleged profits which cannot legitimately accrue under the laws and regulations of the host country.[33]

43. For *an enterprise lacking profitability*, Section 6 of Guideline IV provides as an example of an appropriate valuation method one which looks to the assets' *liquidation value*. This method values an enterprise with demonstrated lack of profitability as the sum of the amounts at which the individual assets comprising the enterprise could be sold less any liabilities that the enterprise might have to meet.

44. For *other assets*, recourse may be had to the *replacement value method*. This method measures value on the basis of the amount of cash that would have been required to purchase the individual assets that have been expropriated at their actual state as of the date of the taking. This method obviously assumes that the assets in question are replaceable, which may not always be the case. In addition, the replacement value may not always reflect the value that individual assets may have had together in an enterprise. This problem may be addressed by using the *book value method*. Book value means the difference between a company's assets and liabilities as recorded in its financial statements, or the amount at which the expropriated asset appears on the enterprise's balance sheet after deducting accumulated depreciation in accordance with generally accepted accounting principles. In the guidelines, this method of valuation is only recommended for cases where such book value has been recently assessed and can therefore be deemed to be a fair substitute for the replacement value. In any case, the 'book value' cannot present a fair methodology if it bears no relationship to the market value.

45. Sections 7 and 8 of Guideline IV consider the two other elements of the general recommendation on appropriate compensation for takings of specific investments, namely the effectiveness and timeliness of such compensation. In both respects, the Sections logically recall the guidelines' recommendations on transfer of capital. It is in this context worth noting that some national investment codes and several bilateral investment treaties explicitly link their provisions on compensation for expropriation with those on transfer. In a manner similar to the transfer provision of Section 6(2) of Guideline III, Section 7 of Guideline IV thus deems compensation to be effective if it is paid in the currency originally imported by the investor (if it remains convertible at the time of transfer), in another currency designated as freely usable by the IMF or in any other currency accepted by the investor, with only the latter two methods applying to investments which do not take the form of monetary contributions.

46. As indicated earlier, many bilateral investment treaties require that compensation for expropriation be paid promptly or without delay. Of course, such treaties are only binding on the States parties to them. Countries not parties to such treaties do not always accept that prompt payment is legally required. Significant numbers of other bilateral treaties and multilateral instruments recognize that there may be reasonable delays in effecting compensation. They accordingly rule out only undue delays in

---

31. See fourth study in *Legal Framework for the Treatment of Foreign Investment*, Vol. I, *supra*, note 12, at 146. See also Westberg, *International Transactions and Claims Involving Government Parties – Case Law of the Iran-U.S. Claims Tribunals* (1991), 252; Amerasinghe, 'Issues of Compensation for the Taking of Alien Property in the Light of Recent Cases and Practice', *International and Comparative Law Quarterly*, 41 (1992), 22.

32. See *Chorzow Factory* case, *PCIJ* Ser. A, No. 17 (1928), at 51; *Amoco International Finance Corporation v. Iran*, *Iran–U.S. C.T.R.*, **15** at 238.

33. See de Laubadère, 2 *Traité des Contrats Administratifs*, **2** (1984), 556 and 1327. The same principle has been reflected in a recent ICSID award.

payment. Elaborating on this, several treaties acknowledge that host countries may face foreign exchange stringencies and therefore allow payment of compensation by installments, subject to the payment of proper interest in respect of the deferred payments. Such circumstances and possibilities are acknowledged within narrow time limits by Section 8 of Guideline IV only as exceptions from the general rule of prompt payment in the cases justifying them. The Section refers in this context to cases where there are arrangements for the use of IMF resources or similar objective circumstances of established foreign exchange stringencies. This elaboration is well justified as Section 8 of Guideline IV, in dealing with compensation for an expropriation, addresses consequences of a deliberate decision by the State.[34] Under both Guidelines III and IV, however, the exceptions should be read as a realistic recognition of inevitable compelling circumstances, not as a permit to avoid transfers where these are possible.

47. The above general principles, which envisage ordinary takings of specific investments, may not be fully applicable in respect of certain other types of takings. For example, a foreign investor may be entitled to lesser compensation or to none at all in respect of an expropriation that results from a breach by the investor of the laws of the host State, as may occur when the investment is used as a conduit for drug trafficking or for other criminal activity, or involves gross violations of anti-trust or environmental laws. This point is made in Section 9 of Guideline IV which of course only envisages cases of sanctions properly imposed by courts of law and assumes a proper application of the principle of proportionality (under which a minor offense, for example, should not provide a basis for such a drastic response as a taking). In this context, the Section raises the possibility of any further claims by the investor for compensation being referred to the mechanisms of settlement of disputes mentioned in Guideline V.

48. Also clearly to be distinguished from takings of specific investments are comprehensive non-discriminatory nationalizations of the kinds that take place in the context of large scale social reforms following the most exceptional circumstances of revolutionary changes, war, and similar exigencies. Many international law writers acknowledge that in such contexts States may be required to pay only partial compensation.[35] Expropriations of these kinds may typically have important international as well as domestic policy dimensions. In view of this, compensation arrangements in such unusual circumstances have in practice often been negotiated between the home and host States of the investors, resulting as a practical matter in partial compensation.[36] Without necessarily suggesting any particular outcome in these circumstances, Section 10 of Guideline IV notes that compensation for such

34. Compare *supra*, paras 31 and 33.

35. See e.g. American Law Institute, Restatement (Third) of Foreign Relations Law 712 cmt. (1987) (suggesting that '[i]n exceptional circumstances, some deviation from the standard of [full] compensation' might be justified, and mentioning in this context takings of alien property 'during war or similar exigency'); 1 Oppenheim, *International Law* 352 (8th ed. Lauterpacht, 1955) (suggesting that, 'in cases in which fundamental changes in the political system and economic structure of the State or far-reaching social reforms entail interference, on a large scale, with private property..., [i]t is probable that, consistently with legal principle, [the] solution must be sought in the granting of partial compensation'). See also other writers cited in *Legal Framework for the Treatment of Foreign Investment*, 1, *supra* note 12, at 142.

36. See e.g. Lillich, 'Lump Sum Agreements', *Encyclopedia of Public International Law*, 8 (1985), 367 (referring to 'the nearly 200 lump sum agreements' that home and host States have negotiated since the Second World War, under which host States have, in settlement of claims occasioned by war, nationalization programs, revolutions, etc., paid fixed amounts to home States for distribution among claimants).

expropriations may more appropriately be determined through negotiations between the States involved or, failing such negotiations, by their submission of the matter to international arbitration. This provision addresses circumstances which rarely occur and which may be expected to become more uncommon in future.

49. Under the laws of most countries, State parties to commercial contracts with foreign nationals are generally bound by such contracts to the same extent as non-State parties would be. However, under many legal systems a State may in the exercise of its sovereign powers, that is, when it acts as a sovereign, not simply as a contracting party, unilaterally change, terminate or repudiate the contract. This practice is tolerated in the practice of States when done in the *bona fide* pursuit of a public purpose, rather than for commercial reasons, and against just compensation. Section 11 of Guideline IV recommends that such practice be subject to the same conditions as expropriation and that in such cases foreign investors should be compensated according to principles similar to those set out in the guidelines for expropriation of specific investments. In this respect, the guidelines reflect the findings of several international arbitral awards and international law writers.

SETTLEMENT OF DISPUTES

50. Particularly in the context of arrangements with States, disputes are normally resolved through negotiations and relatively rarely by recourse to contentious procedures. Section 1 of Guideline V further encourages the negotiated resolution of conflicts between foreign investors and their host States. In case negotiations fail, the courts of the host State will normally and unless otherwise provided have jurisdiction over disputes arising out of investments made in the country. In most countries, it is however possible for States and foreign investors to refer their differences to such alternative mechanisms as conciliation or binding arbitration. Recourse to such mechanisms is dependent on agreement between the parties to make use of the mechanism for the dispute in question. In the field of foreign investment, parties frequently do agree to refer their disputes to arbitration in particular. This practice is endorsed by Section 1 of Guideline V.

51. One of the advantages of arbitration is that it offers parties great scope to structure as they see fit their dispute settlement procedures. Their decisions on such procedures will be embodied in their agreement to have recourse to arbitration. In this context, States in particular may, as a condition of their agreement to refer disputes with foreign investors to arbitration, require the investor to resort to local administrative or judicial remedies before initiating such arbitration. This possibility is recognized by such instruments as the Convention establishing the International Centre for Settlement of Investment Disputes (ICSID) and several bilateral investment treaties. It is not however mentioned in the guidelines as it is rarely pursued in practice.

52. The arbitration that Guideline V envisages as a possible alternative to adjudication before national courts is impartial or independent arbitration. It is widely acknowledged that in the field of international investment arbitration in particular arbitrators should be, and be seen to be, impartial and independent.[37] At the same time, arbitrators are generally chosen through appointments by the parties to the dispute in question. One of the perceived advantages of arbitration is in fact the opportunity that it thus gives

37. See e.g. Redfern and Hunter, *Law and Practice of International Commercial Arbitration*, 2nd edn (1991), 213–25.

parties to have their dispute decided by judges of their own choosing. In appointing arbitrators, each party may naturally wish to select persons who may be expected to be sympathetic to the point of view of the appointing party. To ensure the necessary impartiality of the tribunal as a whole, arbitral tribunals thus commonly consist of one arbitrator appointed by each side and a presiding arbitrator appointed by agreement of the parties or by a neutral appointing authority designated by the parties. An alternative that avoids the costs to the parties of a three-arbitrator panel is to submit the dispute to a sole arbitrator appointed by both parties or by a third party entrusted by them with the role of making such an appointment. Where however the appointment of a sole arbitrator or of a majority of arbitrators is made by one party only, the independence of the tribunal could easily be put in doubt. Section 2 of Guideline V emphasizes the importance of avoiding such a procedure and excludes a tribunal so constituted from the definition of independent arbitration.

53.   The independence and impartiality of arbitrators receive particular emphasis in the rules of ICSID, the international conciliation and arbitration forum sponsored by the World Bank and specially designed to handle disputes between States and foreign investors.[38] Provisions for the resolution of such disputes in bilateral investment treaties, national investment codes and individual investment agreements frequently refer to the arbitration procedures of ICSID. The widespread acceptability of ICSID procedures, indicated by the large number of countries (120) that have so far signed the ICSID Convention, and by the reference to ICSID arbitration in hundreds of large investment contracts, may be due, in addition to its relatively low cost, to the fact that it is the only form of arbitration where awards are not subject to subsequent judicial review in ICSID member countries. ICSID in fact provides two kinds of independent arbitration procedures: ICSID Convention arbitration procedures, which are available for cases where both the home and the host State of the investor are parties to the ICSID Convention; and arbitration procedures under the so-called ICSID Additional Facility, which are available for cases where either the home or the host State is not a party to the Convention. References to both types of procedures are frequently included in the provisions referred to above of bilateral investment treaties and national investment codes. Section 3 of Guideline V further encourages such use, as appropriate, of procedures provided by the ICSID Convention or Additional Facility.

38.   See ICSID Convention at arts 14(1) and 40(2); Shihata, 'The Experience of ICSID in the Selection of Arbitrators', *News from ICSID*, **6**, 1 (1989) at 4. For general descriptions of ICSID and ICSID arbitration, see e.g. Broches, *Arbitration under the ICSID Convention*, ICSID publication (1991); Shihata, *Towards a Greater Depoliticization of Investment Disputes: The Roles of ICSID and MIGA*, ICSID publication (1992); and Paulsson, 'ICSID's Achievements and Prospects', *ICSID Review – Foreign Investment Law Journal*, **6** (1991), 380.

Guidelines on the Treatment of Foreign Direct Investment

The Development Committee

Recognizing

that a greater flow of foreign direct investment brings substantial benefits to bear on the world economy and on the economies of developing countries in particular, in terms of improving the long term efficiency of the host country through greater competition, transfer of capital, technology and managerial skills and enhancement of market access and in terms of the expansion of international trade;

that the promotion of private foreign investment is a common purpose of the International Bank for Reconstruction and Development, the International Finance Corporation and the Multilateral Investment Guarantee Agency;

that these institutions have pursued this common objective through their operations, advisory services and research;

that at the request of the Development Committee, a working group established by the President of these institutions and consisting of their respective General Counsel has, after reviewing existing legal instruments and literature, as well as best available practice identified by these institutions, prepared a set of guidelines representing a desirable overall framework which embodies essential principles meant to promote foreign direct investment in the common interest of all members;

that these guidelines, which have benefitted from a process of broad consultation inside and outside these institutions, constitute a further step in the evolutionary process where several international efforts aim to establish a favorable investment environment free from non-commercial risks in all countries, and thereby foster the confidence of international investors; and

that these guidelines are not ultimate standards but an important step in the evolution of generally acceptable international standards which complement, but do not substitute for, bilateral investment treaties,

therefore *calls the attention* of member countries to the following Guidelines as useful parameters in the admission and treatment of private foreign investment in their territories, without prejudice to the binding rules of international law at this stage of its development.

I   SCOPE OF APPLICATION

1.   These Guidelines may be applied by members of the World Bank Group institutions to private foreign investment in their respective territories, as a complement to applicable bilateral and multilateral treaties and other international instruments, to the extent that these Guidelines do not conflict with such treaties and binding instruments, and as a possible source on which national legislation governing the treatment of private foreign investment may draw. Reference to the 'State' in these Guidelines, unless the context otherwise indicates, includes the State or any constituent subdivision, agency or instrumentality of the State and reference to 'nationals' includes natural and juridical persons who enjoy the nationality of the State.

2.   The application of these Guidelines extends to existing and new investments established and operating at all times as *bona fide* private foreign investments, in full conformity with the laws and regulations of the host State.

3.   These Guidelines are based on the general premise that equal treatment of investors in similar circumstances and free competition among them are prerequisites of a positive investment environment. Nothing in these Guidelines therefore suggests that foreign investors should receive a privileged treatment denied to national investors in similar circumstances.

II   ADMISSION

1.   Each State will encourage nationals of other States to invest capital, technology and managerial skill in its territory and, to that end, is expected to admit such investments in accordance with the following provisions.

2.   In furtherance of the foregoing principle, each State will:
   (a)   facilitate the admission and establishment of investments by nationals of other States, and
   (b)   avoid making unduly cumbersome or complicated procedural regulations for, or imposing unnecessary conditions on, the admission of such investments.

3.   Each State maintains the right to make regulations to govern the admission of private foreign investments. In the formulation and application of such regulations, States will note that experience suggests that certain performance requirements introduced as conditions of admission are often counterproductive and that open admission, possibly subject to a restricted list of investments (which are either prohibited or require screening and licensing), is a more effective approach. Such performance requirements often discourage foreign investors from initiating investment in the State concerned or encourage evasion and corruption. Under the restricted list approach, investments in non-listed activities, which proceed without approval, remain subject to the laws and regulations applicable to investments in the State concerned.

4.   Without prejudice to the general approach of free admission recommended in Section 3 above, a State may, as an exception, refuse admission to a proposed investment:

   (i)   which is, in the considered opinion of the State, inconsistent with clearly defined requirements of national security; or

   (ii)   which belongs to sectors reserved by the law of the State to its nationals on account of the State's economic development objectives or the strict exigencies of its national interest.

5.   Restrictions applicable to national investment on account of public policy (*ordre public*), public health and the protection of the environment will equally apply to foreign investment.

6.   Each State is encouraged to publish, in the form of a handbook or other medium easily accessible to other States and their investors, adequate and regularly updated information about its legislation, regulations and procedures relevant to foreign investment and other information relating to its investment policies including, *inter alia*, an indication of any classes of investment which it regards as falling under Sections 4 and 5 of this Guideline.

III TREATMENT

1.   For the promotion of international economic cooperation through the medium of private foreign investment, the establishment, operation, management, control, and exercise of rights in such an investment, as well as such other associated activities necessary therefor or incidental thereto, will be consistent with the following standards which are meant to apply simultaneously to all States without prejudice to the provisions of applicable international instruments, and to firmly established rules of customary international law.

2.   Each State will extend to investments established in its territory by nationals of any other State fair and equitable treatment according to the standards recommended in these Guidelines.

3.   (a) With respect to the protection and security of their person, property rights and interests, and to the granting of permits, import and export licenses and the authorization to employ, and the issuance of the necessary entry and stay visas to their foreign personnel, and other legal matters relevant to the treatment of foreign investors as described in Section 1 above, such treatment will, subject to the requirement of fair and equitable treatment mentioned above, be as favorable as that accorded by the State to national investors in similar circumstances. In all cases, full protection and security will be accorded to the investor's rights regarding ownership, control and substantial benefits over his property, including intellectual property.

(b) As concerns such other matters as are not relevant to national investors, treatment under the State's legislation and regulations will not discriminate among foreign investors on grounds of nationality.

4.   Nothing in this Guideline will automatically entitle nationals of other States to the more favorable standards of treatment accorded to the nationals of certain States under any customs union or free trade area agreement.

5.   Without restricting the generality of the foregoing, each State will:
   (a)   promptly issue such licenses and permits and grant such concessions as may be necessary for the uninterrupted operation of the admitted investment; and
   (b)   to the extent necessary for the efficient operation of the investment, authorize the employment of foreign personnel. While a State may require the foreign investor to reasonably establish his inability to recruit the required personnel locally, e.g., through local advertisement, before he resorts to the recruitment of foreign personnel, labor market flexibility in this and other areas is recognized as an important element in a positive investment environment. Of particular importance in this respect is the investor's freedom to employ top managers regardless of their nationality.

6.   (1) Each State will, with respect to private investment in its territory by nationals of the other States:
   (a)   freely allow regular periodic transfer of a reasonable part of the salaries and wages of foreign personnel; and, on liquidation of the investment or earlier termination of the employment, allow immediate transfer of all savings from such salaries and wages;
   (b)   freely allow transfer of the net revenues realized from the investment;
   (c)   allow the transfer of such sums as may be necessary for the payment of debts contracted, or the discharge of other contractual obligations incurred in connection with the investment as they fall due;
   (d)   on liquidation or sale of the investment (whether covering the investment as a

whole or a part thereof), allow the repatriation and transfer of the net proceeds of such liquidation or sale and all accretions thereto all at once; in the exceptional cases where the State faces foreign exchange stringencies, such transfer may as an exception be made in installments within a period which will be as short as possible and will not in any case exceed five years from the date of liquidation or sale, subject to interest as provided for in Section 6 (3) of this Guideline; and

(e) allow the transfer of any other amounts to which the investor is entitled such as those which become due under the conditions provided for in Guidelines IV and V.

(2) Such transfer as provided for in Section 6 (1) of this Guideline will be made (a) in the currency brought in by the investor where it remains convertible, in another currency designated as freely usable currency by the International Monetary Fund or in any other currency accepted by the investor, and (b) at the applicable market rate of exchange at the time of the transfer. (3) In the case of transfers under Section 6 (1) of this Guideline, and without prejudice to Sections 7 and 8 of Guideline IV where they apply, any delay in effecting the transfers to be made through the central bank (or another authorized public authority) of the host State will be subject to interest at the normal rate applicable to the local currency involved in respect of any period intervening between the date on which such local currency has been provided to the central bank (or the other authorized public authority) for transfer and the date on which the transfer is actually effected.

(4) The provisions set forth in this Guideline with regard to the transfer of capital will also apply to the transfer of any compensation for loss due to war, armed conflict, revolution or insurrection to the extent that such compensation may be due to the investor under applicable law.

7. Each State will permit and facilitate the reinvestment in its territory of the profits realized from existing investments and the proceeds of sale or liquidation of such investments.

8. Each State will take appropriate measures for the prevention and control of corrupt business practices and the promotion of accountability and transparency in its dealings with foreign investors, and will cooperate with other States in developing international procedures and mechanisms to ensure the same.

9. Nothing in this Guideline suggests that a State should provide foreign investors with tax exemptions or other fiscal incentives. Where such incentives are deemed to be justified by the State, they may to the extent possible be automatically granted, directly linked to the type of activity to be encouraged and equally extended to national investors in similar circumstances. Competition among States in providing such incentives, especially tax exemptions, is not recommended. Reasonable and stable tax rates are deemed to provide a better incentive than exemptions followed by uncertain or excessive rates.

10. Developed and capital surplus States will not obstruct flows of investment from their territories to developing States and are encouraged to adopt appropriate measures to facilitate such flows, including taxation agreements, investment guarantees, technical assistance and the provision of information. Fiscal incentives provided by some investors' governments for the purpose of encouraging investment in developing States are recognized in particular as a possibly effective element in promoting such investment.

IV EXPROPRIATION AND UNILATERAL ALTERATIONS OR TERMINATION OF CONTRACTS

1.   A State may not expropriate or otherwise take in whole or in part a foreign private investment in its territory, or take measures which have similar effects, except where this is done in accordance with applicable legal procedures, in pursuance in good faith of a public purpose, without discrimination on the basis of nationality and against the payment of appropriate compensation.

2.   Compensation for a specific investment taken by the State will, according to the details provided below, be deemed 'appropriate' if it is adequate, effective and prompt.

3.   Compensation will be deemed 'adequate' if it is based on the fair market value of the taken asset as such value is determined immediately before the time at which the taking occurred or the decision to take the asset became publicly known.

4.   Determination of the 'fair market value' will be acceptable if conducted according to a method agreed by the State and the foreign investor (hereinafter referred to as the parties) or by a tribunal or another body designated by the parties.

5.   In the absence of a determination agreed by, or based on the agreement of, the parties, the fair market value will be acceptable if determined by the State according to reasonable criteria related to the market value of the investment, i.e., in an amount that a willing buyer would normally pay to a willing seller after taking into account the nature of the investment, the circumstances in which it would operate in the future and its specific characteristics, including the period in which it has been in existence, the proportion of tangible assets in the total investment and other relevant factors pertinent to the specific circumstances of each case.

6.   Without implying the exclusive validity of a single standard for the fairness by which compensation is to be determined and as an illustration of the reasonable determination by a State of the market value of the investment under Section 5 above, such determination will be deemed reasonable if conducted as follows:

   (i)   for a going concern with a proven record of profitability, on the basis of the discounted cash flow value;

   (ii)   for an enterprise which, not being a proven going concern, demonstrates lack of profitability, on the basis of the liquidation value;

   (iii) for other assets, on the basis of (a) the replacement value or (b) the book value in case such value has been recently assessed or has been determined as of the date of the taking and can therefore be deemed to represent a reasonable replacement value.

For the purpose of this provision:

- a *'going concern'* means an enterprise consisting of income-producing assets which has been in operation for a sufficient period of time to generate the data required for the calculation of future income and which could have been expected with reasonable certainty, if the taking had not occurred, to continue producing legitimate income over the course of its economic life in the general circumstances following the taking by the State;
- *'discounted cash flow value'* means the cash receipts realistically expected from the enterprise in each future year of its economic life as reasonably projected minus that year's expected cash expenditure, after discounting this net cash flow for each year by a factor which reflects the time value of money, expected inflation, and the

risk associated with such cash flow under realistic circumstances. Such discount rate may be measured by examining the rate of return available in the same market on alternative investments of comparable risk on the basis of their present value;

- *'liquidation value'* means the amounts at which individual assets comprising the enterprise or the entire assets of the enterprise could be sold under conditions of liquidation to a willing buyer less any liabilities which the enterprise has to meet;
- *'replacement value'* means the cash amount required to replace the individual assets of the enterprise in their actual state as of the date of the taking; and
- *'book value'* means the difference between the enterprise's assets and liabilities as recorded on its financial statements or the amount at which the taken tangible assets appear on the balance sheet of the enterprise, representing their cost after deducting accumulated depreciation in accordance with generally accepted accounting principles.

7.   Compensation will be deemed 'effective' if it is paid in the currency brought in by the investor where it remains convertible, in another currency designated as freely usable by the International Monetary Fund or in any other currency accepted by the investor.

8.   Compensation will be deemed to be 'prompt' in normal circumstances if paid without delay. In cases where the State faces exceptional circumstances, as reflected in an arrangement for the use of the resources of the International Monetary Fund or under similar objective circumstances of established foreign exchange stringencies, compensation in the currency designated under Section 7 above may be paid in installments within a period which will be as short as possible and which will not in any case exceed five years from the time of the taking, provided that reasonable, market-related interest applies to the deferred payments in the same currency.

9.   Compensation according to the above criteria will not be due, or will be reduced in case the investment is taken by the State as a sanction against an investor who has violated the State's law and regulations which have been in force prior to the taking, as such violation is determined by a court of law. Further disputes regarding claims for compensation in such a case will be settled in accordance with the provisions of Guideline V.

10.   In case of comprehensive non-discriminatory nationalizations effected in the process of large scale social reforms under exceptional circumstances of revolution, war and similar exigencies, the compensation may be determined through negotiations between the host State and the investors' home State and failing this, through international arbitration.

11.   The provisions of Section 1 of this Guideline will apply with respect to the conditions under which a State may unilaterally terminate, amend or otherwise disclaim liability under a contract with a foreign private investor for other than commercial reasons, i.e., where the State acts as a sovereign and not as a contracting party. Compensation due to the investor in such cases will be determined in the light of the provisions of Sections 2 to 9 of this Guideline. Liability for repudiation of contract for commercial reasons, i.e., where the State acts as a contracting party, will be determined under the applicable law of the contract.

V   SETTLEMENT OF DISPUTES

1.   Disputes between private foreign investors and the host State will normally be settled through negotiations between them and failing this, through national courts or

through other agreed mechanisms including conciliation and binding independent arbitration.

2.   Independent arbitration for the purpose of this Guideline will include any *ad hoc* or institutional arbitration agreed upon in writing by the State and the investor or between the State and the investor's home State where the majority of the arbitrators are not solely appointed by one party to the dispute.

3.   In case of agreement on independent arbitration, each State is encouraged to accept the settlement of such disputes through arbitration under the Convention establishing the International Centre for Settlement of Investment Disputes (ICSID) if it is a party to the ICSID Convention or through the 'ICSID Additional Facility' if it is not a party to the ICSID Convention.

Annex 2

Concluding Document of the Hague Conference on the European Energy Charter

The representatives of Albania, Armenia, Australia, Austria, Azerbaijan, Belgium, Byelorussia, Bulgaria, Canada, Czechoslovakia, Cyprus, Denmark, Estonia, The European Communities, Finland, France, Georgia, Germany, Greece, Hungary, Iceland, The Interstate Economic Committee, Ireland, Italy, Japan, Kazakhstan, Kirghizstan, Latvia, Liechtenstein, Lithuania, Luxembourg, Malta, Moldavia, The Netherlands, Norway, Poland, Portugal, Romania, The Russian Federation, Spain, Sweden, Switzerland, Tadjikistan, Turkey, Turkmenistan, Ukraine, The United Kingdom of Great Britain and Northern Ireland, The United States of America, Uzbekistan, Yugoslavia convened in The Hague, The Netherlands, from 16 to 17 December 1991 in order to adopt the European Energy Charter.

The Conference was opened and closed by the Minister of Economic Affairs of The Netherlands.

Her Majesty, Queen Beatrix of The Netherlands, attended the opening of the Conference.

The Prime Minister of the Netherlands and the Commissioner for Energy of the European Commission addressed the Conference.

During the Conference, contributions were received and statements made by delegates of the signatories.

Determined to give full effect to the results of the Conference, the representatives of the signatories adopted the following text for the European Energy Charter:

EUROPEAN ENERGY CHARTER

The representatives of the signatories meeting in The Hague on 16 and 17 December 1991,

Having regard to the Charter of Paris for a New Europe, signed in Paris on 21 November 1990 at the summit meeting of the Conference on security and Co-operation in Europe (CSCE);

Having regard to the document adopted in Bonn on 11 April 1990 by the CSCE Conference on Economic Co-operation in Europe;

Having regard to the declaration of the London Economic Summit adopted on 17 July 1991;

Having regard to the report on the conclusions and recommendations of the CSCE meeting in Sofia on 3 November 1989, on the protection of the environment, as well as its follow-up;

Having regard to the Agreement establishing the European Bank for Reconstruction and Development signed in Paris on 29 May 1990;

Anxious to give formal expression to this new desire for a European-wide and global co-operation based on mutual respect and confidence;

Resolved to promote a new model for energy co-operation in the long term in Europe and globally within the framework of a market economy and based on mutual assistance and the principle of non-discrimination;

Aware that account must be taken of the problems of reconstruction and restructuring in the countries of Central and Eastern Europe and in the [USSR] and that it is desirable for the signatories to participate in joint efforts aimed at facilitating and promoting market-oriented reforms and modernisation of energy sectors in these countries;

Certain that taking advantage of the complementary features of energy sectors within Europe will benefit the world economy; persuaded that broader energy cooperation among signatories is essential for the economic progress and more generally for social development and a better quality of life;

Convinced of the signatories' common interest in problems of energy supply, safety of industrial plants, particularly nuclear facilities, and environmental protection;

Willing to do more to attain the objectives of security of supplies and efficient management and use of resources, and to utilize fully the potential for environmental improvement in moving towards sustainable development;

Convinced of the essential importance of efficient energy systems in the production, conversion, transport, distribution and use of energy for security of supply and for the protection of the environment;

Recognizing State sovereignty and sovereign rights over energy resources;

Assured of support from the European Community, particularly through completion of its internal energy market;

Aware of the obligations under major relevant multilateral agreements, of the wide range of international energy co-operation, and of the extensive activities by existing international organizations in the energy field and willing to take full advantage of the expertise of these organizations in furthering the objectives of the Charter.

Recognizing the role of entrepreneurs, operating within a transparent and equitable legal framework, in promoting co-operation under the Charter;

Determined to establish closer, mutually beneficial commercial relations and promote energy investments;

Aware of the need to promote technological co-operation among signatories;

Affirming that the energy policies of signatories are linked by interests common to all their countries and that they should be implemented in accordance with the principles set out below:

Affirming, finally, their desire to take the consequent action and apply the principles set out below:

HAVE ADOPTED THE FOLLOWING DECLARATION CONSTITUTING THE "EUROPEAN ENERGY CHARTER"

TITLE 1: OBJECTIVES

The signatories are desirous of improving security of energy supply and of maximising the efficiency of production, conversion, transport, distribution and use of energy, to enhance safety and to minimise environmental problems, on an acceptable economic basis.

Within the framework of State sovereignty and sovereign rights over energy resources and in a spirit of practical and economic co-operation, they undertake to promote the development of an efficient energy market throughout Europe, and a better functioning global market, in both cases based on the principle of non-discrimination and on market-oriented price formation, taking due account of environmental concerns. They are determined to create a climate favourable to the operation of enterprise and to the flow of investments and technologies by implementing market principles in the field of energy.

To this end, and in accordance with these principles, they will take action in the following fields:

1. Development of trade in energy consistent with major relevant multilateral agreements such as GATT, its related instruments, and nuclear non-proliferation obligations and undertakings, which will be achieved by means of:

   — an open and competitive market for energy products, materials, equipment and services;
   — access to energy resources, and exploration and development thereof on a commercial basis;
   — access to local and international markets;
   — removal of technical, administrative and other barriers to trade in energy and associated equipment, technologies and energy-related services;
   — modernization, renewal and rationalization by industry of services and installations for the production, conversion, transport, distribution and use of energy;
   — promoting the development and interconnection of energy through appropriate
     existing financial institutions;
   — facilitating access to transport infrastructure, for international transit purposes in accordance with the objectives of the Charter expressed in the first paragraph of this Title;
   — access on commercial terms to technologies for the exploration, development and use of energy resources.

2. Co-operation in the energy field, which will entail:

   — co-ordination of energy policies, as necessary for promoting the objectives of the Charter;
   — mutual access to technical and economic data, consistent with proprietary rights;

— formulation of stable and transparent legal frameworks creating conditions for the development of energy resources;
— co-ordination and, where appropriate, harmonization of safety principles and guidelines for energy products and their transport, as well as for energy installations, at a high level;
— facilitating the exchange of technology information and know-how in the energy and environment fields, including training activities;
— research, technological development and demonstration projects.

3. Energy efficiency and environmental protection, which will imply:

— creating mechanisms and conditions for using energy as economically and efficiently as possible, including, as appropriate, regulatory and market-based instruments;
— promotion of an energy mix designed to minimise negative environment consequences in a cost-effective way through:

(i) market-oriented energy prices which more fully reflects environmental costs and benefits;
(ii) efficient and co-ordinated policy measures related to energy;
(iii) use of new and renewable energies and clean technologies;

— achieving and maintaining a high level of nuclear safety and ensuring effective co-operation in this field.

TITLE II: IMPLEMENTATION

In order to attain the objectives set out above, the signatories will, within the framework of State sovereignty and sovereign rights over energy resources, take co-ordinated action to achieve greater coherence of energy policies, which should be based on the principles of non-discrimination and on market-oriented price formation, taking due account of environmental concerns.

They underline that practical steps to define energy policies are necessary in order to intensify co-operation in this sector and further stress the importance of regular exchanges of views on action taken, taking full advantage of the experience of existing international organizations and institutions in this field.

The signatories recognize that commercial forms of co-operation may need to be complemented by intergovernmental co-operation, particularly in the area of energy policy formulation and analysis as well as in areas which are essential and not suitable to private capital funding.

They undertake to pursue the objectives of creating a broader European energy market and enhancing the efficient functioning of the global energy market by joint or co-ordinated action under the Charter in the following fields:

1. Access to and development of energy resources

Considering that sufficient development of energy resources is a *sine qua non* for attaining the objectives of the Charter, the signatories undertake to facilitate access to and development of resources by the interested operators.

To this end, they will ensure that rules on the exploration, development and acquisition of resources are publicly available and transparent; they recognize the need to formulate such rules wherever this has not yet been done and to take all necessary measures to co-ordinate their actions in this area.

With a view to facilitating the development and diversification of resources, the signatories undertake to avoid imposing discriminatory rules on operators, notably rules governing the ownership of resources, internal operation of companies and taxation.

2. Access to markets

The signatories will strongly promote access to local and international markets for energy products for the implementation of the objectives of the Charter. Such access to markets should take account of the need to facilitate the operation of market forces, and promote competition.

3. Liberalization of trade in energy

In order to develop and diversify trade in energy, the signatories undertake progressively to remove the barriers to such trade with each other in energy products, equipment and services in a manner consistent with the provisions of GATT, its related instruments, and nuclear non-proliferation obligations and undertakings.

The signatories recognize that transit of energy products through their territories is essential for the liberalization of trade in energy products. Transit should take place in economic and environmentally sound conditions.

They stress the importance of the development of commercial international energy transmission networks and their interconnection, with particular reference to electricity and natural gas and with recognition of the relevance of long-term commercial commitments. To this end, they will ensure the compatibility of technical specifications governing the installation and operation of such network, notably as regards the stability of electricity systems.

4. Promotion and protection of investments

In order to promote the international flow of investments, the signatory will at national level provide for a stable, transparent legal framework for foreign investments, in conformity with the relevant international laws and rules on investment and trade.

They affirm that it is important for the signatory States to negotiate and ratify legally binding agreements on promotion and protection of investments which ensure a high level of legal security and enable the use of investment risk guarantee schemes.

Moreover, the signatories will guarantee the right to repatriate profits or other payments relating to an investment and to obtain or use the convertible currency needed.

They also recognize the importance of the avoidance of double taxation to foster private investment.

5. Safety principles and guidelines

Consistent with relevant major multilateral agreements, the signatories will:

— implement safety principles and guidelines, designed to achieve and/or maintain levels of safety, in particular nuclear safety and the protection of health and the environment;

— develop such common safety principles and guidelines as are appropriate and/or agree to the mutual recognition of their safety principles and guidelines.

6. Research, technological development, innovation and dissemination

The signatories undertake to promote exchanges of technology and co-operation on their technological development and innovation activities in the fields of energy production, conversion, transport, distribution and the efficient and clean use of energy, in a manner consistent with nuclear non-proliferation obligations and undertakings. To this end, they will encourage co-operative efforts on:

— research and development activities;
— pilot or demonstration projects;
— the application of technological innovations;
— the dissemination and exchange of know-how and information on technologies.

7. Energy efficiency and environmental protection

The signatories agree that co-operation is necessary in the field of efficient use of energy and energy-related environmental protection. This should include:

— ensuring, in a cost-effective manner, consistency between relevant energy policies and environmental agreements and conventions;
— ensuring market-oriented price formation, including a fuller reflection of environmental costs and benefits;
— the creation of framework conditions for the exchange of know-how regarding environmentally sound technologies and efficient use of energy;
— the creation of framework conditions for profitable investment in energy efficiency projects.

8. Education and training

The signatories, recognizing industry's role in promoting vocational education and training in the energy field, undertake to co-operate in such activities, including:

— professional education
— occupational training
— public information in the energy efficiency field.

TITLE III: SPECIFIC AGREEMENTS

The signatories undertake to pursue the objectives and principles of the Charter and implement and broaden their co-operation as soon as possible by negotiating in good faith a *Basic Agreement and Protocols*.

Areas of co-operation could include:

— horizontal and organisational issues;

- energy efficiency, including environmental protection;
- prospecting, production, transportation and use of oil and oil products and modernization of refineries;
- prospecting, production and use of natural gas, interconnection of gas networks and transmission via high-pressure gas pipelines;
- all aspects of the nuclear fuel cycle including improvements in safety in that sector;
- modernization of power stations, interconnection of power networks and transmission of electricity via high-voltage power lines;
- all aspects of the coal cycle, including clean coal technologies;
- development of renewable energy sources;
- transfer of technology and encouragement of innovation;
- co-operation in dealing with the effects of major accidents, or of other events in the energy sector with transfrontier consequences.

The signatories will, in exceptional cases, consider transnational arrangements. They, in particular, take into account the specific circumstances facing some states of Central and Eastern Europe and the USSR as well as their need to adapt their economies to the market system, and accept the possibility the of a stage-by-stage transition in those countries for the implementation of those particular provisions of the Charter, Basic Agreement and the reflated Protocols that they are, for objectives reasons, unable to implement immediately and in full.

Specific arrangements for coming into full compliance with Charter provisions as elaborated in the *Basic Agreement and Protocols* will be negotiated by each Party requesting transnational status, and progress towards full compliance will be subject to periodic review.

TITLE IV: FINAL PROVISION

The signatories request the Government of The Netherlands, President-in-Office of the Council of the European Communities, to transmit to the Secretary-General of the United nations the text of the European Energy Charter which is not eligible for registration under Article 102 of the Charter of the United Nations.

In adopting the European Energy Charter Ministers or their representatives record that the following understanding has been reached:

The representatives of the Signatories understand that in the context of the European Energy Charter, the principle of non-discrimination means Most-Favoured-Nation Treatment as a minimum standard. National Treatment may be agreed to in provisions of the *Basic Agreement and/or Protocols*.

The original of this Concluding Document, drawn up in English, French, German, Italian, Russian and Spanish texts, will be transmitted to the Government of the Kingdom of The Netherlands, which will retain it in its archives. Each of the Signatories will receive from the Government of the Kingdom of The Netherlands a true copy of the Concluding Document.

In witness whereof, the representatives of the Signatories, mindful of the high political significance which they attach to the results of the Conference, and declaring their determination to act in accordance with the provisions of the European Energy Charter, have subscribed their signatures below:

Annex 3

Energy Charter Treaty
Draft, 20 December 1993

PREAMBLE

The Contracting Parties to this Agreement,

Having regard to the Charter of Paris for a New Europe signed on 21 November 1990,

Having regard to the European Energy Charter signed at The Hague on 17 December 1991,

Aware that all Signatories to the European Energy Charter undertook to agree an Energy Charter Treaty to place the commitments contained in that Charter on a secure and binding international legal basis;

Desiring to establish the structural framework required to implement the principles enunciated in the European Energy Charter;

Whereas Contracting Parties attach the utmost importance to the effective implementation of full National Treatment and this general commitment will be applied with regard to the making of investments according to the provisions of a supplementary Agreement to be negotiated in good faith within three years;

Having regard to the objective of progressive liberalisation of international trade and to the principle of avoidance of discrimination in international trade as enunciated in the General Agreement on Tariffs and Trade and its related instruments and as otherwise provided for in this Agreement;

Determined to remove progressively technical, administrative and other barriers to trade in Energy Materials and Products and related equipment, technologies and services;

Looking to the eventual membership of the General Agreement on Tariffs and Trade of those Contracting Parties which are not currently Contracting Parties to the General Agreement on Tariffs and Trade and concerned to provide interim trade arrangements which will assist those Contracting Parties and not impede their preparation of themselves for such membership;

Having regard to the rights and obligations of certain Contracting Parties who are also parties to the General Agreement on Tariffs and Trade and its related Agreements, as renegotiated from time to time;

Having regard to national competition rules concerning mergers, monopolies, anti-competitive practices and abuse of dominant position where these are already established;

Having regard to the competition rules applicable to member states of the European Community under the Treaty establishing the European Economic Community, the Treaty establishing the European Coal and Steel Community and the Treaty establishing the European Atomic Energy Community;

Having regard to the competition rules applicable to contracting parties to the European Economic Area;

Having regard to the work in the Organisation for Economic Co-operation and Development and the United Nations Conference on Trade and Development to increase co-operation between sovereign states on competition matters;

Having regard to the Treaty on the Non-Proliferation of Nuclear Weapons, the Nuclear Suppliers Guidelines and the obligations of international nuclear safeguards;

Having regard to the necessity of a most efficient exploration, production, conversion, storage, transport, distribution and use of energy;

Having regard to the increasing urgency of measures to protect the environment, *including the decommissioning of energy installations and waste disposal*, and to the need for internationally agreed objectives and criteria for this purpose;

Recalling the United Nations Framework Convention on Climate Change, the ECE Convention on Long-Range Transboundary Air Pollution and its protocols, and other international environmental agreements with energy-related aspects, and recognizing the increasing urgency of measures to protect the environment, including internationally agreed measures;[1]

HAVE AGREED AS FOLLOWS:

CHAIRMAN'S NOTE

For Articles on which full agreement has been reached, or where there are only one or two remaining reservations which have already been exhaustively discussed, the Charter Treaty text contains the note 'Negotiations in the Plenary finished'. This does not mean that delegations are prevented from reopening discussion of a particular Article in the final stages of negotiation. It should be recognised however that there are only two legitimate reasons for requesting such a rediscussion:

(a) because the wording agreed for another Article of the Charter Treaty requires, on grounds of logic or law, a consequential change in the text of an Article which had already been agreed; or

(b) because a delegation feels, at the end of the negotiations of the whole Charter Treaty, that the overall balance needs to be adjusted by making a change in the text of an Article which had previously been agreed.

In the other case described above, where there are only one or two remaining reserves or proposed amendments which have already been discussed, the relevant footnotes have been moved to the end of the Charter Treaty on pages 93 to 96. Again the Plenary should only revert to these Articles for the reasons described above. Delegations with footnotes should of course notify the Secretariat if they have decided on their withdrawal.

PART I DEFINITIONS AND GENERAL PROVISIONS

Article 1 Definitions

For the purposes of this Agreement unless the context otherwise requires:

(1) 'Charter' means the European Energy Charter signed at The Hague on 17 December 1991;

(2) 'Contracting Party' means a State or Regional Economic Integration Organisation which has consented to be bound by the Agreement and for which the Agreement is in force;

(3) ['Regional Economic Integration Organisation' means an organisation constituted by States to which they have transferred competence over certain matters a number of which are governed by this Agreement, including the authority to take decisions binding on them in respect of those matters.]

(4) 'Energy Materials and Products', based on the Harmonised System (HS) of the Customs Cooperation Council and the Combined Nomenclature (CN) of the European Communities, means the items of HS or CN included in Annex EM.

(5) 'Economic Activity in the Energy Sector' means an economic activity in the business of the exploration, extraction, refining production, storage, transport, transmission, distribution, trade, marketing, or sales of Energy Materials and Products except those included in Annex NI.

(6) 'Investment' means every kind of asset, [owned or controlled directly or indirectly by an Investor] [and includes]:

   (a) tangible and intangible, and movable and immovable, property, and any property rights such as leases, mortgages, liens, and pledges;

   (b) a company or business enterprise, or shares, stock, or other forms of equity participation in a company or business enterprise, and bonds, and debt of, a company or business enterprise;

   (c) claims to money and claims to performance pursuant to contract having an economic value [and associated with an Investment];

   (d) Intellectual Property;

   (e) [any right] conferred by law, contract or by virtue of any licences and permits granted pursuant to law.

   A change in the form in which assets are invested does not affect their character as investments and the term 'Investment' includes all investments, whether existing at or made after the later of the dates of entry into force of this Agreement for the Contracting Party of the Investor making the investment and Contracting Party in which the investment is made (hereinafter referred to as the 'effective date') provided that this Agreement shall only apply to matters affecting such investments after the effective date.

   For the purposes of this Agreement, 'Investment' refers to any investment associated with an 'Economic Activity in the Energy Sector.'

(7) 'Investor' means:

(a) with respect to a Contracting Party

   (i) a natural person having the citizenship or nationality of or who is permanently residing in that Contracting Party in accordance with its applicable laws;

   (ii) a company or other organisation organised in accordance with the laws applicable in that Contracting Party

(b) with respect to a 'third state', a natural person, company or other organisation which fulfills, mutatis mutandis, the conditions specified in sub-paragraph (a) for a Contracting Party.]

(8) 'Make Investments' means establishing a new Investment, acquiring all or part of an existing Investment, expanding an existing Investment, or substantially altering the type or the objective of an existing Investment;

(9) 'Returns' means the amounts derived from or associated with an Investment, irrespective of the form in which paid, including profits, dividends, interest, capital gains, royalty payments, management, technical assistance or other fees, and returns in kind.

(10) 'Area' means with respect to a Contracting Party:

(a) the territory under its sovereignty, it being understood that territory includes land, internal waters and the territorial sea, and

(b) subject to and in accordance with the international law of the sea; the sea, sea-bed and its subsoil with regard to which that Contracting Party exercises sovereign rights [and] jurisdiction.

With respect to a Regional Economic Integration Organisation which is or becomes a Contracting Party to this Agreement, Area means the areas of the Member States of such an Organisation, under the provisions laid down in the agreement establishing that Organisation.

(11) 'GATT and Related Instruments' means:

(a) the General Agreement on Tariffs and Trade, done at Geneva October 30, 1947; and

(b) agreements, arrangements, decisions, understandings, or other joint action within the framework of the General Agreement on Tariffs and Trade.

(12) 'Intellectual Property' includes copyright and related rights, trademarks, geographical indications, industrial designs, patents, layout designs of integrated circuits and the protection of undisclosed information.

(13) 'Protocol' means an agreement authorised and adopted by the Charter Conference and entered into by any of the Contracting Parties in order to complement, supplement, extend or amplify the provisions of this Agreement to specific sectors or categories of activity comprised within the scope of this Agreement, including areas of cooperation referred to in Title III of the Charter.

(14) 'Freely Convertible Currency' means a currency which is widely traded in international foreign exchange markets and widely used in international transactions.

Article 2 Purpose of the Agreement

This Agreement establishes a legal framework in order to promote long-term cooperation in the energy field, based on mutual benefits and complementarities, in accordance with the objectives and the principles of the Charter.

PART II COMMERCE

[Article 3] Access to Energy Resources and Markets

(1) The Contracting Parties will strongly promote access to local, export and international markets for the *acquisition and* disposal of Energy Materials and Products on commercial terms and undertake to remove progressively barriers to trade. [*DL*]

(2) *They will, accordingly, seek to ensure* that price formation shall be based on market principles.

[Article 4] Trade in Energy Materials and Products

[Except as otherwise provided in this Agreement trade in Energy Materials and Products between Contracting Parties shall be governed by the provisions of the GATT and Related Instruments, as they are applied under GATT rules between particular Contracting Parties who are members of the GATT].

Article 5 Developments in International Trading Arrangements

Contracting Parties undertake that in the event of the adoption of agreements within the framework [*DL*] of the GATT or other significant and relevant developments in the international trading system, [*DL*] *they will* consider, *within two years of such an adoption or development*, appropriate amendments to this Agreement.

Article 6 Intellectual Property

Deleted

Article 7 Competition

(1) The Contracting Parties agree to work to alleviate market distortions and barriers to competition in [Economic Activity in the Energy Sector.]

(2) Each Contracting Party shall ensure that within its jurisdiction it has and enforces such laws as are necessary and appropriate to address unilateral and concerted anti-competitive conduct in [Economic Activity in the Energy Sector.]

(3) Contracting Parties with experience in applying competition rules shall give full consideration to providing, upon request and within available resources, technical assistance on the development and implementation of competition rules to other Contracting Parties.

(4) Contracting Parties may co-operate in the enforcement of their competition rules by consulting and exchanging information.

(5) If a Contracting Party considers that any specified anti-competitive conduct carried out within the Area of another Contracting Party is adversely affecting an important interest relevant to the purposes identified in this Article, the Contracting Party may notify the other and may request that the other's competition authorities initiate appropriate enforcement action. The notifying Contracting Party shall include in such notification sufficient information to permit the other Contracting Party to identify the anti-competitive conduct that is the subject of the notification and shall include an offer of such further information and cooperation as that Contracting Party is able to provide. The notified Contracting Party or, as the case may be, the relevant competition authorities may consult with the other and shall accord full consideration to the request of the other Contracting Party in deciding whether or not to initiate enforcement action with respect to the alleged anti-competitive conduct identified in the notification. The notified Contracting Party shall inform the other of its decision or the decision of the relevant competition authorities and may inform the other, at the sole discretion of the notified Contracting Party, of the grounds for the decision. If enforcement action is initiated, the notified Contracting Party will advise the notifying Contracting Party of its outcome and, to the extent possible, of significant interim developments.

(6) Nothing in this Article shall require the provision of information by a Contracting Party contrary to its laws regarding disclosure of information, confidentiality or business secrecy.

(7) The procedures set forth in paragraph (5) or in Article 31(1) shall be the exclusive means within this Agreement of resolving any disputes that may arise over the implementation or interpretation of this Article.

[Article 8] Transit

(1) Each Contracting Party shall take the necessary measures to facilitate the Transit of Energy Materials and Products consistent with the principle of freedom of transit and without distinction as to the origin, destination or ownership of such Energy Materials and Products or discrimination as to the pricing on the basis of such distinctions, and without imposing any unreasonable delays, restrictions or charges.

(2) Contracting Parties shall encourage relevant entities to cooperate in:

    (a) modernising Energy Transport Facilities necessary to the Transit of Energy Materials and Products;

    (b) the development and operation of Energy Transport Facilities serving the Area of more than one Contracting Party;

    (c) measures to mitigate the effects of interruptions in the supply of Energy Materials and Products;

    (d) facilitating the interconnection of Energy Transport Facilities.

(3) Each Contracting Party undertakes that its provisions relating to transport of Energy Materials and Products and the use of Energy Transport Facilities shall treat Energy Materials and Products in Transit in no less favourable a manner than its provisions treat such materials and products originating in or destined for its

own Area, except if otherwise provided for in an existing international agreement.

(4) [In the event that Transit of Energy Materials and Products cannot be achieved on commercial terms by means of Energy Transport Facilities the Contracting Parties shall not place obstacles in the way of new capacity being established, subject to applicable legislation which is compatible with paragraph (1) of this Article.]

(5) [A Contracting Party through whose Area Energy Materials and Products may transit shall not be obliged to

    (a) permit the construction or modification of Energy Transport Facilities, or

    (b) permit new or additional Transit through existing Energy Transport Facilities,

which it [demonstrates] to the other Contracting Parties concerned would endanger [the security or efficiency of its energy systems, including the security of supply.]

Subject to paragraphs (6) and (7), Contracting Parties shall secure established flows of Energy Materials and Products to, from or between the Area of other Contracting Parties.]

(6) A Contracting Party through whose Area Energy Materials and Products Transit shall not in the event of a dispute over any matter arising from that Transit interrupt or reduce, nor permit any entity subject to its control to interrupt or reduce, nor require any entity subject to its jurisdiction to interrupt or reduce the existing flow of Energy Materials and Products except where this is specifically provided for in a contract or other agreement governing such Transit or where the procedure in paragraph (7) has been completed.

(7) (a) The parties to a dispute relating to paragraph (6) shall exhaust any contractual or other dispute resolution remedies they have previously agreed;

    (b) If this fails to resolve the dispute, a party to the dispute may refer it to the Secretary General referred to in Article 40 with a note summarising the matters in dispute. The Secretary General shall notify all Contracting Parties of any such referral;

    (c) Within 30 days of receipt of such a note, the Secretary General, in consultation with the parties to the dispute and the Contracting Parties concerned, shall appoint a conciliator. Such a conciliator shall have experience in the matters subject to dispute and shall not be a national or citizen of or resident in the Areas through which the Transit occurs, from which the Energy Materials and Products being transported originate or to which the Energy Materials and Products are being supplied;

    (d) The conciliator shall conciliate between the parties and seek their agreement to a resolution to the dispute or upon a procedure to achieve such resolution. If within 90 days of his appointment he has failed to secure such agreement, he shall recommend a resolution to the dispute or a procedure to achieve such resolution and shall decide the interim tariffs and other terms and conditions to be observed for Transit from a date which he shall specify until such resolution;

    (e) The Contracting Parties undertake to observe and ensure that the entities under their control or jurisdiction observe any interim decision under paragraph (7)(d) on tariffs, terms and conditions for 12 months following the conciliator's decision or until resolution of the dispute, whichever is earlier;

(f) No dispute concerning a Transit which has already been the subject of the conciliation procedures set out in this Article may be referred to the Secretary General under paragraph (7)(b) above unless the previous dispute has been resolved;

(g) Standard provisions on conciliator's expenses, location, etc shall be decided by the Charter Conference.

(8) [This Article shall not derogate from a Contracting Party's rights and obligations under existing bilateral or multilateral agreements [including Articles 4 and 35 of this Agreement.]

(9) This Article shall not be interpreted as to oblige any Contracting Party which does not have a category of Energy Transport Facilities used for Transit to take in relation to that category any measures pursuant to the provisions of this Article. Such Contracting Parties would, however, be obliged to comply with paragraph (4).

(10) For the purpose of this Article:

(a) 'Transit' means the [carriage] through the Area of a Contracting Party, or to or from port facilities in its Area for loading or unloading, of products and materials originating in the Area of another State and destined for the Area of a third State, so long as either the other State or the third State is a Contracting Party. [It also means such [carriage] through the Area of a Contracting Party of products and materials originating in the Area of another Contracting Party and destined for the Area of that other Contracting Party unless the two Contracting Parties concerned decide otherwise and record their decision by a joint entry in Annex N. The two Contracting Parties may delete their listing in Annex N by jointly notifying the Secretary General of that intention who shall notify all other Contracting Parties. The deletion shall take effect four weeks after such former notification without further procedures.]

(b) 'Energy Transport Facilities' consist of high pressure gas transmission pipelines, high voltage electricity transmission grids and lines, crude oil transmission pipelines, coal slurry pipelines, oil product pipelines, and other fixed facilities specifically for handling Energy Materials and Products.

[Article 9] Transfer of Technology

(1) The Contracting Parties agree to promote access to and transfer of technology on a commercial and non-discriminatory basis to assist effective trade and investment and to implement the objectives of the Charter, [in accordance with their laws and regulations] subject to the *protection of the Intellectual Property rights*.

(2) Accordingly to the extent necessary to give effect to paragraph (1), the Contracting Parties shall eliminate existing and create no new obstacles for transfer of technology, in the field of Energy Materials and Products and related equipment and services, subject to non-proliferation and other international obligations.

[Article 10] Access to Capital

(1) Contracting Parties acknowledge the importance of open capital markets in

encouraging the flow of capital to finance trade in Energy Materials and Products and to finance Investment in the Economic Activity in the Energy Sector of Contracting Parties, particularly those with economies in transition. Accordingly each Contracting Party will endeavour to promote conditions for access to its capital market for its companies and nationals and for companies and nationals of other Contracting Parties for Making or assisting Investment in Economic Activity in the Energy Sector in the Area of other Contracting Parties. [Consistent with] existing international agreements, no Contracting Party shall apply terms for access to private sources of finance within its jurisdiction for the purposes of Investment in the Economic Activity in the Energy Sector of another Contracting Party less favourable than those applied in like circumstances for the purposes of Investment by nationals or companies of the Contracting Party in its own energy sector or in that of any other Contracting Party of any third state, whichever is the most favourable.

(2) A Contracting Party which [has] programmes providing for access to public loans [and] grants, guarantees [and] insurance for facilitating trade or Investment abroad shall make such facilities available, consistent with the objectives, constraints and criteria of such programmes, (including but not limited to, on any grounds, objectives, constraints or criteria relating to the place of business of an applicant for any such facility or the place of delivery of goods or services supplied with the support of any such facility) for Investments in the Economic Activity in the Energy Sector of other Contracting Parties or for financing trade in the energy sector with other Contracting Parties.

(3) Contracting Parties shall seek as appropriate to encourage the operations and take advantage of the expertise of relevant international financial institutions in implementing programmes in the Economic Activity in the Energy Sector that endeavour to improve the economic stability and investment climates of the Contracting Parties.

(4) Nothing in this Article shall prevent financial institutions from applying their own lending/underwriting practices based on market principles and prudential considerations or prevent a Contracting Party from taking measures for prudential reasons including for the protection of Investors, consumers, depositors, policy holders or persons to whom a fiduciary duty is owed by a financial service supplier or to ensure the integrity and stability of its financial system and capital markets.

PART III INVESTMENT PROMOTION AND PROTECTION

Article 12 Investment in Energy Resources and Markets

[The Contracting Parties undertake to facilitate investment in and development of energy resources and markets by formulating and applying transparent rules, in accordance with this Part.

Article 13 Promotion, Protection and Treatment of investments

(1) Each Contracting Party shall in accordance with the objectives and principles of

the Charter and the provisions of this Agreement encourage and create stable, equitable, favourable and transparent conditions for investors of other Contracting Parties to Make investments in its Area. Such conditions shall include a commitment to accord at all times to investments of investors of other Contracting Parties fair and equitable treatment. Such investments shall also enjoy the most constant protection and security and no Contracting Party shall in any way impair by unreasonable or discriminatory measures their management, maintenance, use, enjoyment or disposal. [In no case shall such investments be accorded treatment less than that required by international law, including that Contracting Party's international obligations.] [*Each Contracting Party shall observe in good faith obligations it may have entered into with regard to investors of any other Contracting Party.*]

(2) Each Contracting Party shall endeavour *to apply the principle* to permit Investors of other Contracting Parties to Make Investments in its Area on a basis no less favourable than that accorded to its own Investors or to Investors of any other Contracting Party or any state that is not a Contracting Party, [whichever is the most favourable].

(3) A supplementary Agreement shall, [subject to conditions to be laid down therein] commit each party thereto to permit Investors of other parties to Make Investments in its Area on a basis no less favourable than that accorded to its own Investors or to Investors of any other Contracting Party or any state that is not a Contracting Party, and to their respective Investments, whichever is the most favourable. This supplementary Agreement shall be open for signature by the states and Regional Economic Integration Organisations which have signed this Agreement. [The signatories to this Agreement shall commence negotiations not later than 1st January 1996 with a view to concluding, within three years from the date this Agreement is open for signature, the supplementary Agreement.]

(4) Each Contracting Party shall endeavour:

— to reduce progressively existing restrictions which affect the ability of Investors of other Contracting Parties to Make Investments in its Area.
— to limit to the minimum the exceptions to the treatment described in paragraph (2) in any laws and regulations which are enacted after the date of this Agreement is opened for signature and which impose conditions for the Making of Investments. [Such exceptions] shall not apply to Investments existing at the time the exception becomes effective.]

(5) Until such time as the supplementary Agreement shall have been adopted, each Contracting Party shall periodically submit reports to the Charter Conference for a review of the contents of its laws and regulations as they relate to the ability of Investors of other Contracting Parties to Make Investments in its Area. These reports may include the designation of parts of the energy sector where a Contracting Party accords to Investors of other Contracting Parties the treatment described in paragraph (2).

(6) Until such time as the supplementary Agreement shall have been adopted, a Contracting Party may at any time, voluntarily commit itself to all other Contracting Parties not to enact new laws and regulations providing for exceptions to the treatment described in paragraph (2). Any such voluntary commitment shall be declared to the Charter Conference. That Contracting Party may furthermore declare that this voluntary commitment constitutes an obligation to all other Contracting Parties under this Agreement.

(7) In addition each Contracting Party shall in its Area accord to Investments of investors of another Contracting Party, and their [*related activities including*] management, maintenance, use, enjoyment or disposal, treatment no less favourable than that which it accords1 to Investments of its own Investors or of the Investors of any other Contracting Party or any third state, and their management, maintenance, use, enjoyment or disposal, whichever is the most favourable to the investment.

(8) Nothing in this Article shall apply to grants and other financial assistance provided by a Contracting Party for energy technology research and development; or government insurance and loan guarantee programmes for encouraging companies to invest abroad [DL]; [or small business development programmes for socially and economically disadvantaged minorities.]

(9) [Contracting Parties agree that national treatment and/or most favoured nation treatment in relation to the protection of Intellectual Property are exclusively governed by the respective provisions contained in the applicable international agreements for the protection of Intellectual Property rights by which the Contracting Party is bound.]

(10) Without prejudice to Article 16, the provisions of this Article shall also apply to Returns.

(11) Each Contracting Party shall ensure that its domestic law provides effective means for the assertion of claims and the enforcement of rights with respect to Investment, Investment agreements, and Investment authorisations.

Article 13 Bis Key Personnel

(1) A Contracting Party shall, subject to its laws and regulations relating to the entry, stay and work of a natural person, examine in good faith requests by investors of another Contracting Party and key personnel who are employed by such Investors, or by Investments of such Investors, to enter and remain temporarily in its Area to engage in activities connected with the making or the development, management, maintenance, use, enjoyment or disposal of relevant investments, including the provision of advice or key technical services.

(2) A Contracting Party shall permit Investors of another Contracting Party which have Investments in its Area to employ any key person of the Investors' choice regardless of nationality and citizenship provided that such key person has been permitted to enter, stay and work in the Area of the former Contracting Party and that the employment concerned conforms to the terms, conditions and time-limits of, the permission granted to such key person.

[Article 13 Ter] Trade Related Investment Measures

(1) [DL] *Further to* Articles 4 and 35 of this Agreement and *without prejudice to other rights and obligations under those Articles no Contracting Party shall apply any* trade related investment measure [DL] *that is inconsistent with the provisions of article III or article XI of the GATT.*

[DL]

Such measures include any investment measure which is mandatory or enforceable under domestic law or under administrative rulings or compliance with which is necessary to obtain an advantage, and which requires:

(a) the purchase or use by an *investor* of products of domestic origin or from any domestic source, whether specified in terms of particular products, in terms of volume or value of products, or in terms of a proportion of volume or value of its local production;

(b) than an *Investor's* purchase or use of imported products be limited to an amount related to the volume or value of local products that it exports;

or which restricts:

(c) the importance by an *Investor* of products used in or related to its local production, generally or to an amount related to the volume or value of local production that it exports;

(d) the importation by an *Investor* of products used in or related to its local production by restricting its access to foreign exchange to an amount related to the foreign exchange inflows attributable to the *Investor*;

(e) the exportation or sale for export by an *Investor* of products whether specified in terms of particular products in terms of volume or value of products or in terms of a proportion of volume or value of its local production.

(2) Nothing in paragraph (1) shall be construed to prevent a Contracting Party from requiring an Investor or Investment to apply qualification requirements for export promotion, foreign aid, government procurement or preferential tariff or quota programs.

(3) The provisions of Annex TRM shall apply in relation to notification and transitional arrangements for trade related investment measures.

[(4) In the event of a dispute between Contracting Parties over the application of interpretation of this Article, it shall be brought under the GATT and Related Instruments if the parties to the dispute so agree. In the absence of such agreement, Annex D of this Agreement shall apply except that Annex D shall not apply to any dispute between Contracting Parties, the substance of which arises under an agreement that:

(a) has been notified in accordance with and meets the other requirements of Article 35(1); or

(b) establishes a free trade area or customs union as described in Article XXIV of the GATT.]

Annex TRM Notification and Transitional Arrangements (TRIMs)

(1) Contracting Parties shall notify the [Competent Body] of all TRIMs they are applying that are not in conformity with the provisions of Article 13 TER within

(a) 90 days after entering into force of this Agreement if the Contracting Party is a party to the GATT; or

(b) [...] months after entering into force of this Agreement if the Contracting Party is not a party to the GATT.

Such TRIMs of general or specific applications shall be notified along with their principal features.

(2) In the case of TRIMs applied under discretionary authority each specific

application shall be notified. Information that would prejudice the legitimate commercial interests of particular enterprises need not be disclosed.

(3) Each Contracting Party shall eliminate all TRIMs which are notified under paragraph (1) within

   (a) 2 years from the date of entry into force of this Agreement if the Contracting Party is a party to the GATT; or

   (b) [...] years from the date of entry into force of this Agreement if the Contracting Party is not a party to the GATT.

(4) During the periods referred to in paragraph (3) a Contracting Party shall not modify the terms of any TRIM which it notifies under paragraph (1) from those prevailing at the date of entry into force of this Agreement so as to increase the degree of inconsistency with the provisions of Article 13 TER of this Agreement. TRIMs introduced less than 180 days before the signature of this Agreement shall not benefit from the transitional arrangements provided in paragraph (3).

(5) Notwithstanding the provisions of paragraph (4), a Contracting Party, in order not to disadvantage established enterprises which are subject to a TRIM notified under paragraph (1), may apply during the transition period the same TRIM to a new Investment where

   (i) the products or services of such Investment are like products or services to those of the established enterprises; and

   (ii) necessary to avoid distorting the conditions of competition between the new Investment and the established enterprises.

Any TRIM so applied to a new Investment shall be notified to the Secretary-General. The terms of such a TRIM shall be equivalent in their competitive effect to those applicable to the established enterprises, and it shall be terminated at the same time.

Article 14 Compensation for Losses

(1) Except where Article 15 applies, an Investor of any Contracting Party who suffers a loss with respect to any Investment in the Area of another Contracting Party owing to war or other armed conflict, state of national emergency, civil disturbance, or other similar event in that Area, shall be accorded by the latter Contracting Party, treatment, as regards restitution, indemnification, compensation or other settlement, which is the most favourable of that which that Contracting Party accords to any other Investor, whether its own Investor, the Investor of any other Contracting Party, or the Investor of any State that is not a contracting party.

(2) Without prejudice to paragraph (1), an Investor of a Contracting Party who, in any of the situations referred to in that paragraph, suffers a loss in the Area of another Contracting Party resulting from

   (a) requisitioning of its Investment or part thereof by the latter's forces or authorities, or

   (b) destruction of its Investment or part thereof by the latter's forces or authorities, which was not required by the necessity of the situation,

shall be accorded restitution or compensation which in either case shall be prompt, adequate and effective.

Article 15 Expropriation

(1) Investments of Investors of a Contracting Party in the Area of any other Contracting Party shall not be nationalised, expropriated or subjected to a measure or measures having effect equivalent to nationalisation or expropriation (hereinafter referred to as 'expropriation') except where such expropriation is:

    (a) for a purpose which is in the public interest;
    (b) not discriminatory;
    (c) carried out under due process of law; and
    (d) accompanied by the payment of prompt, adequate and effective compensation.

Such compensation shall amount to the fair market value of the investment expropriated at the time immediately before the expropriation or impending expropriation became known in such a way as to affect the value of the Investment (hereinafter referred to as the 'valuation date').

[Such fair market value shall by the election of the Investor be expressed in a Freely Convertible Currency on the basis of the market rate of exchange existing for that currency on the valuation date. Compensation shall also include interest at a commercial rate established on a market basis from the date of expropriation until the date of payment.]

(2) The Investor affected shall have a right to prompt review, under the law of the Contracting Party making the expropriation, by a judicial or other competent and independent authority of that Contracting Party, of its case, of the valuation of its Investment, and of the payment of compensation, in accordance with the principles set out in paragraph (1).

[(3) Where a Contracting Party expropriates the assets of a company or enterprise in its Area in which Investors of any other Contracting Party have Investments, including through shareholding, these provisions shall apply to ensure prompt, adequate and effective compensation for those Investors for any impairment or diminishment of the fair market value of such Investment resulting from such exploration.]

(4) Reversion of properties and rights to a resource owner pursuant to an [investment agreement] and laws and regulations in force in a Contracting Party at the time such agreement was concluded and which are otherwise in conformity with the provisions of this Agreement, shall not in itself be regarded, for purposes of this Agreement, as an act of expropriation or nationalisation or as a measure having effect equivalent to nationalisation or expropriation.]

Article 16 Transfer of Payments Related to Investments

(1) Each Contracting Party shall with respect to Investments in its Area by Investors of any other Contracting Party guarantee the freedom of transfer related to these Investments into and out of its Area, including the transfer of:

    (a) the initial capital plus any additional capital for the maintenance and development of an Investment;
    (b) Returns;
    (c) payments under a contract, including amortisation of principal and accrued interest payment pursuant to a loan agreement;
    (d) unspent earnings and other remuneration of personnel engaged from abroad in connection with that Investment;

(e)   proceeds from the sale or liquidation of all or any part of an investment;

(f)   payments arising out of the settlement of a dispute; and

(g)   payments of compensation pursuant to Articles 14 and 15.

(2)   Transfers of payments under paragraph (1) shall be effected without delay and in a Freely Convertible Currency.

(3)   Transfers shall be made at the market rate of exchange existing on the date of transfer with respect to spot transactions in the currency to be transferred. In the absence of a market for foreign exchange, the rate to be used will be the most recent rate applied to inward investments or the most recent exchange rate for conversion of currencies into Special Drawing Rights, whichever is more favourable to the Investor.

(4)   [A Contracting Party may have laws and regulations requiring reports of currency transfer *provided that such laws and regulations shall not be used to defeat the purpose of paragraphs (1) to (3)*.] Notwithstanding the provisions of paragraphs (1) to (3) a Contracting Party may protect the rights of creditors, or ensure compliance with laws on the issuing, trading and dealing in securities and the satisfaction of judgments in civil, administrative and criminal adjudicatory proceedings, through the equitable, non-discriminatory, and good faith application of its laws and regulations.

(5)   The provisions of paragraph (2) regarding the currency of transfers are applied in relations between Contracting Parties which constituted the former USSR insofar as this does not contradict agreements between them, [provided that such agreements shall not lead to treatment of Investors of other Contracting Parties that is less favourable than that accorded either to Investors of the Contracting Parties which have entered into such an agreement or to Investors of any State that is not a contracting party]. In accordance with Article 36 transitional arrangements may apply in the absence of such agreements, provided that such arrangements accord to Investors of Contracting Parties, not formerly constituting the USSR, treatment that is not less favourable than that accorded either to Investors of the Contracting Party maintaining transitional arrangements or to Investors of any State that is not a contracting party.

(6)   [Notwithstanding the provisions of paragraphs 16(1) and 16(3), [AUS, MOL and RO]4 may in exceptional balance of payments circumstances exercise such controls as are necessary to regulate international capital movements for balance of payments purposes. Any restrictions under this provision shall be temporary and shall be consistent with their obligations under existing international agreements and, in particular, with the responsibilities of IMF membership. In any case, no restrictions under this provision shall affect the making of payments or transfers for current international transactions nor provide for discriminatory treatment between Contracting Parties. In taking a measure pursuant to this paragraph, [AUS, MOL or RO] shall ensure that such measure least infringes the rights of other Contracting Parties and is no broader in scope or duration than necessary.]

Article 17 Subrogation

(1)   If a Contracting Party or its designated agency (the 'Indemnifying Party') makes a payment under an indemnity or guarantee given in respect of an Investment and Returns in the Area of another Contracting Party (the 'Host Party'), the Host Party shall recognise

> (a)   the assignment to the Indemnifying Party by law or by legal transaction of all the rights and claims in respect of such Investment, and
>
> (b)   the right of the Indemnifying Party to exercise all such rights and enforce such claims by virtue of subrogation,

[all without prejudice to the right under Article 30 of the Investor that was given the benefit of the indemnity or guarantee to exercise such rights and enforce such claims [on behalf of and as authorised by the Indemnifying Party.]

(2)   The Indemnifying Party shall be entitled in all circumstances to

> (a)   the same treatment in respect of the rights and claims acquired by it by virtue of the assignment referred to in paragraph (1) above, and
>
> (b)   the same payments due pursuant to those rights and claims,

as the [Party Indemnified] was entitled to receive by virtue of this Agreement in respect of the Investment concerned and its related Returns.

[Article 18] Relation to Other Agreements

Where two or more Contracting Parties have entered into a prior international agreement, or enter into a subsequent international agreement, whose terms in either case concern the subject matter of Part III or V of this Agreement, nothing in Part III or V of this Agreement shall be construed to supersede any incompatible provision of such terms of the other agreement, and nothing in such terms of the other agreement shall be construed to supersede any incompatible provision of Part III or V of this Agreement, where any such incompatible provision is more favourable to the Investor or Investment.

Article 19 Non-Application of Part III in Certain Circumstances

Each Contracting Party reserves the right to deny the advantages of this *Part* to a legal entity if citizens or nationals of a non-signatory country control such entity and if that entity has no substantial business activities in the Area of the Contracting Party in which it is organised or the denying Contracting Party does not maintain diplomatic relationship with the non-signatory or adopts or maintains measures with respect to the non-signatory that prohibit transactions with the Investor *of that State that is not a contracting party* or that would be violated or circumvented if the advantages in *this* Part [DL] were accorded to the Investor *of that State that is not a contracting party* or to its Investments.

PART IV CONTEXTUAL

Article 21 Sovereignty over Energy Resources

The Contracting Parties recognise state sovereignty and sovereign rights over energy resources. They recognise that these are exercised in accordance with and subject to the rules of international law. Each State *accordingly* holds in particular the rights to decide the geographical areas within its Area to be made available for exploration and development of its energy resources and the optimalisation of their recovery and the rate at which they may be depleted or otherwise exploited, to specify and enjoy any taxes, royalties or other financial payments payable by virtue of such exploration and exploitation and to regulate the environmental and safety aspects of such exploration and development within its Area.

Article 22 Environmental Aspects

(1) In pursuit of sustainable development and taking into account its obligations under those international environmental agreements to which it is a party, each Contracting Party shall strive to minimise in an economically efficient manner harmful environmental impacts occurring both within and outside its Area from all operations within the energy cycle in its Area, taking proper account of safety. In doing so each Contracting Party shall act cost-effectively. In its policies and actions each Contracting Party shall strive to take precautionary measures to anticipate, prevent or minimise environmental degradation. They agree that the polluter in the Areas of Contracting Parties, should, in principle, bear the cost of pollution, including transboundary pollution with due regard to the public interest and without distorting Investment in the energy cycle or international trade. Contracting Parties shall accordingly:

   (a) take account of environmental considerations throughout the formulation and implementation of their energy policies;

   (b) promote market-oriented price formation and a fuller reflection of environmental costs and benefits throughout the energy cycle;

   (c) having regard to Article 39(4) encourage cooperation in the [DL] attainment of the environmental objectives of the Charter and in the field of international environmental standards for the energy cycle, taking into account differences in adverse effects and abatement costs between Contracting Parties;

   (d) have particular regard to improving energy efficiency, to developing and using renewable energy sources, to promoting the use of cleaner fuels and to employing technologies and technological means that reduce pollution;

   (e) promote the collection and sharing amongst Contracting Parties of information on environmentally sound and economically efficient energy policies and cost-effective practices and technologies;

   (f) promote public awareness of the environmental impacts of energy systems, of the scope for the prevention or abatement of their adverse impacts, and of the costs associated with various prevention or abatement measures;

   (g) promote and cooperate in the research, development and application of energy efficient and environmentally sound technologies, practices and processes which will minimise harmful environmental impacts of all aspects of the energy cycle in an economically efficient manner;

   (h) encourage favourable conditions for the transfer and dissemination of such technologies consistent with the adequate and effective protection of intellectual property rights;

   (i) promote the transparent assessment at an early stage and prior to decision, and subsequent monitoring, of environmental impacts of environmentally significant energy investment projects;

   (j) promote international awareness and information exchange on Contracting Parties' relevant environmental programmes and standards and on the implementation of those programmes and standards;

(k) participate, upon request, and within their available resources, in the development and implementation of appropriate environmental programmes in the Contracting Parties.

(2) [At the request of one or more Contracting Parties, disputes concerning the application or interpretation of provisions of this Article shall, to the extent that arrangements for the consideration of such disputes do not exist in other appropriate international fora, be reviewed by the Charter Conference aiming at a solution.]

(3) For the purposes of this Article:

(a) 'energy cycle' means the entire energy-chain, including activities related to prospecting for, exploration, production, conversion, storage, transport, distribution and consumption of the various forms of energy, and the treatment and disposal of wastes, as well as the decommissioning, cessation or closure of these activities, minimising harmful environmental impacts.

(b) 'environmental impact' means any effect caused by a given activity on the environment, including human health and safety, flora, fauna, soil, air, water, climate, landscape and historical monuments or other physical structures or the interactions among these factors; it also includes effects on cultural heritage or socio-economic conditions resulting from alterations to those factors.

(c) 'improving energy efficiency' means acting to maintain the same unit of output (of a good or service) without reducing the quality or performance of the output, whilst reducing the amount of energy required to produce that output.

(d) 'cost-effective' means to achieve a defined objective at the lowest cost or to achieve the greatest benefit at a given cost.

[Article 23] Transparency

(1) In accordance with Articles 4 and 35 laws, regulations, judicial decisions and administrative rulings of general application which affect matters covered by Article 4 shall be subject to the transparency disciplines of the GATT and relevant Related Instruments.

(2) Laws, regulations, judicial decisions, and administrative rulings of general application made effective by any Contracting Party, and agreements in force between Contracting Parties, which affect other matters covered by this Agreement shall also be published promptly in such a manner as to enable Contracting Parties and Investors to become acquainted with them. The provisions of this paragraph shall not require any Contracting Party to disclose confidential information which would impede law enforcement or otherwise be contrary to the public interest or would prejudice the legitimate commercial interests of any Investor.

(3) Each Contracting Party shall designate one or more enquiry points to which requests for information about the above mentioned laws, regulations, judicial decisions and administrative rulings may be addressed and shall communicate promptly such designation to the Secretariat which shall make it available on request.

Article 24 Taxation

(1) General Exclusion

Except as set out in this Article, nothing in this Agreement shall apply to impose obligations with respect to taxation measures of the Contracting Parties. In the event of any inconsistency between this Article and any other provision of this Agreement, this Article shall prevail to the extent of the inconsistency.

(2) Application of Provisions Relating to Trade

Notwithstanding paragraph (1),

(a) Articles 4 and 35 shall apply to taxation measures other than those on income or on capital; and

(b) the provisions of this Agreement requiring a Contracting Party to provide most favoured nation treatment relating to trade in goods and services shall apply to taxation measures other than taxes on income or on capital, except that such provisions shall not apply to:

   (i) an advantage accorded by a Contracting Party pursuant to the tax provisions in any convention, agreement or arrangement, described in paragraph (6.1) (b) of this Article; or

   (ii) any taxation measure aimed at ensuring the effective collection of taxes, except where the measure arbitrarily discriminates between goods of the Contracting Parties or arbitrarily restricts benefits accorded under the above-mentioned provisions of this Agreement.

(3) Application of Provisions Relating to Investment

The provisions imposing national treatment obligations or most favoured nation obligations under Part III shall apply to taxation measures of the Contracting Parties other than those on income or on capital, except that such provisions shall not apply to:

(a) impose most favoured nation obligations with respect to advantages accorded by a Contracting Party pursuant to the tax provisions in any convention, agreement or arrangement, described in paragraph (6.1)(b) of this Article [or resulting from membership of any Regional Economic Integration Organisation;] or

(b) any taxation measure concerning the effective collection of taxes, except where the measure arbitrarily discriminates between investors of the Contracting Parties or arbitrarily restricts benefits accorded under the Investment provisions of this Agreement.

(4) Expropriatory and Discriminatory Taxation

(a) Article 15 shall apply to taxes.

(b) Whenever an issue arises under Article 15, to the extent it pertains to whether a tax constitutes an expropriation or whether a tax alleged to constitute an expropriation is discriminatory, the following provisions shall apply:

   (i) the Investor or the Contracting Party alleging expropriation shall refer the issue of whether the tax is an expropriation or whether the tax is discriminatory to the relevant competent tax authority. Failing such referral by the Investor or the Contracting Party, bodies called upon to settle disputes pursuant to Articles 30(2)(c) or 31(2) shall make a referral to the relevant competent tax authorities.

(ii) The competent tax authorities shall, within a period of six months of such referral, strive to resolve the issues so referred. Where non-discrimination issues are concerned, the competent tax authorities shall apply the non-discrimination provisions of the relevant tax convention or, if there is no non-discrimination provision in the relevant tax convention applicable to the tax or no such tax convention is in force between the Contracting Parties concerned, they shall apply the non-discrimination principles under the OECD Model Tax Convention on income and Capital.

(iii) Bodies called upon to settle disputes pursuant to Articles 30(2)(c) or 31(2) may take into account any conclusions arrived at by the competent tax authorities regarding whether the tax is an expropriation. Such bodies shall take into account any conclusions arrived at within the six-month period prescribed in sub-paragraph (ii) above by the competent tax authorities regarding whether the tax is discriminatory. Such bodies may also take into account any conclusions arrived at by the competent tax authorities after the expiry of the six-month period.

(iv) Under no circumstances shall involvement of the competent tax authorities, beyond the end of the six-month period referred to above, lead to a delay of proceedings under Articles 30 and 31.

(5) Withholding Tax

For greater certainty, Article 16 shall not limit the right of a Contracting Party to impose or collect a tax by withholding or other means.

(6) Definitions

(6.1) The term 'taxation measure' includes:

(a) any provision relating to taxes of the domestic law of the Contracting Party or of a political subdivision thereof or a local authority therein; and

(b) any provision relating to taxes of any convention for the avoidance of double taxation or any other international agreement or arrangement by which the Contracting Party is bound.

(6.2) There shall be regarded as taxes on income or on capital all taxes imposed on total income, on total capital or on elements of income or of capital, including taxes on gains from the alienation of property, taxes on estates, inheritances and gifts, or substantially similar taxes, taxes on the total amounts of wages or salaries paid by enterprises, as well as taxes on capital appreciation.

(6.3) 'A competent tax authority' means the competent authority pursuant to a double taxation agreement in force between the Contracting Paries or, when there is no such agreement between the countries in question, the Minister or Ministry responsible for taxes or his or its authorised representatives.

(6.4) For greater certainty, the terms 'tax provisions' and 'taxes' do not include customs duties.

[Article 25] State and Privileged Enterprises

[(1) Each Contracting Party shall ensure that any state enterprise which it maintains or establishes shall conduct its activities in relation to the sale or provision of goods and services in its Area in a manner consistent with the Contracting Party's obligations under Part III of this Agreement.]

(2) No Contracting Party shall encourage or require such a state enterprise to conduct its activities in its Area in a manner inconsistent with the Contracting Party's obligations under other provisions of this Agreement.

(3) Each Contracting Party shall ensure that if it establishes or maintains a state entity and entrusts such entity with regulatory, administrative or other governmental authority, such entity shall exercise such authority in a manner consistent with the Contracting Party's obligations under this Agreement other than obligations arising under Articles 4 and 35.

(4) No Contracting Party shall encourage or require any entity to which it grants exclusive or special privileges to conduct its activities in its Area in a manner inconsistent with the Contracting Party's obligations under this Agreement.

[(5) Any Contracting Party shall be free to participate in Economic Activity in the Energy Sector through, inter alia, direct participation by the government or through state enterprises.]

(6) For the purposes of this Article, entity includes any enterprise, agency or other organisation or individual.

Article 26 Observance by Sub-federal Authorities

[Each Contracting Party shall take all measures available to it within its constitution to ensure observance of the provisions of this Agreement by the regional and local governments and other governmental authorities within its Area.]

Article 27 Exceptions

(1) There shall be no exceptions to Article 4 and 35.

(2) Provisions of this Agreement other than those referred to in paragraph (1) shall not preclude any Contracting Party from adopting or enforcing any measures:

[(a) necessary to protect human, animal or plant life or health;]

(b) essential to the acquisition or distribution of Energy Materials and Products in conditions of general or local short supply arising for reasons outside the control of that Contracting Party, if such measures are consistent with the principle that all other Contracting Parties are entitled to an equitable share of the international supply of such Energy Materials and Products and that any such measures that are inconsistent with this Agreement shall be discontinued as soon as the conditions giving rise to them have ceased to exist;

[provided that such measures shall not constitute disguised restrictions on, Economic Activity in the Energy Sector, or arbitrary or unjustifiable discrimination between Contracting Parties or between Investors or other interested persons of Contracting Parties. Such measures shall be duly motivated and shall not nullify or impair any benefit one or more other Contracting Parties may reasonably expect under this Agreement to an extent greater than is strictly necessary to the stated end.]

(3) Provisions of this Agreement other than those referred to in paragraph (1) shall not be construed:

(a) to prevent any Contracting Party from taking any measure which it considers necessary for the protection of its essential security interests including these;

(i) relating to the supply of Energy Materials and Products to a military establishment; or

(ii) taken in the time of war, armed conflict or other emergency in international relations;

(b) to prevent any Contracting Party from taking any measure in pursuance of its obligations under the United Nations Charter for the maintenance of international peace and security; or

(c) to prevent any Contracting Party from taking any measure that it considers necessary relating to the implementation of national policies respecting the non-proliferation of nuclear weapons or other nuclear explosive devices or needed to fulfil its obligations under the Treaty on the Non-Proliferation of Nuclear Weapons, the Nuclear Suppliers Guidelines, and other international nuclear non-proliferation obligations or understandings;

(d) to prevent any Contracting Party from taking any measure which it considers necessary for the maintenance of public order. [Such measures should not constitute a disguised restriction on Transit.]

[(4) The provisions of this Agreement shall not be construed so as to oblige any Contracting Party member of Regional Economic Integration Organisation (REIO) which aims at liberalising trade and Investment between its members without raising the overall level of barriers to trade and Investment, to extend to another Contracting Party non-member of that REIO the benefit of any treatment or preference resulting from the membership to that REIO.

The same rule will apply to agreements aimed at establishing a customs union or a free-trade area or leading to the accession to a REIO.

PART V DISPUTE SETTLEMENTS

Article 30 Settlement of Disputes between an Investor and a Contracting Party

(1) Disputes between a Contracting Party and an investor of another Contracting Party relating to an investment of the latter in the Area of the former, which concern an alleged breach of an obligation of the former under Part III (except under Article 13(4)), shall, if possible, be settled amicably.

(2) If such disputes can not be settled according to the provisions of paragraph (1) within a period of three months from the date on which either party to the dispute requested amicable settlement, the investor party, to the dispute may choose to submit it for resolution:

(a)   to the courts or administrative tribunals of the Contracting Party party to the dispute;

(b)   in accordance with any applicable, previously agreed dispute settlement procedure; or

(c)   in accordance with the following paragraphs of this Article.

(3) (a)   Subject only to sub-paragraph (b) (i), each Contracting Party hereby gives its unconditional consent to the submission of a dispute to international arbitration or conciliation in accordance with the provisions of this Article.

(b) (i)   The Contracting Parties listed in Annex ID do not give such unconditional consent where the investor has previously submitted the dispute under paragraph (2)(a) or (b).

      (ii)   For the sake of transparency, Contracting Parties that are listed in Annex ID shall state their policies, practices and conditions in this regard to the Secretariat, as soon as possible and in any case no later than the date of the deposit of their instrument of ratification, acceptance or approval in accordance with Article 44.

(4)   In the event an Investor chooses to submit the dispute for resolution under paragraph (2)(c), the Investor shall further provide his consent in writing for the dispute to be submitted to:

(a) (i)   The International Centre for Settlement of Investment Disputes, established pursuant to the Convention on the Settlement of Investment Disputes between States and Nationals of other States opened for signature at Washington, 18 March 1965 (ICSID Convention) if the Contracting Party of the Investor and the Contracting Party party to the dispute are both parties to the ICSID Convention); or

      (ii)   The International Centre for Settlement of Investment Disputes, established pursuant to the Convention referred to in sub-paragraph (a)(i), under the rules governing the Additional Facility for the Administration of Proceedings by the secretariat of the Centre (Additional Facility Rules), if the Contracting Party of the Investor or the Contracting Party party to the dispute, but not both, is a party to the ICSID Convention:

or

(b)   a sole arbitrator or ad hoc arbitration tribunal established under the Arbitration Rules of the United Nations Commission on International Trade Law (UNCITRAL);

or

(c)   an arbitral proceeding under the Arbitration Institute of the Stockholm Chamber of Commerce.

(5) (a)   The consent given in paragraph (3) together with the written consent of the Investor given pursuant to paragraph (4) shall satisfy the requirement for:

      (i)   written consent of the parties to a dispute for purposes of Chapter II of the ICSID Convention and for purposes of the Additional Facility Rules; and

      (ii)   an 'agreement in writing' for purposes of article II of the United Nations

Convention on the Recognition and Enforcement of Foreign Arbitral Awards, done at New York, 10 June, 1958 ('New York Convention').

(b) Any arbitration under this Article shall at the request of any party to the dispute be held in a State that is a party to the New York Convention. Claims submitted to arbitration hereunder shall be considered to arise out of a commercial relationship or transaction for the purposes of article 1 of that Convention.

(6) A tribunal established under paragraph (4) shall decide the issues in dispute in accordance with this Agreement and applicable rules and principles of international law.

(7) An Investor other than a natural person which has the nationality of a Contracting Party party to the dispute on the date of the written request referred to in paragraph (4) and which, before a dispute between it and that Contracting Party arises, is controlled by Investors of another Contracting Party, shall for the purpose of article 25(2)(b) of the ICSID Convention be treated as a 'national of another Contracting State' and shall for the purpose of article 1(6) of the Additional Facility Rules be treated as a 'national of another State'.

(8) [The awards of arbitration, which may include an award of interest, shall be final and binding upon the parties to the dispute. An award of arbitration concerning a measure of a Sub-Federal Government or authority of the disputing Contracting Party shall provide that the Contracting Party may pay monetary damages in lieu of any other remedy granted. Each Contracting Party shall carry out without delay any such award and shall make provision for the effective enforcement in its Area of such awards.]

Article 31 Settlement of Disputes between Contracting Parties

(1) Contracting Parties shall endeavour to settle disputes concerning the application or interpretation of this Agreement through diplomatic channels.

(2) If the dispute has not been settled in accordance with paragraph (1) within a reasonable period of time, either party may, except as otherwise provided in this Agreement or agreed in writing by the Contracting Parties, or as concerns the application or interpretation of Article 7 or 22, by written notice submit the matter to an ad hoc tribunal under this Article.

(3) Such an ad hoc arbitral tribunal shall be constituted as follows:

(a) The Contracting Party instituting the proceedings shall appoint one member of the tribunal within 30 days of delivering the notice in paragraph (2) and inform the other Contracting party of its appointment;

(b) Within 60 days of the receipt of the written notice under paragraph (2), the other Contracting Party to the dispute shall, in turn, appoint one member. If the appointment is not made within the time limit prescribed, the Contracting Party having instituted the proceedings may, within 90 days of the written notice under paragraph (2) request that the appointment be made in accordance with paragraph (3)(d) below:

(c) A third member, who may not be a national or citizen of a Contracting Party to the dispute, shall then be appointed between the Contracting Parties to the dispute. That member shall be the President of the tribunal. If, within 150 days of the delivery of the notice referred to in paragraph (2) above, the

Contracting Parties are unable to agree on the appointment of a third member, that appointment shall be made, in accordance with paragraph (3)(d) below, at the request of either Contracting Party submitted within 180 days of delivery of that notice;

(d) Appointments pursuant to paragraphs (3)(b) or (3)(c) above shall be made by the Secretary-General of the Permanent Court of International Arbitration (PCIA) within 30 days of the receipt of a request to do so. If he is prevented from discharging this task, the appointments shall be made by the First Secretary of the Bureau. If the latter, in turn, is prevented from discharging this task, the appointments shall be made by the most senior Deputy.

(e) Appointments made in accordance with paragraphs (3)(a) to (3)(d) above shall have regard to the qualifications and experience, particularly in matters covered by this Agreement, of the members to be appointed;

(f) In the absence of an agreement between the Contracting Parties to the contrary, the Arbitration rules of the United Nation Commission on International Trade Law (UNCITRAL) shall govern, except to the extent modified by the Contracting Parties to the dispute or by the arbitrators. The tribunal shall take its decisions by a majority vote of its members.

(g) The tribunal shall decide the dispute in accordance with this Agreement and international law.

(h) [The arbitral award shall be final and binding upon the Contracting Parties to the dispute].

(i) The expenses of the tribunal, including the remuneration of its members, shall be borne in equal shares by the Contracting Parties to the dispute. The tribunal may, however, at its discretion direct that a higher proportion of the costs be paid by one of the Contracting Parties parties to the dispute.

(j) Unless the Contracting Parties parties to the dispute agree otherwise, the tribunal shall sit in the Hague, and will use the premises and facilities of the Permanent Court of Arbitration.

(k) A copy of the award shall be deposited with the Secretariat who shall make it generally available.

Article 32 Non-Application of Article 31 to Trade Disputes

To the extent that a dispute between Contracting Parties *concerns* the application of Article 4 *or 35 and no other Article* of this Agreement, it shall not be settled under Article 31 *unless the parties to the dispute agree otherwise.*

Article 33 Settlement of Disputes On Applicability of Article 31

(1) If a disagreement arises over the *application of Article 32 to a dispute a party to the dispute may refer the matter* to an ad hoc arbitration under this Article. *In the light of the overall balance of rights and obligations in the GATT and Related Instruments and in this Agreement, respectively, the arbitration shall determine the existent to which the dispute should be brought under the GATT and Related Instruments or Annex D of this Agreement and to which it should be brought under Article 31 of this Agreement, or both, if the dispute is to be settled under both GATT and Related*

Instruments or Annex D of this Agreement and Article 31 of this Agreement, the arbitrator shall also determine which elements of the dispute are to be considered under which procedure and the sequence of such consideration. Only for compelling reasons should issues in a dispute pertaining to obligations under Article 4 or 35 of this Agreement be considered under Article 31 of this Agreement.

(2) Such an *arbitration* shall be constituted as follows:

   (a) Within 30 days of the *referral* pursuant to paragraph (1), the Contracting Parties parties to the *dispute* shall choose a sole arbitrator who may not be a national or citizen of a Contracting Party party to the dispute. If, within 30 days of the receipt of the request for arbitration, the Contracting Parties are unable to agree on the appointment of a sole arbitrator, that appointment shall be made, in accordance with paragraph (2)(b) below, at the request of any Contracting Party *party to the dispute;*

   (b) An appointment pursuant to paragraph (2)(a) above shall be made by the Secretary-General of the Permanent Court of International Arbitration (PCIA) within 30 days of the receipt of a request to do so. If he is prevented from discharging this task the appointment shall be made by the First Secretary of the Bureau. If the latter, in turn, is prevented from discharging this task the appointment shall be made by the next most senior Deputy;

   (c) Appointments made in accordance with paragraphs (2)(a) and (2)(b) above shall have regard to the qualifications and experience, particularly in matters covered by this Agreement *and by the GATT and Related Instruments,* of the arbitrator to be appointed;

   (d) In the absence of an agreement between the Contracting Parties to the dispute to the contrary, the arbitration rules of the United Nation Commission on International Trade Law (UNCITRAL) shall *apply,* except to the extent modified by the Contracting Parties to the dispute or by the arbitrator;

   (e) *The decisions of the arbitrator under this Article shall be taken within 60 days of this appointment* in accordance with this Agreement and international law *and shall take account of the desirability of an orderly and timely resolution of the dispute;*

   (f) The arbitrator's award shall be final and binding upon the Contracting Parties to the dispute;

   (g) The expenses of the arbitrator, including his remuneration, shall be borne in equal shares by the Contracting Parties parties to the dispute. The arbitrator may, however, at his discretion direct that a higher proportion of the costs be paid by one of the Contracting Parties parties to the dispute;

   (h) Unless the Contracting Parties to the dispute agree otherwise, the arbitrator shall sit in the Hague, and will use the premises and facilities of the Permanent Court of Arbitration;

   (i) A copy of the award shall be deposited with the Secretariat who shall make it generally available.

(3) Neither Contracting Party shall initiate or continue dispute settlement proceedings under the GATT or a GATT Related Instruments *or under Article 35, Annex D of this Agreement* pending the results of arbitration pursuant to this Article.

PART VI TRANSITIONAL

Article 35 Interim Provisions on Trade Related Matters

So long as one or more Contracting Party is not a contracting party to the GATT and Related Instruments, the following provisions shall apply to trade between Contracting Parties at least one of which is not a member of the GATT or a relevant Related Instrument.

(1) [If such trade is governed by an existing bilateral agreement between those Contracting Parties, that agreement shall apply between them following notification to all other Contracting Parties by both Contracting Parties concerned provided that its application does not distort the trade of any third Contracting Party.]

(2) [In all other cases trade in Energy Materials and Products shall be governed by the provisions of the GATT and Related Instruments, as in effect on 1 July 1992, as if all such Contracting Parties were members of GATT and applied the Related Instruments except as provided in Annex G. The Charter Conference may amend Annex G by consensus.]

(3) Each Signatory to this Agreement, and each State or Regional Economic Integration Organisation acceding to this Agreement, shall on the date of its signature or of its deposit of its instrument of accession, deposit with the Depositary a list of all tariff rates and other charges at the level applied on such date of signature or deposit, on Energy Materials and Products imported into its Area.

(4) [Subject to paragraph (5) below, each Contracting Party undertakes not to increase any tariff rates or other charges on Energy Materials or Products above the level applied on the date of its signature or deposit as referred to in paragraph (3).

(5) Notwithstanding paragraph (4), a Contracting Party may maintain limited exceptions to the obligations of paragraph (4), provided that it deposits with the Depositary on the date of signature or deposit as referred to in paragraph (3), along with the list referred to in paragraph (3), a list of such exceptions, specifically identified by reference to the HS or CN items to which such exceptions apply.]

(6) Annex D to this Agreement shall apply to disputes regarding compliance with provisions applicable to trade under this Article, except that Annex D shall not apply to any dispute between Contracting Parties, the substance of which arises under an agreement that:

   (a) has been notified in accordance with and meets the other requirements of paragraph (1) of this Article; or
   (b) establishes a free-trade area or a customs union as described in Article XXIV of the GATT.

Article 36 Transitional Arrangements

(1) In recognition of the need for time to adapt to the requirements of a market economy, a Contracting Party listed in Annex T may temporarily suspend full compliance with its obligations under any one or more of the following provisions of this Agreement, subject to the conditions in paragraphs (3) to (6) of this Article:

Article 7, paragraphs (2) and (5)
Article 23, paragraph (3)

(2) Other Contracting Parties shall assist any Contracting Party which has suspended full compliance under paragraph (1) to achieve the conditions under which such suspension can be terminated. *This assistance will be given in whatever form they consider most effective to respond to the needs notified under paragraph (4)(c) including, where appropriate, through bilateral or multilateral arrangements..*

(3) [The applicable provisions, the stages towards full implementation of each, the measures to be taken and the date or, exceptionally, contingent event, by which each stage shall be completed and measure taken are listed for each Contracting Party claiming transitional arrangements in Annex T to this Agreement. Each such Contracting Party shall take the measures listed by the date (or dates which may differ for different provisions, and different stages) set out in that Annex. Contracting Parties which have temporarily suspended full compliance under paragraph (1) *undertake to comply fully with the relevant obligations by [1 January 1998]. Should a Contracting Party find it necessary, due to exceptional circumstances, to request that the period of such temporary suspensions be extended or that any further temporary suspensions not previously listed in Annex T be introduced, the decision upon such a request shall be made by the Charter Conference.*

(4) A Contracting Party which has invoked transitional arrangements shall notify the Secretariat at least once in every 12 months:

(a) of the implementation of any measures listed in its Annex T and of its general progress to full compliance;

(b) of the progress it expects to make during the next 12 months towards full compliance with its obligations, of any problems it forsees and of its proposals for dealing with those problems;

(c) of the need for technical assistance to facilitate completion of the stages set out in Annex T as necessary for the full implementation of this Agreement, or to deal with any problems noted in subparagraph (b) as well as to promote other necessary market oriented reforms and modernisation of its energy sector;

(d) [DL] *of any possible need to make a request of the kind referred to in paragraph (3).*

(5) The Secretariat shall:

(a) circulate to all Contracting Parties the notifications referred to in paragraph (4);

(b) circulate and actively promote, relying where appropriate on arrangements in other international organisations the matching of needs for and offers of technical assistance referred to in paragraphs (4) (c) and (2);

(c) circulate to all Contracting Parties at the end of each six month period a summary of any notifications made under paragraph (4) (a) above and of any applications under paragraph (4) (d).

(6) The Charter Conference shall annually review the progress by Contracting Parties towards implementation of the provisions of this Article [DL] and the matching of needs and offers of technical assistance referred to in paragraphs (2) and (4)(c). In the course of that review it may decide to take appropriate action. [DL]

PART VII STRUCTURAL AND INSTITUTIONAL

Article 38 Protocols

(1) The Charter Conference may authorise the negotiation of a number of Protocols in order to pursue the objectives and principles of the Charter.

(2) Any Signatory to the Charter may participate in such negotiation.

(3) A State or Regional Economic Integration Organisation shall not become a Contracting Party to a Protocol unless it is, or becomes at the same time, a Signatory to the Charter and a Contracting Party to this Agreement.

(4) Subject to paragraph (3) above, final provisions applying to a Protocol shall be defined in that Protocol.

(5) A Protocol shall apply only to the Contracting Parties which consent to be bound by it, and shall not derogate from the rights and obligations of those Contracting Parties not party to the Protocol.

Article 39 Charter Conference

(1) The Contracting Parties shall meet periodically in a Conference (hereinafter referred to as 'the Charter Conference') at which each Contracting Party shall be entitled to have one representative. Ordinary meetings shall be held at intervals determined by the Charter Conference.

(2) Extraordinary meetings of the Charter Conference may be held at times other than those referred to in paragraph (1) as may be determined by the Charter Conference, or at the written request of any Contracting Party, provided that, within six weeks of the request being communicated to them by the Secretariat, it is supported by at least one-third of the Contracting Parties.

(3) [The Charter Conference shall:]

    (a) carry out the duties assigned it by this Agreement and Protocols;

    (b) keep under review and facilitate the implementation of the principles of the Charter and of the provisions of this Agreement and the Protocols;

    (c) facilitate in accordance with this Agreement and Protocols the co-ordination of appropriate general measures to carry out the principles of the Charter;

    (d) consider and adopt programmes of work to be carried out by the Secretariat;

    (e) consider and approve the annual accounts and budget of the Secretariat;

    (f) consider and approve or adopt the terms of any headquarters or other agreement, including privileges and immunities considered necessary for the Charter Conference and the Secretariat;

    (g) encourage cooperative efforts aimed at facilitating and promoting market oriented reforms and modernisation of energy sectors in those countries of Central and Eastern Europe and the Former Soviet Union undergoing economic transition;

    (h) authorise negotiation of, approve the terms of reference of such negotiation and consider and adopt the text of Protocols;

    (i) authorise the negotiation of and consider and approve or adopt Association Agreements;

    (j) consider and adopt texts of amendments to this Agreement;

(k) appoint the Secretary General and take all decisions necessary for the establishment and functioning of the Secretariat including the structure, staff levels and standard terms of employment of officials and employees.

(4) In the performance of its duties, the Charter Conference, through the Secretariat, shall cooperate with and make as full a use as possible, consistently with economy and efficiency, of the services and programmes of other institutions and organisations with established competence in matters related to the objectives of this Agreement.

(5) The Charter Conference may establish such subsidiary bodies as it considers appropriate for the performance of its duties.

(6) The Charter Conference shall consider and adopt rules of procedure and financial rules.

(7) In 1999 and thereafter at intervals (of not more than 5 years) to be determined by the Charter Conference, the Charter Conference shall thoroughly review the functions provided for in this Agreement in the light of the extent to which the provisions of this Agreement and Protocols have been implemented. At the conclusion of each review the Charter Conference may amend or abolish the functions specified in paragraph (3) and may discharge the Secretariat.

Article 40 Secretariat

(1) In carrying out its duties, the Charter Conference shall have a Secretariat which shall be composed of a Secretary General and such staff as are the minimum consistent with efficient performance.

(2) The Secretary General shall be appointed by the Charter Conference. The first such appointment shall be for a maximum period of 5 years.

(3) In the performance of its duties the Secretariat shall be responsible to and report to the Charter Conference.

(4) The Secretariat shall provide the Charter Conference with all necessary assistance for the performance of its duties and shall carry out the functions assigned to it in this Agreement or in any Protocol and any other functions assigned to it by the Charter Conference.

(5) The Secretariat may enter into such administrative and contractual arrangements as may be required for the effective discharge of its functions.

Article 41 Voting

(1) Unanimity of the Contracting Parties present and voting at the meeting of the Charter Conference where such matters fall to be decided shall be required for decisions by the Charter Conference to:

(a) adopt amendments to this Agreement other than amendments to Articles 39 and 40;

(b) approve accessions to this Agreement under Article 46;

(c) authorize the negotiation of and approve or adopt the text of Association Agreements;

(d) [approve adjustments to Annex B];

(e) approve the adoption of and modification to Annexes EM and NI.

(f)   amend Annex G; and

(g)   approve the Secretary General's nominations of panelists under Annex D, paragraph (7).

The Contracting Parties shall make every effort to reach agreement by consensus on any other matter requiring their decision under this Agreement. If agreement cannot be reached by consensus, paragraphs (2), (3), (4) and (5) shall apply.

(2)   Decisions on budgetary matters referred to in Article 39(3) (e) shall be taken by a qualified majority of Contracting Parties whose assessed contributions as specified in Annex [B] represent, in combination, at least three fourths of the total assessed contributions specified therein.

(3)   Decisions on matters referred to in Article 39(7) shall be taken by a three fourths majority of the Contracting Parties.

(4)   Except in cases specified in paragraphs (1)(a) to (g), (2) and (3) and as otherwise specified in this Agreement, decisions provided for in this Agreement shall be taken by a three fourths majority of the Contracting Parties present and voting at the meeting of the Charter Conference at which such matters fall to be decided.

(5)   For purposes of this Article, 'Contracting Parties present and voting' means Contracting Parties present and casting affirmative or negative votes, provided that the Charter Conference may decide upon rules of procedure to enable such decisions to be taken by Contracting Parties by correspondence.

(6)   Except as provided in paragraph (2), no decision referred to in this Article shall be valid unless it has the support of a simple majority of the Contracting Parties.

(7)   A Regional Economic Integration Organisation shall, when voting, have a number of votes equal to the number of its Member States which are Contracting Parties to this Agreement; provided that such an organisation shall not exercise its right to vote if its Member States exercise theirs, and vice versa.

(8)   In the event of persistent arrears in a Contracting Party's discharge of financial obligations under this Agreement, the Charter Conference may suspend that Contracting Party's voting rights in whole or in part.

Article 42 Funding Principles

(1)   Each Contracting Party shall bear its own costs of representation at meetings of the Charter Conference and any subsidiary bodies.

(2)   The cost of meetings of the Charter Conference and any subsidiary bodies shall be regarded as a cost of the Secretariat.

(3)   The costs of the Secretariat shall be met by the Contracting Parties by assessed contributions payable in the proportions specified in Annex B, which may be adjusted from time to time in accordance with Article 41(2).

(4)   Each Protocol may contain provisions to assure that any costs of the Secretariat arising from a Protocol are borne by the Parties thereto.

(5)   The Charter Conference may accept additional, voluntary, contributions from one or more Contracting Parties or from other sources. Costs met from such contributions shall not be considered costs of the Secretariat for the purposes of paragraph (3).

PART VIII FINAL PROVISIONS

Article 43 Signature

This Agreement shall be open for signature at Lisbon from [ ] to [ ] by the States and Regional Economic Integration Organisations whose representatives signed the Charter.

Article 44 Ratification, Acceptance or Approval

This Agreement shall be subject to ratification, acceptance or approval by Signatories. Instruments of ratification, acceptance or approval shall be deposited with the Depositary.

Article 45 Application to Other Territories

(1) Any State or Regional Economic Integration Organization may at the time of signature, ratification, acceptance, approval or accession declare that the Agreement shall extend to all the *other* territories for the international relations of which it is responsible, or to one or more of them. Such declaration shall take effect at the time the Agreement enters into force for that Contracting Party.

(2) Any Contracting Party may at a later date, by a declaration addressed to the Depositary, extend the application of this Agreement to other territory specified in the declaration. In respect of such territory the Agreement shall enter into force on the ninetieth day following the receipt by the Depositary of such declaration.

(3) Any declaration made under the two preceding paragraphs may, in respect of any territory specified in such declaration, be withdrawn by a notification addressed to the Depositary. The withdrawal shall, subject to the applicability of Article 52(3), become effective upon the expiry of one year after the date of receipt of such notification by the Depositary.

Article 46 Accession

This Agreement shall be open for accession by States and Regional Economic Integration Organisations which have signed the Charter from the date on which the Agreement is closed for signature. The instruments of accession shall be deposited with the Depositary.

Article 47 Amendment

(1) Any Contracting Party may propose amendments to this Agreement.

(2) The text of any proposed amendment to this Agreement shall be communicated to the Contracting Parties by the Secretariat at least three months before the meeting at which it is proposed for adoption.

(3) Amendments to this Agreement texts of which have been adopted [DL] *by the Charter Conference* shall be submitted by the Depositary to all Contracting Parties for ratification, acceptance or approval.

(4) Ratification, acceptance or approval of amendments to this Agreement shall be notified to the Depositary in writing. Amendments shall enter into force between Contracting Parties having ratified, accepted or approved them on the ninetieth day after the receipt by the Depositary of notification of their ratification, acceptance or approval by at least three-fourths of the Contracting Parties. Thereafter the amendments shall enter into force for any other Contracting Party on the ninetieth day after that Contracting Party deposits its instrument of ratification, acceptance or approval of the amendments.

Article 48 Association Agreements

(1) *The Charter Conference may authorize the negotiation of Association Agreements with States or Regional Economic Integration Organizations, or with international organizations, in order to pursue the objectives and principles of the Charter and the provisions of this Agreement or one or more Protocols.*

(2) *The relationship established with and the rights enjoyed and obligations incurred by an associating State, Regional Economic Integration Organization, or international organization shall be appropriate to the particular circumstances of the association, and in each case shall be set out in the Association Agreement.*

Article 49 Entry into Force

(1) This Agreement shall enter into force on the ninetieth day after the date of deposit of the thirtieth instrument of ratification, acceptance or approval thereof.

(2) For each State or Regional Economic Integration Organisation which ratifies, accepts or approves this Agreement or accedes thereto after the deposit of the thirtieth instrument of ratification, acceptance *or* approval [*DL*], it shall enter into force on the ninetieth day after the date of deposit by such State or Regional Economic Integration Organisation of its instrument of ratification, acceptance, approval or accession.

(3) For the purposes of paragraph (1) above, any instrument deposited by a Regional Economic Integration Organisation shall not be counted as additional to those deposited by member States of such organisation.

Article 50 Provisional Application

(1) The Signatories agree to apply this Agreement and any amendments thereto provisionally following signature, to the extent that such provisional application is not inconsistent with their laws or constitutional requirements pending its entry into force in accordance with Article 47 or 49.

(2) Any Signatory may terminate its provisional application of this Agreement. Termination of provisional application for any Signatory shall take effect upon the expiration of one year from the day on which such Signatory's written notice of its intention not to become a party to this Agreement is received by the Depositary.

(3) Notwithstanding that a Signatory terminates its provisional application of this Agreement, Article 1 and Parts III and V of this Agreement shall apply, in accordance with paragraph (1), to any Investment made in the Area of that

Signatory by Investors of other Contracting Parties or in the Areas of other Contracting Parties by Investors of that Contracting Party prior to the effective date of termination of provisional application for a period of [twenty years] from such date.

(4) Before entry into force of this Agreement the signatories shall meet periodically in the provisional Charter Conference, the first meeting of which shall be convened by the provisional Secretariat designated under paragraph (5) not later than ninety days after the closing date for signature of this Agreement as specified in Article 43.

(5) The Secretariat functions will be carried out on an interim basis by a provisional Secretariat until the entry into force of this Agreement pursuant to Article 49 and the appointment of a Secretariat under Article 40.

Article 51 Reservations

No reservations may be made to this Agreement.

Article 52 Withdrawal

(1) At any time after five years from the date on which this Agreement has entered into force for a Contracting Party, that Contracting Party may [DL] give written notification to the Depositary *of its withdrawal from this Agreement.*

(2) Any such withdrawal shall take effect upon expiry of one year after the date of *the* receipt *of the notification* by the Depositary, or on such later date as may be specified in the notification of [DL] withdrawal.

(3) The provisions of this Agreement and the appropriate provisions of any Protocol to which the withdrawing Contracting Party is a party, as defined in that Protocol, shall continue to apply to Investments made in the Area of a Contracting Party *by Investors of other Contracting Parties or in the Area of other Contracting Parties by Investors of that Contracting Party* as of the date when that Contracting Party's withdrawal from this Agreement taxes effect for a period of twenty years from such date.

(4) *[DL] All Protocols to which a Contracting Party is party shall cease to be in force for that Contracting Party on the effective date of its withdrawal from this Agreement.*

Article 53 Depositary

The Government of the Portuguese Republic shall *be the* Depositary of this Agreement.

Article 54 Authentic Texts

In witness whereof the undersigned, being duly authorised to that effect, have signed texts in English, French, German, Italian, Russian and Spanish, of which every text is equally authentic, in one original, which will be deposited with the Government of the Portuguese Republic.

Done at [   ] on the [   ] day of [   ].

Annex 4

Russian Federation Subsoil Law
5 May 1992

The Subsoil Resources are that part of the earth's crust located below the soil layer and reservoirs and reaching depths accessible for geological study and development.

This Act regulates relationships that arise from study, utilization and protection of subsoil resources, mining wastes and connected processing enterprises, and other specific mineral resources on the Russian Federation territory, in the Russian Federation sea exclusive economic zone and continental shelf. The Act includes the juridical and economic basis for complex and rational use and protection of resources, provides defence of interests of the State and citizens of the Russian Federation as well as rights of resources users.

SECTION I GENERAL PROVISIONS

Article 1 Subsoil Resources Legislation

Based on the the respective provisions of the Constitution of the Russian Federation the Subsoil Resources Legislation consists of this Act and co-ordinated with it other legislative Acts of the Russian Federation and republics within it.

State authorities of territories and regions, autonomous formations, as well issue Acts regulating relationships on use of resources with the authority specified in this Act and other federal and republic legislations of the subsoil resources.

The Law applies over the territory of the Russian Federation. Legislative and normative Acts of the republics within the Russian Federation must not contradict this Act.

Land, water, forest relationships, relationships with respect to the use and protection of flora and fauna, atmosphere and other relationships that arise when using mineral resources are governed by special laws of the Russian Federation and republics within it.

Article 2　State Pool of the Subsoil Resources

The State pool of subsoil resources consist of areas in use and unused parts of resources within the State frontiers of the Russian Federation.

The disposal of the State pool of the subsoil resources in the interest of both the peoples inhabiting a relevant territory and all the population of the Russian Federation is realised by joint decision of State governmental bodies of the Russian Federation and republics within it, krays, oblasts, autonomous formations.

Article 3　Competence of the Russian Federation in the Regulation of Relations during Use of Resources

The following is under the Russian Federation authority:

1.　working out and development legislation of the Russian Federation on subsoil resources;
2.　defining the strategy of use, production extension and quality improvement of mineral resources base by means of elaborating and executing of federal programmes;
3.　establishing the procedure of use and protection of resources, including standards (norms and rules);
4.　disposal jointly with the republics within the Russian Federation, krays, oblasts, autonomous formations, of the State pool of the subsoil resources, including those in the continental shelf within the territorial sea of the Russian Federation;
5.　use and management of mineral resources of the continental shelf and the exclusive economic zone;
6.　determination of a list of minerals that belong to the category of generally used one;
7.　determination jointly with republics within the Russian Federation, krays, oblasts, autonomous formations, of the terms and procedures of enforcing payments for use of resources;
8.　making a uniform system of federal and local geological information funds, using information obtained at the expense of federal budgets;
9.　State control of effective application and protection of mineral resources and establishing of its procedures;
10.　maintaining State balance of reserves of minerals, as well as registering areas used for production of minerals, and underground construction not connected with production;
11.　State registration of works on geological study of subsoil resources;
12.　State expertise of information on proved reserves of minerals, other information on resources concerning their value;
13.　introducing restrictions of subsoil resources use on specified areas for the purposes of national security and environmental protection;
14.　entering into international agreements on the use and protection of the subsoil resources;
15.　co-ordination of research and experimental engineering works connected with the subsoil resources use;
16.　protection of rights of users of the subsoil resources and protection of interests of Russian Federation nationals.
17.　settlement of any dispute in relation to the subsoil resources between the subjects of the Federation.

Article 4 Competence of the Republics with the Russian Federation, Krays, Oblasts and Autonomous Formations in the Use and Protection of Subsoil Resources

The following is under the authority of the republics within the Russian Federation, krays, oblasts and autonomous formations:

1. regulation of relationships in the use and protection of subsoil resources within the powers specified under this Act;
2. realization of competence jointly with the Russian Federation with respect to disposal of the joint public pool of the subsoil resources for the purposes of executing common federal policy of its sue, as well as with respect to agreement on conditions subject to which areas of the subsoil resources locating on their territories can be assigned in use, shares of produced raw materials assigned and forms of payment for the right of the subsoil resources use;
3. participation in working out and conducting federal programmes for geological studies of the subsoil resources, expansion and development of the Russian Federation mineral and raw material base;
4. working out and realization of territorial programmes for development and management of the mineral and raw material base;
5. public control of effective application and protection of the Earth's interior;
6. creation of territorial funds of geologic information, disposal of information obtained at the expense of relevant budgets;
7. maintaining local balances of reserves of minerals, as well as registering areas used for underground construction not connected with production;
8. determination of types and procedure of the mineral deposits use, as well as forms and amounts of payments for the use of the subsoil resources;
9. determination of procedure to use the subsoil resources for extraction of generally used minerals and for building the underground constructions for local needs;
10. protection of the rights of the subsoil resources users and protection of interests of citizens and of minorities; settlement of any dispute in relation of the subsoil resources;
11. regulation of other problems in the sphere of the use and protection of mineral resources with the exception of those transferred under the jurisdiction of the Russian Federation;
12. determination of the procedure of reimbursement of any losses to the territory, caused by introducing restrictions provided in Article 12, Point 3 of the present Law.

Article 5 Competence of Regions and Cities in Using and Protecting Mineral Resources

The following is under the authority of cities and regions:

1. participation in solving problems of granting the subsoil resources to be used for concession lands as well as taking account of social, economic and ecological interest of inhabitants on their territory;
2. development of the mineral and raw material base for enterprises of local industry;
3. granting in accordance with established procedure development licenses in relation to generally used mineral deposits, as well as building of underground construction for local needs;
4. suspension of rights of subsoil resources users on production of generally used

mineral deposits on the land plots belonging to them in case of breaking the conditions of production;

5. control of the use and protection of mineral resources in development of generally used mineral deposits, and the use of mineral resources for purposes other than production;

6. introducing restrictions on resources use on the territories of inhabited areas, suburb zones, industrial, communication and transportation units, in case such use can cause the threat to health and life of people, or cause damage to business units or environments.

SECTION II SUBSOIL RESOURCES USE

Article 6 Methods of Using the Subsoil Resources

The subsoil resources are given to be applicable to:

1. geological studies;
2. extraction of minerals, including use of wastes of mining and connected with it processing enterprises;
3. building and exploitation of underground constructions, not connected with production of minerals;
4. creation of specially protected geological objects, having scientific, cultural, sanitary health and other significance, including those for collection of mineralogical, paleontogical and other geological materials.

The subsoil resources may be granted simultaneously for both geological study (exploration) and production of minerals. In such case production may be conducted both during the exploration process and after it.

Article 7 Areas Granted for Use

In accordance with the production license and license for underground construction not connected with production of minerals, or license for creation of specially protected objects, the areas are granted in the form of mining concessions. The area may be as well granted for exploration conducted simultaneously with production of minerals or for production directly following the exploration.

While determining the borders of mining concession the size of an area shall be taken into account, including all zone of works connected with the use of the subsoil resources.

The users of the subsoil resources, who received the mining concession, has the exclusive right to use the subsoil resources within the area in accordance with the license granted to him. Any activity, connected with the use of subsoil resources within the mining concession can be carried out only with the permission of the person to whom the concession was granted.

For the areas granted in accordance with the license for geological study, mining concession is not required. Within the area granted for geological study there may be conducted operations by several users of the subsoil resources. Their relations shall be arranged while granting the area for use.

Article 8   Restrictions on Subsoil Resources Use

Use of the subsoil resources may be restricted or forbidden on specified areas for the purposes of national security and environmental protection.

Use of the subsoil resources may be restricted or forbidden on the territories of inhabited areas, suburb zones, industrial, communication and transportation units, in case such use can cause the threat to health and life of people, or cause damage to business units or environments.

Use of the subsoil resources on specially protected territories shall be conducted in accordance with the status of such territories.

Article 9   Users of the Subsoil Resources

Any subjects of business activities independently of forms of property including artificial persons and foreign citizens may be users of the subsoil resources unless otherwise provided by the Russian Federation Laws. Only State enterprises can be users of resources for the purposes of extracting radioactive raw materials.

Article 10   Terms of Using the Subsoil Resources

The use of the subsoil resources may be termless or provisional.

Terms of the provisional use of the subsoil resources are as follows:

- for geological study up to five years;
- for extraction of minerals and for the purposes not connected with production of minerals up to twenty years.

While conducting both types of act the resources are granted for the term up to twenty five years.

Without preliminary limited term the areas may be granted for the underground construction not connected with production of minerals, and for creation of specially protected geological objects.

Terms of temporary use of the subsoil resources may be prolonged on initiative of the resources user.

Terms are determined from a date when rights for such use are granted.

Article 11   Emergence of Right of the Subsoil Resources Use

The subsoil resources are granted for use by means of special permission (licenses).

A license is meant to be a document identifying rights of a licensee to use the subsoil resources within certain limits for the specified purposes, during set term, keeping preliminary set requirements.

License confirms the right for conducting geological and exploration works, development of mineral deposits, use of wastes of mining and connected with it processing enterprises; use of subsoil resources for creation of specially protected geological objects, for collection of mineralogical, paleontological and other geological materials. It is allowed to grant license for several types of the subsoil resources use.

Granting licenses for the use of the subsoil resources is made simultaneously with granting the land area. Granting the land area is made in accordance with the Land Code of the Russian Federation. Granting licenses for the use of the subsoil resources is made in accordance with the present Law.

Article 12   Content of Licenses

Content of licenses with attached agreements shall include:

1. data on subsoil user who received a license;
2. data on purposes of works to be done connected with the use of the subsoil;
3. description of boundaries of area of the subsoil resources, granted for use;
4. description of boundaries of mining concession, which is necessary for the work, connected with the subsoil resources use;
5. the duration of license, the terms of beginning of works;
6. terms of payments connected with the use of the subsoil resources, land and offshore areas;
7. agreed level of production of minerals, as well as agreement on the sharing of production;
8. rights on geological information obtained while using the subsoil resources;
9. the realization of the requirements on protection of resources and environments, as well as security, which are established by the acting legislation and standards (rules, norms).

The license for the use of subsoil establishes enumerated terms and the form of contract for the use of the subsoil including those on terms of a concession, production sharing contract, service contract (with a risk or without a risk element)

A license may include other provisions, not contradicting the present Law.

Article 13   The Procedure of Granting Licenses

Licenses are granted by means of competitive bidding rounds and auctions.

Determination of the method of holding bidding rounds and auctions for each object or their group shall be carried out by the bodies granting the licenses.

Information on bidding rounds and auctions, as well as their results, shall be published in the press.

Article 14   Refusal of License

Refusal of license shall follow in the case where:

1. an applicant has deliberately submitted incorrect information about himself;
2. an application is not made in compliance with provisions of the legislation;
3. an applicant has not given and can not give proof that he possesses or will possess all necessary financial resources and technical expertise to carry out work effectively and safely.

Article 15   State System of Granting Licenses

Licenses are granted to the resources users by means of the State Licensing System, including research, information, economic institutions, the uniform procedure of granting licenses, institutions providing the management of the licensing process.

The objective of the State Licensing System is to provide:

- practical realization of the State programme of the mining industry development;
- social, economic and other interests of peoples living on the particular territory and on all the territory of the Russian Federation;
- equal opportunities for all juridical and physical persons to receive a license;
- development of market relations in connection with the use of the subsoil resources, and anti-monopoly policy;
- appropriate guarantees and safeguards to license holders (including foreign) and protection of their rights of resources use.

Article 16   Management of the State Licensing System

Providing of functioning of the Licensing System shall be executed by the specially authorized State body for the management of the subsoil resources pool and its territorial divisions.

The State body for the management of subsoil resources and its territorial divisions is [in charge of] carrying out preliminary works connected with holding bidding rounds and auctions and granting of licenses; it agrees the terms of licenses with the governmental bodies for the management of industry, land and wood resources, environmental protection, mining control, and in relation to the payments – with the State bodies for the management of the economy.

Licenses are granted jointly by the representative power body of republics within the Russian Federation, krays, oblasts, autonomous formations, and the State body for the management of the subsoil resources of the Russian Federation.

Procedure of licensing in relation to the subsoil resources shall be approved by the Russian Federation Supreme Soviet.

Article 17   Anti-Monopoly Requirements

Any actions of the governmental or management bodies, as well as business units, including the acts which they issue, are forbidden or shall be regard as not effective in accordance with established procedure, in case they are aimed to:

- restriction of the availability of participation in bidding rounds or auctions of juridical persons and citizens, willing to acquire the rights for the use of the Subsoil Resources in accordance with the present law and in spite of the terms of the bidding round or the auction;
- evasion from granting the license to the winner of the bidding round or auction;
- substitution of the competitive system of granting the Subsoil Resources by direct negotiations except for the cases provided by the present law;
- discrimination of enterprises, creating entities competitive with business units having a dominating position in the use of the Subsoil Resources;
- discrimination while providing availability of transportation and infrastructure.

The State body for the management of the Subsoil Resources has the right to establish the limits for the sizes of areas (mining concessions) granted for use.

Article 18   Granting the Subsoil Resources for the Development of Deposits of Generally Used Minerals

The procedure for granting the subsoil resources for the development of deposits of generally used minerals, as well as the procedure of use of resources by juridical and physical persons within the land plots granted to them, for the purposes of production of generally used minerals, as well as for the purposes, not connected with production, such procedures shall be set by the legal Acts of republics within the Russian Federation, Acts of krays, oblasts and autonomous formations.

The subsoil resources may not be granted for the production of the generally used minerals aimed at manufacturing building materials in the presence of railings and wastes of mining and other production which could be an alternative source of raw materials.

Article 19   Production of Generally Used Minerals by Owners and Users of Land Plots

Proprietors and owners of land areas are entitled at their own discretion within the limits of their areas to produce generally used minerals for their needs not carrying out blasting at depth of up to 5m in the way established by the corresponding Soviets of People's Deputies.

Article 20   Cessation of the Right in relation to the Subsoil Resources Use

A right to use the subsoil resources may be ceased in the following cases:

1. When the term of license is over.
2. When the user relinquishes his rights.
3. When appears a deciding term, fixed in the license, excluding further realization of granted right.

A right to use the subsoil resources may be suspended or revoked ahead of term by the State body for the management of the subsoil resources pool and its territorial divisions, who granted the license, in the following cases:

1. a direct threat to life and health of employees and population due to user's activities;
2. breach of terms of the license;
3. systematic breaking of rules in relation to the subsoil resources and their protection which are determined under legislation being in force;
4. State of emergency (natural calamities, military operations, etc.)
5. where a user during a term specified in a license did not start to use the subsoil resources in envisaged volumes;
6. liquidation of an enterprise or any other subject of economic activity to which the subsoil resources were granted in use;

In the case where a user does not agree with the decision on cessation or restriction of rights of the subsoil resources use, he may appeal against it.

Article 21   Procedure to Cease the Entitlement to the Subsoil Resources Ahead of Term

In all cases subject to sub-section (1) and (4) of Article 19, the entitlement to the subsoil resources is ceased immediately after taking a decision with notice in writing served on a user.

In the cases subject to sub-sections (2), (3) and (5) of Article 19 a decision to cease the entitlement to the subsoil resources is made after the expiration of 3 months after the date of service of the notice of the user about violations committed by him and if he made no arrangements to eliminate them.

Where the entitlement to the subsoil resources was ceased ahead of term, liquidation or temporary closing of an enterprise is made in accordance with the procedure mentioned in Clause 25 of the present Law, on his behalf.

In ceasing the entitlement to the subsoil resources ahead of term for reasons subject to sub-section (1) (through the user's fault), (2) and (3) of the second part of Article 19, or on initiative of the user of the subsoil resources, expenses of liquidation and temporary closing of the enterprise are borne by the user.

In ceasing the entitlement to the subsoil resources ahead of term for reasons subject to sub-section (1) (in case of absence of the user's fault) and (4) of the second part of Article 19, expenses of liquidation and temporary closing of the enterprise are borne by the State.

Where the circumstances or conditions, under which entitlement was suspended or restricted, have been removed it may be wholly restored. Term for which it was suspended shall not be included in the term of the license.

Article 22   Main Rights and Duties of Users of the Subsoil Resources

Users of the subsoil resources have the right:

1. to use the granted areas for performing any act corresponding to the purposes stipulated in a license;
2. to select any type of activity according to the legislation and normative acts;
3. to use results of their activities including manufactured products or produced minerals according to the legislation and the terms of the license;
4. to restrict construction on the areas within the mining concession granted to them;
5. to select any types of activity within the license;
6. to use wastes of own mining and connected with its production, if otherwise not provided in the license;
7. to carry out all types of geological studies of the subsoil resources for their own account within a license area without additional permits;
8. to apply to the body granting the licenses for re-negotiation of the terms of license where the circumstances occur significantly different from those under which the license was granted.

Users of the resources have the priority while prolonging the term of license.

Users of the subsoil resources must provide:

1. keeping the subsoil resources legislation, standards (norms, rules) of technology concerned with the subsoil resources, ratified in the established order;
2. keeping the requirements of the technical projects and programmes of development of mining works;

3. carrying out of work in relation to the subsoil resources safe for employees and population;
4. producing geological information or returns on it to federal and relevant territorial Funds of geological information;
5. informing federal and relevant territorial Funds of geological information recoverable and retained in-situ reserves of host and associated minerals and their components, as well as on application of the subsoil resources for purposes not connected with extraction of minerals;
6. keeping established standards (norms, rules) of protection of the subsoil resources, atmosphere, lands, woods, waters and other environmental objects, as well as buildings and constructions against harmful effects of operations in relation to the subsoil resources;
7. maintaining and preservation of geological, mining and any other documentation obtained during geological study of the subsoil resources;
8. restoration of lands and other nature objects, destroyed while use of subsoil to a normal state, suitable for further use;
9. preservation of mines and drilling wells which can be used during fields development and for other purposes and abandonment in accordance with established procedure of mines and drilling wells not subject to any use;
10. keeping the procedure and terms of the subsoil resources use, specified in the license, including payments for the right of the subsoil resources use and other compulsory payments at the time prescribed.

SECTION III EFFECTIVE USE AND PROTECTION OF SUB-SOIL RESOURCES

Article 23 Main Demands of Effective Use and Protection of Subsoil Resources

Main demands of effective use and protection of the subsoil resources are as follows:

1. maintenance of the legally established order to grant the subsoil resources in use and banning of unwarranted use of the subsoil resources;
2. maintenance of completeness of geological studies, rational complex use and protection of the subsoil resources;
3. head geological studies of the subsoil resources and on their basis ensuring reliable appraisal of mineral reserves, terms of using the subsoil resources for purposes other than mining;
4. public examination and registration of mineral reserves as well as areas of the earth's interior used for purposes not related to mineral mining;
5. provision for most complete recovery of reserves of host and associate minerals and accessory constituents from the subsoil resources;
6. reliable registration of reserves of host and associate minerals and constituents enclosed in them recovered from and remained in the earth's interior in mining of mineral deposits;
7. protection of mineral deposits from flooding water encroachment, fires and other factors deteriorating quality and commercial value of deposits or complicating their exploration;
8. averting pollution of the subsoil resources in carrying out work relating to the subsoil resources as well as by underground storage of oil, gas and other substances and materials, burial of harmful materials and industrial wastes, sewage disposal;

9. maintenance of established order of temporary closing and liquidation of enterprises of mineral industry and underground constructions not related to mining;
10. prevention of unwarranted building in areas of mineral occurrences and maintenance of the established order to use these areas for other purposes;
11. averting accumulation of industrial and domestic wastes in places of underground water occurrences which are used for drinking or industrial water supply.

In the case of violating requirements of this Article the subsoil resources use may be restricted, suspended or prohibited by specially authorized public bodies in compliance with legislation in force.

Article 24 Main Requirements for Safe Operations Relating to the Subsoil Resources Use

Building and exploitation of mining enterprises, underground constructions of any purposes and geological studies of subsoil are permitted only while guaranteeing safety for life and health of employees of the enterprise and population of the zone of impact of works relating to the subsoil use.

Bodies of state power and administration, subsoil users and bodies of state mining inspectors within their competence are obliged to provide fulfilment of requirements of legislation and also of properly established standards (norms, rules) on the safety of carrying out of works relating to subsoil use.

Direct responsibility for providing of safe conditions of works relating to subsoil use is borne by the leaders of these enterprises, irrespective of whether these enterprises work according to licenses granted to them or those which are enlisted for works on contract.

Main requirements for safe operations relating to the subsoil resources use are as follows:

1. only persons specially trained are allowed to conduct mining works;
2. providing the personnel engaged in mining and drilling works with the special clothes and means of individual and collective protection;
3. application of machines, equipments, materials, corresponding to the requirements of safety and sanitarian norms;
4. proper use of mining explosives, their proper storage and registering;
5. carrying out geological, mining and other observations necessary to provide the stability of works and to forecast the situations dangerous for life and health of people and employees;
6. systematic control of the processes in mines, including the contents of oxygen, toxic and explosive gases and dust;
7. carrying out arrangements provided safety of employees and people from dangerous impact of works in normal conditions and in the case of emergency.

The users of the subsoil resources shall create special mining security services on warning and liquidation of open gas and oil gushers, or use such services on a contract basis.

The leaders of enterprises, conducting works connected with the use of subsoil resources, as well as other authorized persons, shall immediately suspend the works and provide the transportation of people to the safe area in case of any danger to health and life of people.

In case of direct danger to life and health of people, living within the area of impact of works connected with the use of subsoil resources, the leaders of corresponding enterprises, shall independently inform the relevant Soviets of People's Deputies.

Article 25   Terms on Construction on the Areas of Mineral Occurrence

Design and construction of settlements, industrial complexes and other national economic objects are carried out after receiving data on lack of minerals in the subsoil resources below the area of forthcoming building.

Building on areas of mineral occurrences as well as siting of underground constructions not connected with extraction of minerals in places of their occurrences is allowed after the permission of authorized public bodies for the management of the subsoil resources pool and mining control.

Article 26   Liquidation and Temporary Closing of Mining Plants and Underground Constructions Not Connected with Mining

Mining plants, underground constructions not connected with mineral extraction and open mining works are liable to be liquidated or temporarily closed after the expiration of the license or on anticipatory ceasing of the subsoil resources use. Until completion of the process of liquidation or temporary closing a user of the subsoil resources bears complete responsibility and all duties put on him under this Act.

With full or partial liquidation or temporary closing of above plants and underground constructions mining workings and drilled wells must be arranged in order to provide safety of population, protection of environment, buildings and constructions, and in temporary closing preservation of fields, mining workings and drilled wells as well as over the time of temporary closing.

In the case of liquidation or temporary closing of a mining plant or its part, as well as underground constructions not connected with extraction of minerals geological, surveying and other documentation is enlarged in completing work and deposited in the established order.

Liquidation and temporary closing of mining plants or underground constructions not connected with extraction of minerals is deemed to be completed after signing a statement of liquidation or temporary closing by public body of direction which has granted a license, and the body of State mining supervision.

Article 27   Geologic Information about Subsoil Resources

Information on the earth's interior geology, minerals available there, conditions of their development, other properties and peculiarities of the subsoil resources as well as contained in geological reports, maps and accompanying materials is property of a customer financing the work as a result of which this information has been received unless otherwise stipulated in a license.

Proprietary right to geologic and other information on the subsoil resources is protected in compliance with provisions of the Russian Federation legislation in relation to other types of property.

An executor has a right to use information about the subsoil resources gained as a result of carrying out work for scientific, teaching and other intellectual act, if interests of a customer mentioned in a contract are not infringed thereby.

Geologic or other information obtained for the account of public resources or other budge funds of reproduction of mineral base, is given in an approved form to territorial and federal funds of geologic information which store and systematize it.

Organizations, enterprises and individual citizens received geologic and other information about the subsoil resources for their own account inform federal and relevant territorial funds of geologic information about obtained data and determine terms of their application. Officials must ensure the confidentiality of information at all stages of its gathering storage, transfer and other application.

Authorized persons shall provide confidentiality of information during its obtaining, keeping, transferring and other use.

The procedure of use of the mentioned information is determined by the State body for the management of the subsoil resources pool in accordance with the Russian Federation legislation.

Article 28   State Records and State Registration

Work on geological study of the Subsoil Resources, areas of the resources granted for the purposes of mineral extraction as well as for purposes other than production are subject to public records and registration.

The State records and registration are carried out in compliance with the system uniform for the Russian Federation according to procedure established by the State body for the management of the Subsoil Resources.

Article 29   State Examination of Mineral Reserves

For the purposes of creation of the conditions for rational and complex use of the Subsoil Resources; for determination of payments for the use of Subsoil Resources and of the borders of areas granted to the users, the reserves of minerals are subject to the State expert examination.

The Subsoil Resources to be used for extraction of minerals are granted after making the State examination of mineral reserves.

A decision of the State examination is a basis to set explored mineral reserves on the State balance.

State examination of initial geological data is made at any stage of geological studies of the deposits proved that the geological information presented to the experts are sufficient for objective estimate of quality and quantity of mineral reserves, their national economic value, mine technical, ecological and other conditions of their exploitation.

While granting the Subsoil Resources to be used for both geological study and simultaneous production of minerals, the users of the Subsoil Resources may start production before the State expert examination of reserves of minerals. The terms of the following presentation of information to the State expert examination and precising the conditions of the license, including payments, shall be set in the license.

Geologic information relating to areas of the Subsoil Resources used for purposes other than development of mineral deposits is also subject to the State examination.

State expert examination of mineral reserves and of geological information concerning areas to be granted, is provided by the State body for the management of the Subsoil Resources pool and its territorial divisions.

Article 30   State Cadastres of Mineral Deposits and Manifestations

State cadastres of mineral deposits and manifestations are kept in order to work out federal, republic and territorial programme on geological studies of the Subsoil Resources, rational location of mining plants, and for other national economic purposes as well.

State cadastres of mineral deposits and manifestations must include information concerning each deposit which characterizes quality and quantity of major and minor minerals, components contained in them, mine technical, hydrogeological and other conditions of exploitation of a deposit and its geologic and economic estimate, as well as information about each manifestation of minerals.

Article 31   State Balances of Mineral Reserves

For the purposes of registering the statement of the mineral raw material base of the Russian Federation, the State balances of mineral reserves shall be maintained.

State balances of mineral reserves must contain evidence on quality, quantity and level of knowledge of mineral reserves with respect to deposits of commercial value, their locations, level of commercial development, production, losses and providing of the industry with explored minerals.

Article 32   Keeping of State Cadastres of Mineral Deposits and Manifestations and State Balances of Mineral Reserves

State federal and territorial cadastres of mineral deposits and manifestations and State Federal and territorial balances of mineral reserves are compiled and kept on the basis of both geologic information submitted by enterprises that study the Subsoil Resources geology to federal and territorial geological funds under this Act, and State accounts of enterprises carrying out development of mineral deposits and their extraction which are submitted to the above funds in accordance with the order established by the Russian Federation Government.

Article 33   Protection of Areas of the Subsoil Resources being of Particular Scientific and Cultural Values

Rare geological outcrops, mineralogical formations, paleontological objects and other zones of the subsoil reserves of particular scientific and cultural values may be announced in the established order reservations or memorials of nature or culture. Any activity breaking preservation of reservations and memorials is prohibited.

In the event of revealing rare geological and mineralogical formations, meteorites, paleontoglogical, archaeological and other objects being of interest for science and culture, users of the Subsoil Resources must suspend the works and inform State bodies which granted the license.

Article 34   Rewards for Discovery of Mineral Deposits

Persons, discovered mineral deposits, rare geological outcrops, mineralogical formations, meteorites, paleontoglogical, archaeological and other objects of particular scientific and cultural values on the areas of the Subsoil Resources not studied earlier, have the right to register the mentioned areas in the State body for the management of the Subsoil Resources pool or its territorial divisions.

In case the value of discovered areas is proved, persons who registered such areas are granted a financial reward.

The procedure and amount of payment is set by the Government of the Russian Federation.

SECTION IV   STATE REGULATION OF THE RELATIONS CONNECTED WITH THE USE OF THE SUBSOIL RESOURCES

Article 35   The Objectives of State Regulation of the Relations Connected with the Use of the Subsoil Resources

The objective of State regulation of the relations connected with the use of the Subsoil Resources is to provide production of the mineral raw material base and its rational use for the benefit of present and future generations of the people of Russian Federation.

State regulation of the relations connected with the use of the Subsoil Resources is executed by means of management, planning system, registering and control.

The following is included in the objectives of the State regulations:

- determination of the volumes of production of the main minerals for the present term and for the future in general for the Russian Federation;
- providing of the development of the mineral raw material base, and creation of the fund of areas to be used for underground constructions, not connected with production of minerals;
- determination of the delivery quotas for mineral raw materials;
- introducing payments, connected with the use of the Subsoil Resources, as well as with introducing of controlled prices for certain minerals;
- establishing standards (rules, norms) in the field of geological study, use and protection of the Subsoil Resources, safety of works, connected with the Subsoil Resources.

Article 36   State Direction of Relations Concerning the Use and Protection of the Subsoil Resources

State direction of relations concerning the use and protection of mineral resources is exercised by the Russian Federation President, Russian Federation Government, Supreme Soviets and governemnts of the Republics within the Russian Federation, Soviets of People's Deputies and administrations of oblasts, okrugs, autonomous formations, as well as by the State body for the management of the Subsoil Resources pool.

The State body for the management of the Subsoil Resources pool creates its territorial divisions.

The State body for the management of the Subsoil Resources pool cannot manage the business activity of the enterprises exploring and developing mineral deposits or constructing and exploiting underground constructions, not connected with production of minerals.

Article 37   State Control of Rational Use and Protection of the Subsoil Resources

The objective of the State control of rational use and protection of the Subsoil Resources is to provide observance of established procedure of the Subsoil Resources use, legislation, standards (rules, norms) in the field of geological study, use and protection of the Subsoil Resources, observance of rules of maintaining the State registering during the process of works, connected with the use of the Subsoil Resources, by all users, irrespectively of subordination, regime of confidentiality and type of ownership.

State control of rational use and protection of the Subsoil Resources shall be executed by the bodies of State geological control in co-operation with the State bodies of mining control, environmental protection and other control bodies.

The powers of the bodies of the State geological control shall be determined by the Statement subject to the approval of the Russian Federation Government.

Article 38   State Supervision of Safe Conducting of Work in Relation to the Subsoil Resources

The objective of the State supervision of safe conducting of works in relation to the Subsoil Resources is to provide observance of the Subsoil Resources legislation, standards, rules and norms relating to rational management and protection of the Subsoil Resources, safety carrying out of works, abandonment of their harmful consequences for population, environments, buildings and constructions, by users of the Subsoil Resources.

State supervision of safe conducting of work connected with the Subsoil Resources use, shall be executed by the bodies of mining supervision. Bodies of State geological control, environmental and other control bodies, trade unions.

The Russian Federation Government approves the statements on competence, rights, duties and procedure of activity of State mining supervision bodies.

SECTION V   PAYMENTS FOR THE SUBSOIL RESOURCES

Article 39   Payment System in the Subsoil Resources Use

The Subsoil Resources use requires payment except cases subject to Article 40 of this Act. Payments payable by a user of the Subsoil Resources available within the limits of the Russian Federation territory, sea economical zone and Russian Federation continental shelf and internal waters of the Russian Federation.

Payment system in the Subsoil Resources use includes:

- payments for the right of use of the Subsoil Resources;
- payments for the reproduction of mineral base;
- fee for licenses granted;
- excise;
- payments for offshore areas and plots of the bottom of the sea.

In addition users of the Subsoil Resources pay other taxes, fees and payments stipulated in the legislation including land rental, payments for geological information, and they may receive allowance for payments for the exhaustion of the resources.

Article 40   Payment Release in the Subsoil Resources Use

The following Subsoil Resources users or types of use are released from payments in the Russian Federation:

- owners and holders of land areas, who are conducting production of generally used minerals on the areas belonging to them or leased by them directly for their needs in accordance with established procedure;
- users of the Subsoil Resources conducting a regional geological-geophysical works, aimed to the general study of the Subsoil Resources, forecasting earthquakes, study of volcanic activity, engineering, paleontological, geo-ecological studies, control of regime of underground waters, other works conducted without breaking the integrity of the Subsoil Resources;
- users of the Subsoil Resources, receiving areas for creation of specially protected objects, having scientific, cultural and other significance.

Supreme Soviets of the republics within the Russian Federation, Soviets of People's Deputies of krays, oblasts and autonomous formations may introduce additional reasons for granting the release to the Subsoil Resources users from payments which are made to a relevant budget.

Normative acts and decisions of government bodies which give some users groundless unilateral advantages at the expense of release from payments for the Subsoil Resources use are invalid under this Act.

Article 41   Payments for the Right of Use of the Subsoil Resources

The Subsoil Resources use is paid by means of collecting mineral prospecting, exploration and production rents, as well as rent for the right to use the Subsoil Resources for the purposes not related to extraction of minerals.

These rents may be enforced in form of single fees, regular payments on their combinations during all the term of the rights granted.

Rentals for the right to conduct prospecting and exploration work are determined depending on the region and area sizes, mineral species, duration of work, degree of geological knowledge and risked value.

Production rentals depend upon species, quantity and quality of minerals, geographical, mining and economic conditions of their development and degree of risk.

Production rentals are paid in the form of initial, and then regular payments starting from the beginning of production. They are determined as percentage of value of minerals produced taking into account liquidation of reserves. Such payments are included in production costs.

After beginning of commercial production of minerals payments for the right of its exploration within the mining concession, granted to the user for such production, shall not be paid.

Subsoil Resources rentals for other purposes, including construction, usage of buildings and structures, storage (burial) of products and wastes are paid as regular payments and as lump sums. The amount of payments is determined depending on size of area to be used, quality of the Subsoil Resources and ecological safety.

The procedure and terms of payments for the right of the Subsoil Resources use, as well as criteria for determination of rates of payments, shall be set by the Russian Federation government. Final amounts of payments for the right of the Subsoil Resources use shall be set while granting the license for such right.

Article 42   Distribution of Subsoil Resources Rental

Rental is distributed between budgets of the Russian Federation, Republics within the Russian Federation, krays, oblasts, autonomous formations, districts (of cities) on which areas the Subsoil Resources use is realized.

The following is paid to the budget of the districts (of cities):

- all payments for the right of exploration of all minerals on their territory;
- all payments for the right of production of generally spread minerals;
- payments for the right of the Subsoil Resources use not connected with production of minerals;
- part of payments for the right of production of minerals except for above mentioned minerals.

Part of payments for the right of production of minerals, excluding those minerals for which payments are made to the budgets of districts (cities) only, is paid to the budgets of Republics within the Russian Federation, krays, oblasts, autonomous formations and to the republican budget of the Russian Federation.

Payments for the right of hydrocarbon production shall be distributed as following:

budgets of districts (cities)	30 per cent
budgets of Republics within the Russian Federation, krays, oblasts, autonomous formations	30 per cent
republican budget of the Russian Federation	40 per cent

Payments for the right of production of other minerals shall be distributed as following:

budgets of districts (cities)	50 per cent
budgets of Republics within the Russian Federation, krays, oblasts, autonomous formations	25 per cent
republican budget of the Russian Federation	25 per cent

For the unique deposits or groups of deposits the distribution of payments between the budgets may be set in another proportion. The proportions shall be set by the agreement of all parties who are interested. In case of disagreement the decision shall be made by the Supreme Soviet of the Russian Federation.

Rental in relation to the Subsoil Resources use in continental shelf within territorial waters shall be distributed as following:

budgets of Republics within the Russian Federation,
krays, oblasts, autonomous formations   60 per cent
republican budget of the Russian Federation   40 per cent

Rental in relation to the Subsoil Resources use within the limits of the sea economic zone of the Russian Federation is payable in full to the Russian Federation budget.

Part of payments made to the budgets of Republics within the Russian Federation, krays, oblasts, autonomous formations, for the Subsoil Resources use in localities of residence of minority peoples and ethnic groups, is used for purposes of social-economic development of these peoples and groups.

Article 43   Forms of Paying Rental in Relation to the Subsoil Resources Use

Rental in relation to the Subsoil Resources use may be taken in the form of:

- payment in cash;
- a share of recovery volume or any other production manufactured by a user;
- carrying out work or giving services;
- a share of the Russian Federation, Republics within the Russian Federation, kray, oblast, autonomous formation or district granting the right to use the Subsoil Resources, in the foundation fund of a joint venture.

Form of payment is established in the license for the right to use subsoil.

It is not allowed to make a call for or accept in payment for the Subsoil Resources use:

- services of military nature radioactive materials, precious metals, diamonds and other materials and products management of which is within the exclusive competence of the Russian Federation in accordance with the Russian Federation legislation;
- information being State secret.

It is not allowed to demand geologic or other information being a commercial secret of a user in payment for the Subsoil Resources use.

Article 44   Payments for Reproduction of Mineral Base

Payments for reproduction of mineral base are collected from users of the Subsoil Resources carrying out extraction of minerals.

Such payments are made to the State outer-budget fund for reproduction of the mineral base.

The fund is used for financing the regional, geological, geophysical, research and other works, connected with geological study of the Subsoil Resources, as well as with completion of exploration within projects approved before the present law is in effect.

Exploration of all other deposits is financed at the expense of enterprises having licenses for development of such deposits. The amounts of payments to the State outer-budget fund for reproduction of mineral-raw material base are made by enterprises financing the completion of exploration projects, approved before adopting the present Law, shall be decreased by the amount of actual financing.

Part of payments for reproduction of mineral-raw material base in amount of 0.5–1.5 per cent is directed for reward for discovery and exploration of mineral deposit.

The amounts of payments for the reproduction of the mineral base, the procedure of making payments, their distribution and use, shall be set by the Supreme Soviet of the Russian Federation.

Article 45   License Grant Fee

The fee is paid for the license for use of the subsoil resources to the bodies granted the license. The amount of fee shall be determined taking into account the expenses on expert examination of applications, organizational and other expenses, connected with the granting of the license.

Article 46   Excise

Excise may be introduced by a special legal Act of the Russian Federation for the specified minerals, produced from deposits in comparatively more favourable mining, geological and economic conditions, when the Subsoil Resources user receives superprofit, included in the price of production.

Article 47   Payments for Use of Offshore Areas and Plots of the Sea Bottom

Payments for the use of offshore areas and plots of the sea bottom are made by users, conducting exploration and production of minerals, as well as other works, within offshore areas and sea economic zones of the Russian Federation.

The amounts of payments depends on areas leased and its form, water depth and the purposes of use. The procedure and terms of making payments shall be set by the Russian Federation Government.

Article 48   Allowance for Payments for the Exhaustion of the Subsoil Resources

Allowance for payments for the exhaustion of the Subsoil Resources may be granted to:

- users, carrying out production of deficit minerals in case the economic efficiency of development of deposits is low due to objective reasons not connected with breaking the conditions of rational use of proved reserves;
- users, carrying out production of minerals from the rest of reserves of low quality, excluding lowering of such quality by reason of selective production.

The decision on such allowance shall be made by the State bodies granting license for the Subsoil Resources use.

SECTION VI   RESPONSIBILITY FOR VIOLATION OF THE LAW ON SUBSOIL

Article 49   Responsibility for Violation of the Subsoil Resources Legislation

Deals directly or indirectly infringing provisions of the present law are invalid.

Persons guilty of making the above deals as well as of:

- non-observance of the established order in relation to the Subsoil Resources use and unwarranted use of resources;
- non-observance of requirements set by the law, standards, rules and norms of safety, concerning the Subsoil Resources use, failure to take necessary measures in case of danger for people's health and life;
- carrying out work connected with the Subsoil Resources use by methods and techniques threatening population's safety and preservation of the environment from pollution;
- violation of the right of ownership of geological and other information and its confidentiality;
- unwarranted building over areas of mineral occurrences;
- not providing protection of buildings, constructions, specially protected areas, and environments during use of the Subsoil Resources;
- destruction or damage of observation regime underground water well holes as well as survey marks and geodetic beacons;
- non-observance of requirements on putting abandoned or temporary closed mine wells and boreholes to a State ensuring the population's safety, as well as requirements on conservation of deposits, mine workings and boreholes within the period of temporary closing;
- not paying regularly for the use of the Subsoil Resources;
- non-fulfilment of obligations on abandonment and re-cultivation of areas and units destroyed during the use of the Subsoil Resources;
- bear criminal responsibility subject to the legislation of the Russian Federation and republics within the Russian Federation. The legislation may determine a responsibility for other violations of Subsoil law.

Article 50   Procedure for Dispute Settlement

The disputes connected with the use of the Subsoil Resources shall be settled by the Soviets of People's Deputies, Court or Arbitration court, in accordance with their competence and in accordance with the procedure established by the legislation of the Russian Federation and Republics within the Russian Federation.

To consideration in court or arbitration court are subject:

- financial, property and other disputes related to the Subsoil Resources use;
- appealing against decisions of governmental bodies contradicting to this law and other Subsoil Resources laws, as well as of the State body for the management of the Subsoil Resources on a cessation of the right in relation to the Subsoil Resources before the appointed time, a refusal of permit (license) in relation to the Subsoil Resources;
- appealing against standards, rules, norms, for the technology of works connected with the use of the Subsoil Resources and environmental protection, that contradict the legislation in force;
- appealing against actions of officials and bodies contradicting this Act and other Subsoil Resources legislation.

Article 51   Compensation for Injury

Injury caused to the user of the Subsoil Resources as a result of activity of enterprises, organizations, institutions, governmental bodies, as well as citizens, which caused damage to the Subsoil Resources, is to be fully reimbursed at the expense of the enterprises, organizations, institutions, as well as budgets of corresponding governmental bodies.

In case the area of subsoil is not granted for use compensation for harmful impact is made by payments to the republican budget of the Russian Federation, budgets of republics within the Russian Federation, budgets of krays, oblasts, autonomous formations.

Compensation in cash by agreement of sides can be substituted by works on reconstruction of violated nature features of subsoils.

Unwarranted use of subsoil and unwarranted building of areas of mineral occurrences is ceased without compensation of expenditures, spent during unwarranted use of subsoil.

SECTION VIII INTERNATIONAL AGREEMENTS

Article 52 International Agreements

If in earlier International Agreements other rules were determined than those established in the present law, the applicability of such rules of the international agreement shall be permitted.

President of the Russian Federation
B. Yeltsin
Moscow, House of Soviets of Russia
21 February 1992, No. 2395-1

LAW OF THE RUSSIAN FEDERATION ON INTRODUCING AMENDMENTS AND ADDITIONS TO THE LAW 'ON SUBSOIL'

Article 1

To introduce the Law of the Russian Federation 'On Subsoils' the following amendments and additions:

1. Article 12 to add a new paragraph 1 in the following form:
    'data about a user of subsoils who was granted a license'
    Paragraphs 1–8 of Article 12 (1) to be changed according to paragraphs 2-9.
2. In the second part of Article 13 the words 'granting a license' are to be substituted by the words 'of holding and terms of tender or auction'.
3. The second part of Article 16, after the words 'Work, connected with' 'holding tenders (auctions) and' is to be added.
4. Article 36 (4) is to be excluded.
5. The last paragraph of the second part of Article 49 is to be stated in the following form 'bear criminal responsibility according to the legislation of the Russian Federation and also administrative responsibility according to the legislation of the Russian Federation and the republics – part of the Russian Federation'.
6. In the first part of Article 51 after the word 'organizations', the word 'citizens' is to be excluded, and after the words 'power and administration' the words 'officials and' are to be added.

Article 2

This Law is to be in effect as from the day of its publication.

President of the Russian Federation
B. Yeltsin
Moscow, The House of Soviets of Russia26 June 1992, No. 3134-1

DECREE OF THE PRESIDENT OF THE RUSSIAN FEDERATION ON INTRODUCTION OF EXCISE FROM THE USERS OF ENTRAILS ON THE TERRITORY OF THE RUSSIAN FEDERATION

In accordance with the Law of the Russian Federation 'On the subsoil' and in connection with the necessity to increase the effectiveness of application of energy resources and also with the purpose of controlling the rise in prices on products, goods and services in the national economy of the Russian Federation I decree the following:

1. To introduce the excise in oil and gas extracting from the deposits with relatively better mining – geological and economical-geographical characteristics.
2. To establish that the excise sums will be collected from the users of the subsoil of the Russian Federation territory and go to the republican budget of the Russian Federation.
3. The Government of the Russian Federation must approve the rates of excise on oil and gas, establish the procedure of collection and differentiate its volumes.
4. The present decree will come into force in the order established by the resolution of the Congress of the People's Deputies of the RSFSR 'On legal ensuring of economic reforms' from 1 November 1991.

President of the Russian Federation
B. Yeltsin
Kremlin, Moscow
14 August 1992, Decree No. 893

RESOLUTION OF THE SUPREME SOVIET OF THE RUSSIAN FEDERATION ON THE PROCEDURE FOR IMPLEMENTATION OF THE LAW OF THE RUSSIAN FEDERATION 'ON RESOURCES'

The Supreme Soviet of the Russian Federation resolves:

1. To implement the Law of the Russian Federation 'On Resources' from the date of its publication.
2. To consider the Code of the RSFSR on resources to have lost its force.
3. That the Committee on Legislation of the Supreme Soviet of the Russian Federation shall bring forward by 1 April 1992 for the consideration of the Supreme Soviet proposals to render the legislative acts of the Russian Federation compatible with the present Law.
4. That the Government of the Russian Federation shall:
   (i) by 1 April 1992 bring its previously adopted normative acts into compatibility with the present Law, and also guarantee the review and rescission by ministries, state committees and departments of the Russian Federation of those of their normative and other acts which conflict with the present Law,

including those on the transfer by them of non-producing fields of mineral resources to the balance sheet of production enterprises;

(ii) establish before the definition for each producing field of the actual amounts of regular payments for the right to use resources temporary minimal rates of payment for all forms of mineral resources and ensure their payment by functioning mining enterprises to the relevant budgets from March 1992.

5. To impose the functions of state administration of the state resources fund on the Committee on Geology and Mineral Resources of the Ministry of Ecology and Natural Resources of the Russian Federation and to instruct it:

(i) by 1 March 1992 to prepare and present to the Supreme Soviet of the Russian Federation a draft Statute on a procedure for licensing the use of resources;

(ii) by 1 July 1992 to ensure the acquisition of licenses by all users of resources.

6. That the Committee of the Supreme Soviet of the Russian Federation on questions of ecology and the rational use of natural resources and the Commission of the Soviet of the Republic of the Supreme Soviet of the Russian Federation on budget, plans, taxes and prices shall develop and present to the Supreme Soviet of the Russian Federation by 25 February 1992 a draft Statute on the state extra-budget fund for the reproduction of the mineral raw material base.

President of the Supreme Soviets of the Russian Federation
R. I. Khasbulatov
Moscow, The House of Soviets of Russia
21 February 1992, No. 2396-1
Text: Rossiiskaia Gazeta, Tuesday, 5 May

LAW OF THE RUSSIAN FEDERATION ON INTRODUCING ALTERATIONS AND ADDITIONS TO THE LAW OF THE RUSSIAN FEDERATION 'ON EXCISE' AND 'ON SUBSOIL' IN CONNECTION WITH REGULATING OF TAX LEGISLATION IN RUSSIA

Article 1

....

Article 2

To introduce in the Law of the Russian Federation 'On Subsoil' the following alterations and additions:

1. In Article 39 the words 'excise duty' to be substituted by 'excises'.
2. Article 46 is to be re-written in the following wording:

'Article 46 Excises

Excises for some kinds of mineral raw materials produced from deposits with relatively better mining geological and economic-geographical characteristics may be introduced by the Government of the Russian Federation in accordance with the Law of the Russian Federation 'On Excise'.

Article 3

The present Law enters into force from 18 September 1992.

President of the Russian Federation
B. Yeltsin
Moscow, The House of Soviets of Russia
25 December 1992, No. 4229-1

Annex 5

Law of the Russian Federation on Oil and Gas
Revised Draft, 14 October 1992[*]

CONTENTS

[*] The Draft has been prepared under the scientific supervision of Dr Gazeev M. Kh.

Revised Draft Law of the Russian Federation on Oil and Gas

The Law of the Russian Federation on Oil and Gas (hereinafter referred to as 'the present Law') has been worked out proceeding from the Treaties of the Federation and the Constitution of the Russian Federation and developing relevant provisions for the Law of the Russian Federation 'On the Subsoil' and other legislative acts of the Russian Federation to the extent affecting the regulation of the relations arising in the process of study, use and protection of oil and gas resources, for the purpose of creation of a legal basis for ensuring comprehensive rational development and protection of oil and gas resources, ecological and technical safety in the process of exploration, production and transportation, protection of interests of the State, regions and citizens of the Russian Federation, as well as the realization of the rights of the subjects of activities in the domain of oil and gas, irrespective of their forms of ownership and citizenship, within the boundaries of the Russian Federation on its continental shelf and in the exclusive (maritime) economic zone.

Section I LEGISLATIVE AND OTHER ACTS ON ACTIVITIES IN THE DOMAIN OF OIL AND GAS OF THE RUSSIAN FEDERATION

Article 1 Legal Status of the Law 'On Oil and Gas' of the Russian Federation

1.1. The present Law with all Annexes hereto shall be a federal law of direct effect and from the moment of its entry into force shall regulate relations arising during the effectuation of activities in the domain of oil and gas within the continental part of the territory of the Russian Federation, including its internal and territorial waters and islands of the Russian Federation, as well as on its continental shelf and exclusive (maritime) economic zone of the Russian Federation, hereinafter all the above mentioned shall be referred to as the Russian territory.

'Oil and gas' in the present Law means all types of naturally occurring liquid and gaseous hydrocarbons and their mixture and other natural hydrocarbon-containing compounds as well as associated substances contained in hydrocarbon compounds and their mixtures.

'Activities in the domain of oil and gas' in the present Law means all types of prospecting exploration and operational activities in the fields of oil and/or gas including transportation of extracted resources to collection points or to main pipelines, preparation and storage of these resources at production sites, their primary processing (reduction of hydrosulphides in their composition, desalting and dehydration, etc.) as well as primary processing of the extracted resources at the deposit for the purpose of fuel production for heating boilers and engines to meet the needs of the licensee within the framework of the license and local needs.

1.2. Relations pertaining to land, water and forest as well as relations regarding use and protection of the environment, vegetation and wild life, property and other relations connected with activities in the domain of oil and gas shall be regulated by appropriate legislative and normative acts of the Russian Federation, republics within the Russian Federation and other subjects of the Federation.

1.3. Changes in the normative documents and acts, supplementing the present Law may be introduced by decision of the government of the Russian Federation on the basis of an appropriate submission of the licensing authority.

Article 2   Relationships of the Present Law with Other Legislative and Normative Acts

2.1. Upon entry into force of the present Law, its provisions shall override the contradicting articles of the previously passed Law of the Russian Federation 'On the Subsoil' and legal acts supplementing the latter, other legislative and normative acts of the Russian Federation, republics within the Russian Federation, other subjects of the Federation related to activities in the domain of oil and gas to the extent contradicting the present Law.

2.2. The provisions of the present Law shall correspond to appropriate articles of other earlier legislative acts of the Russian Federation which regulate relations in the domain of ownership, use of land, ecology, foreign investments, hard currency and export-import operations, taxation, rights of ownership, international law and other spheres to the extent related to activities in the domain of oil and gas.

2.3. Other legislative and normative acts related to the activities in the domain of oil and gas adopted in accordance with Treaties of the Federation at the federal level in republics within the Russian Federation, other subjects of the Federation after coming into force of the present Law should not contradict the present Law.

Section II RIGHT OF OWNERSHIP OF TIIE STATE AND SUBJECTS OF THE FEDERATION TO OIL AND GAS AS WELL AS TO GEOLOGICAL INFORMATION ON OIL AND GAS RESOURCES

Article 3   State's and Subjects' of the Federation Right of Ownership to Oil and Gas Resources Contained in Their Natural State in the Subsoil

3.1. Oil and gas resources contained in their natural state in the subsoil of the territory of the Russian Federation as set forth in Article 1.1 of the present Law shall be inalienable property (title) of the state - the Russian Federation.

The republics within the Russian Federation, other subjects of the Federation together with the state shall also be owners (joint title) of oil and gas resources contained in their natural state in the subsoil of these territories.

3.2. Oil and gas owned by the licensee and returned by him to the subsoil for storage for the purpose of their subsequent realization or for increasing oil production rate and wells output or for prevention of their destruction (including flaring) and for other purposes shall not become property of the state and subjects of the Federation.

3.3. Ownership (title) of oil and gas resources while contained in their natural state in the subsoil of the territory of the Russian Federation as set forth in Article 1.1 of the present Law shall be retained by the state and subjects of the Federation and may not be alienated nor the subject of license or any other agreement on activities in the domain of oil and gas irrespective of the date of its conclusion and its duration.

3.4. Ownership (title) of the subjects of the Federation to oil and gas resources contained in their natural state in the subsoil in the territories may be transferred solely to the Russian Federation given the adoption of an appropriate agreed decision by supreme bodies of the representative power of the parties and in accordance with the Constitution of the Russian Federation.

Article 4 Right of Ownership to Geological, Geophysical and Other Types of Information on Oil and Gas Resources

4.1. Geological, geophysical and other types of information on oil and gas resources contained in their natural state in the subsoil of the Russian territory as set forth in Article 1.1 of the present Law as well as within the continental shelf and exclusive economic zone of the Russian Federation obtained through funding from the federal budget and/or non-budget designated funds to finance prospecting and other operations including information accumulated during the period prior to entry into force of the present Law as well as information acquired from the above sources of financing or transferred to the state free of charge (with the transfer of title) shall be property of the state.

4.2. Geological, geophysical and other types of information on oil and gas resources contained in their natural state in the subsoil of the territory of these subjects of the Federation acquired through financing of prospecting and other types of operations from their own budget or from non-budget funding sources including information accumulated during the period prior to entry into force of the present Law as well as information acquired and owned by them from outside sources which became their property shall be property of subjects of the Russian Federation.

4.3. State's and subjects' of the Federation right of ownership to geological, geophysical and other types of information shall be protected following procedures established by the relevant legislative acts of the Russian Federation.

Article 5 Realization of State's and Subjects' of the Federation Right of Ownership to Oil and Gas

5.1. Owners of oil and gas resources contained in their natural state in the subsoil of the Russian territory as set forth above in Article 1.1 of the present Law shall exercise their right of ownership by the following means:

- transfer of the right to dispose of these resources in the interests of the owner to the relevant bodies of representative and executive power (federal, republic or territorial); in the Russian territory, in its exclusive economic zone and on its continental shelf, the right to dispose of these resources for activities in the domain of oil and gas shall be transferred to the state interdepartmental licensing authority acting in the person of and in the interests of the state;
- recovery of lumpsum and regular payments for activities in the domain of oil and/ or gas, amounts of payments and payment procedures shall be fixed in the terms and conditions of the license;
- of retaining the right of owner (with title) to a certain part (share) of oil and gas extracted within the framework of the license; the size of such share shall be subject to agreement with the licensee and shall be fixed in terms and conditions of the license; right of ownership (title) to the remaining part of the oil and/or gas shall be granted to the licensee (together with the risk of their loss or any other damage) at

the location and time specified in the license but no earlier than the time of their extraction as set forth in Article 29 of the present Law.

'License' in the present Law means agreement (contract) between the licensing authority and the licensee (license owner) which grants the licensee the right to conduct activities in the domain of oil and/or gas which determines its right to production, type of activities, size of the territory, time limits and other conditions of such activities; shall be drawn in the form of a contract (agreement) in an established format.

'Licensee' (or 'license owner') means a legal or natural person with whom the license agreement (license) is concluded, or his legal successor.

Section III   LICENSING OF ACTIVITIES IN THE DOMAIN OF OIL AND GAS

Article 6   Specialized State System for Licensing the Activities in the Domain of Oil and Gas

6.1. In accordance with the Law of the Russian Federation 'On the Subsoil' and with due regard to extreme significance of oil and gas resources for the economy of the country, in the Russian territory , within its continental shelf and in its exclusive economic zone, a specialized state (federal) licensing system for activities in the domain of oil and gas, which assumes appropriate functions and authorities of state licensing system for the use of the subsoil referred to in Section 2 of the Law of the Russian Federation 'On the Subsoil' shall be established.

6.2. Establishment of specialized state licensing system for activities in the domain of oil and gas shall be aimed at providing organizational, economic and legal conditions for rational, economically profitable, meeting the requirements of the normal world practice, safe development of oil and gas resources, control over activities within the framework of the license, preservation of hydrocarbon resources and environmental protection from negative consequences of activities in the domain of oil and gas as well as equality and nondiscrimination of access to activities in the domain of oil and gas for any subjects of activities who meet specified requirements irrespective of their citizenship and the form of ownership.

Article 7   Functions and Structure of the Licensing Authority

7.1. Organization of licensing of activities in the domain of oil and gas, regulation of licensing relationships and control over compliance with the terms and conditions of licenses shall be entrusted to the state interdepartmental licensing authority (hereinafter referred to as 'licensing authority') representing the owner of the subsoil in the capacity of one of the parties involved in the licensing agreement, subordinate to the government of the Russian Federation, which has in its structure a federal service to resolve issues which fall within the competence of the state as well as regional units.

7.2. The licensing authority shall organize and carry out preparatory work for licensing the activities in the domain of oil and gas; shall establish the procedure for concluding license contracts and agree the conditions of licenses, which shall be determined by respective agencies of the representative and executive power of the subjects of the Federation in the territory within their competence with appropriate bodies who manage industry, finances, natural resources and environmental protection, land, water and forest resources, mining supervision, local authorities and so forth shall take other necessary measures to regulate relationships in the domain of use and protection of oil and gas resources in the Russian Federation.

7.3. The licensing authority shall be entitled to issue within the limits of its competence and in accordance with legislation of the Russian Federation instructions and other normative acts which do not contradict the present Law, terms and conditions of the licenses without infringing upon the rights of licensees including establishment of minimal and maximal sizes for land and sea license areas. Instructions issued by the licensing authority as well as normative acts shall come into force upon the approval by the higher licensing authority.

7.4. Funding of the licensing authority shall be provided from the federal budget.

7.5. Participation of the licensing authority in entrepreneurship activities in the domain of oil and gas shall be prohibited.

7.6. Federal service of the licensing authority:

- shall establish and supervise compliance with the unified procedure of licensing and activities in the domain of oil and gas in the Russian territory as set forth in Article 1.1 of the present Law;
- shall execute licensing and supervision over the activities in the domain of oil and gas within license limits on the continental shelf and in the exclusive economic zone of the Russian Federation;
- shall determine within the limits of its competence types, amounts and procedures for payments recovered from licensees;
- shall ensure necessary arrangements of the macroeconomic interbranch level to support activities in the domain of oil and gas in the framework of licenses if these issues cannot be resolved by regional units of the licensing authority;
- shall prescribe unified and valid on the whole of the Russian territory forms for licensing documentation, shall determine the procedure and time framework for considering the documents as well as issue instructions pertaining to relations with regional units;
- shall represent the state as owner of geological, geophysical and other types of information in the domain of oil and gas (except for information which is designated confidential through established procedures), received through the use of the resources from federal budget and/or through other non-budget designated funds;
- shall be entitled at the request of the government of the Russian Federation to establish restrictions or to suspend operations of any license if it is connected with the necessity to ensure national security with the development of ecological emergency as well as the emergence of force majeure circumstances;
- shall keep the register and exercise state registration of licenses within 30 days after the licensing agreement is signed;
- shall take part in conducting by regional units of the licensing authority direct negotiations with regard to operational license;
- shall be entitled to conduct on the entire Russian territory prior to state registration of the licensing agreement, examination on a case-by-case basis and subject to additional examination documents and materials, submitted by contestants of the licensing agreement;
- shall represent the interests of the Russian Federation as well as the subjects of the Federation in the international court of Arbitration, in Russian court of Arbitration, Arbitrage court or People's court and any other judicial institutions;

- shall exercise the functions previously performed by the Central Commission on Oil and Gas Reserves of the Russian Federation (CCR) and the Central Commission on the Development of Oil and Gas Deposits of the Russian Federation;
- shall be entitled to transfer part of its authority to the lower level regional units of the licensing authority if this provides for more effective state regulation of relations associated with oil and gas resources use and protection.

7.7. Regional units of the licensing authority:

- shall conduct licensing of activities in the domain of oil and gas and supervision over activities within the framework of the license in the territory of the region (republic within the Russian Federation, krai, oblast, autonomous territory);
- shall determine within their competence the method of licensing of activities in the domain of oil and/or gas in the territory of the region in each specific instance, types and amounts of payments, provided in the license;
- shall ensure all authorizations necessary for the conduct of activities in the domain of oil and gas within the framework of the license other than those included in the competence of the federal service of the licensing authority;
- shall dispose of accessible geological, geophysical and other types of information representing its owner, other than information recognized through established procedure as confidential, which may not be provided in a routine manner without the consent of the licensee.

7.8. Geological, geophysical and other types of information which the licensing authority has at its disposal (or has access to) regarding oil and gas resources on the license areas may be made available for any subject of activities in the domain of oil and gas without any restrictions at an announced price the size of which shall be determined by the federal licensing authority and may be subject to revision.

Article 8   Types of Licenses, Principles and Methods of Their Issuance

8.1. Activities in the domain of oil and gas in the Russian territory as set forth in Article 1.1 of the present Law, its continental shelf and in the exclusive economic zone shall be allowed solely on the basis of the license agreement (license) concluded with the licensing authority representing the state.

8.2. Noncompliance with the provisions of Article 8.1 shall entail imposition of administrative or material sanctions specified by appropriate bodies of the executive power against the person who violates the provisions of Article 8 at the request of the licensing authority.

8.3. The license depending upon its type shall grant the right to conduct specific types of activities in the domain of oil and gas within a compact, clearly marked territory during a specified period of time on the conditions agreed between the licensing authority and the licensee, fixed in the license.

8.4. In the Russian territory as is defined in Article 1.1 of the present Law, in its exclusive economic zone and on its continental shelf the activities in the domain of oil and gas shall be regulated by licenses of two types: the prospecting license and operational license.

8.5. The federal service of the licensing authority and its regional structures on the basis of the proposals by the Government of the Russian Federation, bodies of representative and/or executive power of the republics within the Russian Federation and other subjects of the Federation and with due regard to the analysis of oil and gas resources, current and prospective needs in these types of energy sources for the economy of the country and regions, consultations with the appropriate bodies of state administration, shall from time to time determine the segments of the subsoil and territories which can be allotted for use within the framework of the license.

8.6. Legal and physical persons irrespective of the forms of ownership and citizenship shall be allowed to take part in the contest or auction if they meet the specified requirements and accept the conditions and terms set by the licensing authority.

8.7. The right to conduct activities in the domain of oil and/or gas within the framework of the license shall be granted by the licensing authority to the winner of the contest or the auction which are accessible to all (provided there are no obstacles for that in the present Law) or on the basis of direct negotiations between the candidate and the licensing authority.

8.8. The means of concluding a license contract in each specific case (contest, auction, direct negotiations) shall be determined by the regional bodies of representative or executive power with the participation of the licensing authority.

8.9. Whenever the license is offered on the production sharing basis, the selection of candidates shall be conducted on the basis of a contest.

In exceptional cases, when the forthcoming activities are connected with great volumes of deposit development work on the deposit with proved oil and/or gas reserves in areas which are difficult to access, as well as in the absence of acceptable offers from candidates for the participation in contest or auction, the operational license may be issued on the basis of direct negotiations.

8.10. The license cannot be granted if the licensing authority has substantiated doubts concerning the candidate's technical, managerial, organizational expertise and financial capabilities for ensuring activities in the domain of oil and/or gas under the terms and conditions of the license and requirements of the present Law.

8.11. Any forms of discrimination of candidates shall not be allowed neither shall be allowed actions of the licensing authority or any other bodies of state power and administration which infringe upon the rights of the candidate without a written notice to him about such intention or without giving him an opportunity to discuss the conflict situation with appropriate agencies.

8.12. General principles, the procedure of organizing and conducting contests and auctions, the contents and the form of announcement of these events, the contents of application to take part in those events and the decision-making procedure to determine the winner shall be regulated by the 'Statute on Conducting Contests and Auctions for Licensing Activities in the Domain of Oil and Gas' which shall constitute an integral part of the present Law (Annex 1).

8.13. Direct negotiations shall be conducted by the licensing authority together with agencies of representative and/or executive power of the region (their duly authorized representatives) on whose territory the license will be valid.

Direct negotiations with regard to the operational license shall be conducted with the participation of a representative of the federal service of the licensing authority.

Article 9   Prospecting License

9.1. Prospecting license which is granted for a term, not exceeding 5 years, gives the licensee a non-exclusive right to conduct geological and geophysical surveys, prospecting and prospecting-estimation operations for oil and/or gas within the limits of the area specified in the license

9.2. Prior to issuing the prospecting license the licensing authority shall ensure its state registration following the procedures established in the present Law but no later than 30 days from the date of the licensing authority's decision about issuing such license.

9.3. The licensing authority shall have the right to issue the prospecting licenses for the same segment of the subsoil to several candidates simultaneously.

9.4. The prospecting license shall be issued on the basis of direct negotiations no later than 90 days from the moment of receiving a duly drawn and legally authentic application of a candidate with the exception of cases stipulated in Article 8.10 of the present Law.

9.5. Prospecting license shall not grant the licensee the right to conduct other activities in the domain of oil and gas or to conduct prospecting operations and extraction of other resources in the license area.

9.6. The licensing authority shall have the right at any moment to include the segment of the subsoil and territory (or its part) for which a prospecting license has been issued into the area of the operational license which is to be issued. The licensee shall be notified about such decision no later than 7 days after the date of such decision. Any other change of the terms and conditions and the duration of the prospecting license shall be possible only on the basis of a written consent of the parties.

9.7. Possession of the prospecting license shall not give the licensee any priority right against other candidates to acquire the operational license if the prospecting license area is included into the area of the operational license which is to be issued.

9.8. Prospecting license shall be terminated from the moment the licensee is notified about the decision taken and the licensee shall be paid back from budget funds part of his previous investments in the amount proportional to the unused duration of the license in the calendar year (proceeding from the amount of his annual contribution).

9.9. The licensee shall be the owner of the geological, geophysical and other types of information acquired by him in the process of prospecting operations within the framework of the license and shall be entitled to dispose of this information at his discretion taking into account the terms and conditions of the license in accordance with the procedure provided for by relevant normative acts of the licensing authority, including submitting to the licensing authority geological data and statements on the results of the completed work within the framework of the prospecting license.

9.10. The licensee shall submit to the licensing authority the information required by it on the intended activities, methods and means thereof in accordance with the procedures provided for by normative acts of the licensing authority.

9.11. The licensee shall be entitled at any moment to waive (entirely or partially) conduct of prospecting operations in licensing area by notifying the licensing authority in writing about such intention 90 days prior to the termination of the operations; this shall not relieve the licensee from the relevant obligations assumed by him before his decision about the waiver and the licensee shall be obliged to fulfil the minimum amount of work provided for in the terms and conditions of the license.

9.12. The licensing authority may provide for a minimal size and configuration of the area to be abandoned by the licensee in the terms and conditions of the license.

9.13. The licensing authority shall determine the list of types of prospecting operations, which the licensee may conduct within the framework of the prospecting license; drilling to the depth exceeding 200 meters from the surface of the earth or of the sea bed shall not be provided for. The licensing authority upon agreement with the licensee may introduce changes into this list proceeding from specific technological conditions and specific features of conducting operations within the framework of the license that emerged after operations were initiated.

9.14. Prospecting license cannot be issued for the operational license area.

9.15. Prospecting license shall not give the licensee the right to sell or alienate in any other form the natural resources extracted in the process of prospecting operations.

9.16. Contents and form of prospecting license shall be described in Annex No 2 'Model Clauses for Documents Included in the Licensing Agreement (License)', which shall constitute an integral part of the present Law.

Article 10   Operational License

10.1. Operational license shall give the licensee the exclusive right to conduct prospecting, exploration and drilling operations, deposits development, oil and/or gas production, construction and operation of pipelines within the oil or gas deposit for oil and/or gas transportation to the collection point, erection of other necessary installations of infrastructure and buildings, use of the subsoil for storage of extracted resources or for the liquidation of production wastes primary processing of the extracted resources (reduction of hydrosulphides in their composition, desalting and dehydration, etc.) as well as their initial refining in the field for the purpose of fuel production for heating boilers and engines to meet the needs of the licensee within the framework of the license, and local needs.

10.2. Contents and form of operational license shall be described in Annex No 2 'Model Clauses for Documents Included in the Licensing Agreement (License)', which shall constitute an integral part of the present Law.

10.3. The licensee shall have the right to dispose of at his discretion of the part of produced oil or gas which are the licensee's property under the terms and conditions of the license including their use to ensure the activities within the framework of the license, processing as is defined in 10.1, transportation, sale and export but other than premeditated destruction unless it is related to production technology or stipulated by force-majeure circumstances.

10.4. The licensee shall also be the owner, together with the State, of any information obtained in the process of activities within the framework of the operational license, related to the license area on the conditions of joint shared ownership (joint title) to the extent stipulated in the terms and conditions of the license regarding participation of the State

10.5. The licensee shall have the right to attract for his entrepreneurship purposes within the framework of the operational license, another subject of activities in the sphere of oil and/or gas irrespective of his form of ownership and citizenship if the latter meets qualification requirements of the licensing authority and assumes obligations to comply with the license terms and conditions.

10.6. The operational license shall become effective on the day of its state registration.

10.7. Prior to issuance of the operational license the licensing authority shall ensure its state registration following the order established by the present Law but no later than 30 days after an appropriate decision is made by the licensing authority.

10.8. The duration of the operational license shall be 25 years and may be prolonged repeatedly (each prolongation period shall be five years) by the licensing authority at the initiative of the licensee up to the termination of commercial production at the deposit site included in the license development area, given the compliance by the licensee with the terms and conditions of the license and a timely submission of an application in due format on the prolongation of the license.

In the present Law 'commercial production' shall mean the extraction of oil and/or gas in amounts ensuring the licensee the return of production costs and taxation payments as well as the normal rate of profit for the capital invested.

'Development area' shall mean part of the license area where geological structures containing oil and/or gas reserves sufficient for their commercial production have been discovered.

Article 11   Licensee's Activities during the Period of Prospecting-Exploration Operations within the Framework of the Operational License

11.1. The period of prospecting-exploration operations shall commence from the moment of state registration and continue up to 8 (eight) years, wherever necessary with the under agreement by the parties the licensing authority may prolong such period, but for no longer than 3 years.

11.2. The operational license terms and conditions shall stipulate that during this period of time the licensee should fulfil in the license area within the framework of the overall programme of prospecting and exploration operations agreed with the licensing authority, an obligatory minimum of such work at the agreed value thereof.

11.3. The licensee's obligations concerning the agreed value of prospecting exploration operations shall reflect all the expenditures related to geology, geophysics, engineering work, equipment, drilling, reasonable costs related to management staff, equipment and employees transportation to and from the license area, as well as other expenses in accordance with the generally accepted world practice in the oil and gas industry.

11.4. Upon completion of the period of prospecting-exploration operations the licensee shall pay to the budget of the Russian Federation the difference (if any) between the amount of money actually spent and agreed value obligations for prospecting-exploration operations for the entire period of the operations.

11.5. The licensee shall be obliged as soon as practically possible prior to the termination of the period of prospecting-exploration operations determine on his own if the discovery made is of commercial nature on the basis of geological, operational and economic information at his disposal, assess the explored discovery and present to the licensing authority a precise description of boundaries and designation of plots of the deposit in the license area included in the development area, as well as geological, technical and economic information related to this area in accordance with normative acts of the licensing authority. All segments of the deposit not included into the development area shall be excluded from the operational license area upon the termination of the period of prospecting-exploration operations.

11.6. If upon expiration of the period of prospecting-exploration operations the licensee has shown no interest in its renewal and has not announced the commercial discovery, he shall be obliged to terminate his operations work and leave the area of the operational license (or part of it) following procedures set forth in the present Law.

In the present Law 'commercial discovery' shall mean that the licensee acknowledges the possibility of the development and operation of such oil and/or gas deposit for commercial purposes.

Article 12   Licensee's Activities during the Development Period within the Framework of the Operational License

12.1. The development period at the sites of the deposit included in the development area shall commence from the moment of announcing by the licensee of the commercial discovery to the licensing authority, and shall end with due regard to possible subsequent prolongations after such exhaustion of oil and/or gas reserves when their commercial production is no longer provided, or earlier at the discretion of the licensee, provided meeting of demands and obligations set forth in the present Law and the license concerning notification time limits about such intention and volumes of minimum obligatory work and their agreed value, or in case of termination of the license on the grounds provided for in Article 23 of the present Law.

12.2. The licensee shall inform the licensing authority about the way the commercial discovery was made, and no later than 90 days after the announcement about it shall submit to the licensing authority for consideration an overall programme and an approximate estimate of expenses for the development area for the entire period of the license.

12.3. The licensing authority if necessary may request the licensee to submit additional information (such request being of mandatory nature) as well as to propose changes in the overall programme and the approximate estimate of expenditures. The licensing authority shall notify the licensee in writing about approval or rejection of the overall programme and the approximate estimate of expenditures within the period not exceeding 90 days from the date of their submission.

12.4. In case of approval of the overall programme and the approximate estimate of expenditures, the licensee shall submit to the licensing authority a working programme and approximate estimate of expenditures for the current and after the 15th of October – for the next calendar year. Annual working programmes and the approximate estimates of expenditures should fit in the main framework of the overall programme and the approximate estimate of expenditures, and should correspond to the generally accepted world practice.

12.5. The licensing authority shall be entitled to propose its modification to the working programme and the approximate estimate of expenditures for the next calendar year. The licensee shall be notified in writing about the approval or rejection of his working programme and the approximate estimate of expenditures for the year within 30 days from the date of their submission.

12.6. Significant amendments, changes and additions proposed by the licensee at any time to overall programme and the approximate estimate of expenditures for the development approved by the licensing authority, as well as to the annual working programmes and the approximate estimate of expenditures shall require agreement with the licensing authority.

12.7. If the licensing authority has serious specific objections with regard to the programme and the approximate estimate of expenditures submitted by the licensee, based on the present Law and terms and conditions of the license, the licensee shall be notified in writing about the essence of the objections and may introduce necessary corrections, changes and additions in order to meet the requirements of the licensing authority or discuss with the licensing authority possibilities of settling the conflict.

12.8. If the parties reach no compromise regarding the programme and the approximate estimate of expenditures within 30 days after their rejection by the licensing authority, each of the parties shall be entitled to bring the matter to the court of arbitration upon their agreement, or the arbitrage court. In this case the licensee shall be entitled to conduct operations within the framework of the license other than operations which caused objections of the licensing authority.

12.9. If arbitrators decide that the programme and expenditures estimate are in conformity with the terms and conditions of the license and generally accepted world practice in the oil and gas industry, they shall be considered approved by the licensing authority. If arbitrators decide that the programme and the expenditures estimate are inadequate, the licensee may either reconsider them taking into account the proposals of the licensing authority and resubmit them for consideration, or waive its right to the license without retaining any obligations or responsibilities for the development area and the right to compensation of expenses according to the terms and conditions of the license and the present Law.

12.10. If after the delineation of the development area the geological structures of the commercial discovery turn out to extend beyond the boundaries of the development area, the development area may be accordingly increased within the area of such license and in accordance with paragraph 12.11. of the present Law.

12.11. If geological structures of the commercial discovery extend beyond the boudaries of such license at the site which was not abandoned by the licensee in the past and which is not related to another operational license, the development area, at the request of the licensee may be enlarged with the consent of the licensing authority, who issued this license but not more than 25%.

12.12. In case the licensee is interested in enlarging the development area in excess of the limits set forth in paragraph 12.11, he shall be entitled to apply to the licensing authority for another (or several) operational licenses within the limits of this deposit on the conditions, specified through direct negotiations.

Article 13   Activities of Different Licensees on One Deposit

13.1. If several operational licenses are valid at an oil and gas deposit, all licensees must carry out their activities in agreement on the basis of jointly developed plans of prospecting, exploration, development and production operations. Joint plans, developed and agreed among all the licensees, shall be submitted for consideration to the licensing authority, who within 30 days after such submission shall notify the licensees about approval or rejection of these plans.

13.2. If the licensees do not come to agreement on the joint plan of operations within one year after such requirement was set, or the licensing authority disagrees with the joint plan of operations, submitted by licensees, the licensing authority shall have the right to demand corrections to the joint plan with due regard to the objections made by the licensing authority, or shall oblige the licensees to conduct operations at such deposit on the terms and according to the plan of the licensing authority, pursuing such aims as rational use of oil and/or gas resources, their preservation, minimizing production wastes, oil reservoirs recovery enhancement, inadmissibility of excessive drilling and other redundant activities, fair establishment of production shares for each licensee as extracted resources diminish.

13.3. The licensing authority shall notify the licensees in advance about its intention regarding the joint plan of operations in order to give them an opportunity to present their reasoning. If any of the licensees expresses disagreement with rejection of the joint plan of the operations or objects to such plan and conditions of operations set by the licensing authority, the licensee whose rights or interests are affected by such a decision of the licensing authority, shall have the right to litigate it in court of arbitration upon agreement of the parties or the arbitrage court.

Article 14   Prolongation of Operational License

14.1. The licensee shall have the right to address the licensing authority with an application for prolongation of the duration of his operational license for the part the development area, where commercial production is carried out, no earlier than two years and no later than one year prior to termination of the current term of the license.

The application shall be drawn in accordance with Annex No 2 to the present Law.

14.2. In case of the prolongation of the license, the licensee shall be charged a special fee, the formula for which shall be set in the terms and conditions of the license.

14.3. Prolongation of the operational license shall not entail any modifications of its original terms and conditions unless otherwise fixed in the license or if there is a consent of the parties to modify the terms and conditions of the license in case of its prolongation. This shall not apply to the part of the license, the rights to which were earlier lost by the licensee or nullified.

14.4. The operational license shall remain in force:

● until its prolongation by the licensing authority in accordance with the duly drawn and timely submitted application of the licensee;
● prior to the decision in court of arbitration upon agreement of the parties, or in the arbitrage court, if the licensee contests the licensing authority' refusal to prolong the license.

Article 15   Granting of License Superceding Rights for Activities in the Domain of Oil and Gas, Valid Prior to the Adoption of the Present Law

15.1. From the time of entry to force of the present Law the requirement for necessity to obtain a license shall also be applied to those subjects of activities (production enterprises, associations, consortia, etc.) in the domain of oil and/or gas, which commenced operation prior to the adoption of the present Law.

15.2. In order to obtain the operational license the acting subject shall submit an application to the licensing authority within 60 days from the entry into force of the present Law in the form, described in Annex No 2 to the present Law certified by notary and also present substantiative documents (their copies) confirming the fact and the grounds for the transfer of the specific deposit of oil and/or gas (or its part) to the given subject of activities and that this deposit contains oil and gas in commercial quantities.

The term for considering the application shall not exceed ninety (90) days from the date of its submission during which the subject of activities shall continue its activities on the earlier terms.

The absence or untimely submission of the application by the subject of activities without a valid objective reason may be considered by the licensing authority as a refusal to obtain the license and may lead to a ban on continuation of operations in this deposit of oil and/or gas.

15.3. If the acting user conducts operations on the site of the deposit, the size of which exceeds the maximum, set for one operational license, an application shall be submitted for the required number of licenses within the boundaries of this site.

15.4. If application and submitted substantiative documents are recognized by the licensing authority as compliant to meeting the requirements of the present Law, the given subject of activities within ninety (90) days after the filing of the application shall be issued the operational license.

15.5. In case there are competitive applications, the license shall be granted to the subject of activities, whose confirmative documents were issued by a higher level state agency with regard to the law previously in effect. In case confirmative documents are equally authoritative, the licensing authority shall grant one operational license to several subjects of activities on terms of joint participatory share ownership which justly take into account their rights and interests.

15.6. Operational license, issued to an acting subject, shall grant him all rights of a licensee in accordance with the present Law; it shall be considered to be valid from the date of its state registration and shall remain in force with due regard to possible prolongation within the period, specified in Article 10.5 of the present Law.

15.7. Decision on refusal to grant the operational license for a deposit under operation or deposit being explored (part of the deposit) by the subject of activities shall be delivered to him with substantiated explanation of the reasons for the refusal no later than 180 days from the date of coming into force of the present Law. Upon expiration of this period of time all his rights to activities in the domain of oil and/or gas at this site of the deposit shall be terminated, if the acting subject within 7 days after this period of time fails to address the court of arbitration or arbitrage court or the ordinary court. If the claim is filed within the established period of time, the subject of activities shall have the right to continue his activities until the court takes a relevant decision.

15.8. Granting an operational license to the acting subject of activities shall preserve valid his current arrangements with his partners concerning joint economic activities and other forms of cooperation in the domain of oil and gas at the licensed site of the deposit.

15.9. The subjects of activities in the domain of oil and/or gas who prior to the adoption of the present Law by the Supreme Soviet of the Russian Federation were granted the right to conduct relevant operations in specified areas, but who for any reason have not started them, may exercise these rights in compliance with the requirements of the present Law through obtaining operational licenses with commencement date license operations, postponed for no longer than 2 years, provided the fulfillment of minimal obligatory scope of work in terms of its agreed cost is agreed with the licensing authority during this period of time.

15.10. Any rights to conduct operations in the domain of oil and/or gas, after the adoption of the present Law by the Supreme Soviet of the Russian Federation, may be granted within only the framework of the appropriate license in compliance with the present Law.

15.11. Arrangements, reached prior to the adoption of the present Law by the Supreme Soviet of the Russian Federation within the framework of the negotiations between acting subjects and any other subjects of activities in the domain of oil and/or gas, concerning joint activities at the sites of the deposits shall remain in force.

15.12. If the acting subject does not intend to conclude the license agreement for the site of the deposit in whose regard an agreement was obtained earlier with any other subjects of activities, in this case, the acting subject shall notify the licensing authority in writing about the availability of such agreement, as well as about his intentions to waive the licensing of the site of the deposit no later than 60 days after coming into force of the present Law.

After such a notification the licensing authority shall be entitled to commence direct negotiations with interested parties concerning the license for this site of the deposit on terms and conditions without infringing upon the interests of the state, and the interested party with maximum approximation to the terms and conditions of the original agreement or offer the given site for a contest or auction in a routine manner.

15.13. In case of competition between the parties concerned the operational license may be granted to a candidate who offered the most advantageous conditions for the state or on terms of joint shared ownership to several candidates as provided for in Article 15.5 of the present Law.

15.14. Contests announced by the decision of competent state bodies before the present Law was adopted by the Supreme Soviet of the Russian Federation for the right to conduct oil and gas production activities in the Russian territory as set forth in Article 1.1 of the present Law in the exclusive economic zone and on the continental shelf of the Russian Federation shall be conducted in accordance with the originally announced terms.

Article 16 Transfer and Assignment of the Rights within Operational License Limits

16.1. The licensee shall have the right to transfer, assign, put in pledge, dispose of as a whole or in any other way his rights (their part), obligations and his share in production distribution within the framework of the license with regard to any subject of activities in the domain of oil and/or gas having received an obligatory written consent of licensing authority to do so.

16.2. Unless otherwise provided for in the terms and conditions of the agreement on rights transfer within the framework of the license, the subject of activities who is granted appropriate rights shall assume at the same time an appropriate part of obligations within the framework of the license.

16.3. The licensing authority cannot impede the transfer of rights by the licensee with the following exceptions:

1. the subject of activities to whom the right is transferred is not, in the opinion of the licensing authority, sufficiently competent technically, organizationally or financially to receive an operational license, and it would fail to obtain the license if he tried to do so on his own;
2. the licensee has not remedied the violations and debts regarding the terms and conditions of the license;
3. the licensee has seriously violated the terms and conditions of the license and the present Law and failed to remedy these violations, whereas the subject of activities who is receiving the right does not assume the obligations to remedy them.

16.4. In case of transfer of rights to a subsidiary the parent company shall retain responsibility and warranties to the licensing authority for the compliance with the terms and conditions of the license by the subsidiary.

The transfer of rights to a subsidiary shall not require consent of the licensing authority, its written notification shall be sufficient.

16.5. The licensing authority shall notify the licensee in writing about consent to transfer or assign the rights, or shall submit a substantiated refusal within sixty (60) days after the receipt of the relevant application by the licensee. The absence of the licensing authority's response after the expiration of this term shall be regarded as consent for the transfer or assignment of rights.

16.6. In case of transfer, assignment or other forms of disposition of the rights of the licensee within the framework of the license including the sale of controlling block of stocks within the framework of the license of an affiliate or any other company, the change of the licensee's title of ownership shall not be allowed except exclusive cases, when the licensee cannot retain the title due to objective reasons; obligatory written consent of the licensing authority to change the title of ownership within the framework of the license.

16.6. Any transfer or assignment of rights conducted in accordance with the present Law shall not require any payment and shall be subject to no taxation.

Article 17   Inspection of Activities within License Limits

17.1. The licensing authority shall have the right to appoint inspectors including persons invited from other authoritative state organizations related to activities in the domain of oil and gas in order to conduct control (monitoring) over the routine activities of the licensee and its compliance with the requirements of the present Law and terms and conditions of the license.

17.2. Inspectors shall have the right of access at any reasonable time to all premises and documentation related to activities within the license to be inspected. They may request suspension or termination of a certain type of activities within the framework of the license if these activities are not provided for by terms and conditions of the license or are conducted with serious violations of terms and conditions of the license and the present Law. The licensing authority shall have the right to allow access to installations together with inspectors to official representative of state power bodies, other state organizations related to the activities in the domain of oil and gas.

17.3. The licensee shall be charged for the necessary (within reasonable limits) expenditures related to inspection of the licensee's activities except the expenditures for salaries or other fees to the inspectors from the budget.

17.4. The inspector shall notify the licensee in writing about the revealed drawbacks and shall warn him of the necessity of their rectification within the shortest period of time technically feasible. Simultaneously the inspector shall inform the licensing authority of the results of the inspection, which in case of gross violations may impose appropriate sanctions up to suspension of the license for a period of time necessary for rectifying the violations (if it is possible) or shall terminate the license; the licensee shall be notified in writing about the intentions of the licensing authority to apply sanctions by the results of the inspection.

Article 18   Granting Rights to Plots of Land

18.1. The availability of the license shall give the licensee the right to use a certain plot of land for activities in the domain of oil and gas in accordance with the Land Code of the Russian Federation unless the licensee is already the owner of the given plot of land.

18.2. Prior to signing the license agreement on the activities in the domain of oil and gas, and later in the course of such activities, the licensing authority obtain all necessary authorizations from the owners and users of land plots, owners of installations located on them within the license area as well as with territorial bodies of state power and administration and shall ensure obtaining authorizations required in such cases and documents including land allotments in accordance with the Land Code of the Russian Federation.

18.3. Bodies of land tenure system at the request of the licensing authority shall allot the required plots of land for activities in the domain of oil and gas within the framework of the license with the exception of cases provided for in the Land Code of the Russian Federation.

18.4. If the licensing authority for some reason has not ensured required consents and authorizations for the use of land within the license limits the licensee shall be entitled to:

- demand that the licensing authority ensure the receipt of necessary consents and arrangements in accordance with the legislation of the Russian Federation proceeding in doing so, if necessary, from state interests and/or social needs of the given territory;
- voluntarily abandon the plot of land within the framework of the license which cannot be used without appropriate consent; in this case at the request of the licensing authority the licensee shall be returned an appropriate part of the bonus and lease payments. The availability of such possibilities for the licensee shall be appropriately reflected in the terms and conditions of the license.

18.5. The licensee shall be obliged to systematically eliminate negative consequences caused by unintentionally inflicted damage to agriculture, water-supply systems, buildings and other installations due to conducting activities within the framework of the license within the shortest period of time possible and to the extent which is practically possible.

Article 19   Use of Infrastructure Facilities within License Area for General Use Purposes

19.1. The licensing authority at the request of the territorial bodies of power may include in the license additional terms concerning obligations of the licensee to place roads, canals and bridges constructed by him for the purpose of general use if such use of these installations is allowed by norms of the operation set in the Russian territory and if it will have no negative consequences for the results of the activities within the framework of the license including the licensee's expenses.

19.2. The licensee shall have the right to use on a general basis the installations of infrastructure and social sphere, designated for general use, located in the license area to ensure the activities within the framework of the license and normal conditions of life for the employees and family members in accordance with the Law of the Russian Federation and instructions of the territorial bodies of power.

Article 20   Use of Local Labour and Material Resources

The licensing authority may provide reasonable requirements in terms and conditions of the license, for attracting local labour for activities within the framework of the license (including organization of training) and the use of local raw materials and other materials, other products and services, affordable to the licensee in terms of prices and with the quality which meets the standards, adopted in the Russian Federation.

Article 21   Participation of the State in the Activities within the Framework of the License

21.1. In the Russian territory as provided for in Article 1.1. of the present Law, on the continental shelf and in the exclusive economic zone of the Russian Federation under terms and conditions of any operational license, with the exception of production sharing type licenses, obligatory participation of the state (the representative appointed by it) on the share basis shall be provided for; the share of state participation shall be determined in each particular case taking into account the interests of the Russian Federation and reasonable limits which correspond to the good world practice.

21.2. Licensee shall be notified by the licensing authority in writing about the state (the representative appointed by it) participation simultaneously with the approval of the overall program and approximate expenses estimate for activities in the development area.

21.3. The state participation shall apply to the development areas within the framework of the license only and shall commence (come into force) no later than in 90 (ninety) days following the approval by the licensing authority of the overall program and approximate expenses estimate for activities in the development area submitted by the licensee.

As soon as the state commences to participate in the activities within the framework of the license it shall acquire the right of owner to part of extracted resources as well as other rights and obligations (including those related to expenditures) proportionally to the share of its participation.

21.4. After the commencement of commercial production within the license limits the state shall compensate to the prime Licensee respectively to the share of its participation the previous expenses (i.e. from the moment of license entry into force prior to the commencement of the state participation), including at the expense of the part of extracted oil and gas which were destined for the state either in kind or in monetary form estimated on the basis of their current market value; conditions and procedure for indemnifying the licensee for the resources spent by the prime licensee (entirely or partially) including in the currency which was used to pay for the expenses shall be provided for in terms and conditions of the license.

Article 22   Voluntary and Forced Abandonment of Territory within Operational License Limits

22.1. At the end of any calendar year within the license duration the licensee shall have the right to voluntarily abandon in full or in part the territory granted to him within the framework of the license by notifying the licensing authority about such intention in writing no at least 90 days before the abandonment.

22.2. Unless otherwise stipulated in the license, the part of the territory to be abandoned shall have without detriment to the licensee as practically feasible, such size and configuration as well as accessibility so that the licensing authority could offer it in the future to other subjects for activities in the domain of oil and/or gas.

22.3. Abandonment of the territory shall neither exempt the licensee from the obligations in respect to the abandoned area set forth in the license, which had not been fulfilled by the moment of the abandonment of the territory, nor shall it diminish his obligations to conduct minimum amount of work in terms of its agreed cost for the entire period of prospecting and exploration work.

If the licensee leaves the license area completely without having fulfilled the obligations on minimum amount of work in terms of its agreed cost, the licensing authority shall oblige him to pay the amount equal to the unspent part of the agreed cost of work, which was planned before the end and of the period of work within the framework of the license in accordance with licensee's obligations.

22.4. Otherwise stipulated in the license, the licensee after (4) years of work on land shall be obliged to abandon 50%, and after six years - 75% of the territory in the license area, at sea - 50% after five years and 75% after 7 years. excluding plots included in the development area.

22.5. The part of the territory in the license area which is abandoned voluntarily in accordance with para 22.1. shall be accounted as included into the territory which is abandoned in accordance with Article 22.4. of the present Law.

22.6. While abandoning the part of the territory included in the development area, the licensee shall submit to the licensing authority a revised overall and annual program as well as approximate general and annual expenditures estimate for in the development area proceeding from the date of abandonment of the territory.

22.7. The licensing authority shall notify the licensee in writing about the approval or denial of the suggested modifications within 30 (thirty) days after their submission; in case of disagreement with the decision of the licensing authority the licensee shall be entitled to apply to the court of arbitration by the agreement of the parties, or arbitrage court.

Article 23　Suspension of the Right to Activities within the Framework of the License

23.1. The licensing authority shall have the right to suspend the license in the case when the licensee:

- violates the terms and conditions of the license and/or does not fulfil the assumed obligations including financial ones;
- conducts the activities within the framework of the license following the program which was not approved by the licensing authority ;
- conducts activities which are not stipulated by the given license;
- impedes by his actions the implementation of other economic activities to the extent exceeding the first necessity for ensuring the normal production process within the framework of the license;
- violates other provisions of the present Law and other legislative and normative acts acting in the Russian Federation.

23.2. The licensing authority shall notify the licensee in writing about its intentions to suspend the license and the reasons which caused it no later than 90 (ninety) days before such intention is realized. If the licensee within this period of time is capable to remove these reasons and brings its activities in accordance with the terms and conditions of the license and the present Law, the licensing authority shall state its waiver of its claim to the licensee.

23.3. The licensee shall have the right in accordance with Article 70 of the present Law to contest the decision of the licensing authority on suspension of the license; in this case entry into force of such a decision on suspension of the license shall be postponed until a decision of the arbitrage or ordinary court whose decision shall be final.

23.4. The licensing authority shall suspend the license in case the reasons for the suspension can be removed by the licensee and for the period of time required for their removal, after which the license is immediately renewed.

Article 24   Termination of License

24.1. The licensing authority shall have the right to terminate the license ahead of time if:

    (a) the fact that deliberately falsified information which had affected the decision in respect of granting the license to the given subject of activities was submitted to the licensing authority has been revealed;

    (b) the licensee was declared bankrupt in court;

    (c) the licensee does not fulfil on a systematic basis the obligations stipulated in the license, the decisions of the court or the court of arbitration and relevant provisions of the present Law including those in the part related to ensuring safety of work, life of the population, protection of the environment and preservation of natural resources;

    (d) in the event force majeur circumstances in accordance with the procedure for activities in force majeur circumstances as set forth in terms and conditions of the license, as well as in other cases, stipulated by the present Law.

24.2. The licensing authority shall notify the licensee about the intention to terminate the license ahead of time, and the licensee shall have the right to contest the decision of the licensing authority in the same procedure as it is provided for in Articles 23.2 and 23.3 of the present Law respectively.

Article 25   Order of Activities, Joint and Several and Individual Responsibility of Licensees Operating within the Framework of One License

25.1. If activities within the limits of one license is conducted by several licensees who have the rights of owners (joint title) they shall be obliged to determine and appoint the licensee-operator who shall be competent enough and meet the technical and financial requirements generally accepted in world practice in the oil and gas industry necessary to fulfil the duties of the operator. The licensee-operator shall perform functions of an organizer and shall administrate the activities within the framework of the license and shall serve as a link between the licensing authority and other licensees. The licensee who is appointed the operator shall immediately inform the licensing authority about his appointment.

25.2. Unless otherwise stipulated in the license terms and conditions, the licensees acting within the framemwork of one license with the rights of owners (joint title) shall be jointly and severely responsible for fulfilling terms and obligations fixed in the license except taxation liabilities.

25.3. Each of the licensees acting within the framework of one license with the rights of owners (joint title) shall bear individual responsibility in regard to payment of any taxes.

25.4. The licensing authority shall bear no responsibility for improper actions or omissions of the licensee or subject whom the rights of the licensee were transferred to, which caused damage to the third party or brought about its substantiated claims.

Article 26   Guarantees

The licensing authority shall have the right to provide for within the license terms and conditions obligations of the licensee to present within the agreed period the guarantees of a specified type in order to ensure fulfilment of the terms and conditions of the license from authoritative legal and/or physical persons including banking and other credit organizations as well as international organizations which are satisfactory to the licensing authority.

Article 27   Confidentiality

27.1. All data, reports and other information related to the license area which the licensee submitted to the licensing authority in accordance with the license terms and conditions shall be confidential within the period agreed in the license terms and conditions.

27.2. The requirement for compliance with the confidentiality in accordance with Article 27.1. in regard to the information obtained from the licensees shall apply to all persons who have access to this information on legal grounds.

27.3. The licensing authority may use these materials for preparation of reports and general informational reviews in regard to activities in the domain of oil and gas in the Russian Federation.

Article 28   Abandonment of Installations within the Framework of the license in Case of Termination of the License

28.1. The licensing authority may provide for in the license the terms and procedure for abandonment by the licensee of his property (abandon) in the form of wells, fixed and other installations and equipment, located in the license area upon expiration of its duration term, as well as in the case of waiver by the licensee of his rights within the framework of the license for the whole area (its part) or in termination of the license ahead of time upon the licensing authority's decision in compliance with Article 23 of the present Law.

28.2. The licensee shall have the right not to leave his property in the territory to be abandoned if he intends to use these installations and equipment in the future within or beyond the area of the given license.

28.3. The licensing authority shall notify in writing the licensee about the future abandonment of the installation as well as about the intentions of the state regarding the future of the installations to be abandoned no later than one year before the license duration term is expired, either simultaneously the notification of intention to terminate the license ahead of time in accordance with Article 23 of the present Law, or immediately upon the receipt of the written notification from the licensee about waiver of his rights for the whole license area or its part.

28.4. Within the time period of no later than six (6) weeks after the receipt of the written notification about abandonment of installations and proceeding from the intent of the state regarding the future of the installations to be abandoned the licensee shall submit to the licensing authority a program of their abandonment, preservation and neutralization in order not to create obstacles or difficulties for any further activities in the area of their location and ensure meeting the environmental protection requirements.

28.5. If the licensing authority notifies the licensee in writing about inexpedience of abandoning installations and equipment, the licensee shall be obliged within the time period of no later than six (6) months after the receipt of the notification to submit to the licensing authority a program for dismantlement of installations and equipment and the neutralization programme for installations to be forcefully abandoned so that in future they do not create obstacles or difficulties for any activities in the area of their location and meet the environmental protection requirements.

Article 29   Import and Export from the Russian Federation to Ensure Activities within the Framework of the License

29.1. The licensee and other subjects of activities to whom the licensee transferred relevant rights in accordance with Article 16 of the present Law as well as his subsidiaries and subcontractors operating in the framework of the license, shall have the right to import from abroad raw materials, materials and equipment as well as consumer goods and foodstuff within the volumes required for ensuring normal activities within the framework of the license without any import fees.

29.2. The licensee and other subjects of activities to whom the licensee transferred relevant rights in accordance with Article 16 of the present Law, shall have the right to export abroad from the Russian Federation their own or acquired on legal grounds raw materials, equipment and materials designated for foreign subsidiaries of the licensee and/or its subcontractors, which are linked with the licensee by the integrated technological process within the framework of the license, within the volumes required for ensuring normal activities within the framework of the license without paying any export fees.

29.3. Foreign citizens hired within the framework of the license, as well as members of their families shall have the right to export and import personal belongings (including automobiles) without paying any import and export fees and taxes.

29.4. Unless otherwise stipulated in the terms and conditions of the license, installations and equipment shall not be exported from the Russian Federation neither may they be sold by the licensee within the Russian Federation in accordance with Article 27 of the present Law, if the licensing authority has notified the licensee about their abandonment in the established procedure.

29.5. All mentioned in Articles 28.2. and 28.3. may be sold in the Russian territory provided appropriate import fees have been paid, with the exception of installations and equipment specified in Article 28.4. of the present Law.

Article 30 Licensee's Right of Ownership to Extracted Oil and Gas

30.1. The right of ownership (the title) to the extracted oil and gas, as well as the risk of their accidental destruction or damage shall be transferred to the licensee at the time and place specified in the license but no earlier than the moment the resource is extracted from the subsoil above the well (wellhead). If the time and place of the transfer of the right of ownership to the licensee's ownership is not specified, the licensee shall become the owner of the extracted oil and gas from the moment of their extraction from the subsoil above the well (wellhead).

30.2. Unless otherwise stipulated in the license, the licensee with the rights of the owner shall have the right to dispose of his due share of oil and gas extracted within the framework of the license including their export without any licenses and quotes, being guided in his other actions by the procedures for carrying out foreign economic activities established in the Russian territory.

Article 31 Deliveries of Oil and Gas Extracted within the Framework of the License for Internal Needs of the Russian Federation

31.1. The licensing authority shall have the right to provide for in the license terms and conditions the licensee's obligations to deliver a certain part of oil and gas extracted within the framework of the license for internal needs of the Russian Federation and conditions of such deliveries.

31.2. Settlements with and payments to Russian licensees and licensees from the states with rouble circulation for the delivered oil and gas shall be exercised in roubles at the internal market prices set at the moment of the deliveries; regarding foreign licensees- at world prices existing at the moment of delivery in a freely convertible currency specified in the license.

31.3. In case of emerging of a situation posing a threat to national security of the Russian Federation and within the whole period until the situation remains the Government of the Russian Federation in order to satisfy the needs of the country shall have the right of requisition of part of oil and gas extracted under all licenses (proportionally to the volume of extraction under each license) with payment to Russian licensees and licensees from the state with rouble circulation in roubles at the internal market prices set at the moment of the requisition; regarding foreign licensees - at current world prices at the moment of the requisition in any freely convertible currency.

Article 32 Currency Operations Conducted by the Licensee to Support the Activities within the Framework of the License

32.1. The licensee as well as the subjects of activities to whom the licensee transferred relevant rights in accordance with Article 16 of the present Law shall conduct in the Russian territory any currency operations within the framework of the license including payment of taxes and transfer of profits earned in foreign currency abroad from the Russian Federation in compliance with the current federal law of the Russian Federation and the rules for currency regulation.

32.2. Foreign licensees and foreign subcontractors as well as foreign subjects of activities to whom the licensee transferred relevant rights in accordance with Article 16 of the present Law shall have the right to export duty-free and without hindrance foreign currency means which were imported into the Russian territory on legal grounds for ensuring activities within the framework of the license, as well as foreign currency earned for obligatory delivery of part of oil and gas extracted for the internal needs of the Russian Federation or as payment for the resources requisitioned in accordance with Articles 31.2 and 31.3 of the present Law respectively.

Article 33   Stability and Invariability of License Terms and Conditions

33.1. All terms and conditions of the license and activities within the framework of the license shall comply with the legislation and normative acts of the Russian Federation and the republics within the Russian Federation which do not contradict Federal laws and acts active at the moment of the license issuance, as well as to the norms of international Law and the good world practice in the domain of oil and gas.

33.2. If after issuing the license the legislation on national security, preservation of resources and environmental protection, as well as other laws are altered, which forces the licensee to bear additional expenses within the framework of the license, the licensing authority may agree with the licensee upon the alterations in the license terms and conditions to reduce for the licensee if necessary, his economic, legal and other losses resulting from the changes in the legislation.

Article 34   Warning about Enforcement Measures and Their Application

34.1. If the licensee fails to fulfil his obligations under the terms and conditions of the license and the requirements of the present Law, the licensing authority shall forward a written notification to him about the intention to take relevant enforcement measures in ninety (90) days after receipt of the notification by the licensee.

34.2. If the licensee refuses to or is not capable of correcting the situation within the specified period, the licensing authority shall be entitled to take a decision on the use of enforcement measures in accordance with Articles 22 and 23 of the present Law, as well as on reimbursing all expenses related to it for the account of the licensee. The licensee shall be entitled to contest the decision of the licensing authority in the court of arbitration by agreement of the parties, arbitrage court or ordinary court in accordance with Article 70 of the present Law.

Section IV PROTECTION OF THE SUBSOIL AND THE ENVIRONMENT

Article 34   Obligations and Responsibility of the Licensee for the Preservation of the Subsoil and Environment

34.1. The licensee shall be obliged to conduct works within the framework of the license with the account of requirements of the present Law and other legislative acts of the Russian Federation with regard to regulation of the responsibility of the subsoil subjects of activities for the preservation of oil and gas resources and the environment. That shall mean:

- that reports be submitted to the licensing authority, showing the location of all oil and gas wells, logs, electrical surveys and other drilling and production records;

- that the drilling, operating, casing, and plugging of wells be done in such a manner as to prevent the escape of oil or gas out of one stratum to another;
- that each dry and abandoned well be plugged and that associated pits be closed;
- that measures be taken to prevent blow outs, caving and seepage;
- that no natural gas be flared or vented except in accordance with procedures and under conditions approved by the licensing authority;
- that enhanced recovery methods, including the introduction of gas, air, water, or other substance into producing formations not be undertaken except at the appropriate stage of development of a deposit so as to obtain maximum economic recovery;
- that the drilling, casing, cementing, disposal interval, monitoring, plugging and permitting of disposal wells which are used to inject waste products into the subsurface be done in such a manner as to prevent the escape of such waste products into a fresh groundwater aquifer or into oil or gas strata;
- that joint exploration and development plans or joint utilization plans be worked out and approved when a reservoir extends across more than one license area with different licensees;
- that documentation of the transportation of oil or gas off the license area be obtained and that the security of facilities be maintained to prevent theft of oil or gas;
- that the siting of facilities and the conduct of petroleum operations be done in a manner that minimizes adverse effects on the environment and natural resources through the use of environmental impact assessment and limits and conditions placed on petroleum operations in exploration and development plans while complying with the Environmental protection act of the Russian Federation, Subsoil Protection Act and Land Code of the Russian Federation;
- that oil spill prevention and countermeasures be properly planned and implemented;
- that a system of liability for offshore oil spills be established and adequacy of funds for liability and restoration be assured.

34.2. The licensee shall conduct activities in compliance with the requirements for protection of oil, gas and other mineral resources and the environment, including air, water, land, forests, animals and vegetation as well as buildings and constructions shall not permit violation and withdrawal of protected woodland and forest resources of the Russian Federation.

34.3. The licensee shall be obliged to have the approved plans for deposits development, their exploration and operation prior to the commencement of any operations. These plans must contain information concerning removing and rendering harmless waste products in the process of exploration and operation. The licensee shall be obliged to ensure compliance with all standards, rules and requirements of the legislative acts and resolutions of the government as well as terms and conditions of the license and the approved plan of search, exploration, and production of oil, disposal of production wastes into the environment in an ecologically safe manner with the consent of the ecological, mining and sanitary supervision bodies.

34.4. The licensee shall keep records and report to the licensing authority about all spills and leakages of oil and gas, produced waters toxic materials and wastes disposed into the environment at the quantities exceeding the permissible quantities, exercise control over withdrawal of contaminating materials and fire fighting.

34.5. The licensee shall have the emergency measures plan containing actions for protection of life, property and the environment against fire, explosions, spills, emergencies, related to interference of health protection bodies.

34.6. The licensee shall be responsible only for ecological violations and pollution of the environment resulted from his own economic activities and shall not be responsible for the baseline background pollution and violation.

34.7. The licensee's responsibility for the damage for the third persons shall be determined by relevant laws of the Russian Federation and the terms and conditions of the license. The damage caused by pollution shall mean: losses and damage to outside installations brought about by the pollution resulted from an oil spill or leakage from the installation and shall include expenses to prevent or minimize the damage caused by pollution; damage or losses outside the installations caused by decontaminating activities.

34.8. The licensee shall be responsible for the safety of all operations. Construction and operation of the enterprises producing mineral resources underground constructions of various designations, conduct of geological survey of the subsoil shall be allowed only if safety of life and health of employees of these enterprises and the population of the impact area of operations related to the use of the subsoil. The licensee shall be directly responsible for ensurance of safe conditions for operations related to use of the subsoil, regardless whether this enterprises conduct operations in compliance with the license granted to him or are employed for fulfilment of the operations under the contract.

34.9. The licensee conducting operations related to the use of the subsoil or other duly authorized officials in case of direct threat to the life and health of employees of these enterprises shall be obliged to suspend without delay the operations and ensure the removal of the people to a safe location.

In case of direct threat to life and health of the local population in the impact area of operations related to the use of the subsoil, managers of relevant enterprises shall be obliged to inform without delay the respective bodies of the state management and local administration about the event.

Compliance with the requirements of health protection and safety of operations shall not exempt the licensee from the responsibility for compliance with other laws and normative requirements.

Article 35   Environment Impact Assessment

35.1. The licensee shall conduct assessment of the impact on the environment which is part of the search and exploration plan and the development and production plan. Specific issues of the environment impact assessment shall be regulated by the current approved normative and legal acts and the present Law.

35.2. Within 90 days following the date of development and production plan receipt, region officials and other relative departments shall submit comments and recommendations to the Licensing authority. The environment protection body and local management bodies shall conduct in the vicinity of the license area public hearings to inform the population of the Assessment of the impact of the oil development and production plan on the environment. The environment protection body shall ensure timely notification of interested persons, public organizations and governmental bodies about such hearings. During public hearing the issues of potential negative impact on the environment shall be discussed including the issues of the use of the subsoil, wells control, air and water pollution protection, wastes withdrawal, restoration of property and the procedure for wells and installations liquidation upon the completion of the operations, training, monitoring and emergency readiness plans.

35.3. The environment protection body shall assess the impact on the environment of all types of activities described in the development and production plan. No later than 60 days after the receipt of the document this body shall take one of the following decisions:

- to approve the plan specifying limitations and conditions of operations by the licensee which diminish negative impact on the environment and the natural resources and prevent waste of oil and gas;
- to demand that the licensee shall alter any plan contradicting the provisions of the license, the present Law, acts (issued under the present Law or any other laws of the Russian Federation;
- disapprove the plan, if the environment protection body finds that the intended activities threatens health or safety of local population or may considerably damage property, the environment, natural resources, other mineral resources or state security and that the intended activities cannot be changed without damage or loss.

35.4. The environment protection body shall notify the licensee in writing about reasons for disapproval of the development and production plan or about requirements to change the plan and conditions which should be met for approval of this plan. The licensee may resubmit his development and protection plan as modified to the environment protection body within 60 days following the 90 day term for submission of comments to the decisions specified in Article 35.6 of the present Law. The environment protection body shall approve, disapprove or demand alterations of the resubmitted plan.

35.5. The licensee in accordance with the new information may at his own initiative change the plan when any activities or intended activities of the licensee can introduce considerable changes to earlier determined and assessed impacts. In addition to such operations the licensee shall annually consider, assess and change the plan and the budget.

35.6. The environment protection body shall periodically consider activities conducted under the approved development and production plan. The frequency and the degree of the analysis of the activities of the licensee by environment protection body shall depend upon considerable changes in the available information and conditions of executing operations aimed at exploration, drilling, development or production, conducted under the plan. If this consideration leads to a decision in favour of changing the plan, the environment protection body shall request the introduction of necessary alterations.

35.7. Alteration of the approved development and production plan or the plan under consideration made by the licensee or required by the environment protection body shall be submitted to the environment protection body for approval. If the environment protection body decides that the proposed alteration may bring about substantial changes in previously determined and assessed impacts, such alterations shall be reflected in all procedures of this article.

35.8. When any alteration of the approved development and production plan is proposed by the licensee, the environment protection body may endorse the alteration provided the alteration is considered as complaint with the objectives of the present Law.

Article 36 Protection of the Subsoil and the Environment in the Search, Exploration, Development and Production Plans

36.1. The licensee shall not commence prospecting operations until the search and exploration plan or the development and production plan is approved. The plans should contain sufficient information to allow the environment protection body:

- to assess whether the planned operations prevent waste of oil and gas and whether they minimize negative impact of oil and gas production on the environment and natural resources;
- to control compliance with the requirement of the present Law for preservation of oil and gas resources and environment protection and any other laws of the Russian Federation on environment protection.

36.2. Entire oil an gas activities of the licensee shall meet requirements, restrictions, and conditions of the search plan and the development and production plan or approved changes of the plans.

36.3. The provisions of this Section and approved plans shall not limit the licensee's responsibility for taking appropriate measures in emergencies.

36.4. The search and exploration plan for exploration licenses should contain precise information regarding the location of surveys, including the description of the intended programme of surveys; description of survey method including technical characteristics of the employed techniques of the survey; the description of vehicles or aircraft used for the survey. The licensee shall submit the search and exploration plan which includes a concise environmental impact assessment in the area of intended seismic operations. Such concise environmental impact assessment shall include:

- any negative impact on the environment, on the land surface, for example the disturbance of soil, vegetation, flora and fauna (including extinct species) as well as impact on archaeological and cultural resources;
- any impact on the local population and their culture and life support means;
- mitigation plan to minimize any negative impact or influence described above;
- requirements regarding training and monitoring for conducting environmental protective and rehabilitation measures.

36.5. If the environment protection body decides that the intended search operation of the licensee does not have negative impact or has minor negative impact on the environment, natural resources or local population, the environment protection body may approve operations proposed in the search and exploration plan without public hearing.

The environment protection body shall submit in writing and make public its arguments for taking a decision regarding the absence of negative impact or minor negative impact.

36.6. The drilling of each well shall be conducted under the provision regarding the location of wells in the approved search and exploration plan or development and production plan or in accordance with the programme of locating the wells approved by the environment protection bodies. The licensee shall submit to the environment protection body notification concerning its intention to drill for each well.

Drilling intention notification shall be submitted no less than 30 days prior to the commencement of the operation. The complete notification shall consist of the form (F-3) which will include information about the surface and the location of the intended zone of completion, necessary geological data and any expected difficulties during drilling operation.

36.7. The licensee may commence drilling wells at any time after 30 days following the submission of drilling intention notification except when the environment protection body informed the licensee concerning its ban on drilling in writing. The reasons for the drilling ban shall include the following:

- location and drilling technique specified in drilling intention notification does not comply with the approved search and exploration plan and the development and production plan;
- location and drilling technique specified in drilling intention notification does not comply with other law or act;
- location and drilling technique specified in drilling intention notification constitutes an imminent threat to environment and this threat was not provided for in approved search and exploration plan and development and production plan.

36.8. The environment protection body shall notify the licensee in writing with regard to reasons of disapproval of drilling intention notification and about any other operations through which the drilling intention notification can be restored.

36.9. The notification concerning operations on wells shall be submitted by the licensee under form 5 to environment protection bodies prior to redrilling, deepening, casing repair, removing from long-term storage, casing modification, conduct of operations which were not planned for partitioning of beds, repumping in a different mode, water shut off, production shifts between regions and/or transfer to drive.

In case of a repeated disturbance of the surface the notification of well operation shall include a working plan for the use of the surface. The consequent report on such activities shall also be submitted in form 5.

36.10. The licensee shall take all necessary precautions for the purpose of permanent supervision of wells and use and store materials and equipment needed for ensuring safety, order and proper working conditions. The licensee shall draw the emergency readiness plan for explosions, raptures and fires.

36.11. The licensee shall conduct drilling in such a way as the well does not considerably deviate vertically except when deviation is specified in the drilling intention notification or in the approved search and exploration plan or development and production plan. The licensee shall isolate seams carrying fresh or any other useable water and other seams carrying minerals and protects them from pollution. Tests and effectiveness survey for such measures shall be conducted by the licensee in accordance with the procedures and practice approved by the environment protection body.

36.12. The licensee without delay shall slush and abandon in accordance with acts or the plan approved by the environment protection body each well which is subject to preservation or repeated preservation in which oil or gas were not discovered in commercial quantities or a production well on which production is completed due to absence of oil and gas in commercial quantities except when environment protection body approves the use of the well for injection for the purpose of extracting additional quantities of oil and gas or for the purpose of removal of oil production wastes under the surface.

36.13. The well cannot be temporarily left without prior approval by the environment protection body. The environment protection body may postpone the target date for final abandonment of the well for twelve months. In the process of removal of drilling and production equipment from the well site which is subject for final abandonment the land surface disturbed by the operations shall be restored to condition suitable for further economic use or to the initial state in accordance with the plan preliminary approved by the environment protection body.

36.14. In case the oil deposit is located in the operation area for several licensees granted to different licensees, the licensees in this case should come to an agreement on search, exploration and production plan for this deposit jointly and in the most effective method.

Article 37   Interaction of the Licensing Authority and Licensee with Territorial Subsoil and Environment Protection Bodies

37.1. Territorial environment protection bodies, the licensing authority and the licensee each of them shall operate within the framework of their authorities.

37.2. Authorized representatives of the government with agreement with the licensing authority shall have the right to conduct inspections of these sites of the license as well as official documents without prior notification including access to guarded facilities at the license sites for the purpose of conducting inspections and investigations and a determining compliance with the provisions of the present Law and any valid acts and decrees.

37.3. The licensing authority shall agree the emergency measures plan with local governmental bodies in order to ensure prompt evacuation in an emergency and conduct of other similar measures.

37.4. In order to respond to emergencies the government of the Russian Federation, the licensing authority, the ecologic supervision body and local management bodies shall establish a special non-budget fund. All licensees shall be obliged to take part in financing the fund in accordance with procedures established by the government of the Russian Federation. If the licensee operates without incidents he may be entitled to refund 90% of his fund donations after the expiration of the license term.

37.5. The state power bodies and management bodies, the subjects of activities of subsoil and state mining supervision bodies within their competence shall be obliged to ensure the observance by the licensee of the requirements of the law as well as safety standards (norms and rules) approved in an established procedure for conduct of operations related to the use of the subsoil.

37.6. Prior to adoption of alterations to or cancellation of any act the licensing authority shall be obliged:

- to issue notification no less than 30 days in advance about its intentions. The notification should include the provision concerning time and location of the implementation of its intentions, the list of operations and the method through which interested persons may express their attitude to it. The notification shall be published in the local press shall be sent to all persons who have forwarded a timely request to the licensing authority;
- to provide for all interested persons to reasonable extent the possibility to submit data, opinion or arguments orally or in writing. The licensing authority shall completely consider everything that has been submitted in writing or orally regarding the proposed action. Upon adoption of the act, the licensing authority shall issue a concise rationale for principle reasons pro and contra such an act including its own reasoning in favour of adoption of the act.

37.7. If the licensing authority decides that imminent threat to health, life and well-being of the population requires an action with the notification issued no less than 30 days in advance and provides its rationale in writing stating its reasons for such a decision, it may without prior notification and without hearing or after any brief notification or hearing to commit an emergency action the time limit for which may not exceed 120 days.

37.8. One year after the adoption of this act any other act which contradicts the provisions of this article shall be cancelled. The acts issued by the licensing authority should be approved by the government of Russian Federation.

37.9. The licensing authority shall register in the territorial management bodies an indorsed copy of each act adopted by it including all acts existing as of the day of coming into force of this act which keeps on a permanent basis a register log for all acts, this register being accessible for public inspection and for copying and publishers and issues copies of acts to all interested authorities, licensees and public groups.

37.10. The licensee may forward a petition to the licensing authority with the request concerning introduction, collection or cancellation of any act. The licensing authority shall issue rules, request form and procedure for their submission, consideration and decision taking. Within 30 days after the submission of the request the licensing authority in case of refusal, shall answer the petition in writing providing rationale for the reasons of the refusal or shall prepare the decision in accordance with this act.

37.11. After the substantiation of the possibility of commercial production reaching agreement on land allotment for development and production, the licensee shall submit for approval the oil development and production plan prepared in accordance with the requirements specified by the environment protection body. Such development and production plan shall be forwarded to the licensing authority together with the development programme and budget required by the law on oil and gas licenses. The plan shall contain a section titled 'Environmental Impact Assessment' which shall be brought to the notice of the environment protection body and the public.

37.12. The licensee shall have the right to receive without delay from the environment protection bodies complete and reliable information concerning environment and existing rules and standards regarding environment protection within their competence.

37.13. The environment protection body shall be obliged to provide the licensing authority with reliable information with respect to the impact of the licensee's operations on all the elements of the environment. The licensee may receive refusal to obtain information or may be denied access to documents containing such information solely in the interests of state security, national defence and private (company) secret. Refusal to have ecological information or denial access to documents containing such information may be appealed against by the licensee in court within 70 days after refusal notification.

37.14. The environment protection bodies shall assess the impact of operations described in exploration and production plan on the environment and take into account the condition of the natural environment in the locations with any object of socioeconomic development of the region and the territory.

37.15. While assessing the search and exploration plan the environment protection bodies shall take into account comments provided by the officials of the region and other interested departments. Environment protection body shall be obliged to consult directly the officials of the region and the territory as well as other interested departments regarding issues contained in the plan. While conducting public hearings all potentially negative impacts on the environment of the planned operations of the licensee shall be discussed including the use of land, well control, air and water pollution prevention, disposal of wastes, restoration of property and well liquidation procedures and installation liquidation procedures after completion of operations, training, monitoring as well as emergency preparedness plan.

37.16. The licensee shall be responsible for his activities in accordance with Section IX of the present Law.

37.17. Disputes between the licensing authority and the territorial environment protection bodies shall be settled in accordance with Article 53 of the present Law.

Article 38 Application of Articles of the Environment Protection Law to the Licensees which Exploit Oil and Gas Deposit

38.1. Upon the issuance of the exploration license the licensee within 60 days shall be obliged to submit a concise report on the environment impact assessment. The licensing authority shall request the licensee to implement all economically acceptable measures to minimize negative impact on the environment, health and culture of the local population within the duration of the search and exploration license.

38.2. Upon the receipt of the license granted to production association for oil production the licensee within one year shall be obliged to submit to the environment protection body the report specifying the environment protection measures at operating deposits. Such a report shall provide the environment protection body with necessary and sufficient information for this body to determine if the licensee complies with the provisions of the present Law. If the licensee fails to provide such a plan within one year the environment protection bodies shall be obliged to assess the activities of the licensee regarding environment protection, resources conservation and safety within 180 days. The environment protection body shall have the right to charge the costs related to the preparation of such a report on the production association as well as to impose the penalty in the amount of triple cost for preparing such a record for the failure to observe the provisions of this paragraph.

38.3. Upon the receipt on the report of the environmental assessment the environment protection bodies shall determine within 60 days if the licensee duly complies to the pro visions of the present Law. If the report shows adequate compliance with the provisions the licensee shall have 90 days at his disposal for submitting its search and exploration plan and development and production plans with regard to his oil and gas activities.

If the report indicates that the owner of the license fails to comply in due manner with the provisions of the present Law the licensee shall submit a temporary plan on meeting established requirements within 120 day. The temporary plan should prove that the licensee shall ensure the compliance with the provisions of the present Law within shortest time possible but in any case no later than 5 years after the date of issuance of the production license. The temporary plan shall at minimum contain:

- baseline data regarding a negative impact on the environment of existing oil and gas activities, safety and preservation of resources in the license area including a precise list of the outflow of contaminating substances from all the installations in the license area as well as oil and gas waste sources;
- the implementation schedule which shows continuous ecologic progress including annual decrease in ejection at the existing installations within the duration of the temporary plan. The schedule shall include the implementation within shortest period of time of control measures and managerial activities in the domain of environment protection, safety and resources conservation.

The system of management, monitoring, planning and implementation of the requirements of the present Law. The management system shall determine persons responsible for such operations and shall ensure personnel training in terms of environment protection, safety and resources conservation. The plan shall also determine financial resources, allotted for the specified purpose required for the implementation of the provisions of the temporary plan.

38.4. In order to prevent major difficulties for the personnel and local population which depend upon the operation of the licensed production association the environment protection bodies with the approval of the government of the Russian Federation after notification and public hearings may relieve the licensee of the existing installations from the requirements of the present Law provided the latter complies with its four following conditions:

- there is no direct threat to health and safety of the personnel and population from continued operation of existing installation;
- there is no economically acceptable and technically feasible method of mitigation of negative impact on the environment or resources conservation of certain types of operations;
- the production association introduced appropriate monitoring system and all possible mitigation techniques and took measures to fulfil its temporary plan of resource saving and environment protecting operations;
- the cost of termination temporarily or finally of certain types or all oil and gas activities of the licensee exceeds advantages of such a termination for environment protection or resource conservation. Exemption cannot be issued for a term exceeding one year.

38.5 The environment protection body prior to approval of any temporary plan or any exemption may request the licensee to allot up to 30% of their revenues from the sale of oil and gas for investments in equipment used for environment protection, safety and resources conservation and training. In excess to that the environment protection body may refuse to indorse any new project including additional well drilling if the licensee fails to submit an acceptable temporary plan which meets established requirements or if it permanently violates the terms and conditions of such a plan.

38.6. The approval of the temporary plan of reaching ecological requirements shall not hamper the environment protection body's exercise of its authorities and suspend operations or production in case there is a direct threat to health and safety of people.

Article 39   Liability and Responsibility for Ecologic Violation

39.1. Ecologic violations shall be considered violations of terms and conditions of license and the provisions of the present Law.

39.2. Responsibility for ecologic violations shall be regulated by the laws of the Russian Federation 'On Environment Protection', 'On Subsoil Protection' (Land Code of the Russian Federation). All claims are filed directly to the licensee in writing within 3 years from the date of the incident. The licensee shall be given 60 days after notification to settle the claim. If the claim is not settled the licensing authority accepts the claim for consideration. The licensee may register any additional material or any comment in writing regarding any pending claim.

39.3. If the licensee refuses to comply with the provisions of the present Law or any other acts or resolutions issued with his agreement the licensing authority may suspend operations or production till the licensee proves its capability to comply with the provisions of the present Law.

39.4. The licensing authority shall notify the licensee in writing regarding any violation of the present Law, acts or resolutions. The notification shall contain the time limit during which the licensee should rectify the violation. Should there be repeated serious violations of the present Law the licensing authority may take measures up to suspension of the license.

Section V OIL AND NATURAL GAS PIPELINE TRANSPORT

Article 40 Object and Scope of the Present Law

40.1. The present Law establishes legal, organizational and economic foundation of the operations of main pipeline transport of oil, gas and products of their processing (hereinafter referred to as 'pipeline transport') as a facility of state importance, of a single state system of continuous oil and natural gas and products of their processing supply, as well as regulates relations in the domain of the use of pipeline transport to provide reliability and safety of main pipelines (hereinafter referred to as 'pipelines') at all the stages of designing, construction and operation and to protect population and natural environment from a possible negative impact of pipeline transport facilities.

40.2. The present Law applies to pipeline transportation of oil and gas and regulates relations between pipeline transport enterprises as well as their relations with licensees, regional authorities and bodies of administration and consumers of oil and gas.

40.3. Facilities of the pipeline transport enterprises shall include:

1. a pipeline (from the place of entering of ready-for-transportation marketable oil and gas to the places of oil processing and shipment, of oil products consumption or of their transshipment to other modes of transport, of the sale of gas to consumers) with ramifications and loopings, locking devices, passages over natural and artificial obstacles, units for linking up pumping and compressor stations, units for setting in motion and reception of cleaning and diagnostic devices, output and quality measurement units, condensate collectors, devices for bringing in inhibitors of hydrate formation, devices for releasing products and blowing through gas pipelines;
2. installations of electrochemical protection of pipelines from corrosion, technological communication lines and facilities, pipeline telemechanics means;
3. electric transmission lines servicing pipelines, electrical supply devices and units for the remote control of locking devices and of pipeline electrochemical protection installations;
4. fire fighting facilities, erosion-control and protection facilities;
5. reservoirs for condensate storage and degassing, waste pits for emergency release of oil, oil products, condensate and liquefied hydrocarbons;
6. facilities of the line service of pipeline operation, along-the-line passages and crossings of pipelines, permanent roads, helicopter landing grounds located along the pipeline and approaches to them, identification and signal signs of pipeline location, information signs in places of pipeline crossings of inland navigable routes;
7. main and intermediate pumping-over, filling-and-pumping and pressure-decreasing stations, oil tank farms, water purification facilities;
8. compressor and gas-distributing stations;
9. stations of underground storage of gas, oil and oil products;
10. gas-filling stations;
11. loading and unloading piers and terminals;
12. points of oil and oil products heating;
13. social institutions, establishments offering everyday services, environment-protection facilities and other facilities pertaining to pipeline transport.

40.4. Normative acts governing the activities of pipeline transport related to operation, occupational safety, fire fighting, protection of facilities and of natural environment shall be mandatory for all state and local authorities and administrative bodies, enterprises, organizations and citizens entering into relationships with enterprises of pipeline transport. The procedure for elaboration and approval of said normative acts shall be established by the Government of the Russian Federation.

Article 41   Ownership to Facilities of Pipeline Transport

41.1. Pipeline transport as a single indivisible technological system having exceptional importance for national economy and defence and imposing rigorous requirements to safe operation shall be primarily property of the state. The property assigned to enterprises of pipeline transport shall belong to them by the right of full economic management according to which they shall own, use and dispose of the said property in accordance with the legislation of the Russian Federation.

41.2. Any interested legal and physical persons can participate with their capital in the development of the state system of pipeline transport. In this case they shall become owners of a section of a separate pipeline (or part of another facility) of the system of pipeline transport on a share basis.

41.3. The state shall have the right to own not less than 51 percent of assets of any separate pipeline or section of the pipeline system constructed on a share basis by legal and physical persons with different types of ownership regardless of their nationality.

41.4. Structures (or facilities) which ensure functioning of several pipeline transport enterprises and which are part of a specific pipeline transport enterprise according to design and construction documentation, shall not be subject to division. The owner of the structure (facility) which ensures functioning of several pipeline transport enterprises shall be obliged to give to another pipeline transport enterprise the right to use part of the structure's capacity he needs with payment of fair tariffs, such capacity not exceeding the pipeline's portion of the throughput flow capacity of the aggregate throughput flow capacity of the pipelines using this structure (facility).

41.5. The owner of the pipeline shall have the rights to liquidate it, decommission or reorient it only by the results of auctions at the real estate exchange which revealed no buyers.

41.6. The owner of the structure (facility) supporting the operation of several pipelines, shall have the right to liquidate or reorient it only after the refusal of owners of other pipelines using this structure to purchase it at residual (with the account of inflation) value.

41.7. Legal and physical persons (bodies of state administration, Russian and foreign enterprises and citizens), organizing in trunk pipelines any forms of individual and joint ownership shall be owners of pipeline transport enterprises.

41.8. The conditions of acquisition of title to a pipeline transport enterprises of state bodies of administration, authorized by the state to dispose of the pipeline transport enterprise (buy-out, presenting, free of charge transfer and others) shall be determined by the Law.

41.9. The owner of the pipeline transport shall have full responsibility, stipulated by the current legislation, related to the non-compliance of the installations with the established operation requirements; pollution of the environment, violation of the title and human rights. The owner of a pipeline transport enterprise running through the Russian territory and a foreign state shall be under the jurisdiction of the foreign state against the part of the property which is located in the territory of this state.

41.10. Owners of the pipeline transport enterprise, passing through the territory of the Russian Federation and a foreign state shall be under the jurisdiction of the foreign state as to the property located on the territory of that state.

Article 42 Lands of Pipeline Transport

42.1. Recognized as lands of pipeline transport shall be:

1. lands allotted for permanent use to site underground, surface and above ground pipeline facilities;
2. lands allotted for temporary use to construct linear parts of pipelines and returned to landowners (land-users) after construction is completed.

The size of the plots of land allotted for these purposes shall be determined in conformity with the standards and design documentation, approved in accordance with the established procedure, and allotment of the plots shall be made with due regard to the order of priority of their development.

Pipeline transport lands shall be in possession and use of the pipeline transport enterprises. Withdrawal of lands allotted for permanent use, shall be made only after decommissioning of the pipeline facility.

42.2. Allotment of new lands for construction of pipeline transport facilities shall be carried out in conformity with the Land Code of the Russian Federation. The time-limits of the temporary allotment of plots of land shall be determined in accordance with the duration of construction of pipeline transport facilities set by approved norms and design documentation. Local authorities, organizations and land users shall not have the right to refuse allotting lands for construction and reconstruction of the pipeline transport facilities. No organization shall have the right to carry out any kind of work on the lands, allotted for permanent or temporary use to the pipeline transport enterprises without their permission.

The pipeline enterprises shall be entitled without new allotment of lands to carry out the work on maintenance, overhaul of the linear part of the pipelines as well as for prevention and elimination of accidents and their consequences, with notification of the land users.

42.3. Compensation for damages by the pipeline transport enterprises to landowners and land users shall be effected in accordance with the Land Code of the Russian Federation.

Article 43 Designing of Pipelines

43.1. The pipeline design shall be carried out with due regard to comprehensive development of the Russian Federation and subjects of the Federation on the basis of development and territorial distribution plans for extraction, pipeline transportation and processing facilities; comprehensive territorial environment protection programs; communications development and location schemes; ensurance of the country's defence potential.

43.2. Pipeline facilities design shall be performed with the account of the evaluation of the facilities impact on the environment, by specialized project institutions, entitled to carry out such work.

43.3. Design and cost estimate documentation for erection and reconstruction of the pipeline transport facilities shall pass, before its approval, a technical, economic and ecological examination according to the established procedure. Examination of the projects of pipeline transport facilities operation shall be performed by bodies of the State committee supervising the safety of operations in industry and mining survey under the President of the Russian Federation or on behalf of them, by independent organizations having the right to perform such examination.

Article 44   Requirements to Supplies of Equipment, Pipes, Materials and Construction Elements for the Pipelines

44.1. The enterprises producing and supplying equipment, pipes, materials and construction elements shall have economic and/or criminal responsibility for concealed defects revealed in the assembly, adjustment and operation during the normative period of service for the equipment, pipes, materials and construction elements, determined by the feasibility study and calculation and shall compensate to construction and assembly organizations and pipeline transport enterprises for the damages caused as a result of accidents, failures and other malfunctions due to mentioned defects.

44.2. The responsibility of foreign suppliers for quality of their equipment, pipes, materials and construction elements for pipeline transport facilities shall be established by terms and conditions of foreign trade contracts.

Article 45   Construction of Pipeline Transport Objects

45.1. Construction of pipeline transport objects shall be carried out by specialized construction and assembly organizations in accordance with the design agreed with the Customer.

45.2. Construction and assembly organizations shall have an obligation to eliminate by their means and at their own expense the defects of construction and assembly nature revealed during the first year of operation, and make post-contraction repair of the pipeline after one year of service. Financing of the post-contraction repair shall be provided by pipeline transport enterprises from the funds provided for by the estimate for the construction.

45.3. Construction and assembly organizations before the pipeline transport objects have been accepted and put into operation shall have an obligation to perform a set of operations provided for by the design to reveal concealed defects of the pipelines and with the application of technical means. Acceptance and putting into service of the pipeline transport objects with deviations from the design not agreed with the customer and the design organization - the author of the project shall be prohibited.

45.4. Construction and assembly organizations shall have economic and other types of liabilities for defects the revealed during the entire service life of the object in construction and assembly; for deviations from the design not agreed with the customer and the design organization; for violations of current construction norms, and shall compensate for damages to the pipeline transport enterprises caused by such violations.

45.5. Construction and assembly organization shall compensate for the local authorities for the damage inflicted upon the natural environment due to their fault.

Article 46 Operation of the Pipeline Transport Objects

46.1. Pipeline transport objects shall be operated in conformity with the approved and the established order safety rules, protection and technical operation of main pipelines, mandatory for all officials, state bodies, enterprises and land users within the Russian territory in their relations with the pipeline transport enterprises.

46.2. The pipeline transport enterprises shall have an obligation to perform:

1. diagnostic control of the technical condition of the pipelines in accordance with the rules of technical operation;
2. periodic technical recertification of the objects in the order set by normative documents.

46.3. The energy supply enterprises shall be prohibited to take operational measures to restrict the established limits of energy consumption by the pipeline transport objects without the consent of the pipeline transport enterprises, and to impose charges on them for the set (declared) capacity.

46.4. The pipeline transport enterprises, together with the local authorities whose territory is crossed by the pipelines, representative offices of the Ministry of Defence of the Russian Federation, bodies of the civil defence, other interested enterprises and organizations, shall work out joint actions to create conditions for safe operation of the pipeline transport objects and liquidation of possible accidents, emergency situations and their consequences.

46.5. The pipeline transport enterprises together with the territorial land-use authorities shall legalize the actual location of the pipelines on the territory and mark their location on the land-use maps.

46.6. In order to protect the pipeline transport facilities and to prevent possible damage to the pipelines in accordance with the current rules of protection of pipelines, security areas shall be established. Any operations and actions conducted without approval of the pipeline transport enterprises shall be prohibited in the security areas.

Article 47 Relations between Enterprises whose Lines of Communication Lie in the Same Technical Corridor or Cross

Relations between enterprises whose lines of communication lie in the same technical corridor or cross shall be established on the basis of mutual agreements on safe and reliable operation of these lines of communication and joint action in case of accidents occurring there.

Article 48 Relations between Pipeline Transport Enterprises and State and Local Bodies of Power and Management

48.1. Local authorities, public and other organizations shall have no right to interfere in regular operational production activities of the pipeline transport related to the process of pumping, storage and distribution of products.

Article 49   Security Arrangements for the Pipeline Transport Facilities

49.1. Security arrangements for the pipeline transport facilities and transported products, fire prevention measures within the system of the pipeline transport shall be performed by the departmental paramilitary guard. The personnel of the departmental pipeline transport guard while on duty shall have a status of legal protection equal to that of militia officers.

49.2. Protection of the most important pipeline transport facilities, including protection against fire, can be secured by the units of militia force, by the fire brigades of the bodies of the Ministry of Internal Affairs and troops of the Ministry of Internal Affairs of the Russian Federation on the basis of contracts concluded in accordance with the established procedure.

Article 50   Organization of Relief Operations in Cases of Accidents and Emergency Situations

50.1. The pipeline transport enterprises shall take immediate and effective measures to eliminate consequences of natural disasters and accidents that have caused disruption of normal functioning of the pipeline transport and shall inform the bodies concerned and the appropriate enterprises in the established order.

50.2. The federal and local authorities and bodies of administration, the pipeline construction and assembly organizations, enterprises, units of the Civil Aviation, railways, Internal Affairs, bodies and units of the Ministry of Defence of the Russian Federation and of Civil Defence must render the pipeline transport enterprises and land users on the territory of which pipeline facilities are located a comprehensive support in the form of personnel, material and technical resources as well as to ensure unimpeded passage and transportation of heavy duty relief and rescue vehicles and equipment along the previously agreed routes in liquidating accidents and elimination of their consequences, consequences of natural disasters and in other emergency situations that pose a threat to life and health of the people, settlements, industrial and other installations and the environment.

The pipeline transport enterprises shall duly reimburse the expenditures incurred by the executive bodies, enterprises and organizations that have assisted in eliminating the consequences of accidents and emergency situations.

50.3. The material losses inflicted upon the pipeline transport as a result of intentional blocking of and damage to the pipeline communications and of other unlawful actions that disrupt its constant and safe functioning shall be reimbursed to the pipeline transport enterprises by the guilty and persons in accordance with the established procedure as well as by the local authorities when they failed to take necessary measures to prevent and stop intentional blocking of the pipeline communications.

Article 51   Responsibility for Violations in the Pipeline Transport

51.1. The pipeline transport enterprises shall be liable for damages caused to enterprises, persons and environment as a result of their operations, against the property in their possession a claim can be made under the Russian Federation legislation.

51.2. Officials and persons guilty of violations of the rules governing the activities in the pipeline security areas, and of non-compliance with the established standards of safe construction distances from the pipeline transport facilities, shall be subject to penalty.

Structures unlawfully constructed in violation of the established norms shall be subject to immediate demolition by the enterprises and persons guilty of the violation, or at their expense. An order by the pipeline transport enterprises shall be the basis for imposition of sanctions and penalties on the guilty persons. The persons guilty of actions disrupting the functioning of the pipeline transport shall be held responsible under the current legislation.

Article 52   Relations between the Pipeline Transport Enterprises and the Consignors

52.1. The economic relations between the pipeline transport enterprises and the consignors shall be determined by the Contract on transportation services.

52.2. The transportation services shall mean the standard business operations that deal with acceptance, drainage, movement, handing-over and pouring of the products at the facilities specially designated for the pipeline transportation, pouring on board (drainage from aboard) a ship and into tank cars (drainage from tank cars). Similar operations of compounding, storing and other processes at specially designated facilities recognized as standard operations shall be included into the list of the transportation services.

52.3. Related to the main activities manufacturing, storage, financial, intermediary operations and information services by the pipeline transport enterprises that do not fall under the statutory activities because they are not inherent to the pipeline transport or are offered as know-how shall not be considered as transportation services.

52.4. Owners of oil and gas shall be recognized as consignors if at the moment of conclusion of a contract they prove their title to the products and state their preparedness to deliver the said products to the main installations of the pipeline transport.

52.5. All the consignors, irrespective of the form of ownership and citizenship as well as the world market situation with the current reserve of the throughput flow capacity of the pipeline shall have equal rights to use the pipelines and shall be in an equal situation regarding access to transportation services and payment for them.

52.6. The pipeline transport enterprise shall be obliged to offer the consignor at his request the optimal possible route for the cargo delivery (with due regard to pumping over costs, reliability of equipment and the conditions of stable handing over of the products). Whenever the pipeline throughput flow capacity does not permit to transport all products of the consignors, each consignor shall be granted the right to use part of the aggregate throughput flow capacity for the quantity of the products he could deliver for transportation pro ratio the quantity of the products that could be delivered to the main installations from all consignors if the pipeline throughput flow capacity were not restricted.

52.7. Matter of preservation and monitoring of quantity and quality of the transported products shall be specified in the contract on transportation services. The consignor cannot claim reimbursement for the losses in terms of the volume and quality of the products (including losses resulting from imperfection of measuring devices) to be paid by the pipeline transport enterprise if these losses meet the technological standards and conditions of pumping-over applicable for the duration of the contract on transportation services.

52.8. The transportation duration of the products through the pipelines shall be specified in the contract on the transpiration services.

Article 53   Payment for the Transportation Services

53.1. The transportation services rendered by the pipeline transport enterprises shall be paid by the consignors according to the current respective tariffs in the tariff sections of the delivery route. Tariffs for transportation services on the Russian territory and the method for calculating them shall be worked out by state pipeline companies, approved by the Ministry of Fuel and Energy of the Russian Federation in agreement with the Ministry of Economy and the Ministry of Finances of the Russian Federation.

53.2. Pipeline transport enterprises shall be obliged to publish in advance and transmit to all potential consignors tariffs corresponding to tariff sections. The tariff shall not force the consignor to pay the costs of the pipeline transport enterprises not related to oil and gas transportation operations at a given route.

53.3. During the year the tariffs may be recalculated on grounds of changes of the workload of the pipeline system, wholesale prices of the products, electricity, materials and services which cause change in the tariff proceeds of a pipeline transport enterprise. Recalculation of a tariff may be done by way of preparation of the tariff ranges with due regard to different volumes of the pipeline deliveries. The pipeline transport enterprise shall be legally responsible for the reliability of the information used for calculation of tariffs. The profit obtained due to distortion of information used in calculation of tariffs, shall be subject to confiscation to the budget of the region where the pipeline transport enterprise is registered.

On the basis of his own information the consignor shall have the right to contest the charged tariffs through a court of arbitration until the court of arbitration passes a ruling the consignor shall pay for the charged tariffs.

53.4. The pipeline transport enterprise shall have the right to establish, upon agreement with the consignors, tariffs that ensure levelling off consumer prices on the products or furnish other corporate advantages. Such average tariffs shall neither lead to higher proceeds for the aggregate of routes to which they apply nor force consignors which are not parties to the relevant agreement to pay higher tariffs.

Taxes on tariff proceeds of pipeline transport enterprises, which participate in the Agreement on average tariffs, shall be levied with the account of deductions from and returns to the tariff proceeds of a pipeline transport enterprise from centralized compensation funds (established to level off tariffs).

No agreements between the owners of main pipeline and consignors with pipeline transport enterprises on transfer of the assets shall be recognized as an increase or a decrease of the tariff proceeds in comparison with the established tariffs and real volume of works on the contracts on transportation services.

53.5. Contract prices shall apply to payments for services of pipeline transport other than transportation services.

Article 54   Pipeline Transport Management

54.1. Management of pipeline transport shall be performed by state pipeline companies authorized to do so by the Government of the Russian Federation. State pipeline companies shall be specialized in transportation of specific types of products and shall unite enterprises technologically integrated in a single system of pipelines.

54.2. State pipeline companies as pipeline transport management bodies shall independently determine its structure, take decisions to establish, to reorganize or to liquidate pipeline transport enterprises; shall provide control over safety of operation effective usage and safety of their property in the interests of the signal system of pipeline transport, and also exercise other powers in accordance with the legislation of the Russian Federation.

Article 55   Time for Record-Keeping and Reporting in Pipeline Transport

In order to ensure efficiency of centralized management of pipeline transport in the Russian territory a uniform time for record-keeping and reporting – Moscow time – shall be established in the pipeline transport enterprises directly involved in the process of products transportation irrespective of their location.

Article 56   Language of Office Record-Keeping and Official Communication in Pipeline Transport

56.1. In pipeline transport in the Russian territory the Russian language shall be the language used for office record-keeping, accounts, reports, commercial and technical documentation, telephone communication, legal, scientific and technological information as well as official communication through dispatcher, telephone, teletype and other means of communication in enterprises, organizations and institutions related to the transportation of products maintenance and repairs.

56.2. All inscription, symbols, signs, information, advertisements on the sites and pipeline transport facilities, as well as the names of enterprises, institutions and organizations of pipeline transport, shall be written both in the language of the republics within the Russian Federation and in the Russian language.

Article 57   International Cooperation

International cooperation in the domain of pipeline transport shall be carried out on the basis of international agreements and direct contracts between enterprises of parties concluded in the established order.

Section VI   TAXATION FOUNDATIONS OF THE ACTIVITIES IN THE DOMAIN OF OIL AND GAS

Article 58   Specificities of Taxation of Activities Related to Oil and Gas

58.1. Taxation of activities in the domain of oil and gas shall not be subject to regulation by the Law 'On the Subsoil' of the Russian Federation due to the specific conditions of this domain of the subsoil usage: volatility of the international oil and gas market; high level of geological risk; uncertain economically justified production period.

58.2. This section sets the system of special payments and taxes which shall be levied only on the subsoil users exercising activities in the domain of oil and gas. The system of payments and taxes shall consist of:

- payments for the license (administrative fee);
- payments for the right to geological survey of the subsoil;
- payments for the right to use the subsoil, including production;
- special taxes on the profit from production of oil and gas;
- customs duty on oil and gas;
- payments for the right to use the subsoil for other purposes, connected with activities in the domain of oil and gas.

Exercising of special payments and taxes shall not release the payer from paying other taxes, duties and payments stipulated in the legislation.

58.3. In accordance with the present Law a special regime to impose the profit tax on licensees exercising activities in the domain of oil and gas. The procedure to determine the taxable basis for the tax of profit, gained from the activities in the domain of oil and gas with due regard to special payments and taxes shall be set in compliance with the Law 'On Taxation in the Oil and Gas Industry'.

58.4. For the purposes of determining the taxable basis of profit tax and tax on superprofit from production the licensees in the domain of oil and gas may use accelerated schemes for writing off capital expenditures. Amortization term can be reduced down to 5 years for all the elements of the fixed assets except the facilities of the trunk pipelines.

The investor shall independently select a write off scheme (uniform or descending). When the descending scale of amortization is used the write off amount in the first year may not exceed 35 percent of the fixed assets value. The elaborated system for writing off capital costs shall be fixed in the license.

58.5. All kinds of special payments and taxes in the activities in the domain of oil and gas, procedure for their determination and payment must be specified in the license.

Article 60   Payments for the License

60.1. Payments for the license for the right to activities in the domain of oil and gas shall be levied in the form of the registration fee and payment for the license. The registration fee shall be paid by all the contestants in submitting an application for the right to activities in the domain of oil and gas irrespective of the method of issuing the license.

Payment for the license shall be levied upon the user in signing the license agreement.

60.2. Amount of the registration fee and payment for the license must compensate the expenditures of the licensing authority for organization of the licensing operations including examination of the applications and projects of usage, or maintenance of the negotiations process. The procedure to determine amounts of the registration fees and payment for the license in each individual case shall be established by the federal service of the licensing authority.

60.3. Registration fees and payment for the license shall be forwarded to the state budget.

Article 61   Payments for the Right to Geological Survey and Development of the Subsoil

61.1. Payments for the right to the geological survey and development of the subsoil (bonus) shall be levied on the users who have received a prospecting or operational license. The bonus shall be a lumpsum payment and shall be levied in the form of an initial payment while receiving the license and can also be levied on achievement of specific conditions of the subsoil development fixed in the license.

61.2. Starting amounts of bonuses shall be determined by the licensing authority in accordance with the government instructions regulating activities of the licensing authorities. Final amounts of bonuses shall be determined proceeding from the results of the contest, auction or direct negotiations. Amounts and forms of payment of initial bonuses or the procedures to determine the amounts of future bonuses shall be fixed in the license.

61.3. Leasing payments for the right to geological survey and development of the subsoil (rentals) shall be levied on all licensees exercising activities in the domain of oil and gas. Rentals shall be regular payments and shall be set with due regard to the acreage of the license area.

61.4. Rates of rentals, form and procedure for their payment shall be set by the licensing authority in compliance with the Law 'On Taxation in the Oil and Gas Industry' and shall depend on economic and geographical conditions of the area and the extent of geological study of it. The use of progressively increasing rates of rentals within the license term shall be allowed.

(In accordance with Article 62 of the present Law) the rentals to be paid shall be set off in determining the amounts of payments from the commencement of paying the royalty.

61.5. The paid bonuses and rentals shall in full be forwarded to the regional budgets.

Article 62   Payments for the Right to Use the Subsoil in the Process of Production

62.1. Payment for the right to use the subsoil in the process of production (royalty) shall be levied on the licensees producing oil and gas. Royalty shall be a guaranteed share of the subsoil's owner in the gross income from production and shall be defined as part of the volume of produced oil and gas or as part of their value in the prices of their actual realization.

Due to specific conditions a method to calculate royalty at the well head royalty for oil and gas shall be determined at the wellhead or in any other convenient point within the framework of the license area shall be specified in the license.

62.2. Royalty rate shall be fixed in the license in the form of a scale, which may be subdivided into three periods of development of the deposit: 'initial,' 'stable production,' 'exhaustion.' Production rate of wells and the achieved level of production shall be the basic parameters for the scale.

A minimum scale of the royalty rates for each license shall be determined by the licensing authority on the basis of the Law 'On Taxation in the Oil and Gas Industry' and the government instructions with due regard to the consultations with experts and representatives of local authorities. Final amounts of royalty may be specified proceeding from the results of the contest or negotiations and shall be fixed in the license.

The maximum royalty rate may not exceed the levels:

- of 15% for production of oil;
- of 12% for production of gas.

62.3. The form of payment of royalty (monetary or in kind) shall be set upon agreement between the licensee and the bodies of local power and shall be fixed in the license. When royalty is paid in kind the license shall specify the point and the terms and conditions of oil and gas deliveries.

62.4. Royalty shall be distributed between the Russian Federation and the subjects of Federation. The share of the Russian Federation shall be 20%.

The remaining part of royalty shall be distributed between the republic within the Russian Federation, krai, oblast, autonomous formation, district (city), upon agreement between the relevant authorities.

Article 63 Special Tax on Profit from Production of Oil and Gas

63.1. Special tax on profit from production of oil and gas shall be levied on the licensees who gain additional profits from activities under relatively better natural conditions or selling oil and gas in relatively better conditions of the market.

63.2. Special tax on profit shall be levied on the licensees when the norm of internal profitability of the invested capital exceeds 15 percent at minimum. The special tax rate on profit shall be set in the form of progressive scale in the interval ranging from 50 to 85% depending on the achieved norm of internal profitability.

63.3. Rules to determine the taxable basis and the special tax rate on the superprofit shall be established by the Law 'On Taxation in the Oil and Gas Industry' and the government instruction in compliance with the following principles:

- the norm of internal profitability shall be determined in respect to the capitalized expenditures;
- special tax on profit shall be charged only for the activities in the domain of oil and gas, accordingly, the norm of return shall be determined only in regard to capital invested in production of oil and gas;
- the mechanism to account for the inflation impact on the amount of the norm of internal profitability shall be provided;
- the special tax rate on profit shall be determined with due regard to the future payment of the total tax on profit in respect to activities of the company in the domain of oil and gas;
- the paid special tax on profit shall be subject to deduction in calculating the taxable basis for the total tax on profit;
- the instruction must contain an unambiguous definition and classification of all elements of profits and expenditures for calculation of special tax on profit which shall be understandable to both domestic and foreign investors;
- the companies carrying out activities in the domain of oil and gas under more than one license may combine the profits and expenditures for the purposes of determination of special tax on profit.

63.4. The special tax on profit from oil and gas production shall be distributed between federal and regional budgets. The share of incomings into the federal budget shall be 85 percent. The remaining amount shall be distributed between budgets of the republics within the Russian Federation, krais, oblasts, autonomous formations and districts (cities) upon agreement between relevant authorities.

63.5. The governmental instructions shall regulate the special regime for determination of rates for special tax on profit under licenses for the deposits, which by the time of adoption of the present Law are already at the stage of oil and gas production.

Article 64   Other Payments

64.1. Customs tax on export of oil and gas shall be introduced as a state regulator for the ratio of prices of oil and gas in the international and domestic markets.

Introduction of the customs tax shall be accompanied by the cancellation of export quotas system, which ensures equal competitive conditions for all licensees in the domain of oil and gas in respect to the access to international and domestic markets.

The customs tax rate shall be set by the Government of the Russian Federation in percentage to the international market price. The federal Government by its decrees shall adjust the customs tax rates in accordance with the change in the real exchange rate of the rouble.

64.2. Payments for the right to use the subsoil for other purposes connected with the activities in the domain of oil and gas (underground storage, disposal of seam waste waters, etc.) shall be charged in the form of regular payments and lumpsum fees.

Amounts of these payments shall be set proceeding from the size of the plots of land allotted for usage, useful properties of the subsoil, volumes of disposal of the seam waste water and the level of ecological safety.

In the cases of the use of seam waste water as a working agent in the systems of reservoir pressure maintenance for injection of reservoir waste water into productive strata of oil and gas deposits no payments shall be levied.

Article 65   Discount for Use of the Oil and Gas Bearing Subsoil

Discount on payments for the right to use the oil and gas bearing subsoil may be granted to:

• the users extracting oil and gas under conditions of objectively substantiated low economic effectiveness of development of oil and gas deposits which is not connected with the violation of the terms of rational use of discovered resources;
• the subjects of activities, extracting oil and gas from the residual reserves of lower quality if the subjects of activities of oil and gas bearing subsoil are not to blame for the deterioration of these reserves of oil and gas as a result of selected development by them of the oil and gas deposits.

The decision to set a discount for usage of such oil and gas bearing subsoil and on the amount of the discount shall be taken by state authorities issuing licenses for the right to use oil and gas bearing subsoil.

Section VII   STATE REGULATION OF RELATIONSHIPS RELATED TO ACTIVITIES IN THE DOMAIN OF OIL AND GAS

Article 66   Tasks of State Regulation

66.1. The aim of state regulation shall be to ensure rational production and usage of resources of oil and gas and restoration of the hydrocarbons raw materials basis with due regard to the current and prospective needs of the economy as well as the requirements for preservation of the environment.

66.2. State regulation shall be exercised through the system of appropriate management, licensing, records keeping and control bodies which:

- shall determine the current and prospective needs of the economy of the Russian Federation and its regions in oil and gas;
- shall determine the volumes of reserves of the hydrocarbons raw materials and their location on the Russian territory ;
- shall outline the directions and the scope for regional prospecting operations including those on the continental shelf and in the exclusive economic zone for the development of the raw materials basis of hydrocarbons as well as for creating the underground facilities for oil and gas;
- shall determine the share of the state participation in the operational licenses, as well as the volume of deliveries of oil and/or gas produced within the framework of the license for the internal needs of the Russian Federation, which shall be reflected in the terms and conditions of the license;
- shall determine the volumes and the procedure for making payments and payment of taxes related to the activities in the domain of oil and gas;
- shall set and monitor compliance with the standards (norms, rules) in carrying out activities in the domain of oil and gas, including those related to ensuring safety of such operations, preservation of resources and the environment.

66.3. State administration of the relationships related to the activities in the domain of oil and gas shall be exercised by President of the Russian Federation, government of the Russian Federation, governments of the republics within the Russian Federation through the specially authorized bodies of state administration within the limits of their competence, determined by the present Law, other legislative acts of the Russian Federation and the republics within the Russian Federation which do not contradict the present Law.

Article 67   State Registration and Inventory

67.1. Reserves of oil and gas on the Russian territory shall be subject to state registration and inventory, as stipulated in Article 1.1 of the present Law, on the continental shelf and in the exclusive economic zone of the Russian Federation as well as the licenses, concluded for carrying out activities in the domain of oil and gas including storage and transportation of the resources produced beyond the deposits and pledge obligations relating to the rights within the framework of the license.

67.2. State registration and inventory shall be carrying out according to the order which shall be uniform for all the regions of the Russian Federation which shall be established by the Government of the Russian Federation in accordance with the present Law and other legislative acts of the Russian Federation, which do not contradict it, through:

- compiling and keeping the state federal, republican (within the Russian Federation) and territorial balance sheets of the reserves of oil and gas;
- forming state, federal, republican (within the Russian Federation) and regional cadasters of oil and gas;
- exercising uniform state (federal) registration of licenses for the activities in the domain of oil and gas, including underground storage and transportation of the extracted resources beyond the production sites.

Article 68   State Control

68.1. State control over the rational usage and preservation of resources of oil and gas with due regard to the requirements for operations safety and ecology protection shall be exercised to ensure compliance by all the subjects of activities with the present Law, other legislative and normative acts of the Russian Federation and the republics within the Russian Federation, pertaining to the activities in the domain of oil and gas and not contradicting the present Law as well as the standards (norms, rules) applied in geological surveys, development and usage of resources of oil and gas, rules for conducting state registration and inventory in the process of exercising activities in the domain of oil and gas.

68.2. State control shall be exercised at the request of the Government of the Russian Federation by the appropriate bodies of state geological, economic, and land control, the bodies supervising over the safety of operations in the industry and the mining supervision to the extent of their competence and in close cooperation with each other.

Article 69   Antimonopoly Objectives

69.1. Exercising uniform state registration of licenses of the activities in the domain of oil and gas including underground storage and transportation of the extracted resources beyond the production deposits shall prevent accumulation in the hands of a single subject of activities, its subsidiaries or the companies under its influence of such quantity of licenses and/or aggregate volume of oil and/or gas which would enable it to become a monopolist in the relevant sphere in violation of the current antimonopoly legislation of the Russian Federation.

This level shall be established by the respective decree of the government of the Russian Federation and may be reviewed if required.

Section VIII   SETTLEMENTS OF DISPUTES

Article 70   The Procedure for Settling Disputes

70.1. No one shall have the right without valid reasons under the present Law to impede the licensee in exercising his rights and activities within the framework of the license.

70.2. Disputes of the licensing authority, the licensee and the subjects of activities to whom the licensee has transferred relevant rights in accordance with Article 16 of the present Law (except foreign subjects of law) regarding any activities of the licensing authority, other bodies of state power or administration, as well as other legal or physical persons (except foreign subjects of law) which have caused or may cause infringement of the title of the licensee or inflicting on him material or morale damage shall be settled in accordance with the current legislation of the Russian Federation in the bodies of arbitration or ordinary court.

70.3. The following matters shall be subject to settlement in court or the arbitrage court:

1. financial, property and other disputes related to the activities within the framework of the license;
2. appealing against decisions, regulations and other normative acts of bodies of state power and administration contradicting the present Law as well as the licensing authority on the current activities within the framework of the license on termination ahead of time or suspension of the license or on the refusal to issue the license;
3. appealing against standards (rules, norms) on the technology of operations related to activities in the domain of oil and/or gas, as well as protection of resources and the environment contradicting the current legislation;
4. appealing against actions of officials and bodies of control which contradict the present Law and infringing on the property and other rights of the licensee. Items 1 and 3 of this Article may be considered in the court of arbitration by agreement of the parties.

70.4. The disputes of the parties specified in Article 70.2 in which foreign subjects of law shall be an interested party or the subjects under the control of a foreign subject of law shall be settled according to the procedure provided for by the license terms and conditions, the present Law and the Law of the Russian Federation on foreign investments, including in a court of arbitration by agreement of the parties.

70.5. Unless otherwise provided in the license the arbitration proceed shall be conducted on the basis of the Rules of Reconciliation and Arbitration of the International Chamber of Commerce or the Rules of Arbitration of the UN Commission on the International Trading Law (UNCITRAL).

70.6. Settlement of international arbitration if required may be introduced as court execution to the bodies of arbitrage or ordinary court on the Russian territory.

70.7. All provisions of Article 70 shall stay in force after termination of the license as well if the terms and the procedure for appeal against a disputable decision have been observed.

Article 71   Liability for Non-Compliance with the Requirements of the Present Law

71.1. Non-compliance with the requirements of the present Law shall entail application of measures of civil, administrative and/or criminal responsibility in accordance with the legislation of the Russian Federation and the republics within the Russian Federation.

71.2. Liabilities and sanctions may be imposed upon the licensees and other subjects of activities in the domain of oil and/or gas, any other legal entities and physical persons, as well as bodies of state power and administration and control, whose actions resulted in violation of provisions of the present Law which caused financial, material of moral damage or infringement on property or other rights for any of the parties engaged or related to the activities in the domain of oil and gas.

71.3. The damage inflicted upon the licensee or the owner of the subsoil caused by actions contradicting the present Law by any other subjects of economic activities, physical persons as well as bodies of state power, administration and control shall be subject to compensation at the expense of the guilty party in the amount and forms agreed by the parties or set upon the decision of the court of arbitration, by agreement of the parties, arbitrage court or ordinary court.

Annex 6

Republic of Kazakhstan Code on Subsurface Resources and Crude Mineral Processing
1992

SECTION I. GENERAL

Article 1 Purpose of the Republic of Kazakhstan Code on Subsurface Resources and Crude Mineral Processing

The purpose of the Republic of Kazakhstan Code on Subsurface Resources and Crude Mineral Processing is to regulate the relations of ownership, use, and management of subsurface resources and crude mineral processing in the interests of the contemporary and future generations and to ensure scientifically grounded, economical, and comprehensive utilization and protection of the subsurface to meet the requirements for minerals, ground water, and other needs of the national economy, to protect the rights of enterprises, organizations, institutions, and individuals, and to ensure compliance with law in this area.

Article 2 The Republic of Kazakhstan Law on Subsurface Resources and Crude Mineral Processing

1. The relations of ownership, use, and management of subsurface resources and crude mineral processing shall be regulated by this Code and other statutory acts of the Republic of Kazakhstan pursuant thereto.
2. The relations of land, water (except the ground and mineral waters), forests, air, wildlife and vegetation protection and utilization shall be regulated by special laws of the Republic of Kazakhstan.

Article 3 Subsurface Resources of the Republic of Kazakhstan

The subsurface constitutes a part of the natural environment which can be used to meet the national economic and other requirements by extracting (recovering) its components, or to locate underground facilities and dispose of hazardous or industrial wastes and waste waters.

Article 4 The Minerals of the Republic of Kazakhstan

In the Republic of Kazakhstan, minerals constitute a part of the subsurface and include solid, liquid, and gaseous substances which can be produced and processed for the purpose of utilization in the area of physical production.

Article 5 Ownership of Subsurface Resources in the Republic of Kazakhstan

1. Subsurface resources in the Republic of Kazakhstan are owned solely and exclusively by the republic and form the physical basis of its sovereignty.
2. The title to the subsurface of the Republic of Kazakhstan shall be exercised by the Supreme Soviet of the Republic of Kazakhstan throughout the republic.
3. No private ownership of the subsurface of the Republic of Kazakhstan shall be permitted, and any purchase, sale, grant, or trade of any part of the subsurface shall be prohibited.
4. Any direct or indirect act in breach of the republic's title to the subsurface shall be prohibited.

Article 6 Principles of Use and Protection of Subsurface Resources and Crude Mineral Processing

The following principles shall be observed in using and protecting subsurface resources and in crude mineral processing:

1. Any special use of the subsurface shall be paid for;
2. Subsurface resources shall be used economically and comprehensively;
3. Any steps to promote efficiency of use and protection of the subsurface shall be encouraged;
4. Waste-free or low-waste processing shall be applied;
5. Government environmental expert examination shall be mandatory for any subsurface use or crude mineral processing projects;
6. National and international goals shall be combined in the area of subsurface use and protection;
7. Any damage to the subsurface and other features of the natural environment through development of mineral deposits and crude mineral processing shall be recovered;
8. Any work associated with subsurface use shall be safe;
9. The impact of subsurface use on the natural environment shall be regulated by norms;
10. Any requirements of laws on subsurface resources and crude mineral processing shall be complied with.

Article 7 Unified National Fund of Subsurface Resources

1. The Unified national fund of subsurface resources of the Republic of Kazakhstan shall include both the used and the unused subsurface areas.
2. The mineral resources of the Republic of Kazakhstan comprise a unified national fund of mineral deposits and technogenic formations (production and processing wastes).

Article 8   State Programs for Development of the Crude Minerals Base, Efficient and Comprehensive Use of Mineral Resources, and Protection of Subsurface Resources

1. State programs for development of the crude minerals base, efficient and comprehensive use of mineral resources, and protection of subsurface resources shall be drafted and implemented to ensure efficient operation of the crude minerals complex of the Republic of Kazakhstan.
2. The procedure for drafting the programs shall be defined by the Republic of Kazakhstan Cabinet of Ministers.

SECTION II   USE OF SUBSURFACE RESOURCES

Article 9   Types of Subsurface Use

The subsurface shall be provided for use for the following purposes:

1. Geological studies.
2. Extraction and production of minerals.
3. Construction and operation of underground facilities not associated with extraction and production of minerals, including underground storage facilities for crude oil, gas, and other materials and substances, for disposal of hazardous materials, industrial wastes, and waste water, and for other purposes.

Article 10   Subsurface Users

1. The subsurface in the Republic of Kazakhstan shall be provided for use to eligible enterprises, organizations and institutions of any form of ownership, as well as to citizens.
2. The procedure for enterprise eligibility shall be determined by the Republic of Kazakhstan Cabinet of Ministers.
3. The subsurface may be provided for use to joint ventures and to foreign legal and physical persons on a contractual or concession basis.

Article 11   Basic Rights and Obligations of Subsurface Users

1. Subsurface users shall have the right to use the subsurface pursuant to the purposes for which the subsurface has been provided.
2. Subsurface users shall be obliged to ensure:

    (1) The full scope of geological studies and surveying services and accurate accounting of produced and processed minerals and components;
    (2) Economical and comprehensive use and protection of subsurface resources;
    (3) Performance of operations associated with the subsurface use which shall be safe for employees and the public;
    (4) Protection of the public, wildlife, air, land, forests, water, and other natural environment, as well as buildings and structures from any harmful impact by operations associated with the subsurface use;
    (5) Integrity of nature preserves, national parks, and historic and cultural monuments;

(6)   Restoration of land parcels and any other natural features to a condition that would permit their use in the national economy in accordance with the laws of the Republic of Kazakhstan;

(7)   Payments made in a timely manner.

3.   In the cases specified by the laws of the Republic of Kazakhstan, the rights of subsurface users may be restricted in the national interests or in the interests of other subsurface users.

Article 12   Allocation of Subsurface Resources for Geological Studies

1.   For the purposes of conducting geological studies, the subsurface shall be awarded, on a tender basis, by the Republic of Kazakhstan to the following entities:

(1)   Enterprises, organizations, institutions, and citizens of the Republic of Kazakhstan based on the plan for geological studies;

(2)   Joint ventures and foreign legal and physical persons, on a contractual or concession basis.

2.   The land relations associated with geological studies of the subsurface shall be regulated pursuant to the land laws of the Republic of Kazakhstan.

3.   Registration with the agencies of Ministry of Geology and Subsurface Protection of plans for geological studies and permissions for obtaining land parcels to be surveyed, as well as contracts and concessions, shall provide basis for commencement of work for geological studies of the subsurface.

Article 13   Allocation of Subsurface Resources for Production of Minerals and Other Uses

1.   The Republic of Kazakhstan Supreme Soviet shall delegate the right of allocation of the subsurface for production of minerals and other uses to the following entities:

(1)   For mineral deposits of national significance, to the Republic of Kazakhstan Cabinet of Ministers;

(2)   For mineral deposits of local significance, including deposits of common minerals, to the local soviets of people's deputies.

2.   Allocation of the subsurface for any use, as well as any other activities related to exercise of the subsurface title, shall be performed with the participation of Ministry of Geology and Subsurface Protection of the Republic of Kazakhstan and its agencies.

3.   Allocation of the subsurface for production of minerals and any other uses shall be performed, for mineral deposits of national significance, by the Republic of Kazakhstan Cabinet of Ministers, and for mineral deposits of local significance, by the local Soviets of People's Deputies.

4.   Allocation of the subsurface for production of mineral waters and medicinal mud shall be performed upon approval by the Republic of Kazakhstan Ministry of Health.

5.   Any legal or physical person previously engaged in financing geological and exploration works shall have a priority right to operate the relevant prospected deposits subject to requirements of this code. This right shall be terminated unless

it has been exercised within two years after the deposits of the prospected field have been approved. In the event of transfer of such field to another organization through a tender, such organization shall reimburse the actual costs to the legal or physical persons that financed the geological exploration.

Article 14   Contract for Use of the Subsurface for the Mineral Production, Crude Minerals Processing, and Other Purposes

1. The right of allocation of the subsurface for purposes of mineral production, crude mineral processing, and other uses shall be exercised by the Republic of Kazakhstan Cabinet of Ministers or local soviets of people's deputies by entering into contracts with the subsurface users.

2. The *contract* for use of the subsurface for the mineral production, crude mineral processing, and other uses shall be entered into provided the subsurface user has obtained mining concession authorization and enterprise plan that has undergone expert evaluation at:

   - The Republic of Kazakhstan Ministry of Geology and Subsurface Protection or its agencies in regard to protection of the subsurface, scope of extraction of subsurface minerals, recovery of useful components in crude mineral processing, and processing waste recycling;
   - The Republic of Kazakhstan Ministry of Ecology and Bioresources in regard to environmental protection;
   - The Republic of Kazakhstan State Committee for Oversight of Work Safety and Mining Inspection or its agencies in regard to safety management;
   - The Republic of Kazakhstan Ministry of Health.

3. The contract for subsurface use shall provide for:

   (1) Duration and conditions of subsurface use and the parties' rights and obligations;
   (2) Ecological requirements subject to which any operations or other activities may be permissible;
   (3) Quotas for the annual quantity of minerals to be used;
   (4) Payment term and amount for use of the subsurface;
   (5) Activities for subsurface protection;
   (6) Scope and conditions of disposal of industrial wastes, payment term and amount for land allocation and conditions of land reclamation;
   (7) Caveats for process technology applied;
   (8) Any bonuses or benefits to be granted;
   (9) Conditions and procedures for application of penalty sanctions for non-economical or non-comprehensive use of the subsurface and environmental pollution;
   (10) The parties' liabilities for failure to comply with the contract terms and conditions;
   (11) Other terms and conditions as deemed necessary by the parties unless in conflict with laws of the Republic of Kazakhstan.

Article 15   Procedure for Allocation of the Subsurface for Production of Minerals and Other Uses

1. Any issue of the subsurface for production of minerals and other uses shall be

performed in accordance with the following procedure which requires that the subsurface user should:

(1) Request and obtain a mining concession authorization from the relevant agencies of the Republic of Kazakhstan Ministry of Ecology and Bioresources;

(2) Arrange for approval of the enterprise and/or facility location and land parcel allocation under the Kazakh SSR Land Code;

(3) Ensure design and survey work, and drafting of a plan for subsurface use and expert review thereof.

2. Registration of a mining concession authorization, a land allocation (concession) permit, subsurface use plan, and subsurface area allocation agreement with agencies of the Republic of Kazakhstan Ministry of Geology and Subsurface Protection shall provide the basis for entitlement to subsurface use for mineral production and other uses.

Article 16   Semicommercial Development of Mineral Deposits

1. Semicommercial development of a mineral deposit or a part thereof shall be performed without issuance of a mining concession authorization for purposes of defining mining, geological, and other conditions, and selection of economical methods of mineral deposit development and effective technologies of crude mineral processing.

2. The right to effect semicommercial development may be granted in exceptional cases. Authorization shall be given by the Republic of Kazakhstan Ministry of Geology and Subsurface Protection upon expert evaluation of the work program as provided by this code.

3. Land relations associated with a semicommercial development shall be regulated in accordance with the land laws of the Republic of Kazakhstan.

4. A subsurface use fee shall be charged for any sales of crude minerals and processed products.

Article 17   Rights of Citizens to Produce Common Minerals and Fresh Ground Water Within Allocated Land Parcels to Satisfy their Own Needs

1. Citizens shall have the right to produce, within land parcels allocated thereto, common minerals and fresh ground water to satisfy their own needs.

2. The right to produce common minerals and fresh ground water arises after permission is obtained from a local soviet of people's deputies registered with the territorial geological organization of the Republic of Kazakhstan Ministry of Geology and Subsurface Protection.

3. Environmental protection requirements and sanitation standards pursuant to the laws of the Republic of Kazakhstan shall be observed in producing common minerals and fresh ground water.

4. A list of common minerals and conditions for use of fresh ground water shall be established by Republic of Kazakhstan Ministry of Geology and Subsurface Protection.

Article 18   Allocation of the Subsurface for Burial of Hazardous Materials and Disposal of Industrial Wastes and Waste Water

1. The subsurface shall be allocated for purposes of burial of hazardous materials and disposal of industrial wastes and waste water by the local soviet of people's deputies upon approval by the Republic of Kazakhstan Ministry of Geology and Subsurface Protection, the Republic of Kazakhstan Ministry of Ecology and Bioresources, and the Republic of Kazakhstan Ministry of Health following notification of the public subject to availability of engineering, geological and hydrogeological data providing assurances that no migration of buried products or any decomposition thereof would be possible outside the burial area.
2. The subsurface shall be allocated for use for burial of radioactive materials by the Republic of Kazakhstan Supreme Soviet, with mandatory notification of the public. Permission may be granted when there is an approved plan that ensures reliable, safe burial and that has been given a positive expert evaluation within the Republic of Kazakhstan Ministry of Geology and Subsurface Protection, the Republic of Kazakhstan Ministry of Ecology and Bioresources, the Republic of Kazakhstan State Committee for Oversight of Work Safety in Industry and for Mining Inspection, and the Republic of Kazakhstan Ministry of Health.

Article 19   Term of Subsurface Use

1. The term of subsurface use may be definite or indefinite.
2. In the event of a definite term of subsurface use such term shall be established by an agreement. The term of subsurface use may be extended if necessary.

[Article 20 to 87]

Article 20   Restrictions on Allocation of Subsurface Resources for Use

1. Any parcels of subsurface resources owned by the Republic of Kazakhstan may be allocated for use except those lying under land excluded from use by the Kazakh SSR Land Code and land parcels on which the use of the subsurface may be restricted, including the following:

    (1) Land parcels located in established boundaries of inhabited points and suburban green zones (park areas);
    (2) Parcels occupied by industrial, communications, and transportation facilities and their protection zones;
    (3) Parcels located within especially valuable agricultural land and lands bearing special land-use designation;
    (4) Parcels intended for nature-conservation, sanative, recreational, historical, and cultural purposes.

2. The boundaries of parcels of subsurface resources that are not subject to transfer for use in accordance with Item 2 of Part 1 of the present article shall be determined by local councils of people's deputies.
3. The parcels of subsurface resources listed in items 1 and 2 of Part 1 of the present article may be transferred for use after the consent of the land users is obtained.

Article 21 Grounds for Termination of the Right to Use the Subsurface

1. The right to use the subsurface shall be terminated by the Republic of Kazakhstan Supreme Soviet, the Republic of Kazakhstan Cabinet of Ministers, and local councils of people's deputies at the representation of state agencies that perform expert review and monitor the use of subsurface resources within their purview in the following cases:

    (1) Expiration of the prescribed term, or passing of the need for use of the subsurface;
    (2) Appearance of a threat to the life or health of workers and the public;
    (3) Violation of the terms and conditions of the contract or document of mining concession;
    (4) Violation of regulations governing the use and protection of subsurface resources;
    (5) Exercise of eminent domain on parcels of subsurface resources for other state and public needs;
    (6) If the user has not undertaken to use the subsurface resources within 1 year;
    (7) Closure of the enterprise or other subject of economic activity to which the subsurface resources were granted for use.

2. Legal and physical persons may be deprived of the right to produce common minerals and fresh ground water within land parcels that belong to them if damage is being sustained by subsurface resources and the surrounding environment.

Article 22 Procedure for Terminating the Use of Subsurface Resources

Use of subsurface resources shall be terminated in the following cases.

1. In the case specified by Item 2 of Part 1 of Article 21, the use of subsurface resources shall be terminated immediately after the decision is made, with written notification of the user of the subsurface resources.
2. In the cases specified by items 3 and 4 of Part 1 of Article 21, the decision to terminate use of subsurface resources may be adopted 1 month after the date of written notification of the user of the subsurface resources of violations committed and of the failure to take steps to correct them.
3. In the case specified in Item 5 of Part 1 of Article 21, use of subsurface resources may be terminated 6 months from the date of written notification of the user.
4. Early termination of the use of subsurface resources at the user's initiative may be carried out 6 months from the date of written notification of the owner of the subsurface resources.
5. In case of early termination of the use of subsurface resources, abandonment or conservation of the using enterprise shall be carried out in accordance with the provisions of the present code.
6. The costs of conservation and abandonment of an enterprise shall be borne by the user of the subsurface resources if the use of the subsurface resources was terminated for the reasons presented in Items 2, 3, and 4 of Part 1 of Article 21, or at the initiative of the user of the subsurface resources.
7. Expenses for conservation and abandonment of the using enterprise shall be reimbursed by the owner of the subsurface resources if the use of the subsurface resources was terminated for the reason indicated in Item 5 of Part 1 of Article 21. Here, the user shall be indemnified for expenses sustained and for losses from the shortfall in profit, at the expense of the new user of subsurface resources.

SECTION III AGENCIES OF STATE AUTHORITY AND CONTROL IN THE AREA OF THE USE AND PROTECTION OF SUBSURFACE RESOURCE AND CRUDE MINERAL PROCESSING

Article 23   Competence of the Republic of Kazakhstan Supreme Soviet in the Area of the Use and Protection of Subsurface Resources and Crude Mineral Processing

1. The following are subject to the jurisdiction of the Republic of Kazakhstan Supreme Soviet in the area of the use and protection of subsurface resources and crude mineral processing:

    (1) Exercise of the right of ownership of subsurface resources directly or through local councils of people's deputies and authorized state agencies;
    (2) Drafting and improvement of legislation on subsurface resources and crude mineral processing;
    (3) Determination of state policy and implementation of international and interstate cooperation in the area of the use and protection of subsurface resources and crude mineral processing;
    (4) Approval of state programs for development of the crude minerals base, rational and complete use of mineral resources, and protection of subsurface resources;
    (5) Determination of the procedure for organization and activity of agencies of state authority and control in the area of the use and protection of subsurface resources and crude mineral processing;
    (6) Approval of lists of mineral deposits (fields) of republican significance;
    (7) Allocation of subsurface resources for use for burial of radioactive substances;
    (8) Approval of fees for the use of subsurface resources;
    (9) Monitoring of the enforcement of legislation on subsurface resources and crude mineral processing;
    (10) Protection of the rights of subsurface-resource users;
    (11) Termination of the right to use subsurface resources.

Article 24   Competence of Local Councils of People's Deputies in the Area of the Use and Protection of Subsurface Resources and Crude Mineral Processing

1. The following are subject to the jurisdiction of local councils of people's deputies in the area of the use and protection of subsurface resources and crude mineral processing

    (1) Allocation of a land parcel to a user of subsurface resources for geological study, mineral production, or use of subsurface resources for other purposes;
    (2) Conclusion of a contract with a user of subsurface resources for mineral production of local significance, and use of subsurface resources for other purposes;
    (3) Granting of common minerals and fresh ground water to citizens for use to satisfy their own needs within their land parcels;
    (4) Participation in the development and implementation, within their territory, of the State Program for Development of the Crude Minerals Base, Rational

and Complete Use of Mineral Resources, and Protection of Subsurface Resources;

(5) Organization and monitoring of the collection of a use fee for subsurface resources;
(6) Monitoring of the use and protection of subsurface resources;
(7) Termination of authorized use of subsurface resources and unauthorized building on sites where minerals occur;
(8) Termination of the right to use subsurface resources within their competence in case of a violation of the requirements of the present code;
(9) Protection of the rights of users of subsurface resources.

2. Delimitation of the competence of local councils of people's deputies at different levels in the area of the use and protection of subsurface resources and crude mineral processing shall be carried out in accordance with legislation of the Republic of Kazakhstan.

Article 25 Competence of the Cabinet of Ministers of the Republic of Kazakhstan in the Area of the Use and Protection of Subsurface Resources and Crude Mineral Processing

The following are subject to the jurisdiction of the Republic of Kazakhstan Cabinet of Ministers in the area of the use and protection of subsurface resources and crude mineral processing:

1. Implementation of the policy defined by the Republic of Kazakhstan Supreme Soviet in the area of the use and protection of subsurface resources and crude mineral processing, and organization of international and intergovernmental cooperation;
2. Drafting of state programs for the development of the crude minerals base, rational and complete use of mineral resources, protection of subsurface resources, and monitoring of their implementation;
3. Coordination of the activity of the crude minerals complex;
4. Determination of the procedure for accounting for and assessment of the state of subsurface resources;
5. Assignment of parcels of subsurface resources to features (objects) that are of particular scientific and cultural value;
6. Approval of lists of mineral deposits (fields) of local significance;
7. Determination of the procedure for certification of users of subsurface resources under all forms of ownership;
8. Conclusion of a contract with a user of subsurface resources for mineral production in fields of republican significance;
9. Setting of quotas on the volume of mineral production;
10. Development of fees and an economic mechanism of the use of subsurface resources;
11. Cessation and prohibition of work in case of violation of requirements of the present code;
12. Monitoring of the protection of subsurface resources and regulation of relations for the use of subsurface resources for geological study and the use of subsurface resources for crude mineral extraction and processing and for other purposes.

Article 26 Competence of the State Commission for Mineral Reserves Under the Republic of Kazakhstan Cabinet of Ministers in the Area of the Use and Protection of Subsurface Resources and Crude Mineral Processing

1. The following are subject to the jurisdiction of the State Commission for Mineral Reserves under the Republic of Kazakhstan Cabinet of Ministers in the area of the use and protection of subsurface resources and crude mineral processing:

    (1) Expert review and approval of the required standards for crude minerals, explored mineral reserves, and deposits of republican significance that are being exploited;

    (2) A description of unconfirmed mineral reserves in deposits of republican significance;

    (3) Abandonment and conservation of mineral deposits of republican and local significance.

2. Expert review of foundation documents and contracts with foreign subjects of foreign economic activity related to exploration for mineral deposits and the extraction and processing of crude minerals.

3. The required standards for crude minerals and mineral reserves approved by the State Commission for Mineral Reserves under the Kazakhstan Cabinet of Ministers are the basis for issuance of a mining concession authorization and conclusion of a contract for the use of subsurface resources for crude mineral production and processing in deposits of republican significance.

4. The expert composition of the State Commission for Mineral Reserves under the Republic of Kazakhstan Cabinet of Ministers shall be formed from representatives of users of the republic's subsurface resources.

Article 27 Competence of the Republic of Kazakhstan Ministry of Geology and Subsurface Protection in the Area of the Use and Protection of Subsurface Resources and Crude Mineral Processing

The following are subject to the jurisdiction of the Republic of Kazakhstan Ministry of Geology and Subsurface Protection in the area of the use and protection of subsurface resources and crude mineral processing:

1. Regulation of relations concerning the geological study of subsurface resources and the use of subsurface resources for mineral extraction and processing and for other purposes;

2. Drafting and implementation of the State Program for Development of the Crude Minerals Base, Rational and Complete Use of Mineral Resources, and Protection of Subsurface Resources;

3. State accounting, registration, and licensing of the use of subsurface resources for geological study, crude mineral extraction and processing, and use for other purposes;

4. State accounting of the degree of study of subsurface resources, and compilation and keeping of the state reserve balance and the register of mineral deposits and mineral wastes;

5. Expert review and approval of required standards and reserves of minerals in deposits of local significance;

6. Description of unconfirmed mineral reserves, and abandonment and conservation of enterprises developing mineral deposits of local significance;
7. Expert review of geological exploration programs, feasibility studies and plans for mining and processing enterprises, and plans for the construction of water intakes for ground water;
8. State monitoring of the observation of the prescribed procedure for the use of subsurface resources by enterprises and organizations, regardless of their forms of ownership, and observance of regulations and standards in the area of the protection of subsurface resources and the rational and complete use of minerals;
9. Drafting of quality requirements for geological exploration and enforceable enactments on the regulation of relations concerning the use of subsurface resources and licensing of geological, mine-survey, and analytical work;
10. Participation in the development of an economic mechanism for the use of subsurface resources, and implementation and monitoring of the use of the fund for protection of subsurface resources and reproduction of mineral resources;
11. Development of republican and regional information services on the state and use of crude mineral reserves and other information on subsurface resources, and licensing of information on subsurface resources;
12. Cessation or prohibition of work in case of violations of the requirements of the present code, and surrender of materials to investigative agencies.

SECTION IV   PROTECTION OF SUBSURFACE RESOURCES

Article 28   Objectives of Protection of Subsurface Resources

1. Protection of subsurface resources is related to the work of [Licensees] of the crude mineral complex who are engaged in the geological study of subsurface resources and the production, processing, and reclamation of crude minerals.
2. The completeness and accuracy of geological, hydrogeologic, engineering-geological, and engineering study of subsurface resources constitute the foundation for the protection of subsurface resources.
3. The objects of the protection of subsurface resources are:

   (1) To ensure completeness of the extraction of minerals and components, as well as rational and complete use thereof;
   (2) Preservation and recultivation of landscapes and individual geomorphic structures;
   (3) Preservation of the properties of the energy balance of the top parts of subsurface resources at a level that prevents the manifestation of technogenic processes: earthquakes, landslides, flooding, and soil subsidence.
   (4) The main subjects of the protection of subsurface resources are:

      (1) All sources and types of crude mineral resources;
      (2) All stages of the production cycle – geological study, production, processing, and storage of crude minerals, and waste recovery.

Article 29   Basic Requirements in the Area of Protection of Subsurface Resources

1. The following are the basic requirements in the field of protection of subsurface resources:

(1) Observance of the prescribed procedure and terms and conditions of the contract for use of subsurface resources;

(2) Creation and introduction of effective systems for working of deposits (fields), and of waste-free and low-waste processes during crude mineral processing;

(3) Accurate accounting of recoverable reserves of basic and associated minerals and their components, the products of crude mineral processing, industrial wastes, and losses;

(4) Prevention of a harmful impact of work related to the use of subsurface resources on the state of the environment, preservation of mine workings and boreholes that are in service or in conservation, and underground structures;

(5) Protection of mineral deposits from depletion, contamination, flooding, inundation, fire, and other harmful factors that diminish the quality of minerals and the commercial value of deposits, or that complicate their development;

(6) Prevention of contamination of subsurface resources during work related to their use, and also in case of underground storage of petroleum and gas, burial of radioactive wastes and other hazardous substances, and the discharge of effluents;

(7) Prevention of unauthorized construction on sites of mineral occurrence, and observance of the prescribed procedure for the use of these sites for other purposes.

2. In case of a violation of the requirements of the present article, the use of subsurface resources may be restricted, suspended, or prohibited by duly empowered state agencies and state monitoring services within their purview.

Article 30   Conditions for Construction on Sites Where Minerals Occur, and for Placement of Underground Structures Unrelated to Mineral Production at Sites Where Minerals Occur

1. Planning and construction (renovation) of industrial and agricultural enterprises, cities and other inhabited points, buildings, structures, and objects on sites where minerals occur, and siting of underground structures unrelated to mineral production at sites where minerals occur are prohibited.

2. Construction on sites where minerals occur and siting of underground structures unrelated to mineral extraction are allowed in exceptional cases by permission of agencies of the Republic of Kazakhstan Ministry of Geology and Subsurface Protection, provided that:

(1) It is possible to extract mineral resources from the subsurface;

(2) Compensation is made for the value of the mineral reserves if it is impossible to extract them from the subsurface.

3. The inadvisability of excavation of mineral reserves beneath sites that have been built on or preservation of the constructed facilities before the promulgation of the present code shall be established by feasibility calculations and a feasibility study.

4. Allocation of sites where minerals occur for construction and siting of underground structures unrelated to mineral extraction shall be carried out in compliance with a regulation approved by the Republic of Kazakhstan Cabinet of Ministers.

5. Unauthorized construction on sites where minerals occur and the siting of underground structures unrelated to mineral extraction shall be halted with indemnification for losses sustained by the subsurface resources and the natural

environment and without reimbursement of expenses incurred.

6. The managers of enterprises, organizations, and institutions and citizens who are guilty of unauthorized construction on sites where minerals occur and of unauthorized siting of underground structures unrelated to mineral extraction and who have committed violations of the terms under which permission was granted shall bear administrative, financial, and criminal responsibility in accordance with laws of the Republic of Kazakhstan.

Article 31   Protection of Parcels of Subsurface Resources of Particular Scientific Value

1. Rare geological outcrops, mineralogical formations, paleontological objects, and parcels of subsurface resources that are of historical, cultural, and special scientific value may be declared nature preserves or natural monuments through the prescribed procedure. Economic activity in the vicinity of such objects shall be regulated by laws of the Republic of Kazakhstan.
2. If rare geological outcrops and mineralogical formations, meteorites, and paleontological, archaeological, and other objects of scientific interest are discovered, the users of subsurface resources shall suspend their work, ensure that these objects are preserved, and report to local councils of people's deputies and interested state agencies.
3. Parcels of subsurface resources shall be classified as objects of special scientific value by the Republic of Kazakhstan Cabinet of Ministers upon the representation of the Republic of Kazakhstan Ministry of Geology and Subsurface Protection, as well as other interested ministries and departments.

SECTION II   USE FEE FOR SUBSURFACE RESOURCES

Article 32   Purpose of the Fee

1. A use fee for subsurface resources shall be introduced to provide economic incentive for rational and complete use of crude mineral resources, protection of subsurface resources and the natural environment, regulation of cost-accounting conditions for mining and processing industries, and the solution of socioeconomic problems of republics and administrative-territorial units within which mineral deposits and technogenic formations are located.
2. Introduction of the fee, the rates, and the collection procedure shall be in compliance with laws of the Republic of Kazakhstan.

Article 33   Types of Use Fee for Subsurface Resources

The following types of use fees for subsurface resources have been established in the Republic of Kazakhstan:

1. A fee for the right to use subsurface resources;
2. A use fee for subsurface resources;
3. A fee for protection of subsurface resources and reproduction of crude mineral resources;
4. Rent payments;

5. A use fee for subsurface resources for purposes unrelated to the mining and processing of crude minerals;
6. A fee for nonrational and incomplete use of crude mineral resources;
7. A fee for alienation of crude mineral resources.

Article 34   Fee for the Right to Use Subsurface Resources

1. A fee for the right to use subsurface resources shall be implemented through the procedure of sale of the right of *ownership of* subsurface resources by the Republic of Kazakhstan, and shall be set only for a foreign user upon conclusion of a contract or concession for geological study or exploitation of subsurface resources. Payments shall be collected as one-time (lump-sum) payments (premiums) and lease payments.
2. The amounts of payments for the right to use subsurface resources shall not be secured legislatively, but shall be governed by a *contract* between the owner of the subsurface resources and the foreign contractor.

Article 35   Use Fee for Subsurface Resources

1. The fee for use of subsurface resources (royalties) provides the right of the owner of subsurface resources to part of the actual product or its economic equivalent obtained in the process of development of mineral deposits, processing of crude minerals, and use of subsurface resources for other purposes.
2. A rate set for a defined period per unit final product obtained from the mineral, or per unit useful component contained in this product, is the basis for the fee.

Article 36   Fee for Protection of Subsurface Resources and Reproduction of Crude Mineral Resources

1. A fee for protection of subsurface resources and reproduction of crude mineral resources shall be collected from users of subsurface resources and shall be the designated source for formation of the state extrabudgetary fund, which is used to finance work aimed at protection of subsurface resources and preparation of the crude minerals base.
2. The fee for protection of subsurface resources and reproduction of crude mineral resources includes withholdings: for geological exploration in all stages, as well as payments for the license for geological study and mining concession documents.
3. Withholdings for protection of subsurface resources and reproduction of mineral resources are reduced by enterprises that have financed geological exploration out of their own funds. The amount of the reduction of withholdings shall be determined by the size of the rates for the stages of geological exploration.
4. The amounts of rates of withholdings for protection of subsurface resources and reproduction of mineral resources and the procedure for collecting, distributing, and using them shall be established by the Republic of Kazakhstan Supreme Soviet.

Article 37   Rent Payments

Rent payments shall be established for enterprises that mine and produce crude minerals for which rental income is formed as a result of especially favorable natural conditions.

Article 38   Use Fee for Subsurface Resources for Purposes Unrelated to the Mining and Processing of Crude Minerals

A use fee for subsurface resources for purposes unrelated to the mining and processing of crude minerals shall be determined by contract, and shall take into account mainly damage inflicted on the natural environment.

Article 39 Fee for Nonrational and Incomplete Use of Crude Mineral Resources

A fee for nonrational and incomplete use of crude mineral resources shall be established for losses of minerals (mineral components) and products of their processing, including wastes, that occur as a result of failure to observe current standards and regulations for protection of subsurface resources and for rational and complete use of mineral resources during their extraction, processing, storage, and recovery.

Article 40   Fee for Alienation of Mineral Deposits

A fee for alienation of mineral deposits that are within a zone affected by military ranges, flooded objects, water reservoirs, and so forth shall be paid to compensate for lost profit as a result of permanent or temporary incapacitation from economic use.

Article 41   Payment Concessions

1. The following are exempt from payments for use of subsurface resources:
    (1) Mineralogical preserves;
    (2) Organizations that use parcels of subsurface resources that are of special scientific and cultural value;
    (3) Scientific research and geological exploration organizations of all forms of ownership in the Republic of Kazakhstan during geological study of subsurface resources.
2. Tax abatements to provide incentives for rational and complete use of technogenic mineral resources shall be established by the Republic of Kazakhstan Cabinet of Ministers and local councils of people's deputies.

SECTION VI   GEOLOGICAL STUDY OF SUBSURFACE RESOURCES

Article 42   Purposes and Objectives of the Geological Study of Subsurface Resources

1. The purpose of geological study is to obtain necessary and sufficient information on subsurface resources for use in the interests of the national economy.
2. The objectives of geological study include: complete geological study, evaluation of the republic's crude mineral potential, discovery of mineral deposits, geological and economic evaluation of their commercial importance, and the acquisition of information ensuring the organization of rational and complete use of subsurface

resources and on possible manifestations of geological processes that impede or hinder their use or that pose a danger to the public and to the conduct of economic activity.

Article 43   Basic Requirements for Geological Study of Subsurface Resources

The following must be secured during the geological study of subsurface resources.

1. The scientifically substantiated advisability of setting up work on geological of subsurface resources.
2. The accuracy and required completeness of the geological study of subsurfaces resources and hydrogeologic, engineering, mining, ecological, and other conditions, including sources of water supply for the development of mineral deposits and for construction and operation of underground structures unrelated to mineral extraction.
3. The accuracy of determination of the physical composition, quality, and quantity of reserves of primary and associated minerals and components present therein, and the conduct of work on geological-engineering mapping.
4. The degree of study of the engineering properties of rocks, development of low-waste and waste-free technologies for crude mineral processing, and compilation of horizon-by-horizon geological-engineering maps.
5. The degree of preservation of geological and other documentation obtained through geological study of subsurface resources, essential exploratory mine workings and boreholes, rock and ore samples, and duplicate mineral samples that can be used in further geological study and development of deposits, and in the use of sub-surface resources for purposes unrelated to mineral extraction.
6. Determination of the quantitative and qualitative characteristics of technogenic formations (products of tailing dumps and slag dumps, off-grade ores and rocks in heaps, etc.).
7. Conduct of exploration by methods that eliminate unwarranted losses of crude minerals and degradation of their quality.
8. Separate storage and preservation of rocks and minerals recovered from subsurface resources during cutting of exploratory workings, and elimination of their adverse impact on the natural environment.
9. Recultivation of disturbed land parcels.

Article 44   Transfer of Explored Deposits (Fields) for Mineral Extraction

1. Transfer of explored deposits for mineral extraction to the user of subsurface resources shall be handled by the Republic of Kazakhstan Ministry of Geology and Subsurface Protection and its agencies through issuance of a mining concession document with complete geological-engineering information, and shall be documented in a contract between the user of the subsurface resources and the Republic of Kazakhstan Cabinet of Ministers or local councils of people's deputies.
2. Geological information on deposits that are being transferred for development shall meet the requirements of the degree of exploration of the deposit and evaluation of reserves by stage.
3. The organization that explored the deposit and approved mineral reserves shall

bear responsibility for the accuracy of geological and other information on an administrative, financial, and criminal basis in accordance with laws of the Republic of Kazakhstan.

Article 45   Discoverers of Mineral Deposits

1. Persons who have discovered a previously unknown field that has commercial value and who have identified additional mineral reserves or new crude minerals in a previously known deposit that significantly increase its commercial value shall be recognized as discoverers of the deposits (fields).
2. The rights and conditions for incentives for discoverers shall be defined by the Republic of Kazakhstan Ministry of Geology and Subsurface Protection, according to the Regulation on Discoverers approved by the Republic of Kazakhstan Cabinet of Ministers.

Article 46   Ownership of Information on Subsurface Resources

1. The results of geological study of the subsurface resources of the Republic of Kazakhstan, as embodied in information carriers (maps, tables, textual attachments, etc.) are the property of the customer funding the work resulting in the given information, unless otherwise specified by contract.
2. The right of ownership of geological and other information on subsurface resources shall be protected through the procedure prescribed by laws of the Republic of Kazakhstan.
3. Geological and other information on the subsurface resources of the Republic of Kazakhstan, regardless of funding sources, shall be transferred free of charge, on a mandatory basis, to agencies of the Republic of Kazakhstan Ministry of Geology and Subsurface Protection that store and systematize it. Information on the subsurface resources of the Republic of Kazakhstan shall be turned over for storage in a form that meets established standards.
4. The terms and conditions of use of information obtained through the internal funds of foreign companies and legal or physical persons shall be defined by contract.
5. The implementer has the right to use information obtained as a result of carrying out work for scientific, pedagogic, and other intellectual activity, provided that the commercial interests of the customer, as stipulated by contract, are not affected.
6. Legal and physical persons, with consideration for their participation in the creation of information on subsurface resources or on funding of research, have a preferential right to use the information.
7. Marketing (transfer, exchange, sale) of information on subsurface resources shall be carried out by the Republic of Kazakhstan Ministry of Geology and Subsurface Protection through the procedure prescribed by the Republic of Kazakhstan Cabinet of Ministers.

SECTION VII   PLANNING, CONSTRUCTION, AND STARTUP OF ENTERPRISES FOR MINERAL EXTRACTION, AND OF UNDERGROUND STRUCTURES FOR OTHER PURPOSES

Article 47   Planning of Enterprises for Mineral Extraction, and of Underground Structures for Other Purposes

1. Planning of enterprises for mineral extraction and subsurface structures for other purposes shall be carried out on the basis of the results of comprehensive study of subsurface resources in the parcel of proposed construction, provided that the results of studies are present without fail in the form of technology and ecology regulations, with consideration for technical and ecological safety and the socioeconomic development of the region.
2. Planning of enterprises and revision of plans for existing enterprises for mineral extraction shall be carried out on the basis of reserves approved on the basis of data from detail survey, additional survey, and development survey. For simple and small deposits it is permitted to plan enterprises using reserves approved on the basis of prospecting, evaluations, and preliminary exploration (survey).
3. Plans for enterprises for mineral extraction, revisions thereof, and plans for underground structures for other purposes are subject to state expert review in accordance with the provisions of the present code.
4. Before the start of planning, the locations of enterprises for mineral extraction or underground structures for other purposes are subject to the consent process with local councils of people's deputies.

Article 48   Peculiarities of the Planning of Enterprises for Mineral Extraction and Underground Structures for Other Purposes Under Complex Forecasting Conditions

1. During planning of enterprises for mineral extraction (production) and underground structures for other purposes in cases where there is a complex prediction of possible adverse ecological and other consequences of the construction and operation of a project, the plan shall undergo comprehensive expert review by a commission specially formed by the Republic of Kazakhstan Cabinet of Ministers. The conclusions of the expert commission shall be made known to the public through agencies and the mass media.
2. The councils of people's deputies shall inform the public of the possible siting of enterprises for mineral extraction and of underground structures for other purposes whose activity affects the social interests of local residents.
3. Planning of underground structures involving the burial of hazardous wastes and industrial wastes, including radioactive wastes, shall be allowed only when reliable geological data are available concerning the possibility of localizing the substances that are to be buried within strictly defined boundaries and when there is a guarantee that precludes the penetration of these substances into neighboring parcels of subsurface resources, ground water, the [day] surface, and the air.

Article 49   Basic Requirements for Planning, Construction, and Startup of Mineral-Extracting Enterprises and Underground Structures for Other Purposes

1. The plan for a mineral-extracting enterprise, including semicommercial development of a deposit, and the plan for underground structures for other purposes shall meet the requirements of the present code and normative planning documents.
2. The plans for enterprises shall provide for:

    (1) An ecological and economic study of enterprises that are under construction and renovation;
    (2) Siting of surface and underground structures of enterprises that will ensure rational and complete use of mineral reserves;
    (3) Methods of penetrating and preparing mineral deposits and systems for developing them that will ensure the most complete, rational, and complete extraction from the subsurface of reserves of primary and associated minerals, and methods of preserving and using country rock that is incidentally separated from its native mass;
    (4) A special 'Protection of Subsurface Resources' section with calculations and a feasibility study to establish rational indices of mineral extraction and ensure complete use of crude minerals with specific measures for achieving them;
    (5) The advisability of using vacated space underground for needs of the national economy;
    (6) Rational use of drain water and overburden in construction and in the development of mineral deposits, separate storage of and accounting for them by type, and prevention of depletion of fresh ground water, mineral water, and therapeutic water;
    (7) Separate storage of, accounting for, and storage of associated minerals that are temporarily not being used, and industrial wastes containing valuable components;
    (8) Further geological study of subsurface resources (additional exploration, development survey), and geological and mine-survey support of work;
    (9) Instruments and automatic monitoring equipment for accurate accounting of the quality and quantity of crude minerals that are to be extracted and processed;
    (10) Measures that ensure the technical safety of work, production personnel, the public, buildings, structures, and environmental features;
    (11) Measures aimed at recultivation of disturbed land;
    (12) Calculations of payments for the use of subsurface resources.

3. Damages sustained by the owner and user of subsurface resources as a result of substandard planning shall be indemnified by the planner.
4. Construction, renovation, and startup of mineral-extracting enterprises and underground structures for other purposes are prohibited:

    (1) If requirements set forth in the present code are not observed during planning;
    (2) If state planning standards and norms are not observed;
    (3) If geological and mine-survey services are not provided for the work.

SECTION VIII USE OF SUBSURFACE RESOURCES FOR MINERAL PRODUCTION AND OTHER RESOURCES

Article 50 Use of Subsurface Resources for Mineral Extraction and Other Purposes

1. Subsurface resources shall be allocated for mineral extraction and other purposes within a mining concession according to the provisions of the present code.
2. The portion of subsurface resources on land that is granted to users for commercial development of the minerals contained therein or for use of subsurface resources for other purposes is called a mining concession.
3. Development of deposits outside of mining concessions is prohibited. The exchange and annexation of parcels of deposits located outside the confines of a mining concession may be carried out through the procedure prescribed for obtaining a new mining concession authorization.

Article 51 Basic Requirements for Development of Mineral Deposits

During the development of mineral deposits, the following must be ensured:

1. Completeness of extraction of resources, and the use of rational, technologically and ecologically safe methods of extraction of primary, associated, and incidental minerals that preclude spoilage of deposits, the formation of above-standard losses, and selective processing of mineral resources;
2. Prevention of spoilage of mineral deposits that are being developed and adjacent deposits, prevention of depletion of groundwater resources as a result of the work carried out, and preservation of mineral reserves preserved within the subsurface for future use;
3. Separate storage, preservation, and accounting of incidentally extracted, temporarily unused minerals and industrial wastes that contain valuable components;
4. Accuracy of geological and mine-survey work during exploration and development;
5. Accurate accounting for and state reporting on matters of the state and migration of reserves, losses and degradation of minerals, extraction of mineral and components, and the use of drain water, as well as allowance for the comprehensive nature of the development and use of crude minerals and evacuated space in the subsurface;
6. Indemnification for damages sustained by the owner of subsurface resources through a decree in the indices of mineral extraction and completeness of utilization, compared with approved figures;
7. Recultivation of disturbed land;
8. Systematic observation of the state of the rock mass.

Article 52 Requirements for Development of Technogenic Formations

1. All technogenic formations of crude minerals extracted from the subsurface and all processing wastes and products (tailing and slag dumps, low-grade orders, rocks, slags, etc.) are subject to classification.
2. Exploration, evaluation, and startup of technogenic formations shall run ahead of this work in fields with analogous minerals.

3. The requirements set forth in sections VI, VII, VIII, and IX of the present code apply to the study, planning, construction, and startup of facilities for crude mineral extraction and processing.

4. Technogenic mineral resources formed before the promulgation of the present code are the property of the Republic of Kazakhstan. The use, purchase, and sale of technogenic formations without a feasibility study are prohibited.

Article 53 Abandonment and Conservation of Enterprises for Mineral Extraction and the Use of Subsurface Resources for Other Purposes

1. Abandonment and conservation of an enterprise for mineral extraction and for the use of subsurface resources for other purposes are allowed in the following cases:

   (1) After complete working of balance mineral reserves, with no prospects for increasing them;
   (2) Substantiation of the impossibility of followup working of the deposit, and of bringing into production of off-balance reserves, provided that reserves that have lost their commercial importance are written off through the prescribed procedure;
   (3) Economic infeasibility of further working of a deposit or a part thereof, and also in case of use of subsurface resources for other purposes;
   (4) Appearance of a threat of flooding or collapse of mine workings prevention of which is technically impossible or economically infeasible;
   (5) The absence of any need to use the subsurface resources for other purposes.

2. Abandonment and conservation of enterprises for mineral extraction and the use of subsurface resources for other purposes shall be carried out by users of subsurface resources according to a special program consented to by the Republic of Kazakhstan Ministry of Geology and Subsurface Protection, the Republic of Kazakhstan Ministry of Ecology and Bioresources, and the Republic of Kazakhstan State Committee for Oversight of Work Safety in Industry and for Mine Inspection.

3. Upon abandonment or conservation of an enterprise for mineral extraction or a part thereof, or use of subsurface resources for other purposes, the user of the *subsurface* resources shall:

   (1) As of the time of completion of work, complete geological and mine-survey documentation and turn it over for storage by agencies of the Republic of Kazakhstan Ministry of Geology and Subsurface Protection;
   (2) Place mine workings and boreholes in a state that ensures public safety, protection of the natural environment, buildings, and structures, and preservation of the deposit;
   (3) Answer the question of possible use of mine workings and boreholes for other national economic purposes;
   (4) Place the ground surface in a condition suitable for use in the national economy;
   (5) Perform expert evaluation of the geological state of the rock mass.

4. Before completion of the abandonment process and during conservation, the user of subsurface resources shall bear all obligations with respect to the use of subsurface resources, as well as full responsibility under the contract and the present code.

SECTION IX   PROCESSING OF CRUDE MINERALS

Article 54   Basic Requirements for Creation of Technologies for Crude Mineral Processing

1. A deposit is considered to have been prepared for commercial development if there is an effective process flow diagram for processing of the crude minerals that can be made the basis for planning of the enterprise, in the form of approved engineering regulations.
2. The degree of engineering study must allow the creation of waste-free and low-waste technologies for ore processing at the level of scientific and technical advances with mandatory resolution of the question of whether to neutralize or bury wastes.
3. For large and unique deposits, a waste-free comprehensive technology for crude mineral processing shall be worked out in two directions:

    (1) On the basis of commercial counterparts and series-produced equipment or equipment that has been prepared for series production;
    (2) Creation of fundamentally new technology for waste-free or low-waste complete processing on the basis of the latest scientific advances.

4. For deposits exploration of which is being conducted to supplement the crude minerals base of existing mining enterprises for the long term, the degree of engineering must provide for:
    (1) Development of the commercial technology without significant renovation of its processing facilities, with mandatory supplementation of the process flow diagram with units for waste-free complete processing;
    (2) Development of a new industrial scheme for waste-free complete ore processing if this scheme ensures a higher level of technical and economic indices of the use of crude minerals.

Article 55   Basic Requirements for Planning of Facilities for Crude Mineral Processing

Industrial facilities for crude mineral processing shall be planned on the basis of an engineering regulation for the planning and construction of these facilities, approved through the prescribed procedure.

1. The plan must provide for the following:

    (1) Ecological and economic substantiation of facilities under construction and renovation;
    (2) Siting of surface and underground service lines so that there is no adverse effect on the completeness of extraction of useful components during processing;
    (3) Use of process flow diagrams that allow the rational and complete extraction of useful components, calculation of a loss allowance, the fullest possible use of circulating water supply, enrichment tailings, slag, dust, slurry, effluents, and other processing products classified as waste;
    (4) Hardware and measures aimed at providing accurate accounting of the quantity and quality of processing products and waste;
    (5) Separate storage, accounting, and preservation of useful components incidentally produced and temporarily unused;

(6) Recultivation of land disturbed as a result of the operations of enterprises.

2. It is not allow to plan and build facilities for crude mineral processing by using processes that leave an ineradicable adverse impact on the environment.

3. Drafted plans for crude mineral processing facilities are subject to expert review by the Republic of Kazakhstan Ministry of Geology and Subsurface Protection, the Republic of Kazakhstan Ministry of Ecology and Bioresources, the Republic of Kazakhstan State Committee for Oversight of Work Safety in Industry and for Mine Inspection. and the Republic of Kazakhstan Ministry of Health, within their respective purviews.

Article 56 Construction and Startup of Facilities for Crude Mineral Processing

1. Facilities for processing of crude minerals may be placed in operation after the complete of construction of all nature-conservation facilities and services that ensure the complete extraction of all components taken into account in approved mineral reserves according to the complete planning program.

2. As an exception, new enterprises and enterprises undergoing renovation may be placed in operation according to process flow diagrams that eliminate the extraction of individual useful components if there are no consumers for their products at the time of acceptance of the construction projects for operation, provided that they are stored, their quality is preserved, and there is no ineradicable adverse impact on the natural environment.

3. The construction, renovation, and startup of enterprises for crude mineral processing are prohibited unless the requirements set forth in the present code are observed during planning.

Article 57 Requirements for the Level of Rational and Complete Use of Crude Minerals During Processing

1. Commercial processing of crude minerals shall be carried out by using waste-free and low-waste processes.

2. As an exception, it may be permitted to use processes in which wastes are formed, provided that there is a positive finding by the ecological and economic expert review, in the following cases:

   (1) There are no areas for use of the processing wastes;
   (2) Reliable storage of wastes, accounting therefor, and preservation of useful minerals and components.

3. It is prohibited to use processing methods on crude minerals that cause harm to the natural environment and that lead to loss of its capacity for self-restoration.

Article 58 Programs for Development of Waste-Free Processes and Complete Processing of Crude Minerals

1. The creation of processes for waste-free and low-waste complete processing of crude minerals is a long-range strategy for the development of all enterprises of processing complexes of the Republic of Kazakhstan. This strategy is being

pursued on the basis of the State Program for the Development of the Crude Minerals Base, Rational and Complete Use of Mineral Resources, and Protection of Subsurface Resources.

2. Programs for creation of waste-free technologies for complete processing of minerals provide for implementation of scientific research, experimental design, and planning work to increase the completeness of utilization of raw materials, determine areas where industrial wastes can be used, create new production equipment, protect the natural environment, rebuild existing facilities, build new ones, and implement other organizational and technical measures that ensure fulfillment of the tasks posed.

3. The programs are periodically supplemented and renewed with consideration for the results of scientific, design, and planning developments and advances of scientific and technical progress.

4. The degree of completeness of the utilization of crude minerals and the level of use shall be determined on the basis of special regulations approved by the Republic of Kazakhstan Cabinet of Ministers.

Article 59   Information on Processing Technology for Crude Minerals

1. Information on processing technology for crude minerals that is developed both during geological exploration and during development of a deposit is the property of the organization that finances its development, and may be used at the discretion of the latter in subordinate industries. Transfer of information on the technology to a third party may be effected by the owner of the information with the consent of the customer and the developer.

2. Individual citizens may have the right of owner of information on crude mineral processing technology in cases where they have funded engineering research or, as the developers of the technology, they carried out research at the level of an invention affirmed through the prescribed procedure.

SECTION X STATE ACCOUNTING OF THE STATE OF SUBSURFACE RESOURCES

Article 60   State Accounting of the State of Subsurface Resources

1. State accounting of the state of subsurface resources is the foundation for elaboration of the strategy and tactics for activities of the crude minerals complex in the republic, and is carried out for the entire production cycle: during geological study, extraction, and processing of crude minerals, the use of subsurface resources for other purposes, and the use of industrial wastes.

2. To ensure planning of work directed at the geological study and rational and complete use of minerals, and also at the fulfillment of other national economic tasks, the following are carried out:

    (1) State registration of work on the geological study and use of subsurface resources for mineral production and other purposes;
    (2) The state registry of deposits and shows of minerals;
    (3) The state registry of wastes from the extraction and processing of crude minerals, and of waste burial;
    (4) State approval of the required standards and reserves of minerals;

(5) State description and conservation of mineral reserves;
(6) The state balance of mineral reserves;
(7) State accounting of losses of crude minerals during extraction and processing;
(8) State accounting of the completeness of utilization of crude minerals.

3. A compilation of state statistical accounting of the status of subsurface resources shall be made annually by agencies of the Republic of Kazakhstan Ministry of Geology and Subsurface Protection on the basis of primary accounting data and data from statistical reporting by users on mineral extraction from the subsurface, the migration of mineral reserves, complete utilization of minerals and components during beneficiation and metallurgical processing, and the use of overburden and industrial wastes, and the reporting balance for minerals, as submitted by all users of the crude minerals complex.

4. State statistical accounting of the status of subsurface resources shall be kept on special forms approved by the Republic of Kazakhstan Cabinet of Ministers.

Article 61 State Registration of Work on the Geological Study and Use of Subsurface Resources for Mineral Extraction and Other Purposes

1. All work by users on the geological study and use of subsurface resources for mineral extraction and other purposes, regardless of the forms of ownership, shall be subject to state accounting and registration for purposes of summarization and use of the results of studies of subsurface resources.

2. State accounting of work on the geological study and use of subsurface resources for mineral extraction and other purposes is based on state registration and is carried out according to the unified system.

3. Performance of work without registration is prohibited.

Article 62 State Registry of Mineral Deposits and Shows

The state registry of mineral deposits and shows contains information on each deposit that characterizes the quantity and quality of reserves of primary and associated minerals and the incidental components contained in them, technical mining, hydrogeologic, and other conditions, a geological-economic evaluation thereof, and information on every show of minerals.

Article 63 State Registries of Wastes From Crude Mineral Extraction and Processing and Waste Burial

The State Registry of Wastes From Crude Mineral Extraction and Processing contains information on every object being stored, characterizing the type or kind of waste and stating their quantitative and qualitative indices and mining conditions of storage, and is kept on the basis of reporting data from users of subsurface resources.

Article 64 State Approval of Standard Requirements for and Reserves of Minerals

1. Upon approval of standard requirements and reserves of minerals in explored fields, their accuracy and the quantity, and quality, mode of occurrence, degree of study, national economic significance, and degree of readiness of the deposit (field)

for commercial development shall be established.

2. The requirements for and quality of minerals shall be defined by standard requirements and by international and state standards.

3. In order to ensure maximal completeness of study of subsurface resources and to organize subsequent complete use thereof, standard requirements shall be established for crude minerals for each deposit or part thereof. When necessary, standard requirements also may be established for fields to which it is possible to apply international and state standards.

4. The standard requirements represent the aggregate of economically substantiated requirements on the quality of minerals and on mining, geological, and other conditions of development of a deposit or individual sections thereof, and shall be drawn up with consideration for the use of primary minerals and associated minerals and the primary and associated components present in the reserves being evaluated.

5. The standard requirements for crude minerals shall be established both in stages of geological exploration (evaluative, temporary, commercial) and during the development of deposits (operational requirements, in the stages of final exploration and development survey).

6. Feasibility studies of the standard requirements, compiled on a competitive basis by geological-exploration and planning organizations and users of subsurface resources, as well as mineral reserves, calculated on their basis, in newly explored and developed deposits shall be subject to approval by the State Commission for Mineral Reserves under the Republic of Kazakhstan Cabinet of Ministers in fields of republican significance and by territorial commissions for reserves of the Ministry of Geology and Subsurface Protection in fields of local significance and common minerals.

Compilation of feasibility studies of standard requirements in fields of republican significance shall be carried out by the planning organizations that carry out planning of facilities.

Article 65   State Writeoff and Conservation of Mineral Reserves

1. Extracted minerals and mineral reserves that have lost their commercial significance and that have been lost during extraction and not confirmed in subsequent geological exploration or the development of the field are subject to writeoff to reflect the corresponding changes in the State Minerals Balance.

2. Permission to write off, with consideration for the indicated reserves (other than unconfirmed minerals), shall be granted by agencies of the Republic of Kazakhstan Ministry of Geology and Subsurface Protection.

Article 66   State Balance of Mineral Reserves

1. The State Balance of Mineral Reserves contains information on the quantity, quality, and degree of study of mineral reserves in deposits, the degree of commercial development, production, losses, and degradation, and the percentage of reserves explored.

2. The State Balance of Mineral Reserves shall be submitted upon request to local councils of people's deputies, planning institutes, and users of subsurface resources through the chain of command, and to interested ministries and departments.

Article 67 State Accounting of Losses of Crude Minerals during Extraction and Processing

State accounting of losses of crude minerals during extraction and processing contains data on the quantity and quality of primary and associated minerals and components that have been lost as a result of development of a deposit and processing of crude minerals.

Article 68 State Accounting of the Completeness of Use of Crude Minerals

State accounting of the completeness of use of crude minerals contains information on the level of extraction of primary and associated minerals and components during processing of crude minerals.

SECTION XI TECHNICAL SAFETY OF WORK RELATED TO USE OF SUBSURFACE RESOURCES

Article 69 Ensuring Technical Safety in Performance of Work Related to the Use of Subsurface Resources

1. Technical safety of production personnel, the public, and the environment must be ensured during construction, renovation, and operation of enterprises for extraction and processing of crude minerals, as well as underground structures unrelated to mineral extraction, and during the performance of geological exploration and other work related to the use of subsurface resources.
2. Permission to carry out work during the use of subsurface resources in regard to ensuring technical safety shall be issued by the Republic of Kazakhstan State Committee for Oversight of Work Safety in Industry and for Mine Supervision and its agencies.
3. The responsibility for the state of technical safety at enterprises, organization, and institutions that use subsurface resources and process crude minerals shall be assigned to their first directors or the owner of the enterprise.
4. State monitoring of the observance of technical safety regulations and standards during the use of subsurface resources and processing of crude minerals shall be provided by the Republic of Kazakhstan State Committee for Oversight of Work Safety in Industry and for Mine Supervision and its agencies to which responsibility for observance of the requirements for ensuring technical safety is assigned.

Article 70 Basic Requirements for Ensuring Safe Conduct of Work Related to the Use of Subsurface Resources

1. During the performance of work related to the use of subsurface resources, regulations and standards concerning technically safe conduct of work must be fulfilled, and measures to prevent and eliminate accidents and mishaps must be implemented.
2. It is prohibited to carry out work on the use of subsurface resources if their condition poses a hazard to human life and health.

SECTION XII STATE MONITORING OF THE PROTECTION AND USE OF SUBSURFACE RESOURCES

Article 71 Tasks of State Monitoring of the Protection and Use of Subsurface Resources

State monitoring of the protection and use of subsurface resources shall be carried out in all stages of activity in the crude minerals complex and shall ensure:

1. Observance of the prescribed procedure for the use of subsurface resources by all users of subsurface resources, regardless of the forms of ownership;
2. Performance of obligations with respect to the completeness and comprehensiveness of the use and protection of subsurface resources;
3. Prevention and elimination of the adverse effect of work on the natural environment, buildings, and structures;
4. Observance of the regulations for state accounting of the state of subsurface resources, the state and migration of mineral reserves and mineral components, losses, completeness of use, and accounting for industrial wastes;
5. The completeness and reliability of geological, mining, and other information obtained during geological study of subsurface resources, the use of subsurface resources, and processing of crude minerals, and observance of other regulations and standards prescribed by the Republic of Kazakhstan Law on Subsurface Resources.

Article 72 State Monitoring of the Protection of Subsurface Resources and the Rational and Complete Use of Crude Minerals

1. State monitoring of the protection of subsurface resources and rational and complete use of crude minerals shall be carried out by the Republic of Kazakhstan Ministry of Geology and Subsurface Protection, and also by geological and mine survey services of extractive and processing enterprises to which responsibility is assigned for observance by enterprises, organizations, and institutions of the requirements of the present code.
2. State monitoring of the geological study and expert review of geological information shall be provided by the State Commission for Mineral Reserves under the Republic of Kazakhstan Cabinet of Ministers with the participation of plan drafters.
3. A regulation on state monitoring of the protection and use of subsurface resources and a regulation on geological and mine survey services of enterprises shall be approved by the Republic of Kazakhstan Cabinet of Ministers.

Article 73 Implementation of the State Monitoring of the Protection and Rational Use of Subsurface Resources and Complete Processing of Crude Minerals

State monitoring of the protection and rational use of subsurface resources and of comprehensive processing of crude minerals shall check the following:

1. Implementation of requirements for protection and rational use of subsurface resources and complete processing of crude minerals;

2. Observance of the prescribed procedure for the use of subsurface resources;
3. The direction, method, comprehensiveness, quality, and accuracy of work on geological study of subsurface resources during all types of use of subsurface resources;
4. Observance of the prescribed procedure and the accuracy of accounting of the quantity and quality of mineral reserves that are being mined and left in the subsurface, processing products, and industrial wastes, as well as parcels of subsurface resources granted for purposes unrelated to mineral extraction;
5. The degree of substantiation of indices of extraction of minerals and components during the extraction and processing of crude minerals, and their actual values;
6. The compliance of technologies used at an enterprise with planning decisions, and the presence and implementation of state programs on these matters;
7. The correctness of collection of the use fee for subsurface resources, and of payments and penalties.

[Such monitoring] also shall check other matters of the protection of subsurface resources and the rational and complete use of mineral resources.

Article 74 Rights of State Monitoring of the Protection and Use of Subsurface Resources

State monitoring of the protection and use of subsurface resources has the right to:

1. Issue instructions, mandatory for execution, for elimination of violations of the present code;
2. Halt work on geological study if the work does not comply with approved plans or is being conducted without state registration, and also in cases of violations of regulations and standards that define the procedure for carrying out this work;
3. Halt work related to the use of subsurface resources during the extraction and processing of crude minerals in cases of violations of the requirements of the present code;
4. Convey to local councils of people's deputies documents concerning authorized use of subsurface resources and unauthorized construction on sites where minerals occur, so that steps can be taken;
5. Following prescribed procedure, apply measures of administrative sanction in the form of fines to officials of enterprises and organizations that use subsurface resources in violation of the requirements of laws on subsurface resources, raise the question of applying disciplinary measures against them with the administrations of enterprises and organizations, and turn over materials to investigative agencies to initiate criminal and financial proceedings against the parties at fault;
6. Submit penalty sanctions for irrational and incomplete use of crude minerals, and the use of subsurface resources in violation of the requirements of the present code.

Article 75 Production Monitoring of the Protection of Subsurface Resources and of Rational and Complete Use of Crude Minerals

1. Responsibility for the state of protection of subsurface resources at enterprises, organizations, and institutions that use subsurface resources and process crude minerals shall be assigned to their first directors or to the owner of the enterprise.
2. At enterprises for extraction and processing of crude minerals, production monitoring shall be supported by engineering personnel and the Technical Monitoring Division.

3. Engineering personnel and technical monitoring divisions of enterprises for extraction and processing of crude minerals shall bear legally prescribed responsibility for nonperformance of their obligations.

SECTION XIII PARTICIPATION OF PUBLIC ORGANIZA-TIONS AND CITIZENS IN THE IMPLEMENTATION OF MEASURES AIMED AT PROTECTION OF SUBSURFACE RESOURCES AND RATIONAL AND COMPLETE USE OF CRUDE MINERALS

Article 76 Promotion by Public Organizations and Citizens of Protection of Subsurface Resources and of Rational and Comprehensive Use of Crude Minerals

1. Public organizations and citizens shall assist state agencies in implementing measures on protection of subsurface resources and the rational and complete use of crude minerals by making recommendations, participating directly in the work, and reporting violations of laws on subsurface resources and on the processing of crude minerals.
2. Public organizations shall take part in activities directed toward ensuring protection of subsurface resources and rational and complete use of crude minerals according to their charters (regulations) and legislation of the Republic of Kazakhstan.
3. State agencies shall take into account the recommendations of public organs and citizens during implementation of measures aimed at protection of subsurface resources and at rational and complete use of crude minerals.

SECTION XIV TEACHING OF THE LAW ON SUBSURFACE RESOURCES AND PROCESSING OF CRUDE MINERALS, AND VOCATIONAL TRAINING FOR MANAGERIAL, ENGINEERING, AND TECHNICAL PERSONNEL OF WORKERS IN THE CRUDE MINERALS COMPLEX

Article 77 Teaching of the Law on Subsurface Resources and Processing of Crude Minerals in Special Educational Institutions

Mandatory teaching of the law on subsurface resources and processing of crude minerals shall be provided in higher and secondary special educational institutions (legal, polytechnical, mining, metallurgical, geological exploration).

Article 78 Vocational Training for Managerial, Engineering, and Technical Personnel at Enterprises and Organizations of the Crude Minerals Complex

Managers and engineering and technical personnel of enterprises and organizations and other forms of ownership of the crude minerals complex must have vocational training on matters of protection of subsurface resources and the rational and complete use of minerals, and must know laws on subsurface resources and on the processing of crude minerals.

SECTION XV   RESOLUTION OF DISPUTES ON MATTERS OF THE USE OF SUBSURFACE RESOURCES AND CRUDE MINERAL PROCESSING

Article 79   Agencies That Resolve Disputes in the Area of the Use of Subsurface Resources and Crude Mineral Processing

Disputes over the possession, use, and disposition of subsurface resources and processing of crude minerals shall be heard by courts and arbitration courts through the procedure prescribed by laws of the Republic of Kazakhstan.

Article 80   Resolution of Disputes between the Republic of Kazakhstan and Other States

1. Disputes between the Republic of Kazakhstan and other states in regard to the use of subsurface resources and the processing of crude minerals shall be heard by a commission of representatives of the parties.
2. If the commission fails to reach an agreed-upon decision, the disputes may be heard on an arbitration tribunal basis.

SECTION XVI   RESPONSIBILITY FOR VIOLATION OF THE LAW ON SUBSURFACE RESOURCES AND CRUDE MINERAL PROCESSING

Article 81   Responsibility of Persons Guilty of Violation of the Law on Subsurface Resources and Crude Mineral Processing

1. Transactions that openly or covertly violate the rights of ownership, disposition, and use of subsurface resources shall be recognized as invalid.
2. Persons guilty of conducting the aforementioned transactions and other violations of laws on subsurface resources and crude mineral processing shall bear the disciplinary, financial, administrative, and criminal responsibility prescribed by law.
3. Legislation of the Republic of Kazakhstan also may establish responsibility for violations of requirements of laws on subsurface resources and crude mineral processing.
4. Institution of disciplinary, administrative, and criminal proceedings shall not relieve guilty parties of their obligation to indemnify for damages caused by them.

Article 82 Disciplinary Responsibility for Violation of the Law on Subsurface Resources and Crude Mineral Processing

Officials and other workers of enterprises, institutions, and organizations guilty of violating the requirements of laws on subsurface resources and crude mineral processing that stem from the work duties and functions, or from their official position, shall bear disciplinary responsibility prescribed by law.

Article 83 Administrative Responsibility for Violation of the Law on Mineral Resources and Crude Mineral Processing

Officials and citizens guilty of the following shall bear the administrative responsibility prescribed by law:

1. Carrying out work on geological study of subsurface resources without state registration;
2. Unsubstantiated refusal to perform work on geological study and to allocate subsurface resources for mineral extraction and use for other purposes;
3. Violation of regulations and requirements for carrying out work on geological study of subsurface resources that leads to inaccurate evaluation of explored mineral reserves or mining and geological conditions for construction and operation of enterprises that extract and process crude minerals, underground structures for burial of industrial wastes, effluent discharge, and other purposes;
4. Violation of regulations and standards during drafting of plans for enterprises engaged in extraction and processing of crude minerals;
5. Nonobservance of planning decisions on the extraction and processing of crude minerals in regard to the completeness of extraction and completeness of use of minerals and components, and separate storage and preservation of industrial wastes;
6. Selective working of rich sections of a deposit, leading to deterioration of the quantity and quality of remaining reserves and unsubstantiated, above-plan and above-allowance losses of minerals;
7. Failure to ensure accurate determination of the quantity and quality of mineral during extraction and processing;
8. Distortion of primary and state reporting intended to account for the extraction and processing of crude minerals;
9. Damage to observation holes running on ground water, and to mine-survey and geodetic signs;
10. Failure to carry out the instructions of agencies of state monitoring of the protection and use of subsurface resources and crude mineral processing.

Article 84 Criminal Responsibility for Violation of the Law on Subsurface Resources and Crude Mineral Processing

Officials and citizens guilty of the following shall bear criminal responsibility in accordance with the Republic of Kazakhstan Criminal Code:

1. Unauthorized extraction of minerals;
2. Unauthorized construction on sites where minerals occur;
3. Failure to carry out the requirements for bringing mine workings and boreholes

that are being abandoned and placed in conservation to a state that will ensure the ecological and technical safety of personnel and the public, and failure to meet the requirements for preservation of deposits, mine workings, and boreholes for the duration of conservation;

4. Failure to carry out the requirements for burial of industrial wastes and effluent discharge;
5. Allowing losses of stored hazardous products and wastes from crude minerals;
6. Violation, loss, destruction, or misappropriation of mine-survey, geological, accounting, and engineering documentation, as well as duplicate samples of minerals and cores necessary for further geological study of subsurface resources and deposit development;
7. Intentional distortion or destruction of primary and state statistical reports used to account for the extraction and processing of crude minerals;
8. Carrying out work related to the use of subsurface resources and methods that create a threat to public safety or a threat of environmental pollution.

Article 85 Indemnification for Damage Sustained as a Result of Violation of the Law on Subsurface Resources and Crude Mineral Processing

1. Enterprises, organizations, institutions, and citizens shall indemnify damages resulting from a violation of the law on subsurface resources and processing of crude minerals in the amounts and through the procedure prescribed by laws of the Republic of Kazakhstan.
2. Officials and other workers through whose fault enterprises, organizations, and institutions have sustained costs related to indemnification for losses shall bear administrative, financial, and criminal responsibility through the procedure prescribed by laws of the Republic of Kazakhstan.

SECTION XVII INTERNATIONAL TREATIES

Article 86 Rules of International Cooperation in the Area of the Use of Subsurface Resources and Crude Mineral Processing

The Republic of Kazakhstan shall conduct international cooperation in the area of the use and processing of crude minerals on the basis of observance of generally recognized norms of international law and recognition of the sovereign rights of states to subsurface resources located within their jurisdiction.

Article 87 Obligations of Legal and Physical Persons in the Area of the Use of Subsurface Resources and Crude Mineral Processing

In the implementation of economic activity within the Republic of Kazakhstan in the area of the use of subsurface resources and crude mineral processing, legal and physical persons of foreign states shall observe the requirements of the present code and other legislative instruments on subsurface resources of the Republic of Kazakhstan.

President of the Republic of Kazakhstan

Annex 7

Petroleum Law of the Republic of Kazakhstan
Draft, 1993

CONTENTS

The present law shall regulate the relationships connected with conducting Oil Operations. The Law shall protect the interests of the Republic of Kazakhstan and its natural resources, define the rights and obligations of contractors, regulate their relations with the government bodies, and act in accordance with the other laws of the Republic of Kazakhstan.

CHAPTER 1 GENERAL PROVISIONS

Article 1 Definitions

'Oil' shall mean Crude Oil and Natural Gas and also hydrocarbons produced from Crude Oil, Natural Gas, oil shale or tar sand.

'Crude Oil' shall mean any hydrocarbons, regardless of their density, produced in liquid state from a well under normal atmospheric temperature and pressure, including liquid hydrocarbons, known under the names of distillate or condensate, which comes from Natural Gas through the process of condensation.

'Natural Gas' Shall mean hydrocarbons which exist in gaseous state under normal atmospheric temperature and pressure, including rich mineral gas, dry mineral gas, associated gas and residual gas which remains after the extraction or separation of liquid hydrocarbons from rich gas, and non-hydrocarbon gas produced together with liquid and gaseous hydrocarbons.

'Associated Components in Oil' shall mean metal-containing and other compounds of various types, which are a constituent part of oil.

'Oil Operations' shall mean all works related to geological exploration, completion, production, processing, enrichment of production (including Natural Gas cleaning and dehydration as well as removal of Associated Components of oil), storage, transportation and sale of hydrocarbons in domestic and foreign markets.

'A Competent Body' shall mean the Government of the Republic of Kazakhstan or another government body to whom it has delegated the rights directly connected with signing and implementation of Contracts for conducting Oil Operations.

'A Contractor' shall mean any legal or natural person, or a consortium of such persons, states and/or international organizations, who carry out Oil Operations in the Republic of Kazakhstan in accordance with the present Law.

'A Contract' shall mean an agreement, between a Contractor and a Competent Body, for conducting Oil Operations.

'A Contract Territory' shall mean a territory allocated, by a Contract, for conducting Oil Operations and defined by geographical co-ordinates.

'Commercial Detection' and 'Commercial Discovery' shall mean a discovery, at a contract territory, of one or several hydrocarbon fields, the development of which is commercially viable.

'A Field' shall mean one or several natural accumulations of hydrocarbons in a geological reservoir of any type.

'A License' shall mean a permission granted by the government of the Republic of Kazakhstan, or, on its behalf, by an appropriate state body, to a contractor for a specific type of Oil Operation within the Contract Territory over a fixed period of time.

'The Main Pipeline' shall mean an engineering installation, consisting of the linear part and overland facilities , communications, remote control and other connection facilities, which is intended for transportation of Oil from the place of production (processing) to the place of transfer to other types of transport or the place of consumption. A pipeline which works as a collector, shall not be regarded as a pipeline.

Article 2   The Right of Ownership of Oil

1. Oil situated in its natural state in the subsoil of the Republic of Kazakhstan shall be the exclusive property of the Republic. The terms of its exploration, development, and production shall be determined by the government of the Republic of Kazakhstan.

2. The right to ownership of the oil delivered to the surface of the earth shall be determined by a Contract which has been worked out on the basis of the present Law.

3. The right to dispose of the Oil delivered to the surface shall belong to the owner, unless other provisions are made in the contract.

CHAPTER 2   STATE BODIES OF REGULATION IN THE SPHERE OF CONDUCTING OIL OPERATIONS

Article 3   Competence of the Government of the Republic of Kazakhstan

1. State regulation of conducting oil operations shall be carried out by the Government of the Republic of Kazakhstan in accordance with its competence. All sub-legislative acts which elaborate provisions of the present Law shall be approved by the Government of the Republic of Kazakhstan.

2. The Supreme Council of the Republic of Kazakhstan, on presentation by the Government of the Republic of Kazakhstan, shall determine the territories where conducting Oil Operations shall be temporarily prohibited for the reasons of national security, for the need to create a strategic reserve or for the threat to the environment.

3. Neither corporate bodies nor natural persons can conduct any Oil Operations in the Republic of Kazakhstan without signing a Contract and receiving a License from the Government or a State Body authorized by it, under the terms stipulated by the Laws of the Republic of Kazakhstan.

Article 4   Competent Body: Its Rights and Obligations

1. **In order to organize Oil Operations the Government of the Republic of Kazakhstan shall determine the competent Body which has the right:**

    *   on behalf of the Government of the Republic of Kazakhstan to determine the areas, fields and types of Oil Operations;
    *   to carry out direct negotiations with a Contractor;
    *   to announce a competition or an auction and its terms for selection of a Contractor;
    *   to determine the forms of co-operation with a Contractor to work out model Contracts which are subject to approval by the Government of the Republic of Kazakhstan;
    *   to carry out independent examination of Contracts and preparation towards a conclusion based on the results of a competition;
    *   on behalf of the Government of Kazakhstan, to sign Contracts with a Contractor;

- to carry out checks on the implementation of the terms of a Contract;
- on behalf of the Government of the Republic of Kazakhstan, to conduct negotiations and to enter into agreements with the relevant bodies of any State for the purpose of acquiring rights which secure the opportunity of building and operating pipelines and other means of transportation on the territory of other States, with the aim of securing the export of Oil.

2. A competent body has an obligation:

- to require the observance of interests of the Republic of Kazakhstan;
- to grant a field to a Contractor for the purpose of its development only upon confirmation of its reserves by the State;
- to observe a Contractor's rights;
- to facilitate the implementation of a Contract;
- to act in strict compliance with the Laws of the Republic of Kazakhstan.

Article 5   Competence of Local Government Bodies

1. Local government bodies shall have the right:

- to allocate to a Contractor an area of land ('zemelny otvod') in order to conduct Oil Operations;
- to participate within their territory in working out and implementation of the State programme for the development of the oil and gas industry of the Republic of Kazakhstan;
- to carry out control over the protection of the areas of land and subsoil allocated for conducting Oil Operations;
- to discontinue unauthorized use of the subsoil for conducting Oil Operations and authorize construction works within the Contract Territory;
- to participate in negotiations with a Contractor in order to make decisions on the issues related to the observance of social, economic and ecological interests of the population and the territory;
- to use at their discretion the taxes which are levied on Contractors and are subject to entering into the local budget in accordance with the current legislation;
- to use at their discretion the payments, including those in hard currency, which are subject, in accordance with a Contract, to entering into the local budget, including all land-lease payments.

CHAPTER 3   CONTRACTS

Article 6   Types of Contracts

1. For carrying out Oil Operations in the Republic of Kazakhstan the following types of Contracts shall be employed in the main:

- Contract on production sharing;
- Contract on supply of services;
- a concession Contract.

2. Depending on the conditions of the specific Oil Operations and other circumstances, combined and other types of Contracts shall be accepted.

Article 7   Duration and Terms of Contracts

1. The duration and terms of Contracts shall be determined by an agreement between the parties in accordance with the Law of the Republic of Kazakhstan which is in force at the time when the Contract is signed.

2. The contents of a Contract, where it regards the use of the subsoil for development of a Field and Oil production, must meet the requirements of the Code of the Republic of Kazakhstan 'On Subsoil and Processing of Mineral Raw Materials' and shall take into account the provisions of this Law.

3. The contents of a Contract for Conducting other Oil Operations shall be determined by standard form contracts.

4. A Contract for conducting Oil Operations concerned with exploration and development of Oil Fields shall include the following periods:

    •   The period of exploration which can consist of one or several stages over a fixed period as determined by the parties' agreement;
    •   The period of development and production over a fixed period as determined by the parties' agreement.

5. Depending on the conditions in which the Oil Operations are carried out, a Contract can include only one of the above stated periods.

6. Upon the exposure of particularly complicated geological conditions or of the impartially recognized need for initiating extra work, the duration of the period of exploration or the period of development and production can be extended with a Contractor's consent and upon the decision of the Competent Body.

7. A Contractor who violated terms and conditions of the Contract shall not be given an extension.

Article 8   Procedure for Signing and Registration of Contracts

1. The procedure for signing Contracts shall be determined by the Government of the Republic of Kazakhstan.

2. Contracts for conducting Oil Operations shall be subject to obligatory State registration in accordance with the procedure established by the Code of the Republic of Kazakhstan 'On Subsoil and Processing of Mineral Raw Materials'.

CHAPTER 4   CONDUCTING OIL OPERATIONS

Article 9   Terms of Conducting Oil Operations

1. Terms of conducting oil operations, including the obligatory work agenda, shall be determined in the Contract in accordance with the Law which is in force.

    If geological prospecting works result in the discovery of an Oil field (fields), the Contractor shall have an obligation to report the discovery to a Competent Body, to make an appraisal of the field and to prepare the assessment of its significance in commercial terms. The deadline for reporting the discovery, the deadline for the appraisal, and the procedure for consideration and pronouncing a judgement upon the commercial viability of the discovery shall be determined in the Contract.

2. In the event of a Commercial Discovery, the Contractor shall be given the right for reimbursement of expenditures in accordance with the terms of the Contract.

3. In the event of the Contractor's refusal to develop the Commercial Discovery, a Competent Body shall have the right to grant this discovery to another Contractor.

4. If the prospecting work did not result in a Commercial Discovery, then the Contractor shall have no right for reimbursement of investments.

Article 10 Dimensions of a Contract Territory and Conditions for its Return

1. A Contract Territory shall be defined in the form of a block (mainly of a rectangular shape) within the system of geographical co-ordinates. The minimum size of a block shall be 10 minutes on a geographical graticule (approximately 350 sq kilometres). A Competent Body shall have the right to make a decision about the quantity of such blocks offered for a tender or for direct negotiations with a Contractor.

   If, in the course of Oil Operations, it is discovered that the geological deposits go beyond the boundaries of the Contract Territory, then the matter of its extension has to be determined by an additional decision or by a separate Contract.

2. The terms of return of the Contract Territories shall be determined by a Contract.

Article 11 Oil Operations in the Territorial Waters

1. The conduct of Oil Operations in the territorial waters of the Republic if Kazakhstan (seas, lakes, rivers) shall be controlled by a special legislation of the Republic of Kazakhstan.

Article 12 The Republic's Right to Purchase Oil

1. The Republic of Kazakhstan has the priority right to purchase Oil from the share of a domestic non-state-owned, or a foreign, Contractor at world market prices. The maximum amount of Oil which can be purchased, the pricing procedure and the form of currency shall be agreed in the Contract.

2. The terms of purchase of Oil from a domestic state-owned Contractor shall be determined by the Government of Kazakhstan.

Article 13 Requisition of Oil and Compensation for it

1. In the event of war, natural disasters or other extraordinary circumstances specified in the Contract, the Republic of Kazakhstan has the right of requisition of a part or of all Oil which belongs to the Contractor. Requisition shall be carried out on a scale necessary for providing the Republic of Kazakhstan's needs during such extraordinary circumstances. The Republic of Kazakhstan shall guarantee to the Contractor a compensation in kind or a financial reimbursement at world market prices which were operating at the time of the extraordinary circumstances.

Article 14   State Control over Conducting Oil Operations

1.   The state control over conducting Oil Operations shall be carried out in accordance with the Law of the Republic of Kazakhstan which is in force.

CHAPTER 5   RIGHTS AND OBLIGATIONS OF A CONTRACTOR

Article 15   Rights of a Contractor

1.   A Contractor has the right:
   - of exclusive conduct of Oil Operations within the Contract Territory if it is provided in a Contract;
   - to use the Contract Territory for conducting the activities indicated in the Contract and in the License;
   - to construct, on the Contract territory, facilities for production and social purposes, which are necessary for conducting the regular progress of work, and also to use, upon an agreement with the owners, the facilities and communications in general use on the Contract Territory as well as outside its borders;
   - to involve Sub-Contractor for performing separate types of work related to conducting Oil Operations;
   - to dispose freely the share of Oil (production) and of Associated Components, which belong to him, in the Republic of Kazakhstan as well as outside its borders. With the exception of the cases stipulated by Article 12 of the present Law;
   - to open its subsidiaries and Representative Offices and to participate in Oil Operations in other Contract Territories of the Republic of Kazakhstan in accordance with the procedure established by the present Law;
   - of priority in the extension of the validity of the Contract;
   - to waive all or part of its rights and to terminate its activities in the Contract Territory as well as in the Republic of Kazakhstan, in accordance with the conditions provided in the Contract.

Article 16   Obligations of a Contractor

1.   In the course of implementation of a Contract the Contractor shall be obliged:
   - to choose the most efficient methods and technology for conducting Oil Operations, based on the standards employed by the world oil industry practices;
   - to use the Contract Territory only for the purposes provided by the Contract;
   - to observe the requirements of the laws of the Republic of Kazakhstan, and in the absence of a law on certain types of activities – the international standards;
   - to conduct Oil Operations in strict accordance with the current legislation of the Republic of Kazakhstan concerning protection of the subsoil and the environment, which includes an obligatory examination of a Contract by ecologists in accordance with the established procedure;
   - not to prevent other persons from moving freely within the Contract Territory, from using the facilities and communications in general use or

from carrying out any types of work, including exploration, development and production of other natural resources, except Oil, on the condition that such activities do not interfere with the conduct of Oil Operations;

- to observe the technological plans and projects for conducting Oil Operations, approved in accordance with the established procedure and securing the safety of the staff, of the population and of the environment;

- to give preference to the equipment, materials and finished products produced in the Republic of Kazakhstan if they are competitive in terms of quality, price, operating parameters, and delivery terms;

- to give priority to services provided by enterprises and organizations of Kazakhstan in the course of conducting Oil Operations, including the use of air, railway, water and other kinds of transport if these services are competitive in terms of price, efficiency and quality;

- in the course of conducting Oil Operations, to give priority to the Kazakhstan personnel and to carry out their training and in-service training at the expense of the Contractor in accordance with a special programme specified by the terms of the Contract;

- to submit to a Competent Body the programme of scheduled work as well as full information during the implementation of the project;

- to provide free access to the necessary documents, information and places of work for the control bodies of the Republic of Kazakhstan during the execution of their official duties;

- to pass on information concerning Oil Operations to a third party if such a necessity arises, solely upon a mutual agreement between the parties unless otherwise provided for by the Contract;

- to submit the geological and geophysical information obtained as a result of activities in the Contract Territory, in accordance with the procedure and terms established by the Code of the Republic of Kazakhstan on 'Subsoil and Processing of Mineral Raw Materials';

- to pay taxes and to make payments in due time;

- to participate in the development of social infrastructures in accordance with a Contract;

- to preserve the places of cultural and historic importance;

- to restore at his own expense the areas of land and other natural facilities, which have been damaged during the period of conducting Oil Operations, to the state which makes them suitable for further use.

CHAPTER 6   MAIN PIPELINE TRANSPORT

Article 17   The Right of Ownership of the Main Pipeline

1. The Main Pipeline shall be an indivisible technological system and can be in state as well as in private ownership.

2. The maintenance of the Main Pipeline shall be carried out by its owner, unless otherwise provided for in the Contract.

Article 18   The Main Pipeline Maintenance

1.   The maintenance of the Main Pipeline's facilities shall be carried out in conformity with the regulations for technical maintenance, safety and security approved in accordance with the established procedure. The regulations shall be obligatory for implementation by all state bodies, enterprises, land users, officials and citizens during the interaction of the owner with the Main Pipeline.

2.   Energy supply enterprises shall be forbidden to carry out regime measures, intended for the restriction of the established limits of energy consumption, if there is no agreement with the owner of the Main Pipeline.

3.   The owner of the Main Pipeline, in agreement with local government bodies and other interested enterprises and organizations, shall work out joint activities which will secure the conditions of safe operation of the Main Pipeline's facilities, for the elimination of possible accidents and for extraordinary situations and their consequences.

4.   The owner of the Main Pipeline shall bear the responsibility for the observation of regulations covering its technical maintenance, safety and security.

5.   In the security zone of the Main Pipeline, there shall be a ban on any type of operations and actions, unless there is an agreement with its owners.

6.   Within the minimal distances established by the building standards and safety regulations, construction of any facilities which are not related to the Main Pipeline shall be forbidden.

Article 19   Relationship between the Owner of the Main Pipeline and the Local Government Bodies and Consignors

1.   Local government bodies have no right to interfere with the operational industrial activities at the Main Pipeline, related to pumping, storage and distribution of Oil.

2.   Employees of emergency services and the emergency and special assignment equipment of the Main Pipeline must not be diverted for other works.

3.   In case if there is a reserve of carrying capacity in the Main Pipeline, its owner shall have no right to refuse the consignors to transport Oil. At the same time the consignors have equal rights for transportation services.

CHAPTER 7   COMMERCIAL TERMS

Article 20   Currency Transactions

1.   The procedure for currency transactions by a Contractor and a Sub-Contractor shall be determined by the Law of the Republic of Kazakhstan which is in force.

2.   A Contractor or a Sub-Contractor shall have the right:

- to allocate freely the currency received as a result of conducting Oil Operations in the Republic of Kazakhstan, including its transfer, saving and use outside the Republic of Kazakhstan, on the condition of fulfillment of

their tax obligations and other payments in accordance with the Contract;
- to settle accounts with the sub-Contractors and to pay wages to resident and non-resident employees, who carry out Oil Operations, in hard currency;
- to open bank accounts in the Republic of Kazakhstan as well as outside its borders;
- to carry out re-export of foreign currency.

3. Re-export of foreign currency brought by a Contractor and a Sub-Contractor into the Republic of Kazakhstan for the purpose of conducting Oil Operations shall not be subject to tax.

Article 21   Customs Procedure

1. The customs procedure shall be carried out in accordance with the Law of the Republic of Kazakhstan which is in force.

Article 22   Taxes and Payments

1. Depending on the type and terms of the Contract, in the course of conducting Oil Operations the Contractor shall make the following payments:
- signature lump sum bonus, the size and dates of payment for which shall be determined by an agreement between the Contractor and the Competent body;
- land lease rent, the size of which shall be determined in a Contract and shall not be below the size of the land tax established by the Laws of the Republic of Kazakhstan;
- production bonus, the size and dates of payment for which shall be determined in the Contract. The first payment shall be made at the moment when Oil production starts. The following payments shall be carried out as the Oil production output grows in accordance with the mutually agreed scale.

2. The Contractor shall also pay the following taxes:
- profit tax

  The procedure for the calculation of taxable profit shall be determined by the Government of the Republic of Kazakhstan in accordance with the Taxation Law of the Republic of Kazakhstan. This order shall form the basis for refining the accounting procedure of a Contract as described in Article 23 of the present Law.

  The profit tax rate, determined in accordance with the established procedure of calculating the taxable profit, shall not be subject to change throughout the duration of a Contract;
- taxes on excess profit from Oil Operations.

  Besides the mentioned taxes a Contractor shall pay other taxes, which are specified by the Law of the Republic of Kazakhstan, taking into account the specific features of taxation of Oil Operations.

3. A Contractor shall not be subject to imposition of new forms of taxes, which have been introduced after the signing of a Contract, except in cases when those taxes are introduced in substitution of the current ones, which are payable by a Contractor in accordance with a Contract.

Article 23   Accounting and Auditing

1. The accounting adopted in the international practice of conducting Oil Operations shall be acceptable. The whole accounting procedure shall be agreed upon during preparation of the provisions of a Contract, and approved by the parties at the time when the Contract is signed.

2. In the course of conducting Oil Operations by a foreign Contractor a US dollar or other freely convertible currency shall be used as an accounting unit, and there will be the simultaneous conducting of comparable accounting in national currency.

3. The auditing of the Contractor's accounting shall be carried out by a Competent Body on a regular basis but not more often than once a year, and for this purpose the latter can invite a specialized auditing organization.

4. Checks on the state of accounting, accuracy of assessments of financial results, and on the completeness and timeliness of payments into the budget and on other issues connected with taxation shall be carried out by the agencies of the State Taxation Department of the Republic of Kazakhstan.

CHAPTER 8   LEGAL PROVISIONS

Article 24   Assignment of Rights and Obligations

1. Only with the written permission of a Competent Body may a Contractor assign to another legal or natural person or an international organization either all or a part of his rights and obligations stipulated in the Contract, including the alienation of the controlling block of shares. The conditions of assignment of rights and obligations to a subsidiary shall be agreed in a Contract.

2. Expenses connected with the assignment of rights and obligations in accordance with Clause 1 of the present Article shall be paid by the Contractor.

3. While a Contractor retains some share in the Contract, he and the person to whom the rights and obligations are being assigned shall bear either joint or separate responsibilities in accordance with the Contract.

Article 25   Compensation for the Use of an Area of Land

1. In the event of a Contractor being provided with the right of access to an area of land for conducting Oil Operations, and if this area of land is the property of, or is used by, another corporate body or natural person, a Contractor must pay compensation to the owner or user for limiting the sphere of his activities as well as the damage inflicted as a result of conducting of Oil Operations.

Article 26   Insurance

1. Insurance cover by a Contractor is compulsory against destruction or damage, as a result of fire or explosion, of the following:

- the property used in the process of conducting Oil Operations and pertaining to the capital assets
- the state property which is on lease to a Contractor;
- the Oil delivered to the surface;
- the Oil transported through the Main Pipeline;
- the pipeline itself which is under the Contractor's full ownership or over which he has full economic authority;

Furthermore, a Contractor shall be obliged to insure:

- the life and health of those of his employees who are citizens of Kazakhstan and participate in conducting Oil Operations, i.e. to provide industrial accident insurance;
- against environmental violations.

The above stated insurance shall be carried out by insurance agencies of the Republic of Kazakhstan. The terms of compulsory insurance shall be determined by the Government of the Republic of Kazakhstan as well as by an insurance agreement concluded between a Contractor and an insurer.

For the purposes of securing his insurance obligations, an insurer shall be allowed to sign reinsurance and co-insurance agreements with other insurance agencies and organizations, including foreign ones.

2.   Parties shall have the right to establish in a Contract other types of insurance which are compulsory for a Contractor.

3.   A Contract, which is not secured by compulsory insurance agreements, shall not be considered signed.

4.   Apart from the above listed cases, a Contractor shall have the right to insure, at his own discretion, against any types of insurance risks.

5.   The insurance shall be carried out in accordance with the Law of the Republic of Kazakhstan and with the universally accepted international practice and standards.

Article 27   Labour – Employer Legal Relations

1.   The terms of the renumeration of labour, operating conditions, terms of holidays, social security and social insurance of the citizens of the Republic of Kazakhstan, working for a Contractor, shall be regulated by the Law of the Republic of Kazakhstan which is in force.

2.   The Law of the Republic of Kazakhstan shall apply to foreign citizens working for a Contractor unless otherwise provided for by an inter-government treaty between the Republic of Kazakhstan and the Contractor's country.

Article 28   Alteration and Termination of a Contract

1.   Any alterations of the terms of a Contract can be carried out only upon mutual agreement between a Contractor and a Competent Body and only in writing.

2.   A Contractor and a Competent Body may terminate the effect of a Contract on the grounds and according to the procedure specified in the Contract. The parties shall not be released from the obligations which existed and remained outstanding at a time when a notification of termination of the Contract was given.

3. In the event of pre-scheduled termination of a Contract a Contractor shall have the right to dispose independently of the assets which are owned by him. In this case a Competent Body shall have the priority right to the acquisition of the above mentioned assets. The issues, related to transfer of the right of ownership of assets belonging to a Contractor during the Contract's validity time, as well as after its validity expires, shall be specified in the Contract. A Contractor shall be obliged to leave the Contract Territory in a state which satisfies the requirements of the State bodies of mining and sanitary inspection and of protection of subsoil and the environment.

Article 29   Grounds for Nullification of Contracts and Licenses

1. The government of the Republic of Kazakhstan shall have the right to declare null and void and to cancel a signed Contract and/or a granted License only in the case if:

   - the information about a Contractor's financial and technical capacity which was given by him and which played a significant role for signing a Contract and/or granting a License, not conforming with the actual facts;
   - after holding a competition or an auction, it was established by a court that the Organization Committee of the competition or the auction had entered into a secret collusion with the future Contractor for the payment to members of the Organizing Committee (or, on their instructions, to a third party) of an illegal reward that resulted in the Contractor gaining privileges over other participants of the competition or the auction.

Article 30   Guarantee of a Contractor's Rights

1. The Republic of Kazakhstan shall guarantee to a Contractor the protection of his rights in accordance with the Laws which are in force.

Article 31   Procedure for Consideration of Disputes

1. Disputes between parties, arising in the course of implementation of a Contract, shall be subject to the settlement by negotiations between themselves. Should no agreement be reached, the dispute shall be submitted for resolution to the court, the Court of Arbitration of the Republic of Kazakhstan or, upon an agreement between the parties, to an arbitration tribunal.

   If an international treaty signed by the Republic of Kazakhstan provides the rules of settlement of disputes, which are different from those provided by the present Law, the rules of the international treaty shall apply.

ENACTMENT

Of the Supreme Council of the Republic of Kazakhstan 'On the Implementation of the Petroleum Law of the Republic of Kazakhstan'

The Supreme Council of the Republic of Kazakhstan enacts the following:

1. To put into effect The Petroleum Law of the Republic of Kazakhstan from 01 January 1993.

2. The Contracts, signed by the Government of the Republic of Kazakhstan before the adoption of the present Law, shall retain their effect.

3. Pending the adoption of the legislative acts, which established tax on excess profit and provide for the specific features of taxation of Oil Operations, the profit tax rate and peculiarities of applying individual types of tax on Oil Operations can be provided by a Contract.

4. The Cabinet of Ministers of the Republic of Kazakhstan [is obliged]:

   - within three months from the moment of publication of the present Law, to prepare and to ratify regulative acts which detail its provisions;
   - to bring the decisions of the Government of the Republic of Kazakhstan in line with the Petroleum Law of the Republic of Kazakhstan;
   - to ensure the revision and repeal by ministries and departments of their regulative acts which contravene the present Law;
   - to present the Draft of the Law of the Republic of Kazakhstan 'Concerning Taxation of Oil Operations' for consideration at the 10th Session of the Supreme Council.

5. To entrust the Committee of the Supreme Council of the Republic of Kazakhstan concerned with the issues of the development of industry, transport and communications to carry out control over the implementation of the present Law.

Chairman of the Supreme Council
of the Republic of Kazakhstan

Index